Self Catering

The Official Where to Stay Guide

SCOTLAND IS SPLIT INTO EIGHT TOURIST AREAS. YOU WILL FIND ACCOMMODATION LISTED ALPHABETICALLY BY LOCATION WITHIN EACH OF THESE AREAS. THERE IS AN INDEX AT THE BACK OF THIS BOOK WHICH MAY ALSO HELP YOU.

Introduction

Welcome to Scotland	ii
Using this book	iii - v
Signs you need to know	vi - xiv
Travellers' Tips	xv - xviii
Maps	xix - xxiv

Accommodation

A	South of Scotland: Ayrshire and Arran, Dumfries and Galloway, Scottish Borders	2
B	Edinburgh and Lothians	39
C	Greater Glasgow and Clyde Valley	57
D	West Highlands & Islands, Loch Lomond, Stirling and Trossachs	67
E	Perthshire, Angus and Dundee and the Kingdom of Fife	128
F	Grampian Highlands, Aberdeen and the North East Coast	174
G	The Highlands and Skye	205
H	Outer Islands: Western Isles, Orkney, Shetland	294

Hostel Accommodation	306
Visitors with Disabilities	312
Index by Location	317
Display Advertisements	324
Books to Help You	325
Publications Order Form	326

Welcome to Scotland | Self Catering

FOR FLEXIBILITY AND INDEPENDENCE THERE'S NOTHING QUITE LIKE A SELF CATERING HOLIDAY. WHETHER YOU WANT AN ACTION-PACKED FAMILY HOLIDAY OR A COSY BREAK FOR TWO, THESE PROPERTIES ARE SOMEWHERE WHERE YOU CAN REALLY FEEL AT HOME. THERE'S NO TIMETABLE TO FOLLOW – MEALTIMES CAN COME AND GO, AND YOU'LL EAT WHEN YOU WANT TO. YOU'LL ENJOY A LIE-IN ONE DAY, SET OFF FOR THE HILLS AT DAWN THE NEXT – IT'S YOUR HOLIDAY!

In Scotland, there's an enticing variety of accommodation, from crofts to castles, with plenty in between, including university residences, pine lodges, caravan holiday homes, and flats. There are some in cities, some in secluded countryside, some in chalet parks where it's ideal for families as it's easy – and safe – for children to wander and make new friends.

And while Scotland offers a host of things to do – hillwalking, historic houses, castles, museums, fishing and golf, to name but a few! – when you're self catering, just a trip to the local shops is an outing. Trying different cakes and breads from the bakery, sampling Scottish cheeses, prime meats and soft fruits – it all makes a treat to enjoy in the comfort of your "own" holiday home.

In the country, the city, or by the seaside, self catering comes in all shapes and sizes – enjoy your holiday the way you want to!

Using this book

Where to Stay...?

Over 1100 answers to the age-old question!

Revised annually, this is the most comprehensive guide to self catering properties in Scotland.

Every property in the guide has been graded and classified by Scottish Tourist Board inspectors. See page vi for details

How to find accommodation

This book split into eight areas of Scotland:

Accommodation

A	**South of Scotland: Ayrshire and Arran, Dumfries and Galloway, Scottish Borders**	**2**
B	**Edinburgh and Lothians**	**39**
C	**Greater Glasgow and Clyde Valley**	**57**
D	**West Highlands & Islands, Loch Lomond, Stirling and Trossachs**	**67**
E	**Perthshire, Angus and Dundee and the Kingdom of Fife**	**128**
F	**Grampian Highlands, Aberdeen and the North East Coast**	**174**
G	**The Highlands and Skye**	**205**
H	**Outer Islands: Western Isles, Orkney, Shetland**	**294**

The map on page xix shows these areas. Within each area section you will find accommodation listed alphabetically by location.

Alternatively there is an index at the back of this book listing alphabetically all accommodation locations in Scotland.

Using this book

Learn to use the symbols in each entry – they contain a mine of information!

There is a key to symbols on the back flap.

Naturally, it is always advisable to confirm with the establishment that a particular facility is still available.

Prices in the guide are quoted per unit and represent the minimum and maximum rentals expected to be charged for one week's let in the low and high season.
They include VAT at the appropriate rate and service charges where applicable. Unless otherwise stated, minimum let is one week.

The prices of accommodation, services and facilities are supplied to us by the operators and were, to the best of our knowledge, correct at the time of going to press. However, prices can change at any time during the lifetime of the publication, and you should check again when you book.

Bookings can be made direct to the establishment, through a travel agent, or through a local Tourist Information Centre.

Self catering in Scotland is very popular, and it is wise to book as early as possible, particularly for the high season months of July and August.

Remember, when you accept accommodation by telephone or in writing, you are entering a legally binding contract which must be fulfilled on both sides. Should you fail to take up accommodation, you may not only forfeit any deposit already paid, but may also have to compensate the establishment if the accommodation cannot be re-let.

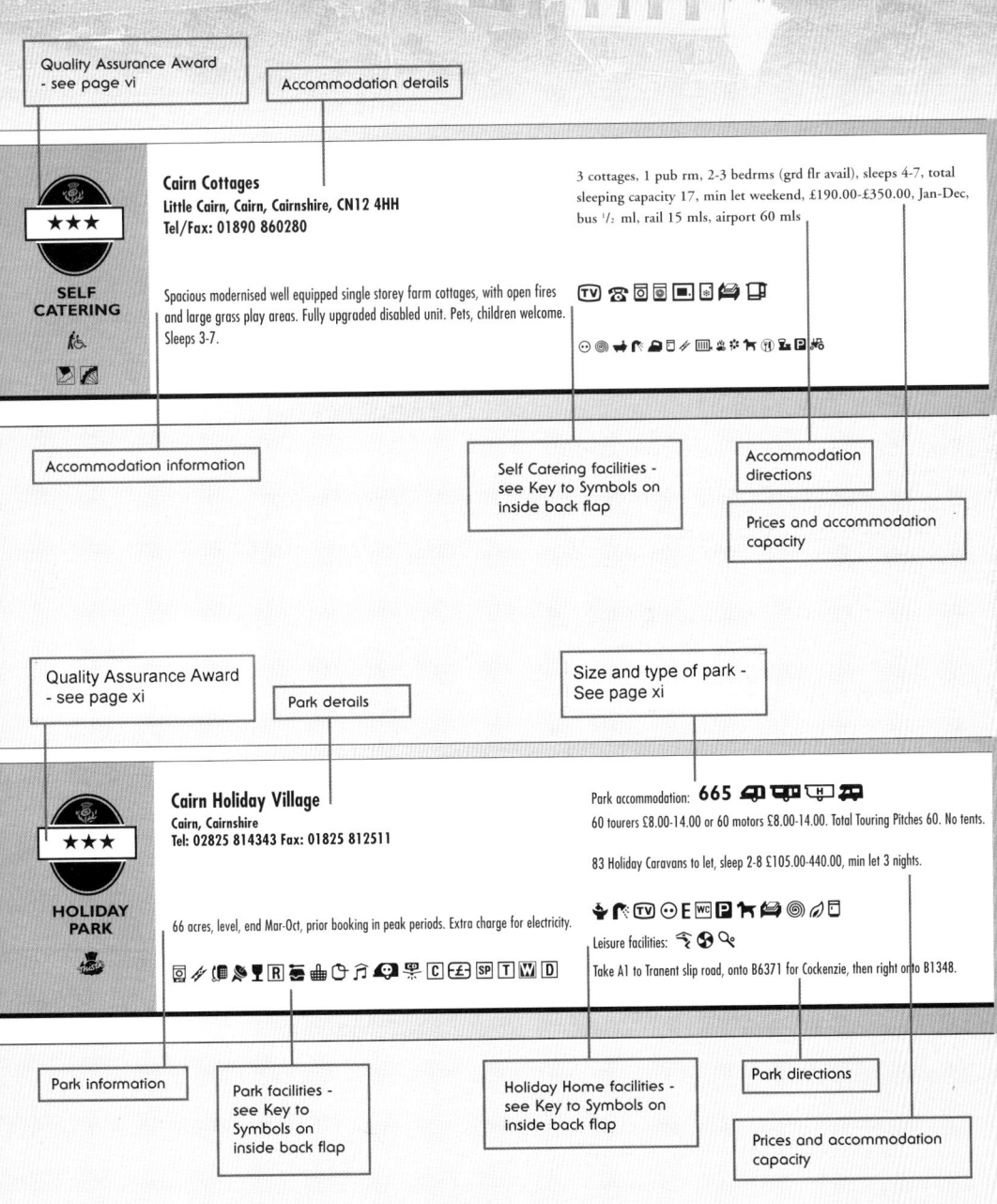

Signs you need to know
Quality Grading

Follow the stars and you won't be disappointed when you get to the inn.

The Scottish Tourist Board Star System is a world-first. Quality is what determines our star awards, not a checklist of facilities. We've made your priorities our priorities.

Quality makes or breaks a visit. This is why it is the most important aspects of your stay; the cleanliness of the property, the condition of the furnishing, fitments, decor and equipment, the welcome touches and the overall ambience which earn Scottish Tourist Board Stars.

This easy to understand system tells you at a glance the quality standard of all types and sizes of accommodation from the smallest B&B and self-catering cottage to the largest country-side and city centre hotels.

The standards you can expect.

★★★★★	Exceptional
★★★★	Excellent
★★★	Very good
★★	Good
★	Fair and Acceptable

A trained Scottish Tourist Board inspector grades each property every year to give you the reassurance that you can choose accommodation of the quality standard you want.

To help you further in your choice the Scottish Tourist Board System also tells you the type of accommodation and the range of facilities and services available.

For further information call into any Tourist Information Centre, or contact the Scottish Tourist Board.

More details available from:

Quality Assurance Department
Scottish Tourist Board
Thistle House
Beechwood Park North
INVERNESS
IV2 3ED

Tel: 01463 716996
Fax: 01463 717244

Look out for this distinctive sign of Quality Assured Accommodation

Signs you need to know
Quality Grading

Accommodation Types

Self Catering
A house, cottage, apartment, chalet or similar accommodation which is let normally on a weekly basis to individuals where facilities are provided to cater for yourselves.

Serviced Apartments
Serviced apartments are essentially self-catering apartments where services such as a cleaning service is available and meals and drinks may be available. Meals and drinks would normally be provided to each apartment or in a restaurant and/or bar which is on site.

Guest House
A Guest House is usually a commercial business and will normally have a minimum of 4 letting bedrooms, of which some will have ensuite or private facilities. Breakfast will be available and evening meals may be provided.

B&B
Accommodation offering bed and breakfast, usually in a private house. B&B's will normally accommodate no more than 6 guests, and may or may not serve an evening meal.

Hotel
A Hotel will normally have a minimum of 6 letting bedrooms, of which at least half must have ensuite or private bathroom facilities. A hotel will normally have a drinks licence (may be a restricted licence) and will serve breakfast and dinner.

International Resort Hotel
A Hotel achieving a 5 Star quality award which owns and offers a range of leisure and sporting facilities including an 18 hole golf course, swimming and leisure centre and country pursuits.

Lodge
Primarily purpose-built overnight accommodation, often situated close to a major road or in a city centre. Reception hours may be restricted and payment may be required on check in. There may be associated restaurant facilities. A car parking space will normally be provided for each bedroom.

Inn
Bed and breakfast accommodation provided within a traditional inn or pub environment. A restaurant and bar will be open to non-residents and will provide restaurant or bar food at lunchtime and in the evening.

Restaurant with Rooms
In a Restaurant with Rooms, the restaurant is the most significant part of the business. It is usually open to non-residents. Accommodation is available, and breakfast is usually provided.

Campus Accommodation
Campus accommodation is provided by colleges and universities for their students and is made available-with meals-for individuals, families or groups at certain times of the year. These typically include the main Summer holiday period as well as Easter and Christmas.

Signs you need to know
Quality Grading

For Self Catering Accommodation Facility and Service Symbols

- TV in self catering unit
- Satellite/cable TV
- Payphone provided
- Ensuite bath and/or shower room(s) in self catering unit
- No TV
- Washing machine
- Tumble dryer
- Laundry facilities on site
- Bed linen provided
- Towels provided
- Microwave
- Telephone in unit
- Hi-fi
- Dishwasher
- Domestic help
- Freezer
- Video

Additional Serviced Apartments Symbols

- Restaurant
- Evening meal available
- Full alcohol drinks licence
- Restricted alcohol drinks licence
- Room service

Signs you need to know
Quality Grading

OVER 900 QUALITY ASSURED ACCOMMODATION PROVIDERS ARE OFFERING AN EXTRA WARM WELCOME FOR VISITORS WHO ARE CYCLING OR WALKING FOR ALL, OR PART, OF THEIR HOLIDAY IN SCOTLAND.

As well as having had the quality of the welcome, service, food and comfort assessed by the Scottish Tourist Board, they will be able to offer the following:-

★ hot drink on arrival
★ packed lunch/flask filling option
★ late evening meal option
★ early breakfast option
★ drying facilities for wet clothes
★ local walking and/or cycling information
★ daily weather forecast
★ local public transport information
★ secure, lockable, covered area for bike storage
★ details of local cycle specialists

 Walkers Welcome Scheme

 Cyclists Welcome Scheme

Look out for the logos in this guide and other accommodation listings.

Green Tourism

In response to the increasing need for businesses throughout the world to operate in an environmentally friendly way, the Scottish Tourist Board has developed the Green Tourism Business Scheme.

Where owners of accommodation are taking steps to reduce waste and pollution, to recycle and to be efficient with resources they are credited in this Scheme with a "Green Award". In our assessment of the degree of environmental good practice the business is demonstrating they are awarded one of the following;

Bronze Award 🌿 BRONZE
for achieving a satisfactory level

Silver Award 🌿🌿 SILVER
for achieving a good level

Gold Award 🌿🌿🌿 GOLD
for achieving a very good level

Signs you need to know
Quality Grading

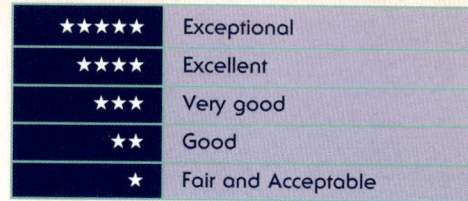

The standards you can expect.

★★★★★	Exceptional
★★★★	Excellent
★★★	Very good
★★	Good
★	Fair and Acceptable

YOU NOT ONLY WANT TO BE SURE OF THE STANDARD OF ACCOMMODATION YOU CHOOSE TO STAY IN, WHICH EVER TYPE IT MAY BE, YOU WANT TO BE SURE YOU MAKE THE MOST OF YOUR TIME.

The Scottish Tourist Board not only inspects every type of accommodation every year, but also a wide range of visitor attractions every second year to grade the quality standards provided for visitors.

The inspection scheme for visitor attractions provides you with the assurance that an attraction has been assessed for the condition and standard of the facilities and services provided – the warmth of welcome, efficiency of service, level of cleanliness, standard of visitor interpretation and of the toilets, restaurant and shop, if provided.

A large world famous castle, or small local museum can attain high grades if their services for the visitor are of a high standard.

In addition to the Star grades, every attraction is categorised under one of the following types to help give the visitor an indication of the type of experience on offer:

Visitor Attraction	Castle	Historic Attraction
Museum	Tour	Garden
Activity Centre	Tourist Shop	Leisure Centre
Arts Venue	Historic House	

Look for the Scottish Tourist Board sign of quality:

Signs you need to know
Quality Grading

When you are looking for a place to stay, you look to the Tourist Board for reassurance.

Every park in this guide is visited every year by Scottish Tourist Board inspectors and assessed for the quality of its facilities and services.

For year 2000, a new grading system has been introduced based on research with visitors staying in parks, where a simple system of Stars tells you the quality standard, replacing the previous Tick scheme.

The new scheme still assesses all aspects of a park for the quality of its visitor provision with particular emphasis on the level of cleanliness of the facilities. It now tells you the standard in the easily understood Star format used by the Scottish Tourist Board for all inspection schemes. Parks can achieve the highest grades regardless of size or range of facilities.

To help give you an indication of the type of park on offer, Stars are awarded alongside three categories:-

Holiday park	a park which offers holiday homes and most likely touring and camping pitches.
Touring park	a park which offers touring pitches and may offer camping pitches
Camping park	a park for camping only

Look out for the Scottish Tourist Board sign of quality:-

The following symbols displayed in each entry in this guide, show you in detail if caravan holiday homes are available for hire, which types of caravans are accepted at the park and if tents are accepted.

The total number of pitches are shown which gives you a good indication of the overall size of the park.

🚐	Pitches for touring caravans
🚐	Caravan holiday-homes on the park
🚐	Caravan holiday-homes for hire
12	Total number of pitches
⛺	Tents Welcome
🚐	Motor caravans welcome

Thistle Awards are issued to individual caravan holiday homes which offer a high standard of accommodation. They are sited on parks with the top gradings under the Scottish Tourist Board Park Grading Scheme – those with three to five stars. They are inspected every year by the Scottish Tourist Board to ensure they offer these standards for the coming holiday season.

Signs you need to know
Mobility Needs

VISITORS WITH PARTICULAR MOBILITY NEEDS MUST BE ABLE TO BE SECURE IN THE KNOWLEDGE THAT SUITABLE ACCOMMODATION IS AVAILABLE TO MATCH THESE REQUIREMENTS. ADVANCE KNOWLEDGE OF ACCESSIBLE ENTRANCES, BEDROOMS AND FACILITIES IS IMPORTANT TO ENABLE VISITORS TO ENJOY THEIR STAY.

Along with the quality awards which apply to all the establishments in this, and every Scottish Tourist Board guide, we operate a national accessibility scheme. By inspecting establishments to set criteria, we can identify and promote places that meet the requirements of visitors with mobility needs.

The three categories of accessibility – drawn up in close consultation with specialist organisations are:

Unassisted wheelchair access for residents

Assisted wheelchair access for residents

Access for residents with mobility difficulties

Look out for these symbols in establishments, in advertising and brochures. They assure you that entrances, ramps, passageways, doors, restaurant facilities, bathrooms and toilets, as well as kitchens in self catering properties, have been inspected with reference to the needs of wheelchair users, and those with mobility difficulties. Write or telephone for details of the standards in each category – address on page vi.

For more information about travel, specialist organisations who can provide information and a list of all the Scottish accommodation which has had the access inspection write (or ask at a Tourist Information Centre) for the Scottish Tourist Board booklet "Accessibility Scotland".

Holiday Care Service
2nd Floor
Imperial Buildings
Victoria Road
Horley
Surrey RH6 7PZ
Tel: 01293 774535
Fax: 01293 784647

In addition, a referral service to put enquirers in touch with local disability advice centres is:-

UPDATE
27 Beaverhall Road
Edinburgh
EH7 4JE
Tel: 0131 558 5200

Signs you need to know
Taste of Scotland

FROM SCOTLAND'S NATURAL LARDER COMES A WEALTH OF FINE FLAVOURS.

The sea yields crab and lobster, mussels and oysters, haddock and herring to be eaten fresh or smoked. From the lochs and rivers come salmon and trout.

Scotch beef and lamb, venison and game are of prime quality, often adventurously combined with local vegetables or with wild fruits such as redcurrants and brambles. Raspberries and strawberries are cultivated to add their sweetness to trifles and shortcakes, and to the home-made jams that are an essential part of Scottish afternoon tea.

The Scots have a sweet tooth, and love all kinds of baking – rich, crisp shortbread, scones, fruit cakes and gingerbreads. Crumbly oatcakes make the ideal partner for Scottish cheeses, which continue to develop from their ancient farming origins into new – and very successful – styles.

And in over a hundred distilleries, barley, yeast and pure spring water come together miraculously to create malt whisky – the water of life.

Many Scottish hotels and restaurants pride themselves on the use they make of these superb natural ingredients – around 400 are members of the Taste of Scotland Scheme which encourages the highest culinary standards, use of Scottish produce and a warm welcome to visitors. Look for the Stockpot symbol at establishments, or write to Taste of Scotland for a copy of their guide.

In Shops		£7.99
By Post:	UK	£8.50
	Europe	£9.50
	US	£11.00

Taste of Scotland Scheme
33 Melville Street
EDINBURGH
EH3 7JF
Tel: 0131 220 1900
Fax: 0131 220 6102
e-mail: tastescotland@sol.co.uk
www.taste-of-scotland.com

Signs you need to know
The Natural Cooking of Scotland

SCOTLAND HAS SOME OF THE FINEST FOOD PRODUCTS IN THE WORLD.

OUR SEAFOOD, BEEF, LAMB, VENISON, VEGETABLES AND SOFT FRUIT ARE RENOWNED FOR THEIR HIGH QUALITY. THESE FINE INDIGENOUS RAW MATERIALS AND A WIDE ASSORTMENT OF INTERNATIONAL FOOD PRODUCTS ARE SKILFULLY COMBINED BY COOKS AND CHEFS INTO THE VAST RANGE OF CUISINE AVAILABLE IN SCOTLAND.

As you travel throughout the country you will find an excellent standard of cooking in all sorts of establishments from restaurants with imaginative menus to tea rooms with simple wholesome home-baking.

You will find some of these culinary gems by reading of their reputation in newspapers and magazines, from advice given by Tourist Information Centre staff, by looking for the Taste of Scotland logo, or by using your own instinct to discover them yourself.

The Scottish Tourist Board has recognised that it would be helpful to you, the visitor, to have some assurance of the standards of food available in every different type of eating establishment; and indeed to be able to find a consistent standard of food in every place you choose to eat.

We launched The Natural Cooking of Scotland as a long-term initiative to encourage eating places to follow the lead of those who are best in their field in providing a consistently high standard of catering.

We have harnessed the skills of chefs, the experience of restaurateurs and the expertise of catering trainers to introduce a series of cooking skills courses which will encourage the use of fresh, local produce, cooked in a simple and satisfying way. We are providing advice and guidance to eating places throughout Scotland on high quality catering and the skills involved in efficient food service and customer care. Many more initiatives are being planned to support this enhancement of Scottish cooking standards and a high dependency on the food available on our own doorsteps.

Whilst you will appreciate the food experiences you will find in eating your way around Scotland this year, the Natural Cooking of Scotland will ensure that the profile of fine Scottish cooking is even greater in future years.

Traveller's Tips
Getting Around

SCOTLAND IS A SMALL COUNTRY AND TRAVEL IS EASY. THERE ARE DIRECT AIR LINKS WITH UK CITIES, WITH EUROPE AND NORTH AMERICA. THERE IS ALSO AN INTERNAL AIR NETWORK BRINGING THE ISLANDS OF THE NORTH AND WEST WITHIN EASY REACH.

Scotland's rail network not only includes excellent cross-border InterCity services but also a good internal network. All major towns are linked by rail and there are also links to the western seaboard at Mallaig and Kyle of Lochalsh (for ferry connections to Skye and the Western Isles) and to Inverness, Thurso and Wick for ferries to Orkney and Shetland.

All the usual discount cards are valid but there are also ScotRail Rovers (multi journey tickets allowing you to save on rail fares) and the Freedom of Scotland Travelpass, a combined rail and ferry pass allowing unlimited travel on ferry services to the islands and all of the rail network. In addition Travelpass also offers discounts on bus services and some air services.

InterCity services are available from all major centres, for example: Birmingham, Carlisle, Crewe, Manchester, Newcastle, Penzance, Peterborough, Preston, Plymouth, York and many others.

There are frequent InterCity departures from Kings Cross and Euston stations to Edinburgh and Glasgow. The journey time from Kings Cross to Edinburgh is around 4 hours and from Euston to Glasgow around 5 hours.

Traveller's Tips
Getting Around

Coach connections include express services to Scotland from all over the UK; local bus companies in Scotland offer explorer tickets and discount cards. Postbuses (normally minibuses) take passengers on over 130 rural routes throughout Scotland.

Ferries to and around the islands are regular and reliable, most ferries carry vehicles, although some travelling to smaller islands convey only passengers.

Contact the Information Department, Scottish Tourist Board, PO Box 705, Edinburgh EH4 3TP, or any Tourist Information Centre, for details of travel and transport.

Many visitors choose to see Scotland by road – distances are short and driving on the quiet roads of the Highlands is a new and different experience. In remoter areas, some roads are still single track, and passing places must be used. When vehicles approach from different directions, the car nearest to a passing place must stop in or opposite it. Please do not use passing places to park in!

Speed limits on Scottish roads:
Dual carriageways 70mph/112kph;
single carriageways 60mph/96kph;
built-up areas 30mph/48kph.

The driver and front-seat passenger in a car must wear seatbelts; rear seatbelts, if fitted, must be used. Small children and babies must at all times be restrained in a child seat or carrier.

Opening times

Public holidays: Christmas and New Year's Day are holidays in Scotland, taken by almost everyone. Scottish banks, and many offices, will close in 2000 on 3 and 4 January, 21 April, 1 May, 7 August, 25 and 26 December. Scottish towns also take Spring and Autumn holidays which may vary from place to place, but are usually on a Monday.

Banking hours: In general, banks open Monday to Friday, 0930 to 1600, with some closing later on a Thursday. Banks in cities, particularly in or near the main shopping centres, may be open at weekends. Cash machines in hundreds of branches allow you to withdraw cash outside banking hours, using the appropriate cards.

Pubs and restaurants: Pubs and restaurants are allowed to serve alcoholic drinks between 1100 hours and 2300 hours Monday through to Saturday; Sundays 1230 hours until 1430 hours then again from 1830 hours until 2300 hours.

Residents in hotels may have drinks served at any time, subject to the proprietors discretion.

Extended licensing hours are subject to local council applications.

Traveller's Tips
Getting Around

Telephone codes
If you are calling from abroad, first dial your own country's international access code (usually 00, but do please check). Next, dial the UK code, 44, then the area code except for the first 0, then the remainder of the number as normal.

Quarantine regulations
If you are coming to Scotland from overseas, please do not attempt to bring your pet on holiday with you. British quarantine regulations are stringently enforced, and anyone attempting to contravene them will incur severe penalties as well as the loss of the animal.

Scotland On The Net
Visit our web site at:

www.visitscotland.com

> THE SCOTTISH TOURIST BOARD IS COMMITTED TO ENSURING THAT OUR NATURAL ENVIRONMENT, UPON WHICH OUR TOURISM IS SO DEPENDANT, IS SAFEGUARDED FOR FUTURE GENERATIONS TO ENJOY.

xviii

Maps
Scotland's Tourist Areas

Accommodation

A	South of Scotland: Ayrshire and Arran, Dumfries and Galloway, Scottish Borders	2
B	Edinburgh and Lothians	39
C	Greater Glasgow and Clyde Valley	57
D	West Highlands & Islands, Loch Lomond, Stirling and Trossachs	67
E	Perthshire, Angus and Dundee and the Kingdom of Fife	128
F	Grampian Highlands, Aberdeen and the North East Coast	174
G	The Highlands and Skye	205
H	Outer Islands: Western Isles, Orkney, Shetland	294

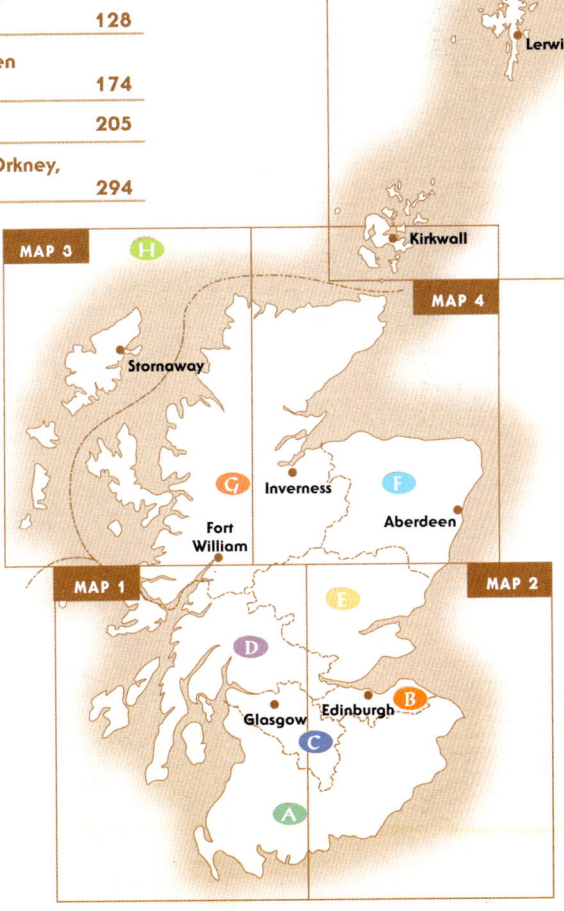

Map 1

A
B
C
D
E
F
G
H
1
2
3
4
5
6
7
8
9
10
11
12
COLL
Arinagour
Tobermory
Glenmore
Strontian
Kentallen
Glencoe
North Ballachulish
Rannoch Sta
Kinloch Rannoch
Glen Lyon
Loch Tay
Calgary
Dervaig
Killundine
Gott Bay
Isle of Tiree
Scarinish
TIREE
Crossapol
Aros
Lochaline
Appin
Barcaldine
Killiechronan
Salen
Gruline
Fishnish
Lismore
Benderloch
North Connel
Lochdon
Killin
MULL
Oban
Lerags
Taynuilt
Lochawe
Dalmally
Crianlarich
Tyndrum
Lochearnhead
Balquhidder
St Fillans
IONA
Fionnphort
Pennyghael
Kinlochspelve
Bunessan
Kilninver
Ardbrecknish
Isle of Seil
Easdale
Balvicar
Strathyre
Cairndow
Inveruglas
Callander
Arduaine
Craobh Haven
Ardfern
Kilmelford
Ford
Loch Awe
Inveraray
St Catherines
Lochgoilhead
Tarbet
Rowardennan
Port of Menteith
Aberfoyle
COLONSAY
Scalasaig
Isle of Colonsay
JURA
Kilmartin
Crinan
Minard
Kilmichael Glen
Lochgilphead
Glendaruel
Inverbeg
Luss
Loch Lomond
Arnprior
Buchlyvie
Fintry
Tayvallich
Ardrishaig
Otter Ferry
Ardentinny
Kilmun
Inchmurrin
Arden
Clynder
Gartocharn
Balloch
Dunoon
Gourock
Greenock
Old Kilpatrick
Bearsden
GLASGOW
Port Askaig
Feolin
Colintraive
Rhubodach
Portavadie
Wemyss Bay
Skelmorlie
ISLAY
Gruinart
Ballygrant
Bruichladdich
Kilchoman
Bridgend
Bowmore
Port Charlotte
Tarbert
Port Bannatyne
Rothesay
Kennacraig
Skipness
Lochwinnoch
Largs
Cambuslang
Cumbrae
Millport
CUMBRAE
Fairlie
Claonaig
BUTE
Lochranza
Port Ellen
Ardminish
Tayinloan
KINTYRE
Pirnmill
Corrie
ARRAN
Carradale
Seamill
Ardrossan
Saltcoats
Kilmarnock
Newmilns
Brodick
Firth of Clyde
Shiskine
Lamlash
Troon
Catrine
Prestwick
Annbank
Ayr
Alloway
Whiting Bay
ATLANTIC OCEAN
Machrihanish
Campbeltown
Dunure
Maybole
Kirkoswald
Straiton
Dailly
Girvan
Barr
Carsphairn
Ballycastle
summer only
Lendalfoot
Pinwherry
Dalry
Ballantrae
Barrhill
New Galloway
Cairnryan
Newton Stewart
Stranraer
Creetown
Gatehouse of Fleet
Larne
Portpatrick
Luce Bay
Sandhead
Port William
Garlieston
BELFAST
To Douglas, Isle of Man
To Liverpool
MAP 1
MAP 2
Car ferries and terminals:
Brodick
Rothesay
Scale 1:1 300 000
0
10
20 miles
© Bartholomew Ltd 1998
These maps are for "Self Catering" locations only. For route planning and touring please use a current road atlas.

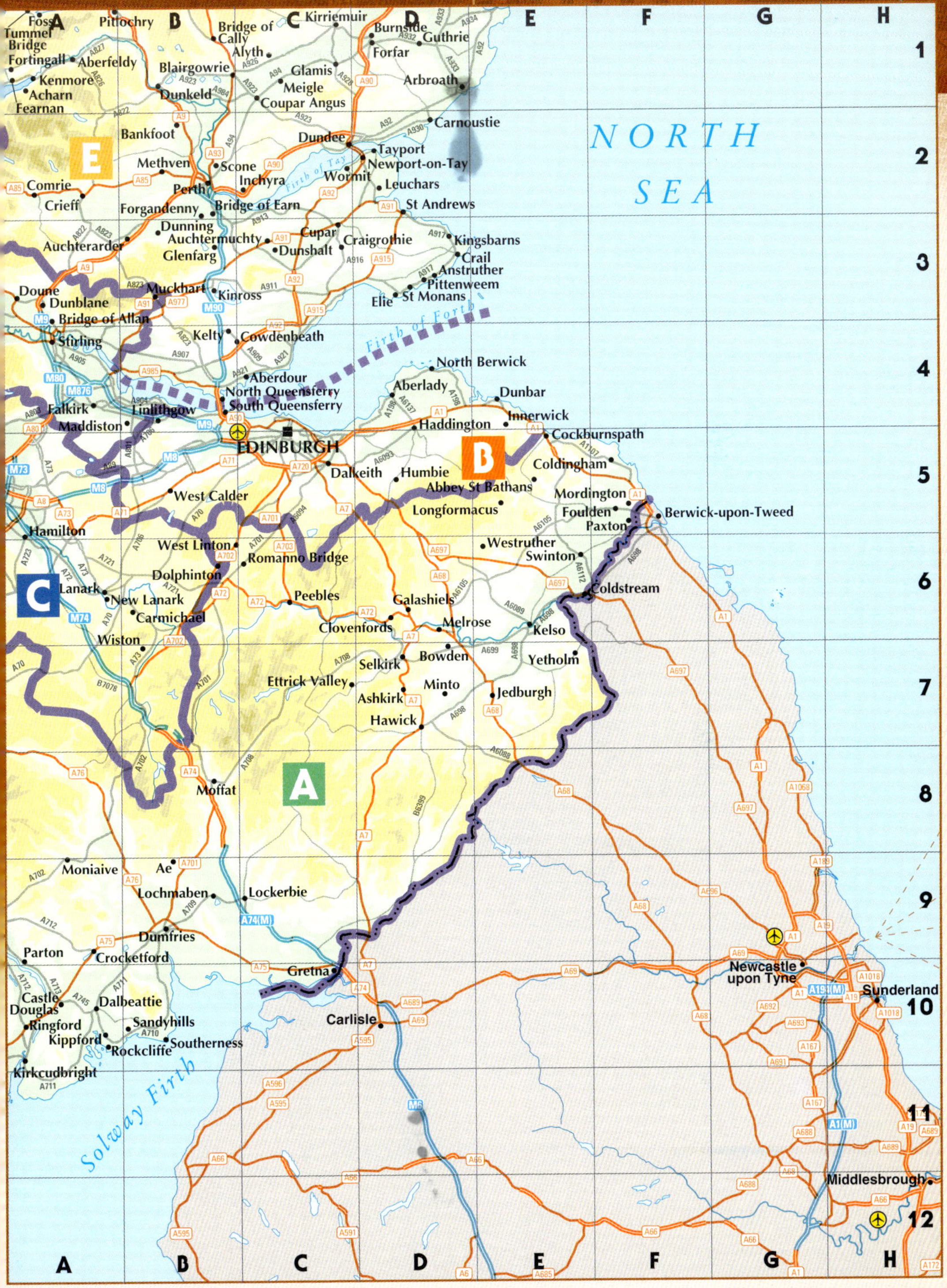
NORTH SEA
Firth of Tay
Firth of Forth
Solway Firth
A
B
C
E
Foss
Tummel Bridge
Fortingall
Aberfeldy
Kenmore
Acharn
Fearnan
Pitlochry
Bridge of Cally
Alyth
Blairgowrie
Dunkeld
Kirriemuir
Glamis
Meigle
Coupar Angus
Burnside
Forfar
Guthrie
Arbroath
Carnoustie
Dundee
Tayport
Newport-on-Tay
Wormit
Leuchars
St Andrews
Bankfoot
Methven
Scone
Inchyra
Perth
Comrie
Crieff
Forgandenny
Bridge of Earn
Dunning
Auchtermuchty
Auchterarder
Glenfarg
Cupar
Dunshalt
Craigrothie
Kingsbarns
Crail
Anstruther
Pittenweem
St Monans
Elie
Doune
Dunblane
Bridge of Allan
Muckhart
Kinross
Stirling
Kelty
Cowdenbeath
Aberdour
North Queensferry
South Queensferry
North Berwick
Aberlady
Dunbar
Innerwick
Falkirk
Maddiston
Linlithgow
EDINBURGH
Haddington
Cockburnspath
Dalkeith
Humbie
Abbey St Bathans
Coldingham
West Calder
Longformacus
Mordington
Foulden
Paxton
Berwick-upon-Tweed
Hamilton
West Linton
Romanno Bridge
Westruther
Swinton
Lanark
Dolphinton
New Lanark
Carmichael
Peebles
Galashiels
Coldstream
Clovenfords
Melrose
Kelso
Wiston
Selkirk
Bowden
Yetholm
Ettrick Valley
Minto
Ashkirk
Jedburgh
Hawick
Moffat
Moniaive
Ae
Lochmaben
Lockerbie
Dumfries
Parton
Crocketford
Gretna
Castle Douglas
Dalbeattie
Ringford
Sandyhills
Kippford
Rockcliffe
Southerness
Kirkcudbright
Carlisle
Newcastle upon Tyne
Sunderland
Middlesbrough

Map 3

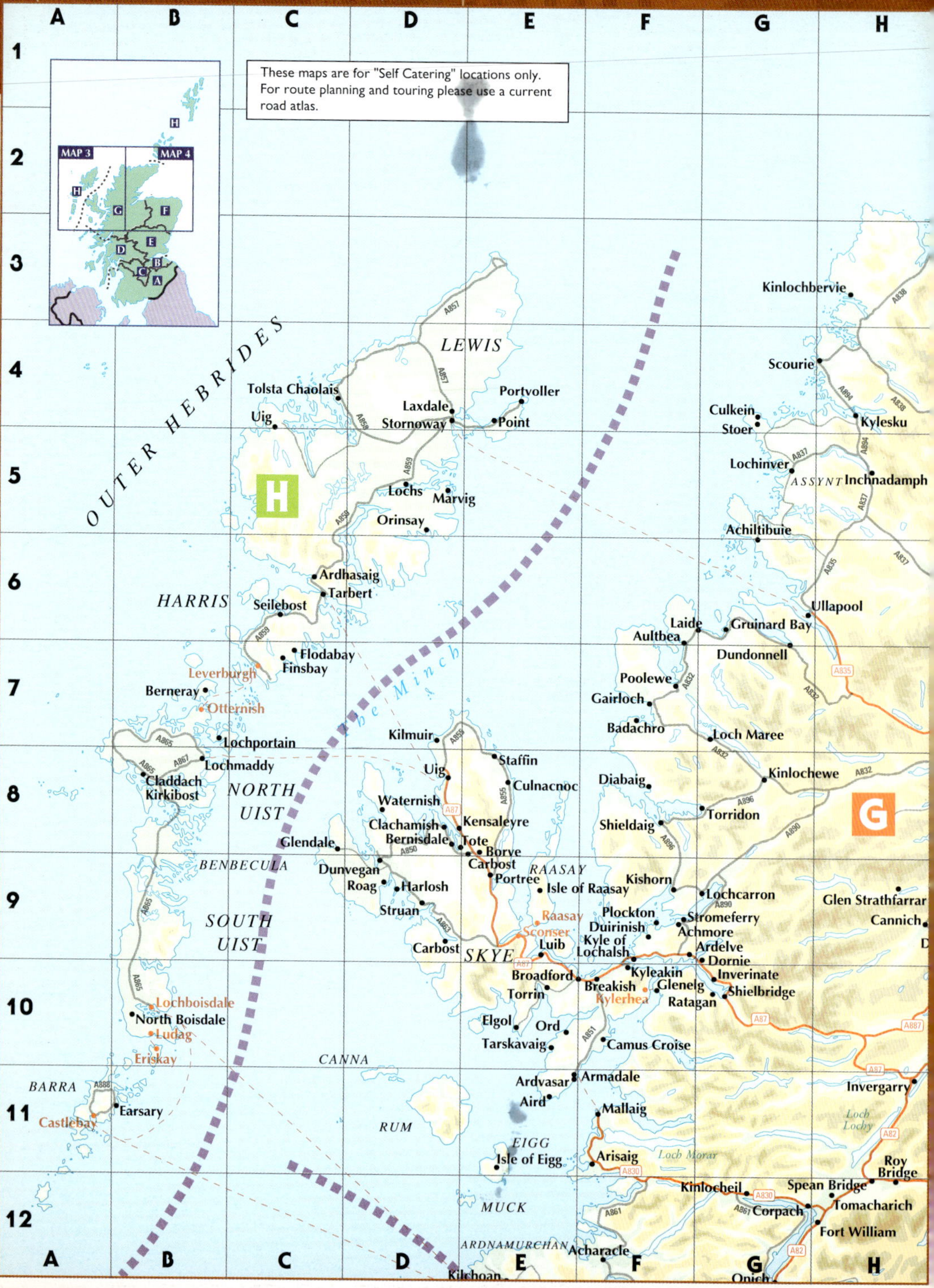
These maps are for "Self Catering" locations only. For route planning and touring please use a current road atlas.
A B C D E F G H
1 2 3 4 5 6 7 8 9 10 11 12
MAP 3
MAP 4
OUTER HEBRIDES
LEWIS
HARRIS
NORTH UIST
BENBECULA
SOUTH UIST
BARRA
SKYE
RAASAY
CANNA
RUM
EIGG
MUCK
ARDNAMURCHAN
ASSYNT
The Minch
Kinlochbervie
Scourie
Culkein
Stoer
Kylesku
Lochinver
Inchnadamph
Achiltibuie
Ullapool
Laide
Gruinard Bay
Aultbea
Dundonnell
Poolewe
Gairloch
Badachro
Loch Maree
Kinlochewe
Diabaig
Torridon
Shieldaig
Kishorn
Lochcarron
Glen Strathfarrar
Cannich
Plockton
Stromeferry
Achmore
Duirinish
Kyle of Lochalsh
Ardelve
Dornie
Kyleakin
Inverinate
Shielbridge
Glenelg
Ratagan
Kylerhea
Breakish
Broadford
Torrin
Luib
Elgol
Ord
Tarskavaig
Camus Croise
Ardvasar
Armadale
Aird
Mallaig
Arisaig
Loch Morar
Isle of Eigg
Kinlocheil
Spean Bridge
Roy Bridge
Tomacharich
Corpach
Fort William
Invergarry
Loch Lochy
Acharacle
Kilchoan
Onich
Tolsta Chaolais
Uig
Laxdale
Stornoway
Portvoller
Point
Lochs
Marvig
Orinsay
Ardhasaig
Tarbert
Seilebost
Flodabay
Finsbay
Leverburgh
Berneray
Otternish
Lochportain
Lochmaddy
Claddach Kirkibost
Kilmuir
Uig
Staffin
Culnacnoc
Waternish
Clachamish
Kensaleyre
Bernisdale
Tote
Borve
Carbost
Portree
Glendale
Dunvegan
Roag
Harlosh
Struan
Carbost
Isle of Raasay
Raasay
Sconser
Lochboisdale
North Boisdale
Ludag
Eriskay
Earsary
Castlebay
A857
A858
A859
A865
A867
A855
A87
A850
A863
A851
A830
A861
A82
A887
A890
A896
A832
A835
A837
A838
A894
A888

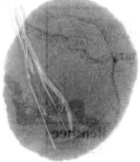

Signs you need to know
Taste of Scotland

FROM SCOTLAND'S NATURAL LARDER COMES A WEALTH OF FINE FLAVOURS.

The sea yields crab and lobster, mussels and oysters, haddock and herring to be eaten fresh or smoked. From the lochs and rivers come salmon and trout.

Scotch beef and lamb, venison and game are of prime quality, often adventurously combined with local vegetables or with wild fruits such as redcurrants and brambles. Raspberries and strawberries are cultivated to add their sweetness to trifles and shortcakes, and to the home-made jams that are an essential part of Scottish afternoon tea.

The Scots have a sweet tooth, and love all kinds of baking – rich, crisp shortbread, scones, fruit cakes and gingerbreads. Crumbly oatcakes make the ideal partner for Scottish cheeses, which continue to develop from their ancient farming origins into new – and very successful – styles.

And in over a hundred distilleries, barley, yeast and pure spring water come together miraculously to create malt whisky – the water of life.

Many Scottish hotels and restaurants pride themselves on the use they make of these superb natural ingredients – around 400 are members of the Taste of Scotland Scheme which encourages the highest culinary standards, use of Scottish produce and a warm welcome to visitors. Look for the Stockpot symbol at establishments, or write to Taste of Scotland for a copy of their guide.

In Shops		£7.99
By Post:	UK	£8.50
	Europe	£9.50
	US	£11.00

Taste of Scotland Scheme
33 Melville Street
EDINBURGH
EH3 7JF
Tel: 0131 220 1900
Fax: 0131 220 6102
e-mail: tastescotland@sol.co.uk
www.taste-of-scotland.com

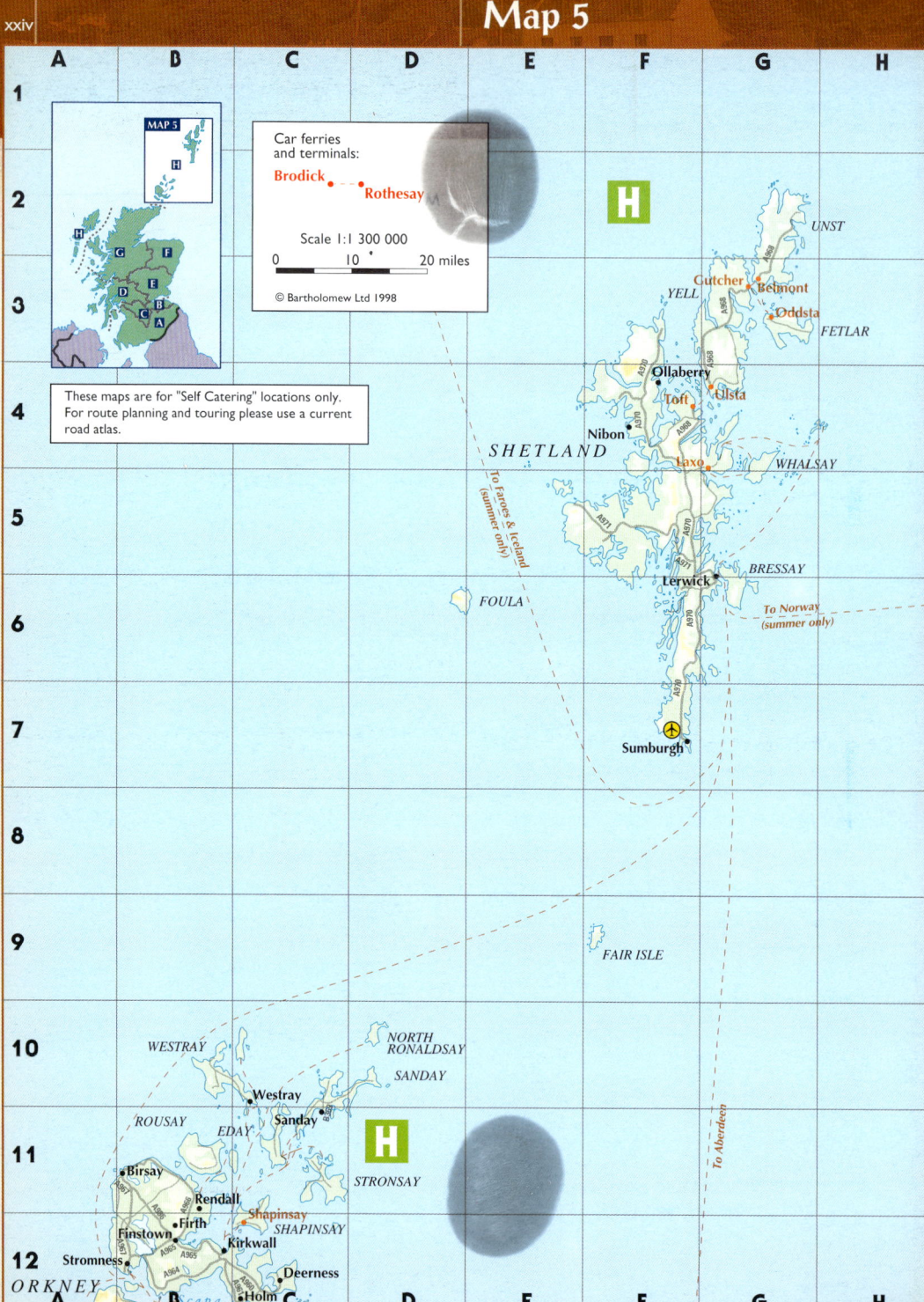

Where to Stay | Self Catering

2000

Welcome to Scotland

South of Scotland: Ayrshire and Arran, Dumfries and Galloway, Scottish Borders

Nestling quietly between the English border and busy central belt of lowland Scotland lies a magical area offering remarkable variety. Stretching from the dramatic coastal headlands of Berwickshire, through the tranquillity of the Tweed Valley, and across the high remote wilderness of the Galloway Hills to the beautiful Clyde coast, there is something for everyone here.

Beginning in the South West there is great walking country to be found, including the 212 mile coast-to-coast, Southern Upland Way, which begins at Portpatrick, and takes you up through the Galloway Forest Park, across the Moffat Hills and past Wanlockhead, Scotland's highest village. Back on the coast the tidal mudflaps and sandy beaches of the Solway Firth are dotted with pretty villages and seaside towns including Kirkcudbright, which has a long tradition of attracting artists. Other outstanding attractions are Caerlaverock Castle, Sweetheart Abbey, Dundrennan Abbey and of course Gretna Green where you can visit the famous Old Smithy.

The Ayrshire coast has some excellent holiday attractions for all the family, including Vikingar! in Largs, which uses the latest multimedia techniques and both the Scottish Maritime Museum and the Magnum Leisure Centre in Irvine. For a taste of some traditional Scottish culture you can visit many attractions connected with Burns including a visit to his birthplace in Alloway, and a chance to relive some of the drama of his life at the Tam O'Shanter Experience. For those who prefer a sporting break there is horse-racing, ice-hockey, football and golf, with over forty golf courses in Ayrshire and Arran, including world famous courses at Troon, Turnberry and Prestwick.

South of Scotland: Ayrshire and Arran, Dumfries and Galloway, Scottish Borders

South of Scotland: Ayrshire and Arran, Dumfries and Galloway, Scottish Borders

The borderlands of Scotland were fought over until the 17th century and the result is a landscape littered with the ruins of magnificent abbeys and towering castles where dark legends and ancient folklore abound. Set within the often wild, hilly countryside are market towns, stately homes and a tapestry of rich agricultural land. The distinctive triple peaks of the Eildon Hills can be seen for many miles standing above the Tweed, one of Scotland's most famous salmon-fishing rivers. Close by are the magnificent ruins of Melrose Abbey. The town also contains Priorwood Garden, the Roman Trimontium Exhibition and is the birthplace of the famous Rugby Sevens tournament.

Close by you can journey back in time by visiting a host of historical sites including Sir Walter Scott's fabulous house at Abbotsford, the graceful ruins of Dryburgh Abbey and Melrose Abbey and Smailholm Tower. The colourful past of the border towns is also brought to life in places like Hawick and Selkirk when the locals re-enact the Common Ridings by dressing up in period costume and riding around the burgh boundaries.

South of Scotland: Ayrshire and Arran, Dumfries and Galloway, Scottish Borders

Further east is the market town of Kelso where the stunning architecture and interiors of Floors Castle and Mellerstain House, are a must-see on any visitors itinerary. The landscape from here offers a beautiful mosaic of farmland, and finally ends at the dramatic cliffs of St Abbs, where the North Sea pounds the towering headland of black volcanic rock.

Events
South of Scotland

Jan-Dec
The Land of Creativity
Scottish Borders
Marking the new millennium, a year long programme of events.
Contact: Scottish Borders Tourist Board
Tel: 01750 20555

29 May - 4 June
Dumfries & Galloway Arts Festival
11 Centres from Moffat to Stranraer.
Contact: Dumfries & Galloway Arts Association
Tel: 01387 260447

5-11 June
Isle of Arran Folk Festival
Various venues around the Isle of Arran.
Contact: Ian or Maggie Frame
Tel: 01770 302623

2-9 Sep
Scottish Borders Festival of Walking
Based in Selkirk
Contact: Roger Smith
Tel: 01896 758991

8-10 Sep
Borders Festival of Jazz & Blues
Weekend of jazz entertainment in various venues in the border town of Hawick.
Contact: Jim Dunlop
Tel: 01450 377278

*provisional dates

Area Tourist Boards

South of Scotland: Ayrshire and Arran, Dumfries and Galloway, Scottish Borders

Ayrshire & Arran Tourist Board

Ayrshire & Arran Tourist Board
Burns House
Burns Statue Square
Ayr KA7 1UP

Tel: (01292) 262555
Fax: (01292) 269555
Web: www.ayrshire-arran.com

Dumfries & Galloway Tourist Board

Dumfries & Galloway
Tourist Board
64 Whitesands
Dumfries DG1 2RS

Tel: (01387) 245550
Fax: (01387) 245551
Web: www.galloway.co.uk

Scottish Borders Tourist Board

Scottish Borders Tourist Board
Shepherds Mills
Whinfield Road
Selkirk TD7 5DT

Tel: (01750) 20555
Fax: (01750) 21886
Web: www.holiday.scotland.net

Tourist Information Centres

South of Scotland: Ayrshire and Arran, Dumfries and Galloway, Scottish Borders

Ayshire & Arran Tourist Board

Ayr
Burns House
Burns Statue Square
Tel: (01292) 288688
Jan-Dec

Brodick
The Pier
Isle of Arran
Tel: (01770) 302140/302401
Jan-Dec

Girvan
Bridge Street
Tel: (01465) 714950
Easter-Oct

Irvine
New Street
Tel: (01294) 313886
Jan-Dec

Kilmarnock
62 Bank Street
Tel: (01563) 539090
Jan-Dec

Largs
Promenade
Tel: (01475) 673765
Jan-Dec

Millport
28 Stuart Street
Isle of Cumbrae
Tel: (01475) 530753
Easter-Oct

Troon
Municipal Buildings
South Beach
Tel: (01292) 317696
Easter-Oct

Dumfries & Galloway Tourist Board

Castle Douglas
Markethill Car Park
Tel: (01556) 502611
Easter-Oct

Dumfries
Whitesands
Tel: (01387) 253862
Jan-Dec

Gatehouse of Fleet
Car Park
Tel: (01557) 814212
Easter-Oct

Gretna Green
Old Blacksmith's Shop
Tel: (01461) 337834

Kirkcudbright
Harbour Square
Tel: (01557) 330494
Easter-end Oct

Moffat
Churchgate
Tel: (01683) 220620
Easter-end Oct

Newton Stewart
Dashwood Square
Tel: (01671) 402431
Easter-Oct

Stranraer
Burns House
28 Harbour Street
Tel: (01776) 702595
Jan-Dec

Scottish Borders Tourist Board

Coldstream
High Street
Tel: (01890) 882607
Easter-Oct

Eyemouth
Auld Kirk
Manse Road
Tel: (018907) 50678
April-Oct

Galashiels
St John Street
Tel: (01896) 755551
Easter-Oct

Hawick
Drumlanrig's Tower
Tel: (01450) 372547
Easter-Oct

Jedburgh
Murray's Green
Tel: (01835) 863435/863688
Jan-Dec

Kelso
Town House
The Square
Tel: (01573) 223464
Easter-Oct

Melrose
Abbey House
Tel: (01896) 822555
Easter-Oct

Peebles
High Street
Tel: (01721) 720138
Jan-Dec

Selkirk
Halliwell's House
Tel: (01750) 20054
Easter-Oct

ANNBANK – CORRIE, ISLE OF ARRAN

SOUTH OF SCOTLAND

Annbank, Ayrshire — Map Ref: 1G7

SELF CATERING ★★★★

Mr & Mrs I Hendry
Gadgirth Estate, Gadgirth Mains, by Ayr, Ayrshire, KA6 5AJ
Tel/Fax: 01292 520721
E-mail: iain/karen@gadgirthestate.freeserve.co.uk

Gadgirth Estate welcome you to its beautiful 28 acres of grounds with a selection of converted stables and courtyard cottages, boasting many features including exposed beams and open fire places. This picturesque setting, only 10 minutes by car from Ayr has lovely picnic areas, wooded riverside walks and estate fishing.

6 log cabins, 6 cottages, 1-2 pub rms, 1-3 bedrms (grd flr avail), sleeps 4-6, total sleeping capacity 26, min let weekend, £120.00-£500.00, Jan-Dec, bus 1 ml, rail 5 mls, ferry 6 mls, airport 5 mls

Brodick, Isle of Arran — Map Ref: 1F7

AUCHRANNIE COUNTRY CLUB
BRODICK, ISLE OF ARRAN KA27 8BZ
Tel: 01770 302020   Fax: 01770 302812
e.mail: info@auchrannie.co.uk Web: www.auchrannie.co.uk
★★★★★ **SELF CATERING**

These exclusive lodges are delightfully situated within Auchrannie's unique estate. The lodges are outstandingly furnished, and equipped with all modern amenities. For dining out there's a choice of the renowned Garden Restaurant or the excellent Brambles Bistro. Complimentary membership of the Country Club's superb swimming pool and leisure facilities included. Price from £330 (winter) and £775 (summer) per unit per week.

SELF CATERING ★★★★★

Auchrannie Country Club
Brodick, Isle of Arran, KA27 8BZ
Tel: 01770 302020/302234 (eve) Fax: 01770 302812
E-mail: info@auchrannie.co.uk Web: www.auchrannie.co.uk

These exclusive lodges are delightfully situated within the unique Auchrannie Estate. The lodges are outstandingly furnished, many with sauna, whirlpool bath. For dining out there's a choice of the renowned Garden Restaurant or the excellent Brambles Bistro. Complimentary membership of the Country Club's superb swimming pool and leisure facilities included.

8 lodges, 1 pub rm, 2-3 bedrms (grd flr avail), sleeps 4-8, total sleeping capacity 40, from £330.00 per week, £120.00 short breaks (off-peak), Jan-Dec, bus 400 yds, ferry 1 ml.

SELF CATERING ★★

Mrs Alison Currie
Castleview, Invercloy, Brodick, Isle of Arran, KA27 8AJ
Tel: 01770 302268

Two flats right on the sea front overlooking Brodick Bay and Goatfell. Close to ferry and local bus stop. Central for all attractions. Private off-street parking.

2 flats, 1 pub rm, 3 bedrms, sleeps 2-5, total sleeping capacity 5, min let weekend, £100.00-£300.00, Jan-Dec, bus nearby, ferry ½ ml

Corrie, Isle of Arran — Map Ref: 1F6

SELF CATERING ★★★ UP TO ★★★★

Mr J Lees
Cir Mhor, Sannox, Isle of Arran, KA27 8JD
Tel: 01770 810248/810661 Fax: 01770 810248
E-mail: jimlees@connectfree.co.uk

Extensively refurbished red sandstone cottages, enclosed rose garden. All rooms have views over Firth of Clyde. Set within the conservation area of Corrie.

1 cottage, 1 pub rm, 3 bedrms (grd flr avail), sleeps 6, £175.00-£345.00, Jan-Dec, bus nearby, ferry 6 mls

Important: Prices stated are estimates and may be subject to amendments

SOUTH OF SCOTLAND — A

CORRIE, ISLE OF ARRAN – LAMLASH, ISLE OF ARRAN

Corrie, Isle of Arran

Mr & Mrs Thorburn
Tigh-na-Achaidh, Corrie, Isle of Arran
Tel/Fax: 01770 810208

★★★★ SELF CATERING

Map Ref: 1F6

1 cottage, sleeps 2, £180.00-£280.00, Jan-Dec, bus nearby, ferry 5 mls

Small cottage adjoining owner's house in elevated position with panoramic views over Firth of Clyde. Private garden available. Off road parking. Non smoking house.

Kildonan, Isle of Arran

Mrs E MacPherson
15f Mariners Whark, North Harbourst, Ayrshire, KA8 8AA
Tel: 01292 611140

★★ SELF CATERING

Map Ref: 1F7

1 house, 2 pub rms, 3 bedrms, sleeps 5, £250.00-£300.00, Easter-Sep, bus nearby

Semi detached house built in the 1880s with south facing views to Pladda, Ailsa Craig and over the Firth of Clyde to the Ayrshire Coast. It has a large garden and is close to the silver sands beach.

Lamlash, Isle of Arran

Middleton Caravan & Camping Park
Lamlash, Isle of Arran, PA27 8NQ
Tel: 01770 600255/600251

★★★ HOLIDAY PARK

Map Ref: 1F7

Park accommodation: 70
15 tourers from £8.00 and 15 motors from £7.50 and 40 tents from £7.50. Total Touring Pitches 70.
7 Holiday Caravans to let, sleep 4-6 £125.00-350.00, total sleeping capacity 36, min let Weekend/Midweek.

7 acres, grassy, level, sheltered, hard-standing, Apr-Oct, latest time of arrival 2130, overnight holding area. Extra charge for electricity, awnings, showers.

Turn left at Ferry at Brodick A841 for 4 miles to Lamlash pass Police Station on left over bridge 1st turn on left ¼ mile to Park.

Schofield
Craig Dhu, Lamlash, Isle of Arran, KA27 8LH
Tel/Fax: 01770 600276

★★★ SELF CATERING

2 cottages, 2 pub rms, 2 bedrms, sleeps 4-6, total sleeping capacity 10, £150.00-£300.00, Jan-Dec, bus 1 ml, ferry 4 mls

Semi-detached two storey cottages adjoining main Edwardian house. On seafront in quiet South East location. 0.5 mile from village centre with tennis courts, bowling green, golf course and bike hire all within walking distance.

Miss E Sloan
Westfield, Lamlash, Isle of Arran, KA27 8NN
Tel: 01770 600428

★★ SELF CATERING

1 cottage, 2 pub rms, 2 bedrms, sleeps 4, £200.00-£300.00, Feb-Nov, bus nearby, rail 18 mls, ferry 4 mls, airport 39 mls

Semi-detached cottage with its own patio. Situated on the south side of the village with views to the hills. Close to all village amenities such as tennis, bowling green and shops. The Lamlash Golf Club is one mile away. B&B also available.

VAT is shown at 17.5%: changes in this rate may affect prices.

Key to symbols is on back flap.

MACHRIE, ISLE OF ARRAN – ASHKIRK

 SOUTH OF SCOTLAND

Machrie, Isle of Arran — Map Ref: 1E7

Mr Simon Boscawen
Jackson's Cottage, Rudgwick, Sussex, RH12 3AB
Tel: 01403 822364 Fax: 01403 823743

3 houses, 2 pub rms, 2-6 bedrms (grd flr avail), sleeps 4-11, total sleeping capacity 27, £210.00-£605.00, Jan-Dec, bus nearby, ferry 10 mls

Three farmhouses, all in their own grounds, with extensive children's play areas. On the west coast of the island, with fabulous views.

Whiting Bay, Isle of Arran — Map Ref: 1F7

Cooper Angus Park
Whiting Bay, Isle of Arran, KA17 8QP
Tel: 01770 700381 Fax: 01770 700370

Park accommodation: 46

18 Holiday Caravans to let, sleep 4-6 from £140.00, total sleeping capacity 96, min let weekend, Mar-Oct.

4½ acres, grassy, level, sheltered, Mar-Oct, prior booking in peak periods.

Leisure facilities:

On disembarkation from ferry head S. 8½ mls to Whiting Bay. Park is on sea shore.

Mr Brian Francis
Heatherhill, Middle Road, Whiting Bay, Isle of Arran, KA27 8PS
Tel: 01770 700355
E-mail: brianfrancis@heatherhill.swinternet.co.uk

2 chalets, 1 pub rm, 3 bedrms, sleeps 6, total sleeping capacity 12, £105.00-£325.00, Jan-Dec, bus nearby, ferry 8 mls

Timber clad chalets, in elevated position, on a small quiet site overlooking the Bay. Many interesting walks in local area.

Pete & Barbara Rawlin
View Bank House, Golf Course Road, Whiting Bay,
Isle of Arran, KA2 8QT
Tel: 01770 700326

1 bungalow, 2 pub rms, 3 bedrms (All grd.floor), sleeps 6, £300.00-£600.00, Jan-Dec, bus nearby, ferry 8 mls

Newly built spacious bungalow in attractive garden with patio areas and barbecue. Only 200 yards from the centre of the village with Bowling Green, Golf Club, restaurant and shops. Situated on a secluded elevated position overlooking Whiting Bay and extensive views towards Ayrshire Coastline.

Ashkirk, Selkirkshire — Map Ref: 2D7

Mr & Mrs Christopher Davies
The Davies Partnership, Synton Mains Farm, Ashkirk,
nr Selkirk, TD7 4PA
Tel/Fax: 01750 32388

2 cottages, 1 pub rm, 3 bedrms (grd flr avail), sleeps 6, total sleeping capacity 12, £140.00-£300.00, Jan-Dec, bus ¼ ml, rail 44 mls, airport 45 mls

Recently renovated semi-detached cottages situated to one side of farm steading. Peaceful setting, yet central for all Borders attractions, including golf, fishing, riding and an ideal situation for touring the Borders. One cottage suitable for guests with mobility difficulties.

Important: Prices stated are estimates and may be subject to amendments

SOUTH OF SCOTLAND

ASHKIRK – AYR

Ashkirk, Selkirkshire

★★ UP TO ★★★★ — SELF CATERING

Mrs Hunter
Headshaw Farm, Ashkirk, by Selkirk, Selkirkshire
Tel: 01750 32233 Fax: 07071 781891
E-mail: headshaw@aol.com

Three traditional, and very well equipped stone terraced cottages on working farm with enclosed garden. Also spacious modern bungalow with own garden, equally well equipped in rural setting close by. Halfway between Selkirk and Hawick. Own fishing loch plus riding and golf nearby. Bicycle hire and stabling available by prior arrangement.

Map Ref: 2D7

3 cottages, 1 bungalow, 1-2 pub rms, 2-3 bedrms (grd flr avail), sleeps 4-7, total sleeping capacity 22, £120.00-£411.00, Jan-Dec, bus ¼ ml, rail 44 mls, airport 45 mls

---

Auchenmalg, Wigtownshire

★★★ — HOLIDAY PARK

Cock Inn Caravan Park
Auchenmalg, Wigtownshire, DG8 0JT
Tel: 01581 500227

7 acres, mixed, Mar-Oct, prior booking in peak periods, latest time of arrival 2200, overnight holding area. Extra charge for electricity.

Map Ref: 1G10

Park accommodation: 120

35 tourers £6.50-8.25 or 35 motors £6.50-8.25 or 35 tents £7.00.
Total Touring Pitches 35.
5 Holiday Caravans to let, sleep 6, total sleeping capacity 30, min let 2 nights.

Leisure facilities:

Park is on A747 Glenluce-Port William road, 5 mls from A75 Newton Stewart-Stranraer road.

Ayr

★★ — SELF CATERING

Mrs J Cochrane
2 Garrock Hill Cottages, Coalhall, Ayr, Ayrshire, KA6 6NA
Tel: 01292 591321

Semi-detached cottage in rural surroundings. Ideally situated for touring Burns Country, Dumfries and Galloway. Bed linen and towels available on request.

Map Ref: 1G7

1 house, 1 pub rm, 3 bedrms, sleeps 6, £200.00-£300.00, Jan-Dec, bus nearby

---

★★★★ — HOLIDAY PARK

Craig Tara Holiday Park
Ayr, KA7 4LB
Tel: 01292 265141 Fax: 01292 445206
Web: www.haven-holidays.co.uk
Booking Enquiries: Haven Reservations 1 Park Lane, Hemel Hempstead, Herts, HP2 4GL
Tel: 0870 242 2222

Easter-Oct, 168 acres, slightly sloping, grassy. Prior booking recommended.

Park accommodation: 875

Caravans and apartments to let. Prices from £175.00-£659.00 approx.

†

Leisure facilities:

Take A77 to Ayr/Stranraer. At Bankfield r/about, take 2nd right into Doonholm Rd. L into Monument Rd, 1st R into Greenfield Av. L at T-junt to Heads of Ayr. Park is 2 mls on right.

★★★ — SELF CATERING

Agnes Y Gemmell
Dunduff Farm, Dunure, Ayr, Ayrshire, KA7 4LH
Tel: 01292 500225 Fax: 01292 500222

Bothy Cottage is ideal for two, situated five miles south of Ayr at the coastal village of Dunure on a working farm, overlooking the Firth of Clyde to Arran. It has a lounge, kitchen, 2 double bedrooms one of which is ensuite. Ideal for Culzean Castle, Burns Heritage, Galloway Forest Farm Park and many more activities. A peaceful retreat for those wishing to capture a country coastal farm atmosphere at its best.

1 cottage, 1 pub rm, 2 bedrms (All grd.floor), sleeps 4, £180.00-£250.00, Jan-Dec, bus 1 ml, rail 6 mls

VAT is shown at 17.5%: changes in this rate may affect prices.

Key to symbols is on back flap.

AYR – BY AYR

SOUTH OF SCOTLAND

Ayr
Map Ref: 1G7

Anne Hardie
Woodcroft, 23 Midton Road, Ayr, KA7 2SF
Tel/Fax: 01292 264383

SELF CATERING ★★★ BRONZE

Cottage with all accommodation on the one level, situated in quiet residential area, yet convenient for the railway station and the town centre with all its amenities. Conservatory at the rear of the cottage overlooking a colourful private garden.

1 cottage, 2 bedrms (All grd.floor), sleeps 4-6, £120.00-£350.00, Jan-Dec, bus nearby, rail nearby, airport 2 mls

---

Heads of Ayr Caravan Park
Dunure Road, Ayr, KA7 4LD
Tel: 01292 442269 Fax: 01292 500298

HOLIDAY PARK ★★★

8 acres, grassy, level, Mar-Oct, prior booking in peak periods, latest time of arrival 2300. Extra charge for electricity, awnings.

Park accommodation: 161
15 tourers £8.50-11.50 or 5 motors £7.50-9.50 or 5 tents £7.50-9.50. Total Touring Pitches 20.
10 Holiday Caravans to let, sleep 4-8 £140.00-340.00, total sleeping capacity 60, min let 2 nights.

Leisure facilities:
5 mls S of Ayr on A719.

Mrs Isla McLellan
5 Park Circus, Ayr, KA7 2DJ
Tel: 01292 287065 Fax: 01292 288228

SELF CATERING ★★★

Spacious first floor apartment in attractive Victorian town house. Situated in quiet tree lined street, close to beach, within walking distance from bus and train station. Ideal base for golfing, fishing, racing, island hopping and exploring Ayrshire and Arran.

1 flat, 2 pub rms, 3 bedrms, sleeps 6, £300.00-£360.00, Jun-Sep, bus 1/2 ml, rail 1/4 ml, ferry 15 mls, airport 6 mls

---

Sundrum Castle Holiday Park
by Ayr, Ayrshire, KA6 5JH
Tel: 01292 570057 Fax: 01292 570065
Booking Enquiries: Haven Reservations 1 Park Lane, Hemel Hempstead, Herts, HP2 4GL
Tel: 0870 242 2222

HOLIDAY PARK ★★★

23 acres, mixed, Apr-Oct, prior booking recommended in peak periods, overnight holding area. Extra charge for electricity, dogs.

Park accommodation: 358
Tourers, motorhomes and tents welcome. Total touring pitches £8.00-£20.50 approx. Contact park direct.
Holiday Caravans to let, sleep 2-8. £141.00-£569.00 per week approx. Contact reservations.

Leisure facilities:
Take A70 from Ayr for approx. 3 mls. Park signposted on road. Or A70 Cumnock to Ayr 1/2 ml W of Coylton.

---

by Ayr
Map Ref: 1G7

Middlemuir Park
Tarbolton, Ayr, Ayrshire, KA5 5NR
Tel: 01292 541647 Fax: 01292 541649

HOLIDAY PARK ★★★

17 acres, grassy, hard-standing, sheltered, Mar-Oct, prior booking in peak periods, overnight holding area. Extra charge for electricity, awnings.

Park accommodation: 161
20 tourers from £7.00 or 20 motors from £7.00. Total Touring Pitches 20. No tents.
12 Holiday Caravans to let, sleep 4-6 £140.00-300.00, total sleeping capacity 58, min let 2 nights.

Leisure facilities:
A75 from Dumfries, then A76 Kilmarnock route to Mauchline traffic lights, turn left onto Ayr rd B743 4 mls on right.

Important: Prices stated are estimates and may be subject to amendments

A SOUTH OF SCOTLAND

BALLANTRAE – CASTLE DOUGLAS

Ballantrae, Ayrshire

Map Ref: 1F9

★★ SELF CATERING

Mrs M Drummond
Ardstinchar Cottage, Ballantrae, Ayrshire, KA26 0NA
Tel: 01465 831343

1 cottage, 1 pub rm, 3 bedrms (grd flr avail), sleeps 6, min let weekend, £130.00–£250.00, Jan-Dec, bus 2 mls, rail 15 mls, ferry 12 mls, airport 35 mls

Balnowlart Lodge is a tastefully furnished cottage offering 'home for home' comforts with superb views. Located in the peaceful Stinchar Valley with panoramic scenery, the cottage is ideal to enjoy beautiful Galloway and Ayrshire Burn's Country. Many golf courses nearby - 2 miles from shops, beach, hotels. Many country walks.

★★ SELF CATERING

Mrs R McKinley
Laggan Dairy, Ballantrae, Ayrshire, KA26 0JZ
Tel: 01465 831426

1 cottage, 1 pub rm, 3 bedrms (All grd.floor), sleeps 8, £120.00-£240.00, Mar-Nov, bus ¼ ml, rail 12 mls, ferry 11 mls, airport 60 mls

The cottage on our working dairy farm offers comfortable accomodation with open fire in the living room. Situated in quiet unspoilt area, 1 mile from Ballantrae and the coast. Ideal for walking with abundant wildlife and birdwatching.

Barr, by Girvan, Ayrshire

Map Ref: 1G8

★★ UP TO ★★★★ SELF CATERING

Mrs V Dunlop
Glengennet Farm, Barr, by Girvan, Ayrshire, KA26 9TY
Tel/Fax: 01465 861220
Web: www.dalbeattie.com/farmholidays/qggfsc.htm

1 house, 1 cottage, 1 pub rm, 1-4 bedrms (grd flr avail), sleeps 2-8, total sleeping capacity 10, min let 2 nights, £150.00–£490.00, Jan-Dec, bus 2 mls, rail 9 mls

Detached renovated period farmhouse and self catering cottage adjoining Glengennet farmhouse situated in a rural location in peaceful Stinchar Valley. Conservation village with hotel and shops nearby. Ideal for walking in the Galloway Forest and Glen Trool. Good base for visiting Culzean Castle, golfing touring or just relaxing in unspoilt south west Scotland.

Cairnryan, Wigtownshire

Map Ref: 1F10

★★★★ HOLIDAY PARK

Cairnryan "Caravan" Park
Cairnryan, Wigtownshire, DG9 8QX
Tel: 01581 200231 Fax: 01581 200207

Park accommodation: 110

15 tourers £8.50 or 15 motors £8.50 or 10 tents £5.00. Total Touring Pitches 15.

5 Holiday Caravans to let, sleep 4 £100.00-245.00, total sleeping capacity 20, min let 1 night.

7½ acres, grassy, level, sheltered, Mar-Oct, latest time of arrival 2200. Extra charge for electricity, showers.

Leisure facilities:

5 mls N of Stranraer on A77 opposite P&O Ferry Terminal, Cairnryan.

Castle Douglas, Kirkcudbrightshire

Map Ref: 2A10

★ UP TO ★★★ SELF CATERING

Mrs Ball
Barncrosh Farm, Castle Douglas, Kirkcudbrightshire, DG7 1TX
Tel: 01556 680216 Fax: 01556 680 442
E-mail: enq@barncros.demon.co.uk

9 flats, 3 cottages, 3 bungalows, 1-2 pub rms, 1-4 bedrms (grd flr avail), sleeps 2-9, total sleeping capacity 68, min let 1 night, £90.00-£500.00, Jan-Dec, bus ½ ml, rail 23 mls, ferry 55 mls, airport 86 mls

Selection of properties on working farm in peaceful country setting just off A75. Castle Douglas 4 miles (6kms).

VAT is shown at 17.5%: changes in this rate may affect prices.

Key to symbols is on back flap.

CASTLE DOUGLAS

SOUTH OF SCOTLAND

Castle Douglas, Kirkcudbrightshire

Map Ref: 2A10

★★ **SELF CATERING**

Mrs Wendy Bendall
Dalvadie, Meikle Knox Farm, Castle Douglas, DG7 1NS,
Tel: 01556 503336

1 cottage, 2 pub rms, 3 bedrms, sleeps 7, £150.00-£250.00, Apr-Oct, bus 1 ml, rail 23 mls, airport 48 mls

Former farm workers cottage situated between Castle Douglas and Kirkcudbright, one mile from the A75, and ideally placed for touring the Solway Coast and the Galloway Hills.

★★ **SELF CATERING**

Mrs Helen Hutton
Crumquhill Bungalow, Ringford, Castle Douglas, DG7 2AF
Tel: 01557 820269

1 chalet, sleeps 2, £80.00-£145.00, Jan-Dec, bus 1 ml

This comfortable and compact chalet with magnificent views over the Galloway countryside is ideally placed for exploring South West Scotland. Equidistant from Kirkcudbright, Castle Douglas and Gatehouse of Fleet.

★★ **SELF CATERING**

Mr & Mrs N McMillan
Old Stakeford, College Road, Dumfries Tel: 01387 254647
E-mail: neil@nandp.demon.co.uk
Web: www.nandp.demon.co.uk

2 separate wings of country house, 2-3 pub rms, 3-5 bedrms (grd flr avail), sleeps 12, total sleeping capacity 24, £325.00-£500.00, Apr-Oct, Xmas/New Year, bus 1 ml, rail 18 mls, ferry 40 mls, airport 70 mls

Ideal for medium to very large parties. Two wings sleep 14 and 12. Total 26. Some disability access - please enquire. Dogs welcome. 40 acres informal wooded grounds, free game fishing. Unspoilt, historic area - coast, hills, wildlife, castles, gardens and golf, riding, cycling and walking. Good shopping, restaurant, pubs 3 miles. Contact Neil and Penny McMillan, tel. 01387 254647.

★★★ **SELF CATERING**

Mrs A Muir
Milton Park Farm, Castle Douglas, Kirkcudbrightshire, DG7 3JJ
Tel: 01556 660212

1 cottage, 1 pub rm, 2 bedrms, sleeps 5, £180.00-£280.00, Mar-Nov, bus 1 ml, rail 16 mls, ferry 55 mls, airport 95 mls

Comfortable semi-detached farm cottage on one level, with own walled patio garden in rural surroundings. Free trout and salmon fishing on River Urr.

★★ **SELF CATERING**

Mrs Ann Nelson
11 Barnton Park Place, Edinburgh, EH4 6ET
Tel: 0131 336 4779
E-mail: f.nelson@cableinet.co.uk

1 house, 2 pub rms, 3 bedrms, sleeps 6-7, £195.00-£240.00, May-end Sep

A 19th century terraced house situated on a side street in the centre of the market town of Castle Douglas and furnished in a warm unostentatious style. The town is at the heart of a beautiful unspoilt area with lots to discover and enjoy.

Important: Prices stated are estimates and may be subject to amendments

A
SOUTH OF SCOTLAND

BY CASTLE DOUGLAS – COLDINGHAM

15

by Castle Douglas, Kirkcudbrightshire

Map Ref: 2A10

Mrs E Millar
Balannan Farm, Ringford, Castle Douglas, Kirkcudbrightshire, DG7 2F
Tel: 01557 820283

★★★ SELF CATERING

1 cottage, 1 pub rm, 3 bedrms (All grd.floor), sleeps 2-6, £180.00-£320.00, Jan-Dec, bus ¼ ml, rail 24 mls, ferry 50 mls, airport 60 mls

Traditional farm cottage set amidst the beautiful Galloway countryside steeped in history and surrounded by castles, abbeys, gardens, nature trails and sandy beaches, yet only a quarter of a mile from the A75 with the nearest town of Castle Douglas and Kirkcudbright only 5 miles away.

Catrine, Ayrshire

Map Ref: 1H7

Mrs Forrest
Bogend Farm, Catrine, Mauchline, Ayrshire, KA5 6NJ
Tel: 01290 551325

★ SELF CATERING

1 bungalow, 1 pub rm, 2 bedrms (All grd.floor), sleeps 6, £258.50, May-Sep, bus ¼ ml, rail 2 ½ mls, airport 15 mls

The bungalow is peacefully situated in the heart of Ayrshire, on a working dairy farm with excellent access to all attractions within Ayrshire. Enclosed garden, ideal for children. Pet donkeys who love visitors. Ample parking. Bed linen and towels provided.

Cockburnspath, Berwickshire

Map Ref: 2E5

Mrs B M Russell
Townhead Farm, Cockburnspath, TD13 5YR Tel: 01368 830 465
E-mail: townhead@telinco.co.uk

★ SELF CATERING

2 cottages, 1 pub rm, 2 bedrms, sleeps 4-6, total sleeping capacity 10, from £200.00, Apr-Dec, bus 1 ½ mls, rail 9 mls, airport 50 mls

Terraced farm cottages on working farm, set high up overlooking the sea. Sandy beaches near by. Only 38 miles (61kms) from Edinburgh.

Coldingham, Berwickshire

Map Ref: 2F5

Joyce McLaren
Crosslea, School Road, Coldingham, Berwickshire, TD14 5NS
Tel: 018907 71558

★★ SELF CATERING

1 cottage, 1 pub rm, 3 bedrms (grd flr avail), sleeps 6, £180.00-£330.00, Jan-Dec, bus nearby, rail 13 mls, airport 50 mls

Recently refurbished 17th Century cottage in the village square. Cliff walks, sandy beach, harbour and National Nature Reserve within 2 miles. One ground floor bedroom with en-suite toilet and basin.

Mr R Penaluna
Press Castle Complex, Coldingham, Eyemouth, Berwickshire, TD14 5TS
Tel: 018907 71257 Fax: 018907 71729

★★ UP TO ★★★ SELF CATERING

6 flats, 1 cottage, 6 pine lodges, 1-2 pub rms, 1-3 bedrms (grd flr avail), sleeps 2-8, total sleeping capacity 51, £142.00-£489.00, Jan-Dec, bus 2 mls, rail 11 mls, ferry 80 mls, airport 45 mls

Fully refurbished apartments within this historic 17th century castle, also secluded pine lodges set in 22 acres of mature wood and parkland. Ideal for golf, fishing, walking etc. Sandy beaches and shops 3 miles.

VAT is shown at 17.5%: changes in this rate may affect prices.   *Key to symbols is on back flap.*

COLDINGHAM – COLMONELL, BY GIRVAN

SOUTH OF SCOTLAND

Coldingham, Berwickshire
Map Ref: 2F5

HOLIDAY PARK ★★★★

Scoutscroft Holiday Centre
Coldingham, Berwickshire, TD14 5NB
Tel: 01890 771338/ Fax: 01890 771746
E-mail: scoutscroft@compuserve.com

15 acres, mixed, Mar-Nov, prior booking in peak periods, latest time of arrival 2400. Extra charge for electricity, awnings, showers.

Park accommodation: 170

30 tourers £7.00-13.00 or 30 motors £7.50-14.50 or 60 tents £6.00-9.00. Total Touring Pitches 60.

20 Holiday Caravans to let, sleep 6 £150.00-305.00, total sleeping capacity 120, min let 2 nights.

Leisure facilities:

12 mls N of Berwick-on-Tweed. Turn N off A1 at Reston-Coldingham. Site on St Abbs side of Coldingham village.

SELF CATERING ★★

Dr & Mrs E J Wise
West Loch Holidays, West Loch House, Coldingham, Berwickshire, TD14 5QE
Tel: 018907 71270

Secluded cottages and chalets, centred on private trout loch in wooded country estate close to sea. Ideal for anglers, naturalists and walkers. An ideal and peaceful base for touring the Borders, Edinburgh and Northumberland.

6 chalets, 3 cottages, 1-2 pub rms, 1-3 bedrms (grd flr avail), sleeps 2-6, total sleeping capacity 42, min let weekend, £165.00-£335.00, Mar-Nov, bus 2 mls, rail 14 mls, airport 50 mls

---

by Coldstream, Berwickshire
Map Ref: 2E6

SELF CATERING ★★★

Sue Brewis
Little Swinton, Coldstream, Berwickshire, TD12 4HH
Tel/Fax: 01890 860280

Spacious modernised well equipped single storey farm cottages, with open fires and large grass play areas. Fully upgraded disabled unit. Pets, children welcome. Sleeps 3-7.

3 cottages, 1 pub rm, 2-3 bedrms (grd flr avail), sleeps 4-7, total sleeping capacity 17, min let weekend, £190.00-£350.00, Jan-Dec, bus ½ ml, rail 15 mls, airport 60 mls

---

SELF CATERING ★★★

Mrs S Walker
Springwells, Greenlaw, Duns, Berwickshire, TD10 6UL
Tel/Fax: 01890 840216

Single storey, semi-detached farm cottage, with own garden area, in peaceful rural setting, with uninterrupted views of the Cheviot Hills. Kelso 8 miles and Edinburgh 42 miles.

1 cottage, 1 pub rm, 3 bedrms (All grd.floor), sleeps 5, from £120.00, Jan-Dec, bus 8 mls, rail 20 mls, airport 52 mls

---

Colmonell, by Girvan, Ayrshire
Map Ref: 1G9

SELF CATERING ★★★

Mrs Dorothy Overend
Dalreoch Lodge, Colmonell, Girvan, Ayrshire, KA26 0SQ
Tel: 01465 881214 Fax: 01465 881282

Detached cottage situated in the grounds of the 2000 acre Dalreoch Sporting Estate in quiet countryside, 1 mile from the village. The cottage has a large enclosed garden, ideal for children. The estate offers fishing, walking, mountain biking routes as well as an abundance of wild life. Golf packages can be arranged.

1 bungalow, 1 pub rm, 3 bedrms (All grd.floor), sleeps 6, £160.00-£255.00, Jan-Dec, bus 1 ml, rail 8 mls, ferry 17 mls, airport 35 mls

---

Important: Prices stated are estimates and may be subject to amendments

SOUTH OF SCOTLAND

COLMONELL, BY GIRVAN – CROCKETFORD

17

Colmonell, by Girvan, Ayrshire

Map Ref: 1G9

SELF CATERING ★★★★

Mrs Anne Shankland
19 Main Street, Colmonell, Girvan
Tel: 01465 881265/881220

1 flat, 1 cottage, 1-2 pub rms, 1-3 bedrms (grd flr avail), sleeps 2-6, total sleeping capacity 8, min let weekend, £100.00-£300.00, Jan-Dec, bus nearby, rail 10 mls, ferry 25 mls, airport 40 mls

Ground floor flat in peaceful country village and traditional stone semi-detached cottage in rural hamlet, both with beautiful views of the River Stinchar and surrounding hills. Sandy beach and Galloway Forest Park within easy reach. Ideal base for touring Ayrshire coast and Galloway.

Creetown, Wigtownshire

Map Ref: 1H10

SELF CATERING ★

Mrs Dawson
70 Coach Road, Brotton, Saltburn-by-Sea, Cleveland
Tel: 01287 676991

2 houses, 1-3 pub rms, 2-3 bedrms, sleeps 4-6, total sleeping capacity 10, £260.00-£360.00, Apr-Oct, bus nearby, rail 40 mls, ferry 40 mls, airport 50 mls

Adjoining stone built terraced houses in residential side street, within easy reach of village centre.

Crocketford, Kirkcudbrightshire

Map Ref: 2A9

HOLIDAY PARK ★★★★

Park of Brandedleys
Crocketford, by Dumfries, Kirkcudbrightshire, DG2 8RG
Tel: 01556 690250 Fax: 01556 690681

Park accommodation: 160

80 tourers £9.00-15.00 or 80 motors £9.00-15.00 or 80 tents £9.00-15.00. Total Touring Pitches 80.

12 Holiday Caravans to let, sleep 2-6 £150.00-370.00, total sleeping capacity 76, min let 3 days.

24 acres, mixed, Jan-Dec, prior booking in peak periods, overnight holding area. Extra charge for electricity, awnings.

Leisure facilities:

From Dumfries take A75 W for 9 mls. Turn left onto unclassified road on leaving Crocketford village. Park is 150 yds on right

PARK OF BRANDEDLEYS
A Holgate Countryside Park
CROCKETFORD, DUMFRIES DG2 8RG
Tel: 01556 690250   Fax: 01556 690681

Beautifully landscaped 24 acre park in south west Scotland set in the midst of uncrowded historic Galloway. Top grade facilities provided in/outdoor pools restaurant and bar. Lodges, cottages, caravans for hire. Pitches for tourers, tents, motor homes. Full facilities. Open all year.
Best Park in Scotland 1995.

SELF CATERING ★★ UP TO ★★★

Linda Purdie
Park of Brandedleys, Crocketford, by Dumfries, DG2 8RG
Tel: 01556 690250 Fax: 01556 690681

3 chalets, 2 cottages, 1-2 pub rms, 1-2 bedrms, sleeps 2-6, total sleeping capacity 30, £260.00-£500.00, Feb-Dec, bus nearby, rail 9 mls

Choice of cottages or pine chalets set in 24 acres of landscaped grounds with views of Auchenreoch Loch and Galloway Hills. Ideal for touring. Golfing paradise with 25 courses in 20 miles radius.

VAT is shown at 17.5%: changes in this rate may affect prices.

Key to symbols is on back flap.

MILLPORT, ISLE OF CUMBRAE – DAILLY

A SOUTH OF SCOTLAND

Millport, Isle of Cumbrae — Map Ref: 1F6

★★ SELF CATERING

Cumbrae Holiday Apartments Ltd
32 Stuart Street, Millport, KA28 0AJ
Tel: 01475 530094

8 flats, 1-2 pub rms, 1-2 bedrms (grd flr avail), sleeps 2-6, total sleeping capacity 34, £80.00-£260.00, Jan-Dec, bus nearby, ferry 3 mls

The apartments are situated in the centre of Millport adjacent to the pier area. All the flats at Quayhead have sea views and ready access to sandy beaches. Linen can be provided if required. Some flats have a bed settee.

★★ SELF CATERING

Mrs P Cusden
4 The Glebe, East Linton, East Lothian, EH40 3EF
Tel: 01620 860045

1 flat, 1 pub rm, 1 bedrm, sleeps 4, £150.00-£210.00, Apr-Oct, bus nearby, ferry nearby

Comfortable, centrally located 2nd floor flat with superb views over bay & harbour to Aryshire and beyond. Large lounge (sleeps 2), spacious fully equipped kitchen/dining area. Twin bedroom, sea facing. Fully equipped bathroom. 24 hours parking on sea front.

★★★ SELF CATERING

Mr & Mrs J Elliott
Ballochmartin Bay, Millport, Isle of Cumbrae, KA28 0HQ
Tel: 01475 530040 Fax: 01475 530317
E-mail: SailawaySeaSchool@btinternet.com

1 cottage, 2 pub rms, 3 bedrms, sleeps 6, £125.00-£300.00, Jan-Dec, bus nearby, rail 3 mls, ferry nearby, airport 40 mls

Semi-detached sandstone house in own grounds with open views over the Largs Channel, less than 1 mile (2kms) from ferry. Full central heating yet coal fire retained.

★★ UP TO ★★★★ SELF CATERING

Mrs B McLuckie
Muirhall Farm, Larbert, Stirlingshire, FK5 4EW
Tel: 01324 551570 Fax: 01324 551223

1 house, 4 flats, 1-2 pub rms, 1-3 bedrms (grd flr avail), sleeps 4-10, total sleeping capacity 32, £110.00-£485.00, Jan-Dec, bus nearby, rail 5 mls, ferry 4 mls, airport 20 mls

Properties that have been in the family since the 18th century with prime position over Millport Bay. All now renovated but individual style and character retained. Many fun features added.

Dailly, Ayrshire — Map Ref: 1G8

★★★★ SELF CATERING — BRONZE

Brunston Castle Holiday Resort
Dailly, Ayrshire, KA26 9RH
Tel: 01465 811589 Fax: 01465 811411

75 bungalows, 1 pub rm, 2-4 bedrms (grd flr avail), sleeps 4-8, min let weekend, £150.00-£395.00, Jan-Dec, bus ¼ ml, rail 5 mls, ferry 35 mls, airport 25 mls

Brunston Castle offers bungalows on a park overlooking the Girvan Valley. There are a wide range of activities/attractions in the area or you can relax at the leisure centre with its indoor heated swimming pool, children's pool, sauna, lounge/bar, games room, children playground and bicycle hire. Adjacent to the holiday resort is Brunston Castle Golf Course with its 6800 yds Burns Championship Course.

Important: Prices stated are estimates and may be subject to amendments

A

SOUTH OF SCOTLAND

DALBEATTIE – DUMFRIES

Dalbeattie, Kirkcudbrightshire

★★★★ SELF CATERING

Mr G Cook
Haywood Property Management Ltd, Barclosh, Dalbeattie, Kirkcudbrightshire, DG5 4PL
Tel: 01556 610380 Fax: 01556 610364

Completely renovated, traditional stone-built cottage. Ideally situated for walking, touring or just relaxing.

Map Ref: 2A10

1 cottage, 1 pub rm, 2 bedrms (All grd.floor), sleeps 4, £150.00-£310.00, Jan-Dec, bus 2 mls, rail 12 mls, ferry 50 mls, airport 80 mls

★★★ UP TO ★★★★ SELF CATERING

Mr & Mrs G C Elkins
Maidenholm Forge Mill, Dalbeattie, Dumfries & Galloway, DG5 4HT
Tel/Fax: 01556 611552

Recent conversion of former stable and barn on site of Maidenholm Forge Mill. Quiet location on banks of Dalbeattie Burn. 10 minutes walk to town.

1 cottage, 2 riverside apartments, 2-4 pub rms, 4 bedrms (All grd.floor), sleeps 2-3, total sleeping capacity 7, £175.00-£390.00, Jan-Dec, bus $^{1}/_{2}$ ml, rail 14 mls

---

Dalry, by Castle Douglas, Kirkcudbrightshire

★★ SELF CATERING

Miss S Harrison
Grennan Mill, St John's Town of Dalry, Kirkcudbrightshire
Tel: 01644 430297

Former gardener's cottage to the rear of Grennan House, overlooking restored watermill.

Map Ref: 1H9

1 cottage, 1 pub rm, 2 bedrms (All grd.floor), sleeps 4, £180.00-£300.00, May-Oct, bus 3 mls, rail 23 mls, ferry 60 mls, airport 90 mls

---

Dolphinton, West Linton, Peeblesshire

★★ SELF CATERING

Mrs Anne Hutchison
Roberton Mains, Dolphinton, West Linton, EH46 7AB
Tel/Fax: 01968 682256

Fully-modernised cottage on a working upland farm. Secluded, yet not isolated, in beautiful countryside. Children and well-behaved pets welcome. Ideal for bird watching. Come and relax in the garden, or fish on the private pond, or take a gentle stroll along the quiet country roads.

Map Ref: 2B6

1 cottage, 2 pub rms, 2 bedrms (All grd.floor), sleeps 4-6, Jan-Dec, bus 1 ml, rail 20 mls, airport 20 mls

---

Dumfries

★★★ HOLIDAY PARK

Barnsoul Farm
Irongray, Shawhead, by Dumfries, DG2 9SQ
Tel/Fax: 01387 730249
E-mail: barnsouldg@aol.com

10 acres, mixed, Easter-Oct, latest time of arrival 2350, overnight holding area. Extra charge for electricity, showers.

Map Ref: 2B9

Park accommodation: **50**

20 tourers £6.00-10.00 or 20 motors £6.00-10.00 or 20 tents £6.00-10.00. Total Touring Pitches 20.

3 Holiday Caravans to let, sleep 4-6 £150.00-250.00, total sleeping capacity 14, min let 4 days.

Leisure facilities:

VAT is shown at 17.5%: changes in this rate may affect prices.

Key to symbols is on back flap.

DUNURE, BY AYR – FAIRLIE

SOUTH OF SCOTLAND

Dunure, by Ayr, Ayrshire
Map Ref: 1G7

SELF CATERING ★★★

Mrs C Montgomerie
Millhouse, Dunure Mains, Dunure, Ayr, Ayrshire, KA7 4LY
Tel/Fax: 01292 500348
E-mail: Montgomerie@mill81.freeserve.co.uk

1 cottage, 1 pub rm, 3 bedrms (All grd.floor), sleeps 4-6, £100.00-£370.00, Jan-Dec, bus 1 ml, rail 6 mls, airport 10 mls

Semi-detached cottage with enclosed garden on working dairy farm, overlooking Firth of Clyde with views westwards to Isle of Arran. Convenient for golfing, fishing and touring the area, with Culzean Castle and Country Park 6 miles.

SELF CATERING ★★★

Mrs Lesley Wilcox
Fisherton Farm, Dunure, Ayrshire, KA7 4LF
Tel/Fax: 01292 500223

1 bungalow, 2 pub rms, 3 bedrms (All grd.floor), sleeps 6, £160.00-£350.00, Jan-Dec, bus nearby, rail 5 mls, airport 8 mls

Modern bungalow with private lawned garden set on a traditional working farm with lovely coastal views to the Isle of Arran and surrounding farmland. Ideal base for touring Burns Country with many activities including golfing, fishing and walking. 5 miles from Ayr and convenient for Prestwick airport.

Ettrick Valley, Selkirkshire
Map Ref: 2C7

HOLIDAY PARK ★★★

Angecroft Caravan Park
Angecroft Caravan Park, Ettrick Valley,
Selkirkshire, TD7 5HY
Tel: 01750 62251/01721 730657 Fax: 01721 730627
E-mail: kevinnewton@compuserve.com

Park accommodation: 49

6 tourers £7.50-9.00 or 6 motors £7.50-9.00 or 6 tents £5.00-7.50. Touring Pitches 6.

4 Holiday Caravans to let, sleep 6 £100.00-295.00, total sleeping capacity 24, min stay weekend.

5 acres, mixed, 5 Feb-15 Jan, prior booking in peak periods, latest time of arrival 2200, overnight holding area. Extra charge for electricity, awnings.

Leisure facilities:

From A74 to Lockerbie, exit J17 follow signs for Eskdalemuir. At Eskdalemuir turn left onto B709. From A7 at Langholm take B709 to park (24mls). From A7 at Hawick take B711. Park 4 mls W of Tushielaw on B709.

SELF CATERING ★★★

Mr K A Newton
Angecroft Caravan Park, Ettrick Valley, Selkirk, Selkirkshire
Tel: 01750 62251/01721 730657 Fax: 01721 730627
E-mail: kevinnewton@compuserve.com

2 holiday lodges, 1 pub rm, 3-4 bedrms, sleeps 6, total sleeping capacity 12, £125.00-£300.00, Jan-Dec, bus 18 mls, rail 24 mls, airport 50 mls

At the edge of the caravan park with its own private garden and parking space, the cottage overlooks Tima water and wooded hills.

Fairlie, Ayrshire
Map Ref: 1G6

SELF CATERING ★★★

Mrs Carol Dunn
32 Greenholm Avenue, Clarkston, Glasgow, G76 7AH
Tel: 0141 571 7417

1 flat, 1 pub rm, 1 bedrm (All grd.floor), sleeps 2-3, £200.00-£300.00, Jan-Dec, bus nearby (100yds), rail ½ ml

Modern ground floor seafront apartment with balcony right on the beach. Views to the Cumbraes, Arran and Isle of Bute. Ideal situation for just sitting out on the balcony.

Important: Prices stated are estimates and may be subject to amendments

SOUTH OF SCOTLAND

FOULDEN – GATEHOUSE OF FLEET

Foulden, Berwickshire

Map Ref: 2F5

★★★ SELF CATERING

Mrs I B Williams
Old Schoolhouse, Foulden, nr Berwick on Tweed, TD15 1UH
Tel: 01289 386332
E-mail: jwfoulden@aol.co.uk

1 house, 1 pub rm, 3 bedrms (All grd.floor), sleeps 6, £180.00-£280.00, Jan-Dec, bus nearby, rail 5 mls, min let 1 week

Sympathetically converted school in the picturesque conservation village of Foulden. Drumoyne enjoys panoramic views across the Tweed Valley to the Cheviot Hills. 1.5 miles from England/Scotland border and 56 miles from Edinburgh.

Galashiels, Selkirkshire

Map Ref: 2D6

★ SELF CATERING

Scottish Borders Events Centre
Heriot-Watt University, Scottish Borders Campus, Tweed Road, Galashiels, TD1 3HE
Tel: 01896 753474 Fax: 01896 755884
E-mail: J.E.Landells@hw.ac.uk

12 flats, 1 pub rm, 6 bedrms (grd flr avail), sleeps 6, total sleeping capacity 72, £230.00-£270.00, Easter, Jul-Sep, bus nearby, rail 34-38 mls, airport 42 mls

Modern and fully equipped flats on College Campus. Ideally situated for touring the Borders. Groups especially welcome.

Gatehead, by Kilmarnock, Ayrshire

Map Ref: 1G6

★★★ SELF CATERING

Mrs Esther Caldwell
Kelk Cottage, Crosshouse, by Kilmarnock, Ayrshire
Tel/Fax: 01563 525269

1 cottage, 1-2 pub rms, 2 bedrms (All grd.floor), sleeps 4-6, £150.00-£250.00, Jan-Dec, bus nearby, rail 2 miles, ferry 12 miles, airport 20 miles

Semi-detached cottage recently converted from a farm building with rural views both back and front. Kilmarnock 2 miles. Ideal for golfers.

Gatehouse of Fleet, Kirkcudbrightshire

Map Ref: 1H10

★★ UP TO ★★★ SELF CATERING

Mrs B Gilbey, (Dept SS/C)
Rusko, Gatehouse of Fleet, Castle Douglas, Kirkcudbrightshire, DG7 2BS
Tel: 01557 814215 Fax: 01557 814679

1 house, 2 bungalows, 1-3 pub rms, 2-5 bedrms (grd flr avail), sleeps 4-10, total sleeping capacity 18, min let weekend, £150.00-£600.00, Jan-Dec, bus 2 mls, rail 35 mls, ferry 45 mls, airport 90 mls

Lovely old farmhouse with beautiful views of 18th century mansion house. Woodland and Garden cottages in the ground. Use of tennis court. Loch and river fishing with tuition given. Member of Scotlands best.

★★★ SELF CATERING

Major & Mrs I A D Gordon
Brownhill, Planetree Park, Gatehouse of Fleet, Kirkcudbrightshire, DG7 2EQ
Tel: 01557 814401

1 house, 1 pub rm, 3 bedrms, sleeps 6, to £320.00, Jan-Dec, bus ½ ml, rail 34 mls, ferry 39 mls, airport 87 mls

Self contained half of owner's house. Peace and quiet, lovely outlook to village and hills beyond. Ideal touring centre.

VAT is shown at 17.5%: changes in this rate may affect prices.

Key to symbols is on back flap.

GATEHOUSE OF FLEET – BY GRETNA

A SOUTH OF SCOTLAND

Gatehouse of Fleet, Kirkcudbrightshire
Map Ref: 1H10

★★★ SELF CATERING

Mr M P Mullan
4 Woodhouse Close, Woodhouse Road, Hove, East Sussex, BN3 5LS
Tel: 01273 413655
E-mail: mit.mullan@dial.pipex.com

1 cottage, 3 pub rms, 2 bedrms, sleeps 4-5, £160.00-£280.00, Jan-Dec, bus nearby, rail 22 mls, ferry 60 mls, airport 62 mls

This two bedroomed terraced cottage with large rear garden and patio area is a Listed building of special architectural and historic interest. Located in the conservation area of Gatehouse, a small country town on the Solway Firth, it is only 5 minutes drive to sandy beaches.

by Gatehouse of Fleet, Kirkcudbrightshire

Auchenlarie Holiday Park
Gatehouse of Fleet, Kirkcudbrightshire DG7 2EX
Telephone: 01557 840251 Fax: 01557 840333

A warm welcome awaits. New for the millennium health and fitness suite incorporating swimming pool, sports hall, gym, sauna and soft play area. Excellent grading. Being situated on the shores of Wigton Bay, we are well placed to enjoy the delights of Dumfries and Galloway. We offer the best in family holidays, fun and facilities.

★★★★ HOLIDAY PARK

Auchenlarie Holiday Park
Gatehouse of Fleet, Kirkcudbrightshire, DG7 2EX
Tel: 01557 840251 Fax: 01557 840333

20 acres, mixed, Mar-Oct, prior booking in peak periods, latest time of arrival 2000, overnight holding area. Extra charge for electricity, awnings, showers.

Park accommodation: 287

49 tourers £5.50-10.00 or 49 motors £5.50-10.00 or 26 tents £5.50-10.00.
Total Touring Pitches 75.

45 Holiday Caravans to let, sleep 4-6 £90.00-390.00, total sleeping capacity 270, min let weekend.

Leisure facilities:

A75 5 mls W of Gatehouse-of-Fleet.

Glenluce, Wigtownshire
Map Ref: 1G10

★★★★ HOLIDAY PARK

Whitecairn Farm Caravan Park
Whitecairn, Glenluce, Wigtownshire, DG8 0NZ
Tel/Fax: 01581 300267

6 acres, grassy, hard-standing, level, Mar-Oct, prior booking in peak periods, latest time of arrival 2200. Extra charge for electricity.

Park accommodation: 50

10 tourers £7.50-8.50 or 10 motors £7.50-8.50 or 10 tents £7.50-8.50.
Total Touring Pitches 10.

12 Holiday Caravans to let, sleep 2-6 £140.00-285.00, total sleeping capacity 72, min let 2 nights.

Leisure facilities:

1 ½ mls north of Glenluce village.

by Gretna, Dumfriesshire
Map Ref: 2C10

★★★ SELF CATERING

Mr & Mrs Read
7 Brow Houses, Eastriggs, Annan, DG12 6TG
Tel: 01461 40873 Fax: 01461 40740
E-mail: mikereadx@cs.com

3 cottages, 3-4 pub rms, 1-2 bedrms (grd flr avail), sleeps 2-4, total sleeping capacity 12, £175.00-£340.00, Jan-Dec, bus 1 ml, rail 3 mls

Modernised, traditional sandstone fisherman's cottages with own secluded gardens. In quiet location on seashore of Solway Estuary.

Important: Prices stated are estimates and may be subject to amendments

SOUTH OF SCOTLAND

HAWICK – ISLE OF WHITHORN

23

Hawick, Roxburghshire

Map Ref: 2D7

★★★ **SELF CATERING**

Mr W Combe
6 Teviot Crescent, Hawick, Roxburghshire, TD9 9RE
Tel: 01450 374258/373237

Second floor flat furnished to high standard, overlooking the river and park, with beautiful garden for tennant's use. Right in the town centre yet with ample free parking.

1 flat, 1 pub rm, 3 bedrms, sleeps 5, £200.00-£350.00, Jan-Dec, bus nearby, rail 50 mls, airport 50 mls

★★★ **SELF CATERING**

Mrs M Scott
Overhall Farm, Hawick, Roxburghshire, TD9 7LJ
Tel: 01450 375045

Comfortable detached cottage on a working farm. Ideal base for touring the Borders. Close to Hawick and all amenities. Attractive gardens front and rear.

1 cottage, 1 pub rm, 3 bedrms (grd flr avail), sleeps 6, £150.00-£230.00, Apr-Oct, bus 1 ml, rail 50 mls, airport 50 mls

---

Houndwood, by Eyemouth, Berwickshire

Map Ref: 2E5

★★ **SELF CATERING**

Mrs H A Argent
25 De Montfort Court, Peterborough, Cambridgeshire, PE2 9DL
Tel: 01733 552219

Stone cottage with fully enclosed garden beside A1, giving easy access to both Edinburgh (25 miles) and Berwick on Tweed (10 miles) approx.

1 house, 2 pub rms, 3 bedrms, sleeps 2-6, £200.00-£275.00, Jan-Dec, bus nearby, rail nearby, airport nearby

---

Isle of Whithorn, Wigtownshire

Map Ref: 1H11

★★★ **HOLIDAY PARK**

Burrowhead Holiday Village
Tonderghie Road, Isle of Whithorn, Wigtownshire, DG8 8JB
Tel: 01988 500252 Fax: 01988 500855

100 acres, mixed, Mar-Oct, prior booking in peak periods, overnight holding area. Extra charge for electricity.

Park accommodation: 560
20 tourers £7.50-9.50 and 10 motors £7.50-9.50 and 10 tents £7.50-9.50. Total Touring Pitches 40.
26 Holiday Caravans to let, sleep 4-6 £140.00-305.00, total sleeping capacity 116, min let weekend.

Leisure facilities:

From Newton Stewart roundabout follow signs for Whithorn. Straight through Whithorn and follow signs for Isle of Whithorn. Site is signposted from Isle of Whithorn village.

★ **SELF CATERING**

Mrs Ann Hammond
58 Sunderton Lane, Clanfield, Waterlooville, Hants, PO8 0NT
Tel: 01705 593468
E-mail: ann@thehammonds.freeserve.co.uk

Detached chalet bungalow on private estate in rural/sea shore location. Close to all village amenities.

1 chalet, 1 pub rm, 2 bedrms (All grd.floor), sleeps 4-5, £140.00-£190.00, Jan-Dec, bus nearby, rail 35 mls, airport 60 mls

---

VAT is shown at 17.5%: changes in this rate may affect prices.

Key to symbols is on back flap.

BY JEDBURGH – BY KELSO

SOUTH OF SCOTLAND

by Jedburgh, Roxburghshire
Map Ref: 2E7

MILLHOUSE, LETTER BOX COTTAGE & STOCKMANS COTTAGE SILVER
OVERWELLS, JEDBURGH, ROXBURGHSHIRE TD8 6LT
Tel: 01835 863020 Fax: 01835 864334

Three quality cottages, each sleeping four, on working farm, three miles from Jedburgh. **Millhouse** – detached house stylishly converted with spectacular views. **Letter Box and Stockmans Cottage** – semi-detached newly modernised in quiet location. All ideal centres for exploring the Borders, sporting holidays or just to "get away from it all".

★★★★ SELF CATERING

Mrs A Fraser
Overwells, Jedburgh, Roxburghshire, TD8 6LT
Tel: 01835 863020 Fax: 01835 864334

3 cottages, 2 pub rms, 2 bedrms (All grd.floor), each sleeps 4, total sleeping capacity 12, £200.00-£320.00, Jan-Dec, bus 3 mls, airport 54 mls

2 recently renovated properties on a working farm. Only 3 miles from Jedburgh yet quiet, peaceful location. Ideal for walking, golf and exploring the Borders country.

★★★★ SELF CATERING

Mrs S Fry
The Spinney, Langlee, Jedburgh, Roxburghshire, TD8 6PB
Tel: 01835 863525 Fax: 01835 864883

2 log cabins, 1 pub rm, 1 bedrm (All grd.floor), sleeps 3, total sleeping capacity 6, min let 1 night, £200.00-£250.00, Jan-Dec, bus 2 mls, rail 50 mls, airport 50 mls

Set in large pleasant garden lying just off main A68 2 miles south of Jedburgh. Two pine cabins, well equipped and with ample parking.

Kelso, Roxburghshire
Map Ref: 2E6

★★★ SELF CATERING

Vicky Broadbent
Clematis Cottage, Ednam, Kelso, Roxburghshire, TD5 7QE
Tel: 01573 224682

1 flat, 1 pub rm, 2 bedrms (All grd.floor), sleeps 4, £200.00-£350.00, Jan-Dec, bus 300 yds, rail 20 mls, airport 50 mls

Attractively refurbished ground floor flat with private parking. Near the centre of Kelso, close to shops and restaurants. Just a five minute walk through this historic town to the banks of River Tweed and riverside walks. Also an ideal base for exploring the Borders.

---

by Kelso, Roxburghshire
Map Ref: 2E6

★★★ SELF CATERING

Mrs Rosalind Aitchison
Karingal, Lochton, Coldstream, Berwickshire
Tel: 01890 830205 Fax: 01890 830210
E-mail: lochton@btinternet.com

1 cottage, 1 pub rm, 3 bedrms, sleeps 2-5/6, min let 2 nights, £200.00-£350.00, Jan-Dec, bus ½ ml, rail 20 mls, airport 50 mls

Traditional, beautifully refurbished stone built semi-detached cottage with open fire, on working farm beside River Tweed. Farm walks, fishing, fine views. Ideally situated for touring.

Important: Prices stated are estimates and may be subject to amendments

A

SOUTH OF SCOTLAND

by Kelso, Roxburghshire

Map Ref: 2E6

BY KELSO

★★★★ SELF CATERING

Peter & Jacqui Hottinger
Houndridge Holiday Cottages, Houndridge, Ednam, Kelso, Roxburghshire, TD5 7QN
Tel: 01573 470 604 Fax: 01573 470604
E-mail: houndridge.holiday@virgin.net
Web: www.touristnet.com/sc/houndridge

Individual character cottages on 50 acre arable farm, 3 miles from Kelso. Indoor heated pool, sauna, games room, tennis court, fitness suite, children's play park, golf chipping range, mountain bike hire and petanque.

5 cottages, 1-2 pub rms, 1-3 bedrms (grd flr avail), sleeps 2-8, total sleeping capacity 28, £100.00-£510.00, Jan-Dec, bus nearby, rail 20 mls, airport 58 mls

★★ SELF CATERING

J Mauchlen
Spotsmains, Kelso, Roxburghshire, TD5 7RT
Tel/Fax: 01573 460226

Comfortable well appointed, semi-detached house on working farm. Within easy reach of all Borders centres and facilities. Fishing can be arranged. Suitable for all ages.

1 cottage, 1 pub rm, 3 bedrms (grd flr avail), sleeps 6, £180.00-£250.00, Jan-Dec, bus 1 ml, rail 25 mls, airport 40 mls

★★★ SELF CATERING

Mrs A Robson
Venchen, by Yetholm, Roxburghshire
Tel: 01573 420207 Fax: 01573 420233

Semi-detached shepherd's cottage fully equipped and with oil fired central heating. Situated in open farm land on a working livestock farm, the cottage gives the impression of seclusion, yet only 2 1/2 miles from the village of Yetholm. Ideal for birdwatching and wildlife, walking and exploring the Borders and Northumberland.

1 cottage, 1 pub rm, 5 bedrms, sleeps 5, min let weekend, £120.00-£300.00, May-Dec, bus 2 1/2 mls, rail 20 mls, airport 60 mls

★★★ SELF CATERING

Pauline Twemlow
Roxburgh Newtown Farm, Kelso, Roxburghshire, TD5 8NN
Tel/Fax: 01573 450250
E-mail: pauline.twemlow@which.net
Web: http://homepages.which.net/~pauline.twemlow

Two attractive, well equipped, semi-detached cottages. Centrally heated with appealing views. Set in the heart of the Borders countryside.

2 cottages, 1 pub rm, 1-3 bedrms (grd flr avail), sleeps 2-6, total sleeping capacity 8, £120.00-£320.00, Jan-Dec, bus 5 mls, rail 30 mls, airport 45 mls

---

VAT is shown at 17.5%: changes in this rate may affect prices.

Key to symbols is on back flap.

KILMARNOCK
Kilmarnock, Ayrshire

SOUTH OF SCOTLAND
Map Ref: 1G6

No 2 Old Rome Mews Cottage
Old Rome Farmhouse, Gatehead, by Kilmarnock KA2 9AJ
Tel: 01563 850265

Superb barn conversion in courtyard off the A759, 5 miles from Troon. Accommodation consists of 2 twin bedded rooms, 1 double bedded room, 2 bathrooms, showers, large lounge, colour TV, video, fully fitted kitchen, oil central heating. Bed linen included, excellent location for touring Ayrshire or golfing. Licensed restaurant serving excellent home-cooked food on site.

★★★ SELF CATERING

Mrs R Elliot
No 2 Old Rome Mews Cottage, Gatehead, Kilmarnock, Ayrshire, KA2 9AJ
Tel: 01563 850265

1 cottage, 1 pub rm, 3 bedrms (grd flr avail), sleeps 6, min let 3 days, £250.00-£450.00, Jan-Dec, bus 350 yds, rail 2 ½ mls, airport 5 mls

Converted barn with full central heating, set on the outskirts of the small village of Gatehead, near to the sea-side town of Troon, and the famous golf courses of Ayrshire.

★★ UP TO ★★★ SELF CATERING

Mrs Mary Howie
Hillhouse Farm, Grassyards Road, Kilmarnock, Ayrshire, KA3 6HG
Tel: 01563 523370

1 house, 1 bungalow, 1 pub rm, 3 bedrms, sleeps 6-9, total sleeping capacity 15, £140.00-£390.00, Jan-Dec, bus 1 ml, rail 2 mls, airport 20 mls

Fully equipped detached farm cottage and farmhouse with lovely views, situated in open quiet countryside on working dairy farm, 1 mile east of Kilmarnock. Safe parking. Storage heaters and open fire. Ideal location for touring west of Scotland and Glasgow.

Important: Prices stated are estimates and may be subject to amendments

SOUTH OF SCOTLAND

A

KIPPFORD, BY DALBEATTIE – KIRKCUDBRIGHT

Kippford, by Dalbeattie, Kirkcudbrightshire   Map Ref: 2A10

Kippford Caravan Park

**Kippford, by Dalbeattie
Kirkcudbrightshire DG5 4LF
Telephone: 01556 620636 Fax: 01556 620636**

Thistle award family owned park in undulating part of wooded setting, rocky outcrops planted with trees and flowering shrubs. Top quality caravan and bungalows for sale or hire, fully serviced with colour TV and fridge. Launderette, public phone. Tents and tourers, electric hook-ups. Free hot showers and covered washing-up areas. Adventure and junior play areas, small shop adjoining 9-hole golf course across road. Fishing, sailing, birdwatching etc, all very local.

SELF CATERING ★★

Kippford Caravan Park
by Dalbeattie, Kirkcudbrightshire, DG5 4LF
Tel/Fax: 01556 620636

6 chalets, 1 pub rm, 3 bedrms, sleeps 4-6, total sleeping capacity 32, £85.00-£325.00, Mar-Oct, bus nearby, rail 17 mls, airport 60 mls

Set in award-winning beautifully landscaped caravan park. Ideal centre for touring or for a relaxing holiday.

Kirkcudbright   Map Ref: 2A10

HOLIDAY PARK ★★★★

Brighouse Bay Holiday Park
Borgue Road, Kirkcudbright, DG6 4TS
Tel: 01557 870267 Fax: 01557 870319
E-mail: T3@brighouse-bay.co.uk
Web: www.brighouse-bay.co.uk

Park accommodation: 240

120 tourers £9.00-12.25 or 120 motors £9.00-12.25 or 120 tents £9.00-12.25. Total Touring Pitches 120.

25 Holiday Caravans to let, sleep 4-8 £145.00-510.00, total sleeping capacity 160, min let 2 nights.

Leisure facilities:

25 acres, mixed, Jan-Dec, prior booking in peak periods, latest time of arrival 2130, overnight holding area. Extra charge for electricity, awnings.

From Kirkcudbright take A755 W for ½ ml, turn left on to B727 signposted Borgue. After 4 mls turn left signposted Brighouse Bay. Park on right of bay behind wood in 2 mls.

SELF CATERING ★★★

Mr & Mrs R G Dunlop
Cannee Farm, Kirkcudbright, DG6 4XD
Tel: 01557 330684

2 cottages, 1 pub rm, 3-5 bedrms (grd flr avail), sleeps 2-10, total sleeping capacity 16, £180.00-£500.00, Jan-Dec, bus 1 ml, rail 30 mls, airport 90 mls

Traditional stone built cottages, recently modernised, double glazed and all electric. On farm in elevated position, 1 mile (2kms) from town.

VAT is shown at 17.5%: changes in this rate may affect prices.   *Key to symbols is on back flap.*

KIRKCUDBRIGHT – LARGS

SOUTH OF SCOTLAND

Kirkcudbright

Map Ref: 2A10

★★★ SELF CATERING

D M Henry
The Grange, Kirkcudbright, DG6 4XG
Tel: 01557 330519

2 flats, 2 pub rms, 2 bedrms, sleeps 4-6, total sleeping capacity 10, £125.00-£240.00, Jan-Dec, bus 2 ½ mls, rail 30 mls, airport 100 mls

Two non self-contained flats on first and second floors of large stonebuilt house standing in it's own 4.5 acres of garden, lawns and woodland. It is an ideal place for those who prefer a quiet holiday. Lawn tennis and croquet. 2.5 miles from Kirkcudbright.

★★ SELF CATERING

Elaine Wannop
Castle Creavie, Kirkcudbright, DG6 1QE
Tel/Fax: 01557 500238

1 flat, 1 pub rm, 1-2 bedrms, total sleeping capacity 4, sleeps 2-4, £140.00-£175.00, Jun-Oct, bus 4 mls, rail 30 mls

Maisonette attached to farmhouse in peaceful rural location, 4 miles from picturesque fishing town of Kirkcudbright. This well equipped property with ensuite bathroom makes this a comfortable base for a couple or a family of four. Available weekly or on a daily basis.

by Kirkcudbright

Map Ref: 2A10

★★★ SELF CATERING

Mrs K A Sproat
Lennox Plunton, Borgue, Kirkcudbrightshire, DG6 4UG
Tel: 01557 870210 Fax: 01557 890210

1 cottage, 1 pub rm, 2 bedrms (All grd.floor), sleeps 4, £160.00-£220.00, Jan-Dec, bus post bus, rail 30 mls, ferry 60 mls

Comfortable, well equipped, traditional cottage in peaceful location. Ideal base for exploring area. Close to coast/beaches.

Largs, Ayrshire

Map Ref: 1F5

★ SELF CATERING

Mrs Rita D Hodsman
2 Sandringham, Largs, Ayrshire, KA30 8BT
Tel: 01475 673387

3 flats, 1-2 pub rms, 1-2 bedrms (grd flr avail), sleeps 3-5, total sleeping capacity 12, £115.00-£300.00, Jan-Dec, bus nearby, rail nearby, ferry nearby, airport 20 mls

The Sandringham self catering apartments occupy the premier position on the seafront and offer panoramic views of the sea, hills and islands. They are within a few minutes of the town centre, pier, shops, railway station and buses.

★★★ SELF CATERING

Mr & Mrs T Marshall
Haus Saron, 106 Greenock Road, Largs, Ayrshire, KA30 8PG
Tel: 01475 673162 Fax: 01475 686244
E-mail: haussaron@aol.com

2 houses, 1 pub rm, 2-3 bedrms (grd flr avail), sleeps 4-6, total sleeping capacity 12, £100.00-£350.00, Apr-Oct, bus 50 yds, rail 1 ml, ferry 1 ml, airport 25 mls

Flat in almost two acres of secluded surroundings of lawns, gardens and mature woodlands. 10 minute walk from Largs.

Important: Prices stated are estimates and may be subject to amendments

SOUTH OF SCOTLAND

LARGS – BY LOCKERBIE

Largs, Ayrshire

Mrs Seona Mills
6 Buchanan Street, Largs
Tel: 01475 674290

★★★ SELF CATERING

Map Ref: 1F5

1 flat, 1 pub rm, 3 bedrms, sleeps 5, £150.00-£300.00, Jan-Dec, bus ½ ml, rail ½ ml, ferry ½ ml, airport 30 mls

2nd floor flat in 19th century villa with views over the Clyde to the islands. Access via main house. Ideal touring base even without a car.

Lendalfoot, by Girvan, Ayrshire

Mrs Moyra M Hay
50 Dalrymple Street, Girvan, Ayrshire, KA26 9BT
Tel/Fax: 01465 714421

★★ SELF CATERING

Map Ref: 1F9

1 cottage, 1 pub rm, 2 bedrms, sleeps 5, £95.00-£290.00, Jan-Dec, bus ½ ml, rail ½ ml

Modernised cottage on shore line with fine views to Ailsa Craig and Firth of Clyde. Own steps to beach and rocky shore. Peaceful setting.

Lilliesleaf, by Melrose, Roxburghshire

Mrs Susan Manners
Deanfoot Farm, Denholm, by Hawick, Roxburghshire, TD9 8SH
Tel: 01450 870229

★ SELF CATERING

Map Ref: 2D7

1 cottage, 1 pub rm, 2 bedrms (grd flr avail), sleeps 5, £150.00-£250.00, Apr-Oct, bus 4 mls, rail 50 mls, airport 50 mls

Charming semi-detached country farm cottage nestling in the peaceful and fascinating Scottish Borders. South facing view to Minto Hill.

Lochmaben, Dumfriesshire

Mrs E Maxwell & Mr R Thorburn
Railway Inn, Barras, Lochmaben, Dumfriesshire
Tel: 01387 810296

★ SELF CATERING

Map Ref: 2B9

1 flat, sleeps 6-11, £220.00-£300.00, Jan-Dec, bus ½ ml, rail 4 mls, ferry 90 mls, airport 75 mls

First floor flat with a private entrance, situated within the Royal Burgh of Lochmaben. Suitable for families, golfing and fishing parties.

by Lockerbie, Dumfriesshire

Mr & Mrs Finch
Dalton Pottery, Meikle Dyke, Dalton, nr Lockerbie
Tel: 01387 840236

★★★ SELF CATERING

Map Ref: 2C9

1 flat, 1 pub rm, 2 bedrms, sleeps 4-6, to £250.00, Jan-Dec, bus nearby, rail 5 mls, ferry 80 mls, airport 80 mls

Stylish conversion from an old farmhouse, this self contained first floor apartment is at the gable end of the owners courtyard style house and pottery. With it's own private entrance it offers accommodation of a high standard enjoying peace and quiet. Rolling countryside all around with a pleasant 500 metre walk to the village pub. Enclosed childrens play area, and pottery making available.

VAT is shown at 17.5%: changes in this rate may affect prices.

Key to symbols is on back flap.

MAYBOLE – MELROSE

SOUTH OF SCOTLAND

Maybole, Ayrshire
Map Ref: 1G8

★★★ SELF CATERING

Mrs Margaret Johnstone Duncan
4 Arrol Drive, Ayr, Ayrshire, KA7 4AF
Tel: 01292 264022

1 cottage, 2 pub rms, 2 bedrms (All grd.floor), sleeps 2-4, £140.00-£250.00, Jan-Dec, bus 2 mls, rail 4 mls, ferry 20 mls, airport 12 mls

Recently renovated traditional cottage 10 miles (16kms) south of Ayr en route to Turnberry, by the Electric Brae.

★★★ SELF CATERING

Mrs L Wallace
Lyonston, Maybole, Ayrshire, KA19 7HS Tel/Fax: 01655 883176
E-mail: laurenwallace@lyonston.freeserve.co.uk

2 cottages, 1 pub rm, 2 bedrms (All grd.floor), sleeps 2-5, total sleeping capacity 8-10, from £140.00, Jan-Dec, bus nearby, rail ¼ ml, ferry 40 mls, airport 12 mls

Two cottages approx. 6 miles South of Ayr, each with their own private enclosed garden and parking. Tastefully decorated and furnished with many extras for all year comfort. Shops, restaurants within walking distance. An ideal location within short travelling distance to many places of interest, coastal, country leisure and historic. In the heart of Burns Country and world famous golf courses. Glasgow 40 miles.

Melrose, Roxburghshire
Map Ref: 2D6

★★★★ SELF CATERING

Mrs Jill Hart
Eildon Holiday Cottages, Dingleton Mains, Melrose,
Roxburghshire, TD6 9HS
Tel/Fax: 01896 823258
E-mail: EHCottages@aol.com
Web: www.aboutscotland.co.uk/eildon/cottages.html

1 flat, 5 cottages, 1 pub rm, 1-3 bedrms (grd flr avail), sleeps 1-6, total sleeping capacity 25, £240.00-£520.00, Jan-Dec, bus ½ ml, rail 35 mls, airport 42 mls

Award winning farm steading conversion adjacent to Melrose 9 hole golf course and just ½ mile from the centre of historic Melrose and Abbey. Edinburgh 40 miles. Views over Tweed Valley. Five cottages are fully equipped for disabled visitors, two with hoists.

★★★★ SELF CATERING

Mr John Pygott
Cherry Trees, Roxham Road, Leasingham, by Sleaford,
Lincolnshire, N34 8NQ
Tel: 01529 414555 Fax: 01529 414759
E-mail: sleaford@pygott-crone.com
Web: www.pygott-crone.com

1 cottage, 1 pub rm, 3 bedrms (grd flr avail), sleeps 6, £300.00-£450.00, Jan-Dec, bus nearby, rail 38 mls, airport 40 mls

Well furnished 2/4 bedroom property in quiet residential area of historic Melrose, with open views to Eildon Hills. Fully equipped, double glazed and gas central heating. Garage and enclosed garden.

★★ SELF CATERING

Mrs E Rodger
BRAIP Ltd, Abbey Place, Cloisters Road, Melrose, TD6 9LQ
Tel: 01896 822595

1 house, 1 pub rm, 3 bedrms, sleeps 4, £206.00-£360.00, Apr-Nov, bus nearby, rail 40 mls, airport 40 mls

Attractive, compact Edwardian cottage, peacefully hidden behind Abbey, yet within 4 minutes of shops, hotels and restaurants.

Important: Prices stated are estimates and may be subject to amendments

SOUTH OF SCOTLAND

BY MELROSE – NEW GALLOWAY

31

by Melrose, Roxburghshire

Map Ref: 2D6

★★★ SELF CATERING

Mrs Jane Cameron
Dimplenowe, Lilliesleaf, Melrose, TD6 9JU
Tel/Fax: 01835 870333

1 bungalow, 1 pub rm, sleeps 5-6, £120.00-£300.00, Apr-Oct

Modern detached cottage on 200 acre mixed sheep and arable farm over looking the beautiful valley in the heart of Border country, near to Melrose.

Moffat, Dumfriesshire

Map Ref: 2B8

★★★★ SELF CATERING

Mrs Elizabeth Edwards
Waterside Coach House, Moffat, Dumfriesshire, DG10 9LF
Tel: 01683 220092

1 cottage, 1 pub rm, 3 bedrms (grd flr avail), sleeps 6, £200.00-£400.00, Jan-Dec, bus 3 mls, rail 16 mls, airport 55 mls

Traditional stone built coach house, fully renovated and set in courtyard off Waterside House, sharing 12 acres of woodland garden and river. Located in the lovely Moffat Water Valley. 3 miles from Moffat. Fishing, golf, birdwatching and walking. No-smoking. Brochure available.

Moniaive, Dumfriesshire

Map Ref: 2A9

★★ UP TO ★★★ SELF CATERING

Sue Grant/Glenluiart Holidays
Glenluiart House, Moniaive, Dumfriesshire, DG3 4JA
Tel: 01848 200331 Fax: 01848 200675
E-mail: sue@badpress.demon.co.uk

4 cottages, 1 pub rm, 1-4 bedrms (grd flr avail), sleeps 2-6, total sleeping capacity 14, £120.00-£340.00, Jan-Dec, bus ½ ml, rail 20 mls

Four well-equipped cottages set around a shared courtyard in the grounds of a large country house half a mile from the village of Moniaive. Convenient for walking the Southern Upland way or visiting Drumlanrig Castle and the marbles of Durisdeer Church.

Mordington, Berwickshire

Map Ref: 2F5

★★ SELF CATERING

Mrs J Trotter
Mordington House, Berwick-upon-Tweed,
Northumberland, TD15 1XA
Tel/Fax: 01289 386470
E-mail: j.trotter@btinternet.com

1 bungalow, 2 pub rms, 2 bedrms, sleeps 4, £150.00-£210.00, Mar-Dec, bus ½ ml, rail 4 mls, airport 60 mls

Stone built lodge to Mordington House, set in 70 acres of woodland. Excellent views over surrounding countryside. 4 miles (6kms) from Berwick.

New Galloway, Kirkcudbrightshire

Map Ref: 1H9

★★★ SELF CATERING

Glenlee Holiday Houses
New Galloway, Castle Douglas, Kirkcudbrightshire, DG7 3SF
Tel: 01644 430212 Fax: 01644 430340

5 cottages, 1-2 pub rms, 2-3 bedrms, sleeps 4-7, total sleeping capacity 28, £200.00-£380.00, Mar-Nov, bus 2 mls, rail 28 mls, airport 45 mls

Five charming cottages around a central courtyard, converted from the former home farm of Glenlee Estate, 2 miles (3km) from New Galloway and Dalry in a peaceful woodland setting. Each spacious cottage has its own character. Magnificent walks around a wooded glen with dramatic waterfalls. Free trout fishing. Pets welcome.

VAT is shown at 17.5%: changes in this rate may affect prices.

Key to symbols is on back flap.

NEWTON STEWART – PEEBLES

SOUTH OF SCOTLAND

Newton Stewart, Wigtownshire — Map Ref: 1G10

Creebridge Caravan Park
Newton Stewart, Wigtownshire, DG8 6AJ
Tel: 01671 402432 Fax: 01671 402324
Booking Enquiries: Creebridge Caravan Park Newton Stewart, DG8 6AJ
Tel/Fax: 01671 402324

★★★ HOLIDAY PARK

4 ½ acres, mixed, Mar-Oct, prior booking in peak periods, latest time of arrival 2000, overnight holding area. Extra charge for electricity, awnings, showers.

Park accommodation: 86
25 tourers £8.00 and 5 motors £7.70 and 10 tents £7.20. Total Touring Pitches 40.
5 Holiday Caravans to let, sleep 6 £160.00-245.00, total sleeping capacity 30, min let 1 night.

Leisure facilities:

¼ ml E of Newton Stewart off A75, or through centre of Newton Stewart over bridge to Minnigaff, 300 mtrs on right.

by Newton Stewart, Wigtownshire — Map Ref: 1G10

Mrs Janet Adams
Clugston Farm, Kirkcowan, Newton Stewart,
Wigtownshire, DG8 9BH
Tel: 01671 830338

★★ UP TO ★★★ SELF CATERING

Newly created from wing of owner's farmhouse in quiet country location on beef and sheep farm. Level access to lower flat. 5 mls (8 kms) off the A75.

2 flats, 1 pub rm, 1 bedrm (All grd.floor), sleeps 2, total sleeping capacity 4, £100.00-£160.00, Jan-Dec, bus 3 mls, rail 25 mls, ferry 25 mls, airport 60 mls

---

Mr & Mrs H Hall
East Kirkland Farm, Newton Stewart, Wigtownshire, DG8 9TA
Tel: 01988 402266
Web: www.wm.hall @virgin.net

★★ SELF CATERING

Courtyard cottages on beautifully situated farm. Own heated indoor swimming pool, games room and quiet pony. Ideal for children and touring.

4 cottages, 1 pub rm, 1-3 bedrms (grd flr avail), sleeps 2-7, total sleeping capacity 22, £150.00-£340.00, Jan-Dec, bus 6 mls, rail 55 mls, ferry 19 mls, airport 60 mls

Peebles — Map Ref: 2C6

Mrs Loraine Chisholm
Ferndene, 93 Edinburgh Road, Peebles, Tweeddale, EH45 8ED
Tel/Fax: 01721 720501

★★★ SELF CATERING

Deceptively spacious dormer bungalow on A703 on outskirts of Peebles. Double glazing and full central heating. Bedroom and bathroom available on ground floor.

1 bungalow, 2 pub rms, 3 bedrms (grd flr avail), sleeps 5, £185.00-£250.00, Jan-Dec, bus nearby, rail 23 mls, airport 23 mls

---

Mrs Janice Haydock
Winkston Farmhouse, Peebles, Tweeddale, EH45 8PH
Tel: 01721 721264

★★★ SELF CATERING

The original byre of Winkston Farm has been carefully converted to form two charming semi-detached cottages which retain the original character of the rhine-stone building, with its natural wood interior and pine floors. Open plan design and tastefully decorated with spiral staircase to upper sleeping area.

2 cottages, 1 pub rm, 2 bedrms, sleeps 4, total sleeping capacity 8, min let weekend, £165.00-£295.00, Jan-Dec, bus 100yds

---

Important: Prices stated are estimates and may be subject to amendments

SOUTH OF SCOTLAND — PEEBLES

Peebles — Map Ref: 2C6

★★★★ SELF CATERING

Mrs Holmes
Kerfield Cottage, Innerleithen Road, Peebles, EH45 8BG
Tel: 01721 720264

Original coach house c1750 with views of Glentress Forest. Fully modernised, peaceful courtyard setting with own walled garden and stream yet less than a mile to the centre of historic Peebles.

1 coach house, 1 pub rm, 2 bedrms (grd flr avail), sleeps 4, £250.00-£350.00, Apr-Oct, bus nearby, rail 23 mls, airport 24 mls

---

★★★ SELF CATERING

Miss Evelyn Inglis
46 Edinburgh Road, Peebles, EH45 8EB
Tel/Fax: 01721 720226

Cosy cottage style upper flat over looking the ^Cuddy Burn^ in the centre of this historic town. Walking distance to all amenities and restaurants.

1 flat, from £180.00, Jan-Dec, bus ¼ ml

★★★★ SELF CATERING

Mrs Mundy
Eldercroft House, Springhill Road, Peebles, Peeblesshire, EH45 9ER
Tel: 01721 724427

Upper apartment of detached Victorian house, with open outlook. Tastefully refurbished to a high standard, easy access to all amenities.

1 house, 2 pub rms, 2 bedrms, sleeps 4, £250.00-£325.00, Apr-Oct, bus nearby, airport 45 mls.

★★★ SELF CATERING

Mr & Mrs R K Walkinshaw
The Glack Farm, Manor, Peebles, EH45 9JL
Tel: 01721 740277

Whinstone built lower flat in residential area of Peebles, also centrally located flat with sunny rear garden. Ideal touring base. Varied local amenities.

2 flats, 1 pub rm, 4 bedrms, sleeps 6, total sleeping capacity 12, £200.00-£325.00, Jan-Dec, bus ¼ ml, rail 24 mls, airport 24 mls

---

★★★ SELF CATERING

Dr J Young
Liddisdale, Millfield Road, Riding Mill, Northumberland, NE44 6DL
Tel/Fax: 01434 682220
E-mail: jacyoung@yahoo.co.uk

Upper floor flat in detached house of traditional style, with external stone stairway. Furnished to a high standard and ideal for the town centre. Non-smoking.

1 flat, 1 pub rm, 1 bedrm, sleeps 3, £120.00-£200.00, Apr-Oct, bus nearby, rail 23 mls, airport 25 mls

---

VAT is shown at 17.5%: changes in this rate may affect prices.

Key to symbols is on back flap.

BY PEEBLES – PRESTWICK

A SOUTH OF SCOTLAND

by Peebles
Map Ref: 2C6

★★ SELF CATERING

Mrs Arran Waddell
Lyne Farmhouse, by Lyne Station, Peebles, EH45 8NR
Tel/Fax: 01721 740255

1 cottage, 1 pub rm, 4 bedrms (grd flr avail), sleeps 8, £200.00-£375.00, Jan-Dec, bus 4 mls, rail 23 mls, airport 24 mls

Cottage on 1300 acre farm, in area of scenic beauty. Ideal base for touring and walking. 4 miles (6 kms) from Peebles. 23 miles from Edinburgh.

Pinwherry, by Girvan, Ayrshire
Map Ref: 1G9

★★ SELF CATERING

Mrs P Guthrie
The Manse, Kirkoswald, by Maybole, Ayrshire, KA19 8JA
Tel: 01655 760210

1 cottage, 2 pub rms, 3 bedrms (grd flr avail), sleeps 6, £180.00-£200.00, Jan-Dec, bus nearby, rail 7 mls

Spacious detailed house with extensive enclosed woodland gardens with river boundary on the edge of the village. Ideal for those interested in outdoor pursuits, walking & fishing.

Portpatrick, Wigtownshire
Map Ref: 1F10

★★★ HOLIDAY PARK

Sunnymeade Caravan Park
Portpatrick, Stranraer, DG9 8LN
Tel/Fax: 01776 810293
E-mail: info@sunnymeade98.freeserve.co.uk
Web: www.sunnymeade98.freeserve.co.uk

Park accommodation: 90

15 tourers £7.00-9.00 or 15 motors £7.00-9.00 or 15 tents £7.00-9.00. Total Touring Pitches 15.
5 Holiday Caravans to let, sleep 6 £140.00-300.00, total sleeping capacity 30, min let 2 nights.

8 acres, grassy, hard-standing, level, Mar-Oct, prior booking in peak periods. Extra charge for electricity, showers.

Leisure facilities:

Take A77 to Portpatrick, on entering the village turn left. Park ¼ ml on left.

Port William, Wigtownshire
Map Ref: 1G11

★★ SELF CATERING

Hon Mrs Andrew Agnew
Sweethaws Farm, Crowborough, Sussex, TN6 3SS
Tel: 01892 655045

2 cottages, 1 pub rm, 2 bedrms (All grd.floor), sleeps 4-5, total sleeping capacity 13, £150.00-£400.00, Jan-Dec, bus nearby, rail 17 mls, ferry 17 mls, airport 100 mls

Comfortable cottages from Lermay close to the shore with views over Luce Bay to the Mull of Galloway.

Prestwick, Ayrshire
Map Ref: 1G7

★★ SELF CATERING

The Fairways
19 Links Road, Prestwick, Ayrshire, KA9 1QG
Tel/Fax: 01292 470396

1 cottage, 1 pub rm, 1 bedrm, sleeps 2-4, £150.00-£200.00, Jan-Dec, bus nearby, rail ¼ ml, airport 1 ml

Self-contained cottage all on ground floor in gardens of hotel with private parking. Short distance from town centre, railway station, golf course and beaches. Close to airport.

Important: Prices stated are estimates and may be subject to amendments

SOUTH OF SCOTLAND — A

RINGFORD – SALTCOATS

Ringford, Kirkcudbrightshire
Map Ref: 2A10

★★★ SELF CATERING

Queenshill Country Cottages
Fellend, Ringford, Castle Douglas, DG7 2AT
Tel/Fax: 01557 820227

6 chalets, 1 flat, 5 cottages, 1 8 bed dormitory, 1 estate house, sleeps 12, total sleeping capacity 66, from £160.00, Jan-Dec, bus 1 ml, rail 30 mls

At Queenshill we offer holidays to suit all tastes. Our visitors can enjoy either a quiet relaxing "get away from it all" holiday or one with more activity. Available to our visitors on site are: farm tours, bicycles for hire, pony trekking, fishing, clay pigeon shooting, tennis and nature trails.

Rockcliffe, by Dalbeattie, Kirkcudbrightshire
Map Ref: 2A10

★★★★ HOLIDAY PARK

Castle Point Caravan Site
Rockcliffe, by Dalbeattie, Kirkcudbrightshire, DG5 4QL
Tel: 01556 630248

Park accommodation: 37
29 tourers £7.75-10.20 or 29 motors £7.75-10.20 or 29 tents £7.75-10.20. Total Touring Pitches 29.
6 Holiday Caravans to let, sleep 6 £150.00-280.00, total sleeping capacity 36, min let 1 night.

3 acres, grassy, level, sloping, Mar-Oct, prior booking in peak periods. Extra charge for electricity, awnings.

From Dalbeattie take A710 S for 5 mls, turn right to Rockcliffe, then after 1 ml turn left down signposted road to Site.

Romanno Bridge, Peeblesshire
Map Ref: 2C6

★★ SELF CATERING

Dr Margaret Habeshaw
Damside, Romanno Bridge, West Linton, Peeblesshire, EH46 7BY
Tel/Fax: 01968 660887

1 cottage, 2 pub rms, 1 bedrm (All grd.floor), sleeps 2, £140.00-£180.00, May-Sep, bus 3 ½ mls, rail 17 mls, airport 20 mls

Traditional semi-detached stone cottage, spacious, comfortable and warm with beautiful views over fields and hills. Free fishing in half mile stretch of River Lyne. Ideally placed for exploring Borders or Edinburgh. Available May - September. Prices £140 -£180 including electricity.

St Boswells, Roxburghshire
Map Ref: 2D7

★★ UP TO ★★★★ SELF CATERING

Rosemary Joy Dale
The Holmes, St Boswells, Roxburghshire, TD6 0EL Tel: 01835 822356

3 flats, 2 cottages, 1 pub rm, 2-3 bedrms, sleeps 4-6, total sleeping capacity 22, £120.00-£360.00, Easter-Oct, Xmas/New Year, bus ½ ml, rail 40 mls, airport 37 mls

Cottages plus flats set in the spacious grounds of a delightful country mansion, bordered by the beautiful River Tweed, trout fishing available. Riverside walks, collection of farm animals and rare breeds and its own "Site of Special Scientific Interest".

Saltcoats, Ayrshire
Map Ref: 1G6

★★ SELF CATERING

Mrs Anne Hogarth
Knockrivoch Farm, Saltcoats, Ayrshire, KA21 6NH
Tel/Fax: 01294 463052

1 house, 3 pub rms, 3 bedrms, sleeps 7, £150.00-£300.00, Apr-Oct, bus 1 ml, rail 2 mls, ferry 3 mls, airport 20 mls

Spacious family house on dairy farm, with open views over the Firth of Clyde towards Arran. Large sun porch and separate dining room add to the large public areas.

VAT is shown at 17.5%: changes in this rate may affect prices.   *Key to symbols is on back flap.*

SANDHEAD – BY STRAITON, BY MAYBOLE

A SOUTH OF SCOTLAND

Sandhead, Wigtownshire — Map Ref: 1F11

Sands of Luce Caravan Park
Sandhead, by Stranraer, Wigtownshire, DG9 9JR
Tel/Fax: 01776 830456
Booking Enquiries: Mr & Mrs J W Sime

★★★★ HOLIDAY PARK

12 acres, mixed, mid Mar-Oct, prior booking in peak periods, latest time of arrival 2200, overnight holding area. Extra charge for electricity, awnings.

Park accommodation: 90
50 tourers £7.00-9.00 or 50 motors £6.50-8.50 or 10 tents £7.00-9.00. Total Touring Pitches 50.
6 Holiday Caravans to let, sleep 4-6 £145.00-295.00, total sleeping capacity 26, min let 2 days.

Leisure facilities:

From Stranraer take A77/A716 S for 7 mls. Entrance at junction of A716/B7084 approx. 1 ml N of Sandhead.

by Selkirk — Map Ref: 2D7

Mrs P Millar
Nether Whitlaw, Selkirk, TD7 4QN
Tel: 01750 21217/01896 754842

★★ SELF CATERING

Situated 4 miles (6kms) from Selkirk, this secluded detached cottage on a working farm has extensive views of the Cheviot and Eildon Hills, within 15 minutes drive of fishing on the River Tweed, Teviot, Ettrick and Yarrow, excellent walking country and golf courses.

1 cottage, 1 pub rm, 3 bedrms (grd flr avail), sleeps 6, £150.00-£350.00, Jan-Dec, bus 3 ½ mls, rail 40 mls, airport 40 mls

Southerness, Dumfriesshire — Map Ref: 2B10

Mrs J H Harris
North End Cottage, Damerham, Fordingbridge, Hants, SP6 3HA

★★ SELF CATERING

Spacious terraced cottage situated on the seashore of the Solway coast with superb views. Ideal for children, golfers, walkers and for touring the area. Shops & leisure of cumbrian hills across the solway. Facilities nearby.

1 cottage, 2 pub rms, 3 bedrms, sleeps 6, £250.00-£260.00, Jan-Dec, bus nearby, rail 15 mls, airport 70 mls

Lighthouse Leisure
Southerness, Dumfriesshire, DG2 8AZ
Tel: 01387 880277 Fax: 01387 880298

★★★ HOLIDAY PARK

8 ½ acres, grassy, level, Mar-Oct, prior booking in peak periods. Extra charge for electricity, awnings.

Park accommodation: 200
15 tourers £6.50-8.00 or 15 motors £6.50-8.00 or 15 tents £6.50-8.00. Total Touring Pitches 15.
5 Holiday Caravans to let, sleep 4-6 £95.00-280.00, total sleeping capacity 30, min let 1 night.

Leisure facilities:

From Dumfries take A710 S for 15 mls. Turn left at Southerness sign for 2 mls. Park office by first house on right.

by Straiton, by Maybole, Ayrshire — Map Ref: 1G8

Mrs A Hay
Blairquhan Estate Office, Maybole, Ayrshire, KA19 7LZ
Tel: 01655 770239 Fax: 01655 770278
E-mail: enquiries@blairquhan.co.uk Web: www.blairquhan.co.uk

★★ UP TO ★★★ SELF CATERING

Blairquhan is surrounded by a country estate in the beautiful wooded valley of the Water of Girvan. The Dower House and 7 holiday cottages are available all year round. Our guests can enjoy walks and picnics anywhere on the 2,000 acre estate or fish in the river lochs. Ayrshire is a world centre for golf. Local places of interest include Crossraguel Abbey, Culzean Castle and its country park, Loch Doon and the seaside resorts of Ayr and Girvan.

5 houses, 1 flat, 2 cottages, 1-4 pub rms, 1-10 bedrms (grd flr avail), sleeps 5-18, total sleeping capacity 60, £127.00-£1400.00, Jan-Dec, bus 4 mls, rail 7 mls, airport 20 mls

---

Important: Prices stated are estimates and may be subject to amendments

SOUTH OF SCOTLAND

BY STRANRAER – WEST LINTON

by Stranraer, Wigtownshire

Map Ref: 1F10

★★★ SELF CATERING

Wm McCormack
Kathleen Cottage, Lochnaw, Stranraer, by Stranraer
Tel: 01776 870635

1 cottage, 1 pub rm, sleeps 1-4, £135.00-£299.00, Jan-Jun, Aug-Dec, bus 2 mls, rail 5 mls, ferry 5 mls, airport 60 mls

Former gamekeepers cottage, dating from circa 1900, on a country estste. Quiet rural area, only 3 miles form the coast and renowned for a mild climate.

Thornhill, Dumfriesshire

Map Ref: 2A8

★★★ SELF CATERING

Mrs Craig
The Garth, Tynron, Thornhill, Dumfriesshire, DG3 4JY
Tel/Fax: 01848 200364

1 bothy cottage, 1 pub rm, 1 bedrm, sleeps 2, min let 3 days, to £182.00, Jan-Dec, bus ½ ml, rail 15 mls

Adjoining the owners large country house is this small cottage in a quiet peaceful situation with a river bordering the owners garden. A modern conversion of a high standard offering cosy accommodation for one couple with a Scandinavian type 'closet' bed, stylish kitchen and shower room. An ideal holiday home in a lovely rural farm with Thornhill approx 6 miles distance.

Troon, Ayrshire

Map Ref: 1G7

★★★ SELF CATERING

The Cherries
50 Ottoline Drive, Troon, Ayrshire, KA10 7AW
Tel: 01292 313312 Fax: 01292 319007
E-mail: andrew@scotsec.demon.co.uk
Web: www.smoothhound.co.uk/hotels/cherries.html

1 flat, 1 pub rm, 2 bedrms, sleeps 2-6, £160.00-£320.00, Jan-Dec, bus nearby, rail ½ ml, airport 3 mls

Second floor top flat on seafront with magnificent views over beach and sea. Near shops and transport. On street parking.

★★ SELF CATERING
BRONZE

Marion I Gibson
16 Harling Drive, Troon, Ayrshire, KA10 6NF
Tel: 01292 312555

2 flats, 1 pub rm, 2 bedrms, sleeps 4-5, total sleeping capacity 10, £130.00-£250.00, Jan-Dec, bus nearby, rail ½ ml, airport 5 mls

Two first floor flats situated in town centre, convenient for local shops. Close to local beaches and golf courses. Both flats have telephones which receive incoming calls only.

West Linton, Peeblesshire

Map Ref: 2B6

★★★ SELF CATERING

Mrs C M Kilpatrick
Slipperfield House, West Linton, Peeblesshire, EH46 7AA
Tel/Fax: 01968 660401
E-mail: hols@kilpat.demon.co.uk
Web: www.kilpat.demon.co.uk

2 cottages, 1 pub rm, 2-3 bedrms (grd flr avail), sleeps 4-6, total sleeping capacity 10, from £310.00, Jan-Dec, bus nearby, rail 18 mls, airport 24 mls

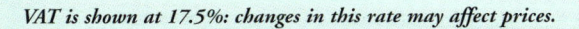

Attractive individual cottages one of which is attached to owner's house, set in 100 acres of woodlands overlooking stocked private fishing loch. Secluded location, yet only 19 miles from central Edinburgh.

VAT is shown at 17.5%: changes in this rate may affect prices.

Key to symbols is on back flap.

WESTRUTHER, BY GORDON – YETHOLM, BY KELSO

Westruther, by Gordon, Berwickshire
Map Ref: 2E6

★★ SELF CATERING

Mrs M MacFarlane
Flass, Westruther, Gordon, Berwickshire, TD3 6NJ
Tel/Fax: 01578 740215

1 cottage, 1 pub rm, 3 bedrms (All grd.floor), sleeps 5, £180.00-£230.00, May-Nov, bus 6 mls, rail 25 mls, airport 40 mls

Modern semi-detached single storey cottage on large mixed farm. Superb view of surrounding countryside. Westruther 1.5mls (3kms), Edin 40mls (64kms).

Yarrow, Selkirkshire
Map Ref: 2C7

★★ SELF CATERING

Mrs Caryl Thompson
Whitehope, Yarrow, Selkirk, Selkirkshire, TD7 5LA
Tel/Fax: 01750 82221

1 cottage, 1 pub rm, 3 bedrms (grd flr avail), sleeps 6, £120.00-£300.00, Jan-Dec, bus ¼ ml, rail 43 mls, airport 43 mls

Well equipped, traditional stone cottage in secluded location on working hill farm with panoramic views. 0.25 mile from main road through the beautiful Yarrow Valley. Enclosed grassy garden.

Yetholm, by Kelso, Roxburghshire
Map Ref: 2E7

★ SELF CATERING

Mrs A Freeland-Cook
Cliftoncote Farm, Yetholm, Kelso, Roxburghshire, TD5 8PU
Tel/Fax: 01573 420241

2 cottages, 1 pub rm, 2-3 bedrms (grd flr avail), sleeps 5-7, total sleeping capacity 12, min let weekend (low season), £80.00-£200.00, Jan-Dec, bus 2 ½ mls, rail 20 mls, airport 50 mls

Homely terraced cottages on a typical Borders sheep farm in the Cheviot Hills commanding excellent views. Ideal hillwalking/touring base.

Important: Prices stated are estimates and may be subject to amendments

Welcome to Scotland | Edinburgh & Lothians

DOMINATED BY ITS MIGHTY CASTLE PERCHED ON A HIGH CRAGGY RIDGE, EDINBURGH, THE CAPITAL CITY OF SCOTLAND, SURELY HAS ONE OF THE MOST DRAMATIC SETTINGS IN THE WORLD. BUILT AROUND AN EXTINCT VOLCANO, THE CITY CENTRE IS DIVIDED INTO TWO DISTINCT PARTS, CREATING A GREAT JUXTAPOSITION OF ARCHITECTURE BETWEEN ITS RAMBLING MEDIEVAL OLD TOWN AND ITS CLASSICAL GEORGIAN NEW TOWN.

Edinburgh is also a World Heritage City, hosts the world's largest annual arts festival and is now home to the new Scottish Parliament.

The city is steeped in history and culture, from the Palace of Holyrood where the tragic story of Mary Queen of Scots unfolded, to the once dark and cramped alleys of the Old Town which were the inspiration for Robert Louis Stevenson's novel Dr Jekyll and Mr Hyde. There are also scores of historic buildings along the length of the famous Royal Mile including John Knox's House, St Giles Cathedral and Gladstone's Land. In fact, history can be traced back through the entire history of Scotland at the Museum of Scotland, while the Dynamic Earth experience goes even further, by telling the concise evolution of the earth!

The Capital is known around the globe for its spectacular International Festival and Fringe but there is also a Science Festival, Film Festival and Folk Festival as well as the biggest street party in the world, to celebrate the New Year. As a major cultural centre, Edinburgh has numerous galleries, theatres and cinemas which offer all-year-round entertainment. Street cafes and restaurants specialising in both international cuisine and traditional Scottish cooking flourish, while over 700 bars can offer local beers and a wide range of malt whiskies.

Edinburgh & Lothians

Edinburgh & Lothians

Some of the best traditional and modern shopping in the country can be found in the city with the Waverley Shopping Centre enhancing the numerous department stores of Princes Street and the designer labels of George Street. Edinburgh has grown into a fast-paced cosmopolitan city, but at heart it still remains a collection of villages like those of Stockbridge and Cramond, where small shops and friendly welcomes are guaranteed. A relaxing alternative within the bustling city are the many quiet green spaces including Holyrood Park, Calton Hill, Dean Village and the Royal Botanical Gardens, whose horticultural delights include the world's largest collection of rhododendrons.

Within a few miles of the city centre are the Lothians, a haven for the outdoor enthusiast, with splendid hill-walking in the surrounding Pentlands, Moorfoots and Lammermuir Hills. There are almost seventy miles of coastline along the Firth of Forth combining nature reserves, sandy beaches and seaside resorts to satisfy most tastes. In the west, South Queensferry has the most dramatic location, with its cramped main street running under the gigantic structures of the famous Forth Bridges, while in the east, Dunbar has been officially recorded as Scotland's driest and sunniest town.

Edinburgh & Lothians

Experience and enjoy one of Europe's most exciting areas, by combining city and countryside, with easy access by air, rail and road. Edinburgh and Lothians can offer something for everyone, throughout the year.

Events
Edinburgh and Lothians

22-23 Jan
A Century of Farm Power
A static indoor exhibition illustrating the development of power on the farms of Scotland throughout the century. Royal Highland Showground, Ingliston, Edinburgh.
Tel: 01573 410354

8-23 Apr
Edinburgh International Science Festival
Tel: 0131 473 2070

22-25 Jun
Royal Highland Show
Contact: Lara Kirkpatrick
Tel: 0131 333 2444

1-31 Jul
Festival of Scottish Craft
Royal Museum/Museum of Scotland, Edinburgh
A month-long festival celebrating Scottish indigenous crafts including demonstrations, workshops and related events from boat building to bagpipe making.
Tel: 0131 247 4219

4-26 Aug
Edinburgh Military Tattoo
Tel: 0131 225 1188

Area Tourist Boards

Edinburgh & Lothians

43

Edinburgh & Lothians Tourist Board

Edinburgh & Lothians
Tourist Board
4 Rothesay Terrace
Edinburgh EH3 7RY

Tel: (0131) 473 3600
Fax: (0131) 473 3616
Web: www.ayrshire-arran.com

Tourist Information Centres

Edinburgh & Lothians

Edinburgh & Lothians Tourist Board

Dunbar
143 High Street
Tel: (01368) 863353
Jan-Dec

Edinburgh
Edinburgh and Scotland Information Centre
3 Princes Street
Tel: (0131) 473 3800
Jan-Dec

Edinburgh Airport
Tourist Information Desk
Tel: (0131) 333 2167
Jan-Dec

Linlithgow
Burgh Halls
The Cross
Tel: (01506) 844600
April-Oct

Newtongrange
Scottish Mining Museum
Lady Victoria Colliery
Tel: (0131) 663 4262
Easter-Oct

North Berwick
Quality Street
Tel: (01620) 892197
Jan-Dec

Old Craighall
Granada Service Area
A1
Musselburgh
Tel: (0131) 653 6172
Jan-Dec

Penicuik
Edinburgh Crystal Visitor Centre
Eastfield
Tel: (01968) 673846
Easter-Sept

B

EDINBURGH AND LOTHIANS

DUNBAR – EDINBURGH

Dunbar, East Lothian

Map Ref: 2E4

★★★ SELF CATERING

Mrs E Cox
26 Minto Street, Edinburgh, EH9 1SB
Tel: 0131 667 0880

1 house, 1 pub rm, 3 bedrms, sleeps 5, £200.00-£280.00, Jan-Dec, bus $1/4$ ml, rail $1/2$ ml, airport 30 mls

House full of character on harbour location with excellent views. Fitted to a high standard. Close to leisure centre.

Edinburgh

Map Ref: 2C5

★★★ UP TO ★★★★ SELF CATERING

Ronald Aitken
St Margarets Cottage, 32 Duddingston Park, Edinburgh, EH15 1JU
Tel: 0131 669 8327 Fax: 0131 661 9762

1 cottage, 1 pub rm, 2 bedrms, sleeps 4, £250.00-£400.00, Apr-Sep, bus nearby, rail 4 mls, airport 14 mls

Refurbished cottage adjacent to owners house with rear patio and garden. Easy access to local amenities and on main bus route to city centre. Also, luxury apartment close to Royal Mile and Holyrood Palace. Rooms warm and light with views to Arthurs Seat. All tourist attractions, and choice of fine restaurants close by. Secure parking and video entry system.

★★★ SELF CATERING

Baronscourt
7 Milton Road East, Edinburgh, EH15 2ND
Tel/Fax: 0131 669 6900

1 flat, 1 pub rm, 1 bedrm, sleeps 4, £180.00-£280.00, Jan-Dec, bus nearby, rail 3 $1/2$ mls, airport 10 mls

Compact self-contained flat in large house, with excellent coastal views. Excellent bus service to city centre (15 minutes). Off street parking. 5 - 10 minutes walk to Joppa Beach, and within easy access of East Lothian.

BOTANIC GARDEN APARTMENT

PO Box 12302, Edinburgh EH12 5LX
Tel: 0131 552 3260 Fax: 0131 347 9001
e.mail: BGA@netcomuk.co.uk Web: www.netcomuk.co.uk/~BGA

Beautifully renovated garden apartment in Georgian Villa next to Royal Botanic Garden. 15 minute walk or frequent bus service to city centre. Deluxe kitchen, large washer, dryer. Linens, towels provided. Twin beds convert to kings. Non-smoking. Telephone, satellite TV, video, CD. Landscaped deck with original well. Off street parking.

★★★★★ SELF CATERING

Botanic Garden Apartment
Po Box 12302, Edinburgh, EH12 5LX
Tel: 0131 552 3260 Fax: 0131 347 9001
E-mail: BGA@netcomuk.co.uk
Web: www.netcomuk.co.uk/~BGA

1 luxury garden flat, 1 pub rm, 3 bedrms, sleeps 6, £700.00-£950.00, Jan-Dec, bus nearby, rail 3 kms, ferry 6 kms, airport 10 kms.

Garden flat with secluded private garden with original well and deck area. Many original features of Georgian house retained. Close to Royal Botanic Garden. Private car parking space.

VAT is shown at 17.5%: changes in this rate may affect prices.

Key to symbols is on back flap.

EDINBURGH

EDINBURGH AND LOTHIANS

Edinburgh — Map Ref: 2C5

★★★★ SELF CATERING

Muriel Brattisani
13 Blackford Hill View, Edinburgh, EH9 3HD
Tel: 0131 667 7161 Fax: 0131 667 7042

Modernised apartment close to Queen's Park, Royal Commonwealth Pool and Edinburgh University residences. Easy access to city centre. Plus spacious house in quiet residential area within easy reach of all the amenties of Scotland's Historic Capital. Superb views of the city and Arthur's Seat.

2 flats, 2 pub rms, 2 bedrms (All grd.floor), sleeps 6, total sleeping capacity 12, £190.00-£700.00, Jan-Dec, bus nearby

★★★★ SELF CATERING

Mrs Lindsay Burge
Heathbank, Boat of Garten, Inverness-shire, PH24 3BD
Tel: 0131 332 0515/07711 317401
E-mail: raphaelle@hbank77.freeserve.co.uk

Beneath the castle in the heart of the Old Town this non smoking apartment is the ideal pied-a-terre for couples with its stylish rooms containing many thoughtful extras. The lounge overlooks the lively cosmopolitan Grassmarket, while the bedroom is quietly situated to the rear. Within 10 minutes walk are the Castle, Royal Mile, Princes Street and many Festival venues. The area teams with restaurants, characterful old inns and intriguing shops.

1 flat, 1 pub rm, 1 bedrm, sleeps 2, min let 3 nights, £300.00-£500.00, Dec-Oct, bus nearby, rail 1/2 ml, airport 6 mls

---

★★★★ SELF CATERING

Calton Apartments
44/1-8 Annandale Street, Edinburgh, EH7 4AY
Tel: 0131 556 3221
E-mail: Caltonapts@ednet.co.uk
Web: www.townhousehotels.co.uk

Perfectly situated near the top of Leith Walk, in the heart of Scotland's Capital. Only a short walk away from Princes Street, Calton Hill, Playhouse Theatre and Edinburgh Castle. Calton Apartments are furnished to an excellent standard and are the ideal base to explore historic Edinburgh.

8 apartments in 1 block, lounge, 2 bedrms, sleeps max. 6, min.let 2 nights, £300.00-£950.00, Jan-Dec, bus 1 ml, rail 1/2 ml, ferry 1 ml, airport 9 mls.

★ SELF CATERING

Mr A Cameron
51/2 Cockburn Street, Edinburgh, EH1 1BS
Tel: 0131 225 4772

Studio flat with own entrance from the communal stair, close to all city centre amenities. Views of Scott Monument and Princes Street.

1 flat, 1 pub rm, sleeps 1-4, £245.00-£490.00, Jan-Dec

★★★★ SELF CATERING

Capital Vacations
28 Braid Crescent, Edinburgh, EH10 6AU
Tel: 0131 447 1450 Fax: 0131 446 9393
E-mail: capitalvacations@dial.pipex.com
Web: www.capitalvacations.co.uk

Luxurious modern, fully equipped, apartment in attractive docklands location with large external balcony overlooking the Water of Leith river. Facilities include lift (elevator) and private off road parking. Local attractions include the Royal Yacht Britannia and a wide range of restaurants and pubs.

1 first floor apartment, 2 pub rms, 2 bedrms, sleeps 4, min let 2 nights, £504.00-£625.00, Jan-Dec, bus 5 min, rail 15 min, airport 25 min

Important: Prices stated are estimates and may be subject to amendments

EDINBURGH AND LOTHIANS

B

EDINBURGH

Edinburgh

Map Ref: 2C5

DUNSTAFFNAGE HOUSE
12 Regent Terrace, Edinburgh EH7 5BN
Tel: 0131 556 8309 Fax: 0131 478 0251

Central yet quietly located luxury apartments only eight minutes walk from Princes Street and the Royal Mile. These apartments are furnished to a high standard and accommodate a maximum of 5 people. The house retains many original features and the owner lives on the premises. £45-£90 per night. Dunstaffnage House has a no smoking policy.

★★★★
SELF CATERING

John Crooks
Dunstaffnage House, 12 Regent Terrace, Edinburgh, EH7 5BN
Tel: 0131 556 8309 Fax: 0131 478 0251

Impressive first floor Georgian flat with many period features. Peaceful location in a prestigious area just 10 minutes' walk from Princes St and Royal Mile.

1 house, 2 pub rms, 2 bedrms, sleeps 1-4, £280.00-£650.00, Jan-Dec, bus nearby, rail nearby, airport 8 mls Nightly rate £45.00-£90.00.

★★★★
SELF CATERING

Mrs Mary Curran
8 East Bay, North Queensferry, Fife, KY11 1JX
Tel: 01383 413242

Attractive 2-storey mews cottage in the heart of the Georgian new town. 5 minutes walk from Princes Street. Ideal location to explore Edinburgh on foot.

1 cottage, 1 pub rm, 3 bedrms, sleeps 4, min let 4 days, £250.00-£600.00, Jan-Dec, bus ¼ ml, rail ¼ ml, airport 10 mls

---

★
SELF CATERING

Sheila Donachie
64 St John's Road, Edinburgh, EH12 8AT
Tel/Fax: 0131 334 2860

In centre of Corstorphine, close to zoo, this semi-detached house is an ideal base for exploring Edinburgh and its surroundings.

1 house, 1 cottage, 1 pub rm, 2-3 bedrms, sleeps 5-6, total sleeping capacity 11, £380.00-£420.00, Jan-Dec, bus nearby, rail 5 mls, airport 5 mls

---

★★
SELF CATERING

Mr J Donaldson
Invermark, 60 Polwarth Terrace, Edinburgh, EH11 1NJ
Tel: 0131 337 1066

First floor flat in residential area, with local bus routes to city centre. Good restaurants, cinemas and theatres all in walking distance. Unrestricted on-street parking.

1 flat, 2 pub rms, 3 bedrms, sleeps 5, £300.00-£485.00, Jan-Dec, bus 500 yds, rail 1 ml, airport 4 mls

---

VAT is shown at 17.5%: changes in this rate may affect prices.

Key to symbols is on back flap.

EDINBURGH

EDINBURGH AND LOTHIANS

Edinburgh
Map Ref: 2C5

★★ UP TO ★★★★ SELF CATERING

Mrs Elizabeth Epps
3d Scotland Street, Edinburgh, EH3 6PP
Tel: 0131 556 9797

2 flats, 1 pub rm, 1 bedrm, sleeps 2, total sleeping capacity 2, £320.00-£385.00, Jan-Dec, bus 200 yds, rail 1 mls, airport 5 mls

Garden and main door flats, centrally situated in Edinburgh New Town, close to city centre and major bus routes. Variety of restaurants nearby.

★ UP TO ★★ SELF CATERING

Mrs Hilary Forbes
20 Parrotshot, Edinburgh, EH15 3RU
Tel: 0131 6697692
E-mail: h@forbes200.freeserve.co.uk

2 studio flats, 1 room with en-suite, sleeps 2, total sleeping capacity 4, £250.00-£350.00, Jan-Dec, bus nearby, rail 1 ml, airport 6 mls

Self contained studio flatlets with ensuite shower rooms in quiet Georgian square 2 minutes walk from Princes Street with all its amenities and attractions. Numerous restaurants in the immediate vicinity.

★★ SELF CATERING

Aileen Gilchrist
7/8 St Clair Avenue, Edinburgh
Tel: 0131 553 6239

1 flat, 1 pub rm, 1 bedrm, sleeps 4, min let weekend, £200.00-£480.00, Jan-Dec, bus nearby, rail nearby

First floor flat situated close to castle and a few minutes walk to Princes St. Leisure facilities and laundry available.

Glen House Apartments
101 Lauriston Place, Tollcross, Edinburgh EH3 9JB
Telephone: 0131 228 4043 Fax: 0131 229 8873
e.mail: info@edinburgh-apartments.co.uk
Web: www.edinburgh-apartments.co.uk

We offer a welcome to our wide range of city centre apartments; comfortable, modernised, fully furnished, from studio to 3-bedrooms – some with private parking – for business and holidays. Individuals, families and groups.
Housekeeping services available if required.
TV, telephones, central heating and washing machines. Full linen service.

★★★ SELF CATERING

Glen House Apartments
101 Lauriston Place, Edinburgh, EH3 9JB
Tel: 0131 228 4043 Fax: 0131 229 8873
E-mail: info@edinburgh-apartments.co.uk
Web: www.edinburgh-apartments.co.uk

See details of properties in display advertisement above.

Important: Prices stated are estimates and may be subject to amendments

EDINBURGH AND LOTHIANS

EDINBURGH

Map Ref: 2C5

★★ SELF CATERING

Karen & Gerry Johnstone
Adam Drysdale Apartment, 42 Gilmore Place, Edinburgh, EH3 9NQ
Tel/Fax: 0131 228 8952

Cottage style apartment in central location. Close to Kings Theatre and Conference Centre, within walking distance of Princes Street and the Castle. Private parking. Majority of property on ground level.

1 cottage style apartment, 2 pub rms, 2 bedrms (All grd.floor), sleeps 4, min let 3 nights, £50.00-£90.00 per night, £250.00-£500.00 per week. Please contact the establishment, bus nearby, rail 1 ml, airport 8 mls.

★★★★ SERVICED APARTMENTS

Kew Serviced Apartments
1 Kew Terrace, Edinburgh, Lothian, EH12 5JE
Tel: 0131 313 0700 Fax: 0131 313 0747
E-mail: kewhouse@compuserve.com
Web: www.kewhouse.co.uk

Modern luxury penthouse flat near historic Dean Village in west end of city centre. Fully equipped and serviced. All bedding and towels supplied. Continental breakfast on first morning. Lounge with balcony. Private garage.

1 penthouse flat, 2 pub rms, 2 bedrms, sleeps 2-4, min let 2 nights, £450.00-£720.00, Jan-Dec, bus ¾ ml, rail 1 ml, airport 4 mls

---

★★★ SELF CATERING

Sally le Bert - Francis
4 Regent Terrace, Edinburgh, EH7 5BN
Tel: 0131 558 9536

Garden flat in prestigious Georgian Terrace skirting Calton Hill. Five minutes walk to Princes Street. Access to extensive Calton Hill Gardens.

1 flat, 1 pub rm, 2 bedrms (All grd.floor), sleeps 5-6, min let 2 nights, £325.00-£625.00, Jan-Dec, bus 150 yds, rail ¾ ml

---

★★★★ SELF CATERING

Mrs Janet Linney
3 Redford Grove, Colinton, Edinburgh, EH13 0AH
Tel: 0131 441 6984

Luxury family accommodation, sleeps 6. Close to Murrayfield rugby ground and 10 min walk to city centre. On main bus routes. Modern sunny flat with views of Pentland Hills. Private parking.

1 self catering apartment, 1 pub rm, 2 bedrms, sleeps 6, £360.00-£560.00, Jan-Dec, bus 200 mtrs, rail 800 mtrs, airport 4 mls

---

★ UP TO ★★ SELF CATERING

Linton Court Apartments
Linton Court, Murieston Road, Edinburgh, EH11 2JJ
Tel: 0131 337 4040 Fax: 0131 337 8547
E-mail: lintoncourt@enterprise.net
Web: www.accomodata.co.uk

Selection of serviced flats and apartments, 1 mile (2kms) south-west of centre. Convenient bus routes to city. Resident caretaker. Entryphone system.

39 flats, 5 bedsit complex, 1 pub rm, 1-3 bedrms (grd flr avail), sleeps 1-7, total sleeping capacity 173, min let 1 day, £90.00-£575.00, Jan-Dec, bus nearby, rail 1 ml, airport 5 mls

---

VAT is shown at 17.5%: changes in this rate may affect prices.

Key to symbols is on back flap.

EDINBURGH AND LOTHIANS

Edinburgh

Map Ref: 2C5

★★★ SELF CATERING

Mrs M MacDougall
10 Player Green, Deer Park, Livingston, EH54 8RZ
Tel: 01506 438900 Fax: 01506 432117
E-mail: meg@castlettes.demon.co.uk

3 flats, 1 pub rm, 1 bedrm, sleeps 2-4, total sleeping capacity 10, £195.00-£420.00, Jan-Dec, rail ½ ml

Compact apartments, ideal location in the heart of Edinburgh's historic Grassmarket. Minutes walk from Princes Street and the castle.

★★★★ SELF CATERING

Mr L E MacIntosh
42 Inverleith Row, Edinburgh, EH3 5PY
Tel/Fax: 0131 552 2954

1 main door flat, 2 pub rms, 3 bedrms (All grd.floor), sleeps 6, min let 4 days, £450.00-£800.00, Jan-Dec, bus nearby, rail ½ ml, airport 5 mls

Spacious and attractively furnished new town apartment. Ideally situated for all city centre amenities.

★★★ UP TO ★★★★ SELF CATERING

MacRae Capital & Country Holidays
45 Eskbank Road, Dalkeith, Midlothian, EH22 3BH
Tel/Fax: 0131 663 3291
E-mail: edinvac@email.menet.net
Web: www.scotland2000/morningside

3 flats, 2 pub rms, 4-6 bedrms (grd flr avail), sleeps 4-5, total sleeping capacity 15/16, £250.00-£650.00, Jan-Dec, bus nearby, rail 7 mls, airport 8 mls

3 self catering apartments. Two in up market residential area of Edinburgh and the other in the conservation area of Eskbank. Ideal for the capital experience and country touring.

★★★★ SELF CATERING

Joanne Mower
5 Royal Terrace, Edinburgh, EH7 5AB
Tel: 0131 557 5778 Fax: 0131 557 1215
E-mail: jo_mower@ednet.co.uk Web: www.ednet.co.uk/~jo_mower

1 house, 2 pub rms, 3 ensuite bedrms, sleeps 2-8, min.let 2 nights, £300.00-£800.00, Jan-Dec, bus nearby, rail nearby, airport 15 mls.

Central garden flat in fine Georgian town house. 3 bedrooms, 1 ensuite, sleeps 2-8 people. Well equipped, newly refurbished. Spacious and comfortable accommodation. Access to 12 acres of beautiful private gardens with swings tennis courts and putting green which leads to Calton Hill and Princes Street 5 mins walk, all major sites of interest in walking distance, 15 mins walk to Arthurs Seat.

★★ SELF CATERING

Napier University
St Andrews Hall, 219 Colinton Road, Edinburgh, EH14 1DJ
Tel: 0131 455 4291 Fax: 0131 455 4411
E-mail: j.grieve@napier.ac.uk
Web: www.vacation.lets@napier.ac.uk

3 houses, each 1-2 pub rms, 7-9 bedrms (grd flr avail), sleeps total sleeping capacity 38, £115.00-£130.00 per person per week, Jul-Sep, bus nearby, rail 2 mls, airport 5 mls

Victorian terraced villas in quiet location close to town centre.

Important: Prices stated are estimates and may be subject to amendments

EDINBURGH AND LOTHIANS

Edinburgh

Map Ref: 2C5

SELF CATERING — UP TO ★★

Napier University
219 Colinton Road, Edinburgh, EH14 1DJ
0131 455 4331 Fax: 0131 455 4411
E-mail: d.stratton@napier.ac.uk
Web: www.vacation.lets@napier.ac.uk

Self-contained university flats in central area with nearby bus routes, restaurants, cinema and the Kings Theatre.

81 flats, 1 pub rm, 3-5 bedrms (grd flr avail), sleeps 3-5, total sleeping capacity 382, min let 3 nights, £300.00-£450.00, early Jul-3rd.wk Sep, bus nearby, rail 1 ml, airport 5 mls

SELF CATERING — ★★★ UP TO ★★★★

Newbank Lettings
c/o Dunstane House Hotel, 4 West Coates, Edinburgh, EH12 5JQ
Tel/Fax: 0131 337 6169
E-mail: smowat@compuserve.com
Web: http://members.edinburgh.org/mowat

Newly refurbished detached houses in garden grounds with ample private parking. Quiet residential area. Approx 1 mile to city centre and 5 mins walk to Royal Botanical Gardens.

2 houses, 2 pub rms, 3 bedrms (grd flr avail), sleeps 5-6, total sleeping capacity 11, min let 2 nights, £450.00-£790.00, Jan-Dec, bus 1 1/2 mls, rail 1 1/2 mls, airport 7 mls

SELF CATERING — ★ UP TO ★★★

No 5, 5 Abercorn Terrace
Portobello, Edinburgh, EH15 2DD
Tel/Fax: 0131 669 1044

Good quality, budget priced self catering offering a range of singe, double and twin bedded units. Each unit is fully equipped. Some have ensuite bathrooms, others share four bath/shower rooms. Some off-road parking, also unrestricted street parking. Frequent buses to city centre and well kept beach 200 metres distance.

2 flats, 5 studio apartments, 1 pub rm, 1 bedrm, sleeps 1-3, total sleeping capacity 18, £60.00-£350.00, Jan-Dec, bus nearby, rail 4 mls, airport 6 mls

CANON COURT
20 CANONMILLS, EDINBURGH EH3 5LH
Tel: 0131-474 7000   Fax: 0131-474 7001
e.mail: canon.court@dial.pipex.com   Web: www.canoncourt.co.uk

A modern complex of 43 apartments in an ideal city centre location, offering flexible and secure quality accommodation. Purpose built in 1997, the apartments are bright and comfortable with 1 or 2 bedrooms, lounge/dining room, bathroom and fitted kitchen. Close to the Royal Botanic Gardens and excellent local amenities. Lift. On-site parking.

SERVICED APARTMENTS — ★★★★

N Paul
Canon Court Apartments, 20 Canonmills, Edinburgh, EH3 5LH
Tel: 0131 474 7000 Fax: 0131 474 7001
E-mail: canon.court@dial.pipex.com
Web: www.canoncourt.co.uk

Modern complex of apartments in City centre location. Facilities include reception on site, complimentary parking, security entry 'phone and 24hr laundry service available. Other limited services available at extra cost.

43 flats, 1-2 pub rms, 1-2 bedrms (grd flr avail), sleeps 1-4, total sleeping capacity 122, min let 1 night, £413.00-£1260.00, Jan-Dec, bus nearby, rail nearby, airport nearby

VAT is shown at 17.5%: changes in this rate may affect prices.

Key to symbols is on back flap.

EDINBURGH

EDINBURGH AND LOTHIANS

Edinburgh — Map Ref: 2C5

SELF CATERING ★

Mrs C F Peters
Wester Bavelaw, Balerno, Edinburgh, EH14 7JS
Tel: 0131 449 5515

1 cottage, 2 pub rms, 2 bedrms (All grd.floor), sleeps 5, £245.00-£405.00, Jan-Dec, bus 4 mls, rail 12 mls, airport 8 mls

Traditional farm cottage on sheep farm in the Pentlands. Hillwalking from the doorstep yet only 12 miles (19kms) from Edinburgh and 5 miles to motorway.

SELF CATERING ★★★★

Premier Vacations
5 St Peters Buildings, Edinburgh, EH3 9PG
Tel: 0131-221 9001 Fax: 07000 777577
E-mail: reservations@premiervacations.net
Web: www.premiervacations.net

2 flats, 1 pub rm, 1 bedrm (All grd.floor), sleeps 2-4, total sleeping capacity 8, min let 3 days, £280.00-£560.00, Jan-Dec, bus nearby, rail 2 mls, airport 5 mls

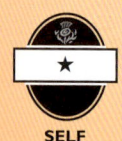

An upmarket conversion of a former bonded warehouse into stylish modern apartments close to the Waterfront of Leith. An old port makes this a fascinating destination for both business and leisure trips.

SELF CATERING ★

Queen Margaret University College
Clerwood Terrace, Edinburgh, EH12 8TS
Tel: 0131 317 3310 Fax: 0131 317 3169
E-mail: k.sampson@mail.qmced.ac.uk
Web: www.qmuc.ac.uk

37 flats, 3-4 bedrms (grd flr avail), sleeps 3-4, total sleeping capacity 138, £380.00-£485.00, Jun-Sep, bus nearby, rail 3 mls, airport 3 mls

Holiday flats in a secluded campus with an 18c flower garden. 20 minutes from city centre. On site leisure facilities, including indoor swimming pool.

Royal Garden Apartments

York Buildings, Queen Street, Edinburgh EH2 1HY
Tel: 0131 625 1234 Fax: 0131 625 5678
e.mail: reservations@royal-garden.co.uk Web: www.royal-garden.co.uk

Luxury serviced apartments in a 'B' listed Georgian building, offering a range of one or two bedrooms with a spacious lounge, dining area, fully fitted kitchen and ensuite bathroom. Two penthouse suites with private balcony. Ideal for leisure or business for any length of stay.
Prices from £60-£73.75 sharing per person per night.

SERVICED APARTMENTS ★★★★

Royal Garden Apartments
York Buildings, Queen Street, Edinburgh, EH2 1HY
Tel: 0131 625 1234 Fax: 0131 625 5678
E-mail: reservations@royal-garden.co.uk
Web: www.royal-garden.co.uk

30 luxury serviced apartments, 1 pub rm, 1-2 bedrms, sleeps 1-6, min let 1 night, £595.00-£1,505.00, Jan-Dec, bus nearby, rail ½ ml, airport 8 mls.

Conveniently situated near the city centre this large 'B' listed Georgian Building offers a range of luxury one or two bedrooms Serviced Apartments. 24 hour reception, cleaning service, laundry & stylish cafe for breakfast and lunch. Lift to all floors modern kitchens, cable TV fax modem points, dishwashers, microwaves and traditional oven & Hob.

Important: Prices stated are estimates and may be subject to amendments

B

EDINBURGH AND LOTHIANS **EDINBURGH**

53

Edinburgh   Map Ref: 2C5

SELF CATERING ★★★★

Eleanor Simpson
97 Market Street, Musselburgh, EH21 6PY
Tel: 0131 665 7140

2 flats, 1 pub rm, 1 bedrm (All grd.floor), sleeps 4, total sleeping capacity 4, £180.00-£500.00, Jan-Dec, bus 200 yds, rail 1 ml

New housing development 1 mile south of Princes Street, adjacent to Holyrood Park. Central yet peaceful location. Private Parking. Lady Wynd is situated off the grassmarket and overlooked by Edinburgh Castle. A five minute walk through the gardens to Princes Street with its exclusive shopping facilities. Central location for all of Edinburghs cultural and historical attractions.

SELF CATERING ★★★

Mrs F Speight
5 Inverleith Row, Edinburgh, EH3 5LP
Tel: 0131 558 1653 Fax: 0131 624 0015

1 house, 2 flats, 1 pub rm, 2 bedrms, sleeps 4, total sleeping capacity 8, £361.00-£682.00, Jan-Dec, bus nearby, rail 1 ml, airport 10 mls

Lower ground flat with traditional character in listed Georgian villa. On main bus route, adjacent to the Botanic gardens in this prestigious area. Also 4th floor flat in the area of Arthurs Seat and beside Holyrood. Views across Firth of Forth as far as North Berwick.

Sibbet House Apartments
c/o 26 Northumberland Street, Edinburgh EH3 6LS
Tel: 0131 556 1078 Fax: 0131 557 9445
e-mail: sibbet.house@zetnet.co.uk
Web: http://www.sibbet-house.co.uk

Two central but quiet apartments, both looking towards private gardens in Edinburgh's prestigious New Town. Close to Princes Street with many attractions nearby plus serious shopping and restaurants. Spacious, with full facilities – cable TV, radio, telephone, laundry. All linen and towels provided. Car parking available. *Suitable for vacation or business.*

SELF CATERING ★★★★

Mr & Mrs Steffen
Sibbet House, 26 Northumberland Street, Edinburgh
Tel: 0131 556 1078 Fax: 0131 557 9445
E-mail: sibbet.house@zetnet.co.uk
Web: www.sibbet-house.co.uk

1 flat, 1 pub rm, 3 bedrms (grd flr avail), sleeps 5, min let 4 days, £480.00-£700.00, Jan-Dec, bus ½ ml, rail ½ ml, airport 8 mls

Newly refurbished, ground and basement luxury flat in Edinburgh New Town. In the centre of the city but in quiet area. Princes Street 7 minutes walk.

SELF CATERING ★★★★

Gillian Stephens
23 Dublin Street, Edinburgh, EH1 3PG
Tel: 0131 556 7081 Fax: 0131 623 7123
E-mail: edinburgh.accommodation@cableinet.co.uk
Web: http://wkweb4.cableinet.co.uk/edinburgh_accommodation

1 flat, 2 pub rms, 2 bedrms, sleeps 6, min let 2 nights, £504.00-£630.00, Jan-Dec, bus nearby, rail ½ ml, airport 8 mls

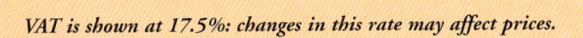

Very comfortable spacious second floor flat in a substantial stone built gracious Georgian crescent. Ideally located for all amenities including theatres, excellent shopping and transport facilities. A short walk to the conference centre, Edinburgh Castle and Princes Street.

VAT is shown at 17.5%: changes in this rate may affect prices.   *Key to symbols is on back flap.*

EDINBURGH — EDINBURGH AND LOTHIANS

Edinburgh
Map Ref: 2C5

★★★★ SELF CATERING

Sandra Tully
Dunalton, 43 Braid Farm Road, Edinburgh, EH10 6LE
Tel: 0131 447 3065 Fax: 0131 452 8497
E-mail: sandra_tully@edinhire.demon.co.uk
Web: www.edinhire.demon.co.uk

Self contained flat adjoining owners house with access to garden, in quiet residential area on South side of Edinburgh. Private parking.

Quiet comfortable fully equipped ground floor flat lovely views 3 mls city centre (bus nearby, rail 3 mls, airport 5 mls). Sleeps 1-4, £300 per week £50 per night. Min charge 2 nights.

Edinburgh First — Holyrood Park Road, Edinburgh EH16 5AY
University of Edinburgh

Well-equipped self-catering flats and houses for 3 to 6 persons in convenient city locations at great value for money prices. Weekly terms (Saturday to Saturday) from £280 fully inclusive.
Tel: 0800 028 7118   Fax: 0131 667 7271
e.mail: Edinburgh.First@ed.ac.uk   Web: www.EdinburghFirst.com

★ SELF CATERING

Vacation Letting
30 Buccleuch Place, Edinburgh, EH8 9JS
Tel: 0131 650 4669 Fax: 0131 650 6867
E-mail: accommodation@ed.ac.uk

A range of 58 flats accommodating 3-5 persons, converted from a former school and overlooking the Meadows and Bruntsfield Links. Some flats have views of Edinburgh Castle. Convenient for the city centre with good public transport links. Restaurants, cafes, delicatessens and theatres nearby. Putting, tennis, swimming in the close vicinity. 10 minutes Edinburgh cycle way, cycle hire locally.

38 flats, 1 pub rm, 3-5 bedrms (grd flr avail), sleeps 3-5, total sleeping capacity 140, £280.00-£420.00, Jul-Sep, bus nearby, rail 2 mls, airport 6 mls

---

★★★ SELF CATERING

Dr Julie Watt
630 Lanark Road, Edinburgh, EH14 5EW
Tel: 0131 538 0352 Fax: 0131 453 4088

First floor flat in picturesque old town of Edinburgh. Formerly an 18th century coaching inn, restored by a conservation trust. Kitchen window overlooks ancient Greyfriars Church and Kirkyard.

1 flat, 1 pub rm, 1 bedrm, sleeps 2-4, £250.00-£520.00, Jan-Dec, bus nearby, rail 1/2 ml, airport 5 mls

---

★★★ UP TO ★★★★ SELF CATERING

West End Apartments
2 Learmonth Terrace, Edinburgh, EH4 1PQ
Tel: 0131 332 0717/226 6512 Fax: 0131 226 6513
E-mail: brian@sias.co.uk

Apartments and studio apartments situated in elegant Victorian terraced house, close to West End and city centre. Unrestricted parking close by and frequent bus services.

5 flats, 1 pub rm, 1-2 bedrms, sleeps 2-5, total sleeping capacity 13, min let 2 nights, £200.00-£800.00, Jan-Dec, bus nearby, rail 1 ml, airport 7 mls

Important: Prices stated are estimates and may be subject to amendments

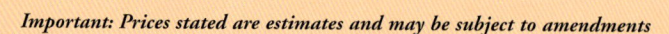

EDINBURGH AND LOTHIANS

HADDINGTON – NORTH BERWICK

Haddington, East Lothian
Map Ref: 2D4

The Monks' Muir ★★★★ HOLIDAY PARK
Haddington, East Lothian, EH41 3SB
Tel: 01620 860340 Fax: 01620 861770
E-mail: monksmuir@aol.com

7 acres, grassy, level, sheltered, Jan-Dec, prior booking in peak periods, latest time of arrival 2400. Extra charge for electricity, awnings.

Park accommodation: 93
40 tourers £11.40-12.00 or 40 motors £11.40-12.00 or 40 tents £8.40-9.90. Total Touring Pitches 40.
8 Holiday Caravans to let, sleep 2-6 £130.00-440.00, total sleeping capacity 40, min let 1 night.

On A1 midway between Haddington and East Linton, signposted on A1 in advance.

Humbie, East Lothian
Map Ref: 2D5

Fiona Lewis ★★ SELF CATERING
10 Kippithill, Humbie, East Lothian, EH36 5PP
Tel: 01875 833323

Former gate lodge, 15 miles (24kms) from Edinburgh, in quiet countryside offering peace and tranquility. Ideal for hillwalking, golfing and outdoor pursuits.

1 cottage, 2 pub rms, 2 bedrms (All grd.floor), sleeps 5, £130.00-£290.00, Jan-Dec, bus 2 mls, rail 17 mls, airport 20 mls

Linlithgow, West Lothian
Map Ref: 2B4

Craigs Chalet Park, John & Greetje Howie ★★ SELF CATERING
Williamcraigs, Linlithgow, West Lothian, EH49 6QF
Tel/Fax: 01506 845025
E-mail: info@craigslodges.freeserve.co.uk
Web: www.craigslodges.freeserve.co.uk

Nine chalets set in 8.5 acres of wooded hillside, on the outskirts of historic Linlithgow. Extensive views over the Forth Valley. Children's play area. Two country parks within walking distance as are Linlithgow Sports Centre and swimming pool. Convenient access to Glasgow and Edinburgh via motorway.

9 chalets, 1 pub rm, 2 bedrms, sleeps 4-5, total sleeping capacity 43, from £159.00, Jan-Dec, bus 1 ml, rail 1½ mls, airport 14 mls

Longniddry, East Lothian
Map Ref: 2D4

Seton Sands Holiday Village ★★★ HOLIDAY PARK
Longniddry, East Lothian
Tel: 01875 813333 Fax: 01875 813531

66 acres, level, end Mar-Oct, prior booking in peak periods. Extra charge for electricity.

Park accommodation: 665
60 tourers £8.00-14.00 or 60 motors £8.00-14.00. Total Touring Pitches 60. No tents.
83 Holiday Caravans to let, sleep 2-8 £105.00-440.00, min let 3 nights.

Leisure facilities:

Take A1 to Tranent slip road, onto B6371 for Cockenzie, then right onto B1348.

North Berwick, East Lothian
Map Ref: 2D4

Mr I Kirkpatrick ★ SELF CATERING
2 Hillview Road, Edinburgh, EH12 8QN
Tel: 0131 334 5951

2nd floor family flat in the town centre close to sandy beaches and town harbour. ½ hour by train from Edinburgh. Suitable for family and golfing holidays.

1 flat, 1 pub rm, 2 bedrms, sleeps 4, £100.00-£200.00, Jan-Dec, bus nearby, rail ¼ ml, airport 30 mls

VAT is shown at 17.5%: changes in this rate may affect prices.

Key to symbols is on back flap.

NORTH BERWICK – BY WEST CALDER

EDINBURGH AND LOTHIANS

North Berwick, East Lothian — Map Ref: 2D4

★★★ SELF CATERING

Mrs E M MacDonald
Blake Holt, Browsea View Avenue, Lilliput, Poole, Dorset, BH14 8LQ
Tel: 01202 707894

1 house, 1 pub rm, 3 bedrms (grd flr avail), sleeps 6, £125.00-£425.00, Jan-Dec, bus nearby, rail nearby, airport 30 mls

Traditional Scottish home in sheltered walled garden with garden furniture and private parking. It has immediate access on to the golf course (18th green) and nearby sandy beach. Convenient for rail station and local amenities in town.

★★★★ SELF CATERING

Mrs M Stamp
10 Westgate, North Berwick, East Lothian, EH39 4AF
Tel/Fax: 01620 893785

1 garden studio apartment, sleeps 2, £160.00-£220.00, Jan-Dec, bus 50 yds, rail 1/2 ml, airport 26 mls

Self contained south facing comfortable garden studio situated within our garden with its own patio, furnished to a high standard. Close to beach and nearby golf courses. Private parking. Only 2 minutes walk from the shops and restaurants.

Penicuik, Midlothian — Map Ref: 2C5

★★ UP TO ★★★★ SELF CATERING

Mrs Susan Cowan
Eastside Farm, Penicuik, Midlothian, EH26 9LN
Tel/Fax: 01968 677842

2 cottages, 1 pub rm, 1-2 bedrms (grd.flr avail), sleeps 2-4, min.let 4 days, £220.00-£450.00, Jan-Dec, bus 1 ml, rail 9 mls, airport 12 mls.

Two 18c converted cottages side by side on working sheep farm in Pentland Hills Regional Park. Hillside location but within easy commuting distance of Edinburgh.

---

by West Calder, West Lothian — Map Ref: 2B5

★★★ UP TO ★★★★ SELF CATERING

Mrs Geraldine Hamilton
Crosswoodhill Farm, West Calder, West Lothian, EH55 8LP
Tel: 01501 785205 Fax: 01501 785308
E-mail: crosswd@globalnet.co.uk
Web: www.users.globalnet.co.uk/~crosswd/index.html

2 cottages, 1 apartment, 1-2 pub rms, 2-3 bedrms (grd flr avail), sleeps 5-6, total sleeping capacity 17, £260.00-£550.00, Jan-Dec, bus 6 mls, rail 6 mls, airport 6 mls

Enviable location on Pentland Hills, 35 mins drive from the heart of Edinburgh. Within an hour's drive of Glasgow, Rob Roy, Braveheart and Border Country. This is the perfect place to relax. Our 1700 acre sheep farm offers 3 very special 200 year old properties: two imaginatively designed cottages (one isolated) and a farmhouse "wing". Cosy peat/coal fires. CH. Thoughtfully equipped. 3 bedrooms each. Car essential. Photographic brochure.

Important: Prices stated are estimates and may be subject to amendments

Welcome to Scotland | Greater Glasgow & Clyde Valley

SINCE THE DAWN OF THE 1990'S WHEN GLASGOW PUT ON ITS MANTLE AS THE EUROPEAN CITY OF CULTURE, THERE'S BEEN NO HOLDING IT BACK. ONCE SEEN ONLY AS AN INDUSTRIAL GIANT SET ON THE BANKS OF THE RIVER CLYDE, GLASGOW HAS BEEN REBORN AS A VIBRANT, FASHIONABLE METROPOLIS, WHICH POSITIVELY HUMS WITH ENTERPRISE AND VITALITY.

This is one of Europe's most eclectic and stylish cities whose architecture, ranging from the magnificent Gothic style of Glasgow Cathedral to the imposing Italian Renaissance of the City Chambers, resulted in the accolade of UK City of Architecture and Design in 1999.

Britain's finest Victorian city offers a welcoming ambience of 19th-century grandeur in its streets, squares and gardens while the fashionable and elegant terraces of the West End have been restored to their former glory. In the revamped Merchant City you will find cafes and boutiques, and a visit to the chic Italian Centre will reveal lots of exclusive, designer labels. The largest city in Scotland has the widest choice of shopping, and you can browse in St Enoch's Shopping Centre, the largest glass-covered building in Europe, Princes Square or the new Buchanan Galleries, or look for bargains in the famous Barras market.

Glasgow is a synthesis of architecture, heritage and culture, with an unrivalled selection of more than 20 art galleries and museums to discover from the innovative Gallery of Modern Art to the internationally renowned Burrell Collection. Throughout the city, the unmistakeable influence of one of the city's greatest sons, Charles Rennie Mackintosh, can also be seen especially at the Glasgow School of Art and the beautifully restored Willow Tearooms. Perhaps most outstanding of all, however, is his Art Nouveau creation, in Bellahouston Park, where the House for an Art Lover was painstakingly constructed 95 years after Mackintosh designed it as a winning competition entry.

Greater Glasgow & Clyde Valley

Greater Glasgow & Clyde Valley

A year-round programme of events including Celtic Connections, Glasgow Folk Festival and the International Jazz Festival takes centre stage in the city, which is also home to Scottish Opera, Scottish Ballet and the Royal Scottish National Orchestra. The true magic of Glasgow, however, is really to be found in its cafes, bars and nightclubs where the warm character of the locals can be seen at its best. Glaswegians have a genius for instant friendship and the city offers some of Scotland's best nightlife to suit every party animal.

One of the great joys of Glasgow is its easy access to some of Scotland's most beautiful countryside such as the wide open hills of Renfrewshire, the Inverclyde coastline and the Clyde Valley. Downriver at Paisley you can visit the restored 12th-century abbey and explore the story of the famous Paisley pattern. Head upriver and the Clyde changes its character tumbling over waterfalls into a rocky gorge at New Lanark, a World Heritage Site.

Greater Glasgow & Clyde Valley

Events
Greater Glasgow & Clyde Valley

12-30 Jan
Celtic Connections
Glasgow
Contact: Colin Hynd
Tel: 0141 353 4137

15 Apr-7 Oct
Superdays
A series of specific events centred around various populations in the Glasgow area. Each day will allow that targeted audience to take physical activity in the various forms designed for that group.
Contact: Tony McKay, Cultural & Leisure Services Department, Glasgow
Tel: 0141 287 5527

1-9 Apr
Curling World Championships
Braehead, Glasgow
Contact: Richard Harding
Tel: 0141 561 2000

1 June-1 Oct
"On a Million Tables everyday"
Paisley Museum & Art Gallery,
High Street, Paisley.
Exhibition on "Robertsons" marmalade.
Contact: Anne Phillips
Tel: 0141 842 5414

12 Aug
World Pipe Band Championships
Glasgow Green
Contact: Royal Society Pipe Band Association.
Tel: 0141 221 5414

Area Tourist Boards

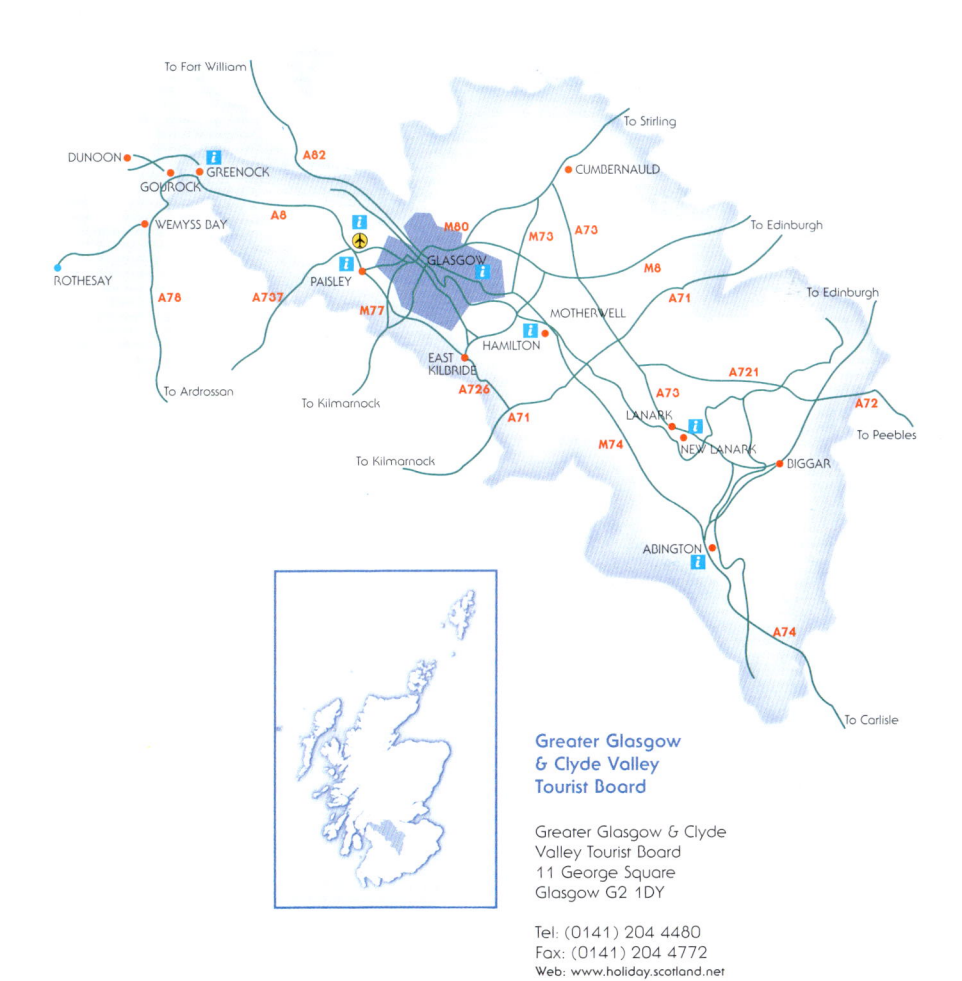

Greater Glasgow & Clyde Valley

**Greater Glasgow
& Clyde Valley
Tourist Board**

Greater Glasgow & Clyde
Valley Tourist Board
11 George Square
Glasgow G2 1DY

Tel: (0141) 204 4480
Fax: (0141) 204 4772
Web: www.holiday.scotland.net

Greater Glasgow & Clyde Valley

Tourist Information Centres

**Greater Glasgow
& Clyde Valley
Tourist Board**

Abington
Welcome Break Service Area
Junction 13, M74
Tel: (01864) 502436
Jan-Dec

Biggar
155 High Street
Tel: (01899) 221066
Easter-Oct

Glasgow
11 George Square
G2 1DY
Tel: (0141) 204 4400
Jan-Dec

Glasgow Airport
Tourist Information Desk
Tel: (0141) 848 4440
Jan-Dec

Greenock
7a Clyde Square
Renfrewshire
Tel: (01475) 722007
Jan-Dec

Hamilton
Road Chef Services
M74 Northbound
Tel: (01698) 285590
Jan-Dec

Lanark
Horsemarket
Ladyacre Road
ML11 7LQ
Tel: (01555) 661661
Jan-Dec

Paisley
9a Gilmour Street
Tel: (0141) 889 0711
Jan-Dec

GREATER GLASGOW AND CLYDE VALLEY

BEARSDEN – EAGLESHAM, BY GLASGOW

Bearsden, East Dumbartonshire
Map Ref: 1H5

SELF CATERING ★★★

Kilmardinny Estate
Milngavie Road, Bearsden, Glasgow, G61 3DH
Tel: 0141 943 1310

3 cottages, 1 pub rm, 1-2 bedrms (grd flr avail), sleeps 2-6, total sleeping capacity 12, £220.00-£400.00, Jan-Dec, bus nearby, rail 500 yds, airport 9 mls

Modern terraced cottages in residential area 6 miles (10 kms) from Glasgow city centre. On main bus route. Close to railway station.

Cambuslang, Glasgow
Map Ref: 1H5

SELF CATERING ★★★★

Mrs Anne M Leggat
Greenleeshill Farm, Cambuslang, Glasgow, G72 8YL
Tel/Fax: 0141 641 3239
E-mail: aml@greenleeshill.prestel.co.uk
Web: www.commercepark.co.uk/greenleeshill

2 self-contained apartments, 1 pub rm, 1-2 bedrms, sleeps 2-4, total sleeping capacity 6, min let 3 nights (low season), £195.00-£375.00, Jan-Dec, bus 300 yds, rail 1 1/2 mls, airport 12 mls

Unique apartments within 18c building. Relaxed setting yet offering close proximity to shops, restaurants and sports facilities, situated in green belt area. 5 miles from Glasgow, Edinburgh, Burns Country and Loch Lomond within easy reach.

Carmichael, Lanarkshire
Map Ref: 2B6

CARMICHAEL COUNTRY COTTAGES
Carmichael Estate, by Biggar, Clydesdale
Tel: 01899 308336   Fax: 01899 308481
e.mail: chiefcarm@aol.com
web: www.carmichael.co.uk/cottages
Centrally situated in the heart of southern Scotland, Carmichael is the perfect touring base. Four miles from M74 motorway, yet set in luxurious wooded countryside, our historic stone-built cottages offer private tennis, fishing and fine walking in a unique unspoilt

SELF CATERING ★★ UP TO ★★★★

Mr Richard Carmichael of Carmichael
Carmichael Estate Office, West Mains, Carmichael, by Biggar, Lanarkshire, ML12 6PG
Tel: 01899 308336 Fax: 01899 308481
E-mail: chiefcarm@aol.com
Web: www.carmichael.co.uk/cottages

15 cottages, 1 farmhouse apartment, 1-2 pub rms, 1-3 bedrms (grd flr avail), sleeps 2-7, total sleeping capacity 65, min let 2 nights, £180.00-£500.00, Jan-Dec, bus 1/2 ml, rail 5 mls, ferry 90 mls, airport 30 mls

Attractive 18c stone cottages on historic wooded estate. Ideal touring base. Farm visitor centre, shop, restaurant and wax museum. Tennis, fishing, pony trekking, and off-road buggy racing all available. Some no-smoking cottages.

Eaglesham, by Glasgow, Renfrewshire
Map Ref: 1H6

SELF CATERING ★★★★

Mrs F Allison
New Borland, Glasgow Road, Eaglesham, Glasgow, G76 0DN
Tel/Fax: 01355 302051
E-mail: newborland@dial.pipex.com

1 house

Former threshing mill one of only his in the area sympathetically converted into a modern family home yet retaining many of the original features. All bedrooms ensuite mahogany feature staircase. 3 night lets sometimes available.

VAT is shown at 17.5%: changes in this rate may affect prices.   *Key to symbols is on back flap.*

GLASGOW

GREATER GLASGOW AND CLYDE VALLEY

Glasgow — Map Ref: 1H5

★★★ SELF CATERING

Mr H Bain & Mr A E Mole
The Knowes, 32 Riddrie Knowes, Glasgow, G33 2QH
Tel: 0141 770 5213 Fax: 0141 770 0955
E-mail: stay@theknowes.sol.co.uk
Web: www.sol.co.uk/t/theknowes

Studio flat with separate kitchen in distinctive 1920's bungalow. Easy access from M8 junction 12. Spacious garden and use of picnic table. B&B also available.

1 studio flat with sep.kitchen, (grd flr), sleeps 2-3, £210.00, Jan-Dec, bus nearby

★ SELF CATERING

Conference & Visitor Services
Univ.of Glasgow, 81 Great George Street, Glasgow, G12 8RR
Tel: 0141 330 5385/Freephone 0800 0272030
Fax: 0141 334 5465
E-mail: conf@gla.ac.uk Web: www.gla.ac.uk/Otherdepts/Accom

Modern halls of residence located in the west end of Glasgow in a quiet area, yet providing easy acess to the city centre. Regular bus service nearby. A short walk from Kelvin Grove, art galleries and museums and the S.E.C.C, nearby Byres Road offers a selection of cafes, bars and restaurants. A comfortable base for exploring Glasgow, or touring west / central Scotland.

156 self catering rooms, 1 pub rm, 1 bedrm (grd flr avail), sleeps 1-2, total sleeping capacity 242, from £81.00 per week, £13.50 pppn, Jul-Sep, bus nearby, rail 2 mls, airport 9 mls

★ UP TO ★★ SELF CATERING

Mrs Helen A McAdam
Comrie Farm, Keltheyburn, Aberfeldy, PH15 2LS
Tel/Fax: 01887 830261

Top & ground floor flats with security access to communal stairway centrally situated in Glasgows West End. Convenient for the subway. Walking distance to Kelvingrove Art Gallery, the Glasgow University Campus, Botanic Gardens and BBC.

2 flats, 2 pub rms, 3-5 bedrms (grd flr avail), sleeps 6, total sleeping capacity 12, £300.00-£400.00, Jul-Sep, bus nearby, rail nearby, airport 10 mls

---

★ SELF CATERING

University of Strathclyde
Residence & Catering Services, 50 Richmond Street, Glasgow, G1 1XP
Tel: 0141 553 4148 Fax: 0141 553 4149
E-mail: rescat@mis.strath.ac.uk
Web: www.strath.ac.uk/Departments/RESCAT/sales/index.htm

Purpose built modern flats within hall of residence on campus. Centrally situated for all amenities.

20 flats, 1 pub rm, 4-6 bedrms, sleeps 4-6, total sleeping capacity 104, min let 3 nights, £250.00-£310.00, Jun-Sep, bus nearby, rail 1/2 ml, airport 8 mls

★★★★ SELF CATERING

West End Apartments
401 North Woodside Road, Kelvinbridge, Glasgow, G20 6NN
Tel: 0141 342 4060 Fax: 0141 334 8159

Newly refurbished studio apartments in Victorian terrace. Within easy reach of University, museums, Botanic Gardens and main routes North and West. Handy for all forms of public transport.

4 flats, 1 pub rm, 1 bedrm (grd flr avail), sleeps 1-4, total sleeping capacity 10, from £252.00, Jan-Dec, bus nearby, rail nearby, airport 5 mls

---

Important: Prices stated are estimates and may be subject to amendments

GREATER GLASGOW AND CLYDE VALLEY

GREENOCK – BY LOCHWINNOCH

Greenock, Renfrewshire

★★ SELF CATERING

Angela Hurrell
James Watt College, Roseath Hall, Waterfront Campus, Customhouse Way, Greenock, PA15 1EN
Tel: 01475 731360

Map Ref: 1G5

7 flats, 7 pub rms, 7 bedrms (grd flr avail), sleeps 7, total sleeping capacity 49, £100.00-£140.00, Jan-Dec, bus nearby, rail 200 yds, ferry 2 mls, airport 14 mls

Modern purpose-built campus accommodation on waterfront. Many ground floor flats. Ideally placed for Dunoon & Rothesay ferries. Two minutes walk from town centre, swimming pool & cinema.

Lanark

★★★★ TOURING PARK

Newhouse Caravan & Camping Park
Ravenstruther, Lanark, ML11 8NP
Tel/Fax: 01555 870228

Map Ref: 2A6

Park accommodation: 22

25 tourers from £6.50 or 25 motors from £6.50 or 25 tents from £6.50. Total Touring Pitches 45.

4 Holiday Caravans to let, sleep 2-6 from £160.00, total sleeping capacity 20, min let 3 days.

8 acres, mixed, mid Mar-mid Oct, latest time of arrival 2200, overnight holding area. Extra charge for electricity, awnings, showers.

Leisure facilities:

Site on A70, ½ ml W of Carstairs village, 3 mls E of Lanark.

Lochwinnoch, Renfrewshire

★★★★ SELF CATERING

Mrs J Anderson
East Lochhead Farm, Largs Road, Lochwinnoch, PA12 4DX
Tel: 01505 842610 Fax: 01505 814610
E-mail: winnoch@aol.com
Web: www.self-catering.co.uk

Map Ref: 1G5

3 cottages, 1 pub rm, 1-3 bedrms (grd flr avail), sleeps 2-6, total sleeping capacity 12, £200.00-£480.00, Jan-Dec, bus 1 ml, rail 1 ml, airport 7 mls

A courtyard of cottages and a studio overlooking Loch Barr and the Renfrewshire countryside. Set in two acres of gardens and ideally positioned for the Ayrshire coast, Burns country, Glasgow and Loch Lomond.

by Lochwinnoch, Renfrewshire

★★ SELF CATERING

Mrs Janet MacGregor
Barrs of Cloak, Calderside Road, by Lochwinnoch, PA12 4LB
Tel: 01505 842252 Fax: 01505 843001
E-mail: j-r-macg@dircon.co.uk
Web: www.j-r-macg.dircon.co.uk

Map Ref: 1G5

2 flats, 1 pub rm, 1 bedrm (All grd.floor), sleeps 4, total sleeping capacity 8, £95.00-£205.00, Jan-Dec, bus 1 ml, rail 3 mls, ferry 15 mls, airport 10 mls

Two converted byres attached to former farmhouse. In idyllic location with fine views, yet only half an hour's drive from Glasgow. Close to Muirshiel Country Park, North Ayrshire, Burns Country and Loch Lomond.

VAT is shown at 17.5%: changes in this rate may affect prices.

Key to symbols is on back flap.

NEW LANARK, BY LANARK

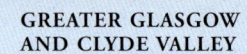

New Lanark, by Lanark, Lanarkshire

GREATER GLASGOW AND CLYDE VALLEY

Map Ref: 2A6

The Waterhouses at New Lanark

Mill One, New Lanark ML11 9DB
Tel: 01555 667200 Fax: 01555 667222
e.mail: hotel@newlanark.org
Web: www.newlanark.org

On the banks of the River Clyde in the heart of the 200-year-old village of New Lanark, The Waterhouses offer a unique opportunity to experience beauty, history and peace. The views from the cottages over the river are unrivalled and the facilities of the New Lanark Mill Hotel are only a few steps away. Less than an hour from Glasgow, Edinburgh and the Borders.
A unique experience.

★★★★
SELF CATERING

Mr Stephen Owen
New Lanark Mill Hotel, New Lanark, Lanark, ML11 9DB
Tel: 01555 667200 Fax: 01555 667222
E-mail: hotel@newlanark.org
Web: www.newlanark.org

Recently renovated row of millhouses situated on the banks of the River Clyde on the lane behind the New Lanark Mill Hotel.

8 houses, 1-2 pub rms, 1-2 bedrms, sleeps 4-6, total sleeping capacity 28, £250.00-£700.00, Jan-Dec, bus ½ ml, rail 1 ml, airport 40 mls

Important: Prices stated are estimates and may be subject to amendments

Welcome to Scotland

West Highlands & Islands, Loch Lomond, Stirling and Trossachs

From the green slopes of the Ochil Hills in the east, through to the far-flung islands in the western ocean, you will find a remarkably diverse country, steeped in history and mystery, all set within a glorious natural environment, where the Great Highland Line divides the lowland south from the mountainous north. In fact, scenically, the area has just about everything, from the bonny banks of Loch Lomond, a playground for generations of visitors, to the empty mountains of Breadalbane, a paradise for walkers and climbers.

The region is the very birthplace of Scotland, and has seen in its time, the Picts, Romans and Vikings all come and go, and been the setting for Clan feuds, the arrival of Christianity and the fight for nationhood. A good place to begin is the Royal Burgh of Stirling, which has been at the centre of Scotland's turbulent history, repelling invaders down the centuries. Now it offers a friendly welcome as an all-year-round destination and as well as its historic Old Town and cliff-top castle, you will find excellent shopping, indoor leisure facilities and a nearby golf course. Close to the town is the National Wallace Monument, where you can visit the hall of heroes and learn the true story of Braveheart.

The Trossachs, celebrated as "The Highlands in Miniature", are plainly visible from the ramparts of Stirling Castle, and the gateway to this area is the bustling and friendly town of Callander. At the Rob Roy and Trossachs Visitor Centre, you can uncover the legend of this celebrated folk hero and outlaw who once roamed these magical hills and wooded glens. A wonderful way to view this captivating beauty is on board the unique Victorian steamship, the SS Sir Walter Scott, which makes daily cruises across the placid waters of Loch Katrine.

West Highlands & Islands, Loch Lomond, Stirling and Trossachs

West Highlands & Islands, Loch Lomond, Stirling and Trossachs

Further west is the delightful Cowal Peninsula and the lovely Isle of Bute known as Scotland's Festival Isle. Across the sheltered waters of Loch Fyne sits the Georgian planned village of Inveraray from where the road meanders into the beautiful peninsula of Kintyre offering miles of shoreline and beaches with unsurpassed views to the Inner Hebrides. Regular ferry services can take you to the lively island of Islay, famed the world over for its peaty malt whisky and then to neighbouring Jura, which in contrast, has one road, one distillery, one hotel, and lots of space.

The road west will take you through a panorama of awesome mountains which sweep down to the coastal resort of Oban. Romantic names and romantic places like Tobermory, with its picture postcard harbour, await the visitor on Mull, while saintly Iona and musical Staffa are close by. For a real experience of island life you could venture further west to Colonsay, Tiree or Coll, where the rhythm of life is governed by tide and ferry timetables. But wherever you choose to go, there is one thing you can be sure of, you will find a warm welcome and a true celebration of Scottish culture in this, the heartland of Scotland.

Events
West Highlands & Islands, Loch Lomond, Stirling and Trossachs

Events
West Highlands & Islands
Loch Lomond, Stirling Trossachs

*May-Jan 2001
The Stirling Story
Stirling Smith Art Gallery & Museum
Exhibition celebrating 1000 years of Stirling's history as a strategic town up to present day.
Contact: Elspeth King
Tel: 01786 4721917

27 May-1 June
Loch Fyne Sea Food Fair
Loch Fyne, Cairndou, Argyll
Feast of West Coast Sea Food, live music, children's entertainments, specially selected wines and beers in an idyllic setting.
Contact: Virginia Sumsion
Tel: 01499 600264

27 May - 1 June
Isle of Bute Jazz Festival
Various venues throughout the island.
Contact: Ray Bruce
Tel: 01700 502800

16-18 Jun
Royal Rothesay Regatta
Rothesay, Isle of Bute
A celebration of the millenium for the yacht clubs of the Clyde and their friends worldwide.
Contact: Tourist Information Centre, Rothesay
Tel: 01700 502151

11-13 Aug
Lomond Folk Festival
Various venues in Balloch, Loch Lomond
Festival of traditional and contemporary music with various attractions for all the family.
Contact: Stewart Davidson
Tel: 01389 757561

4-9 Sep
Helensburgh Millennium Visual Arts Festival 2000
Victoria Halls, Helensburgh
Festival week of workshops and demonstrations and lectures.
Contact: Rev Jill Locock
Tel: 01436 671252

13 Oct
Philips Tour of Mull
Popular Car Rally on the demanding Isle of Mull.
Contact: Neil Molyneux
Tel: 01254 826564

Area Tourist Boards

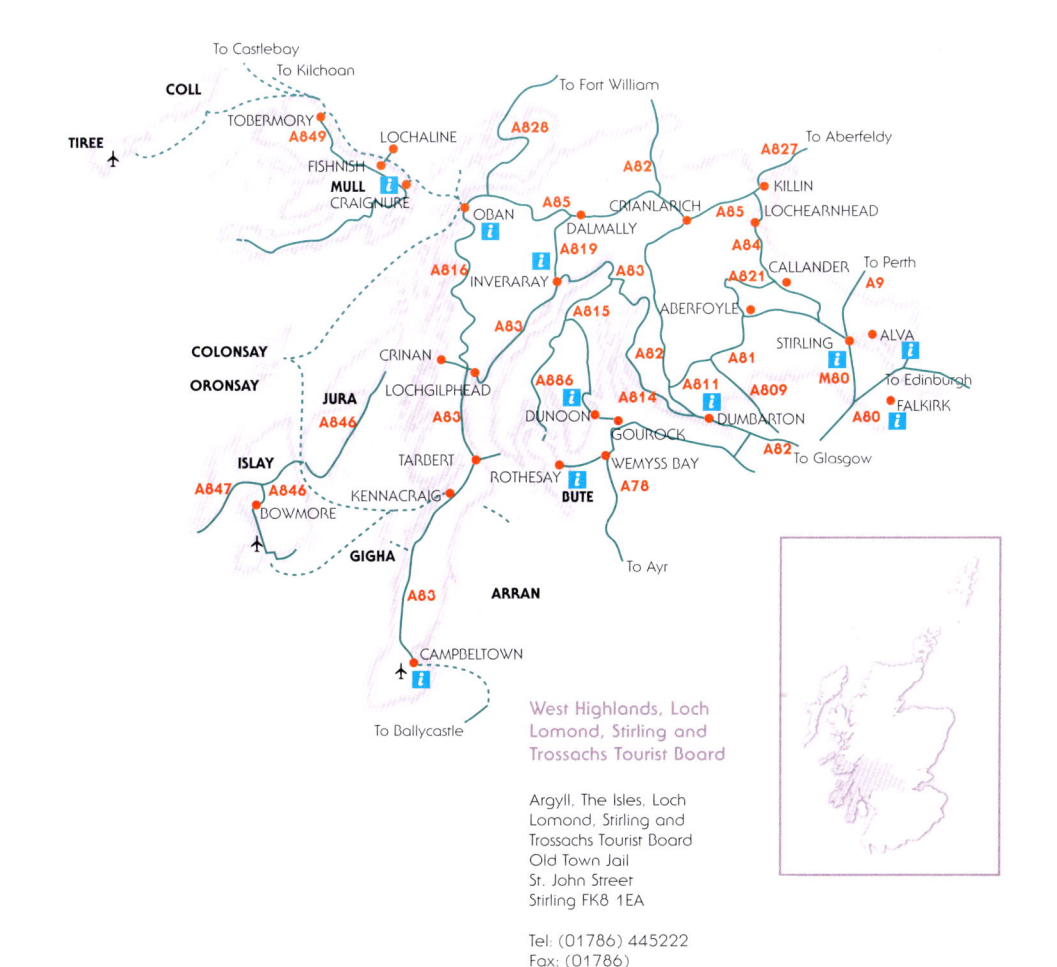

West Highlands & Islands, Loch Lomond, Stirling and Trossachs

71

West Highlands, Loch Lomond, Stirling and Trossachs Tourist Board

Argyll, The Isles, Loch Lomond, Stirling and Trossachs Tourist Board
Old Town Jail
St. John Street
Stirling FK8 1EA

Tel: (01786) 445222
Fax: (01786) 471301/446325
Web: www.holiday.scotland.net

Tourist Information Centres

West Highlands & Islands, Loch Lomond, Stirling and Trossachs

West Highlands, Loch Lomond, Stirling and Trossachs Tourist Board

Aberfoyle
Trossachs Discovery Centre
Main Street
Tel: (01877) 382352
Jan-Dec

Alva
Mill Trail Visitor Centre
Tel: (01259) 769696
Jan-Dec

Ardgartan
Arrochar
Tel: (01301) 702432
April-Oct

Balloch
Balloch Road
Tel: (01389) 753533
April-Oct

Bo'ness
Seaview Car Park
Tel: (01506) 826626
April-Sept

Bowmore
Isle of Islay
Tel: (01496) 810254
Jan-Dec

Callander
Rob Roy and Trossachs Visitor Centre
Ancaster Square
Tel: (01877) 330342
Mar-Dec
Jan and Feb weekends only

Campbeltown
Mackinnon House
The Pier
Argyll
Tel: (01586) 552056
Jan-Dec

Craignure
The Pier
Isle of Mull
Tel: (01680) 812377
Jan-Dec

Drymen
Drymen Library
The Square
Tel: (01360) 660068
May-Sept

Dumbarton
Milton
A82 Northbound
Tel: (01389) 742306
Jan-Dec

Dunblane
Stirling Road
Tel: (01786) 824428
May-Sept

Dunoon
7 Alexandra Parade
Argyll
Tel: (01369) 703785
Jan-Dec

Falkirk
2-4 Glebe Street
Tel: (01324) 620244
Jan-Dec

Helensburgh
The Clock Tower
Tel: (01436) 672642
April-Oct

Inveraray
Front Street
Argyll
Tel: (01499) 302063
Jan-Dec

Killin
Breadalbane Folklore Centre
Tel: (01567) 820254
March-end Oct
Feb weekends only

Lochgilphead
Lochnell Street
Argyll
Tel: (01546) 602344
April-Oct

Oban
Argyll Square
Argyll
Tel: (01631) 563122
Jan-Dec

Rothesay
15 Victoria Street
Isle of Bute
Tel: (01700) 502151
Jan-Dec

Stirling
Dumbarton Road
Tel: (01786) 475019
Jan-Dec

Stirling (Royal Burgh)
The Esplanade
Tel: (01786) 479901
Jan-Dec

Stirling
Pirnhall Motorway
Service Area
Juntion 9, M9
Tel: (01786) 814111
April-Oct

Tarbert
Harbour Street
Argyll
Tel: (01880) 820429
April-Oct

Tarbet-Loch Lomond
Main Street
Tel: (01301) 702260
April-Oct

Tobermory
Isle of Mull
Tel: (01688) 302182
April-Oct

Tyndrum
Main Street
Tel: (01838) 400246
April-Oct

D

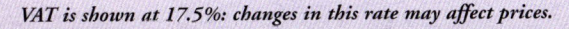

WEST HIGHLANDS & ISLANDS,
LOCH LOMOND, STIRLING & TROSSACHS

ABERFOYLE

Aberfoyle, Perthshire | Map Ref: 1H3

★★★ **SELF CATERING**

Ingrid Anderson
Lochside Cottages, Kinlochard, by Aberfoyle
Tel/Fax: 01877 387212
E-mail: ingrid.anderson@virgin.net

2 cottages, 1 pub rm, 1-2 bedrms (grd flr avail), sleeps 4-6, total sleeping capacity 10, £175.00-£375.00, Jan-Dec, bus ¼ ml, rail 25 mls, airport 30 mls

Newly renovated cottages with log burning stoves. Set beside the River Chon, in the scenic foothills of the Trossachs, at the head of Loch Ard.

★★★ **SELF CATERING**

Harry & Gill Forster
Springburn House, Craignavie Road, Killin, Perthshire, FK21 8SH
Tel/Fax: 01567 820371

1 cottage, 2 pub rms, 2 bedrms, sleeps 4-5, £250.00-£300.00, Apr-Nov, bus 2 ½ mls, rail 18 mls, airport 40 mls

Completely renovated cottage of traditional Scottish style, set amidst spectacular scenery at the top of the Dukes Pass in the heart of the Trossachs and Queen Elizabeth National Parklands.

★★★ **SELF CATERING**

David & Melanie McNeil
Blarnaboard Farm, Gartmore, Aberfoyle, Stirlingshire, FK8 3SE
Tel: 01877 382374

1 converted barn, 1 pub rm, 3 bedrms (grd flr avail), sleeps 8, £195.00-£475.00, Jan-Dec, bus 1 ml, rail 15 mls, airport 26 mls

Totally refurbished former mill in secluded 35 acre site. 1.5 miles from Gartmore. Near Aberfoyle and Rob Roy country.

★★★ **SELF CATERING**

Oak Royal Coach House
Aberfoyle, Perthshire
Tel: 01877 382633/0411 649720 (mobile)
Fax: 01877 382633

1 cottage, 1 pub rm, 2 bedrms (All grd.floor), sleeps 4, £275.00-£375.00, Jan-Dec, bus nearby

Reconstructed traditional coach house c1900 in own grounds with barbecue area. One mile from the village. Pets by arrangement.

★★★★ **SELF CATERING**

Anita & Paul Wilson
Braeval, Main Street, Gartmore, Stirlingshire, FK8 3RW
Tel/Fax: 01877 382346
E-mail: anita.wilson@braeval.com
Web: www.braeval.com

1 converted barn, 1 pub rm, 1 bedrm, sleeps 4, £195.00-£325.00, Jan-Dec, bus nearby, rail 15 mls, airport 20 mls

Former village dairy attached to owner's home but completely self-contained. Comfortably furnished in contemporary style with large open-plan living/kitchen area. Centrally situated in the picturesque village of Gartmore and an ideal base for exploring the Trossachs. 16 miles from Stirling.

VAT is shown at 17.5%: changes in this rate may affect prices.

Key to symbols is on back flap.

APPIN

Appin, Argyll — Map Ref: 1E1

WEST HIGHLANDS & ISLANDS, LOCH LOMOND, STIRLING & TROSSACHS

APPIN HOLIDAY HOMES ★★ UP TO ★★★ SELF CATERING

Excellent choice of lodges and caravans, set apart near lochside. Magnificent situation. Ideal for families. Also honeymoons! Good touring centre midway Oban-Fort William. Free fishing. Boats available. Licensed Inn, pony trekking nearby. Lovely walks. Sleeps 2-5. *Free Colour Brochure* £155-£375 per unit weekly with reductions to couples.
Residential proprietors: Mr & Mrs I Weir, Appin Holiday Homes, APPIN, ARGYLL PA38 4BQ   Tel: 01631 730287
e-mail: appinholidayhomes@tesco.net   Web: http://www.oban.org.uk

---

★★ UP TO ★★★ SELF CATERING

Appin Holiday Homes
Appin, Argyll, PA38 4BQ Tel: 01631 730287
E-mail: appinholidayhomes@tesco.net
Web: www.oban.org.uk

Timber bungalows with excellent views over Loch Creran to the hills beyond. Free fishing, boat hire and access to safe beach.

10 chalets, 1-2 pub rms, 1-2 bedrms (grd flr avail), sleeps 2-5, total sleeping capacity 40, £155.00-£375.00, Jan-Dec exc Nov, bus nearby, rail 16 mls

★★★★ HOLIDAY PARK

Appin Lochside Caravan Park
Appin, Argyll, PA38 4BQ
Tel: 01631 730287
E-mail: appinholidayhomes@tesco.net
Web: www.oban.org.uk

2 acres, Apr-Oct.

Park accommodation: 8

5 Holiday Caravans to let, sleep 2-5 from £135.00, total sleeping capacity 20, min let weekend (low season), Apr-Oct.

Leisure facilities:

10 mls N of Connel Bridge. 15 mls S of Ballachulish Bridge, on A828.

★★★★ SELF CATERING

Mrs Ann Calvert
The Cottage, Inverfolla Mill Croft, Appin, Argyll
Tel: 01631 730360
E-mail: wasvet@aol.com

Two recently completed cottages, quietly situated on a 40 acre croft on the banks of the An Iola River. Ideal for all outdoor pursuits. Plenty of flora and fauna in the area, yet only 28 miles to Oban and 34 miles to Fort William. Glencoe and Ben Nevis within an hours drive.

2 cottages, 2 pub rms, 2 bedrms (All grd.floor), sleeps 6, total sleeping capacity 12, £240.00-£370.00, Jan-Dec, bus nearby, rail 30 mls, ferry 30 mls

---

★★ SELF CATERING

Donal & Susie Hutchison (Wts)
Kinlochlaich House, Appin, Argyll, PA38 4BD
Tel: 01631 730342 Fax: 01631 730482
E-mail: 101602.3101@compuserve.com
Web: www.robbins-associates.co.uk/kinlochlaich

Beautifully situated in its own grounds in Strath of Appin overlooking Loch Linnhe, midway between Oban and Fort William.

4 flats, 1 cottage, 1 pub rm, 1-2 bedrms, sleeps 2-5, total sleeping capacity 17, £129.00-£384.00, Jan-Dec, bus nearby, rail 13 mls

---

Important: Prices stated are estimates and may be subject to amendments

WEST HIGHLANDS & ISLANDS, LOCH LOMOND, STIRLING & TROSSACHS

APPIN – ARDFERN

Appin, Argyll — Map Ref: 1E1

APPIN HOUSE – APARTMENTS AND LODGES APPIN HOUSE, APPIN, ARGYLL PA38 4BN
Tel: 01631 730207   Fax: 01631 730567

Set in its own large, beautifully laid out garden, commanding spectacular views across Loch Linnhe to Lismore, Mull, and the Morvern Hills. There are 6 individual and well-appointed apartments and two luxury lodges, each offering pleasing aspects of garden and countryside. Brochure available on request.

★★ TO ★★★★ SELF CATERING

★★ UP TO ★★★★ SELF CATERING

Mrs Mathieson
Appin House, Appin, Argyll PA38 4BN
Tel: 01631 730207 Fax: 01631 730567

Apartments of individual character and design adjoining historic country house and two lodges in large garden with superb views. Barbecue.

2 chalets, 2 flats, 4 apartments, 1-2 pub rms, 1-3 bedrms, sleeps 2-6, total sleeping capacity 28, min let 3 nights, £130.00-£390.00, Dec-Oct, bus nearby, rail 20 mls, ferry 5 mls, airport 100 mls

---

Arden, Argyll & Bute — Map Ref: 1G4

★★★★ SELF CATERING

Mr Andrew MacLeod
The Gardeners Cottages, Arden House, Arden,
Dunbartonshire, G83 8RD
Tel/Fax: 01389 850601
E-mail: andymacleod@sol.co.uk
Web: www.vacations-scotland.co.uk/gardeners.html

Three cottages of high quality and comfort in secluded wooded grounds including Victorian Walled Garden, wooded glen and putting green by the shores of Loch Lomond and near by Loch Lomond golf course.

3 cottages, 1 pub rm, 1-2 bedrms (grd flr avail), sleeps 2-6, total sleeping capacity 10, min let 3 days, £160.00-£500.00, Jan-Dec, bus nearby, rail 3 mls, airport 15 mls

---

Ardentinny, by Dunoon, Argyll — Map Ref: 1F4

★★ SELF CATERING

Stronchullin Holiday Cottages
Ardentinney, by Dunoon, Argyll, PA23 8TP
Tel/Fax: 01369 810246

Modern cottages, built in traditional style, on working hill farm. Magnificent views over Loch Long.

4 cottages, 1 pub rm, 3 bedrms (grd flr avail), sleeps 5-7, total sleeping capacity 23, £160.00-£424.00, Mar-Feb, bus ¼ ml, rail 12 mls, ferry 9 mls, airport 29 mls

---

Ardfern, Argyll — Map Ref: 1E3

★★★★ SELF CATERING

Alison Campbell
Aird Farm, Ardfern, Argyll, PA31 8QS
Tel/Fax: 01852 500224

The farmhouse is situated at Craignish Point with panoramic views of Jura, Scarba, Mull and Luing. Also the Straits of Corryvrechan. Beautiful walks with coves and bays, offering peace and tranquility.

1 house, 2 pub rms, 4 bedrms (grd flr avail), sleeps 6, £180.00-£450.00, Jan-Dec

---

VAT is shown at 17.5%: changes in this rate may affect prices.   Key to symbols is on back flap.

ARDFERN – ARDLUI

D WEST HIGHLANDS & ISLANDS, LOCH LOMOND, STIRLING & TROSSACHS

Ardfern, Argyll
Map Ref: 1E3

Loch Craignish Cottages
ARDFERN, by LOCHGILPHEAD, ARGYLL PA31 8QN
Telephone/Fax: 01852 500671
Eight beautifully appointed cottages in private grounds beside the sea, offering all-year-round comfort. Superb scenery for many outdoor (and indoor) activities, pets welcome. Excellent shop(s), restaurant and PO in village. A wonderful holiday experience. Linen, towels, high chairs and cots included in rent. Mastercard and Visa. *Colour brochure.* **Prices: £190 min – £520 max per week.**

★★★★ SELF CATERING

Loch Craignish Cottages
Ardfern, by Lochgilphead, Argyll, PA31 8QN
Tel/Fax: 01852 500671

8 cottages, 1 pub rm, 1-3 bedrms, sleeps 2-6, total sleeping capacity 32, £190.00-£520.00, Jan-Dec, bus 2 mls, rail 25 mls, ferry 25 mls, airport 98 mls

White washed cottages overlooking Loch Craignish on 3.5 acre private site in the village of Ardfern.

Ardlui, Argyll
Map Ref: 1G3

Ardlui Hotel, Marina & Holiday Home Park
Ardlui, Loch Lomond, Argyll
Tel: 01301 704243   Fax: 01301 704268
e-mail: reservations@ardlui.prestel.co.uk
Web: www.ardlui.co.uk

Nestling in the midst of magnificent scenery at the head of Loch Lomond, the Ardlui Caravan Park stands on the shore commanding a superb panoramic view of this most famous of Scottish lochs. Our fleet of luxury holiday caravans are 6 or 8 berth, well equipped and connected to mains services with W.C., shower, fridge and colour TV. Hotel on site is fully licensed with two lounge bars serving meals and restaurant open to non-residents. Laundry, children's play area, sheltered marina, boat hire, slipway, moorings, floating fuel dock and shop. Ardlui is an ideal centre for touring, water ski-ing, fishing, hill-walking and mountaineering.

Brochure on request to:
Ardlui Hotel and Caravan Park, Loch Lomond, Argyll G83 7EB
Tel: 01301 704243

★★★ HOLIDAY PARK

Ardlui Caravan Park
Ardlui, Loch Lomond. G83 7EB
Tel: 01301 704243 Fax: 01301 704268
E-mail: reservations@ardlui.prestel.co.uk
Web: www.ardlui.co.uk

Park accommodation: **96**
10 tourers £10.00-11.00 or 10 motors £10.00-11.00 or 10 tents. Total Touring Pitches 20.
5 Holiday Caravans to let, sleep 6-8 £235.00-310.00, total sleeping capacity 36, min let 2 nights.

Leisure facilities:

Situated on A82 at Ardlui.

5 acres, mixed, Jan-Dec, latest time of arrival 2000, overnight holding area. Extra charge for electricity, awnings, showers.

Important: Prices stated are estimates and may be subject to amendments

D

WEST HIGHLANDS & ISLANDS, LOCH LOMOND, STIRLING & TROSSACHS

ARDRISHAIG, BY LOCHGILPHEAD – BALLOCH

Ardrishaig, by Lochgilphead, Argyll

SELF CATERING — UP TO ★★★★

Mrs MacDonald
Brenfield Croft, Ardrishaig, Argyll
Tel: 01546 603284

Four star - modern terraced cottages built on traditional croftland with open views over Loch Fyne. Also, luxury pine lodge, lochside location with private beach and panoramic views to Isle of Arran and Cowal peninsula. One star - chalet accommodation available.

Map Ref: 1E4

3 cottages, 1 pub rm, 3 bedrms (All grd.floor), sleeps 6, total sleeping capacity 18, to £420.00, Jan-Dec, bus nearby

---

Arnprior, by Kippen, Stirlingshire

SELF CATERING — ★★★

Thorntree Barn, Carol Seymour
Thorntree, Arnprior, Stirlingshire, FK8 3EY
Tel/Fax: 01786 870710

Tastefully converted spacious barn with stunning rural views and magnicifent sunsets. Centrally situated for touring. Variety of leisure activities in the area.

Map Ref: 1H4

1 converted barn, 1 pub rm, 3 bedrms, sleeps 6-7, £200.00-£475.00, Jan-Dec, bus ½ ml, rail 11 mls

---

Arrochar, Argyll

SELF CATERING — ★★★

Douglas Fraser
Cairndow Stagecoach Inn, Cairndow, Argyll, PA26 8BN
Tel: 01499 600286 Fax: 01499 600220

Completely renovated ex-forestry cottage just 0.5 mile from village, at the head of Loch Long, providing an excellent base for climbing, hill walking and touring.

Map Ref: 1G3

1 house, 2 pub rms, 3 bedrms (grd flr avail), sleeps 6, min let weekend, £220.00-£520.00, Jan-Dec, bus ¼ ml, rail 1 ml, airport 32 mls

---

Balloch, Dunbartonshire

Map Ref: 1G4

Tullichewan Holiday Park

Old Luss Road, Balloch, Loch Lomond G83 8QP
Tel: 01389 759541 Fax: 01389 755763
e.mail: tullichewan@holiday-parks.co.uk Web: www.holiday-parks.co.uk

Nestling in the hills and woodlands surrounding Loch Lomond our "Four Star" pine lodges are perfect for relaxing and enjoying the freedom of a self catering holiday on our beautifully landscaped family holiday park. Superb leisure suite with sauna, jacuzzi and sunbed, games room mountain bike hire etc. Free colour brochure.
OPEN ALL YEAR.   ★★★★ **SELF CATERING**

SELF CATERING — ★★★★

Tullichewan Holiday Park
Old Luss Road, Balloch, Loch Lomond, Dunbartonshire, G83 8QP
Tel: 01389 759541 Fax: 01389 755763
E.mail: tullichewan@holiday-parks.co.uk
Web: www.holiday-parks.co.uk

Pine lodges with high level of insulation and feature pine decoration situated in family holiday park by Loch Lomond. Leisure suite and games room available.

6 pine lodges, 1 pub rm, 3 bedrms (All grd.floor), sleeps 4-6, total sleeping capacity 36, min let 3 nights, £180.00-£510.00, Jan-Dec, bus ¼ ml, rail ¼ ml, airport 15 mls

VAT is shown at 17.5%: changes in this rate may affect prices.

Key to symbols is on back flap.

BALQUHIDDER – BENDERLOCH, BY OBAN

WEST HIGHLANDS & ISLANDS, LOCH LOMOND, STIRLING & TROSSACHS

Balquhidder, Perthshire

Map Ref: 1H2

★★★ SELF CATERING

Mrs F M Allan
Castlandhill Farm, Rosyth, Fife, KY11 2UX
Tel/Fax: 01383 412829

1 cottage, 2 pub rms, 3 bedrms, sleeps 6, min let weekend, £140.00-£420.00, Jan-Dec, bus nearby, rail 28 mls, airport 60 mls

Tastefully renovated secluded cottage situated in the delightful Braes of Balquhidder. Ideal for touring, walking and water sports.

★★★ SELF CATERING

Dunollie Cottage
Balquhidder, Perthshire, FK19 8NY
Tel: 01877 384659

1 guest wing, 1 pub rm, 1 bedrm, sleeps 2-4, £110.00-£240.00, Jan-Dec, bus 1 ml, rail 28 mls, airport 60 mls

Charming self contained wing of traditional country cottage in peaceful glen with wonderful mountain scenery. Ideal for outdoor pursuits.

★★★★ SELF CATERING

Mr K P Horsley, Rob Roy Workshop
Balquhidder, Lochearnhead, Perthshire, FK19 8NX
Tel: 01877 384274 Fax: 01877 384252
(after 6.30pm 01877 330780)

1 cottage, 1 pub rm, 2 bedrms (All grd.floor), sleeps 4, £180.00-£310.00, Jan-Dec, bus nearby, rail 24 mls, airport 40 mls

Semi detached cottage surrounded by woods, in the heart of Rob Roy country. Centrally located for both outdoor activities and touring.

★★★ SELF CATERING

Loraine Telfer
Uam-Vaar, Balquhidder Station, Lochearnhead, Perthshire, FK19 8NX
Tel/Fax: 01567 830262

1 cottage, 1 pub rm, 2 bedrms (All grd.floor), sleeps 4, Jan-Dec

Modern country cottage with own grounds, in peaceful rural area. Ideally situated for walking, touring or just relaxing.

Benderloch, by Oban, Argyll

Map Ref: 1E2

★★★ SELF CATERING

Tralee Bay Holidays
Benderloch, by Oban, Argyll
Tel: 01631 720255 Fax: 01631 720545
E-mail: tralee@easynet.co.uk
Web: www.tralee.com

16 log cabins, 1 pub rm, 2-3 bedrms, sleeps 4-6, total sleeping capacity 96, min let 2 days, £225.00-£525.00, Feb-Dec, bus 1 ml, rail 3 mls, ferry 5 mls, airport 2 mls

Eighteen lodges in woodland setting with views to Tralee Beach. Part of Tralee Holiday Park with full access to all its facilities.

Important: Prices stated are estimates and may be subject to amendments

WEST HIGHLANDS & ISLANDS, LOCH LOMOND, STIRLING & TROSSACHS

BRIDGE OF ALLAN – PORT BANNATYNE, ISLE OF BUTE

Bridge of Allan, Stirlingshire

Map Ref: 2A3

★★★ SELF CATERING

Isobel Johns
3 Wolsey Close, Kingston upon Thames, Surrey, KT2 7ER
Tel/Fax: 0181 942 7203
E-mail: 106362.1201@compuserve.com

Modern ground floor flat in quiet residential area, close to Stirling University Campus. Centrally situated for touring.

1 flat, 2 pub rms, 2 bedrms (All grd.floor), sleeps 4, £200.00-£350.00, Jan-Dec, bus nearby, rail 1 ml, airport 30 mls

---

Bridge of Orchy, Argyll

Map Ref: 1G1

UP TO ★★★★ SELF CATERING

D M Mackinnon & Co (Auch)
Bank of Scotland Buildings, Oban, Argyll, PA34 4LN
Tel: 01631 566122/01631 563014 Fax: 01631 564754

3 cottages, 1 pub rm, 3 bedrms, sleeps 6-8, total sleeping capacity 20, £150.00-£550.00, Jan-Dec, bus nearby, rail 3 1/2 mls

---

Buchlyvie, Stirlingshire

Map Ref: 1H4

★★ SELF CATERING

Mrs Rosemary Rollinson
Ballamenoch, Buchlyvie, Stirlingshire, FK8 3NX
Tel: 01360 850577 Fax: 01360 850535

Most attractive detached cottage in its own garden with accommodation all on one level. About 10 minutes walk to village. Ideal base for touring central Scotland and walking parts of the West Highland Way.

1 cottage, 1 pub rm, 1 bedrm (All grd.floor), sleeps 4, £110.00-£250.00, Jan-Dec, bus 1/4 ml, rail 14 mls, airport 27 mls

---

Kilchattan Bay, Isle of Bute

Map Ref: 1F6

★★★ SELF CATERING

Mrs Marian McDougall
Birgidale Crieff Farmhouse, Kilchattan Bay, Isle of Bute, PA20 9PE
Tel: 01700 831236

Wing of a traditional Victorian Farmhouse set in own garden with lovely views over surrounding farmland and sea views accross to the Isle of Arran. Close to safe beaches and golf courses. Ideal cycling and walking holiday base in peaceful location.

1 semi detached farmhouse, 2 pub rms, 2 bedrms, sleeps 2-5, £150.00-£250.00, Mar-Nov, ferry 4 mls

---

Port Bannatyne, Isle of Bute

Map Ref: 1F5

★★★ SELF CATERING

Kames Castle
Port Bannatyne, Isle of Bute, PA20 0QP
Tel: 01700 504500 Fax: 01700 504554
E-mail: kames-castle@easynet.co.uk
Web: http://www.kames-castle.co.uk

Traditional stone built cottages comfortably furnished. Perfect for family holidays. Tranquil setting in 20 acres of grounds with large walled garden and 14c Keep. Ideal for walking, cycling and birdwatching. Pets welcome.

6 cottages, 1-2 pub rms, 2-4 bedrms (grd flr avail), sleeps 2-9, total sleeping capacity 33, min let 2 nights, £225.00-£590.00, Jan-Dec, bus nearby, ferry 3 mls, airport 35 mls

---

VAT is shown at 17.5%: changes in this rate may affect prices.

Key to symbols is on back flap.

ROTHESAY, ISLE OF BUTE – CAIRNDOW

WEST HIGHLANDS & ISLANDS, LOCH LOMOND, STIRLING & TROSSACHS

Rothesay, Isle of Bute
Map Ref: 1F5

Ardencraig Self Catering Holidays
UP TO ★★★★ SELF CATERING
Ardencraig House, High Craigmore, Rothesay, Isle of Bute, PA20 9EP
Tel/Fax: 01700 504550

7 chalets, 5 Apartments, 1 pub rm, 1-2 bedrms, sleeps 2-6, total sleeping capacity 64, £145.00-£430.00, Jan-Dec, bus 400 yds, ferry 1 ½ mls

Built in 1829 this Palladian style mansion, now converted into luxury apartments, enjoys superb views over the Firth of Clyde. Set within 9 acres of mature garden and woodland we also offer comfortable detached chalet accommodation. Ideal base for touring and enjoying outdoor activities.

The Commodore
★★★ SELF CATERING
12 Battery Place, Rothesay, Isle of Bute, PA20 9DP
Tel/Fax: 01700 502178

1 flat, 1 pub rm, 1 bedrm (All grd.floor), sleeps 2-3, £120.00-£198.00, Jan-Dec, bus nearby, ferry 400 yds

Walking distance from town centre. On seafront with panoramic view of Rothesay Bay. Rear garden, patios and BBQ area available.

Mr S T Shaw
★★★ SELF CATERING
Morningside, Mount Pleasant Road, Rothesay, Isle of Bute, PA20 9HQ
Tel/Fax: 01700 503526
E-mail: islebute@aol.com
Web: www.isle-of-bute.com

5 flats, 1 cottage, 1 pub rm, 1-2 bedrms (grd flr avail), sleeps 2-5, total sleeping capacity 18, min let 3 days, £189.00-£359.00, Jan-Dec, bus nearby, ferry 1 ml

Two individual complexes in conservation area, one with cottage on the sea front with its own garden and private parking; the other in town centre overlooking Loch Striven and the Cowal hills. Within easy walking distance of golf course.

Cairndow, Argyll
Map Ref: 1F3

Achadunan Estate
★★★ SELF CATERING
c/o Mrs Delap, Little Armsworth, Alresford, Hampshire, SO4 9RH
Tel/Fax: 01962 732004

2 cottages, 1-2 pub rms, 2-3 bedrms (grd flr avail), sleeps 4-6, total sleeping capacity 10, £220.00-£525.00, Jan-Dec, bus 350 yds, rail 11 mls, airport 50 mls

Two individual cottages in beautiful position on privately owned Highland estate overlooking the estuary at head of Loch Fyne. Good walking country, with abundant wildlife.

Mr J M McCluskey
★ SELF CATERING
3 St Margaret's Road, Twickenham, Middlesex, TW1 2LN
Tel: 0181 892 5704

1 cottage, 2 pub rms, 2 bedrms, sleeps 4, £250.00-£270.00, Jan-Dec, bus 1 ml, rail 10 mls, ferry 24 mls, airport 62 mls

Traditional, detached country cottage, set in 3.5 acres of hill land, in elevated position overlooking Loch Fyne. Inveraray 11 miles (18kms).

Important: Prices stated are estimates and may be subject to amendments

WEST HIGHLANDS & ISLANDS, LOCH LOMOND, STIRLING & TROSSACHS

CALLANDER

Callander, Perthshire — Map Ref: 1H3

Invertrossachs Country House
Nr CALLANDER, PERTHSHIRE FK17 8HG
Telephone: 01877 331126   Fax: 01877 331229
e-mail: res@invertrossachs.freeserve.co.uk
Web: www.invertrossachs.co.uk

This elegant lochside Edwardian Mansion offers superior, spacious apartments amidst 33 acres of outstanding natural beauty and privately managed grounds. Cottage available. All units have dish-washer, laundry, microwave, TV/video, CD/cassette, telephone, plus the 1st class facilities you would expect in this prestigious country house. Classified 4 Stars – Serviced Apartments. Enjoy memorable views and an ideal touring base. Loch/woodland walks, fishing, cycling on site. Nearby golf and other activities offered. Enjoy the original flair, hospitality and personal attentions of resident proprietors and staff dedicated to your comfort and privacy. Exquisite country house bedrooms and suites for B&B also available.

Contact Iain H. Aitchison, BA. Ref. ESC.

As featured in BBC "Summer Holiday" TV Programme.

★★★★ SERVICED APARTMENTS

★★★★ SERVICED APARTMENTS

Mr Iain Aitchison B.A.
Invertrossachs Country House, Invertrossachs, by Callander, Perthsire, FK17 8HG
Tel: 01877 331126 Fax: 01877 331229
E-mail: res@invertrossachs.freeserve.co.uk
Web: www.invertrossachs.co.uk

Separate cottage and spacious self-contained mansion apartments within a former Edwardian Hunting Lodge; enjoying a secluded lochside position in the midst of an area of breathtaking natural beauty.

1 log cabin, 4 flats, 1 cottage, 1-2 pub rms, 1-3 bedrms (grd flr avail), sleeps 2-8, total sleeping capacity 31, min let 2 nights, £195.00-£1500.00, Jan-Dec, bus 4 mls, rail 20 mls, airport 40 mls

---

★★★★ SELF CATERING

Mr & Mrs B Barker
Mid Torrie Farm, Callander, Perthshire, FK17 8JL
Tel: 01877 330 203 Fax: 01877 330203

Charming two-storey stonebuilt cottage on small livestock farm, in peaceful setting with superb views.

1 cottage, 2 pub rms, 3 bedrms (grd flr avail), sleeps 6, £220.00-£470.00, Jan-Dec, bus 3 mls, rail 12 mls, airport 40 mls.

★★★ SELF CATERING

Mrs Janette Donald
Trean Farm, Callander, Perthshire, FK17 8AS
Tel/Fax: 01877 331160

Modern bungalow on a farm, situated on the outskirts of Callander, with magnificent views to Ben Ledi.

1 bungalow, 2 pub rms, 4 bedrms, sleeps 7, £200.00-£360.00, Jan-Dec, bus ¼ ml, rail 16 mls, airport 45 mls

---

VAT is shown at 17.5%: changes in this rate may affect prices.   Key to symbols is on back flap.

CALLANDER

WEST HIGHLANDS & ISLANDS, LOCH LOMOND, STIRLING & TROSSACHS

Callander, Perthshire — Map Ref: 1H3

★★★ SELF CATERING

Mr & Mrs J Greenfield
Annfield, North Church Street, Callander, Perthshire, FK17 8EG
Tel: 01877 330204

1 bungalow, 1 pub rm, 2 bedrms (All grd.floor), sleeps 3, £190.00-£230.00, Jan-Dec, bus nearby, rail 12 mls, airport 40 mls

Modern semi-detached bungalow in quiet residential area yet only minutes walk from the town centre.

★★★★ SELF CATERING

Andrew Little
Auld Toll Cottages, Riverview, Leny, Callander, FK17 8AL
Tel: 01877 330635

2 cottages, 1 pub rm, 2 bedrms (All grd.floor), sleeps 3-4, total sleeping capacity 7, £150.00-£320.00, Jan-Dec, bus 1 ml, rail 16 mls

Former toll house and cottage comprising 2 semi-detached stone cottages sleeping 3/7 in beautiful rural setting, yet only a mile from Callander town centre. The Callander/Strathyre track is close by providing attractive riverside walks and cycleways. Within easy walking distance of a good inn and 2 woollen mills with tea rooms.

★★ SELF CATERING

Mrs Michie
Drumardoch Farm, Callander, Perthshire, FK17 8LT
Tel: 01877 330568

2 houses, 1 pub rm, 2 bedrms (All grd.floor), sleeps 4-5, total sleeping capacity 9, £210.00-£300.00, Jan-Dec, bus ½ ml, rail 14 mls

Detached cottages of character in own parkland at entrance to Pass of Leny.

Important: Prices stated are estimates and may be subject to amendments

WEST HIGHLANDS & ISLANDS, LOCH LOMOND, STIRLING & TROSSACHS

CALLANDER – CAMPBELTOWN

Callander, Perthshire Map Ref: 1H3

Leny Estate Lodges

Leny House, Callander, Perthshire FK17 8HA
Tel: 01877 331078 Fax: 01877 331335
e.mail: res@lenyestate.demon.co.uk
Web: www.lenyestate.demon.co.uk

Six new solid spruce lodges and cottages set in parkland on the Leny Estate near Callander. The private Leny Glen, in which visitors may walk, and where deer safely graze, contains much wildlife. Within the grounds of Leny House itself, which dates from 1513, there is a small goat herd and horses. Every luxury including washing/drying machine, dishwasher, colour TV and telephone. The ONLY self-catering accommodation in Scotland awarded Four to Five Stars – Self Catering and recommended by the television travel programme "Wish You Were Here". Own picnic area and barbecue. Perfect centre for touring. Open all year, weekends available. Colour brochure.

Winner of Antartex "Best Self-Catering" award.

★★★★★ SELF CATERING

Roebuck

Leny House, Leny Estate, Callander, Perthshire, FK17 8HA
Tel: 01877 331078 Fax: 01877 331335
E-mail: res@lenyestate.demon.co.uk
Web: www.lenyestate.demon.co.uk

Spruce lodges and stone cottages on a small peaceful site set in acres of parkland on Leny Estate, with superb views to the Trossachs. Our own private, unspoilt glen to enjoy walks amongst the plentiful wildlife. Paddocks with angora goats. Tranquil estate but only 2 miles from Callander, the gateway to the Highlands. Beautiful at any time of the year. Central location with good access to both Scottish coasts.

6 log cabins, 2 cottages, 2 pub rms, 2 bedrms (All grd.floor), sleeps 4-6, total sleeping capacity 48, min let 2 nights, £333.00-£610.00, Jan-Dec, bus 1 ml, rail 15 mls, airport 36 mls

Campbeltown, Argyll Map Ref: 1D7

Col & Mrs W T C Angus

Kilchrist Castle, Campbeltown, Argyll, PA28 6PH
Tel: 01586 553210 Fax: 01586 551852
E-mail: william.t.c.angus@btinternet.com
Web: www.oas.co.uk/ukcottages/kilchrist/index.htm

Friendly welcome, comfortable, all electric cottage accommodation in castle grounds. Campbeltown amenities and beaches within short distance. Bed linen included.

6 cottages, 1 pub rm, 1-2 bedrms (grd flr avail), sleeps 2-6, total sleeping capacity 22, £135.00-£299.00, Apr-Oct, bus 600 yds, airport 3 mls

---

Mrs C McArthur

Booking Enquiries: Mrs C McArthur
Fort Argyll, High Askomil, Campbeltown, Argyll, PA28 6EN
Tel: 01586 552087

Park accommodation:

Holiday Caravan to let, sleeps 6 from £100.00, min let weekend, Jan-Dec.

HOLIDAY CARAVAN

VAT is shown at 17.5%: changes in this rate may affect prices. Key to symbols is on back flap.

CARRADALE

WEST HIGHLANDS & ISLANDS, LOCH LOMOND, STIRLING & TROSSACHS

Carradale, Argyll

Map Ref: 1E6

Mrs Campbell
Gorton House, Gorton Wood, Carradale, Argyll
Tel: 01583 431641

★★ SELF CATERING

1 house, 1 pub rm, 4 bedrms (grd flr avail), sleeps 8, from £175.00, Jan-Dec, bus nearby, ferry 16 mls, airport 14 mls

Detatched house commanding views over Carradale Bay to Arran and Ailsa Craig from a secluded, elevated position. Abundance of birds and wildlife. Area rich in archaeology.

Mr M Hurst
The Steading, Carradale, Argyll, PA28 6QG
Tel: 0800 581259

★★★★ SELF CATERING

3 cottages, 1-2 pub rms, sleeps 2-4, total sleeping capacity 8, min let 2 nights, £150.00-£250.00, Jan-Dec, bus nearby, airport 15 mls

Very attractive and comfortable studio cottages recently converted from former steading. Traditional box bedroom off living area. Extremely well equipped to a high standard. Ideal for romantic breaks, single occupancy lets available. An attractive garden and barbecue area.

Mrs M MacAlister Hall
Torrisdale Castle, Carradale, by Campbeltown, Argyll, PA28 6QT
Tel/Fax: 01583 431233
E-mail: machall@torrisdalecastle.freeserve.co.uk

★★ UP TO ★★★ SELF CATERING

2 houses, 3 flats, 3 cottages, 1-3 pub rms, 1-5 bedrms (grd flr avail), sleeps 2-10, total sleeping capacity 42, min let 3 nights, £120.00-£410.00, Jan-Dec (flat), Apr-Oct (cottages), bus 800 yds, ferry 16 mls, airport 13 mls

A varied selection of properties on beautiful, peaceful estate halfway down the Mull of Kintyre. Own sandy bay and rowing boat. All cottages set in individual location in natural woodland with many rhododendrons.

D & P Washington
Lag Kilmichael, Carradale, Argyll, PA28 6QJ
Tel: 01583 431626

★★★★ SELF CATERING

3 cottages, 1 pub rm, 1-4 bedrms (grd flr avail), sleeps 2-8, total sleeping capacity 16, £250.00-£620.00, Jan-Dec, bus 2 mls, ferry 10 mls, airport 15 mls

Two detached cottages and converted byre peacefully situated in Carradale Glen yet only 1.5 miles (2.5kms) from village. Fishing and golfing available locally. Pony Trekking. Children welcome, pets corner and adventure play area.

Ruth Watson
Carradale Chalets, Carradale Bay Caravan Park, Carradale, Argyll, PA28 6QG
Tel: 01583 431665

★★★ SELF CATERING

3 log cabins, 1 pub rm, 2 bedrms (All grd.floor), sleeps 5, total sleeping capacity 15, min let 3 nights, £120.00-£325.00, Apr-Oct, bus ½ Mile, rail 60 Miles, ferry 15 Miles, airport 25 Miles

Pine lodges in quiet area of caravan park, with own safe sandy beach. Canoeing instruction. Trout and salmon fishing available. Forest walks, abundance of wildlife and 9-hole golf course all nearby. All village amenities, restaurant and shop within 1 mile.

Important: Prices stated are estimates and may be subject to amendments

WEST HIGHLANDS & ISLANDS, LOCH LOMOND, STIRLING & TROSSACHS

CARRICK CASTLE, LOCH GOIL – COLONSAY, ISLE OF

Carrick Castle, Loch Goil, Argyll

Map Ref: 1F4

★★ SELF CATERING

Mrs J Murray
Darroch Mhor Chalets, Carrick Castle, Loch Goil, Argyll, PA24 8AF
Tel: 01301 703249/703432 Fax: 01301 703348

3 chalets, 1 pub rm, 2 bedrms, sleeps 4, total sleeping capacity 12, £110.00-£300.00, Jan-Dec, bus nearby, rail nearby

Three cedar wood chalets set in a peaceful location in the heart of Argyll Forest Park, with panoramic views over Lochgoil. Pets welcome, ideal location for a relaxing peaceful holiday.

Clynder, Argyll & Bute

Map Ref: 1G4

★★★★ SELF CATERING

Mrs Lulu Staahl
Bella Vista, Annachmor Road, Clynder, G84 0QD
Tel/Fax: 01436 831312

1 bungalow, 1 pub rm, 1 bedrm, sleeps 4, £150.00-£250.00, Jan-Dec, bus nearby, rail 11 mls, ferry 3 mls, airport 36 mls

Bungalow centrally located for touring, sea-fishing and walking. Lovely views of the Gare Loch. Non-smoking property.

Colonsay, Isle of, Argyll

Map Ref: 1C4

★★ SELF CATERING

Isle of Colonsay Chalets
Argyll, PA61 7YR
Tel: 01951 200320 Fax: 01951 200242
E-mail: chalets@colonsay.org.uk
Web: www.colonsay.org.uk

3 chalets, 1 pub rm, 1-2 bedrms, 1-2 bedrms (grd flr avail), sleeps 3-6, total sleeping capacity 15, £145.00-£495.00, Jan-Dec, ferry 1/4 ml

Comfortable chalets on Hebridean Island, within grounds of hotel. Near church, shop and beach.

★★ UP TO ★★★ SELF CATERING

Mr and Mrs W Lawson
Seaview, Isle of Colonsay, Argyll, PA61 7YR
Tel: 01951 200315

1 cottage, 1 studio flat, 1-3 pub rms, 1-3 bedrms (grd flr avail), sleeps 2-5, total sleeping capacity 8, £95.00-£450.00, Jan-Dec, ferry 3 1/2 mls

A former byre, this charming cottage has been refurbished in character, with comfort and warmth foremost. Small studio adjoins. Brand new large cottage with balcony, set above, in hillside. Enjoy the peace and tranquility of this unique island, sandy beaches, woodland gardens, moorland, cliffs and lochs. This varied scenery gives you the opportunity to enjoy walking, cycling, golf, bird watching or just relaxing in unspoilt surroundings.

VAT is shown at 17.5%: changes in this rate may affect prices.

Key to symbols is on back flap.

COLONSAY, ISLE OF –
CRAOBH HAVEN, BY LOCHGILPHEAD

D WEST HIGHLANDS & ISLANDS,
LOCH LOMOND, STIRLING & TROSSACHS

Colonsay, Isle of, Argyll

Map Ref: 1C4

Isle of Colonsay Estate Cottages
Machrins Farm, Isle of Colonsay, Argyll PA61 7YR
Tel: 01951 200312   Fax: 01951 200312   Web: www.colonsay.org.uk

Peaceful and unspoilt island of outstanding natural beauty. Stunning scenery, magnificent sandy beaches, abundant wildlife, famous gardens, trout fishing, 18-hole golf course, tennis, cycling, wonderful walks. Traditional farmhouses and cottages with spectacular views scattered throughout island. Flats in Colonsay House overlooking garden. Art Courses. Regular car ferry from Oban. Brochure.

UP TO ★★★ SELF CATERING

Mrs E McNeill
Machrins Farm, Isle of Colonsay, Argyll
Tel/Fax: 01951 200312

Traditional houses, cottages and flats on island of outstanding natural beauty. Famous for sunshine, sandy beaches, woodland gardens and wildlife.

7 houses, 6 flats, 8 cottages, 3 bungalows, 2-3 pub rms, 1-5 bedrms (grd flr avail), sleeps 2-12, total sleeping capacity 156, min let 2 nights, £180.00-£850.00, Mar-Nov, Xmas/New Year, ferry 3 ½ mls

---

Craobh Haven, by Lochgilphead, Argyll

Map Ref: 1E3

★★★★ SELF CATERING

Croabh Haven Cottages
17 Brunton Terrace, Edinburgh, EH7 5EH
Tel: 0131 661 2783 Fax: 0131 478 0566
E-mail: stb@craobh.demon.co.uk
Web: www.craobh.demon.co.uk

Traditionally built with open fires and timber beams, the cottages combine the warmth and comfort of home with wonderful, unspoilt views of the islands. Right beside the sea and a short stroll from the village, they make a cosy and well equipped base for walking, touring or just relaxing. Website - http://www.craobh.demon.co.uk

2 cottages, 1 pub rm, 2-3 bedrms, sleeps 4-6, total sleeping capacity 10, £320.00-£520.00, Jan-Dec, bus ¼ ml, rail 20 mls, ferry 20 mls, airport 100 mls

LUNGA ESTATES
CRAOBH HAVEN, ARGYLL PA31 8QR

Telephone: 01852 500237   Fax: 01852 500639   e.mail: colin@lunga.demon.co.uk

LUNGA overlooks the islands of the Firth of Lorne. It has been run by the same family for 300 years who offer rooms for B&B and nearby cottages and flats which share the many facilities of this 3,000-acre coastal estate. Sailing, riding, fishing, candlelit dinners.
UTTERLY SECLUDED AND PEACEFUL.

★ SELF CATERING

Mr C Lindsay MacDougall
Lunga, Ardfern, Argyll, PA31 8QR
Tel: 01852 500237 Fax: 01852 500639
E-mail: colin@lunga.demon.co.uk

18c mansion house on 3000 acre private coastal estate. Two flats and two converted cottages on the estate. Superb views over Sound of Jura and Firth of Lorne. Ideal for sailing, riding and fishing.

1 house, 2 flats, 2 cottages, 1-2 pub rms, 1-3 bedrms, sleeps 2-8, total sleeping capacity 20, min let 3 days, £96.50-£415.00, Jan-Dec, bus 2 mls, rail 20 mls, airport 90 mls

---

Important: Prices stated are estimates and may be subject to amendments

WEST HIGHLANDS & ISLANDS, LOCH LOMOND, STIRLING & TROSSACHS

CRIANLARICH

Map Ref: 1G2

Mrs C S R Christie
Lochdochart, Crianlarich, Perthshire, FK20 8QS
Tel/Fax: 01838 300274

2 chalets, 1 wing of house, 1 pub rm, 2-3 bedrms, sleeps 6-9, total sleeping capacity 21, £160.00-£350.00. Jan-Dec, bus ½ ml, rail 1 ½ mls, airport 55 mls

UP TO ★★ — SELF CATERING

Inverhaggernie chalets:- two cedarwood cottages at Inverhaggernie Farm, two miles outside the village of Crianlarich. Well behaved dogs allowed. North wing of Lochdochart House:- wing of large mansion house situated a half mile from the main road near loch and river. Bed linen can be hired if desired. Regret no dogs in north wing.

Mr W J C & Mrs J Christie
Inverardran, Crianlarich, Perthshire, FK20 8RS
Tel: 01838 300240 Fax: 01838 300363
E-mail: john@inverardran.demon.co.uk
Web: www.inverardran.demon.co.uk

1 house, 1 cottage, 1-3 pub rms, 2-4 bedrms (grd flr avail), sleeps 4-8, total sleeping capacity 12, £220.00-£360.00. Jan-Dec, bus nearby, rail 1 ml, ferry 45 mls, airport 50 mls

★★ — SELF CATERING

Former shooting lodge and courtyard cottage situated back from the main road, 0.25 miles (0.5km) from village. Superb mountain views. Satellite television.

Portnellan Lodges

Crianlarich, Perthshire FK20 8QS
Telephone: 01838 300284   Fax: 01838 300332
e.mail: lodges@portnellan.demon.co.uk
Web: www.portnellan.demon.co.uk

Luxury Lodges in the Heart of the Scottish Highlands, set in elevated positions with views over our lochs and glen.

'Best Self Catering Holiday Homes Award.'

Every home comfort including dishwasher, microwave, toasted sandwich maker ... TV/satellite/video/stereo ... private balcony with garden furniture and barbeque. New ultimate luxury lodges with en-suite bathrooms, some with spa-bath and sauna. Free fishing, boats, bikes, canoes. Golf packages available. Sleeps 2 to 8 persons. Open all year.

Portnellan Lodges
Crianlarich, Perthshire, FK20 8QS
Tel: 01838 300284 Fax: 01838 300332
E-mail: lodges@portnellan.demon.co.uk
Web: www.portnellan.demon.co.uk

16 chalets, 3 cottages, 1-2 pub rms, 1-4 bedrms (grd flr avail), sleeps 2-8, total sleeping capacity 82, min let 3 days, £225.00-£1095.00. Jan-Dec, bus nearby, rail 2 mls, airport 45 mls

★★★★ UP TO ★★★★★ — SELF CATERING

Spacious well appointed lodges, each with provate patio/deck & gas barbecue, set in a 70 acre private estate. Spectacular Highland views. The ideal centre for touring the Highlands. Free fishing/boating on private loch.

VAT is shown at 17.5%: changes in this rate may affect prices.

Key to symbols is on back flap.

CRINAN, BY LOCHGILPHEAD – BY DALMALLY

D

WEST HIGHLANDS & ISLANDS, LOCH LOMOND, STIRLING & TROSSACHS

Crinan, by Lochgilphead, Argyll — Map Ref: 1E4

KILMAHUMAIG BARN FLATS

Kilmahumaig, Crinan, by Lochgilphead, Argyll PA31 8SW
Tel: 01546 830238 Fax: 01546 830238

Kilmahumaig Barn Flats provide 3 self-contained flats accommodating 2/6 in one or two-bedroomed units. This is an ideal place for all the usual country pursuits and just what you need for a truly relaxing holiday.

★★ SELF CATERING

Daphne Murray
Kilmahumaig, Crinan, by Lochgilphead, Argyll, PA31 8SW
Tel/Fax: 01546 830238

3 flats, 1-2 pub rms, 1-2 bedrms, sleeps 2-6, total sleeping capacity 14, £100.00-£375.00, Jan-Dec, bus nearby, rail 35 mls, airport 80 mls

Apartments of individual character and style, converted from farm steading. Peaceful location under 1/2 mile (1km) from Crinan.

★★ SELF CATERING

Mrs Walker
The Change House, Crinan Ferry, by Lochgilphead, Argyll, PA31 8QH
Tel: 01546 510232 Fax: 01546 510249

1 cottage, 3 pub rms, 3 bedrms, sleeps 6, £230.00-£475.00, Jan-Dec, bus 8 mls, rail 30 mls

Modernised stone built cottage on isolated peninsula, surrounded by sandy beaches. Ideal for quiet holiday, bird watching, fishing and walking.

Dalmally, Argyll — Map Ref: 1F2

★★★ SELF CATERING

Ms Irene Chapman
Troughwood, Kippen, Stirlingshire, FK8 3HU
Tel: 01786 870778

1 cottage, 2 pub rms, 2 bedrms, sleeps 4, £230.00-£325.00, Jan-Dec, bus 1/2 ml, rail 1/2 ml

Delightful stone cottage on the banks of the River Orchy. Perfect for fishing, hillwalking and family activities. Ideal for touring the Western and Central Highlands. Coal/Log fire.

---

by Dalmally, Argyll — Map Ref: 1F2

★★ UP TO ★★★ SELF CATERING

Mrs E Fellowes
Inistrynich, Lochaweside, by Dalmally, Argyll, PA33 1BQ
Tel: 01838 200256 Fax: 01838 200253

3 cottages, 2 pub rms, 2-4 bedrms, sleeps 4-8, total sleeping capacity 16, £150.00-£480.00, Apr-Nov, bus 1/4 ml, rail 5 mls, ferry 28 mls, airport 70 mls

Traditional cottages on private estate overlooking Loch Awe. Magnificent scenery. All electric. Fishing, walking, golf, ferries from Oban to Islands.

Important: Prices stated are estimates and may be subject to amendments

WEST HIGHLANDS & ISLANDS, LOCH LOMOND, STIRLING & TROSSACHS

D

BY DOUNE – DUNOON

89

by Doune, Perthshire

Map Ref: 2A3

SELF CATERING ★★★★

Mrs F J R Graham
Mackeanston House, Doune, Perthshire, FK16 6AX
Tel: 01786 850213 Fax: 01786 850414
E-mail: mackean.house@cwcom.net
Web: www.aboutscotland.com/stirling/mackeanston/gled.html

Luxurious, pretty cottage with spectacular views south to Gargunnock Hills in central rural location at the Gateway to the Highlands. Ideal base for Trossachs, Loch Lomond, Perth, Glasgow, Edinburgh and Stirling. Hill and mountain walking, historic sights. Own garden. Open fire. Ensuite bathrooms. Easy reach of airports. Available all year for short or long lets.

1 cottage, 1 pub rm, 2 bedrms (All grd.floor), sleeps 4, min let weekend, £150.00-£425.00, Jan-Dec, bus 2 mls, rail 5 mls, 40 mls

Dunblane, Perthshire

Map Ref: 2A3

SELF CATERING ★★★

Mrs A Wordie
The Row, Dunblane, Perthshire, FK15 9WZ
Tel: 01786 841200 Fax: 01786 842162

In grounds of large country house with magnificent open views. Peaceful, yet only 2 miles (3kms) from Doune. Easy access to M9, A9 and airports.

1 cottage, 1 pub rm, 2 bedrms, sleeps 4-5, £210.00-£250.00, Jan-Dec exc Xmas/New Year, bus 2 mls, rail 7 mls, airport 30 mls

---

Dunoon, Argyll

Map Ref: 1F5

HOLIDAY PARK ★★★★

Cowal Caravan Park
Hunters Quay, Dunoon, Argyll, PA23 8JY
Tel: 01369 704259

1½ acres, sloping, sheltered, Jan-Dec, prior booking in peak periods, latest time of arrival 2230.

Park accommodation: 32

3 Holiday Caravans to let, sleep 6, £150.00-220.00, total sleeping capacity 18, min let 2 nights, Jan-Dec.

2 mls from Dunoon pier off A815, signposted at Western Ferry terminal, Hunters Quay.

SELF CATERING ★★★★

Mr A C Gordon
Ri Cruin, Kilmartin, by Lochgilphead, Argyll, PA31 8QF
Tel: 01546 510316
E-mail: gordon@ri-cruin.freeserve.co.uk

Clyde Cottage is a 19C Listed Building situated on the sea front with wonderful views of the Firth of Clyde and hills beyond. Completely renovated and furnished to a very high standard. Private enclosed garden with patio and furniture. Private parking to rear. Town centre, restaurants, pub, cinema and ferry within 5 minutes walk. Come "Doon the Watter", explore the hills and lochs of the Cowal penisula, cruise on the Firth, enjoy the fresh air.

1 house, 2 pub rms, 3 bedrms, sleeps 6, £190.00-£482.00, Jan-Dec, ferry ½ Mile

---

SELF CATERING ★★★

Mr Lawson
The Close, Mill Lane, Cloughton, nr Scarborough, N. Yorkshire, YO1 0AB
Tel: 01723 870455 Fax: 01723 870349

Located on the outskirts of Dunoon adjacent to the 18-hole Cowal golf course and bowling club. On the door step of this lovely home are mountains, fells,hills,forests to walk, cycle, climb and enjoy. There are many roads, lochs and views to view with pleasure. This is an area of outstanding natural beauty.

1 house, 2 pub rms, 2 bedrms, sleeps 4-6, £150.00-£250.00, Apr-Oct, bus nearby, rail 6 mls, ferry 2 mls, airport 20 mls

---

VAT is shown at 17.5%: changes in this rate may affect prices.

Key to symbols is on back flap.

DUNOON – FINTRY

WEST HIGHLANDS & ISLANDS, LOCH LOMOND, STIRLING & TROSSACHS

Dunoon, Argyll — Map Ref: 1F5

★ UP TO ★★ — SELF CATERING

Mr John Quirk
Dunmore Holiday Flats, Alexandra Parade, Kirn, Dunoon, Argyll, PA2 8DX
Tel: 01369 704205

5 flats, 1 pub rm, 1-2 bedrms (grd flr avail), sleeps 2-5, total sleeping capacity 22, min let weekend (low season), £90.00-£240.00, Jan-Dec, bus nearby, ferry 1 ml, airport 12 mls

Victorian villa of character tastefully converted to holiday apartments with additional units in rear gardens. Located on the sea front at Kirn close to ferry terminals and all amenities. All flats are fully self contained comprising hall, lounge, kitchen, bathroom and bedrooms (s) sleeping 5. The front flats enjoy panoramic views of the Firth of Clyde. Free ferry pickup for foot travellers. Ideal for touring the unspoilt Argyll countryside.

by Dunoon, Argyll — Map Ref: 1F5

★★ — SELF CATERING

Mrs G Cox
Blairmore Holidays Ltd, 22 Victoria Park Gardens North, Glasgow, G11 7EJ
Tel: 0141 337 6669 Fax: 07070 604089
E-mail: blairmore.house@unforgettable.com

1 house, 4 pub rms, 8 bedrms (grd flr avail), sleeps 16, £795.00-£1550.00, Jan-Dec, bus nearby, rail 10 mls, ferry 10 mls, airport 30 mls

Spacious house recently built in traditional style and set back from coastal road overlooking Loch Long. Eight bedrooms and four bathrooms make this property ideal for large groups or several families holidaying together. Sauna, jacuzzi and pool table.

Easdale, by Oban, Argyll — Map Ref: 1D3

★★ — SELF CATERING

Mrs J Forster
Kilchurn, Killin, Perthshire, FK21 8TN
Tel: 01567 820298

1 cottage, 1 pub rm, 2 bedrms, sleeps 5, £220.00-£240.00, Jan-Dec, bus 500 yds, rail 16 mls

150 year-old cottage, modernised yet retaining original character, in peaceful village with views of the Atlantic Ocean and Inner Hebrides. Ideal for fishing, walking, birdwatching, photography. Wonderful sunsets!

Fintry, Stirlingshire — Map Ref: 1H4

★★★★ — HOLIDAY PARK

Balgair Castle Caravan Park
Overglinns, Fintry, Stirlingshire, G63 0LP
Tel: 01360 860283/860399 (9-5pm) Fax: 01360 860300

Park accommodation: 234
63 tourers £9.95 or 10 motors £8.95-9.95 or 6 tents from £8.00.
Total Touring Pitches 63.
10 Holiday Caravans to let, sleep 6-8 £130.00-340.00, total sleeping capacity 18, min let weekend.

35 acres, grassy, Mar-Oct (tourers), Mar-Nov (homes), prior booking in peak periods, latest time of arrival 2100, overnight holding area. Extra charge for electricity, awnings.

Leisure facilities:

B822 Fintry-Kippen, 1 ½ mls N of Fintry.

Important: Prices stated are estimates and may be subject to amendments

WEST HIGHLANDS & ISLANDS, LOCH LOMOND, STIRLING & TROSSACHS

FINTRY – FORD, BY LOCHGILPHEAD

Fintry, Stirlingshire   Map Ref: 1H4

Culcreuch Castle Lodges

Culcreuch Castle and Country Park
Fintry, Stirlingshire G63 0LW
Tel: 01360 860555   Fax: 01360 860556

Set in magnificent 1,600-acre parkland estate, surrounded by breathtaking scenery, eight Scandinavian-style lodges. Sleep 6 in 3 bedrooms. Modern, tastefully furnished, fully carpeted, central heating, colour TV. Free fishing. Cosy bar, licensed restaurant in castle. Adjacent squash courts, children's play area. Central for all Scotland's attractions including Edinburgh (55 minutes by road).

For free accommodation brochure and free fishing and golf brochures contact:
Laird of Culcreuch, Culcreuch Castle, Fintry, Stirlingshire G63 0LW.   Tel: 01360 860555.

★★★ SELF CATERING

Culcreuch Castle Lodges
Culcreuch Castle & Country Park, Fintry, Stirling, G63 0LW
Tel: 01360 860228/860555 Fax: 01360 860556

Lodges on elevated site with impressive views over 1600 acre parkland.

8 lodges, 1 pub rm, 2-3 bedrms (grd flr avail), sleeps 4-6, total sleeping capacity 40, £169.00-£429.00, Jan-Dec, bus 1 ml, rail 17 mls, airport 30 mls

★★★ SELF CATERING

Mrs Helen Morris
Netherton of Glenboig, Fintry, Stirlingshire, G63 0YH
Tel/Fax: 01360 860242
E-mail: morrish2@aol.com

Recently renovated farm workers cottage. Cosy lounge with wood burning stove. In a quiet peaceful location it offers picturesque views across the surrounding countryside to the Campsie Fells. Ideally situated for touring the Trossachs. Private trout and salmon fishing available.

1 cottage, 1 pub rm, 2 bedrms (All grd.floor), sleeps 4, min let 3 nights, £145.00-£320.00, Jan-Dec, bus 3 mls, rail 18 mls, airport 25 mls

---

Ford, by Lochgilphead, Argyll   Map Ref: 1E3

★★★ SELF CATERING

Mrs W Cairns
Finchairn, Ford, by Lochgilphead, Argyll, PA31 8RJ
Tel: 01546 810 223

Three comfortable and warm traditional stonebuilt highland cottages, all recently refurbished and equipped, situated in various locations on extensive working estate. An abundance of wildlife, different habitats, ancient chaple, burial site and castle all to be explored on the estate.

3 cottages, 1 pub rm, 1-4 bedrms, sleeps 2-7, total sleeping capacity 16, £165.00-£390.00, Jan-Dec, bus 1 ml, ferry 20 mls

---

VAT is shown at 17.5%: changes in this rate may affect prices.   *Key to symbols is on back flap.*

GARTOCHARN – INVERBEG

D — WEST HIGHLANDS & ISLANDS, LOCH LOMOND, STIRLING & TROSSACHS

Gartocharn, Dunbartonshire — Map Ref: 1G4

★★★★ SELF CATERING

Lomond Luxury Lodges
Oakwoods Farm, Gartocharn, Alexandria, G83 8SB
Tel: 01360 660054
E-mail: lodges@globalnet.co.uk
Web: www.users.globalnet.co.uk/~lodges

New spacious Scandinavian lodges with open views across farmland to the Endrick Water. Ideal base for Loch Lomond and the Trossachs.

2 lodges, 1 pub rm, 2 bedrms (All grd.floor), sleeps 6, total sleeping capacity 12, min let 2 days, £220.00-£460.00, Jan-Dec, bus nearby, rail 6 mls, airport 18 mls

---

Glendaruel, Argyll — Map Ref: 1F4

★★ SELF CATERING

Mrs S MacKellar
Ardacheranmor, Glendaruel, Argyll, PA22 3AE
Tel: 01369 820209

A south facing picturesque situation in a rural Glen with views to hills of Cowal and across green fields to the small village of Glendaruel. In the area is an extensive choice of country pursuits, Loch and sea sailing, sailboarding and diving tuition. Just off the A886, a central base for touring gardens, castles and museums.

1 farmhouse, 2 pub rms, 5 bedrms (grd flr avail), sleeps 9, from £180.00, May-Sep, bus 1 ml, rail 40 mls, ferry 8 mls, airport 60 mls

Inveraray, Argyll — Map Ref: 1F3

★★★ SELF CATERING

Mrs Crawford
Brenchoille Farm, Inveraray, Argyll, PA32 8XN
Tel/Fax: 01499 500662

19c stone building carefully restored to provide three houses peacefully situated with views to the Cowal Hills. Area rich in archaeology and natural history.

3 houses, 2 pub rms, 1-2 bedrms (grd flr avail), sleeps 2-5, total sleeping capacity 11, £111.00-£367.00, Jan-Dec, bus ½ ml, rail 23 mls, airport 70 mls

---

Inverbeg, Argyll — Map Ref: 1G4

★★★ UP TO ★★★★ SELF CATERING

Inverbeg Holiday Park
Inverbeg, Luss, Dunbartonshire, G83 8PD
Tel: 01436 860267 Fax: 01436 860266
E-mail: inverbeg-holidays@swinternet.co.uk
Web: www.inverbeg-holidays.swinternet.co.uk

Chalets on large holiday park on the shore of Loch Lomond. All park facilities available to chalet guests.

1 chalet, 1 pub rm, 3 bedrms (All grd.floor), sleeps 8, £250.00-£485.00, Mar-Oct, bus nearby, rail 6 mls, airport 20 mls

---

★★★ HOLIDAY PARK

Inverbeg Holiday Park
Inverbeg, by Luss, Argyll, G83 8PD
Tel: 01436 860267 Fax: 01436 860266

13 acres, hard-standing, level, sheltered, 1 Mar-31 Oct, prior booking in peak periods, latest time of arrival 2200. Extra charge for electricity, awnings.

Park accommodation: 181

20 tourers £9.50-10.75 or 10 motors £9.50-10.75. Total Touring Pitches 20. No tents.

12 Holiday Caravans to let, sleep 4-6 £150.00-450.00, min let 3 nights.

Leisure facilities:

Take M8 through Glasgow. Go over Erskine Bridge, take A82 for Crianlarich. Park is 4 mls N of Luss on right hand side, beside Loch Lomond.

Important: Prices stated are estimates and may be subject to amendments

LOCH LOMOND
INVERBEG HOLIDAY PARK
• 01436 860 267 •
CARAVANS & CHALETS FOR HIRE

Most with loch view (most chalets are beach front). The park is located on a promontary which stretches into the loch, and has the River Douglas flowing down one side of it. The position and the view across the loch to Ben Lomond (3198ft) is fabulous. Stirling and much of the West Coast can be reached by car in under an hour.

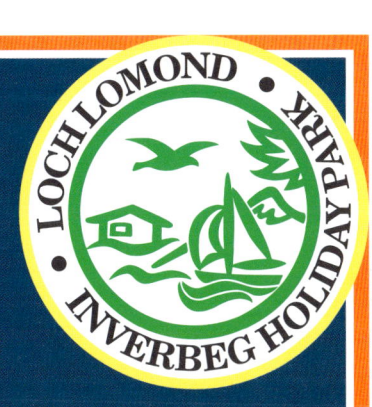

★ **FISHING FROM SHORE**
★ **HARBOUR & SLIPWAY**
★ **CYCLE HIRE**

Thistle
COMMENDATION AWARD

All our chalets, Gold, Silver & Bronze Caravans surpass the "Thistle" requirements.

Loch Lomond (from the South)

★ **PRIVATE BEACH**
★ **LAUNDRETTE**
★ **FAMILY RESTAURANT (200 YARDS)**
★ **FERRY (200 YARDS), BOAT TRIPS (4 MILES)**
★ **TRAIN (6 MILES), CITYLINK BUSES (AT GATE)**

Looking across the harbour

INVERBEG HOLIDAY PARK
Inverbeg, Luss,
Dumbartonshire G83 8PD.

01436 860 267
Brochure will be sent by return.

A Lochside Chalet

INVERUGLAS – BOWMORE, ISLE OF ISLAY

WEST HIGHLANDS & ISLANDS, LOCH LOMOND, STIRLING & TROSSACHS

Inveruglas, Argyll & Bute

Map Ref: 1G3

★★★★ SELF CATERING

Loch Lomond Holiday Park
Inveruglas, by Tarbet, Argyll & Bute, G83 7DW
Tel: 01301 704224 Fax: 01301 704224/704206
E-mail: inveruglas@aol.com

4 chalets, 1 cottage, 9 luxury lodges, 1 pub rm, 2-3 bedrms, sleeps 4-6, total sleeping capacity 52, £180.00-£625.00, Jan-Dec, exc Nov/Feb, bus ¼ ml, rail 4 mls, airport 35 mls

Chalets, luxury lodges and a cottage; situated on the lochside in this peaceful 13 acre park, with superb open views.

★★★★ HOLIDAY PARK

Loch Lomond Holiday Park
Inveruglas, by Tarbet, Argyll & Bute, G83 7DW
Tel: 01301 704224 Fax: 01301 704206

Park accommodation: **90**

18 tourers £7.00-12.50 or 18 motors £7.00-12.50. Total Touring Pitches 18. No tents.

13 Holiday Caravans to let, sleep 6 £140.00-325.00, total sleeping capacity 78, min let 3 days.

13 acres, hard-standing, level, Dec-Jan, Mar-Oct, prior booking in peak periods, latest time of arrival 2100. Extra charge for electricity, awnings.

Leisure facilities:

From Dumbarton take A82 N following W side of Loch Lomond. Take right fork at Tarbet Hotel, park is on Lochside, 3 ½ mls N of Tarbet.

Ballygrant, Isle of Islay, Argyll

Map Ref: 1C5

★★ SELF CATERING

Catriona Bell
Knocklearach, Ballygrant, Isle of Islay, Argyll, PA45 7QL
Tel/Fax: 01496 840209

3 flats, 1 pub rm, 1-4 bedrms (grd flr avail), sleeps 3-8, total sleeping capacity 17, £120.00-£250.00, Jan-Dec, bus nearby, ferry 3 mls, airport 11 mls

Three flats in stonebuilt house situated in the centre of a small village. An ideal base for walkers and nature lovers. Short lets available.

Bowmore, Isle of Islay, Argyll

Map Ref: 1C6

★★ SELF CATERING

Islay Rhind, c/o Mrs F McNeill
19 Elder Crescent, Bowmore, Isle of Islay, Argyll
Tel: 01496 810532

4 flats, 1 pub rm, 1-2 bedrms, sleeps 4-6, total sleeping capacity 22, £130.00-£275.00, Jan-Dec, bus nearby, ferry 10 mls, airport 6 mls

Four modernised flats overlooking the bay in the centre of the village.

★★ SELF CATERING

Mr & Mrs L MacLean
Distillery House, School Street, Bowmore, Islay, PA43 7JS
Tel: 01496 810630

1 house, 1 pub rm, 3 bedrms, sleeps 7, £100.00-£250.00, Jan-Dec, bus nearby, ferry 10 mls, airport 6 mls

Traditional island welcome awaits you in our spacious, family home centrally situated in Bowmore. Stones throw from the harbour, shops, restaurants, swimming pool, tourist information centre and distillery all within 5 minutes walking distance. Ideal centre for touring island. Parking available on street in front of house. Fully double glazed and centrally heated.

Important: Prices stated are estimates and may be subject to amendments

WEST HIGHLANDS & ISLANDS, LOCH LOMOND, STIRLING & TROSSACHS

BY BOWMORE, ISLE OF ISLAY – BRUICHLADDICH, ISLE OF ISLAY

95

by Bowmore, Isle of Islay, Argyll

SELF CATERING ★★

W Murray
Clachan, Bowmore, Isle of Islay, Argyll
Tel: 01496 810440

Map Ref: 1C6

2 cottages, 1 pub rm, 1-2 bedrms, sleeps 4-6, total sleeping capacity 10, £85.00-£260.00, Jan-Dec, bus nearby, rail 100 mls, ferry 8 mls, airport 4 mls

These well-equipped cottages are situated one and a quarter miles from Bowmore the islands capital, in open countryside and are ideally placed for shopping and exploring all quarters of Islay. Children and pets are especially welcome.

Bridgend, Isle of Islay, Argyll

SELF CATERING ★★★★

Liz Cuninghame
Neriby Farm, Bridgend, Isle of Islay, Argyll, PA44 7PZ
Tel: 01496 810274

Map Ref: 1C5

1 cottage, 1 pub rm, 3 bedrms (All grd.floor), sleeps 6, £220.00-£390.00, Jan-Dec, bus 2 mls, ferry 10 mls, airport 6 mls

Modern cottage, 2 miles from Bridgend in peaceful, rural setting with panoramic views of the surrounding countryside. Real fire.

SELF CATERING ★

Mrs M Dunne
Chadshunt, Kineton, Warwickshire, CV35 0EQ
Tel/Fax: 01926 640215

1 house, 6 bedrms (grd flr avail), sleeps 12, £550.00-£600.00, Jan-Dec, bus 1 ml, ferry 10 mls, airport 7 mls

Owners own holiday home. Spacious, comfortable accommodation. Set in its own grounds. Ideal for two families. View of the sea. Three quarters of a mile from Bridgend village, with shops and hotel. Sleeps twelve. Centrally heated and carpeted throughout.

SELF CATERING ★★★★

Mrs Johanna Mottram
Briar Lea, Jamieson Street, Bowmore, Isle of Islay, PA43 7HL
Tel: 01496 810547/810212 (work)

1 house, 2 pub rms, 3 bedrms, sleeps 5, £325.00-£350.00, bus ½ ml, ferry 10 mls, airport 6 mls.

Cnoc Ard boasts a magnificent view overlooking Loch Indaal. This recently renovated cottage is ideally and centrally situated for those wishing a quiet, tranquil holiday or for the more active walker, angler or bird watcher.

Bruichladdich, Isle of Islay, Argyll

SELF CATERING ★★

Mrs D H Doyle
Foreland Estate, Bruichladdich, Isle of Islay, Argyll, PA49 7UU
Tel: 01496 850211 Fax: 01496 850337

Map Ref: 1B5

3 bungalows, 1-2 pub rms, 2-3 bedrms (grd flr avail), sleeps 4-6, total sleeping capacity 16, £220.00-£300.00, Jan-Dec, bus 1 ¼ mls, ferry 20 mls, airport 18 mls

Cottages individual in character and location on 6000 acre private estate. Fishing on trout loch, boat available. Pony-trekking.

VAT is shown at 17.5%: changes in this rate may affect prices.

Key to symbols is on back flap.

BRUICHLADDICH, ISLE OF ISLAY – KILCHOMAN, ISLE OF ISLAY

WEST HIGHLANDS & ISLANDS, LOCH LOMOND, STIRLING & TROSSACHS

Bruichladdich, Isle of Islay, Argyll — Map Ref: 1B5

★★★ SELF CATERING

Mr R E R Falconer
Rose Cottage, Odiham Woods, Odiham, Hants, RG29 1JQ
Tel/Fax: 01256 704178 E-mail: Rob.Falconer@tesco.net

1 cottage, 2 pub rms, 3 bedrms (grd flr avail), sleeps 1-6, £200.00-£325.00, Jan-Dec, bus nearby, ferry 16 mls, airport 12 mls

A comfortable traditional style cottage in a quiet village location with uninterrupted views of Loch Indaal. The cottage is attached to our main house but is completely self contained in every aspect. Ample off-road car parking. Conservatory and secure garden. The cottage has 2 main bedrooms, a spacious kitchen with dining for 6, bathroom and a comfortable lounge with open fire. An additional bedroom on the 1st floor is available if required.

★★★ SELF CATERING

Mrs Pat Jones
Coull Farm, Kilchoman, Bruichladdich, Isle of Islay, Argyll, PA49 7UT
Tel/Fax: 01496 850317

1 flat, 1 cottage, 1 pub rm, 1-2 bedrms, sleeps 2-6, total sleeping capacity 8, £175.00-£290.00, Jan-Dec, bus 8 mls, ferry 20 mls, airport 20 mls

Modern cottage and spacious apartment with wonderful views on busy working farm on the west coast. 5 minutes from sandy beach. Non-smokers preferred.

Caol Ila, Isle of Islay, Argyll — Map Ref: 1C6

★★★ SELF CATERING

Mrs M Carmichael
Sonas, Bridgend, Isle of Islay, PA44 7PX
Tel: 01496 810784

1 house, 1 pub rm, 2 bedrms, sleeps 4, £200.00-£275.00, Apr-Sep, bus ½ ml, ferry 2 mls, airport 16 mls

Situated in the picturesque distillery village of Caol Ila. No 16 offers magnificent views over the Sound of Islay to the islands of Jura and Mull. Islay is the ideal location for a wide variety of outdoor activities including fishing (coarse, fly and loch) shooting, cycling, walking, climbing, birdwatching and golf.

Gruinart, Bridgend, Isle of Islay, Argyll — Map Ref: 1C5

★★★ SELF CATERING

Mr & Mrs J Adamson
Newton House, Bridgend, Isle of Islay, Argyll, PA44 7PD
Tel: 01496 810293

1 cottage, 2 pub rms, 3 bedrms, sleeps 6, £230.00-£350.00, , bus 3 mls, ferry 16 mls, airport 12 mls

Modern detached cottage with garden in quiet location close to RSPB Reserve on north side of island.

Kilchoman, Isle of Islay, Argyll — Map Ref: 1B5

★★★ UP TO ★★★★ SELF CATERING

Ian & Margaret Brooke
Kilchoman House Cottages, Bruichladdich, Isle of Islay, Argyll, PA9 7UY
Tel: 01496 850382 Fax: 01496 850277

5 cottages, 1-2 pub rms, 2-3 bedrms (grd flr avail), sleeps 2-6, total sleeping capacity 22, £200.00-£450.00, Jan-Dec, ferry 19 mls, airport 15 mls

Overlooked by magnificient crags that run down to a mile long dune-fringed sandy Atlantic beach, Kilchoman House with its five self-catering cottages offers a truly peaceful location, but only 15 minutes from nearby villages. Choughs for birdwatchers, trout for fishermen, hills for walkers, safety for children. Adjacent pony trekking. Open fires. Short breaks offered September to May.

Important: Prices stated are estimates and may be subject to amendments

WEST HIGHLANDS & ISLANDS, LOCH LOMOND, STIRLING & TROSSACHS

PORT CHARLOTTE, ISLE OF ISLAY

Port Charlotte, Isle of Islay, Argyll

Map Ref: 1B6

SELF CATERING — UP TO ★★

Mrs C Barlow
An Cala Holiday Cottages, 70 Marchmont Crescent,
Edinburgh, EH9 1HD
Tel: 0131 667 7347

1 house, 1 annexe, 2 pub rms, 1-3 bedrms, sleeps 2-7, total sleeping capacity 7, min let weekend, £210.00-£300.00, Jan-Dec

This double glazed white-washed stone build house and apartment in terrace overlooking Loch Indaal is ideal for families. The rocky shore is a favourite with children. The village with its shape and choice of eating establishments is a good base for touring the island.

SELF CATERING — ★★★

J M Bricknell
The Corran, School Street, Port Charlotte, Islay, Argyll, PA48 7TW
Tel/Fax: 01496 850434

1 house, 2 pub rms, 4 bedrms, sleeps 6, £150.00-£350.00, Jan-Dec, bus nearby, ferry 15 mls, airport 13 mls

Carefully renovated 19c house situated in picturesque conservation village. Sandy beach, fishing pier, well stocked shop, post office and 2 hotels all within 100 yards. Centrally heated sunny patio area to rear. Parking/garage beside property available. Pets by arrangement, ideal centre for touring island and bird watching.

SELF CATERING — ★★★

James & Sheila Brown
Octomore Farm, Port Charlotte, Isle of Islay, PA48 7UD
Tel: 01496 850235

1 cottage, 1 pub rm, 3 bedrms (All grd.floor), sleeps 6, £200.00-£350.00, Jan-Dec, bus ¼ ml, ferry 20 mls, airport 15 mls

A renovated traditional cottage close to Octomore, a working farm overlooking Loch Indaal, a large sea loch in the south west of the island. There are nesting owls and chuffs in nearby farm buildings and the adjacent field is home to migrating geese during the winter months.

SELF CATERING — ★★

Mrs Emily Daniel
Flat 2, 3 Earlham Street, London, WC2H 9LL
Tel: 0171 836 3232

1 house, 2 pub rms, 6 bedrms, sleeps 6, £280.00-£320.00, Mar-Dec, ferry 16 mls, airport 12 mls

Traditional family home in centre of village. Ideally situated for relaxing or exploring the Island.

SELF CATERING — ★★★ UP TO ★★★★

Lorgba Holiday Cottages
Port Charlotte, Isle of Islay, Argyll, PA48 7UD
Tel/Fax: 01496 850208

5 cottages, 1 pub rm, 1-2 bedrms (grd flr avail), sleeps 2-6, total sleeping capacity 22, £105.00-£365.00, Jan-Dec, bus nearby, ferry 20 mls, airport 18 mls

Semi-detached cottages of individual character in picturesque setting with direct access to safe sandy beach. Superb views across the loch.

VAT is shown at 17.5%: changes in this rate may affect prices.

Key to symbols is on back flap.

PORT CHARLOTTE, ISLE OF ISLAY – PORT ELLEN, ISLE OF ISLAY

D WEST HIGHLANDS & ISLANDS, LOCH LOMOND, STIRLING & TROSSACHS

Port Charlotte, Isle of Islay, Argyll — Map Ref: 1B6

Mrs G Roy
Sgioba House, Port Charlotte, Isle of Islay, Argyll
Tel: 01496 850334

★★★ SELF CATERING

1 cottage, 2 pub rms, 1 bedrm, sleeps 2-4, £120.00-£280.00, Jan-Dec, bus nearby, ferry 15 mls, airport 15 mls

Comfortable cottage within picturesque conservation village. Suntrap garden adjoining safe sandy beach. Restaurants close by. Perfect base for relaxing holiday.

Mrs M Shaw
10 An-Creagan Place, Port Charlotte, Isle of Islay
Tel: 01496 850355

★★ UP TO ★★★ SELF CATERING

2 flats, 1 pub rm, 2 bedrms, sleeps 4, total sleeping capacity 8, £185.00-£300.00, Jan-Dec, bus nearby, ferry 20 mls, airport 16 mls

Flats in centre of Port Charlotte, close to seafront and local sandy beach.

Port Ellen, Isle of Islay, Argyll — Map Ref: 1C6

Glenmachrie Riverside Caravan
Booking Enquiries: Glenmachrie Riverside Caravan
Glenmachrie Farm, Port Ellen, Isle of Islay, Argyll, PA42 7AW
Tel/Fax: 01496 302560

SCOTTISH TOURIST BOARD INSPECTED
HOLIDAY CARAVAN

Park accommodation:

Holiday Caravan to let, sleeps 6 £180.00-200.00, min let Day, Jan-Dec.

Midway between Bowmore and Port Ellen on A846

Pat & John Kent
Tighcargaman, Port Ellen, Isle of Islay, Argyll, PA42 7BX
Tel/Fax: 01496 302345

★ UP TO ★★ SELF CATERING

3 cottages, 1-2 pub rms, 1-2 bedrms (grd flr avail), sleeps 2-4, total sleeping capacity 10, £100.00-£300.00, Jan-Dec, bus nearby, ferry 1/2 ml, airport 4 mls

3 Individual stone built cottages situated in grounds to rear of Tighcargamon House. Two overlook the bay with magnificent views to Ireland. Garden cottage is compact; sleeping 2 only.

Mrs H Roxburgh
Ballivicar Farm, Port Ellen, Isle of Islay, Argyll, PA42 7AW
Tel/Fax: 01496 302251

★★ SELF CATERING

3 apartments, 1 pub rm, 1-2 bedrms, sleeps 2-6, total sleeping capacity 8, min let weekend (low season), £90.00-£215.00, Jan-Dec, bus 2 mls, ferry 2 mls, airport 5 mls

Apartments in converted farm buildings on 250 acre stock farm. Pony-trekking centre, bird-watching, golf, diving within easy access.

Important: Prices stated are estimates and may be subject to amendments

WEST HIGHLANDS & ISLANDS, LOCH LOMOND, STIRLING & TROSSACHS

PORT ELLEN, ISLE OF ISLAY – KILLIN

Port Ellen, Isle of Islay, Argyll

Map Ref: 1C6

★★★★ SELF CATERING

Mr J & Mrs A Toland
133 Lathro Park, Kinross, Perthshire, KY13 8RU
Tel: 01577 863658

1 bungalow, 2 pub rms, 2 bedrms (All grd.floor), sleeps 4, £200.00-£360.00, Jan-Dec, bus 500 yds, ferry ¼ ml, airport 5 mls

Spacious and very comfortable quiet cul-de-sac. Private garden, driveway, patio. Village 2 mins. Beach 150 yds. Tennis, putting, bowling adjacent. Golf 4 miles.

Isle of Seil, Argyll

Map Ref: 1D3

★★★★ SELF CATERING

Mr Donald J MacDougall
Oban Seil Croft, Isle of Seil, Argyll, PA34 4TN
Tel/Fax: 01852 300457

1 cottage, 2 pub rms, 2 bedrms, sleeps 4, £260.00-£350.00, Jan-Dec, bus ½ ml, rail 14 mls, ferry 14 mls, airport 100 mls

Renovated traditional cottage situated in peaceful surroundings, with excellent facilities including open fire, parking and garden with views to the sea.

Kilchrenan, Argyll

Map Ref: 1F2

SCOTTISH TOURIST BOARD INSPECTED
HOLIDAY CARAVAN

Mrs MacDougall
Booking Enquiries: Mrs MacDougall
Cuilreoch, Kilchrenan, Taynuilt, Argyll, PA35 1HG
Tel: 01866 833236

Park accommodation:

Holiday Caravan to let, sleeps 4 £120.00-150.00, May-Oct.

Map Ref: (not shown)

★★★★ SELF CATERING

Gerald Moncrieff
20 Lowther View, Leadhills, Biggar, ML12 6XZ
Tel: 01659 74286

1 bungalow, 2 pub rms, 4 bedrms (All grd.floor), sleeps 7, £275.00-£550.00, Jan-Dec, bus 300 yds, rail 6 mls, ferry 18 mls, airport 80 mls

Spacious, nicely appointed single storey bungalow in secluded countryside situation by Loch Awe, set in one acre of well landscaped gardens. Beautiful views of surrounding countryside and Ben Cruachan.

Killin, Perthshire

Map Ref: 1H2

★★ SELF CATERING

Mrs K Dowling
Gardeners Cottage, Kinnell Estate, Killin, Perthshire, FK21 8SR
Tel: 01567 820814 Fax: 01567 820590

1 cottage, 1 pub rm, 1 bedrm, sleeps 4-6, £120.00-£280.00, Jan-Dec, bus ½ ml, rail 14 mls, airport 65 mls

Listed traditional stone and harl building which forms part of one side of steading. Own fishing available, river and hill walks.

VAT is shown at 17.5%: changes in this rate may affect prices.

Key to symbols is on back flap.

KILLIN – BY KILLIN

WEST HIGHLANDS & ISLANDS, LOCH LOMOND, STIRLING & TROSSACHS

Killin, Perthshire — Map Ref: 1H2

Mrs Dani Grant
Fernbank, Main Street, Killin, Perthshire, FK21 8UW
Tel/Fax: 01567 820386

★★★ UP TO ★★★★
SELF CATERING

2 houses, 2 pub rms, 3 bedrms (All grd.floor), sleeps 4-7, total sleeping capacity 11, £150.00-£350.00, Jan-Dec, bus nearby, rail 13 mls, ferry 60 mls, airport 60 mls

Houses, both with all rooms on the one level, centrally situated in Killin. Enclosed garden with swings and barbecue.

J D Howe
Finlarig, Killin, Perthshire, FK21 8TN
Tel: 01567 820259

★★★
SELF CATERING

1 cottage, 2 pub rms, 2 bedrms, sleeps 6, £275.00-£375.00, Jan-Dec, bus ½ ml, rail 15 mls

Traditional country cottage on 200 acre estate surrounded by spectacular Highland scenery at the head of Loch Tay. Fishing available, with golf, watersports and hill walking close by.

Mr & Mrs D K Mardon
Fagus, Manse Road, Killin, Perthshire, FK21 8UY
Tel: 01567 820248

★★
SELF CATERING

1 cottage, 1 pub rm, 3 bedrms (All grd.floor), sleeps 6, £145.00-£240.00, Jan-Dec, bus nearby, rail 13 mls

Traditional stone cottage with enclosed garden situated close to the Falls of Dochart. Short walk to village centre.

Mr A Whitehead
Shieling Accommodation, Killin, Perthshire, FK21 8TX
Tel/Fax: 01567 820334

★★★
SELF CATERING

8 chalets, 1 bungalow, 1 pub rm, 2-4 bedrms (grd flr avail), sleeps 4-8, total sleeping capacity 40, min let 1 night, £150.00-£550.00, Jan-Dec, bus 1 ml, rail 14 mls, airport 50 mls

Log chalets in woodland setting overlooking the rolling hills at the west end of Loch Tay.

---

by Killin, Perthshire — Map Ref: 1H2

Loch Tay Highland Lodges
Milton Morenish, by Killin, Perthshire, FK21 8TY
Tel: 01567 820323 Fax: 01567 820581
E-mail: info@lochtay-vacations.co.uk
Web: www.lochtay-vacations.co.uk

★★★★
SELF CATERING

35 log cabins, 1 house, 1 cottage, 1 pub rm, 2-3 bedrms (grd flr avail), sleeps 4-6, total sleeping capacity 168, £224.00-£688.00, Jan-Dec, bus 3 mls, rail 8 mls, airport 80 mls

Timber lodges on the shores of Loch Tay. Trout and salmon fishing, boat hire, horse riding and other activities available.

Important: Prices stated are estimates and may be subject to amendments

WEST HIGHLANDS & ISLANDS, LOCH LOMOND, STIRLING & TROSSACHS

D BY KILLIN

by Killin, Perthshire

Map Ref: 1H2

Loch Tay Highland Lodges

– OPEN ALL YEAR –

Forty luxury pine lodges set in a beautiful, well-maintained, 160-acre private estate on the shore of Loch Tay. The lodges have 2 or 3 bedrooms sleeping 4 to 6 people. There is also a superior waterside bunkhouse which sleeps 8. All lodges are warm, comfortable and fully-equipped (some with en-suite, dishwasher, microwave and pay phone) for an enjoyable trouble-free holiday. Loch Tay is in the heart of Scotland, ideal for touring or relaxing. There is a private harbour with boats for hire, salmon and trout fishing are available on the loch. On the estate is the Equestrian Centre with new, purpose-built olympic size indoor riding school for all year round riding. (All-inclusive riding short breaks available.) Novice and experienced riders welcome, guests may bring own horse, pony trekking, expert tuition and childrens' pony rides are available. Other on-site facilities include a putting green, clay pigeon shooting and private 4 mile hill-track for walking, riding and mountain-biking. Golf, watersports, swimming and skiing are available nearby. New heated wooden wigwams with colour TV, fridge, barbeque, cooking facilities, toilet and shower. Excellent budget accommodation. (Tent pitches). We have 40 log cabins, 1 bunkhouse and wooden wigwams, sleeping a total of 200 people. **Prices for 2000 – Lodges £224-£688, Bunkhouse £10 per person per night (min £40), Wigwams £8 per person per night. Group bookings welcome.**

Also for sale: 2 and 3 bedroom Pine Lodges as a whole, $\frac{1}{2}$ or $\frac{1}{4}$ share (Freehold – not Time-share). Management Letting/Cleaning Service available.

Contact below for further details.

★★★★ SELF CATERING

For full details and colour brochure, please contact: Mr and Mrs J. C. Booth
Milton Morenish Estate, Killin, Perthshire FK21 8TY

Tel: 01567 820323   Fax: 01567 820581
e.mail: info@lochtay-vacations.co.uk
Web: www.lochtay-vacations.co.uk

VAT is shown at 17.5%: changes in this rate may affect prices.

Key to symbols is on back flap.

KILMARTIN, BY LOCHGILPHEAD

WEST HIGHLANDS & ISLANDS, LOCH LOMOND, STIRLING & TROSSACHS

Kilmartin, by Lochgilphead, Argyll — Map Ref: 1E4

SELF CATERING ★★★★

Sandy Gordon
Ri Cruin West, Kilmartin, by Lochgilphead, Argyll, PA31 8QF
Tel: 01546 510316
E-mail: gordon@ri-cruin.freeserve.co.uk

1 cottage, 1 wing of large house, 1 pub rm, 2-3 bedrms (grd flr avail), sleeps 4-6, total sleeping capacity 10, £190.00-£504.00, Jan-Dec, bus 1 ml, rail 30 mls, airport 85 mls

Very comfortably and tastefully renovated stable buildings on 100 acre working sheep farm in historic Kilmartin Glen. Sandy beaches and Crinan Canal nearby. Very quiet rural location, ideal base for walking, nature watching or simple relaxing holidays.

DUNTRUNE CASTLE
KILMARTIN, ARGYLL PA31 8QQ
Telephone: Susan Malcolm on 01546 510283

6 traditional stone-built cottages in the extensive grounds of this 12th-century fortress beside Loch Crinan. Each cottage of individual character and with private garden. Enjoy solitude and spectacular scenery with abundant wildlife on our 5,000 acre estate, or tour Argyll from this central point.

SELF CATERING ★★★★

Mrs Malcolm
Duntrune Castle, Kilmartin, Argyll, PA31 8QQ
Tel: 01546 510283 Fax: 01546 510335
E-mail: duntrune@msn.com
Web: www.vital.co.uk/gallanach

6 cottages, 1-2 pub rms, 1-3 bedrms (grd flr avail), sleeps 2-5, total sleeping capacity 26, £200.00-£375.00, Mar-Nov, car essential

Individually sited stone built cottages and honeymoon bothy on 4500 acre estate with 6 miles (10 kms) of coastline. Country pursuits and fishing. Area rich in pre-history. Excellent restaurants and hotels within a short driving distance.

SELF CATERING ★★★★

Tibertich
Kilmartin, Argyll, PA31 8RQ
Tel/Fax: 01546 810281
E-mail: tibertich@hotmail.com

2 cottages, 1 pub rm, 1-2 bedrms (grd flr avail), sleeps 2-4, total sleeping capacity 6, £135.00-£295.00, Jan-Dec

Two renovated stone cottages providing all modern facilities yet retaining their original charm and character. Nestling in the hills Tibertich is a working farm with a flock of Blackface sheep and a small herd of Luing Suckler cows. Beautiful scenery.

Important: Prices stated are estimates and may be subject to amendments

WEST HIGHLANDS & ISLANDS, LOCH LOMOND, STIRLING & TROSSACHS

Kilmelford, by Oban, Argyll
Map Ref: 1E3

Ardenstur Cottages

Mrs Atkinson, Woodside, Park Avenue, Hartlepool, TS26 0EA
Tel: 01429 267266 Fax: 01429 267266

Be at one with nature in this secluded site overlooking and leading to Loch Melfort. Own headland bay, hill and forest walks. An area of great natural beauty is the setting for our attractive stone cottages. Fishing, sailing, and bird watching. Excellent touring centre. Beautiful views over loch and hills. Cottages equipped to a high standard. Linen supplied. Colour TV. Prices from £110 per week. Available throughout the year. Units sleep 2 to 10. Enjoy the open log fire, the serenity of the site. Nature abounds. History surrounds. Gardens to see, cuisine for all tastes within reach.

UP TO ★★★★
SELF CATERING

Ardenstur Cottages
Park Avenue, Hartlepool, Co Cleveland, TS26 0EA
Tel/Fax: 01429 267266

Range of properties, from 200 year old full modernised and comfortable principle residence, with panoramic views overlooking lochs and mountains, to converted cottages close to farm, all with views of loch Melfort. All properties are within 12,000 acre estate, with wonderful walks, mountains and island views. Abundance of wildlife, flora and fauna. Private slipway to loch. Pony trekking, bike hire close by. Idyllic setting yet ideal for touring.

4 houses, 4 cottages, 1-2 pub rms, 1-4 bedrms (grd flr avail), sleeps 2-10, total sleeping capacity 36, £110.00-£630.00, Jan-Dec, bus 3 mls, rail 21 mls, ferry 18 mls, airport 21 mls

★★
SELF CATERING

Mrs G H Dalton
Maolachy, Lochavich, Taynuilt, Argyll, PA35 1HJ
Tel: 01866 844212 Fax: 01866 844295

Comfortably converted stable cottage within a small farm courtyard, built c 1780. Set in a peaceful and beautiful remote glen, close to Loch Alrich, it is the perfect base for those with interests in the great outdoors. Rich in bird and wildlife, fishing by permit locally. Watersports can be arranged in the village of Kilmelford 6 km (4 miles).

1 cottage, 1 pub rm, 2 bedrms, sleeps 4, min let 3 days, £220.00-£346.00, Apr-Oct, bus 4 mls, rail 18 mls, ferry 18 mls, airport 100 mls

★★
SELF CATERING

Eleraig Highland Chalets
Kilninver, by Oban, Argyll, PA34 4UX
Tel/Fax: 01852 200225
Web: www.scotland2000.com/eleraig

Widely spaced Norwegian chalets set in magnificent scenery in secluded private glen 12 miles south of Oban. Close to Loch Tralaig, with free trout fishing and boating. Children and pets welcome. Parking by each chalet. Walking and birdwatching. Pony-trekking, sailing, golf and other sports can be arranged locally. Evening entertainment locally and in Oban - open March to October. Prices include electricity. Brochure from resident owners.

7 chalets, 1 pub rm, 2-3 bedrms (grd flr avail), sleeps 4-6, total sleeping capacity 40, £195.00-£445.00, Mar-Oct, bus ½ ml, rail 12 mls, ferry 12 mls, airport 100 mls

---

VAT is shown at 17.5%: changes in this rate may affect prices.

Key to symbols is on back flap.

KILMELFORD, BY OBAN

Kilmelford, by Oban, Argyll — Map Ref: 1E3

Melfort Pier & Harbour
★★★★★ SELF-CATERING

Kilmelford, by Oban, Argyll PA34 4XD
Tel: 01852 200333 Fax: 01852 200329
e.mail: melharbour@aol.com Web: scotland2000.com/melfort

If you want the best call us . . . Relax and pamper yourself in The Highlands. Harbour houses each with sauna, spa-bath, satellite TV, telephone. Some with sunbed, logfire. Enjoy spectacular views over Loch Melfort and surrounding hills. Boats and pets welcome. Excellent base for touring. Restaurants/shops nearby. Enquire for promotions. Minimum 2 nights. From £75–£185 per house per night.

Melfort Pier & Harbour
Kilmelford, by Oban, Argyll, PA34 4XD
Tel: 01852 200333 Fax: 01852 200329
E-mail: melharbour@aol.com
Web: www.scotland2000.com/melfort

Private fully ensuite harbour houses, at the waters edge, each with saunas and spa baths. Views across Loch Melfort.

10 houses, 1-3 bedrms (grd flr avail), sleeps 2-6, total sleeping capacity 48, min let 2 nights, £75.00-£185.00 per house/night, Jan-Dec, bus 1½ mls, rail 16 mls, ferry 16 mls, airport 100 mls

Melfort Village
Kilmelford, by Oban, Argyll PA34 4XD
Telephone: 01852 200257 Fax: 01852 200321

Luxury 19th century Gunpowder Village at the head of Loch Melfort amidst beautiful walking and touring scenery. Carefully restored cottages providing comfortable accommodation with dishwashers, microwaves, colour television, video recorders, central heating. Linen and towels provided. On-site facilities include indoor swimming pool, sauna, solarium, games rooms, children's playground and horse riding. Our restaurant and bar, **The Shower of Herring Inn**, offers excellent, reasonably priced meals with entertainment a regular feature throughout the year. Water sports and boat trips nearby.
Ideal for families. Pets most welcome.

Melfort Village
Kilmelford, by Oban, Argyll, PA34 4XD
Tel: 01852 200257 Fax: 01852 200321

★★★ UP TO ★★★★ SELF CATERING BRONZE

Comfortable, spacious, 19th century cottages set amidst beautiful walking and touring scenery. Peaceful setting. Cottages have dishwasher, microwave, colour TV and video, central heating, linen, on-site indoor swimming pool, sauna, solarium, tennis, games rooms, horse riding, restaurant, bar. Pets welcome.

10 houses, 5 flats, 17 cottages, 2 pub rms, 1-3 bedrms, sleeps 2-8, total sleeping capacity 146, £280.00-£865.00, Jan-Dec, bus 1½ mls, rail 16 mls, ferry 16 mls, airport 100 mls

Important: Prices stated are estimates and may be subject to amendments

WEST HIGHLANDS & ISLANDS, LOCH LOMOND, STIRLING & TROSSACHS

KILNINVER, BY OBAN – LOCHAWE

Kilninver, by Oban, Argyll

UP TO ★★
SELF CATERING

Mrs J Handley
Bragleenbeg, Kilninver, by Oban, Argyll, PA34 4UU
Tel: 01852 316283

Map Ref: 1E2

2 flats, 1 pub rm, 2-3 bedrms, sleeps 4-9, total sleeping capacity 15, £130.00-£320.00, Jan-Dec, bus 5 mls, rail 15 mls, ferry 15 mls

Two spacious well equipped apartments in secluded Victorian shooting lodge, sleeping 6 + 9. Situated at head of Loch Scammadale. Take the opportunity to enjoy magnificent scenery and wildlife with free fishing to guests including boat. Ideal location for visiting Mull, Iona and Staffa. Perfect for large and small families. Dogs welcome. TV, laundry room. Linen can be supplied. Car essential.

★★★★
SELF CATERING

Mrs D A Macdonald
21 Lindisfarne Road, Newcastle-upon-Tyne, NE2 2HE
Tel: 0191 281 1695 Fax: 0191 281 1253
E-mail: dacmac@btinternet.com

1 house, 2 pub rms, 3 bedrms (grd flr avail), sleeps 6, £295.00-£575.00, Apr-Oct, Xmas, N/Year, bus nearby, rail 12 mls, ferry 12 mls

Traditional spacious stone cottage, with open fire. In own fenced and extensive grounds overlooking trout stream. 12 miles (19 kms) south of Oban. 2 bathrooms. An excellent location for exploring this beautiful part of Scotland with easy access to the islands of Gigha, Jura, Mull and Iona.

Kippen, Stirlingshire

★★★
SELF CATERING

Roberta Nicoll
Ballimore Farm, Balquhidder, FK19 8PE
Tel: 01877 384255

Map Ref: 1H4

1 house, 1 pub rm, 2 bedrms, sleeps 5, £250.00-£300.00, Jan-Dec, bus ¼ ml, rail 10 mls, airport 26 mls

A well-equipped semi-detached house situated in a quiet residential estate in the picturesque village of Kippen. Garden to front and rear. A home from home.

Lochawe, Argyll

★★
SELF CATERING

Sheena Anderson
St Conan's Tower, Loch Awe, Argyll, PA33 1AH
Tel/Fax: 01838 200342

Map Ref: 1F2

3 flats, 2-4 bedrms, sleeps 2-4, total sleeping capacity 7, £170.00-£310.00, Jan-Dec, bus ¼ ml, rail ¼ ml.

Second and third floor apartments in this six storey granite tower house. Magnificent views over Loch Awe.

★★★
SELF CATERING

Ardbrecknish House
South Lochaweside, by Dalmally, Argyll, PA33 1BH
Tel/Fax: 01866 833223
E-mail: ardbreck01@aol.com
Web: www.loch-awe.com/ardbrecknish/default.htm

8 flats, 5 cottages, 3 pub rms, 1-5 bedrms (grd flr avail), sleeps 2-12, total sleeping capacity 77, min let weekend, £175.00-£840.00, Jan-Dec, bus 6 mls, rail 6 mls, ferry 30 mls, airport 65 mls

Ardbrecknish house dating back to the 16th Century is set in 20 acres of woodland gardens on the south shore of spectacular Loch Awe. Carefully converted to provide spacious self catering apartments with splendid views. A paradise for angling, sailing, walking, cycling and bird watching, deer stalking by arrangement. Licensed bar and games room with log fires, evening meal served. Visit our Web site www.loch-awe.com/ardbrecknish/default.htm.

VAT is shown at 17.5%: changes in this rate may affect prices.

Key to symbols is on back flap.

LOCHEARNHEAD – BY LOCHGILPHEAD

D — WEST HIGHLANDS & ISLANDS, LOCH LOMOND, STIRLING & TROSSACHS

Lochearnhead, Perthshire — Map Ref: 1H2

Hoseasons Holidays ★★★ SELF CATERING
Sunway House, Lowestoft, Suffolk, NR32 3LT
Tel: 01502 500500

8 log cabins, 1 pub rm, 2-3 bedrms, sleeps 4-6, total sleeping capacity 36, £130.00-£470.00, Jan-Dec, bus nearby, rail 16 mls, airport 60 mls

Modern Danish pine cottages in elevated position overlooking Loch Earn, alongside hotel. Mooring and jetty facilities included and water sports centre. Ideal centre for golfing, touring, fishing and cycling.

Loch Eck, by Dunoon, Argyll — Map Ref: 1F4

Lamont Lodges ★★ SELF CATERING
Rashfield, By Dunoon, Argyll, PA23 8QT
Tel/Fax: 01369 840205

17 log cabins, 1 pub rm, 2-3 bedrms, sleeps 4-6, total sleeping capacity 92, min let 2 nights, £200.00-£450.00, Jan-Dec, bus nearby, rail 6 mls, ferry 5 mls, airport 35 mls

Small development of log cabins magnificently set in Argyll Forest Park. Forest walks, trails and near the Younger Botanic Garden. For touring Oban, Glencoe, Loch Lomond and The Kyles of Bute are all easy distances and comparatively free of traffic. Glasgow and Edinburgh are also within reach for a days outing.

Millar ★ SELF CATERING
14 Vancouver Road, Scotstoun, Glasgow, G14 9HJ
Tel: 0141 950 1290

1 chalet, 1 pub rm, 2 bedrms, sleeps 4, £100.00-£200.00, Apr-Oct, Dec

Timber built lodge with its own verandah nestling on the hillside overlooking Loch Eck on the Cowal Peninsula. Ideal base for the outdoor enthusiast and exploring the Western Highlands of Scotland.

Stratheck Caravan Park ★★★ HOLIDAY PARK
Loch Eck, by Dunoon, Argyll, PA23 8SG
Tel/Fax: 01369 840472

Park accommodation: 150

70 tourers £7.00-9.00 or 70 motors £7.00-9.00 or 70 tents £6.00-8.00. Total Touring Pitches 70.

4 Holiday Caravans to let, sleep 6 £140.00-290.00, total sleeping capacity 24, min let 2 nights.

13 acres, grassy, hard-standing, level, Mar-Dec, prior booking in peak periods, latest time of arrival 2200, overnight holding area. Extra charge for electricity, awnings.

Leisure facilities:

From Dunoon take A815 N for 7mls. Park on left of road ½ mile beyond Younger Botanic Gardens.

by Lochgilphead, Argyll — Map Ref: 1E4

Cnoc-na-Coille ★★★ SELF CATERING
6 Port Ann, by Lochgilphead
Tel: 01546 603640

1 house, 1 pub rm, 3 bedrms, sleeps 6, £175.00-£325.00, Apr-Sep, bus nearby, rail 40 mls, ferry 40 mls, airport 83 mls

Home situated in quiet hamlet with beautiful views overlooking the sea loch fyne. Beach within 10 minutes walk. Shrub garden provides parking, picnic and barbeque areas. Ideal rural central location.

Important: Prices stated are estimates and may be subject to amendments

WEST HIGHLANDS & ISLANDS, LOCH LOMOND, STIRLING & TROSSACHS

LOCHGOILHEAD – MACHRIHANISH

Lochgoilhead, Argyll

Map Ref: 1F3

SELF CATERING ★

Mr G E F Johnston
Upper Dunard, Station Road, Rhu, Dunbartonshire, G84 8LW
Tel: 01436 820563
E-mail: geoffrey@dunard.demon.co.uk

1 house, 2 pub rms, 5 bedrms, sleeps 12, £220.00-£600.00, Jan-Dec, bus ½ ml, rail 7 mls, airport 30 mls

Spacious Victorian lochside house with 5 bedrooms, sleeping 12. Large grounds with superb west facing views. ½ mile to village. Golf, water sports and walking locally. Coal, electricity and linen included. Cot available, Pets by arrangement.

Luss, Argyll & Bute

Map Ref: 1G4

SELF CATERING ★★★

Mrs Anne Lennox
Shantron Farm, Luss, by Alexandria, Dunbartonshire, G83 8RH
Tel/Fax: 01389 850231
E-mail: rjlennox@shantron.u-net.com
Web: www.webscape.co.uk/farmaccom/scotland/argyll+stirling/shantron/index.htm

1 cottage, 1 pub rm, 2 bedrms (All grd.floor), sleeps 6, min let weekend, £150.00-£375.00, Jan-Dec, bus ½ ml, rail 6 mls, airport 20 mls

Traditional stone cottage on hill sheep farm. Superb views over Loch Lomond. Ideal for touring, hill walking and water sports.

SELF CATERING ★★★

Mrs Clare Rankin
Edentaggart, Glen Luss, Luss, Alexandria, Dunbartonshire, G83 8PB
Tel: 01436 860226

1 cottage, 2 pub rms, 2 bedrms, sleeps 4, £260.00-£300.00, May-Oct, bus 3 mls, rail 11 mls, airport 25 mls

Bungalow with large enclosed garden on working sheep farm. 3 miles (5 kms) from Luss. Superb loch and mountain views.

SELF CATERING ★★★★

Mrs C Wishart
Shegarton Farm, Luss, Loch Lomond, G83 8RH
Tel: 01389 850269

2 cottages, 1 pub rm, 1-2 bedrms (grd flr avail), sleeps 2-5, total sleeping capacity 7, £200.00-£450.00, Jan-Dec, bus ½ ml, rail 5 mls, airport 20 mls

Newly converted courtyard cottages in quiet rural situation. Within walking distance of Loch Lomond Golf Course.

Machrihanish, Argyll

Map Ref: 1D7

SELF CATERING ★★

Mrs M Craig
The Garth, Tynron, Thornhill, Dumfriesshire, DG3 4JY
Tel/Fax: 01848 200364

1 house, 2 pub rms, 4 bedrms, sleeps 5-6, £292.00-£344.00, mid Mar-mid Oct, bus nearby, ferry nearby, airport 5 mls

Victorian stone built house of character with own garden and open views across Machrihanish Bay to Islay and Jura. Fine sandy beach and local golf links. Ideal for walkers and birdwatchers.

VAT is shown at 17.5%: changes in this rate may affect prices.

Key to symbols is on back flap.

MADDISTON – MUCKHART

WEST HIGHLANDS & ISLANDS, LOCH LOMOND, STIRLING & TROSSACHS

Maddiston, Stirlingshire

Map Ref: 2B4

★★★ SELF CATERING

Avon Glen Chalets
Melons Place, Maddiston, FK2 0BT
Tel: 01324 861166/861242

3 chalets, 2 bedrms, sleeps 6, total sleeping capacity 6, min let weekend, £185.00-£385.00, Jan-Dec, bus 1 ml, rail 4 mls, airport 15 mls

Newly built pine chalets situated in forty acres of beautiful surroundings, overlooking the River Avon. Kids play park. Free fishing on the River Avon. An ideal base for touring Scotland, with easy access to all major routes.

Minard, by Inveraray, Argyll

Map Ref: 1E4

★★ SELF CATERING

R Gayre
Minard Castle, Minard, Argyll, PA32 8YB
Tel/Fax: 01546 886272
E-mail: reinoldgayre@bizonline.co.uk

2 flats, 1 bungalow, 1 pub rm, 2 bedrms (All grd.floor), sleeps 4-6, total sleeping capacity 16, min let weekend, £100.00-£370.00, Jan-Dec, bus ¾ ml, rail 35 mls, airport 75 mls

Two courtyard flats and modern bungalow situated in the private grounds of Minard Castle. Salmon fishing in season. 13 miles (20km) from Inveraray.

★★ SELF CATERING

Mrs H D McNab
Fox Hill, Closworth Road, Halstock, Somerset, BA22 9SZ
Tel: 01935 872353
E-mail: v.mcn@lineone.net

1 cottage, 2 pub rms, 2 bedrms, sleeps 6, £180.00-£280.00, Jan-Dec, bus ¼ ml

Modernised former crofter's cottage, situated above village of Minard with excellent views over loch and hills.

Muasdale, by Tarbert, Argyll

Map Ref: 1D6

★★ SELF CATERING

Mrs Linda Bryce
Crubasdale Lodge, Muasdale, by Tarbert, Argyll, PA29 6XD
Tel: 01583 421358 Fax: 01583 421322
E-mail: KenBryce@aol.com

1 chalet, 1 pub rm, 3 bedrms (All grd.floor), sleeps 6, min let 4 days, £175.00-£375.00, Jan-Dec

Detached 3 bedroom timber chalet with private garden. Wonderful views of the Isles of Islay, Gigha and Jura. This charming property has been modernised to provide comfortable holiday accommodation. Great area for walking, wildlife, archaeology or a peaceful relaxing holiday.

Muckhart, Clackmannanshire

Map Ref: 2B3

★★ SELF CATERING

H Maak
The Old Schoolhouse, Pool of Muckhart,
Clackmannanshire, FK14 7JN
Tel: 01259 781527

1 cottage, 1 pub rm, sleeps 2, £125.00-£140.00, Jan-Dec, bus nearby, rail 17 mls, airport 28 mls

Private self-catering accommodation in the heart of Scotland. Ideally suited as a base for walking, fishing and golfing holidays. Studio type accomodation.

Important: Prices stated are estimates and may be subject to amendments

WEST HIGHLANDS & ISLANDS, LOCH LOMOND, STIRLING & TROSSACHS

AROS, ISLE OF MULL – BUNESSAN, ISLE OF MULL

Aros, Isle of Mull, Argyll

Map Ref: 1D1

UP TO ★★
SELF CATERING

Ursula Bradley
The Old Byre, Dervaig, Isle of Mull, Argyll, PA75 6QR
Tel: 01688 400229

Two properties 7 miles apart – 1. Converted farmhouse on working farm, 5 miles (8km) from Salen. Magnificent views over Glen Aros. 2. Bothy beside heritage centre, 2 miles (3km) from Dervaig with views over Glen Bellart.

1 cottage, 1 bothy, 1 pub rm, 1-3 bedrms, cottage sleeps 2-5, bothy sleeps 2, total sleeping capacity 5, Mar-Oct, bus 3 mls, ferry 25 mls

---

★★ UP TO ★★★
SELF CATERING

G Forster
Kentallen Farm, Aros, Isle of Mull, PA72 6JS
Tel: 01680 300427 Fax: 01680 300489

Four individual units in secluded rural positions on family farm, with outstanding views of the sea and mountains. Centrally located for touring.

1 log cabin, 1 flat, 2 cottages, sleeps 2-8, total sleeping capacity 20, £100.00-£500.00, bus $^{1}/_{4}$ ml, ferry 11 mls

---

★★
SELF CATERING

Mr & Mrs C B Scott
Kilmore House, Kilmore, by Oban, Argyll, PA34 4XT
Tel: 01631 770369 Fax: 01631 770329
E-mail: glenaros@tesco.net

The cottages are situated on a 2000 acre estate, 1 $^{1}/_{2}$ miles north of Salen, overlooking Aros Castle and the Sound of Mull. Magnificent views, attractive woodland and hillwalks. Abundant wildlife and sites of historic interest within walking distance of the cottages. Fly fishing available on Aros River & Trout Pond. The five cottages, of individual character are comfortable & well equipped. Open fires and electric heating. Pets by arrangement.

1 house, 4 cottages, 2 pub rms, 2-4 bedrms (grd flr avail), sleeps 4-7, total sleeping capacity 26, £210.00-£350.00, Jan-Dec, bus 500 yds, ferry 12 mls

---

Bunessan, Isle of Mull, Argyll

Map Ref: 1C3

★★★
SELF CATERING

Ardachy House Hotel Apartment
Uisken, by Bunessan, Isle of Mull, Argyll, PA67 6DS
Tel/Fax: 01681 700505

Quietly located ground floor garden apartment with own entrance, attached to private hotel. Unforgettable seascape views to Colonsay, Jura and Islay from lounge. Sleep 3. Twin bedded room with ensuite bathroom. Lounge with single divan. Modern fully fitted kitchen. Located only 7 miles from Iona & Staffa ferries and a short stroll to white sandy beach. Car parking immediately adjacent.

1 flat, 1 pub rm, 1 bedrm (All grd.floor), sleeps 3, £250.00-£275.00, Apr-Sep, bus 2 mls, ferry 32 mls

---

★★★
SELF CATERING

Ardfenaig Farmhouses
Tiraghoil, Bunessan, Isle of Mull, Argyll, PA67 6DU
Tel: 01681 700260 Fax: 01681 700260

Two traditional granite farmhouses located on scenic Ross of Mull. Secluded location with views over surrounding hills. Convenient for boat trips to Staffa and Treshnish Isles. 10 minute drive to Iona Ferry. Comfortable, well appointed accommodation offering a perfect base for a holiday on Mull.

2 houses, 2 pub rms, 2-3 bedrms (grd flr avail), sleeps 4-6, total sleeping capacity 10, £195.00-£425.00, Jan-Dec, bus nearby, ferry 35 mls

---

VAT is shown at 17.5%: changes in this rate may affect prices.

Key to symbols is on back flap.

BUNESSAN, ISLE OF MULL – CALGARY, ISLE OF MULL

D WEST HIGHLANDS & ISLANDS, LOCH LOMOND, STIRLING & TROSSACHS

Bunessan, Isle of Mull, Argyll — Map Ref: 1C3

★★★ SELF CATERING

Donald & Fiona Black
26 Broom Drive, Inverness, IV2 4EG
Tel: 01463 231127 Fax: 0870 05529
E-mail: donald@blackshouse.demon.co.uk

1 cottage, 1 pub rm, 3 bedrms (grd flr avail), sleeps 5-6, £165.00-£290.00, Jan-Dec excl Xmas, bus ¼ ml

House in the family since the early 19th century. Recently restored. Secluded. Fenced garden. Convenient for Iona.

★★ SELF CATERING

Mr & Mrs Mathie
Welwyn, Firpark Terrace, Cambusbarron, Stirling, FK7 9ND
Tel/Fax: 01786 472900
E-mail: hm@hmathie.freeserve.co.uk

1 cottage, 1 pub rm, 2 bedrms (All grd.floor), sleeps 4-5, £150.00-£300.00, Jan-Dec, bus 1 ½ mls, ferry 30 mls

Comfortable cottage 1.5 miles from Bunessan. Beautiful quiet surroundings. Easy access to safe sandy beaches and the islands of Iona and Staffa.

---

by Bunessan, Isle of Mull, Argyll — Map Ref: 1C3

★★★★ SELF CATERING

Mr and Mrs Davidson
Ardfenaig House, By Bunessan, Isle of Mull, Argyll, PA67 6DX
Tel/Fax: 01681 700210
E-mail: davidson@ardfenaig.demon.co.uk

1 house, 1 pub rm, 2 bedrms, sleeps 4-6, £370.00-£550.00, Jan-Dec, bus Nearby, rail 40 mls, ferry 35 mls, airport 100 mls

In the grounds of Ardfenaig House hotel but quite separate. Completely rebuilt to highest standards in 1994 and with extensive views over sea loch and moorland. Ardfenaig is close to the boats to Iona and Staffa and there are many walks across deserted moors to hidden white sandy beaches. Hotel facilities and restaurant are all available to Coach House guests.

Calgary, Isle of Mull, Argyll — Map Ref: 1C1

★★★ SELF CATERING

J E G Bartholomew
Calgary, Isle of Mull, PA75 6QT
Tel/Fax: 01688 400240

1 cottage, 2 pub rms, 3 bedrms (grd flr avail), sleeps 6, £200.00-£395.00, Jan-Dec, bus nearby, rail 45 mls, ferry 28 mls, airport 20 mls

Traditional modernised Highland cottage in 0.5 acre fenced garden with magnificent views over the white sands of Calgary Beach. 0.5 mile to local hotel for evening meals. 3 double rooms, one en-suite, one with baby room. Seperate bathroom/WC. A birdlovers paradise.

★ SELF CATERING

Dr Morgan
Tigh-na-Drochaid, Salen, Aros, Isle of Mull, Argyll, PA72 6JB
Tel/Fax: 01680 300536

1 house, 2 pub rms, 4 bedrms (grd flr avail), sleeps 6, £300.00-£430.00, Jan-Dec, bus nearby, ferry 30 mls

Secluded, fully modernised warm stone-built house with large comfortable lounge. 1 ½ miles from Calgary beach (sandy, safe for bathing). Dervaig 3 ½ miles, Tobermory 13 miles. Ideal family spot - see eagles, puffin, otter, seals, deer etc. Local riding, mountain biking, sailing, boat trips, fishing, wildlife trips. Hill-walking, bird-watching and beaches all accessible on foot from the doorstep. Plenty to fill a fortnight or more.

Important: Prices stated are estimates and may be subject to amendments

WEST HIGHLANDS & ISLANDS, LOCH LOMOND, STIRLING & TROSSACHS

BY CALGARY, ISLE OF MULL – DERVAIG, ISLE OF MULL

111

by Calgary, Isle of Mull, Argyll

Map Ref: 1C1

Carolyne Charrington
House of Treshnish, by Calgary, Isle of Mull, PA75 6QX
Tel/Fax: 01688 400249
E-mail: treshnish.farm@virgin.net
Web: www.zynet.co.uk/mull/members/tresh.html

SELF CATERING — ★★ UP TO ★★★ — SILVER

Four modernised farm cottages, equipped to a high standard. Also, three fully refurbished, gas powered crofters blackhouses, situated on working farm. All have modern amenities. Each cottage has an outstanding sea & island view. Four miles of spectacular coastal walking. An abundance of wildlife, birdlife, flora & fauna and several sites of historic interest (Pets by arrangement) (Open fires).

3 comfortable cottages, 4 crofters' blackhouses, sleep 2-6, prices £100.00-£260.00, bus 3 mls, ferry 29 mls.

Dervaig, Isle of Mull, Argyll

Map Ref: 1C1

Mr Sid Austin
Brow Top Farm House, Bothel, Carlisle, CA5 2HS
Tel/Fax: 016973 22843

SELF CATERING — ★★★

Refurbished traditional cottage in centre of conservation village and within walking distance of all amenities.

1 cottage, 2 pub rms, 2 bedrms, sleeps 4, £120.00-£330.00, Jan-Dec, bus nearby, ferry 22 mls

---

Mrs Galbraith
Croig, Dervaig, Isle of Mull, Argyll, PA75 6QS
Tel: 01688 400219

SELF CATERING — ★★★

Traditional stone built croft house over 300 years old right on the harbour at the road end, with spectacular views to Outer Isles. 500m to owner's nearest sandy bay. In-tune piano in lounge for guests' use.

1 house, 2 pub rms, 3 bedrms (1 bedroom and bathroom on ground floor), sleeps 6, £100.00-£340.00, Jan-Dec, bus 1 ml, ferry 26 mls

---

Mr & Mrs J Matthew
Ardrioch Farm, Dervaig, Isle of Mull, Argyll, PA75 6QR
Tel/Fax: 01688 400264

SELF CATERING — ★★

Ardrioch is a cedarwood bungalow set in its own croftland with lovely views over Loch and Thus. A mile from the village, 4 miles from Calgary beach and 2 miles from Croig Harbour where our own inter island cruises depart daily. Ideal family accommodation.

1 bungalow, 1 pub rm, 4 bedrms (All grd.floor), sleeps 7, min let 2 nights, £325.00-£395.00, Mar-Oct, bus nearby, ferry 24 mls

---

Mrs E M Smith
Achnacraig, Dervaig, Isle of Mull, Argyll, PA75 6QW
Tel: 01688 400309

SELF CATERING — ★★★★

Recently converted stone farmhouse, centrally heated. Situated 4 miles (6 Kms) from Dervaig in tranquil Glen Bellart. Courtesy mountain bikes available.

1 house, 1 pub rm, 3 bedrms, sleeps 6, £250.00-£365.00, Feb-Nov, bus 4 mls, ferry 12 mls

---

VAT is shown at 17.5%: changes in this rate may affect prices.

Key to symbols is on back flap.

DERVAIG, ISLE OF MULL – GRULINE, ISLE OF MULL

WEST HIGHLANDS & ISLANDS, LOCH LOMOND, STIRLING & TROSSACHS

Dervaig, Isle of Mull, Argyll

Map Ref: 1C1

★★★★ SELF CATERING

Jim Spence
Penmore, Dervaig, Isle of Mull, Argyll, PA75 6QS
Tel: 01688 400235 Fax: 01688 400235
E-mail: penmore@mull.com
Web: www.penmore.mull.com

1 house, 2 pub rms, 5 bedrms (grd flr avail), sleeps 10, £500.00-£690.00, Jan-Dec, bus ½ ml, ferry 25 mls, airport 20 mls

---

★★ SELF CATERING

P J C Sumner
Buttercliff, Winscombe Hill, Winscombe, Somerset, BS25 1DQ
Tel: 01934 842219

Modern bungalow in elevated position with fine views towards the sea.

1 bungalow, 3 pub rms, 3 bedrms (All grd.floor), sleeps 6, £280.00-£380.00, Apr-Oct, bus ½ ml, ferry 26 mls

Fionnphort, Isle of Mull, Argyll

Map Ref: 1C2

★★ SELF CATERING

Ms A Rimell
Dungrianach, Fionnphort, Isle of Mull, Argyll, PA66 6BL
Tel: 01681 700417

Comfortable and spacious accommodation. Superb views to Iona across the sound. Direct access to the sandy beach below the home, through garden gate. Dungrianach is secluded, yet conveniently near the village. It's an ideal base for exploring Iona, the beautiful coastal scenery and abundant wildlife on Mull. In summer months, boat trips to Staffa and the Treshnish Isles can be taken from the village pier. Brochure available.

1 bungalow, 1 pub rm, 3 bedrms, sleeps 6, £198.00-£380.00, Jan-Dec, bus nearby, rail 45 mls, ferry 500 yds, airport 140 mls

Gruline, Isle of Mull, Argyll

Map Ref: 1D2

★★★ SELF CATERING

Diana McFarlane
Torlochan, Gruline, Isle of Mull, Argyll, PA71 6HR
Tel/Fax: 01680 300380

Centrally situated on our working croft, the 2 log cabins, and 2 stone cottages are surrounded by beautiful scenery and unusual animals such as Kune Kune pigs and llamas.

2 log cabins, 2 cottages, 1 pub rm, 1-2 bedrms (all grd flr), sleeps 2-4, total sleeping capacity 14, £205.00-£295.00, Jan-Dec, bus 2 mls, ferry 13 mls

---

Important: Prices stated are estimates and may be subject to amendments

WEST HIGHLANDS & ISLANDS, LOCH LOMOND, STIRLING & TROSSACHS

KILLIECHRONAN, ISLE OF MULL – LOCHDON, ISLE OF MULL

Killiechronan, Isle of Mull, Argyll — Map Ref: 1D2

KILLIECHRONAN
Isle of Mull

With spectacular views over Loch Na Keal – this former farmhouse and steading have been tastefully converted to provide seven cottages and one house. Centrally situated on the island, Killiechronan can offer fishing, pony trekking and hill walking and has active farming and forestry enterprises.

Highland Holidays, 1 Springkerse Road, Stirling FK7 7SN.
Tel: 01786 462519   Fax: 01786 471872

★★ SELF CATERING

Killiechronan
1 Springkerse Road, Stirling, FK7 7SN
Tel: 01786 462519 Fax: 01786 471872

1 house, 7 cottages, 1-2 pub rms, 1-3 bedrms, sleeps 2-6, total sleeping capacity 32, min let 2 nights (low season), £120.00-£410.00, Mar-Nov, ferry 12 mls, airport 5 mls

Comfortable cottages centrally situated on a mixed agricultural estate overlooking Loch Na Keal. Pony trekking available on site. 12 miles (19 km) from Craignure ferry.

Kinlochspelve, Isle of Mull, Argyll — Map Ref: 1D2

★★★★ SELF CATERING

Mrs G M Railton-Edwards
The Barn, Barrachandroman, Kinlochspelve, Lochbuie, Isle of Mull, Argyll, PA62 6AA
Tel: 01680 814220 Fax: 01680 814247
E-mail: spelve@aol.com

1 house, 4 pub rms, 4 bedrms, sleeps 8, £200.00-£750.00, Jan-Dec, bus 4 mls, ferry 11 mls, airport 80 mls

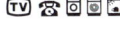

Former farmhouse of character, dating from 1600, situated at the head of Loch Spelve. Excellent scenery and interesting wildlife.

Lochbuie, Isle of Mull, Argyll — Map Ref: 1D2

★★★ SELF CATERING

Mrs J Corbett
Lochbuie House, Lochbuie, Isle of Mull, PA62 6AA
Tel/Fax: 01680 814214

2 cottages, 3 pub rms, 3 bedrms (grd flr avail), sleeps 5, total sleeping capacity 7, £185.00-£350.00, Jan-Dec, bus 7 mls, ferry 14 mls

Mabel & Kathleen Cottages are situated on Lochbuie Estate, 21,000 acres of farmland. They sleep 2 and 5 people respectively and are charming and comfortable, with wonderful sea views, surrounded by hills and a sandy beach nearby. Fishing, Hill Walking and Birdwatching available.

Lochdon, Isle of Mull, Argyll — Map Ref: 1D2

★★ SELF CATERING

Mrs G M Railton-Edwards
Kinlochspelve, Isle of Mull, PA62 6AA
Tel: 01680 814220 Fax: 01680 814247
E-mail: spelve@aol.com

1 bungalow, 2 pub rms, 2 bedrms (All grd.floor), sleeps 4, £150.00-£400.00, Jan-Dec, bus 300 yds, ferry 3 mls

Modern bungalow near the shore of Lochdon with its own garden and uninterrupted views over the water. 3 miles (5kms) from ferry at Craignure.

VAT is shown at 17.5%: changes in this rate may affect prices.   *Key to symbols is on back flap.*

PENNYGHAEL, ISLE OF MULL – SALEN, AROS, ISLE OF MULL

WEST HIGHLANDS & ISLANDS, LOCH LOMOND, STIRLING & TROSSACHS

Pennyghael, Isle of Mull, Argyll

Map Ref: 1C2

UP TO ★★ — SELF CATERING

Sue Morgan
Ormsaig, Pennyghael, Isle of Mull, Argyll, PA70 6HF
Tel: 01681 704230

1 cottage, 1 bungalow, 1-2 pub rms, 1-5 bedrms, sleeps 2-8, total sleeping capacity 12, £100.00-£400.00, Jan-Dec, bus nearby, ferry 30 mls

One cedar bungalow on elevated position with magnificent views over Loch Scridain. Ideal for family holidays. One converted Byre bungalow, ideal for couples. ½ way between Bunessan and Pennyghael.

Pennyghael Hotel & Cottages
Pennyghael, Isle of Mull PA70 6HB
Tel: 01681 704288 Fax: 01681 704205

Converted from a 17th century farmhouse, the cottages are in a lochside setting of unparalleled beauty. Ideally situated for visiting Iona and Staffa and overlooking 'Ben More' there is walking and wildlife in abundance. Comfortably furnished and very well equipped, each cottage has superb loch views, especially sunsets. Own beach.

★★★ — SELF CATERING

Pennyghael Hotel & Cottages
Pennyghael, Isle of Mull, Argyll, PA70 6HB
Tel: 01681 704288 Fax: 01681 704205

3 cottages, 1 pub rm, 2-3 bedrms (grd flr avail), sleeps 4-6, total sleeping capacity 14, £200.00-£400.00, Jan-Dec, ferry 20 mls

The cottages are in an idyllic situation right on the shores Loch Scridain, with stunning panoramic views from Iona to Ben More. South Mull is a walkers paradise with flowers and wildlife in abundance, a lot of which can be seen from your window. All cottages are spacious, comfortable and have modern kitchens and bathrooms and recently refurbished lounge and bedrooms.

Salen, Aros, Isle of Mull, Argyll

Map Ref: 1D1

★★★ — SELF CATERING

Mrs Angela Boocock
Gruline Home Farm, Gruline, By Salen, Isle of Mull, PA71 6HR
Tel: 01680 300581 Fax: 01680 300573
E-mail: gruline@ukonline.co.uk

1 cottage, 2 pub rms, 2 bedrms (grd flr avail), sleeps 4, total sleeping capacity 4, £160.00-£375.00, Jan-Dec, bus 2 ½ mls, 20 mls, ferry 8 mls, airport 3 mls

Former School now converted into a two bedroom cottage situated on a quiet road, in the centre of the Island, 2 miles (4km) from Salen. Ideal base for touring, nature lovers and walkers (Ben More, 5 miles).

★★★★ — SELF CATERING

Mrs Moisey
7 Combe Park, Bath, Avon, BA1 3NP
Tel: 01225 332996

1 cottage, 3 pub rms, 2 bedrms (All grd.floor), sleeps 4, £160.00-£260.00, Jan-Dec, bus nearby, ferry 11 mls

Traditional stone built detached cottage close to the sea, modernised and extended but maintaining character and providing spacious accommodation in easy walking distance of the local shops and hotel. The attractive private garden alongside the burn has views of Salen Bay. Burnside is situated at the narrow neck of the island, making it an ideal centre for touring the whole island.

Important: Prices stated are estimates and may be subject to amendments

WEST HIGHLANDS & ISLANDS, LOCH LOMOND, STIRLING & TROSSACHS

SALEN, AROS, ISLE OF MULL – TOBERMORY, ISLE OF MULL

Salen, Aros, Isle of Mull, Argyll

Map Ref: 1D1

★★★ SELF CATERING

Steve and Alison Willis
Argyll House, Salen, Isle of Mull, Argyll
Tel/Fax: 01680 300555 E-mail: argyllhse@aol.com
Web: www.holidaymull.org/members/argyll.html

2 cottages, 2 studio apartments, 1-2 pub rms, 1-2 bedrms, sleeps 2-6, total sleeping capacity 12, £150.00-£315.00, Jan-Dec, bus nearby, ferry 10 mls

Argyll House offers a range of 3 star Cottage and Studio Apartment Accommodation sleeping 2-6. The quiet village of Salen, centrally situated on Mull, is ideally placed to explore the whole island, all year. For guests convenience, the Coffee Pot is situated on the ground floor of Argyll House where tasty snacks, coffees and other hot and cold drinks are available from Easter to October.

by Salen, Aros, Isle of Mull, Argyll

Map Ref: 1D1

★★★ SELF CATERING

Mrs MacPhail
Callachally Farm, Glenforsa, Salen, Isle of Mull, Argyll, PA72 6JN
Tel/Fax: 01680 300424

1 cottage, 2 pub rms, 3 bedrms (All grd.floor), sleeps 8, from £150.00, Jan-Dec, bus nearby, ferry 8 mls

This cottage with all rooms on the ground floor has views over the Sound of Mull and is a mere 100yds, (100 m) from the beach. Around 1 mile to Salen and shop.

Tobermory, Isle of Mull, Argyll

Map Ref: 1C1

★★★ SELF CATERING

Mrs Gallagher
Raraig House, Tobermory, Isle of Mull, Argyll
Tel/Fax: 01688 302390
E-mail: paul@scotshop.demon.co.uk

1 flat, 1 pub rm, 1 bedrm (All grd.floor), sleeps 2, £160.00-£190.00, Jan-Dec, bus ½ ml, ferry ½ ml, airport 12 mls

A modern, ground floor appartment which sits in 2 acres of grounds. With panoramic views over Tobermory Bay, Sound of Mull and to Morven Hills beyond. The apartment offers spacious, comfortable and well appointed accommodation for two. 5 mins walk from Tobermory. An ideal base for touring Mull and enjoy the atmosphere of Tobermory. Golf course adjacent, ample safe parking.

★★★★ SELF CATERING

Mrs Marian Hands
19 Orwell Road, Walsall, West Midlands, WS1 2PJ
Tel: 01922 624091

1 cottage, 1 pub rm, 3 bedrms, sleeps 5, min let 7 Days, £280.00-£375.00, Mar-Oct, bus nearby, ferry 21 mls

Exceptionally comfortable traditional cottage in upper Tobermory, with stunning views over the bay, to the Morven Hills. Private garden and parking.

★★ SELF CATERING

Mrs Janet Nelson
Glengorm Castle, by Tobermory, Isle of Mull, Argyll, PA75 6QE
Tel: 01688 302321
E-mail: janetn@sol.co.uk
Web: www.glengormcastle.co.uk

2 flats, 6 cottages, 1-2 pub rms, 2-4 bedrms (grd flr avail), sleeps 4-8, total sleeping capacity 31, £170.00-£475.00, Mar-Nov, bus 4 mls, ferry 25 mls

Castle c1860 and cottages on 5000 acre farming estate, 4 miles (6km) from Tobermory. Fishing, walking and wildlife in abundance. Garden produce and plants available for sale from June each year. Views to small outer isles.

VAT is shown at 17.5%: changes in this rate may affect prices.

Key to symbols is on back flap.

BY TOBERMORY, ISLE OF MULL – OBAN

WEST HIGHLANDS & ISLANDS, LOCH LOMOND, STIRLING & TROSSACHS

by Tobermory, Isle of Mull, Argyll — Map Ref: 1C1

Achnadrish House
by Tobermory, Isle of Mull, PA75 6QF
Tel: 01688 400388 Fax: 01688 400413 e.mail: achnadrish@hotmail.com

A lovingly restored 17th century former shooting lodge set in 8 acres of private grounds with waterfall and mixed woodlands. Comprising 2 charming self-catering wings of house sleeping 2-6. All linen included and guest sauna available. Experience a tranquil and quality break in a traditional island house and setting.

UP TO ★★★ SELF CATERING

Achnadrish House
by Tobermory, Isle of Mull, PA75 6QF
Tel: 01688 400388 Fax: 01688 400413
E-mail: achnadrish@hotmail.com

Lovingly restored former shooting lodge set in 8 acres of private grounds. Boasting stream and waterfall, surrounded by mixed woodlands. Ideal for wildlife, walking, cycling and exploring Mull.

1 chalet, 1 house, 1-2 pub rms, 1-3 bedrms (grd flr avail), sleeps 2-6, total sleeping capacity 8, £200.00-£500.00, Feb-Nov, bus nearby, rail 30 mls, ferry 20 mls, airport 90 mls

---

North Connel, Argyll — Map Ref: 1E2

★★ SELF CATERING

Mrs Isobel Campbell
Druimbhan, North Connel, Argyll, PA37 1RA
Tel/Fax: 01631 710424

Modern bungalows, beautifully situated overlooking Loch Etive. Ideal base for touring and visiting the islands.

2 bungalows, 1 pub rm, 3 bedrms, sleeps 6, total sleeping capacity 12, £110.00-£320.00, Jan-Dec, bus 1 ml, rail 2 mls, airport 1 ml

---

UP TO ★★★ SELF CATERING

Mrs D Campbell
Achnacree Bay, North Connel, Argyll, PA37 1QZ
Tel: 01631 710288 Fax: 01631 710799

The Grianach is a modernised croft cottage with a magnificent view of Loch Etive and Ben Cruachan: Rhonelin is a semi-detached bungalow with a loch view, both in an ideal location for exploring the west coast.

1 cottage, 1 bungalow, 1 pub rm, 3 bedrms, sleeps 6, total sleeping capacity 12, £110.00-£320.00, Jan-Dec, bus 2 mls, rail 3 mls

---

Oban, Argyll — Map Ref: 1E2

★★ SELF CATERING

Mrs Adams
Westmount, Dalriach Road, Oban, Argyll
Tel: 01631 562884

End terraced house in residential area within walking distance of swimming pool and tennis courts. 10 minutes walk from town centre shops.

1 house, 1 pub rm, 2 bedrms, sleeps 5, £180.00-£290.00, Apr-Oct

---

Important: Prices stated are estimates and may be subject to amendments

WEST HIGHLANDS & ISLANDS, LOCH LOMOND, STIRLING & TROSSACHS

OBAN

Oban, Argyll
Map Ref: 1E2

★★ UP TO ★★★ SELF CATERING

Ardoran Marine
Lerags, Oban, PA34 4SE
Tel: 01631 566123 Fax: 01631 566611
E-mail: anne@ardoran.freeserve.co.uk

2 chalets, 1 pub rm, 2-3 bedrms (grd flr avail), sleeps 5-6, total sleeping capacity 11, min let weekend, £200.00-£350.00, Mar-Dec, bus 2 1/2 mls, rail 5 mls, ferry 5 mls, airport 8 mls

Two modern comfortable chalets, situated on shore with superb views of Loch Feochan. Ardoran Marine is also a 200 acre farm, breeding pedigree Highland Cattle. Offering walks to observe abundant wildlife and Flora & Fauna. A quiet peaceful base for touring yet only 10 mins by car from Oban. Launch slipway and moorings adjacent to chalets, launch facilities free of charge to guests.

★★★★ SELF CATERING

Mrs Dorothy Bingham
Glenara, Rockfield Road, Oban, Argyll, PA34 5DQ
Tel: 01631 563172 Fax: 01631 571125
Web: www.smoothhound.co.uk/hotels/glenara.html

1 flat, 1 pub rm, 1 bedrm, sleeps 2, £260.00, Jan-Dec, rail nearby, ferry nearby, airport 90 mls

Modern 4th floor apartment within an attractive development adjacent to the seafront and close to the town centre and all amenities. Excellent views across Oban Bay and towards McCaigs Tower. Lift access, secure entry, private parking. Non-smoking.

Cologin Farm Holiday Chalets
Lerags Glen, by Oban, Argyll PA34 4SE
Tel: 01631 564501 Fax: 01631 566925
e.mail: cologin@oban.org.uk Web: www.oban.org.uk/accommodation/cologin/index.htm

An old farmyard setting – lovely hill views – just three miles from bustling Oban. Excellent facilities on-site: country pub/restaurant games room, laundry, play-park, duck-pond and library. Free rods and loch fishing. Wonderful walking. Pets welcome. Short breaks. Senior citizens discounts, and other low season deals available. Weekly lets from £120 to £430.

★★ SELF CATERING

Cologin Farm Holiday Chalets
Lerags Glen, by Oban, Argyll, PA34 4SE
Tel: 01631 564501 Fax: 01631 566925
E-mail: cologin@oban.org.uk
Web: www.oban.org.uk/accommodation/cologin/index.htm

18 chalets, 1 cottage, 1-2 pub rms, 1-2 bedrms (grd flr avail), sleeps 2-6, total sleeping capacity 92, min let 2 days, £65.00-£430.00, Jan-Dec, bus 1 ml, rail 3 mls, ferry 3 mls, airport 90 mls

Discover the secret world of Lerags Glen. Chalets, farmyard animals, country pub and restaurant, fishing, walking, peace and tranquility only minutes from Oban's bustling centre.

★★★ SELF CATERING

Mr & Mrs Eccleston
Braeside, Soroba Road, Oban, Argyll, PA34 4SA
Tel: 01631 563303

1 flat, 1 pub rm, 2 bedrms, sleeps 2-3, min let 3 days, £120.00-£250.00, Jan-Dec, bus 300 yds, rail 1 ml, ferry 1 ml

Purpose built self-catering unit in owners garden, quiet location on outskirts of Oban, with south facing sun terrace and private parking. Ideal location for visiting historic sights, with scenic walks and numerous castles and gardens within the Oban/ Lochaber area.

VAT is shown at 17.5%: changes in this rate may affect prices.

Key to symbols is on back flap.

OBAN

Oban, Argyll

Map Ref: 1E2

★★★ UP TO ★★★★
SELF CATERING

Esplanade Court Apartments
The Esplanade, Oban, Argyll, PA34 5PW
Tel/Fax: 01631 562067

28 flats, 1 pub rm, 1-3 bedrms, sleeps 1-4, total sleeping capacity 82, £225.00-£405.00, Apr-Nov, bus ¼ ml, rail ¼ ml, ferry ¼ ml

Central, modern apartment block with superb views of sea and islands. Elevator to all floors. Walking distance to all transport terminals. Private parking for all units. Ideal base for enjoying Oban and all surrounding areas.

★★
SELF CATERING

Mrs D McDougall
Harbour View, Shore Street, Oban, Argyll, PA34 4LQ
Tel: 01631 563462

1 flat, 2 pub rms, 2 bedrms (All grd.floor), sleeps 4-6, £150.00-£300.00, Jan-Dec, bus nearby, rail nearby, ferry nearby

Ground floor flat with seaview, convenient for ferry, railway and town centre. Flat has its own front door.

★★★
SELF CATERING

McDougalls of Oban Ltd
32 Combie Street, Oban, Argyll, PA34 4HT
Tel: 01631 562304 Fax: 01631 564408

5 flats, 1 pub rm, 2-3 bedrms, sleeps 4, total sleeping capacity 20, £120.00-£350.00, Jan-Dec, bus nearby, rail 500 yds, ferry 500 yds, airport 96 mls

Comfortable accommodation, airy, spacious with open plan kitchen/lounge area. Each flat has direct views over harbour and the neighbouring Islands. In central shopping area close to ferry, bus and railway station. Lift access. Restaurant on first floor. Lift.

★★★
SELF CATERING

Mrs R Miller
Creag Mhor, Connel, Argyll, PA37 1PH
Tel: 01631 710508

1 flat, 1 pub rm, 1 bedrm, sleeps 2, Jan-Dec, bus 300 yds, rail 300 yds, ferry 200 yds, airport 5 mls

This first floor modern flat is centrally located on the level within easy walking distance of all amenities and public transport, including the ferry terminal to Mull and the Islands. There are nice walks from the flat which take you around the bays and piers. Restaurants and hotels are also nearby.

Important: Prices stated are estimates and may be subject to amendments

WEST HIGHLANDS & ISLANDS, LOCH LOMOND, STIRLING & TROSSACHS

OBAN – BY OBAN

Oban, Argyll

Map Ref: 1E2

Lagnakeil Highland Lodges
★★★ SELF CATERING

LERAGS, OBAN, ARGYLL PA34 4SE

Tel: 01631 562746   Fax: 01631 570225   e.mail: lagnakeil@aol.com

Our timber lodges are nestled in 7 acres of scenic wooded glen 3½ miles from Oban *"Gateway to the Isles"*. Fully equipped to high standard, country pub serving fine ales and good food a short walk up the Glen. Pets welcome. OAP discount, free loch fishing. Safe for children. **Special breaks from £35.00 per night, weekly from £145.00 to £535.00.**

★★★ SELF CATERING

Colin Mossman
Lagnakeil Highland Lodges, Lerags, Oban, Argyll, PA34 4SE
Tel: 01631 562746 Fax: 01631 570225
E.mail: lagnakeil@aol.com

Timber lodges nestling in 7 acres of scenic wooded glen overlooking Loch Feochan only 3.5 miles (6 kms) from the picturesque harbour town of Oban "Gateway to the Isles".

17 timber lodges, 1-3 bedrms, sleeps 2-6, Jan-Dec, £145.00-£535.00, nightly from £35.00.

★★★★ HOLIDAY PARK

Oban Caravan & Camping Park
Gallanachmore Farm, Gallanach Road, Oban, Argyll, PA34 4QH
Tel: 01631 562425 Fax: 01631 566624
E-mail: obancp@aol.com

15 acres, grassy, hard-standing, level, Apr-mid Oct, latest time of arrival 2300, overnight holding area. Extra charge for electricity, awnings.

Park accommodation: 120
50 tourers £7.00-8.00 or 150 motors £7.00-8.00 or 150 tents £7.00-8.00. Total Touring Pitches 50.
10 Holiday Caravans to let, sleep 6-8 £160.00-350.00, total sleeping capacity 64, min let weekend (low season).

Leisure facilities:

2 mls S of Oban on coast road from town centre. Follow signs to Gallanach.

★★★★ SELF CATERING

G Strachan
Glenburnie, Esplanade, Oban, PA34 5AQ
Tel/Fax: 01631 562089

Well appointed modern apartment close to all public transport links and within a short walk from Oban town centre. Restaurants, hotels and leisure facilities nearby.

1 flat, 1 pub rm, 1 bedrm, sleeps 2, £150.00-£350.00, Jan-Dec, bus ¼ ml, rail ¼ ml, ferry ¼ ml

---

by Oban, Argyll

Map Ref: 1E2

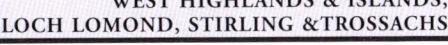

★ SELF CATERING

Mrs M R Whitton
Kilbride Farm, Lerags, by Oban, Argyll, PA34 4SE
Tel: 01631 562878

Modernised, traditional country cottage in a pleasant, secluded glen within 3 miles (5 kms) of Oban. Birdwatching, fishing, walking in the immediate vicinity. Popular country pub/restaurant close by. Come along and enjoy the peace and tranquility of this beautiful part of Argyll.

1 house, 1 pub rm, 2 bedrms, sleeps 8, £150.00-£290.00, Jan-Dec, bus 3 mls, rail 3 mls, ferry 3 mls

---

VAT is shown at 17.5%: changes in this rate may affect prices.

Key to symbols is on back flap.

OLD KILPATRICK – PORT OF MENTEITH

D WEST HIGHLANDS & ISLANDS, LOCH LOMOND, STIRLING & TROSSACHS

Old Kilpatrick, Dunbartonshire
Map Ref: 1H5

★★ SELF CATERING

Mrs S Fleming
Gavinburn Farm, Old Kilpatrick, Glasgow, G60 5NH
Tel: 01389 873058/0831 383084

2 houses, 1 pub rm, 2-4 bedrms, sleeps 4-8, total sleeping capacity 12, min let weekend, £100.00-£320.00, Jan-Dec, bus 1 ml, rail 1 ml, airport 5 mls

Two adjoining cottages beautifully situated overlooking the Clyde Estuary. Totally rural, yet only 20 minutes from both Glasgow city centre and Loch Lomond. Ideal base for trips to Stirling and Edinburgh.

Otter Ferry, Argyll
Map Ref: 1E4

★★ UP TO ★★★★ SELF CATERING

Largiemore Holiday Estate
Otter Ferry, Loch Fyne, by Tighnabruaich, Argyll, PA21 2DH
Tel/Fax: 01700 821235

7 chalets, 1 farmhouse annexe, 1 pub rm, 2-3 bedrms (grd flr avail), sleeps 4-6, total sleeping capacity 34, min let 3 nights, £180.00-£350.00, Jan-Dec, bus 18 mls, rail 26 mls, ferry 20 mls, airport 90 mls

Individually owned cedar chalets and a traditional farmhouse annexe forming part of a family run estate on the east shore of Loch Fyne. South west facing with superb views and sunsets. Slipway and moorings available. Ideal base for sea and loch fishing, scuba diving, hill walking, cycling and water sports. Boat hire and fishing trips available on site. Shop on site, pub and restaurant nearby. Tighnabruaich 25 mins and Dunoon 45 mins by car.

Peninver, by Campbeltown, Argyll
Map Ref: 1E7

★★★★ HOLIDAY PARK

Peninver Sands Caravan Park
Craigview, Campbeltown, Argyll, PA28
Tel/Fax: 01586 552262

Park accommodation: 25
6 tourers £6.00-9.00 or 6 motors £6.00-8.00. Total Touring Pitches 6. No tents.

6 Holiday Caravans to let, sleep 6 from £120.00, total sleeping capacity 36, min let 2 nights.

2 ¾ acres, mixed, Apr-Oct, latest time of arrival 2100. Extra charge for electricity, awnings.

From Campbeltown take B842 N for 4 ½ mls. Site on right as you enter Peninver.

Port of Menteith, Perthshire
Map Ref: 1H3

★★ SELF CATERING

Mrs E Forbes
Glenny, Port of Menteith, Perthshire, FK8 3RD
Tel: 01877 385229

2 cottages, 1 pub rm, 1-2 bedrms (grd flr avail), sleeps 2-7, total sleeping capacity 9, £165.00-£290.00, Apr-Oct, bus ½ ml, rail 15 mls, airport 25 mls

Renovated cottages with magnificent views over the Lake of Menteith. Peaceful yet convenient for many local attractions, including fishing on Lake of Menteith.

★★★★ SELF CATERING

Mrs K MacPhail
Mondhui Farm, Port of Menteith, by Stirling, Perthshire, FK8 3RD
Tel: 01877 385273

1 farmhouse extension, 1 pub rm, 1 bedrm (All grd.floor), sleeps 2, £190.00-£240.00, Jan-Dec, bus ½ ml, rail 15 mls, airport 30 mls

Farmhouse apartment with superb views over Lake of Menteith, on working sheep farm.

Important: Prices stated are estimates and may be subject to amendments

WEST HIGHLANDS & ISLANDS, LOCH LOMOND, STIRLING & TROSSACHS

PORTSONACHAN – ST CATHERINES

Portsonachan, Argyll

Map Ref: 1F3

★★★★ SELF CATERING

Mrs Isabella Crawford
Blarghour Farm, by Dalmally, Argyll, PA33 1BW
Tel: 01866 833246 Fax: 01866 833338

3 houses, 1 bungalow, 1 pub rm, 1-3 bedrms (grd flr avail), sleeps 2-8, total sleeping capacity 19, £160.00-£530.00, Jan-Dec, bus 16 mls, rail 16 mls, airport 70 mls

A selection of properties of individual character and design, most with extensive views over Loch Awe.

Rowardennan, Stirlingshire

Map Ref: 1G3

ROWARDENNAN LODGES

18 CROWHILL ROAD, BISHOPBRIGGS, GLASGOW G64 1QY
Telephone: 0141 762 4828 Fax: 0141 762 1625

Situated at Rowardennan on the Bonnie Banks of Loch Lomond with Ben Lomond and the breathtaking Queen Elizabeth Forest Park as a backdrop. The development is only a short drive away from the spectacular scenery of the Scottish Highlands.

★★★★ SELF CATERING

Rowardennan Lodges (Loch Lomond)
18 Crowhill Road, Bishopbriggs, Glasgow, G64 1QY
Tel: 0141 762 4828 Fax: 0141 762 1625

6 pine lodges, 1 pub rm, 2-3 bedrms (grd flr avail), sleeps 4-6, total sleeping capacity 32, £250.00-£575.00, Jan-Dec, bus 6 mls, rail 15 mls, airport 30 mls

Lodges on 10 acre site on the shore of Loch Lomond. Free mooring and landing facilities for the boaters.

St Catherines, Argyll

Map Ref: 1F3

Halftown Cottages, St Catherines

Two semi-detached historical cottages near Loch Fyne, Argyll opposite Inveraray and 54 miles from Glasgow. Each cottage is completely refurbished, sleeps four, TV, washing machine and is set in secluded woodland, on site of ancient township. Many interesting activities available in the surrounding area including golf, walking, fishing.

CONTACT: CROITACHONIE, CAIRNDOW, ARGYLL PA26 8BH
Tel/Fax: 01499 600239

★★★ SELF CATERING

Halftown Cottages
Croitachonie, Cairndow, Argyll, PA26 6BH
Tel/Fax: 01499 600239

2 cottages, 1 pub rm, 2 bedrms (grd flr avail), sleeps 4, total sleeping capacity 8, £180.00-£400.00, Jan-Dec, bus ½ ml, rail 12 mls, ferry 20 mls, airport 45 mls

Two semi detached cottages by Loch Fyne. Set in natural woodland on site of ancient township as described by author Neil Munro. The cottages are completely restored and refurbished with natural wood and open fires secluded and surrounded by natural rural woodland, of special scientific interest.

VAT is shown at 17.5%: changes in this rate may affect prices.

Key to symbols is on back flap.

ST CATHERINES – STIRLING

WEST HIGHLANDS & ISLANDS, LOCH LOMOND, STIRLING & TROSSACHS

St Catherines, Argyll — Map Ref: 1F3

★★★★ SELF CATERING

Mrs C E Mactavish
Strathalmond, Clenches Farm Lane, Sevenoaks, Kent, TN13 2LX
Tel: 01732 461318

Tastefully refurbished, traditional two-bedroomed cottage, in quiet position on old Shore Road with uninterrupted views of Loch Fyne. Secure parking.

1 cottage, 2 pub rms, 2 bedrms, sleeps 4, £230.00-£330.00, Jan-Dec, bus 1 ml, rail 16 mls, ferry 16 mls, airport 50 mls

Clachan Seil, by Oban, Isle of Seil, Argyll — Map Ref: 1E3

★★★★ SELF CATERING

Bette and Nick
Oban Seil Farm Steadings, Isle of Seil, by Oban, Argyll, PA34 4TN
Tel/Fax: 01852 300245

Farm steading, beautifully converted. Spectacular views to the islands. Hillwalking, sailing and ponies. Breakfast/Evening meals available. Babysitting. Pets by arrangement. Private marina. Free brochure.

3 cottages, 1-3 pub rms, 2 bedrms, sleeps 4-6, total sleeping capacity 16, £120.00-£500.00, Jan-Dec, bus nearby, rail 13 mls

Skipness, Argyll — Map Ref: 1E5

★ SELF CATERING

Sophie James
Skipness Castle, nr Tarbert, Argyll, PA29 6XU
Tel: 01880 760207 Fax: 01880 760208

Individual cottages in quiet seaside village with views over Kilbrannan Sound to Arran beyond. Open fires. Ideal for quiet relaxing holidays, dogs and children welcome.

1 house, 4 cottages, 1-3 pub rms, 2-4 bedrms, sleeps 4-10, total sleeping capacity 40, £100.00-£450.00, Jan-Dec, bus ½ ml, rail 60 mls, ferry 2 mls, airport 30 mls

Stirling — Map Ref: 2A4

University of Stirling

Vacation Campus, University of Stirling, Stirling FK9 4LA
Tel: 01786 467141 Fax: 01786 467143
e. mail: holidays@stir.ac.uk Web: www.stir.ac.uk/theuni/vacation

With a superb range of chalets, flats and apartments, Stirling Vacation Campus provides the perfect holiday setting for individuals, families and groups. (Accommodation available June–September). The University boasts excellent sports and leisure facilities, including a 25m indoor swimming pool, and provides the ideal base from which to explore the very best of Scotland. *Prices from £150–£415 per unit per week* (ref:SC00).

★★★ SELF CATERING

Conference and Vacation Campus
University of Stirling, Stirling, FK9 4LA
Tel: 01786 467141/467142 Fax: 01786 467143
E-mail: holidays@stir.ac.uk
Web: www.stir.ac.uk/theuni/vacation

Scandinavian type timber chalets in quiet location on University Campus. Access to sports and leisure facilities, which are available at additional cost.

32 chalets, 80 flats, 71 apartments, 1 pub rm, 2-7 bedrms, sleeps 2-7, total sleeping capacity 1250, £150.00-£415.00, Jun-Sep, bus nearby, rail 1 ½ mls, airport 33 mls

---

Important: Prices stated are estimates and may be subject to amendments

WEST HIGHLANDS & ISLANDS, LOCH LOMOND, STIRLING & TROSSACHS

STIRLING – TARBERT, LOCH FYNE

Stirling
Map Ref: 2A4

SELF CATERING ★★★★

Mrs S Dempster
McNair House, The Square, Gargunnock, by Stirling, FK8 3BH
Tel: 01786 860668 Fax: 01224 699424

1 cottage, 2 pub rms, 2 bedrms, sleeps 4, min let weekend, £225.00-£375.00, Jan-Dec, bus nearby, rail 5 mls

Late 18th century mid-terraced cottage overlooking the attractive village square, 6 miles west of Stirling in an area of great natural beauty.

Strathyre, Perthshire
Map Ref: 1H3

SELF CATERING ★★

Mrs L Beale
Newlands, 23 The Sands, Long Clawson, Melton Mowbray, Leicestershire, LE14 4PA
Tel: 01664 822247

1 cottage, 1 pub rm, 3 bedrms (grd flr avail), sleeps 6-8, min let weekend, £150.00-£295.00, Jan-Dec, bus 100 yds

Newly-renovated, traditional stone house in centre of village. Conveniently situated for walking and touring.

Tarbert, Loch Fyne, Argyll
Map Ref: 1E5

SELF CATERING ★★★

Mr & Mrs Arnold
Holmes Farm, Long Bennington, Newark, Nottinghamshire, NG23 5EB
Tel/Fax: 01400 281282

1 cottage, 3 pub rms, 3 bedrms, sleeps 7, £200.00-£500.00, Jan-Dec, bus nearby, rail 50 mls, ferry 1 ml, airport 33 mls

Stonebuilt, traditional family house standing in own grounds within 5 minutes walk of harbour and shops. Views over Loch Fyne.

SELF CATERING ★★★

Bowmore Farm
Tarbert, Argyll, PA29 6YJ
Tel: 01880 820222

2 flats, 4 cottages, 1-2 pub rms, 1-2 bedrms, sleeps 4-6, total sleeping capacity 22, £180.00-£580.00, Jan-Dec, bus nearby, rail 50 mls, ferry 1/2 ml, airport 38 mls

Recently renovated Listed farm steadings grouped around landscaped central courtyard. 1.5 miles (3kms) from Tarbert. Childrens play area. Horse-riding, mountain bike hire, boat trips and clay pigeon shooting all available by arrangement.

SELF CATERING ★

Mrs Una Coombs
25 Higher Knutsford Road, Grappenhall, Warrington, Cheshire, WA4 2JS
Tel/Fax: 01925 261695

1 flat, 1 pub rm, 3 bedrms, sleeps 6, £125.00-£600.00, Apr-Oct, bus nearby

VAT is shown at 17.5%: changes in this rate may affect prices.

Key to symbols is on back flap.

TARBERT, LOCH FYNE – TARBET, BY ARROCHAR

WEST HIGHLANDS & ISLANDS, LOCH LOMOND, STIRLING & TROSSACHS

Tarbert, Loch Fyne, Argyll — Map Ref: 1E5

★★★ SELF CATERING

Mrs Elizabeth Jessiman
75A Craigcrook Road, Edinburgh, EH4 3PH
Tel: 0131 332 6678

1 flat, 1 pub rm, 3 bedrms, sleeps 5, £200.00-£350.00, Jan-Dec, bus nearby, rail 35 mls, airport 75 mls

First floor flat in conversion of Scottish baronial house in elevated position overlooking Loch Fyne. A central base for exploring the unspoilt landscape of Mid-Argyll.

★★★★ SELF CATERING

West Loch Tarbert Holiday Park
West Loch, Tarbert, Argyll, PA29 6YF
Tel: 01880 820873

2 log cabins, 1 pub rm, 2 bedrms (All grd.floor), sleeps 4-6, total sleeping capacity 12, £90.00-£420.00, Apr-Oct, bus at park entrance, rail 45 mls, ferry 3 mls

Two newly built pine lodges located within West Loch Holiday Caravan Park, situated 1.5 miles south from Tarbert village overlooking West Loch Tarbert, the Park is an excellent home for exploring Argyll and the Kintyre Peninsula. Good access to all ferries.

---

by Tarbert, Loch Fyne, Argyll — Map Ref: 1E5

★★ SELF CATERING

Mrs Meg MacKinnon
Dunmore Home Farm, Dunmore, nr Tarbert, Argyll, PA29 6XZ
Tel: 01880 820654

1 house, 4 cottages, 2-3 pub rms, 2-5 bedrms (grd flr avail), sleeps 5-10, total sleeping capacity 43, £165.00-£750.00, Jan-Dec, bus 7 mls

Architect designed courtyard conversion of former steading. Secluded modern family villa on edge of loch with unrestricted views. Both properties on estate of over 1000 acres including large areas of natural oak woodland. Use of private harbour area suitable for day boats. Boats also available to hire.

Tarbet, by Arrochar, Dunbartonshire — Map Ref: 1G3

★★★ SELF CATERING

Mr S J MacDonald
9 Rannoch Road, Kilmacolm, Renfrewshire, PA13 4LT
Tel: 01505 872923
E-mail: jmacd3@csi.com

1 house, 3 pub rms, 3 bedrms (grd flr avail), sleeps 6, £210.00-£380.00, Jan-Dec, bus 1/2 ml, rail nearby, airport 30 mls

Semi-detached traditional stone cottage in village of Tarbet. Large private garden. 0.25 mile (1 km) from shores of Loch Lomond.

★★★ SELF CATERING

Elizabeth McMillan
5a Bellevue Road, Kirkintilloch, Glasgow, G66 1AL
Tel: 0141 775 1432/578 1039

1 cottage, 1 pub rm, 2 bedrms, sleeps 6, £290.00-£360.00, Apr-Oct, bus nearby, rail 1 ml, airport 30 mls

Modern cottage converted from 200 year old smiddy. Enclosed garden with stream and wooden bridges. Loch view. Ideal base for touring.

Important: Prices stated are estimates and may be subject to amendments

WEST HIGHLANDS & ISLANDS, LOCH LOMOND, STIRLING & TROSSACHS

TAYNUILT

Taynuilt, Argyll
Map Ref: 1F2

★★★★ SELF CATERING

Mrs Lucy Beaton
Dalry, Kirkton, Taynuilt, Argyll, PA35 1HW
Tel: 01866 822657

Newly-built timber chalet and brick cottage in peaceful rural environment. Spectacular mountain scenery.

1 chalet, 1 cottage, 1 pub rm, 1-2 bedrms (grd flr avail), sleeps 2-4, total sleeping capacity 6, £130.00-£310.00, Jan-Dec, bus ¼ ml, rail ½ ml

---

★★ SELF CATERING

John Garvie
Sliabh, Bridge of Awe, Taynuilt, Argyll, PA35 1HU
Tel: 01866 822637
E-mail: jgarvie@aol.com

Semi-detached bungalow with enclosed back garden in small hamlet, 14 miles (22kms) from Oban. Ideal centre for touring, walking and fishing.

1 cottage, 1 pub rm, 2 bedrms (All grd.floor), sleeps 4-6, min let 3 nights not Fri/Sat incl, £130.00-£290.00, Apr-Oct, bus nearby, rail 2 mls, ferry 12 mls, airport 100 mls

---

★★ SELF CATERING

Mrs Anne Hay
Airds Cottage, Taynuilt, Argyll, PA35 1JW
Tel: 01866 822349

Airds cottage flat is a modern extension to our traditional cottage with its own private entrance situated on the outskirts of the village, set back from the road the flat offers magnificent views over Loch and Glen Etive. Most facilities ie. local shops, hotel etc and within walking distance.

1 flat, 1 pub rm, 1 bedrm, sleeps 2, £100.00-£180.00, Mar-Oct, bus 400 yds, rail 400 yds

---

★★★ SELF CATERING

Mrs Jan McGougan
Brackendale, Taynuilt, Argyll, PA35 1JQ
Tel: 01866 822365 Fax: 01866 822548

Spacious first floor flat in a rural position 1 mile (2kms) from Taynuilt with panoramic views towards Ben Cruachan, Loch Etive and Glen Lonan.

1 flat, 1 pub rm, 2 bedrms, sleeps 5, £125.00-£275.00, Jan-Dec, rail 1 ml

---

★★★ SELF CATERING

Mrs Olsen
Airdeny Chalets, Airdeny, Taynuilt, Argyll, PA35 1HY
Tel: 01866 822648 Fax: 01866 822665

Wooden chalets in peaceful rural setting. Fine views to mountains and close to village shops and Oban.

4 chalets, 1 pub rm, 2 bedrms, sleeps 4, total sleeping capacity 16, £165.00-£320.00, Mar-Nov, bus 1 ml, rail 1 ml

---

VAT is shown at 17.5%: changes in this rate may affect prices.

Key to symbols is on back flap.

WEST HIGHLANDS & ISLANDS, LOCH LOMOND, STIRLING & TROSSACHS

Taynuilt, Argyll
Map Ref: 1F2

BONAWE HOUSE
TAYNUILT, NR OBAN, ARGYLL, PA35 1JQ   Tel: 01866 822309
e.mail: Damon.Powell@btinternet.com   Web: www.btinternet.com/~bonawe.house

18th century listed country house in 12 acres of mature grounds. Magnificent rural setting overlooking Loch Etive and Ben Cruachan. Six cottages and three apartments, forming a pleasant courtyard, converted to maintain former character and provide comfortable accommodation. Shops, hotels, train and bus within easy walking distance. Open all year. Prices from £110 to £370 per week. Short stays in off-season.

★★ UP TO ★★★ SELF CATERING

Renate Powell
Bonawe House, Taynuilt, nr Oban, Argyll, PA35 1JQ
Tel: 01866 822309
E-mail: Damon.Powell@btinternet.com
Web: www.btinternet.com/~bonawe.house

Flats in converted 18 century country house set amidst parkland about 1 mile (2kms) from Taynuilt village and shops. Bonawe Iron Furnace under the care of Historic Scotland is close by.

1 house, 2 flats, 6 cottages, 1 pub rm, 1-3 bedrms (grd flr avail), sleeps 2-6, total sleeping capacity 31, min let 2 nights (low season), £110.00-£370.00, Jan-Dec, bus ¼ ml, rail ½ ml

---

Gott Bay, Isle of Tiree, Argyll
Map Ref: 1A1

★ SELF CATERING

Tiree Lodge Hotel
Gott Bay, Isle of Tiree, PA77 1TN
Tel: 01879 220368 Fax: 01879 220884

Flat adjoining the hotel. Beach for wind surfing and other water sports facilities available nearby.

1 flat, 2 pub rms, 2 bedrms (All grd.floor), sleeps 7, £125.00-£300.00, Jan-Dec, ferry 2 mls, airport 7 mls

---

Scarinish, Isle of Tiree, Argyll
Map Ref: 1A2

★★★★ SELF CATERING

Mrs Rosemary M Omand
Scarinish Villa, Scarinish, Isle of Tiree, Argyll, PA77 6UH
Tel: 01879 220307 Fax: 01879 220607

Recently converted croft house with large kitchen/dining extension and garden area. Centrally situated 1 mile from shop and many beaches.

1 house, 2 pub rms, 4 bedrms (grd flr avail), sleeps 8, min let weekend, £200.00-£350.00, Jan-Dec, ferry 4 mls, airport 1 ml

---

★★★ SELF CATERING

Mrs Janet Paterson
6 Crossapol, Isle of Tiree, Argyll
Tel: 01879 220429

Traditional croft house with kitchen extension in centre of island, 4 miles (7 km) to ferry. Ideal base for families. Short stroll to sandy beach.

1 house, 1 pub rm, 4 bedrms (grd flr avail), sleeps 7, £140.00-£170.00, Jan-Dec, ferry 3½ mls, airport 1¾ mls

---

Important: Prices stated are estimates and may be subject to amendments

WEST HIGHLANDS & ISLANDS, LOCH LOMOND, STIRLING & TROSSACHS

TIREE, ISLE OF – TYNDRUM, BY CRIANLARICH

Tiree, Isle of Tiree, Argyll

Map Ref: 1A1

★★ SELF CATERING

Mrs Susan Atkins
Bloxham House, Highbridge Road, Wappenham, Towcester,
Northants, NN12 8SL
Tel/Fax: 01327 860102

Traditional Hebridean thatched cottage within walking distance of beach at Sandaig and the magnificent Kenavara.

1 cottage, 1 pub rm, 1 bedrm (grd.flr), sleeps 2+cot, £125.00-£175.00, Jan-Dec, ferry 8 mls, airport 6 mls

★★ SELF CATERING

Mrs G Latham
Baugh, Isle of Tiree, Argyll, PA77 6UN
Tel: 01879 220538

South facing property with all rooms on ground floor. Open views to neighbouring islands. 2 miles from ferry and airport.

1 cottage, 1 pub rm, 1 bedrm, sleeps 2, £160.00-£190.00, Apr-Oct, bus nearby, ferry 2 mls, airport 2 mls

Tyndrum, by Crianlarich, Perthshire

Map Ref: 1G2

★★ SELF CATERING

Christina Honeybone
11 Park Lane, Roundhay, Leeds, LS8 2EX
Tel: 0113 2668456

Cosy traditional stone built cottage in a small terrace. On West Highland Way. Near junction for Oban and Fort William roads.

1 cottage, 2 pub rms, 4 bedrms (All grd.floor), sleeps 6, £160.00-£300.00, Jan-Dec, bus nearby, rail ½ ml

★ SELF CATERING

Diane & Jim Mailer
Glengarry House, Tyndrum, Perthshire, FK20 8RY
Tel: 01838 400224
E-mail: glengarry@altavista.net
Web: www.jmailer.freeserve.co.uk

The West Highland Way passes close to this chalet which has magnificent views, being set above the A82. Evening meals provided by prior arrangement.

1 chalet, 1 pub rm, 2 bedrms, sleeps 4, £200.00-£220.00, Jan-Dec, bus ¼ ml, rail ¼ ml, ferry 38 mls, airport 45 mls

---

VAT is shown at 17.5%: changes in this rate may affect prices.

Key to symbols is on back flap.

Welcome to Scotland

Perthshire, Angus & Dundee and The Kingdom of Fife

THIS IS AN AREA OFFERING PLENTY OF CONTRASTS: FROM THE WHITE WALLED HARBOURFRONT HOUSES OF THE EAST NEUK OF FIFE FISHING VILLAGES TO THE WINDY SILENCES OF THE EDGE OF RANNOCH MOOR, FROM THE PUBS AND UPBEAT NIGHTLIFE OF THE CITY OF DUNDEE TO THE UPLAND TRANQUILLITY OF THE ANGUS GLENS. IT MAKES A GOOD CHOICE IF YOUR SCOTTISH BREAK SHOULD HAVE A LITTLE OF EVERYTHING.

Here you will find within one square mile, a royal palace, a 12th-century abbey and the fortified tower where King Malcolm held court after the death of Macbeth. This thriving city is also a great base for touring the region with good hotels and restaurants, superb shops, and excellent leisure facilities.

Further afield, history unfolds in the nearby Royal Burgh of Falkland, the one-time favourite holiday home of of Mary Queen of Scots, and nearby Culross, a 17th-century town of narrow cobbled alleyways and white-washed, red tiled houses. The eastern most corner of the Kingdom teems with subjects for artists and photographers, amongst the seashore villages of St Monans, Pittenweem and Crail, while Anstruther chronicles past struggles with the sea in its Scottish Fisheries Museum. St Andrews, the home of golf, attracts both amateurs and champions of the sport to its famous Old Course, and there are another 40 courses throughout Fife, as well as the fascinating British Golf Museum for the enthusiast to visit.

Perthshire, Angus & Dundee and The Kingdom of Fife

Perthshire, Angus & Dundee and The Kingdom of Fife

Across the River Tay is Dundee, home to Captain Scott's Antarctic exploration vessel RRS Discovery, and the innovative Verdant Works, which tells the moving story of the city's Victorian industrial heritage. The city is also the gateway to the upland tranquillity of Angus, where the unspoilt landscapes of its beautiful glens offer wonderful walking country. The coast has good beaches, seaports and dramatic cliffs, while the farming hinterland is dotted with numerous small market towns such as Kirriemuir, which was the birthplace of one of Scotland's most celebrated playwrights, J. M. Barrie, the creator of Peter Pan. Close by are Edzell Castle, the House of Dun and Glamis Castle, whose towered and turreted profile was the childhood home of the Queen Mother.

From the gleaming white edifice of Blair Castle to the crowning glory of Scone Palace, Perthshire can claim to have more castles and stately homes than any other region in Scotland, but there is also much more to see and do. Blairgowrie, with its antique shops and bistros, lies in the heart of fruit growing country and is the gateway town to Glenshee, one of Scotland's five ski areas. The Victorian spa town of Pitlochry has the multi-attractions of its Festival Theatre, Dam Visitors Centre and salmon ladder and Aberfeldy, the quintessential highland town, has a water mill and white-water rafting on the River Tay.

In fact, there are literally dozens of sports and pastimes to be found in Perthshire throughout the year, including fishing, golf, horse-riding, mountain biking or even heading out on a wildlife safari with an expert driver-guide. Perthshire can claim to have Scotland's longest glen, Britain's tallest tree and the world's oldest distillery, and with such a wealth of wonders, the decision is surely not whether to come, but when.

Perthshire, Angus & Dundee and The Kingdom of Fife

Events
Perthshire, Angus & Dundee and the Kingdom of Fife

2-4 Mar
Dunfermline Abbey Sound & Light 2000
Dunfermline Abbey
Sound and light performance in Dunfermline Abbey, the burial place of old Scottish kings and queens, illustrating 2000 years of Christian history.
Contact: Mrs Cunningham
Tel: 01383 721271

25 Mar
Millennium Champions Challenge
Blair Castle
Highland Dancing competition for champions/international choreography competition.
Tel: 01796 481207

1-2 Apr
City of Dundee Flower Show
Dick McTaggart Centre, Dundee
Contact: Vic Stuart
Tel: 01382 433435

1-5 May
Celtic Fayre
Scottish Crannog Centre, Loch Tay
Displays depicting the lifestyle of the ancient Crannog dwellers, watch craftsmen at work, try your hand at spinning, weaving, wood turning, etc. Become immersed in Celtic folk tales. In other words – travel back in time.
Tel: 01887 830583

2-9 Jul
The Thrie Estates
Castlehill, Cupar, Fife
Large scale production of Scotland's greatest play on its original outdoor site.
Tel: 0141 339 9210

20-23 Jul
The Open Golf Championship
Old Course, St Andrews, Fife
This famous major golf competition will take on more significance due to the Millennium. The QEII is due to berth off St Andrews offering the cruise of a lifetime in celebration of the Millennium.
Tel: 01334 472112 Fax: 01334 475483

1-3 Sept
Kirriemuir Festival of Traditional Music & Song
Contact: Mr Newman
Tel: 01575 540261

25-30 Nov
St Andrew's Week
Festivities celebrating St Andrew's Day and the best of Scottish culture and cuisine.
Contact: St Andrew's TIC
Tel: 01334 472021

Perthshire, Angus & Dundee and The Kingdom of Fife

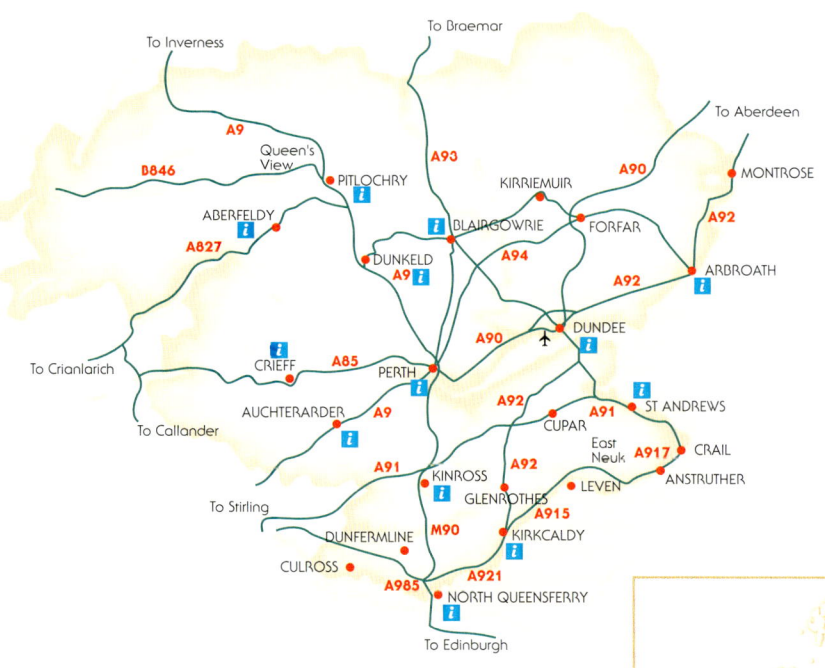

Area Tourist Boards

Angus & City of Dundee Tourist Board

Angus & Dundee
Tourist Board
21 Castle Street
Dundee DD1 3AA
Perth PH1 5QP

Tel: (01382) 527540
Fax: (01738) 527550
Web: www.carnoustie.co.uk/.

Kingdom of Fife Tourist Board

Kingdom of Fife
Tourist Board
Haig House
Haig Business Park
Markinch KY7 6AQ

Tel: (01592) 750066
Fax: (01592) 611180
Web: www.standrews.co.uk

Perthshire Tourist Board

Perthshire Tourist Board
Lower City Mills
West Mill Street
Perth PH1 5QP

Tel: (01738) 627958
Fax: (01738) 630416
Web: www.perthshire.co.uk

Perthshire, Angus & Dundee and The Kingdom of Fife

Tourist Information Centres

Angus & City of Dundee Tourist Board

Arbroath
Market Place
Tel: (01241) 872609
Jan-Dec

Brechin
St Ninians Place
Tel: (01356) 626838
April-Sept

Carnoustie
1b High Street
Tel: (01241) 852258
April-Sept

Dundee
7-21 Castle Street
Tel: (01382) 527527
Jan-Dec

Forfar
40 East High Street
Tel: (01307) 467876
April-Sept

Kirriemuir
St. Malcolm's Wynd
Tel: (01575) 574097
April-Sept

Montrose
Bridge Street
Tel: (01674) 672000
April-Sept

Kingdom of Fife Tourist Board

Anstruther
Scottish Fisheries Museum
Tel: (01333) 311073
Easter-Sept

Crail
Museum and Heritage Centre
Marketgate
Tel: (01333) 450859
Easter-Sept

Dunfermline
13/15 Maygate
Tel: (01383) 720999
April-Oct

Forth Bridges
by North Queensferry
Tel: (01383) 417759
Jan-Dec

Kirkcaldy
19 Whytecauseway
Tel: (01592) 267775
Jan-Dec

St Andrews
70 Market Street
Tel: (01334) 472021
Jan-Dec

Perthshire Tourist Board

Aberfeldy
The Square
Tel: (01887) 820276
Jan-Dec

Auchterarder
90 High Street
Tel: (01764) 663450
Jan-Dec

Blairgowrie
26 Wellmeadow
Tel: (01250) 872960
Jan-Dec

Crieff
Town Hall
High Street
Tel: (01764) 652578
Jan-Dec

Dunkeld
The Cross
Tel: (01350) 727688
Jan-Dec

Kinross
Kinross Service Area
off Junction 6, M90
Tel: (01577) 863680
Jan-Dec

Perth
45 High Street
Tel: (01738) 638353
Jan-Dec

Perth (Inveralmond)
Caithness Glass
Inveralmond
A9 Western City Bypass
Tel: (01738) 638481
Jan-Dec

Pitlochry
22 Atholl Road
Tel: (01796) 472215/472751
Jan-Dec

PERTHSHIRE, ANGUS AND DUNDEE AND THE KINGDOM OF FIFE

Aberdour, Fife — Map Ref: 2C4

★★★ SELF CATERING

Mrs Flora Dickson
6 Glamis Place, Dalgety Bay, Fife, KY11 5UA
Tel: 01383 823448
E-mail: stay@aberdour-holidays.co.uk
Web: www.aberdour-holidays.co.uk

1 flat, 3 bedrms, sleeps 5-7, £350.00, Jan-Dec

Top-floor spacious flat overlooking the High Street. Aberdour is a lively village with a safe sandy beach, makes this an ideal base for family holidays. Less than half hour by train to Edinburgh - rail station only 2 mins walk away. Ideal for golfers and fishermen.

★★★★ SELF CATERING

Mrs W Henderson
6 Campbell Avenue, Edinburgh, EH12 6DS
Tel: 0131 337 5844 Fax: 0131 313 1464

1 studio cottage, 1 pub rm, 1 bedrm, sleeps 2, £350.00-£440.00, Jan-Dec, bus ¼ ml, rail ¼ ml, airport 14 mls

This unique seaside studio cottage has been built and equipped to exceptionally high standard. Located within a conservation village, overlooking the harbour and Inchcolm Abbey. Within easy reach of Edinburgh and St Andrews.

---

by Aberdour, Fife — Map Ref: 2C4

★★★★★ SELF CATERING

Mrs June Weatherup
Parkend Farm, Crossgates, Cowdenbeath, KY4 8EX
Tel/Fax: 01383 860277

1 cottage, 2 pub rms, 3 bedrms (All grd.floor), sleeps 5-6, min let 3 nights, £225.00-£500.00, Jan-Dec, bus 2 mls, rail 2 mls, airport 14 mls

Peacefully located on working dairy farm with panoramic views to Firth of Forth. The centre of Edinburgh is only 25 minutes by car or train. All ground floor accomodation.

Aberfeldy, Perthshire — Map Ref: 2A1

★★★★ SELF CATERING

Angela Delph
Distillery Cottage, The Lagg, Aberfeldy, Perthshire, PH15 2ED
Tel: 01887 820754 Fax: 01887 829116

1 cottage, 3 bedrms (grd flr avail), sleeps 6, £245.00-£430.00, Jan-Dec

Picturesque victorian cottage refurbished to a high standard. Large traditional country kitchen with a wood burning pot-belly stove and open fire in sitting room. Woodland garden with patio and garden furniture.

★★★★ SELF CATERING

Mrs Isobel S Kerr
17 Buchanan Drive, Cambuslang, Glasgow, G72 8BD
Tel: 0141 641 2856
E-mail: 101461.3151@compuserve.com

1 cottage, 2 pub rms, 1 bedrm, sleeps 2-4, min let 3 nights, £160.00-£275.00, Jan-Dec, bus nearby, rail 15 mls, airport 75 mls

Cottage, tastefully renovated, conveniently situated near the town centre and adjacent to the Birks of Aberfeldy.

Important: Prices stated are estimates and may be subject to amendments

PERTHSHIRE, ANGUS AND DUNDEE AND THE KINGDOM OF FIFE

ABERFELDY – BY ABERFELDY

Aberfeldy, Perthshire — Map Ref: 2A1

★ SELF CATERING

Mr & Mrs J H Macnaughton
50 Brownside Road, Cambuslang, Glasgow, G72 8NJ
Tel/Fax: 0141 641 2699

1 flat, 2 pub rms, 2 bedrms, sleeps 5, £150.00-£220.00, Mar-Oct, bus ¼ ml, rail 15 mls, airport 70 mls

Ground floor flat, conveniently situated in town centre and near the entrance to the Birks walk.

★★★ UP TO ★★★★ SELF CATERING

Mrs D D McDiarmid
Castle Menzies Home Farm, Aberfeldy, Perthshire, PH15 2LY
Tel: 01887 820260 Fax: 01887 829666
E-mail: ddmcd@farmline.com

2 houses, 1-2 pub rms, 2-3 bedrms (grd flr avail), sleeps 4-6, total sleeping capacity 10, min let weekend (low season), £150.00-£550.00, Jan-Dec, bus 2 mls, rail 15 mls

Two stone built, well equipped cottages. All located separately on farm. 2 miles (3 kms) west of Aberfeldy.

★★★★ SELF CATERING

Nicky & Calum McDiarmid, Drumcloy Lodges
Mains of Murthly, Aberfeldy, Perthshire, PH15 2EA
Tel: 01887 820978
E-mail: nickymcdiarmid@compuserve.com

4 chalets, 6 pub rms, 2 bedrms (All grd.floor), sleeps 4-6, total sleeping capacity 24, min let weekend (low season), £180.00-£380.00, Jan-Dec, bus 1 ml, rail 15 mls, airport 90 mls

Four chalets in stunning rural setting with spectacular views over the River Tay and Highland Perthshire, one mile from picturesque village of Aberfeldy. On site nature walks, fishing, shooting and mountain bike rides.

★★★ SELF CATERING

Pamela McDiarmid
Mains of Murthly, Aberfeldy, Perthshire, PH15 2EA
Tel/Fax: 01887 820427

2 cottages, 1 pub rm, 2 bedrms (All grd.floor), sleeps 3-5, total sleeping capacity 9, £160.00-£300.00, Jan-Dec, bus 1 ml, rail 14 mls

On working farm, 2 miles (3kms) from the town centre in quiet and peaceful situation, two cottages adjacent to farm steading.

---

by Aberfeldy, Perthshire — Map Ref: 2A1

★★★ SELF CATERING

"The Weem"
Weem, by Aberfeldy, Perthshire, PH15 2LD
Tel: 01887 820381 Fax: 01887 829720
E-mail: weem@compuserve.com

3 flats, 1 pub rm, 2 bedrms, sleeps 2-5, total sleeping capacity 5, £203.00-£525.00, Jan-Dec, bus ¼ ml, rail 13 mls, airport 60 mls

Self contained apartments on upper floors of 17th Century Inn situated in the delightful Tay Valley in a peaceful and tranquil setting.

VAT is shown at 17.5%: changes in this rate may affect prices.

Key to symbols is on back flap.

Acharn, by Kenmore, Perthshire — Map Ref: 2A1

Loch Tay Lodges
Mrs M. G. Millar, Acharn, Aberfeldy, Perthshire PH15 2HR
Telephone: 01887 830209 Fax: 01887 830802
e.mail: remony@btinternet.com   Web: www.fishingnet.com/remony.htm

These top-quality, self-catering cottages sleeping 2-8, are beside Loch Tay, on edge of village, set in beautiful countryside. They are totally modernised and fully equipped, including linen and towels. Log fires, TV, etc., children and dogs welcome. Boats available. Also suitable for sailing, golfing, hill-walking and touring. **Prices from £180–£485 per lodge.**

SELF CATERING ★★★★

A & J Duncan Millar
Loch Tay Lodges, Remony, Aberfeldy, Perthshire, PH15 2HR
Tel: 01887 830209 Fax: 01887 830802
E-mail: remony@btinternet.com
Web: http://www.fishingnet.com/remony.htm

Converted Listed stone buildings in quiet picturesque Highland village. Sailing, fishing, bird watching and many lovely country walks.

4 houses, 2 flats, 1 pub rm, 2-3 bedrms (grd flr avail), sleeps 4-8, total sleeping capacity 32, min let weekend, £180.00-£485.00, Jan-Dec, bus 7 1/2 mls, rail 21 mls, airport 80 mls

Alyth, Perthshire — Map Ref: 2C1

SELF CATERING ★★

Mr & Mrs Brian Groom
East Tullyfergus Farm, Alyth, Perthshire, PH11 8JY
Tel: 01828 633251

Traditional stone-built cottage in rural setting on a working farm. Peaceful, but convenient for touring and all outdoor activities.

1 cottage, 1 pub rm, 2 bedrms (All grd.floor), sleeps 4, £200.00-£250.00, Jan-Dec, bus 2 mls, rail 20 mls

---

Anstruther, Fife — Map Ref: 2D3

SELF CATERING ★★★★

Paul Capaldi
The Great Lodging, 21 High Street, Anstruther, Fife, KY10 3DJ
Tel/Fax: 01333 312389

16th Century restored town house featuring four large bedrooms and top floor open plan lounge with uninterrupted seaviews. Separate garden flat would suit couples, with double bedroom and bed settee in living room.

1 house, 1 flat, 1-3 pub rms, 1-5 bedrms (grd flr avail), sleeps 2-8, total sleeping capacity 10, £140.00-£475.00, Jan-Dec, bus 1/2 ml, rail 15 mls, airport 50 mls

---

SELF CATERING ★★★

Mr & Mrs Warman
17 Greenways, Abbots Langley, Herts, WD5 0EU
Tel: 01923 265258
E-mail: arradoul@aol.com
Web: www.about-scotland.co.uk/fife/arradoul.html

Semi-detached granite house renovated and refurbished to a high standard, 9 miles (14kms) south of St Andrews, close to beach and harbour. Excellent choice of restaurants, hotels and bus within a few miles distance.

1 house, 1 pub rm, 3 bedrms, sleeps 6, £300.00-£600.00, Jan-Dec, bus nearby, rail 9 mls, airport 50 mls

Important: Prices stated are estimates and may be subject to amendments

PERTHSHIRE, ANGUS AND DUNDEE AND THE KINGDOM OF FIFE

AUCHTERARDER – BANKFOOT

Auchterarder, Perthshire

Morrison's Holiday Homes
Ben Lawers, Townhead Dairy, Auchterarder, Perthshire, PH3 1JG
Tel/Fax: 01764 662369
E-mail: mhh3star@aol.com
Web: www.scottish-towns.co.uk

★★★ SELF CATERING

Apartments in tastefully renovated cottage dating back to 1709. Convenient for town, shops and park. Ideal for golfers, as at least a dozen courses within half an hour.

Map Ref: 2B3

2 apartments, 2 pub rms, 2 bedrms (All grd.floor), sleeps 4-6, total sleeping capacity 12, £185.00-£310.00, Jan-Dec, bus 50 yds, rail 1 ml, airport 60 mls

---

by Auchterarder, Perthshire

Muriel Donald
Old House Of Orchil, Braco, Perthshire, FK15 9LF
Tel/Fax: 01764 682373
E-mail: john@rushworth.co.uk

★★★★ SELF CATERING

Compact apartment in recently restored Jacobite mansion. Set in 25 acres of woodland with superb views. Gleneagles 6 miles. Peacocks and small lake with swans nearby. Within 20 minutes of Stirling and 30 minutes of Perth. Ideal golfing or touring base.

Map Ref: 2B3

1 flat, 1 pub rm, 1 bedrm, sleeps 2, £195.00-£320.00, bus 1 ml, rail 9 mls, airport 42 mls

---

Auchtermuchty, Fife

Auchtermuchty Holiday Homes
6 Gladgate, Auchtermuchty, Fife, KY14 7AY
Tel: 01337 828496 Fax: 01592 751911
E-mail: auchtermuchty-holiday@dial.pipex.com
Web: www.auchtermuchty-holiday.com

★★★ UP TO ★★★★ SELF CATERING

Warm comfortable traditional style houses with private gardens. In a friendly rural town. Ground floor accommodation available.

Map Ref: 2C3

3 houses, 1-2 pub rms, 3 bedrms, sleeps 5-6, total sleeping capacity 16, £240.00-£540.00, Jan-Dec, bus nearby, rail 5 mls, airport 40 mls

---

Ballintuim, by Blairgowrie, Perthshire

Ballintuim Caravan Park
Ballintuim, Blairgowrie, PH10 7NH
Tel: 01250 886276

★★★ HOLIDAY PARK

18 acres, grassy, level, sloping, Jan-Dec, prior booking in peak periods, latest time of arrival 2200, overnight holding area. Extra charge for electricity, showers.

Map Ref: 2B1

Park accommodation: 90
24 tourers £8.00 or 6 motors £8.00 or 20 tents £5.00-£6.00. Total Touring Pitches 30.

4 Holiday Caravans to let, sleep 6 £150.00-£240.00, total sleeping capacity 24, min let 2 nights.

Leisure facilities:

Leave Blairgowrie on A93 to Braemar. Turn left at Bridge of Cally for 3 mls on A924 heading for Pitlochry.

Bankfoot, Perthshire

Mrs C McKay
Blair House, Main Street, Bankfoot, Perth, Perthshire, PH1 4AB
Tel/Fax: 01738 787338

★★ SELF CATERING

Stone built period cottage with modern interior. Spacious tiled and pine lined kitchen. Off street parking, and garden to rear. At centre of small village with hotels, restaurants, shops and hairdresser in walking distance. 10 miles N of Perth.

Map Ref: 2B2

1 cottage, 1 pub rm, 2 bedrms (All grd.floor), sleeps 5, from £200.00, Jan-Dec, bus 500 yds, rail 8 mls

VAT is shown at 17.5%: changes in this rate may affect prices.

Key to symbols is on back flap.

BLAIR ATHOLL

PERTHSHIRE, ANGUS AND DUNDEE AND THE KINGDOM OF FIFE

Blair Atholl, Perthshire

Map Ref: 4C12

BLAIR CASTLE CARAVAN PARK
BLAIR ATHOLL, PERTHSHIRE PH18 5SR
Tel: 01796 481263 for colour brochure **Fax: 01796 481587**

Have an unforgettable holiday in Highland Perthshire in one of our fully equipped luxury caravan holiday homes. All caravans are fully serviced with all mod cons, kitchen, shower room, lounge and up to three bedrooms.

Fishing, golf, pony trekking, mountain bikes available.

★★★★★ HOLIDAY PARK

Blair Castle Caravan Park
Blair Atholl, Perthshire, PH18 5SR
Tel: 01796 481263 Fax: 01796 481587

32 acres, mixed, Apr-Oct, prior booking in peak periods, latest time of arrival 2130, overnight holding area. Extra charge for electricity, awnings.

Park accommodation: 377

178 tourers £8.50-£10.00 and 35 motors £8.50-10.00 and 70 tents £8.50-10.00. Total Touring Pitches 283.

28 Holiday Caravans to let, sleep 2-6 £160.00-£350.00, total sleeping capacity 144, min let 3 nights.

Leisure facilities:

Take A9 N from Pitlochry. Turn off for Blair Atholl after 6 mls.

★★★ SELF CATERING

The Firs Lodge
The Firs, St Andrews Crescent, Blair Atholl, Perthshire, PH18 5TA
Tel: 01796 481256 Fax: 01796 481661

Lodge set in its own garden with off street parking.

1 log cabin, 1 pub rm, 2 bedrms (All grd.floor), sleeps 4, £170.00-£375.00, Jan-Dec, bus nearby, rail 500 yds

---

★★★ SELF CATERING

Mrs M MacDonald
Auchleeks, Trinafour, Pitlochry, Perthshire, PH18 5UF
Tel: 01796 483263 Fax: 01796 483337
E-mail: angus_macdonald@btconnect.com

Attractively furnished traditional stone cottage in Georgian stable block. Set amidst extensive grounds and beautiful scenery.

1 cottage, 2 pub rms, 3 bedrms (grd flr avail), sleeps 5-6, £230.00-£437.00, Jan-Dec, bus 5 mls, rail 8 mls

---

★★ SELF CATERING

Mrs Sandy Smith
Kincraigie Farm, Glen Fender, Blair Atholl, Perthshire, PH18 5TU
Tel: 01796 481286

Traditional stone built farm house set in open hill ground. Spectacular views. Convenient for fishing and all outdoor activities.

1 house, 1 pub rm, 3 bedrms (grd flr avail), sleeps 6, £200.00-£350.00, Jan-Dec, bus 2 mls, rail 2 mls, airport 90 mls

---

Important: Prices stated are estimates and may be subject to amendments

PERTHSHIRE, ANGUS AND DUNDEE AND THE KINGDOM OF FIFE

BLAIRGOWRIE

Blairgowrie, Perthshire Map Ref: 2B1

Blairgowrie Holiday Park
Rattray, Blairgowrie, Perthshire PH10 7AL
Telephone: 01250 872941 Fax: 01250 874535
e.mail: blairgowrie@holiday-parks.co.uk
Web: www.holiday-parks.co.uk

★★★★ SELF CATERING

Set in the heart of Perthshire our superb quality pine lodges are perfect for relaxing and enjoying the freedom of a self catering holiday on our beautifully landscaped holiday park. Ideal for touring the hills, lochs and glens of Perthshire or taking part in the huge range of activities locally.
Open all year.

★★★★ SELF CATERING

Blairgowrie Holiday Park
Rattray, Blairgowrie, Perthshire, PH10 7AL
Tel: 01250 872941 Fax: 01250 874535
E.mail: blairgowrie@holiday-parks.co.uk
Web: www.holiday-parks.co.uk

Pine lodges with high level of insulation and feature pine decoration situated in 15 acre holiday park with own supermarket, laundry facility, putting green and children's play area.

9 pinelodges, 1 pub rm, 2-3 bedrms, sleeps 4-6, total sleeping capacity 48, min let 3 nights, £215.00-£530.00, Jan-Dec, bus ½ ml, rail 14 mls, airport 50 mls

★★★ SELF CATERING

Mr Bradley
Glenshieling Lodge, Rattray, Blairgowrie, PH10 7HZ
Tel: 01250 874605

Conversion of former lodge in 2.5 acres of gardens and woodland of Glenshieling House Hotel. Town centre within easy reach.

1 house, 2 bedrms, sleeps 5, min let weekend, £150.00-£295.00, Jan-Dec, bus ½ ml, rail 16 mls

---

★★ SELF CATERING

Eastfield
New Road, Rattray, Blairgowrie, Perthshire, PH10 DJ
Tel/Fax: 01250 872105
E-mail: efield@globalnet.co.uk
Web: www.users.globalnet.co.uk/~efield

Stone built terraced cottage with private garden in quiet location close to town centre.

1 cottage, 1 pub rm, 2 bedrms, sleeps 4, min let weekend, £200.00-£389.00, Jan-Dec, bus nearby, rail 18 mls, airport 20 mls

★★ SELF CATERING

Mrs P J Elder
Pondfauld, Alyth Road, Blairgowrie, Perthshire, PH10 7HF
Tel: 01250 873284

Stone cottage and timber chalet on small holding situated on outskirts of Blairgowrie. Open views to beautiful countryside, ample space for children to play.

1 chalet, 1 cottage, 1 pub rm, 1 bedrm, sleeps 3-5, total sleeping capacity 8, min let 2 nights, £110.00-£185.00, Apr-Oct, bus 140 yds, rail 16 mls, airport 19 mls

---

VAT is shown at 17.5%: changes in this rate may affect prices. *Key to symbols is on back flap.*

BLAIRGOWRIE – BY BLAIRGOWRIE

PERTHSHIRE, ANGUS AND DUNDEE AND THE KINGDOM OF FIFE

Blairgowrie, Perthshire

Map Ref: 2B1

★★★★ SELF CATERING

Mrs Catharine Jones
Brooklinn Mill, Blairgowrie, Perthshire, PH10 6TB
Tel: 01250 873090

1 house, 2 pub rms, 4 bedrms, sleeps 8, £300.00-£515.00, Jan-Dec, bus 1 ml, rail 18 mls, airport 40 mls

Spacious modernised conversion of an old flax mill situated on the banks of the River Ericht. 1 mile (2kms) from the town. Owners live adjacent.

★★ SELF CATERING

Jean L Paterson
31 Mart Lane, Northmuir, Kirriemuir, Perthshire DD8 4TL
Tel/Fax: 01575 572506

1 cottage, 1 pub rm, 3 bedrms, sleeps 5, £120.00-£280.00, Jan-Dec, bus nearby

Cosy single storey cottage near centre of town. Sunny, enclosed patio to rear.

★★ UP TO ★★★ SELF CATERING

Mrs Catherine Peebles
Ericht Holiday Lodges, Balmoral Road, Blairgowrie, PH10 7AN
Tel: 01250 874686 Fax: 01250 875616
E-mail: ericht@compuserve.com

6 chalets, 1 pub rm, 2 bedrms, sleeps 4-6, total sleeping capacity 30, £190.00-£405.00, Jan-Dec, bus 500 yds

Lodges in quiet location 10 minutes walk from town centre and its amenities. Ideal base for touring Perthshire, hillwalking and skiing.

★★★ SELF CATERING

Mrs N Poole
Woodville, Mount Ericht Road, Rattray, Blairgowrie, Perthshire, PH10 7HS
Tel: 01250 875364

1 cottage, 1 pub rm, 2 bedrms, sleeps 5, £190.00-£230.00, Jan-Dec, bus 200 yds, rail 16 mls, airport 40 mls

Detached traditional stone built cottage with own garden in quiet location close to town centre. Non-smoking house.

---

by Blairgowrie, Perthshire

Map Ref: 2B1

UP TO ★★ SELF CATERING

Mrs Elizabeth Church
Rannagulzion House, Bridge of Cally, Blairgowrie, Perthshire, PH10 7JR
Tel: 01250 886359

2 cottages, 1 pub rm, 2-3 bedrms (grd flr avail), sleeps 5-6, total sleeping capacity 11, £160.00-£200.00, Apr-Jan, Xmas/New Year, bus 4 1/2 mls, rail 23 mls, airport 23 mls

Two semi-detached cottages on working hill farm set amidst rolling Perthshire countryside. Use of tennis court. Fishing available.

Important: Prices stated are estimates and may be subject to amendments

PERTHSHIRE, ANGUS AND DUNDEE AND THE KINGDOM OF FIFE

BRECHIN – CARNOUSTIE

Brechin, Angus

Map Ref: 4F12

★★ SELF CATERING

Mrs Stewart Sandeman
East Kintrockat, Brechin, Angus, DD9 6RP
Tel/Fax: 01356 622739

1 flat, 1 pub rm, 2 bedrms, sleeps 4, £200.00, Jan-Dec, bus ¼ ml, rail 10 mls

Pleasant, sunny, first floor conversion in 18th C courtyard, with river and farm walks. Ideal for Deeside castles and nearby beaches. Plenty of golf courses within easy reach.

Bridge of Cally, Perthshire

Map Ref: 2B1

★★ SELF CATERING

Patrick Dean Ltd
Estate Office, East Mere, Bracebridge Heath, Lincoln, LN4 2HU
Tel/Fax: 01250 886250

3 cottages, 1 pub rm, 2-3 bedrms (grd flr avail), sleeps 4-6, total sleeping capacity 15, £185.00-£350.00, Jan-Dec, bus 9 mls, rail 23 mls, airport 68 mls

Three cottages in picturesque countryside on a mixed livestock hill farm. Superb views down Glenshee, 3 miles (5kms) north of Bridge of Cally.

Bridge of Earn, Perthshire

Map Ref: 2B2

★★★★ SELF CATERING

River Edge Lodges (Mary McKay)
Bridge of Earn, Perth, Perthshire, PH2 9AB
Tel: 01738 812370 Fax: 01738 813161

11 log cabins, 1-2 pub rms, 1-3 bedrms, sleeps 2-8, total sleeping capacity 66, £155.00-£400.00, Jan-Dec, bus nearby, rail 4 mls, airport 40 mls

Comfortably furnished cedar lodges overlooking the River Earn and set in the scenic splendour of Perthshire. Situated in secluded grounds with outdoor pursuits such as cycling, walking, fishing, golf and other sports nearby. Four miles from Perth and easy access to St Andrews and Edinburgh.

Carnoustie, Angus

Map Ref: 2D2

★★★ SELF CATERING

Mrs McLean
45 Taymouth Street, Carnoustie
Tel: 01241 854546 Fax: 01241 410480
E-mail: thomas.mclean@virgin.net

1 cottage, 1 pub rm, 2 bedrms (All grd.floor), sleeps 4, min let weekend, £100.00-£320.00, Jan-Dec, bus 200 yds, rail ½ ml, airport 16 mls

Very comfortable furnished cottage. Ground level, recently modernised. Close to rail, bus, shops and golf courses. Ideal for golfing, family holiday or as a touring base for Angus hills and glens.

★★★★ SELF CATERING

Mr D Milne
11 Little Carron Gardens, St Andrews, Fife, KY16 8QL
Tel: 01334 479821
E-mail: doug@milne32.freeserve.co.uk
Web: www.milne32.freeserve.co.uk/index.htm

1 flat, 1 pub rm, 2 bedrms (All grd.floor), sleeps 4, £175.00-£300.00, Jan-Dec, bus nearby, rail ¼ ml

Spacious bright new ground floor apartment with private parking, situated adjacent to the golf course. Spectacular views, overlooking 18th green, and first tee of Carnoustie Championship Course.

VAT is shown at 17.5%: changes in this rate may affect prices.

Key to symbols is on back flap.

PERTHSHIRE, ANGUS AND DUNDEE AND THE KINGDOM OF FIFE

Carnoustie, Angus
Map Ref: 2D2

Mr & Mrs S Pape ★★★ SELF CATERING
The Old Manor, Panbride, Carnoustie, Angus, DD7 6JP
Tel: 01241 854804
E-mail: papemhr@btinternet.com

1 cottage, 1 pub rm, 2 bedrms (All grd.floor), sleeps 4-6, min let 1 night, £175.00-£400.00, Jan-Dec, bus ¼ ml, rail 1 ml

Attractive cottage in restored Manor House. Rural location convenient for town centre, golf and beach. Very well equipped with plenty extras. Ideal base for Tayside and the beautiful Angus Glens. Large garden and patio area with parking.

Mrs E Watson ★★ UP TO ★★★ SELF CATERING
Balhousie Farm, Carnoustie, Angus, DD7 6LG
Tel: 01241 853533 Fax: 01241 857533
E-mail: balhousie@msn.com

2 cottages, 1 pub rm, 2 bedrms (All grd.floor), sleeps 5, total sleeping capacity 5, from £170.00

Stone built detached adjacent farm cottages with small enclosed gardens situated on working farm 0.75 miles (1km) off main Dundee - Arbroath road (A92). Rural views, peaceful location within easy reach of numerous golf courses and many tourist attractions.

---

by Cellardyke, by Anstruther, Fife
Map Ref: 2D3

Mrs Catherine Greig, (The Loft) ★★★ SELF CATERING
Glenbervie, 29 Eastforth Street, Cellardyke, Anstruther, Fife, KY10 3AR
Tel: 01333 311065

1 cottage, 1 bedrm, sleeps 4, £175.00-£225.00, Jan-Dec

The loft is a converted former fisher dwelling nestling on a slope one hundred metres from the sea, in the East Neuk fishing village of Cellardyke. Excellent views across the Forth estuary towards the Isle of May. A short stroll from the harbour, Haven Pub and restaurant. Anstruther village is within one mile. Outdoor activities available.

Comrie, Perthshire
Map Ref: 2A2

Mrs Rosemary Dundas ★★★★ SELF CATERING
Comrie House, Comrie, Crieff, Perthshire, PH6 2LR
Tel/Fax: 01764 670640

1 self-contained wing of house, 2 pub rms, 2 bedrms, sleeps 4, min let 3 days, £190.00-£320.00, Jan-Dec, bus ¼ ml, rail 18 mls, airport 60 mls

Recently modernised and attractively furnished east wing of Comrie House. Situated beside the River Lednock and over the Lade stream which was used to generate electricity in earlier days. Access to garden, own entrance and completely self contained.

Mrs Susan Dyer ★★★★ SELF CATERING
Culticheldoch, Muthill, Crieff, Perthshire, PH5 2DD
Tel: 01764 681543
E-mail: sue.dyer@muthill.demon.co.uk
Web: http://rowallan.unitech.net.uk

1 cottage, 2 pub rms, 3 bedrms (All grd.floor), sleeps 6, £220.00-£400.00, Jan-Dec, bus nearby, rail 15 mls, airport 55 mls

Charming detached cottage situated in the delightful conservation village of Comrie. Tastefully furnished and decorated throughout, with all modern appliances provided. Private parking and large secure garden.

Important: Prices stated are estimates and may be subject to amendments

PERTHSHIRE, ANGUS AND DUNDEE AND THE KINGDOM OF FIFE

Comrie, Perthshire — Map Ref: 2A2

HOLIDAY PARK ★★★

West Lodge Caravan Park
Comrie, Perthshire, PH6 2LS
Tel/Fax: 01764 670354

Park accommodation: 60
20 tourers £9.00 or 20 motors £7.00-9.00 or 20 tents £8.00-9.00.
Total Touring Pitches 20.
6 Holiday Caravans to let, sleep 4-6 £100.00-200.00, total sleeping capacity 30, min let 1 night.

3½ acres, grassy, sheltered, Apr-Oct, prior booking in peak periods, latest time of arrival 2200, overnight holding area. Extra charge for electricity, awnings.

On A85 1 ml E of Comrie, 5 mls W of Crieff.

Cowdenbeath, Fife — Map Ref: 2B4

SELF CATERING ★★★

Mrs I Wilson
Lumphinnans Farm, Cowdenbeath, Fife, KY4 8HN
Tel/Fax: 01592 780279
E-mail: lumfarm@globalnet.co.uk

1 cottage, 1 pub rm, 3 bedrms (All grd.floor), sleeps 6, £200.00-£325.00, Jan-Dec, bus ½ ml, rail 2 mls, airport 20 mls

Comfortable cottage with enclosed garden on working mixed farm. Historic sites, golf and other sports, nature and eating out all within 6 mile radius. Centrally located, only 45 minutes drive to Edinburgh, St. Andrews and Stirling. 15 minutes to Dunfermline/Kirkcaldy.

Craigrothie, by Cupar, Fife — Map Ref: 2C3

SELF CATERING ★★★

Mr and Mrs A Oliphant
Shillinghill, Old Mill Road, Craigrothie, Fife, KY15 5PZ
Tel: 01334 828361 Fax: 01334 828088

1 cottage, 1 pub rm, 2 bedrms (All grd.floor), sleeps 4-5, £200.00-£250.00, Jan-Dec, bus 600 yds, rail 2½ mls, airport 40 mls

Well equipped modern cottage in quiet village, 8 miles (13 kms) from St Andrews and close to the quaint harbours of East Fife. Secure garage parking available.

Crail, Fife — Map Ref: 2D3

SELF CATERING ★★★

Mrs A Duffy
35 Rose Street, Dunfermline, Fife, KY12 0QT
Tel: 01383 723366

1 cottage, 2 pub rms, 2 bedrms (All grd.floor), sleeps 2-5, £200.00-£450.00, Mar-Nov, bus 1 ml, rail 10 mls

Charming country cottage with sea views and large garden. Convenient for village, golf and beaches. Easy access to Kingdom of Fife's coastal port walk and cycle routes. Child friendly garden and children's playhouse.

SELF CATERING ★★★

Mrs Margaret Muir
7 Lyle Green, Livingston, West Lothian, EH54 8QE
Tel: 01506 433678 Fax: 01506 441149

1 house, 2 pub rms, 3 bedrms, sleeps 6, min let 3 nights, £210.00-£410.00, Jan-Dec, bus ¾ ml, rail 15 mls, airport 50 mls

Attractive new, semi-detached villa in quality development, adjacent to open countryside and looking towards the sea, at edge of fishing village.

VAT is shown at 17.5%: changes in this rate may affect prices.

Key to symbols is on back flap.

CRAIL – BY CRIEFF

PERTHSHIRE, ANGUS AND DUNDEE AND THE KINGDOM OF FIFE

Crail, Fife — Map Ref: 2D3

★★ SELF CATERING

Mrs P L Taylor
20A Langhouse Green, Crail, Fife, KY10 3UD
Tel: 01333 450845

1 bungalow, 2 pub rms, 2 bedrms (All grd.floor), sleeps 4, min let 2 nights, £140.00-£295.00, Jan-Dec, bus nearby, rail 15 mls, airport 50 mls

Modern, centrally heated bungalow with small enclosed private garden. Quiet position in picturesque fishing village. All rooms on ground floor.

Crieff, Perthshire — Map Ref: 2A2

Loch Monzievaird Norwegian Chalets
Crieff, Perthshire PH7 4JR Tel: 01764 652586 Fax: 01764 652555
e.mail: monchalets@aol.com Web: www.monzievaird.com

The beautiful mature grounds at Loch Monzievaird are hidden away just two miles from the highland town of Crieff. Our Norwegian chalets are laid out amongst ancient oak, beech and scots pine. The chalets are private and well spread out, and all take advantage of differing elevated positions to enjoy the magnificent views over the loch. Walks right from your door, space and privacy.

Weekly rates from £225 (low season) to £575 (high season).

★★★★ SELF CATERING

★★★★ SELF CATERING

Mr S J S & Mrs D S Brown
Loch Monzievaird Chalets, Ochtertyre, Crieff, Perthshire, PH7 4JR
Tel: 01764 652586 Fax: 01764 652555
E-mail: monchalets@aol.com
Web: www.monzievaird.com

23 chalets, 2 pub rms, 2-3 bedrms (grd flr avail), sleeps 2-8, total sleeping capacity 136, min let 2 nights, £225.00-£575.00, Jan-Dec, bus 500 yds, rail 10 mls, airport 30 mls

Quiet relaxation or an active holiday are both assured on this magnificent setting of 40 acres of parkland overlooking Loch Monzievaird. A mature wooded site offering seclusion to a range of pine chalets, all with open plan kitchen/living/dining area and covered deck. Tennis court, fishing, childrens play area on site and wide range of activities in area.

★★★ UP TO ★★★★★ SELF CATERING

Crieff Hydro Ltd
Crieff, Perthshire, PH7 3LQ
Tel: 01764 655555 Fax: 01764 653087

15 chalets, 8 cottages, 1-2 pub rms, 2-3 bedrms (grd flr avail), sleeps 1-6, total sleeping capacity 142, min let 2 nights, from £100.00, Jan-Dec, bus 1 ml, rail 17 mls, airport 60 mls

Chalets, cottages and lodges in hillside woodland setting in grounds of hotel. Sporting and leisure facilities of hotel available free to occupants.

by Crieff, Perthshire — Map Ref: 2A2

★ SELF CATERING

Mrs R E MacAskill
Kaimknowe, Glendevon, by Dollar, Clackmannanshire, FK14 7JZ
Tel: 01259 781331

1 cottage, 2 pub rms, 2 bedrms, sleeps 4, £140.00-£180.00, Apr-Oct, bus 800 yds, rail 9 mls, airport 50 mls

Fifty year old cottage on working farm. Peaceful setting. 2 miles (3kms) out of Crieff. Ideal for touring, golfing, walking, and fishing.

Important: Prices stated are estimates and may be subject to amendments

PERTHSHIRE, ANGUS AND DUNDEE AND THE KINGDOM OF FIFE

CUPAR – BY CUPAR

Cupar, Fife — Map Ref: 2C3

Hilton of Carslogie

Booking Enquiries: J G Lang & Son, Hilton of Carslogie, Cupar, Fife, KY15 4NG
Tel: 01334 652113 Fax: 01334 656710

SCOTTISH TOURIST BOARD INSPECTED — HOLIDAY CARAVAN

Park accommodation:

2 Holiday Caravans to let, sleep 6 £130.00-210.00, total sleeping capacity 12, min let weekend, Apr-Oct.

2 mls W of Cupar on A91, opposite Scotts Porridge Oats factory.

---

by Cupar, Fife — Map Ref: 2C3

C B Addison-Scott

Kinloss House, Cupar, Fife, KY15 4ND
Tel: 01505 654169 Fax: 01505 613304

★★★★ SELF CATERING

Clinkmill Cottage is tastefully modernised, situated in a grade B listed building on a working farm near the market town of Cupar.

2 cottages, 2 pub rms, 2-3 bedrms, sleeps 4-6, total sleeping capacity 10, £250.00-£450.00, Jan-Dec, bus 1 ml, rail 1 1/2 mls

---

Morna Chrisp

Scotstarvit Farm, by Cupar, Fife, KY15 5PA
Tel/Fax: 01334 653591

★★ SELF CATERING

Spacious, stone-built cottage set in beautiful countryside beside a working farm. Enclosed sheltered gardens with garden furniture. Scotstarvit Tower and Hill of Tarvit Mansion House are on the doorstep. Well placed for golfing or touring. All ground floor rooms.

1 cottage, 1 pub rm, 3 bedrms (All grd.floor), sleeps 4-5, £160.00-£300.00, Jan-Dec, bus 1/2 ml, rail 2 mls, airport 40 mls

---

Mrs A Fotheringham

Rumgally House, by Cupar, KY15 5SY
Tel/Fax: 01334 653388
E-mail: cbf@sol.co.uk
Web: www.sol.co.uk/r/rumgally/

★★ SELF CATERING

An attractive white washed cottage tucked away in the historic town centre yet with a quiet secluded garden. Restaurants and shops are on the doorstep. Golf and beach a 10 minute walk.

1 cottage, 2 pub rms, 2 bedrms (grd flr avail), sleeps 6, £250.00-£350.00, mid Jun-mid Sep, bus nearby, rail 3 mls, airport 10 mls

---

Mr & Mrs Wedderburn

FREEPOST, Mountquhanie Estate, Cupar, KY15 4BR
Tel: 01382 330318 Fax: 01382 330480
E-mail: enquiries@standrews-cottages.com
Web: www.standrews-cottages.com

★★★ UP TO ★★★★★ SELF CATERING

Idyllic cottages and luxury farmhouses. Private walks. Abundant wildlife. Blazing log fires. Relax explore or golf.

6 houses, 3 flats, 3 cottages, 1-2 pub rms, 2-6 bedrms (grd flr avail), sleeps 4-14, total sleeping capacity 140, £195.00-£955.00, Jan-Dec, bus 2 mls, rail 5 mls, airport 45 mls

---

VAT is shown at 17.5%: changes in this rate may affect prices.

Key to symbols is on back flap.

DUNDEE – BY DUNKELD

PERTHSHIRE, ANGUS AND DUNDEE AND THE KINGDOM OF FIFE

Dundee, Angus
Map Ref: 2C2

UP TO ★★ SELF CATERING

Accommodation Office
University of Abertay Dundee, Bell Street, Dundee, DD1 1HG
Tel: 01382 308059 Fax: 01382 308877
E-mail: accommo@tay.ac.uk

Centrally located accommodation in the University Residences. Three sites esily accessible by public transport. Private parking at Alloway site. All sites within distance of shops. Carnoustie, St Andrews and Perth all within a half hour drive.

30 flats, 1 pub rm, 2-9 bedrms (grd flr avail), sleeps 2-9, total sleeping capacity 350, min let 1 night, from £80.50, Jun-Aug, bus 500 yds, rail 3 mls, airport 4 mls

---

★★ SELF CATERING

Mrs S E Baird
Scotston, Auchterhouse, Dundee, Angus, DD3 0QT
Tel: 01382 320286

Secluded log house on working farm. 9 miles (14kms) north west of Dundee. Panoramic views to Sidlaw Hills, sheltered south facing garden.

1 log cabin, 1 pub rm, 3 bedrms (All grd.floor), sleeps 6, £155.00-£295.00, Jan-Dec, bus 2 mls, rail 10 mls, airport 9 mls

---

★★★★ SELF CATERING

Kingennie Woodland Lodges
Kingennie Fishings, Kingennie, Broughty Ferry, Dundee, DD5 3RD
Tel: 01382 350777 Fax: 01382 350400
E-mail: kingennie@easynet.co.uk

New lodges, equipped to a high standard, in 12 acre woodland setting, overlooking idyllic trout fishing lochs. One lodge kitted out for disabled use.

3 chalets, 4-5 pub rms, 2-3 bedrms (grd flr avail), sleeps 6-8, total sleeping capacity 20, £200.00-£470.00, Jan-Dec, bus ½ ml, rail 6 mls, airport 7 mls

---

by Dunkeld, Perthshire
Map Ref: 2B1

Wester Riechip
Laighwood, Butterstone, Dunkeld, Perthshire PH8 0HB
Telephone: 01350 724241   Fax: 01350 724259

Self-cater in style in this superior detached house set amidst the Perthshire Hills. Spectacular panoramic views.
Comfortably accommodating eight for a holiday to remember.
For smaller groups requiring a cottage or flat see Laighwood Self-Catering.

★★★★ SELF CATERING

W & W I Bruges
Laighwood, Dunkeld, Perthshire, PH8 0HB
Tel: 01350 724241 Fax: 01350 724259

Former 19c shooting lodge in a remote situation with stunning views. Very comfortable. Shooting, fishing, squash available. Dunkeld 6 miles (10kms).

1 house, 3 pub rms, 4 bedrms, sleeps 8, £384.00-£570.00, Jan-Dec, bus 1½ mls, rail 6 mls, airport 70 mls

---

Important: Prices stated are estimates and may be subject to amendments

PERTHSHIRE, ANGUS AND DUNDEE AND THE KINGDOM OF FIFE

BY DUNKELD

by Dunkeld, Perthshire **Map Ref: 2B1**

★★★★ SELF CATERING

Mrs D B Court
51 Bennochy Road, Kirkcaldy, Fife, KY2 5QZ
Tel/Fax: 01592 264369
E-mail: 105527.1042@compuserve.com

1 cottage, 1 pub rm, 2 bedrms, sleeps 4, £195.00-£330.00, Jan-Dec, bus ¼ ml, rail ½ ml

Former coach house, now a Listed building with sheltered patio and south facing garden, on edge of small village.

★★★ UP TO ★★★★ SELF CATERING

Kinnaird
Kinnaird Estate, by Dunkeld, Perthshire
Tel: 01796 482440
E-mail: enquiry@kinnairdestate.com
Web: www.kinnairdestate.com

7 cottages, £375.00-£900.00, Jan-Dec, bus 3 mls, rail 7 mls, airport 50 mls

Eight charmingly furnished individually styled cottages in secluded locations in a 9000 acre estate, set in the spectacular Perthshire countryside. Many of the facilities and services available to guests at Kinnaird luxury hotel, are also available to cottage guests.

★★★ SELF CATERING

Laighwood Self-Catering
Laighwood, Dunkeld, Perthshire, PH8 0HB
Tel: 01350 724241 Fax: 01350 724259

2 flats, 2 cottages, 1-2 pub rms, 2-3 bedrms (grd flr avail), sleeps 3-4, total sleeping capacity 15, £130.00-£275.00, Apr-Oct, bus 4 mls, rail 5 mls

Two flats adjoining Butterglen House and two houses, all in idyllic tranquil settings. Central for touring. Ideal for walking and fishing.

★★★ SELF CATERING

Mrs S Mason
North Moor House, North Moor Road, Walkeringham, Doncaster, DN10 4W
Tel/Fax: 01427 890680

1 cottage, 1 pub rm, 3 bedrms (grd flr avail), sleeps 6, £200.00-£350.00, Jan-Dec

Sympathetically renovated Victorian farm cottage with magnificent rural views. Accessed by 1 mile of bumpy farm track. Superb peaceful situation, yet only 15 min drive from Dunkeld.

★★★ SELF CATERING

Mrs G Scott
Craig View, 17 West Shore, St Monans, Fife, KY10 2BT
Tel: 01333 730893

1 cottage, 2 pub rms, 3 bedrms, sleeps 6, £240.00-£350.00, Jan-Dec, bus 2 mls, rail 2 mls

Renovated cottage, a mixture of old and new, in 1 acre of garden opening out onto extensive woodland walks. Open log fires in the lounge.

VAT is shown at 17.5%: changes in this rate may affect prices.

Key to symbols is on back flap.

BY DUNKELD – DYKEHEAD

PERTHSHIRE, ANGUS AND DUNDEE AND THE KINGDOM OF FIFE

---

by Dunkeld, Perthshire — Map Ref: 2B1

★★ SELF CATERING

Mrs M Thomson
135 Grahamsdyke Street, Laurieston, Falkirk, Stirlingshire, FK2 9LP
Tel: 01324 625019
E-mail: destecroix@aol.com

Log cabin on secluded wooded site close to small village of Butterstone. 4 miles (6kms) from Dunkeld. Ideal for fishing, shooting and walking.

1 log cabin, 1 pub rm, 3 bedrms, sleeps 6, £200.00-£395.00, Jan-Dec, bus 4 mls, rail 4 mls, airport 60 mls

---

Dunning, Perthshire — Map Ref: 2B3

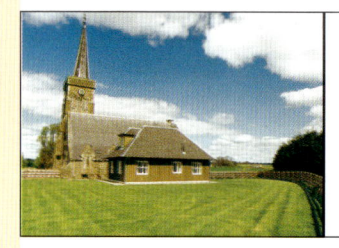

DUNCRUB HOLIDAYS
Dalreoch, Dunning, Perthshire PH2 0QJ
Tel: 01764 684368   Fax: 01764 684633
e.mail: dalreoch@globalnet.co.uk   Web: www.duncrub-holidays.com

A warm welcome awaits visitors to our family run holiday homes. Historic chapel apartments and farm cottages sleeping 2-6. Set in the beautiful Strathearn Valley, this is the ideal setting from which to explore Scotland's glorious scenery, historic and culture. Excellent golf locally (Gleneagles courses 7 miles). Short breaks available.

★★★ UP TO ★★★★★ SELF CATERING

Duncrub Holidays
Dalreoch, Dunning, Perthshire, PH2 0QJ
Tel: 01764 684368 Fax: 01764 684633
E-mail: dalreoch@globalnet.co.uk
Web: www.duncrub-holidays.com

Selection of family run properties set in parklands and farm in rural Perthshire. Indoor facilities on site. Country sports by arrangement. Golf nearby. Two properties form part of a unique 19th century listed chapel.

3 houses, 1 cottage, 1-2 pub rms, 1-3 bedrms (grd flr avail), sleeps 2-6, total sleeping capacity 16, min let 2 nights, £120.00-£480.00, Jan-Dec, bus ½ ml, rail 10 mls, airport 40 mls

---

Dunshalt, Fife — Map Ref: 2C3

★★★★ SELF CATERING

Mrs F Watson
Homelands, Auchtermuchty Road, Dunshalt, Fife, KY14 7ET
Tel: 01337 828874

Recently converted stable adjacent to owner's house. Pleasant private garden and gazebo. Easy access to East Neuk villages and many golf courses and M90 to Perth. Tay Bridge 20 minutes and Forth Road Bridge 35 mins drive. Shop 500 yards, pub 1 mile.

1 cottage, 1 pub rm, 1 bedrm (All grd.floor), sleeps 2, £160.00-£322.00, Jan-Dec, bus nearby, rail 2 mls, airport 30 mls

---

Dykehead, Cortachy, Angus — Map Ref: 4E12

★★ SELF CATERING

Mr R MacAlister
St Kessog's Rectory, High Street, Auchterarder Perthshire, PH3 1AD
Tel/Fax: 01764 662525

Traditional cottages, now tastefully modernised, in a rural setting. Centrally located for touring the castles of Angus and Deeside.

3 cottages, 1 pub rm, 2-4 bedrms (grd flr avail), sleeps 4-6, total sleeping capacity 14, £240.00-£465.00, Apr-Oct, bus nearby, rail 20 mls, airport 20 mls

---

Important: Prices stated are estimates and may be subject to amendments

PERTHSHIRE, ANGUS AND DUNDEE AND THE KINGDOM OF FIFE

ELIE – FEARNAN, BY KENMORE

Elie, Fife

Map Ref: 2D3

★★★★ SELF CATERING

Mrs Sally Pattullo
The Park, Bank Street, Elie, Fife, KY9 1BW
Tel: 01333 330219

Variety of self catering cottages situated in small coastal village yards from long sandy beach and with two golf courses close by. Easy access to coastal path and cycle way also tennis and watersports. Plenty to do for all members of the family with many diverse activities on the door step plus good pubs and restaurants with excellent seafood.

4 cottages, 1-2 pub rms, 2-4 bedrms, sleeps 2-8, £100.00-£480.00pw, Jan-Dec, bus ½ ml, rail 16 mls, airport 45 mls.

★★ SELF CATERING

Tom D R Reekie
22 Carlton Place, Aberdeen, AB15 4BQ
Tel: 01224 642263 Fax: 01224 639773

Comfortably furnished with own garden. Off street parking available. Excellent location, 50 metres from beach. Close to golf course and other sports facilities.

1 cottage, 2 pub rms, 2 bedrms, sleeps 5, min let weekend, £150.00-£320.00, Jan-Dec, bus 200 yds, rail 15 mls, airport 40 mls

---

Enochdhu, by Pitlochry, Perthshire

Map Ref: 4D12

★★ SELF CATERING

Ardle Crichton
Cleireach, Middle Road, Rattray, Blairgowrie
Tel: 01250 874880 Fax: 01250 876622

A characterful stone built traditional farm cottage with two bedrooms, lounge with open fire, and a spacious kitchen. A fenced garden with barbeque. Winter lets get free oil fired stove and heating. A lovely peaceful retreat in a scenic area with a wide range of outdoor activities available. Pitlochry 10 miles, Blairgowrie 15 miles.

1 cottage, 1 pub rm, 2 bedrms, sleeps 4, min let weekend, £120.00-£360.00, Jan-Dec, bus 10 mls, rail 10 mls, ferry 200 mls, airport 30 mls

---

Fearnan, by Kenmore, Perthshire

Map Ref: 2A1

★★★ SELF CATERING

Mr MacLean
Clach an Tuirc, Fearnan, Aberfeldy, Perthshire, PH15 2PG
Tel/Fax: 01887 830615

Early 19c cottage situated on edge of scenic Fearnan on Loch Tayside. Ideal location for all outdoor pursuits. Coal or wood fire.

1 cottage, 2 pub rms, 2 bedrms, sleeps 4, £150.00-£300.00, Jan-Dec, rail 25 mls, airport 75 mls, cot available

---

★★ SELF CATERING

Mr McLaren
Pier View, Fearnan, Aberfeldy, Perthshire, PH15 2PF
Tel: 01887 830676

Tigh Beag, a single storey flat adjacent to owners dwelling, is situated on the north side of the Kenmore to Killin road within its own garden area. On the south side of the road the garden extends down to the shore of Loch Tay from which boats may be launched and fishing is permitted.

1 cottage, 1 pub rm, 1 bedrm (All grd.floor), sleeps 2, £140.00-£210.00, Jan-Dec, bus 10 mls, rail 25 mls, airport 70 mls

---

VAT is shown at 17.5%: changes in this rate may affect prices.

Key to symbols is on back flap.

FORFAR – FORTINGALL

PERTHSHIRE, ANGUS AND DUNDEE AND THE KINGDOM OF FIFE

Forfar, Angus

Mrs Patricia Gandy
Castle Cottage, Balgavies, Forfar, Angus, DD8 2TH
Tel: 01307 818535 Fax: 01334 838899
E-mail: bruce.gandy@curtisfinepapers.com

★★★ SELF CATERING

Comfortable and spacious single storey 3 bedroomed cottage enjoying 13 acres of pasture and woodland in lovely Angus countryside. Ideal base for touring, recreation or just relaxing.

Map Ref: 2D1

1 cottage, 1 pub rm, 3 bedrms (All grd.flr), sleeps 6, £180.00-£280.00, Jan-Dec, bus 1/2 ml, rail 10 mls, airport 20 mls.

Mrs Jane Skea
Dykehead, Burnside, by Forfar, Angus, DD8 2RY
Tel: 01307 818900 Fax: 01307 818149

★★★★ SELF CATERING

Recently renovated small farm house on working farm. Rural location yet only 3 miles from Forfar. Loch fishing and golfing nearby. Woodland walks within the farm. Games room with pool table, darts and table tennis, adjacent to property. Ideal for family holidays.

1 house, 1 pub rm, 3 bedrms (grd flr avail), sleeps 6, £250.00-£350.00, Jan-Dec, bus 1 1/2 mls, rail 12 mls, airport 70 mls

---

by Forfar, Angus

Hunter Cabins, Bruce Hunter
Forfar, Angus, DD8 2SZ Tel/Fax: 01307 463101
E-mail: hunter@spero.demon.co.uk
Web: www.scotland2000.com/hunters

★★★ SELF CATERING

Family run cedarwood cabins 5 miles North of Forfar, set in a tranquil elevated meadow overlooking the South Esk with glorious panoramic views of the Angus Glens. Ideal location for touring, golf, fishing, rambling, bird watching and castle haunting. Two or three bedroomed units, all linen provided, cots, video available but cost extra, pets welcome. Fully equipped kitchen with microwave. Ample play area for children also BBQ.

Map Ref: 2D1

3 chalets, 1 pub rm, 2-3 bedrms (grd flr avail), sleeps 6-8, total sleeping capacity 22, £180.00-£390.00, Jan-Dec, bus 2 mls, rail 15 mls, airport 15 mls

---

Fortingall, Perthshire

Mrs Anne Stark
Craigard, Aberfeldy, Perthshire, PH15 2LB
Tel: 01887 829767

★★★★ SELF CATERING

Thatched cottage with quiet enclosed garden situated in historic village at the foot of Glen Lyon. Loch Tay 2 miles (3kms).

Map Ref: 2A1

1 cottage, 2 pub rms, 2 bedrms, sleeps 4-5, £175.00-£375.00, Jan-Dec, bus 10 mls, rail 20 mls

---

Important: Prices stated are estimates and may be subject to amendments

Foss, by Pitlochry, Perthshire — Map Ref: 2A1

Drumnakyle Farmhouse
Drumnakyle, Foss, Pitlochry, Perthshire PH16 5NJ
Tel: 01882 634281   Web: come.to/drumnakyle

Fairytale Highland Farmhouse in stunning location. Panoramic views over Loch Tummel (Queens view in reverse). Sleeps 8 spaciously in four bedrooms (one en-suite). Large conservatory south-facing to forest and Schiehallion (1083 m). Well-appointed open-plan kitchen. Woodburning stove $1/4$ mile along hillside track. Ospreys and wondrous wildlife in vicinity.

★★★★ SELF CATERING

Dr & Mrs Allan Forsyth
Drumnakyle, Foss, Pitlochry, Perthshire, PH16 5NJ
Tel: 01882 634281
Web: http://come.to/drumnakyle

An early 18c stone built farmhouse of interesting character, lovingly restored. In isolated position with superb views.

1 house, 2 pub rms, 4 bedrms (grd flr avail), sleeps 8, £540.00-£790.00, Apr-Oct, bus 2 mls, rail 11 mls, airport 75 mls

---

Glenesk, by Edzell, Angus — Map Ref: 4F12

★ UP TO ★★ SELF CATERING

Blakes Cottages (Ref SM16)
Stoneybank Road, Earby, Colne, Lancashire, BB8 6PR
Tel: 01282 445544 Fax: 01356 623725

A selection of cottages, rural locations in scenic Glenesk. Plenty of walks, fauna, wildlife and boat fishing on Loch Lee. Summer events include sheep dog trials and ceilidhs.

3 cottages, 1 pub rm, 2-4 bedrms, sleeps 3-6, total sleeping capacity 13, £190.00-£470.00, Jan-Dec, bus 19 mls, rail 30 mls, airport 90 mls

---

Glenfarg, Perthshire — Map Ref: 2B3

★★★ SELF CATERING

Mrs J D S Baillie
Colliston, Glenfarg, Perthshire, PH2 9PE
Tel: 01577 830434

Comfortable cottage with full central heating set on working farm amidst scenic countryside. Good location for touring. 10 miles (16kms) south of Perth and under an hours drive to the centre of Edinburgh. Secluded garden with picnic table.

1 cottage, 1 pub rm, 2 bedrms (All grd.floor), sleeps 4, £150.00-£398.00, Jan-Dec, bus $1/4$ ml, rail 10 mls, airport 25 mls

---

VAT is shown at 17.5%: changes in this rate may affect prices.   *Key to symbols is on back flap.*

GLENFARG – GLENISLA

PERTHSHIRE, ANGUS AND DUNDEE AND THE KINGDOM OF FIFE

Glenfarg, Perthshire

Map Ref: 2B3

Glenfarg Properties Ltd
Glenfarg House, Glenfarg, Perthshire PH2 9PT
Tel: 01738 850708 Fax: 01738 850661
e.mail: Biddlecombe@glenfarg-house.demon.co.uk

East wing of Scottish country house plus two converted coach houses set in eight acres of private grounds with spectacular views over the surrounding hills.

Ideal touring base within easy reach of Edinburgh, St Andrews and the Highlands. 10 minutes from Perth, all properties have large living areas, modern kitchens with automatic washing machines and tumble driers.

Cottages can be adapted to suit parties or families of ten people.

Price includes lighting, heating and bed linen. Sorry no pets.

Open January to December, £275 to £650 per week.

★★★ SELF CATERING

Glenfarg Properties
Glenfarg House, Glenfarg, Perthshire, PH29PT
Tel: 01738 850708 Fax: 01738 850661
E-mail: Biddlecombe@glenfarg-house.demon.co.uk

Beautifully restored, Scottish country house and courtyard development, with extensive grounds. Spectacular views over the surrounding area. Perth 8 miles, Edinburgh 40 miles. St Andrews 30 miles.

2 cottages, 1 east wing of house, 1-3 pub rms, 2-5 bedrms (grd flr avail), sleeps 4-10, total sleeping capacity 18, £275.00-£650.00, Jan-Dec, bus ½ ml, rail 6 mls, airport 30 mls

★★ SELF CATERING

Mrs M MacLean
Arngask House, Glenfarg, Perth, PH2 9QA
Tel/Fax: 01577 830311

Traditional stone semi-detached cottage, sleeps 2/3. Quiet outlook with private area in front. One mile from Glenfarg village. Central for touring in any direction - Edinburgh, St Andrews, Perth and Stirling. The cottage is all on one floor.

1 bungalow, 1 pub rm, 1 bedrm, sleeps 2-3, £120.00-£210.00, Jan-Dec, bus ½ ml, rail 10 mls, airport 30 mls

---

Glenisla, Angus

Map Ref: 4D12

★★★ UP TO ★★★★ SELF CATERING

Mrs M Clark
Purgavie Farm, Glenisla, Kirriemuir, Angus, DD8 5HZ
Tel: 01575 560213/0860 392794 (mobile)
Fax: 01575 560213
E-mail: purgavie@aol.com

Log chalet and bungalow, on mixed farm at the foot of Glen Isla, close to Lintrathen Loch. Ideal base for touring and all outdoor pursuits. Many golf courses within easy reach. 7 miles from Kirriemuir - home of J M Barrie (Peter Pan).

1 log cabin, 1 bungalow, 1 pub rm, 2-3 bedrms (grd flr avail), sleeps 4-6, total sleeping capacity 12, £200.00-£400.00, Jan-Dec, bus 7 mls, rail 23 mls, airport 23 mls

---

Important: Prices stated are estimates and may be subject to amendments

PERTHSHIRE, ANGUS AND DUNDEE AND THE KINGDOM OF FIFE

GLENLYON – GLENSHEE

153

Glenlyon, Perthshire   Map Ref: 1H1

Innerwick Estate
Innerwick Garden Flat, Glen Lyon, Aberfeldy, Perthshire PH15 2PP
Tel: 01887 866222 Fax: 01887 866301
Three traditional stone-built self-catering cottages offering peace without isolation in National Scenic Area. Good for walkers, birdwatchers and botanists. Fishing in River Lyon during season. Tennis court available. Water sports and golf within 30 minutes. Open all year. Prices from £150-£420. Weekends (Nov-March) from £100. Brochure available.

★★★★ SELF CATERING

Mrs M Marshall
Garden Flat, Innerwick, Glenlyon, Aberfeldy, Perthshire, PH15 2PP
Tel: 01887 866222 Fax: 01887 866301

1 house, 2 cottages, 1-2 pub rms, 2-3 bedrms (grd flr avail), sleeps 4-6, total sleeping capacity 16, £150.00-£400.00, Jan-Dec, bus 18 mls, rail 33 mls, airport 95 mls

Stone built cottages and farmhouse with open fires, situated in a national scenic area. Peaceful but not isolated.

★ SELF CATERING

S Chesthill Est, per Mrs Pirie
Keepers Cottage, Chesthill, Glenlyon, Perthshire, PH15 2NH
Tel: 01887 877233

1 cottage, 2 pub rms, 2 bedrms, sleeps 4, £175.00-£225.00, Jan-Dec, bus 11 mls, rail 28 mls

Former gardener's cottage on privately owned sporting estate, set amidst rugged scenery of Glen Lyon, 12 miles (19kms) from Aberfeldy.

Glenshee, Perthshire   Map Ref: 4D12

★★★ SELF CATERING

Mrs Burke
Dalnaglar Castle, Glenshee, Blairgowrie, Perthshire, PH10 7LP
Tel: 01250 882232 Fax: 01250 882277
E-mail: dalnaglar@zetnet.co.uk
Web: www.castles-scotland.com

1 east wing of castle, 3 pub rms, 11 bedrms, sleeps 20, min let 2 nights, from £2100.00, Jan-Dec, bus 14 mls, rail 30 mls, airport 70 mls

East wing of baronial style castle set amidst beautiful scenery of Glenshee.

★★★ SELF CATERING

The Compass Christian Centre
Glenshee Lodge, Glenshee, Blairgowrie, Perthshire, PH10 7QD
Tel: 01250 885209 Fax: 01250 885309
E-mail: compass@compasschristian.co.uk
Web: www.compasschristian.co.uk

1 flat, 3 bed sitting rooms, 1-2 bedrms (grd flr avail), sleeps 2-5, total sleeping capacity 14, £56.00-£302.00, Jan-Dec, bus 17 mls, rail 35 mls

Refurbished 19c former coach house set in 14 acres of Highland estate. Wide range of indoor and outdoor sporting activities.

VAT is shown at 17.5%: changes in this rate may affect prices.   *Key to symbols is on back flap.*

GLENSHEE – KELTY

PERTHSHIRE, ANGUS AND DUNDEE AND THE KINGDOM OF FIFE

Glenshee, Perthshire
Map Ref: 4D12

Dalmunzie Highland Cottages
Spittal o' Glenshee, Blairgowrie, Perthshire PH10 7QG
Telephone: 01250 885226   Fax: 01250 885225
e.mail: dalmunzie@aol.com

Seven traditional stonebuilt cottages set on 6,000-acre sporting estate with log fires, well-equipped kitchens, bed linen included. Ideal base for touring the Highlands or for shooting, fishing, tennis, walking, pony-trekking, and our own 9-hole golf course. Excellent catering at nearby Dalmunzie House Hotel.

★★ SELF CATERING

Dalmunzie Highland Cottages
Spittal of Glenshee, Blairgowie, PH10 7QG
Tel: 01250 885226 Fax: 01250 885225
E-mail: dalmunzie@aol.com

Stone built cottages of individual style and character on 6000 acre shooting estate. 9 hole golf course, shooting, fishing, pony trekking, tennis and hill walking.

7 cottages, 1-2 pub rms, 1-3 bedrms (grd flr avail), sleeps 2-6, total sleeping capacity 30, £150.00-£430.00, Jan-Dec, bus 22 mls, rail 36 mls, airport 80 mls

---

UP TO ★★ SELF CATERING

Finegand Estate Ltd
Finegand Farm, Glenshee, Perthshire, PH10 7QB
Tel/Fax: 01250 885234

Traditional cottages individually sited on working farm in famous Highland Glen. Ideal for fishing, walking and skiing. Most have wonderful views, and are accessed by rough farm track.

5 cottages, 1-3 pub rms, 2-4 bedrms, sleeps 3-8, total sleeping capacity 29, £136.30-£258.50, Jan-Dec, bus 15 mls, rail 30 mls, airport 70 mls

---

Guthrie, by Forfar, Angus
Map Ref: 2D1

★★★★ SELF CATERING

Mrs C Shand
Crosshill, Guthrie, Forfar, Angus, DD8 2TL
Tel: 01241 828548

Pretty and charming set in private garden with magnificent views across valley. Completely modernised and refurbished to an excellent and luxurious standard. Ideal base for recreation and touring. St Andrews, Dundee and Aberdeen all within an hours drive.

1 cottage, 2 pub rms, 2 bedrms (All grd.floor), sleeps 4, £175.00-£300.00, Jan-Dec, bus nearby, rail 8 mls

---

Kelty, Fife
Map Ref: 2B4

★★ SELF CATERING

Mrs B Constable
Benarty House, Kelty, Fife, KY4 0HT
Tel/Fax: 01383 830235

Steading cottage on farm. Peaceful woodland setting in country park. Fishing, golf, gliding, water sports, riding and adventure playground all close by. Convenient for travel to Dundee, Edinburgh, Stirling, Perth and St. Andrews.

1 cottage, 1 pub rm, 3 bedrms (All grd.floor), sleeps 6, £175.00-£300.00, Jan-Dec, bus 1 1/2 mls, rail 6 mls, airport 20 mls

---

Important: Prices stated are estimates and may be subject to amendments

PERTHSHIRE, ANGUS AND DUNDEE AND THE KINGDOM OF FIFE

KENMORE – KINLOCH RANNOCH

Kenmore, Perthshire

SELF CATERING ★★★★

D Menzies and Partners
Taymouth Farm Cottages, Mains of Taymouth, Kenmore, Aberfeldy, Perthshire, PH15 2HN
Tel: 01887 830226 Fax: 01887 830211
E-mail: cottages@taymouth.co.uk
Web: www.taymouth.co.uk

Stone built cottages in courtyard setting close to loch/village. Own golf course, bowling and putting greens. Bistro Bar with games room.

Map Ref: 2A1

4 cottages, 1-3 pub rms, 2-4 bedrms (grd flr avail), sleeps 3-8, total sleeping capacity 27, £300.00-£900.00, Jan-Dec, bus 6 mls, rail 30 mls, airport 80 mls

---

Kilconquhar, by Elie, Fife

SELF CATERING ★★★★

Mrs Patricia McCune
28 Colquhoun Street, Helensburgh, G84 8UJ
Tel: 01436 671362 Fax: 01436 674576
E-mail: emcairns@aol.com

Terraced cottage in picturesque village. Quiet location yet easy access to many local attractions. St Andrews 11 miles. Edinburgh within 1 hours drive.

Map Ref: 2D3

1 cottage, 1 pub rm, 2 bedrms (All grd.floor), sleeps 4, £250.00-£350.00, Jan-Dec, bus nearby

---

Killiecrankie, Perthshire

SELF CATERING ★★★

Old Faskally Chalets
Old Faskally, Killiecrankie, Pitlochry, Perthshire, PH16 5LR
Tel/Fax: 01796 473436

Timber chalets in woodland setting, with fine views to Blair Atholl and the Grampians. Blair Atholl 4 miles (5kms), Pitlochry 4 miles (6kms).

Map Ref: 4C12

5 chalets, 1 pub rm, 2 bedrms, sleeps 4, total sleeping capacity 20, £230.00-£355.00, Jan-Dec, bus 4 mls, rail 4 mls, airport 75 mls

---

SELF CATERING ★★★★

Joan Troup
The Old Mill, Acharn, Aberfeldy, PH15 2HS
Tel: 01887 830644 Fax: 01887 830732

Traditional stone cottage (built 1812) in own grounds, peaceful but not isolated situation. Glorious open views to the hills.

1 cottage, 2 pub rms, 2 bedrms, sleeps 5, £294.00-£534.00, Jan-Dec, bus nearby, rail 2 mls, airport 70 mls

---

Kinloch Rannoch, Perthshire

SELF CATERING ★★★

Dr Hazel Campbell
Drumashie Lodge, Dores, Inverness-shire, IV2 6TR
Tel/Fax: 01463 751202

Comfortable, traditional stone cottage on quiet country road at edge of attractive village. Sleeps 4 and 2 in 2 bedrooms. Open fire, electric central heating. Sunny enclosed garden with views of Schiehallion. Close to Loch. Beautiful walking country in all seasons. Not suitable for very young children. No smoking or pets.

Map Ref: 1H1

1 cottage, 1 pub rm, 2 bedrms (All grd.floor), sleeps 4+2, £200.00-£260.00, Apr-Oct, bus nearby, rail 17 miles

---

VAT is shown at 17.5%: changes in this rate may affect prices.

Key to symbols is on back flap.

KINLOCH RANNOCH – BY KINROSS

PERTHSHIRE, ANGUS AND DUNDEE AND THE KINGDOM OF FIFE

Kinloch Rannoch, Perthshire — Map Ref: 1H1

SELF CATERING ★★★★

Mrs Susan Churchill
Lassintullich Lodge, Kinloch Rannoch, Perthshire, PH16 5QE
Tel: 01882 632330 Fax: 01882 632431

2 cottages and grd.flr apartment, 1 pub rm, 1-2 bedrms, sleeps 2-3, total sleeping capacity 8, £140.00-£295.00, Jan-Dec, rail 18 mls

Two cottages (with woodburners) and ground floor converted Stable apartment. Spectacular Highland scenery. Ideal for peaceful, relaxing holidays, excellent for Highland pursuits; walking, fishing, cycling, wildlife. No smoking/pets. Open all year.

SELF CATERING ★★

James Stewart
2 Ashton Villas, Edinburgh, EH15 2QP
Tel/Fax: 0131 657 1718
E-mail: stewart@sol.co.uk

1 flat, 1 pub rm, 3 bedrms, sleeps 10, £210.00-£450.00, Jan-Dec, bus nearby, rail 18 mls

Totally refurbished apartment in centre of quiet Highland village. Within walking distance of all local amenities.

---

by Kinloch Rannoch, Perthshire — Map Ref: 1H1

Dunalastair Holiday Houses

Dunalastair Estate, Kinloch Rannoch, By Pitlochry PH16 5PD
Telephone: 01882 632491   Fax: 01882 632469
e.mail: dunalastair@sol.co.uk   Web: www.dunalastair.com

Comfortable, secluded, traditional cottages set amongst spectacular Highland scenery. Abundant wildlife: deer, eagles, osprey, red squirrels. Fishing, boat-use and tennis – FREE. Central for touring, castles, woollen shops, golf and leisure centre nearby. Electric heating, open fires. Sleeping 2-8. Pets welcome. Open Jan – Dec.
Prices: **from £219 weekly (includes electricity).** *Short breaks available.* **Colour brochure.**

SELF CATERING ★★ UP TO ★★★★

Mrs M A MacIntyre
Dunalastair Holiday Houses, Dunalastair Estate, Kinloch Rannoch, Perthshire, PH16 5PD
Tel: 01882 632491 Fax: 01882 632469
E-mail: dunalastair@sol.co.uk Web: www.dunalastair.com

7 cottages, 1-2 pub rms, 1-4 bedrms (grd flr avail), sleeps 2-8, total sleeping capacity 34, min let weekend, £219.00-£556.00, Jan-Dec, bus upto 3 mls, rail 18 mls, airport 80 mls

Eight Victorian cottages of unique charm and character, individually sited on family run highland estate with working farm. Wonderful views. All are very well equipped and have log fires. One romantic 2-person cottage has four-poster bed, ideal for honeymoons. Fishing, boat-use and tennis free.

---

by Kinross, Perthshire — Map Ref: 2B3

SELF CATERING ★★ UP TO ★★★

Linda Bayne
Gospetry, Milnathort, Kinross, Kinross-shire, KY13 7SW
Tel/Fax: 01577 862052

1 cottage, 1 pub rm, 3 bedrms, sleeps 6, £180.00-£280.00, Jan-Dec, bus 2 mls, rail 5 mls, airport 20 mls

Two well equipped, semi-detached cottages 1600 acre working farm. Open views to the Lomond Hills, including West Lomond - highest hill in Fife. Close to the most westerly point of the new Fife cycle route. Access via the farm. Edinburgh and Perth within a 30 min drive. Glasgow and other major centres and attractions within an hour.

Important: Prices stated are estimates and may be subject to amendments

PERTHSHIRE, ANGUS AND DUNDEE AND THE KINGDOM OF FIFE

BY KINROSS – KIRKMICHAEL

by Kinross, Perthshire

Map Ref: 2B3

★★ SELF CATERING

Loch Leven Chalets
Stan-ma-Lane, Balgedie, Kinross, KY13 9HE
Tel: 01592 840257

18 chalets, 1 pub rm, 2-3 bedrms, sleeps 4-6, total sleeping capacity 86, min let 3 nights, £140.00-£360.00, Jan-Dec, bus 3 mls, rail 12 mls, airport 28 mls

Situated at the foot of the Lomond Hills, overlooking Loch Leven, you'll really enjoy a holiday in this quiet and unspoilt area. Ideally positioned for Scotland's main tourist attractions, Edinburgh, Stirling, Perth, St Andrews and Fife are within easy reach. Dundee, Crieff and Pitlochry are all within a relaxed hours drive.

by Kirkcaldy, Fife

Map Ref: 2C4

★★★ SELF CATERING

Margaret Cunningham
Lawers, Main Street, Auchtertool, Fife, KY2 5XJ
Tel: 01592 781656

1 bungalow, 1 wing of bungalow, 1 pub rm, 2 bedrms, sleeps 2-4, total sleeping capacity 6, min let 2 days, £150.00-£280.00, Jan-Dec, bus nearby, rail 4 mls, airport 15 mls

Very comfortable bungalow situated in a quiet cul-de-sac in the small village of Auchtertool. Also self-contained east wing at end of owners bungalow. Catering for two-twin bedded for breaks or weekly lets - all year round. 4 miles from Kirkcaldy. Breakfast available on request.

Kirkmichael, Perthshire

Map Ref: 4D12

★★★★ SELF CATERING

Mrs M C Hilton
18 The Glen, Endcliffe Vale Road, Sheffield, S10 3FN
Tel: 01142 663188 Fax: 0114 268 7088
E-mail: hilton@bratach.freeserve.co.uk

1 bungalow, 2 pub rms, 3 bedrms (All grd.floor), sleeps 5, £240.00-£360.00, 1 Jun-end Sep, bus nearby, rail 12 mls, airport 45 mls.

Detached modern house with own garden and private parking. In peaceful location overlooking Bannerfield, with easy access to village and facilities.

★★ SELF CATERING

Jean C Keiro
The Firs, Kirkmichael, by Blairgowrie, Perthshire, PH10 7LY
Tel: 01250 881334

1 cottage, 1-3 pub rms, 2 bedrms (All grd.floor), sleeps 4-6, £80.00-£210.00, Jan-Dec, rail 12 mls

Self contained bungalow cottage and garden adjoining owners house. Set in a lovely peaceful area within easy walking distance of the village centre. Pitlochry 12 miles, Blairgowrie 12 miles, Braemar 28 miles distance.

SCOTTISH TOURIST BOARD INSPECTED
HOLIDAY CARAVAN

Mrs Jean Keiro
Booking Enquiries: Mrs Jean Keiro
The Firs, Kirkmichael, by Blairgowrie, Perthshire, PH10 7LY
Tel: 01250 881334

Park accommodation:

Holiday Caravan to let, sleeps 4-6 £70.00-110.00, min let weekend, Jan-Dec.

VAT is shown at 17.5%: changes in this rate may affect prices.

Key to symbols is on back flap.

KIRKMICHAEL – BY KIRRIEMUIR

PERTHSHIRE, ANGUS AND DUNDEE AND THE KINGDOM OF FIFE

Kirkmichael, Perthshire — Map Ref: 4D12

J & I Milne, Kirkmichael Village Cottages
Main Street, Kirkmichael, Blairgowrie, Perthshire, PH10 7NT
Tel/Fax: 01250 881385
Web: www.accomodata.co.uk/020496.htm

★★★ SELF CATERING

1 house, 2 cottages, 1-2 pub rms, 2-3 bedrms (grd flr avail), sleeps 4-6, total sleeping capacity 14, min let 2 nights, £144.00-£390.00, Jan-Dec, bus nearby, rail 12 mls, airport 60 mls

Traditional stone built cottages of individual character and style, situated in centre of small Perthshire village. Kirkmichaels central location is a perfect base for touring Scotland but particularly for walkers with many local routes and easy access to the hills.

Mrs Helen Reid
Balnakilly, Kirkmichael, Blairgowrie, Perthshire, PH10 7NB
Tel/Fax: 01250 881281
E-mail: balnakilly@webscot.net

★★ SELF CATERING

4 log cabins, 2 houses, 2 cottages, 1-3 pub rms, 2-3 bedrms (grd flr avail), sleeps 2-7, total sleeping capacity 50, £140.00-£440.00, Jan-Dec, bus 1/2 ml, rail 12 mls, airport 28 mls

Charming traditional cottages and Norwegian log cabins on a private 1200 acre Highland Estate. All the properties are spread over a wide area, and provide individual settings, space and privacy, amid fantastic scenery and amazing varied wildlife flora and fauna. Facilities on the Estate include swimming, tennis, croquet and fishing.

Kirriemuir, Angus — Map Ref: 2C1

Mr & Mrs H G McCrum
92 Glamis Road, Kirriemuir, Angus, DD8 5DF
Tel: 01575 572085

★★ SELF CATERING

2 cottages, 1-2 pub rms, 2 bedrms (All grd.floor), sleeps 4-5, total sleeping capacity 9, min let weekend, £170.00-£260.00, Jan-Dec, bus nearby, rail 15 mls, airport 60 mls

Terraced former weavers cottages with own gardens in quiet residential area, on south side of town centre. Ideal base for touring Angus Glens. Both properties have private parking and open fires, for which a starter pack of coal and logs will be provided.

---

by Kirriemuir, Angus — Map Ref: 2C1

Mrs R Findlay
3 Taylor Street, Forfar, Angus, DD8 3JQ
Tel: 01307 461052

★ SELF CATERING

1 cottage, 2 pub rms, 2 bedrms, sleeps 6-8, £150.00-£250.00, Jan-Dec

Roadside cottage in Hamlet of Criagon of Airlie. Panoramic views over open countryside and Sidian Hills. Ideal for the Castle Trail and all outdoor persuits.

Mrs Maureen Marchant
The Welton of Kingoldrum Holiday Properties, Kingoldrum, Kirriemuir, Angus, DD8 5HY
Tel/Fax: 01575 574743
Web: www.angusanddundee.co.uk/members/562.htm

★★★ UP TO ★★★★ SELF CATERING

1 flat, 1 cottage, 1 house, sleeps 2-4, total sleeping capacity 10, min let weekend, to £320.00, bus 6 mls, rail 22 mls, airport 25 mls

Three luxurious self catering properties on a secluded working farm, situated in a spectacular setting with panoramic views. Ideal for hill walking and bird watching and an excellent base for golf, fishing, riding, shooting, skiing etc, coast, castles and touring the glens. Pets are welcomed.

Important: Prices stated are estimates and may be subject to amendments

PERTHSHIRE, ANGUS AND DUNDEE AND THE KINGDOM OF FIFE

LADYBANK – METHVEN, BY PERTH

Ladybank, Fife

SELF CATERING ★★★

David & Catherine Collins
Greyfriars Manse, 2 Friarsdene, Lanark, ML11 9EJ.
Tel: 01555 663363
E-mail: greyfriars@webartz.com
Web: www.webartz.com/eden

Spacious cottage in a quiet village a few minutes drive from Cupar. Convenient for Ladybank Railway Station giving easy access to Edinburgh, Dundee and Perth. 20 minutes from the M90 and central in Fife for golf, fishing and visiting St Andrews, East Neuk fishing villaes and Falkland.

Map Ref: 2C3

1 cottage, 3 pub rms, 4 bedrms, sleeps 5+cot, £200.00-£350.00, Jan-Dec, bus nearby, rail ¼ ml

---

by Leven, Fife

SELF CATERING ★★★

Mrs E Todd
Blacketyside Farm, by Leven, Fife, KY8 5PX
Tel/Fax: 01333 423034

Refurbished farm cottages in open farmland on working farm. Close to golf course, beaches and East Neuk of Fife. 5 minutes from easy road systems.

Map Ref: 2C3

2 cottages, each 1 pub rm, 3 bedrms (All grd.flr), sleeps 6, £175.00-£275.00, Jan-Dec, bus 250 yds, rail 10 mls, airport 30 mls.

Methven, by Perth, Perthshire

SELF CATERING ★★

Mr David M A Smythe
Cloag Farm, Methven, Perthshire, PH1 3RR
Tel: 01738 840239 Fax: 01738 840156
E-mail: cloagfarm1@cs.com
Web: www.destination-scotland.com/cloagfarm

Cottages with extensive southerly views over Perthshire and beyond. Open fires. Ideal base for touring Perthshire. Shooting and fishing available.

Map Ref: 2B2

3 cottages, 1 pub rm, 2 bedrms (All grd.floor), sleeps 4, total sleeping capacity 12, £275.00-£350.00, Jan-Dec, bus 1 ml, rail 8 mls, airport 30-50 mls

Strathearn Holidays Ltd.

Hilton House, Methven, Perth PH1 3QX
Telephone: 01738 633322 (day)/01738 840263 (eve) Fax: 01738 621177
e.mail: bookings@scotland-holidays.com
Web: www.scotland-holidays.com

In the very heart of Scotland. Enjoy our home from home holidays in fully equipped and beautifully furnished south facing properties on our 710 acre farm. The ideal base for sporting or touring holidays. Each property has colour TV, microwave, dishwasher, etc. Price includes linen and electricity. Call for brochure.

SELF CATERING ★★★★

Strathearn Holidays
Kilda Way, North Muirton Industrial Estate, Perth, PH1 3XS
Tel: 01738 633322/(office hours) 01738 840263
(eve) Fax: 01738 621177
E-mail: bookings@scotland-holidays.com
Web: www.scotland-holidays.com

Traditional farm cottages on 700 acre mixed arable farm in Strathearn. Golf, shooting, fishing and riding available. Open all year.

3 cottages, 1 pub rm, 1-2 bedrms (grd flr avail), sleeps 2-6, total sleeping capacity 14, £200.00-£395.00, Jan-Dec, bus ½ ml, rail 6 mls, airport 40 mls

VAT is shown at 17.5%: changes in this rate may affect prices.

Key to symbols is on back flap.

NEWPORT-ON-TAY – PERTH

PERTHSHIRE, ANGUS AND DUNDEE AND THE KINGDOM OF FIFE

Newport-on-Tay, Fife — Map Ref: 2D2

★★★ SELF CATERING

Mr & Mrs A Ramsay
Mrs B L Ramsay, Newport-on-Tay, DD6 8HH
Tel: 01382 542274 Fax: 01382 542927

Self-contained wing of large Listed house, standing in its own grounds in Newport-on-Tay. 3 miles (5kms) from Dundee and 10 miles (16kms) from St Andrews.

1 house, 3 pub rms, 3 bedrms (All grd.floor), sleeps 5-6, £170.00-£350.00, Jan-Dec, bus 200 yds, rail 3 mls, airport 5 mls

---

★★★★ SELF CATERING

Mrs P Scott
Forgan Steading, Forgan, Newport-on-Tay, Fife, DD6 8RB
Tel/Fax: 01382 542760

A traditional stone built cottage dated to c1800 between Dundee and St Andrews, former steadings CC1730 in 5 acres with walled garden. Attractive interior finish with french windows open to the south facing garden. Sitting rooms incorporate part of the original stone wall into which are built open fires. Ensuite master bedroom. Spacious and fully equipped kitchen/diner. Next to golf course and 15 minutes woodland drive to a wonderful beach.

1 cottage, 1 pub rm, 3 bedrms (grd flr avail), sleeps 6, min let 2 days, £195.00-£450.00, Jan-Dec, bus ¼ ml, rail 3 mls, airport 40 mls

---

North Queensferry, Fife — Map Ref: 2B4

★★ SELF CATERING

Mrs E R Anderson
1 Inverkeithing Road, Crossgates, Fife, KY4 8AL
Tel/Fax: 01383 510666

Secluded, centrally located 19c mansion house with superb view of the River Forth and its famous bridges. Within easy reach of Edinburgh and Glasgow. Perth, the gateway to the Highlands is less than 30 minutes away by road.

6 flats, 2 cottages, 1 pub rm, 1-3 bedrms (grd flr avail), sleeps 2-6, total sleeping capacity 33, £160.00-£400.00, Jan-Dec, bus nearby, rail nearby, ferry nearby, airport 7 mls

---

★★★ SELF CATERING

Mrs E Stirrat
Fingask Farm, Rhynd, by Perth, Perthshire, PH2 8QF
Tel: 01738 812220 Fax: 01738 813325

Two traditional, stone built semi-detached cottages on working farm. On an elevated site overlooking the Rivers Tay and Earn and the Ochil Hills. 5 miles south east of Perth in a peaceful haven of Perthshire.

2 cottages, 1 pub rm, 1-2 bedrms (grd flr avail), sleeps 2-6, total sleeping capacity 8, min let weekend, £120.00-£300.00, Jan-Dec, bus 3 mls, rail 5 mls, airport 38 mls

---

Perth — Map Ref: 2B2

★★ SELF CATERING

Anderson
Deer Bank, Fairmount Road, Perth, PH2 7AW
Tel: 01738 622272

Spacious first floor flat in the centre of the city. Short distance from bus and train stations and easy access to shops, theatre, cinema, many leisure activities and many restaurants.

1 flat, 1 pub rm, 3 bedrms, sleeps 5, min let weekend, £155.00-£350.00, Jan-Dec, bus nearby, rail ½ ml

---

Important: Prices stated are estimates and may be subject to amendments

PERTHSHIRE, ANGUS AND DUNDEE AND THE KINGDOM OF FIFE

PERTH – BY PERTH

Perth

★★ SELF CATERING

Mrs Ailsa McKee
Rosemount, Pittenzie Road, Crieff, PH7 3JN
Tel: 01764 653981 Fax: 01764 655584

Map Ref: 2B2

2 flats, 4-6 bedrms, sleeps 6, total sleeping capacity 12, £200.00-£420.00, Jun-Aug, bus 1/2 ml, rail 1/2 ml, airport 20 ml

Three spacious apartments in a converted stone granary in the centre of the city. Restaurants and shops on the doorstep. Parks, swimming pool and attractions within a five minute walk. Off street private parking. Rail and bus stations 7 mins walk. An ideal base for walking, fishing and golfing.

★★★ SELF CATERING

Queens Hotel
Leonard Street, Perth, PH2 8HB
Tel: 01738 442222 Fax: 01738 638496
E-mail: email@lovat.co.uk

1 house, 1 pub rm, 2 bedrms, sleeps 4, £200.00-£450.00, May-Oct, bus nearby, rail 2 mls

Nicely furnished lodge house within 3 acres of grounds on the banks of the River Tay. Conveniently situated for all city centre amenities, (10 minute walk). Trout fishing from the bank. Scone Palace close by. Many other activities are available.

★★ SELF CATERING

Mrs A E Roberts
Jessamine House, Hamsterley, Bishop Auckland,
Co. Durham, DL13 3QF
Tel: 01388 488280

1 flat, 2 pub rms, 1 bedrm, sleeps 2, £150.00-£180.00, Jan-Dec, bus nearby, rail 1 ml, airport 15 mls

Top floor flat accessed by communal stairway, conveniently situated in town centre near main shopping areas.

---

by Perth

Map Ref: 2B2

★★★ SELF CATERING

Mrs Christine Jeffrey
Airntully, Stanley, Perth, PH1 4PH
Tel: 01738 828463

1 house, 1 cottage, 1 pub rm, 2-3 bedrms, sleeps 4-6, total sleeping capacity 6, £175.00-£400.00, Jan-Dec

Spacious well furnished cottage with a large secluded lawned garden and putting green. Panoramic views from Strathmore valley. Plus semi-detached villa on the edge of Stanley. Comfortably furnished and with a lawned garden. Views over open countryside to the rear.

★★★ SELF CATERING

Mrs Susan Leadbitter
The Old Post Office, Caroline Place, Wolfhill, by Perth,
Perthshire, PH2 6DA
Tel: 01821 650468

1 cottage, 1 pub rm, 1 bedrm (All grd.floor), sleeps 4, from £170.00, Jan-Dec, bus 50 yds, rail 8 mls

Tastefully renovated former post office dating from 1820, situated in quiet village midway between Perth and Blairgowrie. Use of large garden and off street parking. Fishing, walking, golfing and other sporting activities nearby. Perth 15 mins, Edinburgh, Aberdeen, Glasgow all within 1 1/2 hours drive.

VAT is shown at 17.5%: changes in this rate may affect prices.

Key to symbols is on back flap.

PERTHSHIRE, ANGUS AND DUNDEE AND THE KINGDOM OF FIFE

by Perth

Map Ref: 2B2

A C Miller & MacKay
63 Scott Street, Perth, PH2 8JN
Tel: 01738 620087 Fax: 01738 621225

★★★★ SELF CATERING

Beautifully constructed, comfortable cottage overlooking River Tay. Set in nicely maintained gardens. Private parking. Six miles North of Perth. Edinburgh, Glasgow and the best of Scotland's tourist attractions are within an hours drive.

1 cottage, 2 pub rms, 2 bedrms (grd flr avail), sleeps 4, £300.00-£400.00, short brk £60.00 per night, min stay 3 nights, Mar-Nov, bus ½ ml.

Mr A M Threipland
Fingask Castle, Rait, by Perth, Perthshire, PH2 7SA
Tel: 01821 670777 Fax: 01821 670755
E-mail: fingask@dial.pipex.com
Web: www.tayside-online.com/fingask

★ UP TO ★★★ SELF CATERING

Individual cottages within the estate of Fingask Castle, 70 acres of wood and parkland. Located 12 miles from Perth/Dundee it is an excellent base for exploring the area and for enjoying outdoor persuits including walking, fishing and golfing.

5 cottages, 1 pub rm, 2-4 bedrms (grd flr avail), sleeps 4-6, total sleeping capacity 24, min let 3 nights, £160.00-£400.00, Jan-Dec

Pitlochry, Perthshire

Map Ref: 2A1

Mrs Sheena Brennan
Bonnethill Property Co, 30a Bonnethill Road, Pitlochry, Perthshire, PH16 5BS
Tel: 01796 472532 Fax: 01796 474060

★★★ SELF CATERING

Apartments, one on the ground floor, conveniently situated close to town centre.

4 flats, 1 pub rm, 1-2 bedrms, sleeps 2-6, total sleeping capacity 15, £125.00-£325.00, Apr-Oct, bus 300 yds, rail ½ ml, airport 60 mls

---

Burnside Apartment Hotel
19 West Moulin Road, Pitlochry, Perthshire, PH16 5EA
Tel: 01796 472203 Fax: 01796 473586
E-mail: burnsideapts@sol.co.uk
Web: www.sol.co.uk/b/burnsideapartments

★★★★ SERVICED APARTMENTS

Modern and comfortable apartments with a self catering and serviced element. Central quiet location. Bistro-coffee shop open 10.00 - 21.00 April-October.

2 cottages, 9 serviced apartments, 1 pub rm, 1-2 bedrms (grd flr avail), sleeps 2-6, total sleeping capacity 34, £225.00-£435.00, Jan-Dec, bus ¼ ml, rail ¼ ml, airport 65 mls

Craigroyston Lodge
2 Lower Oakfield, Pitlochry, Perthshire, PH16 5HQ
Tel/Fax: 01796 472053
E.mail: sandra.crowe@lineone.net

★★★ SELF CATERING

Tastefully restored cottage with own small garden and private car park. Situated in the grounds of Craigroyston Guest House, with direct access to Pitlochry town centre. South facing views over the town to the hills beyond. Open all year.

1 cottage, 2 pub rms, 2 bedrms, sleeps 4, £150.00-£390.00, Jan-Dec, bus ¼ ml, rail ¼ ml, airport 65 mls

---

Important: Prices stated are estimates and may be subject to amendments

PERTHSHIRE, ANGUS AND DUNDEE AND THE KINGDOM OF FIFE

PITLOCHRY

Pitlochry, Perthshire | Map Ref: 2A1

★★★★ SELF CATERING

Derrybeg
18 Lower Oakfield, Pitlochry, Perthshire, PH6 5DS
Tel/Fax: 01796 472070

Stonebuilt house, totally rebuilt with three apartments situated in quiet location in elevated position, close to the town centre with fine views of hills and Tummel Valley.

3 flats, 1 pub rm, 2 bedrms (All grd.floor), sleeps 4, total sleeping capacity 12, min let 1 night, £150.00-£400.00, Jan-Dec, bus 500 yds, rail ½ ml, airport 63 mls

---

★★★ SELF CATERING

Mr I Hendry
Oakbank, 20 Lower Oakfield, Pitlochry, Perthshire, PH16 5DS
Tel: 01796 472080/0411 580127 Fax: 01796 473502
E-mail: ian@oakburn.clara.co.uk

Self contained flat with conservatory, on ground floor of traditional, fully modernised Victorian villa, 150 metres from town centre (no gradients).

1 flat, 1 bedrm (All grd.floor), sleeps 2-4, £205.00-£250.00, Apr-Oct, bus nearby, rail nearby

---

★★★★ SELF CATERING

Mrs Carolyn Hohman
Balrobin Hotel, Higher Oakfield, Pitlochry, Perthshire, PH16 5HT
Tel: 01796 472901 Fax: 01796 474200
E-mail: balrobin@globalnet.co.uk
Web: www.milford.co.uk/scotland/accom/r-l-2013.html

Modern flat in new residential area, overlooking surrounding hills. 10 minutes walk from the town centre.

1 flat, 1 pub rm, 2 bedrms, sleeps 4, £210.00-£320.00, Jan-Dec, bus ½ ml, rail ½ ml

★★ SELF CATERING

Mrs Howman
Auchnahyle, Pitlochry, Perthshire, PH16 5JA
Tel: 01796 472318 Fax: 01796 473657
E-mail: howmana@aol.com

Traditional stone built cottage of unique charm and character, situated across courtyard from main farmhouse. 15 minutes walk to Pitlochry.

1 cottage, 2 pub rms, 2 bedrms, sleeps 5, £180.00-£355.00, Jan-Dec, bus ½ ml, rail 1 ml, airport 40 mls

VAT is shown at 17.5%: changes in this rate may affect prices.

Key to symbols is on back flap.

PITLOCHRY

PERTHSHIRE, ANGUS AND DUNDEE AND THE KINGDOM OF FIFE

Pitlochry, Perthshire — Map Ref: 2A1

★★★★ SELF CATERING

Kinnaird Woodland Lodges
Kinnaird House, Kirkmichael Road, Pitlochry, Perthshire, PH16 5JL
Tel: 01796 472843
E-mail: kinnaird@hotmail.com
Web: www.scotland2000.com/kinnairdlodges

Comfortable cottage, attached to Victorian house, in rural setting with superb views of the golf course and Craigower Hill.

1 log cabin, 1 pub rm, 2 bedrms, sleeps 4-6, min let weekend, £250.00-£500.00, Jan-Dec, bus 1 1/2 mls, rail 1 1/2 mls

---

★★★★ SELF CATERING

Mrs Leaman
The Well House, 11 Toberargan Road, Pitlochry, Perthshire, PH16 HG
Tel: 01796 472239
E-mail: arrochar@btinternet.com
Web: www.btinternet.com/~arrochar

Three bedroomed modern house with private garden. Situated within walking distance of Pitlochry town centre. Refurbished to provide facilities for both able bodied and disabled. One ground floor bedroom and shower room.

1 house, 2 pub rms, 3 bedrms (grd flr avail), sleeps 6, £250.00-£370.00, Jan-Dec, bus nearby, rail 1/2 ml, airport 80 mls

---

★★★ SELF CATERING

Neil & Laurie Macdonald
140 Atholl Road, Pitlochry, Perthshire, PH16 5AG
Tel: 01796 472170
E-mail: macdonalds.pitlochry@usa.net

Treasaite, which means 'the third place', is a fully furnished Victorian end terrace house of architectural interest with a pleasant garden. Centrally located, with easy access to shops, theatres & attractions. Secluded garden with flower beds and car parking available.

1 house, 1 pub rm, 2 bedrms, sleeps 4, £250.00-£350.00, Jan-Dec, bus 400 yds, rail 400 yds, airport 69 mls

---

★★★ SELF CATERING

Colin & Marleen Mackay
25 Atholl Road, Pitlochry, PH16 5BX
Tel: 01796 472065/473000 (eve) Fax: 01796 472065

Bungalow situated on outskirts of Pitlochry. Open view to hills and golf course to front. Easy access to town centre and ideal for day trips within Perthshire.

1 bungalow, sleeps 8 in 1 dbl and 3 twin rooms, tv lounge and sep. dining room, £325.00-£525.00, Jan-Dec, bus 200 yds.

★★★★ SELF CATERING

Mr & Mrs G W Morison
Cruachan, Golf Course Road, Blairgowrie, Perthshire, PH10 6LQ
Tel: 01250 875191 Fax: 01250 873786

Carefully modernised apartment within a nicely situated Victorian house within easy access of the shops, local services and amenities. The accommodation combines old world charm with modern conveniencies and is suitable for those looking for a peaceful holiday in this beautiful area.

1 flat, 2 pub rms, 3 bedrms (grd flr avail), sleeps 6, min let weekend, £180.00-£340.00, Jan-Dec, bus nearby, rail nearby

---

Important: Prices stated are estimates and may be subject to amendments

PERTHSHIRE, ANGUS AND DUNDEE AND THE KINGDOM OF FIFE

PITLOCHRY – BY PITLOCHRY

Pitlochry, Perthshire

★★★ SELF CATERING

Woodburn Self Catering
Ferry Road, Pitlochry, PH16 5DE
Tel: 01796 473818
E-mail: woodburn@breathemail.net

Map Ref: 2A1

1 flat, 1 pub rm, 2 bedrms (All grd.floor), sleeps 2-4, min let weekend, £200.00-£250.00, Apr-Oct, bus 800 yds, rail 900 yds, airport 70 mls

Comfortable two bedroomed ground floor flat, adjacent to family run B&B. Open views, private parking.

---

by Pitlochry, Perthshire

★★ SELF CATERING

Mrs F Davidson
Tigh-na-Cnoc, Logierait, Pitlochry, Perthshire, PH9 0LH
Tel/Fax: 01796 482240

Map Ref: 2A1

1 cottage, 2 pub rms, 2 bedrms (All grd.floor), sleeps 4, £225.00-£275.00, Jan-Dec, bus nearby, rail 6 mls

Attractive stone built cottage with views over the River Tay. Five miles south of Pitlochry off the A827 Aberfeldy road. Garden with lovely views.

★★★ SELF CATERING

Eleanor Howie
Moulinearn, by Pitlochry, Perthshire, PH9 0NB
Tel/Fax: 01796 482248

1 cottage, 1-2 pub rms, 2 bedrms, sleeps 3, £155.00-£245.00, Jan-Dec, bus nearby

Picturesque rose covered cottage near the River Tummel. Peaceful secluded setting one and a half miles south of Pitlochry.

★★★ SELF CATERING

Mrs E H Laing
Auchanross House, Strathtay, by Pitlochry, Perthshire, PH9 0PG
Tel: 01887 840374

2 cottages, 2 pub rms, 2 bedrms, sleeps 4, total sleeping capacity 8, £135.00-£350.00, Jan-Dec, bus 550 yds, rail 9 mls, airport 70 mls

Two cottages (one with central heating and open hearth fire) in courtyard of Victorian Villa. Guests have full access to the secluded south facing gardens and wooded grounds overlooking the River Tay. Pitlochry 10 miles (4 by hill path), Aberfeldy 5 miles. Ideal base for touring or activity holidays. 2 mins walk to golf course (6 other courses within 1/2 hour drive). Good walks - maps, advice and guide books provided.

VAT is shown at 17.5%: changes in this rate may affect prices.

Key to symbols is on back flap.

BY PITLOCHRY – PITTENWEEM

PERTHSHIRE, ANGUS AND DUNDEE AND THE KINGDOM OF FIFE

by Pitlochry, Perthshire — Map Ref: 2A1

Logierait Pine Lodges ★★★ SELF CATERING
Logierait, by Pitlochry, Perthshire PH9 0LH
Telephone: 01796 482253 Fax: 01796 482253
Resident Proprietors: Mr & Mrs E Brodie

So peaceful with wonderful views, these chalets are beautifully situated on the banks of the River Tay. All are fully equipped and have electric heating. This is an ideal location for touring, golfing, walking and fishing which is free to residents. Please call for a colour brochure.

★★★ SELF CATERING

Logierait Pine Lodges
Logierait, Pitlochry, Perthshire, PH9 0LH
Tel: 01796 482253

Lodges located in a beautiful riverside setting, yet only a few minutes drive from Pitlochry.

15 chalets, 1 pub rm, 1-3 bedrms, sleeps 2-8, total sleeping capacity 82, £160.00-£500.00, Jan-Dec, bus nearby, rail 5 mls, airport 60 mls

---

★★ SELF CATERING

Mrs Catherine J Michie
Clunskea Farmhouse, Enochdhu, by Blairgowrie, Perthshire, PH10 7PJ
Tel: 01250 881358/881361

Situated on working sheep farm, set back from A924, affording scenic views over Strathardle, 6 miles (10kms) from Pitlochry.

1 house, 1 pub rm, 3 bedrms, sleeps 4-6, £175.00-£325.00, Jan-Dec, bus 6 mls, rail 6 mls

★★★ SELF CATERING

Kathleen Yates
Cherry Cottage, Ballinluig, by Pitlochry, Perthshire, PH9 0LG
Tel/Fax: 01796 482409
E-mail: kathleenyates@btinternet.com

Semi-detached Victorian stone built cottage retaining some period features, set in small village with hotel and bar nearby. Only a four mile drive takes you to Pitlochry's Festival Theatre providing seasonal culture. Watersports at Grantully with other outdoor activities nearby, fantastic local walks and skiing. The Tay & Tummel rivers are a stones throw away with fishing permits available locally.

1 cottage, 2 pub rms, 2 bedrms, sleeps 4, £190.00-£300.00, Jan-Dec, bus nearby, rail 5 mls

Pittenweem, Fife — Map Ref: 2D3

★★★ SELF CATERING

Mrs Nancy I Sneddon
Glenlusset, 21 Redwood Crescent, Bishopton, Renfrewshire, PA7 5DJ
Tel: 01505 862398/0141 887 9866 Fax: 0141 887 9993

19c semi-detached house in East Neuk village centre, with large south facing garden. Quality garden furniture. Fine views over Firth of Forth. Easy access to the new Fife Coastal Path Walk.

1 house, 2 pub rms, 2 bedrms, sleeps 5-7, £190.00-£320.00, Jan-Dec, bus nearby

---

Important: Prices stated are estimates and may be subject to amendments

PERTHSHIRE, ANGUS AND DUNDEE AND THE KINGDOM OF FIFE

RANNOCH STATION – ST ANDREWS

Rannoch Station, Perthshire
Map Ref: 1G1

SELF CATERING ★★

Mrs Shirley Somerville
10 Park Road, Twickenham, Middlesex, TW1 2PX
Tel/Fax: 0181 892 1803

2 houses, 1 cottage, 1-2 pub rms, 2 bedrms, sleeps 4, total sleeping capacity 12, min let 2 nights, £165.00-£300.00, Jan-Dec, bus 200 yds, rail 5 mls

Cottages individual in character, on a 25 acre estate, with direct access to lochside. Boats for hire.

St Andrews, Fife
Map Ref: 2D2

Eve Brown Holiday Properties
23 Argyle Street, St. Andrews, Fife KY16 9BX
Telephone: 01334 478800   Fax: 01334 478855
e.mail: post@EveBrown.co.uk Web: www.EveBrown.co.uk

Contact the regions largest self catering agency for the widest selection of town centre apartments, town houses, family houses and cottages available. Indulge in the atmosphere of this historic Royal Burgh, acknowledged as the 'Jewel of Northeast Fife', with its rich history, ancient university and recognised as the home of golf. Visit one of Scotland's accredited E.U. 'Blue Flag' beaches, absorb the bracing fresh air, savour the restaurants and coffee houses or tour the Scottish Highlands and glens. *It's yours to discover.* Free brochure upon request. **Booking now for 'The Open' 2000.**

SELF CATERING ★★★★

Eve Brown Holiday Properties
23 Argyle Street, St Andrews, Fife, Fife KY16 9BX
Tel: (St Andrews) 01334 478800 Fax: 01334 478855

A variety of properties in the St Andrews area. Ideal location for golfing and touring. Blue pendant award for beach. Some properties STB inspected.

SELF CATERING ★★★

Mrs V Browning
2 Sinclair Avenue, Bearsden, Glasgow, G61 3BT
Tel: 0141 942 7498 Fax: 0141 563 9946

1 flat, 1 pub rm, 2 bedrms, sleeps 4, £200.00-£375.00, Jan-Dec, bus nearby, rail 5 mls, airport 40 mls

Ground floor flat of a detached villa, south facing with conservatory and garden complete with garden furniture. Newly refurbished throughout. Modern kitchen and bathroom with bath and shower. All linen and towels supplied. Ideal for families young and old or golfers. Only 7 mins walk from the beach and the 1st tee of the R.&A. golf course and 2 mins. walk from all the towns amenities, yet in a quiet secluded spot with car parking facilities.

VAT is shown at 17.5%: changes in this rate may affect prices.   *Key to symbols is on back flap.*

ST ANDREWS

PERTHSHIRE, ANGUS AND DUNDEE AND THE KINGDOM OF FIFE

St Andrews, Fife Map Ref: 2D2

★★ SELF CATERING

Mrs Cheng
Pagan Osborne, South Street, St Andrews, KY16
Tel: 01334 475001 Fax: 01334 476322

Terraced town house, central close to shops, restaurants, beach and golf course. Ideal for families or golfers.

1 house, 1 pub rm, 3 bedrms, sleeps 5, £320.00-£400.00, Jun-Aug, bus nearby, rail 5 mls

---

★★★★★ SELF CATERING

Mr S Fleming
Law Park House, 120 Hepburn Gardens, St Andrews, Fife, KY16 9LT
Tel: 01334 477991 Fax: 01334 477371

Self-contained cottage, forming part of Law Park House. 1 mile from the centre of St Andrews, with it's beautiful beaches and famous golf courses. South facing sun terrace. Private parking.

1 house, 1 pub rm, 5 bedrms (All grd.floor), sleeps 7, £350.00-£550.00, Jan-Dec, bus at door, rail 5 mls

---

★★ UP TO ★★★ SELF CATERING

Anne R Hippisley
Rockview, 15 The Scores, St Andrews, Fife, KY16 9AR
Tel: 01334 475844

Attractive Victorian town house on the cliff above St Andrews bay and overlooking the Old Course. Peaceful setting and private parking in large secluded garden.

1 house, 1 flat, 1 cottage, 1 pub rm, 2-5 bedrms (grd flr avail), sleeps 5-10, total sleeping capacity 21, £250.00-£1200.00, Jun-Sep, bus ¼ ml, rail 4 mls

---

★★★★ SELF CATERING

Lady Hirst
Glentirran, Kippen, Stirlingshire, FK8 3JA
Tel: 01786 870283 Fax: 01786 870679

A Listed, terraced house of character in the centre of St. Andrews. Restored period features. Gardens. Only 3 minutes from the beach, golf and all town's amenities.

1 house, 2 pub rms, 4 bedrms (grd flr avail), sleeps 7-9, £500.00-£600.00, Jun-Sep, bus nearby, rail 5 mls, airport 40 mls

---

★★★ SELF CATERING

Mrs L Kinsley
The Hirsel, 50 The Scores, St Andrews, KY16 9AS
Tel: 01334 472578/470442 Fax: 01334 470442

The cottage is a wing of the Hirsel 19th century house, but is totally self contained with a pleasant side garden. Car parking and direct access to St Andrews foreshore, close to old course and sealife centre, families and dogs welcome.

1 cottage, 1-2 pub rms, 4 bedrms (grd flr avail), sleeps 6, to £400.00, Jun-Sep, bus ¼ ml, rail 5 mls, airport 50 mls

---

Important: Prices stated are estimates and may be subject to amendments

PERTHSHIRE, ANGUS AND DUNDEE AND THE KINGDOM OF FIFE

ST ANDREWS

St Andrews, Fife   Map Ref: 2D2

★★ UP TO ★★★ SELF CATERING

Mrs Margaret Pirie
Argyle Properties, 14 Albert Place, Stirling, FK8 2RE
Tel: 01786 478655 Fax: 01786 475859

Three well furnished centrally located flats, sleep 2 to 5. Shared garden with garden furniture and off street parking. Five minutes walk to town centre. Golf courses and beaches within an easy walk.

2 flats, 1 pub rm, 1-3 bedrms (grd flr avail), sleeps 2-6, total sleeping capacity 11, £200.00-£300.00, Jun-Aug, bus 500 yds

---

★ SELF CATERING

Ken Prudhoe
29 L'Arbre Cres, Whickham, Newcastle-upon-Tyne, NE16 5YQ
Tel: 0191 488 6273 Fax: 0191 461 0106
E-mail: kenprudhoe@aol.com

Central well equipped three bedroomed flat overlooking St Andrews market place and with secure city centre parking. Within walking distance of all amenities including shops, restaurants, churches, golf courses, beaches and leisure centre.

1 flat, 3 bedrms, sleeps 4-6, £250.00-£330.00, Jun-Sep

★★★ SELF CATERING

Miss F Robertson
Rathcluan, Carslogie Road, Cupar, KY15 4HY
Tel/Fax: 01334 650000
E-mail: rathcluan@rathcluan.co.uk

Quietly located town house with south facing walled garden. Only minutes from Byre Theater, cinemas and shops. In free parking zone. Available all year. Pets by arrangement.

1 house, 1 pub rm, 3 bedrms, sleeps 4-5, £250.00-£480.00, Jan-Dec, bus ½ ml, rail 6 mls

---

★ SELF CATERING

Susan & Jim Sinclair
The Thistles, 7 Albany Place, St Andrews, Fife, KY16 9HH
Tel/Fax: 01334 479823
E-mail: Thethistles@btinternet.com.uk

Five bedroomed Town House in town centre. Close to Old Course, beach, university and all amenities.

1 house, 1 pub rm, 5 bedrms (grd flr avail), sleeps 9, £400.00-£450.00, Jun-Sep, bus 500 yds, rail 4 mls, airport 14 mls

---

★★★★ SELF CATERING

Mrs G Stephen
Inchdairnie Properties, 9 Bell Street, St Andrews, Fife, KY16 9UR
Tel: 01334 477011 Fax: 01334 478643

Spacious farmhouse situated on working farm, recently refurbished to high standard with fine views over surrounding countryside. Approx 2 miles (3kms) from St Andrews.

1 house, 2 pub rms, 4 bedrms, sleeps 8, min let 3 days, £395.00-£595.00, Jan-Dec, bus nearby, rail 5 mls, airport 50 mls

---

VAT is shown at 17.5%: changes in this rate may affect prices.   *Key to symbols is on back flap.*

ST ANDREWS

PERTHSHIRE, ANGUS AND DUNDEE AND THE KINGDOM OF FIFE

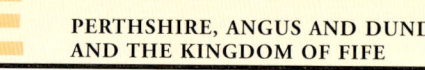

St Andrews, Fife Map Ref: 2D2

★★★ SELF CATERING

Mr & Mrs A J Strang
31 Bradenham Beeches, Walter's Ash, High Wycombe,
Bucks, HP14 4XQ
Tel/Fax: 01494 562073
E-mail: alanstrang@hotmail.com

1 flat, 1 pub rm, 4 bedrms, sleeps 8, £350.00-£800.00, Jun-mid Sep

A modern, spacious apartment in the centre of St Andrews. Restaurants, shops and the Old Course are all within a 5 minute walk. Beaches and attractions are nearby. Private parking space.

★★★ SELF CATERING

Mrs E M Thomson
Ravenswood, Tighnabruaich, Argyll, PA21 2EE
Tel: 01700 811603
E-mail: liz@tighnabruaich.demon.co.uk

1 house, 1 pub rm, 2 bedrms, sleeps 4, £275.00-£375.00, Jan-Dec, bus 1 ml, rail 10 mls

Tastefully modernised and refurbished terraced cottage in quiet residential street. Close to the town centre with enclosed rear garden. Parking space in grounds.

★★ SELF CATERING

Dr & Mrs D P Tunstall
4 West Acres, St Andrews, Fife, KY16 9UD
Tel: 01334 473507

1 flat, 1 pub rm, 1 bedrm (All grd.floor), sleeps 3, £160.00-£170.00, Apr-Oct, bus 1 ml, rail 6 mls, airport 60 mls

Comfortable sunny flat forming part of large family house. Quiet residential area, 1 mile (2kms) from town centre. Private entrance with direct access to large sunny garden and open country beyond.

ST ANDREWS COUNTRY COTTAGES

FREEPOST by CUPAR, Nr ST. ANDREWS, FIFE KY15 4BR
Freephone: 0808 1002464   Fax: 01382 330480
e.mail: enquiries@standrews-cottages.com   Web: www.standrews-cottages.com

Idyllic cottages and luxury farmhouses on a beautiful country estate. Private walks. Abundant wildlife. Blazing log fires.
Relax, explore or golf. Children and pets welcome. Short breaks available. Colour brochure.

★★★★ SELF CATERING

Mr & Mrs Wedderburn
FREEPOST, Mountquhanie Estate, Cupar, by St Andrews,
Fife, KY15 4BR
Tel: 01382 330318 Fax: 01382 330480 Freephone: 0808 1002464
E-mail: enquiries@standrews-cottages.com
Web: www.standrews-cottages.com

4 houses, 6 cottages, 1-2 pub rms, 2-6 bedrms, sleeps 4-14, total sleeping capacity 65, £195.00-£955.00, Jan-Dec, bus 2 mls, rail 5 mls, airport 50 mls

A choice selection of quality properties in St Andrews or on our private country estate nearby. Real country living for country lovers. A home for all seasons. Doo'cot cottage is equipped for guests with disabilities and has wheelchair facilities.

Important: Prices stated are estimates and may be subject to amendments

PERTHSHIRE, ANGUS AND DUNDEE AND THE KINGDOM OF FIFE

BY ST ANDREWS

by St Andrews, Fife   Map Ref: 2D2

★★★★ SELF CATERING

Mr Graham Drummond
17 St Ronan's Circle, Peterculter, Aberdeen, AB14 0NE
Tel/Fax: 01224 732874
E-mail: drummond@cwcom.net

1 house, 3 pub rms, 3 bedrms, sleeps 6, £350.00-£650.00, Jan-Dec, bus 1 ml, rail 4 mls, airport 15 mls

Victorian school, tastefully converted. Set in an acre of grounds with a conservatory surrounded by an attractive and peaceful garden. Country setting yet only 4 miles (6km) from the historic town of St Andrews. Craigton Country Park within 1 mile. Convenient for the Dukes Golf Course. Discounts available for couples in low season.

★★ UP TO ★★★ SELF CATERING

Mr Peter Erskine
Cambo House, Kingsbarns, by St Andrews, Fife, KY16 8QD
Tel: 01333 450313 Fax: 01333 450987
E-mail: 100130.1660@compuserve.com

4 flats, 2 cottages, 1-2 pub rms, 1-4 bedrms (grd flr avail), sleeps 2-8, total sleeping capacity 42, £190.00-£695.00, Jan-Dec, bus ¼ ml, rail 13 mls, airport 60 mls

Flats in Victorian mansion and cottages in grounds of wooded, lowland coastal estate. Extensive gardens, activities and walks to sandy beaches.

★★ SELF CATERING

J L W Foster & Co (Estate Office)
Craigie Farm, Leuchars, Fife, KY16 0DT
Tel: 01334 839218 Fax: 01334 839503
E-mail: brochures@craigie.co.uk
Web: www.craigie.co.uk

5 cottages, 1 pub rm, 2-4 bedrms (grd flr avail), sleeps 4-8, total sleeping capacity 29, £205.00-£385.00, Jun-Oct, bus 2 mls, rail 3 mls, airport 45 mls

Situated on a small promentory between the Tay and the Eden Estuaries, with easy access to forest and beaches. Modernised farm cottages 15 minutes drive from St Andrews. Just a stepping stone to the historic East Neuk fishing villages and over the Tay to Dundee and Perth.

★★ UP TO ★★★ SELF CATERING

Mrs Joan Inglis
8 Dunure Place, Newton Mearns, Glasgow, G77 5Z
Tel/Fax: 0141 616 3491

3 houses, 3 cottages, 1-2 pub rms, 2-4 bedrms (grd flr avail), sleeps 2-8, total sleeping capacity 31, min let 2 nights, £165.00-£575.00, Jan-Dec, bus nearby, rail 3 mls

Converted farmhouse and steadings in natural stone, each of individual character and design, situated around landscaped courtyard.

★★★★ SELF CATERING

Mrs L Logan
Kingask Country Cottages, Kingask House, by St Andrews, Fife, KY16 8PN
Tel: 01334 472011 Fax: 01334 470900
E-mail: kcc@easynet.co.uk
Web: easyweb.easynet.co.uk/kcc/index.htm

1 house, 9 cottages, 2-3 pub rms, 1-6 bedrms (grd flr avail), sleeps 2-12, min let 3 nights, £250.00-£1300.00, Jan-Dec, rail 15 mls

Traditional farm cottages and old large farmhouse refurbished to a high standard, many with open fireplace. Rural location yet ideal for St Andrews, Crail and Fife coast.

VAT is shown at 17.5%: changes in this rate may affect prices.   Key to symbols is on back flap.

BY ST ANDREWS – ST MONANS
PERTHSHIRE, ANGUS AND DUNDEE AND THE KINGDOM OF FIFE

by St Andrews, Fife
Map Ref: 2D2

★★★★ SELF CATERING

John Parker
Morton of Pitmilly, Kingsbarns, St Andrews, Fife, KY16 8QF
Tel: 01334 880466 Fax: 01334 880437
E-mail: mop@sol.co.uk
Web: www.pitmilly.co.uk

Small award winning complex of converted farm buildings in courtyard setting. Heated indoor pool, sauna, gym, tennis court and children's play areas.

10 houses, 1 pub rm, 1-4 bedrms, sleeps 2-10, total sleeping capacity 60, £265.00-£1010.00, Jan-Dec, bus $1/2$ ml, rail 9 mls, airport 55 mls

★★ SELF CATERING

Miss Pamela Smith, Woodland Holidays
Kincaple Lodge, Kincaple, St Andrews, Fife, KY16 9SH
Tel/Fax: 01334 850217

Nine Scandinavian lodges in rolling countryside with panoramic views towards the sea and St Andrews. The comfortable lodges are well spaced and provide the ideal base for golf, touring or just tom relax. Home cooking available. Play areas. Groups welcom. Sorry no pets. They frighten the Rabbits.

9 log cabins, 1 pub rm, 2 bedrms, sleeps 4, total sleeping capacity 36, £200.00-£415.00, Jan-Dec, bus $1/2$ ml, rail 2 mls, airport 40 mls

---

★★ SELF CATERING

Mrs C Wright
Croft Butts, Kingsbarns, by St Andrews, Fife, KY16 8SN
Tel: 01334 880247

Comfortably appointed traditional cottage which dates to the early 18th century. Set in a peaceful location on the edge of the Conservation village of Kingsbarns it is within easy access of St Andrews (7 miles) and the fishing villages of the East Neuk its the perfect place for low level walking, golfing or beachcombing, exploring the area or just to relax.

1 cottage, 1 pub rm, 2 bedrms (All grd.floor), sleeps 5-7, min let 3 days, £165.00-£275.00, Jan-Dec, bus 200 yds

---

St Monans, Fife
Map Ref: 2D3

★★★ SELF CATERING

Mrs B Wallace
16 Inglis Road, Colchester, Essex, CO3 3HU
Tel: 01206 547835
E-mail: wallace@anglia.net.co.uk

Fisherman's cottage with garden gate onto the village green. Quiet position in picturesque fishing village. 100 yards from Fife Coastal Path Walk.

1 house, 2 pub rms, 3 bedrms, sleeps 6, £250.00-£375.00, Jan-Dec, bus 200 yds, rail 16 mls, airport 45 mls

---

Important: Prices stated are estimates and may be subject to amendments

PERTHSHIRE, ANGUS AND DUNDEE AND THE KINGDOM OF FIFE

SCONE, BY PERTH – TUMMEL BRIDGE

Scone, by Perth, Perthshire
Map Ref: 2B2

SCONE PALACE HOLIDAYS
ESTATES OFFICE, SCONE PALACE, PERTH PH2 6BD
Tel: 01738 552308 (24 hrs)   Fax: 01738 552588

Located in the beautiful grounds of Scone Palace, a short distance from historic Perth, is one of Britain's idyllic holiday areas. Luxury modern fully fitted caravans that sleep up to 8 persons. Ideal for fishing, golf, touring, walking or simply relaxing in beautiful surroundings. Write or phone for free colour brochure.

★★★★ TOURING PARK

Scone Palace Holiday Caravans
Booking Enquiries: Balformo Enterprises Ltd Estate Office, Scone Palace, Scone, Perth, PH2 6BD
Tel: 01738 552308 Fax: 01738 552588

Park accommodation: 165

20 Holiday Caravans to let, sleep 4-8 £140.00-400.00, total sleeping capacity 160, min let 2 nights.

From Perth take A93. Turn onto Stormontfield road then onto drive to racecourse.

Spittal of Glenshee, Perthshire
Map Ref: 4D12

★ UP TO ★★★ SELF CATERING

Mr D Stewart
Glenbeag Mountain Lodges, Spittal of Glenshee, Blairgowrie, Perthsire
Tel: 01250 885204 Fax: 01250 885261

Modern log cabins with magnificent all round views of the glen. Very quiet situation. Ideal for skiing, walking, birdwatching or touring.

3 chalets, 2 log cabins, 1 pub rm, 2-3 bedrms, sleeps 2-6, total sleeping capacity 24, £185.00-£405.00, Jan-Dec, bus 19 mls, rail 36 mls, airport 80 mls

Tummel Bridge, Perthshire
Map Ref: 2A1

★★★★ HOLIDAY PARK

Tummel Valley Holiday Park
near Pitlochry, Perthshire, PH16 5SA
Tel: 01882 634221 Fax: 01882 634302
Booking Enquiries: Haven Reservations PO Box 218, 1 Park Lane, Near Pitlochry, Herts, HP2 4GL
Tel: 0870 242 2222

55 acres, level, sloping, Apr-Oct, prior booking recommended in peak periods, latest time of arrival 2100, overnight holding area. Extra charge for electricity, dogs.

Park accommodation: 180

Tourers and motorhomes welcome. No tents. Total touring pitches 40. £8.00-£16.00 per night approx. Contact park direct.

Caravans and lodges to let, sleep 4-8. £160.00-£619.00 per week approx. Contact reservations.

Leisure facilities:

Take B8019 to Tummel Bridge, by leaving A9 1 ½ mls N of Pitlochry. The park is 11 mls on left.

VAT is shown at 17.5%: changes in this rate may affect prices.

Key to symbols is on back flap.

Welcome to Scotland

Grampian Highlands, Aberdeen and the North East Coast

From the heather-clad hills and high peaks of the Grampian Mountains, to the dramatic North Sea coast at Kinnaird Head, lies a rich tapestry of river valleys, wooded countryside, characterful towns and rolling farmland. In contrast, set between the rivers Dee and Don, is the "Granite City" of Aberdeen, famous for its magnificent floral displays, the third city of Scotland which makes an ideal base for exploring this delightful area.

Throughout the northeast you will find family attractions, sporting activities and leisure pursuits, as well as a proud welcoming people who will delight in sharing their unique traditions, language and culture.

Close to the attractive coastal town of Stonehaven is the huge fortress of Dunnottar Castle which, surrounded on three sides by the sea, was dramatic enought to be chosen as the setting for Zeffirelli's film "Hamlet". Long empty beaches stretch north from here to the popular seaside resort of Cruden Bay and beyond, heading up the entire eastern seaboard to the port of Fraserburgh. The bustling harbour here is always full of activity and the town is home to Scotland's Lighthouse Museum, which gives a fascinating portrait of the mariners' constant struggle with the sea.

Heading westwards along the sheltered Moray Firth, keeping an eye open for the resident population of dolphins offshore, you will encounter secret coves, caves and cliffs around the pretty villages of Pennan and Crovie, once the haunt of smugglers. The maritime theme continues at the Buckie Drifter, a salty, tarry-roped evocation of the local herring industry, which uses the latest hands-on interpretative technology to delight kids of all ages.

Grampian Highlands, Aberdeen and the North East Coast

Grampian Highlands, Aberdeen and the North East Coast

At Spey Bay you can walk the forty-eight mile Speyside Way and follow Scotland's fastest flowing river all the way back inland to its Highland source on the very edge of the empty Cairngorms.

Nowhere in Grampian gets crowded, even in the height of the season and Royal Deeside, to the west of Aberdeen, is as attractive today as it was in 1848, when Queen Victoria decided she was going to build her Scottish holiday home at Balmoral. There are, in fact, countless fortresses, castles and mansions conveniently linked together in a Castle Trail throughout the region. Duff House is an outstanding example of architecture by William Adam, which is now an "outstation" of the National Gallery of Scotland exhibiting many fine paintings.

Another innovative route to follow is the Malt Whisky Trail, which is clearly signposted to help you track down Speyside's eight major distilleries, whose visitor centres have audio-visual, historical displays and a wee dram, for the non-drivers, at the end of the tour. Climate plays its part in the production of barley, the main ingredient in whisky making, and Speyside has low rain and plenty of sunshine, the perfect combination. In fact the whole region is sheltered from most Atlantic south-westerlies throughout the year, which may explain why Queen Victoria, with the entire Empire to choose from, built her holiday home in the centre of this wonderful area.

Grampian Highlands, Aberdeen and the North East Coast

Events
Grampian Highlands, Aberdeen and the North East Coast

Jan-Sep
Banff 2000
Banff 2000 – the alternative Olympics involving children/veterans/disabled. Three-week Olympics culminates a year long programme of training, festivals, international events and coaching.
Contact: Marion Philip
Tel: 01261 818303 Fax: 01261 818489

28 April-8 May
Spirit of Speyside Whisky Festival
Various venues in Speyside
Festival celebrating malt whisky in its spiritual home.
Contact: Elgin TIC
Tel: 01343 542666
e.mail: elgin@agtb.ossian.net

15-17 Jul
Stonehaven Folk Festival
Various venues, Stonehaven
Three-day festival of contemporary and traditional music.
Mrs Pat Cruise
Tel: 01569 765063
e.mail: pat.cruise@virgin.net

3-6 Aug
Speyfest, Fochabers
A pan-Celtic festival of music and dance including concerts, ceilidhs, workshops and craft fair.
Mr Paul Devine
Tel: 01343 820951

4-6 Aug
Gordon Gathering
Huntly, Aberdeenshire
A celebration of Huntly's historical status as the ancient seat of the mighty Clan Gordon when it is planned to attract Gordons from all over the world back to celebrate their heritage and roots in North-East Scotland.
Contact: Lyndsay Clark
Tel: 01466 799178

15-23 Oct
Aberdeen Alternative Festival
Various venues throughout Aberdeen
The north of Scotland's biggest and longest running festival, featuring jazz, rock, world music, comedy, drama, children's events and much more.
Contact: Festival office
Tel: 01224 635822

Area Tourist Boards

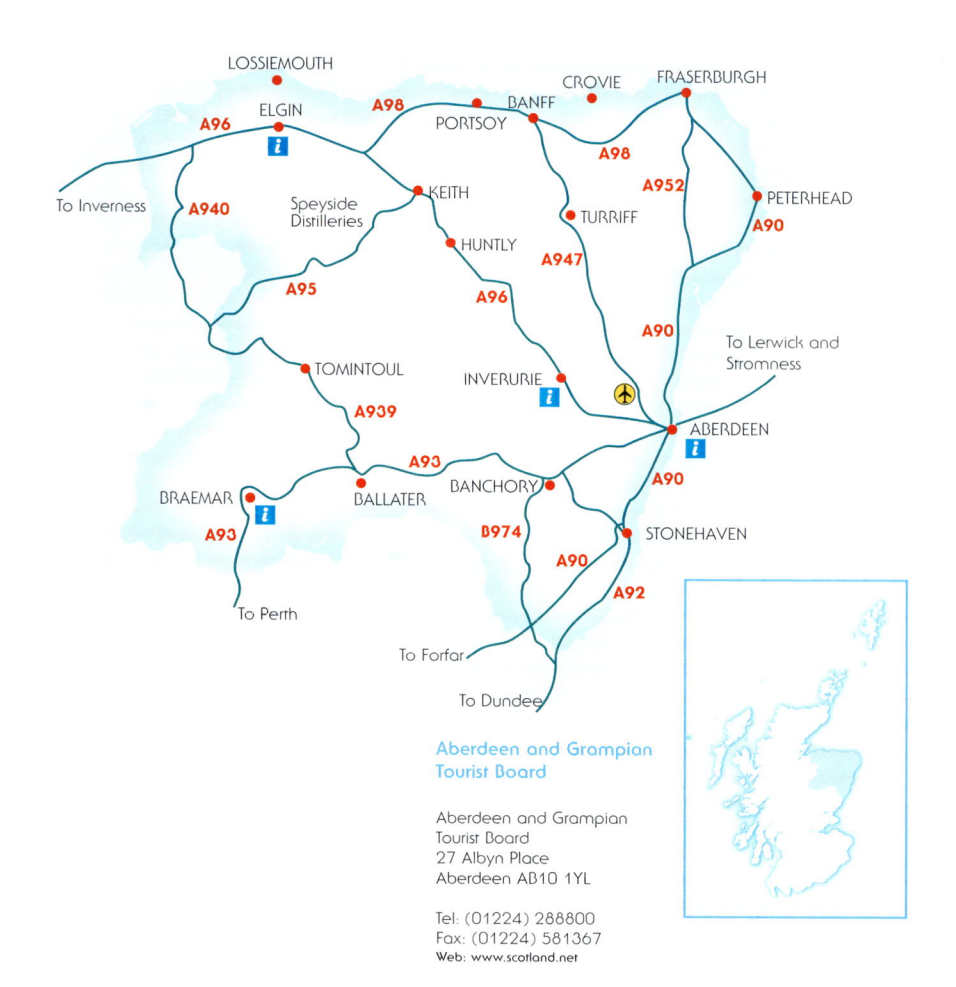

Grampian Highlands, Aberdeen and the North East Coast

Aberdeen and Grampian Tourist Board

Aberdeen and Grampian Tourist Board
27 Albyn Place
Aberdeen AB10 1YL

Tel: (01224) 288800
Fax: (01224) 581367
Web: www.scotland.net

Tourist Information Centres

Grampian Highlands, Aberdeen and the North East Coast

Aberdeen and Grampian Tourist Board

Aberdeen
St Nicholas House
Broad Street
Tel: (01224) 632727
Jan-Dec

Alford
Railway Museum
Station Yard
Tel: (019755) 62052
Easter-Sept

Ballater
Station Square
Tel: (013397) 55306
Easter-end Oct

Banchory
Bridge Street
Tel: (01330) 822000
Easter-Oct

Banff
Collie Lodge
Tel: (01261) 812419
Easter-Sept

Braemar
The Mews
Mar Road
Tel: (013397) 41600
April-Oct

Crathie
Car Park
Balmoral Castle
Tel: (013397) 42414
Easter-Oct

Dufftown
Clock Tower
The Square
Tel: (01340) 820501
Easter-Oct

Elgin
17 High Street
Tel: (01343) 542666/543388
Jan-Dec

Forres
116 High Street
Tel: (01309) 672938
Easter-Oct

Fraserburgh
Saltoun Square
Tel: (01346) 518315
Easter-Sept

Huntly
The Square
Tel: (01466) 792255
Easter-Oct

Inverurie
18 High Street
Tel: (01467) 625800
Jan-Dec

Stonehaven
66 Allardice Street
Tel: (01569) 762806
Easter-Oct

Tomintoul
The Square
Tel: (01807) 580285
Easter-Oct

GRAMPIAN HIGHLANDS, ABERDEEN AND THE NORTH EAST COAST

Aberchirder, by Huntly, Banffshire
Map Ref: 4F8

Mrs A Hay
Mill of Auchintoul, Aberchirder, by Huntly, Aberdeenshire, AB54 7RF
Tel: 01466 780349

★★ SELF CATERING

1 house, 2 pub rms, 3 bedrms, sleeps 6-8, £160.00-£250.00, Feb-Nov, bus nearby, rail 10 mls, airport 40 mls

Extensively refurbished holiday house on working farm. Centrally heated and double glazed. Plenty local interests including distilleries and castles.

Aberdeen
Map Ref: 4G10

Mrs I Clarke
Paddockhurst, Kemnay, Inverurie, AB51 5LN
Tel: 01467 642425

★★★ SELF CATERING

1 cottage, 1 pub rm, 1 bedrm (All grd.floor), sleeps 2, min let 4 days, £160.00-£240.00, Jan-Dec, bus 3 mls, rail 3 mls, ferry 12 mls, airport 4 mls

An attractive lodge bungalow with lovely views of woods and fields. Warm, comfortable and charmingly decorated it is a cosy hideaway for two. Within the half acre of fenced garden is a paved picnic spot with table and benches. A multitude of activities with golf, horse riding and castle trails in easy driving distance. Aberdeen 9 miles, Dyce Airport 3 miles.

Lower Deeside Holiday Park
Maryculter, Aberdeen, AB12 5FX
Tel: 01224 733860 Fax: 01224 732490

★★★★ HOLIDAY PARK

Park accommodation: 75

45 tourers £8.00-10.00 or 45 motors £8.00-10.00 or 45 tents £4.00-10.00. Total Touring Pitches 45.

10 Holiday Caravans to let, sleep 6 £175.00-300.00, total sleeping capacity 60, min let 2 nights.

14 acres, grassy, hard-standing, level, Jan-Dec, prior booking in peak periods, overnight holding area. Extra charge for electricity, awnings.

Leisure facilities:

Take B9077 from Aberdeen for 6 mls, or B976 from Stonehaven for 10 mls, or B9077 from Banchory for 10 mls. Park is behind hotel.

The Robert Gordon University
Business & Vacation Accommodation Service
Customer Services Department, Schoolhill, Aberdeen AB10 1FR
Telephone: 01224 262134   Fax: 01224 262144
e.mail: accommodation@rgu.ac.uk   Web: www.scotland2000.com/rgu

Fully equipped, comfortable, self-catering flats at various city locations. All flats have 6/8 single bedrooms with shared kitchen/living areas. All units have TVs provided and some have microwave facilities. Ensuite rooms available. Ideal for city centre and countryside. Large groups welcome. Available June to August. Prices on request.

Peggy McInnes
Business & Vacation Accommodation Service,
The Robert Gordon University, Schoolhill, Aberdeen AB10 1FR
Tel: 01224 262134 Fax: 01224 262144
E-mail: accommodation@rgu.ac.uk
Web: www.scotland2000.com/rgu

★ UP TO ★★ SELF CATERING

64 flats, 1 pub rm, 6-8 bedrms (grd flr avail), sleeps 1-8, total sleeping capacity 400, £225.00-£435.00, end May-Aug, bus nearby

Student flats at separate locations, all on or near to main bus routes for city centre. Use of sports facilities.

Important: Prices stated are estimates and may be subject to amendments

GRAMPIAN HIGHLANDS, ABERDEEN AND THE NORTH EAST COAST

F

ABERDEEN – ABOYNE

Aberdeen

Nether Don Ltd
Don Street, Old Aberdeen, AB24 1XP
Tel: 01224 488321 Fax: 01224 488650
E-mail: info@prosyst.co.uk

SELF CATERING ★★★

Map Ref: 4G10

1 cottage, 1 pub rm, 2 bedrms (All grd.floor), sleeps 2-4, £220.00-£330.00, Jan-Dec, bus ½ ml, rail 2 mls, ferry 2 mls, airport 5 mls

A small charming cottage in a unique spot beside the River Don and Brig O' Balgowmie. Quiet tranquility and wildlife right on your doorstep. Seals, geese, ducks and birdlife in abundance, this area is designated number one conservation area. 2 miles to city centre, 5 miles to airport. Fishing available.

Skene House
96 Rosemount Viaduct, Aberdeen, AB25 1NX
Tel: 01224 645971 Fax: 01224 626866
E-mail: reservations@skene-house.co.uk
Web: www.skene-house.co.uk

SERVICED APARTMENTS ★★★ UP TO ★★★★

117 suites, 1 pub rm, 1-3 bedrms, sleeps 2-6, total sleeping capacity 400, £66.00-£150.00 per day per suite, Jan-Dec

A "home away from home" located in the heart of Aberdeen, Skene House provides a range of 1 to 3 bedrooms. Suites individually furnished and decorated offering comfort and space with independence. Daily maid service and off street parking. Shops and restaurants nearby.

Skene House Holburn
6 Union Grove, Aberdeen, AB10 6SY
Tel: 01224 580000 Fax: 01224 585193
E-mail: holburn@skene-house.co.uk
Web: www.skene-house.co.uk

SERVICED APARTMENTS ★★★★

39 Suites, 2 pub rms, 1-3 bedrms (grd flr avail), sleeps 2-5, total sleeping capacity 80, £75.00-£195.00, Jan-Dec, bus nearby, rail 1 mile, ferry 1 mile, airport 8 mls

A "home away from home" located in the heart of Aberdeen, Skene House provides a range of 1 - 3 bedroom suites individually furnished and decorated offering comfort and space with independence. Daily maid service, off street parking, shops and restaurants nearby.

---

by Aberlour, Banffshire

Aberlour Gardens Caravan Park
Aberlour, Banffshire, AB38 9LD
Tel/Fax: 01340 871586
E-mail: Abergard@compuserve.com

HOLIDAY PARK ★★★★★

Map Ref: 4D8

Park accommodation: 56

30 tourers £7.00-9.00 or 30 motors £7.00-9.00 or 30 tents £3.25-9.00. Total Touring Pitches 30.
Holiday Caravan to let, sleeps 4-6 £150.00-325.00, min let 3 days.

5 acres, mixed, Apr-Oct, prior booking in peak periods. Extra charge for electricity, showers.

Signposted off A95 midway between Aberlour and Craigellachie onto unclassified road. Vehicles over 10'6 use A941 Craigellachie to Dufftown. Site is sign posted.

Aboyne, Aberdeenshire

Glen Tanar Estate
Brooks House, Glen Tanar, Aboyne, Aberdeenshire, AB34 5EU
Tel: 013398 86451/86305 Fax: 013398 86047

SELF CATERING ★★★ UP TO ★★★★

Map Ref: 4F11

2 houses, 2 cottages, 1-2 pub rms, 1-6 bedrms, sleeps 2-12, total sleeping capacity 30, £150.00-£820.00, Feb-Dec, bus 5 mls, rail 35 mls, airport 40 mls

Tastefully refurbished cottages, individual in character, on Highland estate. Wide range of leisure activities available on site and nearby.

VAT is shown at 17.5%: changes in this rate may affect prices.

Key to symbols is on back flap.

ABOYNE – BY ABOYNE

GRAMPIAN HIGHLANDS, ABERDEEN AND THE NORTH EAST COAST

Aboyne, Aberdeenshire

Map Ref: 4F11

★★★ SELF CATERING

Mary Levie
Gordon Lodge, Aboyne, Aberdeenshire, AB34 5EL
Tel: 013398 86466
E-mail: kbv73@dial.pipex.com

Comfortable garden flat, located within easy walking distance of village centre. Convenient for walking, fishing, golf and tourist attractions.

1 house, 1 pub rm, 3 bedrms, sleeps 4-6, £250.00-£300.00, Apr-Oct, bus 1/2 ml, rail 30 mls, airport 30 mls

★★★★ SELF CATERING

Mrs K M White
Craig Eunan House, St Eunan's Road, Aboyne, Aberdeenshire, AB34 5HH
Tel: 013398 86577

Traditional sporting lodge, fully modernised, situated in quiet location in centre of Aboyne within walking distance of all village facilities.

1 cottage, 1 pub rm, 1 bedrm (All grd.floor), sleeps 2, Jan-Dec, bus 300 yds, rail 30 mls, airport 30 mls

---

by Aboyne, Aberdeenshire

Map Ref: 4F11

★★★ SELF CATERING

Mr R W Russell
3 Norman Terrace, Cranbrook Road, Hawkhurst, Kent, TN18 4AU
Tel/Fax: 01580 754370

A former Schoolhouse, this large traditional granite bungalow cottage offers spacious accommodation in a delightful peaceful location. Set in a quiet rural village surrounded by farmland, it is an ideal holiday base. Aboyne 9 miles, Ballater and Banchory approx 14 miles each.

1 cottage, 3 bedrms (All grd.floor), sleeps 6, £190.00-£390.00, Jan-Dec, bus 2 mls, rail 30 mls, airport 30 mls

---

★★★ SELF CATERING

Anne & Donald Silcock
Oldyleiper Farmhouse, Birse, Aboyne, Aberdeenshire, AB34 5BY
Tel: 013398 86332 Fax: 013398 87261
E-mail: 101526.2537@compuserve.com

Converted steading in rural deeside, original farmhouse just beside. Ideal area for outdoor pursuits, hills and rivers, bring yer boots.

1 cottage, 1 pub rm, 1 bedrm, sleeps 2, £100.00-£200.00, Jan-Dec, bus nearby, rail 30 mls, airport 30 mls

★★★★ SELF CATERING

Mrs I Strachan
Dorevay, Birse, Aboyne, Aberdeenshire, AB34 5BT
Tel: 013398 86232

A cosy east wing of a large granite-built house with extensive landscaped and wooded garden. Lovely scenic views over Aboyne to hills beyond.

1 wing of house, 1 pub rm, 1 bedrm, sleeps 2, min let 3 nights, £138.00-£240.00, Jan-Dec, bus 1 1/2 mls, rail 30 mls, airport 30 mls

---

Important: Prices stated are estimates and may be subject to amendments

GRAMPIAN HIGHLANDS, ABERDEEN AND THE NORTH EAST COAST

F

BY ABOYNE – ARCHIESTOWN

183

by Aboyne, Aberdeenshire

Map Ref: 4F11

★★★★ SELF CATERING

Tillypronie Estate
c/o Strutt & Parker, 68 Station Road, Banchory,
Kincardineshire, AB31 5YJ
Tel: 01330 824888 Fax: 01330 825577
E-mail: banchory@struttandparker.co.uk

A substantial detached cottage situated on the extensive Tillypronie Estate in Upper Deeside. A magnificent panoramic vista over the farmland and wooded countryside to distant hills. Loch and river fishing.

1 house, 3 pub rms, 4 bedrms, sleeps 8, £310.00-£740.00, Jan-Dec, bus 4 mls, rail 45 mls, airport 40 mls

---

by Alford, Aberdeenshire

Map Ref: 4F10

★★★ SELF CATERING

Mr Mark Tennant
30 Abbey Gardens, London, NW8 9AT
Tel: 0171 624 3200

16c Baronial Castle, restored 1968. Modern comforts with domestic help. Open fire, grand piano. Set in quiet rural setting with hill views.

1 castle, 3 pub rms, 5 bedrms, sleeps 9, £650.00-£750.00, Jan-Dec, bus 1 ml, rail 12 mls, airport 27 mls

---

★★ SELF CATERING

Mrs P Thomas
Roughhaugh, Midmar, by Inverdurie, AB51 7QB
Tel: 01330 833455

Traditional cottage in quiet rural Donside. Ideal for peaceful relaxing stay - yet not isolated. Whisky and castle trails nearby. Also plenty of golf courses, fishing and walking.

1 cottage, 2 pub rms, 2 bedrms, sleeps 4-5, £150.00-£225.00, Apr-Oct, bus 1½ mls

---

Archiestown, Moray

Map Ref: 4D8

★★ SELF CATERING

Mrs Marian B Mansfield
3A Resaurie, Smithton, Inverness, IV1 2NH, IV2 7NH
Tel: 01463 791714

Traditional cottage with pleasant garden in quiet village. On Whisky Trail and central for Speyside area. Short stroll to Post Office and Hotel.

1 cottage, 1 pub rm, 3 bedrms (grd flr avail), sleeps 4, £90.00-£225.00, Jan-Dec, bus nearby, rail 18 mls, airport 45 mls

---

VAT is shown at 17.5%: changes in this rate may affect prices.

Key to symbols is on back flap.

BALLATER

Ballater, Aberdeenshire

GRAMPIAN HIGHLANDS, ABERDEEN AND THE NORTH EAST COAST

Map Ref: 4E11

Sydney Cottage (Ballater)

Reservations: 70 Cluny Gardens, Edinburgh EH16 6BR
Tel: 0131 447 1055   e.mail: chadwickap@aol.com

Wonderful holiday cottage of character. 100 years old. Clean and warm. Open fires and central heating. Well equipped kitchen. Master bedroom with four poster and fire. Three comfortable twin rooms. Garden with patio furniture and barbeque. Fabulous base for skiing, walking, golf, tennis, fishing, cycling or relaxing. Lots to see and do.

SELF CATERING ★★★

Dr Paul Chadwick
70 Cluny Gardens, Edinburgh, EH10 6BR
Tel: 0131 447 1055

1 cottage, 1 pub rm, 4 bedrms (grd flr avail), sleeps 8, £250.00-£580.00, Jan-Dec, bus nearby

Surprisingly spacious traditional stone built cottage set at the heart of this peaceful Royal Deeside village. A fine holiday home and base for a wide range of leisure and sporting activities available in the area.

SELF CATERING ★★★★

Dr C W Gosden
Catbells, Orestan Lane, Effingham, Leatherhead, Surrey, KT24 5SN
Tel: 01372 459123 Fax: 01372 456784
E-mail: cliff@cwgo.freeserve.co.uk
Web: www.cwgo.freeserve.co.uk

1 cottage, 1 pub rm, 3 bedrms (grd flr avail), sleeps 6, £300.00-£450.00, Jan-Dec, bus 1 1/2 mls

Traditional, stone built cottage renovated to a very high standard. One of four in this secluded sunny, south facing spot. Balmoral Castle 7 miles away, Ballater 2 miles. An ideal holiday home set in a wonderfully peaceful situation yet with a wide range of sporting activities including golf, gliding and hillwalking.

SELF CATERING ★★★★

Mrs Harrison
P.O. Box 24, Inchbroom, Nigg, Aberdeen, AB12 3GF
Tel: 01224 897278 Fax: 01224 896954

1 house, 3 pub rms, 3 bedrms (grd flr avail), sleeps 6, £375.00-£550.00, Jan-Dec, bus 1/2 ml, rail 35 mls, airport 35 mls

Stone built house on outer edge of village, large garden and spectacular views over 15th fairway to the hills.

SELF CATERING ★★

Ian A Hepburn
Gairn Lodge, 67 Golf Road, Ballater, Aberdeenshire, AB35 5RU
Tel: 013397 56025

1 bungalow, 2 bedrms (All grd.floor), sleeps 6, £140.00-£295.00, Jan-Dec, bus 300 yds

Cosy bungalow cottage set in garden of owners house. Peaceful situation overlooking golf course with club house only 100 meters distance. Easy walking distance of village centre. Numerous leisure activities available in area.

Important: Prices stated are estimates and may be subject to amendments

GRAMPIAN HIGHLANDS, ABERDEEN AND THE NORTH EAST COAST

F

BALLATER – BALLINDALLOCH

Ballater, Aberdeenshire — Map Ref: 4E11

SELF CATERING ★★★★

Mairi MacLeod
1 Bridge Square, Ballater, Aberdeenshire, AB35 5QJ
Tel: 013397 55056/020 7403 7760

A stylish conversion to a traditional georgian cottage with many artistic touches in centre of Ballater with views of River Dee. Sauna and jacuzzi, sun terrace and private garden.

1 house, 2-3 pub rms, 4-5 bedrms, 2 bathrooms, sleeps 7-8, £450.00-£750.00, Jan-Dec, bus nearby, rail 42 mls, airport 40 mls

---

SELF CATERING ★★★

Mr and Mrs Middleton
255 Holburn Street, Aberdeen, AB10 7FL
Tel: 01224 315607/591787 Fax: 01224 591787

Cosy semi detached cottage in picturesque Highland town. Ideal for touring and walking, in Royal Deeside.

1 cottage, 2 pub rms, 2 bedrms, sleeps 4-6, £200.00-£450.00, Jan-Dec, bus nearby, rail 40 mls, airport 40 mls

---

SELF CATERING ★★★★

Mr James Wimpenny
49 Blackmoorfoot, Linthwaite, Huddersfield, Yorkshire, HD7 5TR
Tel: 01484 847283 Fax: 01484 846969
E-mail: james.wimpenny@wimpenny.co.uk

Traditional Victorian cottage lovingly restored to a bright stylish and comfortable holiday home with safe, sunny enclosed garden.

1 house, 3 pub rms, 3 bedrms (grd flr avail), sleeps 5-6, min let long weekend, £211.00-£520.00, Jan-Dec, bus ½ ml, airport 40 mls

---

by Ballater, Aberdeenshire — Map Ref: 4E11

SELF CATERING ★★★★

David Young
Honey Cottage, Dinnet, nr Aboyne, Aberdeenshire, AB34 5JY
Tel: 013398 87473 Fax: 013398 87427

Recently renovated stone-built, semi-detached cottage in peaceful small rural village. 4 miles (7km) to Aboyne with shops, etc. Local village pub offers excellent fayre. Suitable cottage for a family holiday.

1 cottage, 1 pub rm, 2 bedrms, sleeps 4, £200.00-£300.00, Jan-Dec

---

Ballindalloch, Banffshire — Map Ref: 4D9

SELF CATERING ★★★★

Mrs A Jenkins
Ashwell House Home Farm, Little Walden, Saffron Walden, Essex, CB10 1XE
Tel/Fax: 01799 524038

Purpose built lodge with excellent views over the River Spey, which is only 100yds away. "Speyside Way" passes nearby. Sauna available.

1 lodge, 1 pub rm, 3 bedrms (grd flr avail), sleeps 6-8, £250.00-£550.00, Jan-Dec, bus 1 ml, rail 20 mls, airport 50 mls

---

VAT is shown at 17.5%: changes in this rate may affect prices.

Key to symbols is on back flap.

BALLINDALLOCH – BY BANCHORY

GRAMPIAN HIGHLANDS, ABERDEEN AND THE NORTH EAST COAST

Ballindalloch, Banffshire — Map Ref: 4D9

★★★★ SELF CATERING

Mr Pottinger
Baille Farm, Bridge of Westfield, Thurso, Caithness, KW14 7QW
Tel: 01847 871200 Fax: 01847 871222

1 lodge, 1 pub rm, 3 bedrms (grd flr avail), sleeps 8, £250.00-£650.00, Jan-Dec, bus 1 ml, rail 20 mls, airport 50 mls

Scandinavian Lodge situated in spectacular scenery and offering many sporting opportunities. Ideal for skiing, fishing, touring or just resting.

Banchory, Aberdeenshire — Map Ref: 4F11

★★ SELF CATERING

Mrs M Bolland
Arbeadie House, Station Road, Banchory, Kincardineshire, AB31 5YA
Tel: 01330 825898

1 flat, 3 pub rms, 2 bedrms, sleeps 4-6, £290.00-£400.00, Jan-Dec, bus nearby, rail 17 mls, airport 17 mls

Comfortable flat adjoining owners Victorian house in peaceful situation with large garden. Within 200 meters of the centre of Banchory with shops, bars and restaurants in easy walking distance.

★★★★ SELF CATERING

Rosalind Holmes
Village Guest House, 83 High Street, Banchory, Kincardineshire, AB31 5TJ
Tel/Fax: 01330 823307
E-mail: 106053.2144@compuserve.com

1 cottage, 1 pub rm, 2 bedrms (grd flr avail), sleeps 4-5, £225.00-£425.00, Jan-Dec, bus nearby, rail 17 mls, airport 17 mls

Traditional cottage, situated within heart of Royal Deeside village, offering charm and comfort. Conveniently situated for castle, whiskey and victorian trails, fishing, walking and many other outdoor activities. Oil capital of Aberdeen and Dyce airport 30 minutes away.

★★★★ HOLIDAY PARK

Silver Ladies Caravan Park
Strachan, Banchory, Aberdeenshire, AB31 6NL
Tel: 01330 822800 Fax: 01330 825701

Park accommodation: 103
18 tourers £5.75-8.00 or 18 motors £5.75-8.00 or 18 tents £4.75-6.50. Total Touring Pitches 18.
15 Holiday Caravans to let, sleep 6-8 £115.00-285.00, total sleeping capacity 108, min let 2 nights.

7.5 acres, grassy, level, sloping, Apr-Oct, prior booking in peak periods, latest time of arrival 2000. Extra charge for electricity, awnings.

Leisure facilities:

2 miles South of Banchory on left of B974 Fettercairn Road

by Banchory, Aberdeenshire — Map Ref: 4F11

★★ SELF CATERING

Mrs J Hutton
Borrowstone House, Kincardine O'Neil, Aboyne, Aberdeenshire, AB34 5AP
Tel/Fax: 013398 84264

1 flat, 1 pub rm, 3 bedrms, sleeps 5, £175.00-£250.00, Mar-Oct, bus ¼ ml, rail 20 mls, airport 20 mls

Former coach house in grounds of large private house, with own secluded area. Steep stairs to charming first floor flat. 0.25 mile to village, pub and shop.

Important: Prices stated are estimates and may be subject to amendments

F

GRAMPIAN HIGHLANDS, ABERDEEN AND THE NORTH EAST COAST

BY BANCHORY – BANFF

by Banchory, Aberdeenshire

Map Ref: 4F11

Woodend Chalet Holidays
Rose Cottage, Glassel, by Banchory, Aberdeenshire AB31 4DD
Telephone: 013398 82562   Fax: 013398 82845

In quiet woodland setting, three miles from Banchory, a spacious and south-facing site with views to hills. Seven clean and well-maintained chalets. We provide a large grassed area for children's play with swings and small recreation hut. Car parking on site.

Chalet prices from £99-£272 per week (long lets £55).

★★

SELF CATERING

Mr & Mrs A Kostulin
Woodend Chalet Holidays, Rose Cottage, Glassel, by Banchory, Aberdeenshire, AB31 4DD
Tel: 013398 82562 Fax: 013398 82845

A selection of timber cabins set in a peaceful woodland setting with views across fields to hills beyond. A beautiful part of the Royal Deeside region with forest walks, castles and gardens. A wide range of outdoor activities available in the area.

7 chalets, 1 pub rm, 1-2 bedrms (grd flr avail), sleeps 3-5, total sleeping capacity 32, £99.00-£272.00, Jan-Dec, bus on route, rail 20 mls, airport 20 mls

---

★★★★

SELF CATERING

Mrs M Watson
3 William Street, Torphins, by Banchory, Kincardineshire, AB31 4FR
Tel: 013398 82277
E-mail: john.watson@torphins45.freeserve.co.uk

Detached Victorian garden cottage renovated to a high standard. Situated in owners garden in a peaceful secluded spot. The centre of Torphins village is within easy strolling distance. All accommodation is on the ground floor.

1 cottage, 2 pub rms, 1 bedrm (All grd.floor), sleeps 2, £160.00-£260.00, Jan-Dec, bus nearby, rail 22 mls, airport 22 mls

---

Banff

Map Ref: 4F7

SCOTTISH TOURIST BOARD — INSPECTED

HOLIDAY CARAVAN

Banff Links Caravan Park
Booking Enquiries: Heather Ewen 1 Penny Place, Middlegrange, Peterhead, Aberdeenshire, AB42 2RP
Tel: 01779 470934/01261 818897 (weekends)

Park accommodation:

5 Holiday Caravans to let, sleep 6-8 £130.00-225.00, total sleeping capacity 36, min let weekend (low season), Apr-Oct.

From Banff take A98 W for 1 ml. Turn right. Signposted 300 yds.

VAT is shown at 17.5%: changes in this rate may affect prices.

Key to symbols is on back flap.

BY BANFF – BRAEMAR

GRAMPIAN HIGHLANDS, ABERDEEN AND THE NORTH EAST COAST

by Banff — Map Ref: 4F7

Strocherie Farm

Strocherie Farm, King Edward, Banff, Aberdeenshire AB45 3PL
Tel: 01888 551220 Fax: 01888 551220

Honeysuckle and Pinetree cottages offer you the delights of peace and seclusion. Recently refurbished, well-equipped, cosy, log-burning fires. Ideal for touring, beaches, golf, horse-riding, whisky and castle trails, Pennan nearby, walking, romantic weekend breaks, enjoy fishing from our trout loch or browse round the farm.

★★★ SELF CATERING

Mrs W M Anderson
Strocherie Farm, King Edward, by Banff, Aberdeenshire, AB45 3PL
Tel/Fax: 01888 551220

2 cottages, 2 pub rms, 4 bedrms, sleeps 8, total sleeping capacity 4, £150.00-£300.00, Jan-Dec, bus ¼ ml, rail 40 mls, airport 40 mls

Traditional farm cottage. Recently refurbished in quiet location. Trout fishing and clay pigeon shooting available. 7 miles from Banff and 4 miles from Turiff. Ideal for castle and whisky trails. Many golf courses within easy reach.

★ SELF CATERING

Mrs E Davidson
Mill of Alvah, Banff, AB45 3UT
Tel/Fax: 01261 821609

1 flat, 1 pub rm, 2 bedrms, sleeps 4-6, £80.00-£140.00, Jan-Dec, bus 3 mls, rail 27 mls, airport 46 mls

Flat on working farm. Quiet sheltered location. Close to River Deveron and Bridge of Alvah. Idea for scenic country walks. 3miles from Banff.

★★★ SELF CATERING

Mrs M Kitchen
Wood of Shaws, Alvah, Banff, AB45 3UL
Tel/Fax: 01261 821223

1 cottage, 2 pub rms, 2 bedrms (All grd.floor), sleeps 4, £210.00-£310.00, Jan-Dec, bus 5 mls, rail 18 mls, airport 40 mls

Lovely cottage peacefully situated among lawns and woodland beside River Deveron. The abundance of wildlife and the peaceful environment makes badger cottage ideal for country Lovers and fishermen. Residential painting holidays and courses available.

Braemar, Aberdeenshire — Map Ref: 4D11

★★★ UP TO ★★★★ SELF CATERING

Mrs Maria Franklin, Callater Lodge Hotel
9 Glenshee Road, Braemar, Aberdeenshire, AB35 5YQ
Tel: 013397 41275 Fax: 013397 41345
E-mail: maria4@hotel-braemar.co.uk
Web: www.hotel-braemar.co.uk

1 chalet, 1 cottage, 1 pub rm, 1-2 bedrms (grd flr avail), sleeps 2-4, total sleeping capacity 6, min let weekend (low season), £180.00-£330.00, Jan-Dec, bus ½ ml, rail 49 mls, airport 58 mls

Cottage (Twin/Double bedrooms) and Chalet (Sleeps 2). Fully equipped to high standard, linen supplied. Situated in quiet corner of spacious garden with mature trees. Cottage has open fire. Close to centre of village, nature reserves, Balmoral and Glenshee ski slopes.

Important: Prices stated are estimates and may be subject to amendments

GRAMPIAN HIGHLANDS, ABERDEEN AND THE NORTH EAST COAST

BRAEMAR – BRODIE

Braemar, Aberdeenshire — Map Ref: 4D11

★★ UP TO ★★★ SELF CATERING

Mrs A M Cheyne
Fife Cottages, Braemar, AB35 5YT
Tel: 013397 41608

Stone built house with attached cottage and large garden in quiet location on edge of village. Plenty of car parking.

1 house, 1 cottage, min let weekend, £250.00-£500.00, Jan-Dec, bus ½ ml, rail 60 mls, airport 60 mls

---

★★★ SELF CATERING

Mr Moore
Braemar Lodge, Glenshee Road, Braemar, Aberdeenshire, AB35 5YQ
Tel/Fax: 013397 41627

Modern fully equipped log cabins in hotel grounds, within easy walking distance of village and its Royal connections. Excellent base for touring, walking and winter activities.

4 log cabins, 1 pub rm, sleeps 6, total sleeping capacity 24, £200.00-£450.00, Jan-Dec, bus ¼ mile, rail 49 miles, airport 59 miles

---

★★★★ SELF CATERING

Mrs Jessie Smith
10 Leighton Gardens, Ellon, Aberdeenshire, AB41 9BH
Tel: 01358 720346

A stylish well appointed one bedroom apartment with additional sofabed. Peacefully situated this impressive conversion of a former church is within easy walking distance of shops and restaurants. A small but renowned highland village with a wide variety of sporting activities including golf, gliding and hill walking available in this beautiful region.

1 1st floor flat ensuite, 1 pub rm, 1 bedrm, sleeps 2-4, min let 3 nights, £125.00-£290.00, Jan-Dec, bus nearby, rail 65 mls, airport 65 mls

---

by Braemar, Aberdeenshire — Map Ref: 4D11

★★ SELF CATERING

Helen Stuart
8 Hilltop Crescent, Westhill, Aberdeen
Tel: 01224 741787
E-mail: helen_stuart@yahoo.com

Country cottage in small hamlet 4 miles from Ballater. Quiet, rural position. A good base for exploring Royal Deeside and surrounding countryside.

1 cottage, 1 pub rm, 3 bedrms (grd flr avail), sleeps 6, £260.00-£280.00, Jan-Dec, bus 5 mls, rail 60 mls, airport 60 mls

---

Brodie, Moray — Map Ref: 4C8

★★★★ HOLIDAY PARK

Old Mill Caravan Park
Brodie, Forres, Moray, IV36 0TD
Tel: 01309 641244

7 acres, grassy, level, sheltered, Apr-Oct, prior booking in peak periods, latest time of arrival 2200. Extra charge for electricity, awnings.

Park accommodation: 74
27 tourers or 27 motors or 12 tents. Total Touring Pitches 27. Charges on application.

11 Holiday Caravans to let, sleep 4-6, total sleeping capacity 58, min let 3 nights.

Leisure facilities:
On left of A96, 3mls from Forres, on A96 main road.

VAT is shown at 17.5%: changes in this rate may affect prices.

Key to symbols is on back flap.

BUCKIE – CULLEN

GRAMPIAN HIGHLANDS, ABERDEEN AND THE NORTH EAST COAST

Buckie, Banffshire — Map Ref: 4E7

★★ SELF CATERING

Mr James Merson Grant
8 Great Eastern Road, Portessie, Buckie, Banffshire, AB56 1SL
Tel: 01542 831277

1 flat, 1 pub rm, 1 bedrm (All grd.floor), sleeps 2, min let weekend, £160.00–£190.00, Jan-Dec, bus nearby, rail 14 mls, airport 60 mls

Ground floor flat with south facing garden in quiet location close to sea in picturesque village of Portessie. Ideal for golf courses and beaches.

by Buckie, Banffshire — Map Ref: 4E7

★★ SELF CATERING

Mr J Forbes
Maryhill Farm, Drybridge, Buckie, Banffshire, AB56 2JB
Tel: 01542 831284

2 log cabins, 1-2 pub rms, 2 bedrms, sleeps 2-6, total sleeping capacity 10, £121.00–£305.00, Jan-Dec, bus 4 mls, rail 12 mls, airport 55 mls

Finnish log cabins in peaceful rural setting, close to stock farm with magnificent views over the Moray Firth.

Burghead, Moray — Map Ref: 4D7

★★★ SELF CATERING

Mrs Mhairi Mackenzie
2 Distillery Cottages, Teaninich Distillery, Alness, Rossshire, IV17 0XB
Tel: 01349 885013

1 cottage, 1 pub rm, 3 bedrms (All grd.floor), sleeps 4, £180.00–£280.00, mid Jan-mid Dec, rail 9 mls

Traditional stonebuilt semi-detached cottage with large enclosed garden and off road parking for 2 cars. 3 bedroom accommodation on one level. Sleeps 4, pets welcome.

Colpy, Aberdeenshire — Map Ref: 4F9

★★★★ SELF CATERING

Greg Manning
Snipefield, Culsalmond, Insch, Aberdeenshire
Tel: 01464 841394

1 cottage, 2 pub rms, 2 bedrms (All grd.floor), sleeps 4, min let 3 days, £100.00–£370.00, Jan-Dec, bus 1 ml, rail 4 mls, airport 26 mls

Rebuilt farmhouse providing compact holiday cottage of a high standard. Quiet location, with panoramic views.

Cullen, Banffshire — Map Ref: 4E7

★★★ SELF CATERING

Mrs W Grant
Lesina, Kennethmont, Huntly, Aberdeenshire, AB54 4NN
Tel: 01464 831696
E-mail: jas1@grantken.freeserve.co.uk
Web: www.grantken.freeserve.co.uk

1 house, 2 pub rms, 2 bedrms, sleeps 5, min let 3 nights, £150.00–£330.00, Jan-Dec, bus ¼ ml, rail 12 mls, airport 56 mls.

Traditional renovated fisherman's house in conservation area, close to sea and sandy beach. Shops, pubs, restaurants nearby. Ideal for coast or country.

Important: Prices stated are estimates and may be subject to amendments

GRAMPIAN HIGHLANDS, ABERDEEN AND THE NORTH EAST COAST

CULLEN – DINNET, BY ABOYNE

Cullen, Banffshire

Map Ref: 4E7

SELF CATERING ★★

Mrs W Grant
Lesina, Kennethmund, Huntly, Aberdeenshire, AB54 4NN
Tel: 01464 831696
E-mail: Jas1@Grantken.Freeserve.co.uk

1 house, 2 pub rms, 2 bedrms, sleeps 5, £150.00-£330.00, Jan-Dec, bus nearby, rail 12 mls, airport 55 mls

Traditional fisherman's house in conservation village close to beach, harbour and golf courses. Watch bottle-nose dolphins at play, tour whisky and castle trails, ideal base for walking in coast or country.

SELF CATERING ★★★

Mrs Evelyn Taylor
Buschweide, Pitkeathly Wells Road, Bridge of Earn,
Perthshire, PH2 9HA
Tel: 01738 812862

1 cottage, 1 pub rm, 1 bedrm (All grd.floor), sleeps 4, £120.00-£240.00, Jan-Dec, bus nearby, rail 16 mls, airport 60 mls

Modernised fisherman's cottage in coastal village close to sandy beaches.

Dinnet, by Aboyne, Aberdeenshire

Map Ref: 4E11

GLENDAVAN HOUSE
DINNET, Nr ABOYNE, ABERDEENSHIRE AB34 2SL
Tel/Fax: 01569 730693

Set in woodland grounds of seven acres, comfortable and well-appointed family home overlooking Davan Loch and high hills of Royal Deeside. Each season brings its own beauty and changing wildlife. A warm welcome awaits those seeking quiet retreat, reunion and exploration of the countryside and its activities (angling, gliding, golfing, climbing, pony trekking, ski-ing, cycling, clay pigeon shooting, castle and whisky "trails", Highland Games).
High quality accommodation (recommended maximum 10) includes generous heating, etc. –
We believe everything you would wish.
Terms: parties up to 10 – £700–£900 per week.
Additional £50–£70 per week, per person parties over 10.

SELF CATERING ★★★★

Dr Milne
North Cookney Croft, Muchalls, Stonehaven,
Kincardineshire, AB39 3SB
Tel/Fax: 01569 730693

1 house, 2-3 pub rms, 8 bedrms, sleeps 10, min let weekend, £700.00-£900.00, Jan-Dec, bus 1/2 ml, rail 37 mls, airport 42 mls

Set in the heart of Royal Deeside this former victorian shooting lodge has been refurbished with attention to detail emphasising the unique character and ambience of this large and spacious holiday home. Standing in it's own extensive 7 acres of woodland, the house overlooks Loch Davan, a bird sanctuary settled at times by greylag geese, whooper swans, mallards, moorhens and a family of otters.

VAT is shown at 17.5%: changes in this rate may affect prices.

Key to symbols is on back flap.

DUFFTOWN – BY ELGIN

GRAMPIAN HIGHLANDS, ABERDEEN AND THE NORTH EAST COAST

Dufftown, Banffshire

Map Ref: 4E9

★★★ SELF CATERING

Mrs Margaret J Brown
Ashville, Church Street, Dufftown, Keith, Banffshire, AB55 4AR
Tel: 01340 820265/820342 Fax: 01340 820265

Holiday flat with superb views. Ideally situated for Whisky Trail and Speyside Way. Dogs welcome.

1 flat, 1 pub rm, 2 bedrms, sleeps 4-5, £110.00-£130.00, Jan-Dec, bus nearby, rail 9 mls, ferry 54 mls, airport 54 mls

Elgin, Moray

Map Ref: 4D8

★★ SELF CATERING

Mr Graham Broad
Windmill Lodge, Gordonstoun School, Elgin, IV30 5RF
Tel: 01343 837880/830250 Fax: 01343 837879
E-mail: gb@gordonstoun.org.uk

Recently converted old steading building, to provide facilities for two persons in secluded grounds and gardens, 3 miles (5km) from Hopeman. Ideal base for family holidays.

2 cottages, 1 pub rm, 4 bedrms (grd flr avail), sleeps 1-3, total sleeping capacity 14, £175.00-£250.00, Jan-Dec, bus 1 ml, rail 6 mls, airport 25 mls

★★★ SELF CATERING

Mr & Mrs F Duncan
Westbank House, College of Roseisle, Elgin, Morayshire, IV30 5YD
Tel/Fax: 01343 835604
E-mail: fduncan@globalnet.co.uk

Stone built semi-detached cottages with enclosed garden in rural setting overlooking open farmland. Elgin 5 miles, coast 1 mile.

2 cottages, 1 pub rm, 2 bedrms (grd.flr avail), sleeps 4+baby, total sleeping capacity 8, £170.00-£270.00, Jan-Dec, bus 1 ml, rail 5 mls, airport 30 mls.

by Elgin, Moray

Map Ref: 4D8

★★ SELF CATERING

Mrs E Albiston
Little Buinach, Kellas, Elgin, Moray, IV30 8TS
Tel: 01343 890233

Detached modern house in rural farmland setting convenient for all local amenities.

1 house, 1 pub rm, 3 bedrms (grd flr avail), sleeps 6, £200.00-£250.00, Jan-Dec, bus 7 mls, rail 7 mls, airport 32 mls

★★★ SELF CATERING

Mr John A Christie
Blackhills House, Elgin, Moray, IV30 3QU
Tel/Fax: 01343 842223
E-mail: holcots@aol.com
Web: www.blackhills.co.uk

Well-appointed houses in magnificent woodland water garden on private estate with own tennis court. Secluded walks in exquisite natural surroundings.

5 cottages, 1-2 pub rms, 2-4 bedrms (grd flr avail), sleeps 3-8, total sleeping capacity 26, £160.00-£500.00, Jan-Dec, bus 1 ml, rail 6 mls, airport 40 mls

---

Important: Prices stated are estimates and may be subject to amendments

GRAMPIAN HIGHLANDS, ABERDEEN AND THE NORTH EAST COAST

F

BY ELGIN – FORRES

193

by Elgin, Moray

SELF CATERING ★★

North East Farm Chalets
Sheriffston, Elgin, Moray, IV30 8LA
Tel/Fax: 01343 842695

Map Ref: 4D8

1 chalet, 1 pub rm, 2 bedrms (grd flr avail), sleeps 6, £170.00-£300.00, Jan-Dec, bus ¼ ml

Substantial cottage in mature garden behind hotel in the historic and picturesque coastal village of Hoswick, 15 miles south of Lerwick and 12 miles north of Sumburgh Airport. Ideal base for birdwatching and handy for boat trips to Mousa island.

SELF CATERING ★★★ UP TO ★★★★ BRONZE

Springburn Log Cabins
Springburn, Miltonduff, Elgin, Moray, IV30 3TL
Tel: 01343 541939 Fax: 01343 548863
E-mail: enquiries@springburncabins.free-online.co.uk
Web: www.springburncabins.free-online.co.uk

Map Ref:

3 log cabins, 1 pub rm, 2 bedrms, sleeps 4, total sleeping capacity 4, £160.00-£360.00, Mar-Jan, bus ½ ml, rail 3 ½ mls, airport 36 mls

3 beautiful pine log cabins each standing on their own private location within 60 acres of natural surroundings. Ideal setting for a relaxing holiday. Fly-fishing on Springburn loch. Central for whisky trail, castles and gardens. Clean sandy beaches closeby.

Findhorn, Moray

SELF CATERING ★

Mr D M Sinclair
Balmalcolm, Kinrossie, Perth, Perthshire, PH2 6JA
Tel: 01821 650253

Map Ref: 4C7

1 house, 2 pub rms, 3 bedrms, sleeps 6, £230.00-£470.00, Jan-Dec, bus nearby, rail 5 mls, airport 40 mls

Traditionally furnished cottage, overlooking Findhorn Bay. Safe, sandy beaches nearby.

---

by Fochabers, Moray

SELF CATERING ★★

Mr A A Mitchell
2 South March, Bogmoor, Spey Bay, Fochabers, Moray, IV32 7PU
Tel: 01343 820459

Map Ref: 4E8

1 flat, 1 pub rm, 1 bedrm, sleeps 4, £150.00-£190.00, Jan-Dec, bus 2 ½ mls, rail 11 mls, airport 60 mls

A modern bungalow annex in a peaceful rural setting, sheltered garden with private patio and panoramic views up the River Spey valley to Ben Rinnes. Excellent location for walking, fishing, golf & beaches. Pets and children welcome.

Forres, Moray

SELF CATERING ★★★

Wellside Farmhouse
Kincorth Estate, Forres, Moray, IV36 2SP
Tel/Fax: 01309 674132

Map Ref: 4C8

1 house, 2 pub rms, 4 bedrms, sleeps 8, £323.00-£622.00, Jan-Dec, bus 2 mls, rail 2 mls, airport 20 mls

Recently converted stone built farmhouse, 4 miles (7 km) from Forres. Ideal base for group/family holidays.

VAT is shown at 17.5%: changes in this rate may affect prices.

Key to symbols is on back flap.

BY FORRES – GLENLIVET

GRAMPIAN HIGHLANDS, ABERDEEN AND THE NORTH EAST COAST

by Forres, Moray
Map Ref: 4C8

SELF CATERING ★

Mrs Jean M Taylor
Wellhill Farm, Dyke, Forres, Moray, IV36 2TG
Tel: 01309 641205

1 cottage, 1 pub rm, 3 bedrms (All grd.floor), sleeps 6, £180.00-£250.00, Apr-Oct, bus ¼ ml, rail 5 mls, airport 15 mls

Country cottage in its own large grounds near pleasant woodland walks. Castles, fishing, golf, beaches, hill-walking, distilleries and beautiful gardens also within easy reach. Ideal for family holidays.

Fraserburgh, Aberdeenshire
Map Ref: 4G7

SELF CATERING ★★★

Mr & Mrs E Simpson
89 Saltoun Place, Fraserburgh
Tel/Fax: 01346 518626

1 flat, 1 bedrm, sleeps 4-5, £150.00-£250.00, Jan-Dec, bus nearby, rail 42 mls, airport 40 mls

Self-contained flat on two floors, close to town amenities and beach areas. Ideal base for touring. Come and see the lighthouse museum. Car parking available.

Gardenstown, Banffshire
Map Ref: 4G7

SELF CATERING ★★★

Mr M French
Old Mill Inn, South Deeside Road, Maryculter, Aberdeen, Aberdeenshire, AB12 5FX
Tel: 01224 733212 Fax: 01224 732884

1 house, 5 pub rms, 2 bedrms, sleeps 4, £165.00-£335.00, Jan-Dec, bus nearby, rail 30 mls, ferry 40 mls, airport 40 mls

Traditional 2 storey cottage, completely renovated, in heart of village. Superb views from secluded rear terrace over Gamrie Bay.

SELF CATERING ★★

R L Morris
White Horse, Briningham, Melton Constable, Norfolk, NR24 2PY
Tel/Fax: 01263 860514

1 cottage, 2 pub rms, 3 bedrms, sleeps 5, £160.00-£300.00, Jan-Dec, bus nearby

Two-storey fisherman's cottage situated close to the sea in this spectacular cliffside village.

Glenlivet, Banffshire
Map Ref: 4D9

SELF CATERING ★★

Mrs Jo R Durno
Deepdale, Glenlivet, Ballindalloch, Banffshire, AB37 9EJ
Tel/Fax: 01807 590364

1 bungalow, 1 pub rm, 3 bedrms, sleeps 8, £270.00-£370.00, Jan-Dec

Cosy semi-detached bungalow with Rayburn stove in kitchen and open fire in sitting room. Local facilities within 5 miles. Good garden with barbecue, suitable for children playing.

Important: Prices stated are estimates and may be subject to amendments

GRAMPIAN HIGHLANDS, ABERDEEN AND THE NORTH EAST COAST

GLENLIVET – HOPEMAN

Glenlivet, Banffshire — Map Ref: 4D9

★★ UP TO ★★★ — SELF CATERING

Glenlivet Holiday Lodges
Glenlivet, Ballindalloch, AB37 9DR
Tel: 01807 590209 Fax: 01807 590401

10 chalets, 1 cottage, 1 pub rm, 2-3 bedrms, sleeps 2-8, total sleeping capacity 72, £200.00-£450.00, Dec-Oct, bus 8 mls, rail 17 mls, airport 53 mls

Lodges and a cottage recently completely refurbished, situated amidst rolling upland scenery, with spectacular views. Bar/Restaurant and laundry on site, also open to non-residents.

★★★ — SELF CATERING

Jenny & Stewart Grant
Easter Corrie Holidays, Tomnavoulin, Glenlivet, Banffshire, AB37 9JB
Tel: 01807 590241 Fax: 01807 590741

4 cottages, 1 pub rm, 2-3 bedrms (grd flr avail), sleeps 2-6, total sleeping capacity 18, min let 2 nights, £200.00-£400.00, Jan-Dec

Converted farm steadings with superb views over Glen Livet. Easy access for all outdoor pursuits and touring.

★ UP TO ★★ — SELF CATERING

Jaqui White
The Post Office, Tomnavoulin, Ballindalloch, AB37 9JA
Tel/Fax: 01807 590220

4 cottages, 2 pub rms, 1 bedrm, sleeps 2-4, total sleeping capacity 14, £240.00-£260.00, Jan-Dec, bus on bus route, rail 25 mls, airport 60 mls

Converted cottages in contrasting situations. One secluded, near river, with fenced garden, other in village centre, annexed to owners' house. Others in own grounds close to village.

---

by Glenlivet, Banffshire — Map Ref: 4D9

★★ UP TO ★★★ — SELF CATERING

Mrs Innes
Deskie Farm, Glenlivet, Ballindalloch, Banffshire, AB37 9BX
Tel: 01807 590207

1 cottage, 1 annex, 1 pub rm, 2 bedrms, sleeps 4-6, total sleeping capacity 10, £220.00, Jan-Dec, rail 24 mls, airport 55 mls

Converted farm cottages on working farm. Fine views of the surrounding hills. Situated right on the Speyside Way. 8 miles (14km) to Lecht ski area.

Hopeman, Moray — Map Ref: 4D7

★ — SELF CATERING

Hopeman Lodge
Hopeman, Elgin, Moray, IV30 2YA
Tel: 01343 830245

3 flats, 1 pub rm, 1-2 bedrms, sleeps 4-6, total sleeping capacity 14, £110.00-£210.00, Apr-Oct, bus 1/2 ml, rail 6 mls, airport 40 mls

Flats on top floor of Listed building. Sited on a sandstone ridge adjacent to sandy beach and golf courses.

VAT is shown at 17.5%: changes in this rate may affect prices.

Key to symbols is on back flap.

HUNTLY – KEMNAY

GRAMPIAN HIGHLANDS, ABERDEEN AND THE NORTH EAST COAST

Huntly, Aberdeenshire — Map Ref: 4F9

★★★★ SELF CATERING

Mrs Rhona Cruickshank
Logie Newton, Huntly, Aberdeenshire, AB54 6BB
Tel: 01464 841229 Fax: 01464 841277
E-mail: davidln@aol.com
Web: www.assc.co.uk/logienewton/

Two charming traditional semi-detached cottages, on working farm, 8 miles (13kms) east of Huntly. Ideal centre for holiday pursuits, Castle and Whisky Trails. Children welcome.

2 cottages, 1 pub rm, 2-3 bedrms (grd flr avail), sleeps 4-6, total sleeping capacity 10, £200.00-£390.00, Jan-Dec, bus 1½ mls, rail 10 mls, airport 30 mls

---

★★★ SELF CATERING

Mrs T Ingleby
Aswanley, Glass, Huntly, Aberdeenshire, AB54 4XJ
Tel: 01466 700262 Fax: 01466 700222

Stone cottages with panoramic views over hills and River Deveron. Modern, comfortable furnishings. Private stretch of water. Fishing available. Varied moorland and woodland wildlife. Ideal for all outdoor pursuits. Barbeque in each garden.

1 house, 2 cottages, 1-3 pub rms, 2-5 bedrms (grd flr avail), sleeps 4-8, total sleeping capacity 18, min let weekend, £150.00-£500.00, Mar-Dec, bus 1 ml, rail 6 mls, airport 45 mls

---

by Huntly, Aberdeenshire — Map Ref: 4F9

★★ SELF CATERING

Mrs A J Morrison
Haddoch Farm, Huntly, Aberdeenshire, AB54 4SL
Tel: 01466 711217

Stone built cottage with own garden, situated on B9022 only 3 miles (5kms) from Huntly and on Castle and Whisky Trails.

1 cottage, 1 pub rm, 3 bedrms (grd flr avail), sleeps 6, £100.00-£250.00, Jan-Dec, bus 3 mls, rail 3 mls, airport 40 mls

---

by Keith, Banffshire — Map Ref: 4E8

★★ SELF CATERING

Mrs Lorna Milne
Whitehillock, Keith, Banffshire, AB55 3PH
Tel: 01466 760221
E-mail: dmilne@globalnet.co.uk

A traditional stone built farmhouse with own garden, on owners' farm, 3 miles (5kms) from Keith just off the A96.

1 house, 2 pub rms, 3 bedrms (grd flr avail), sleeps 7, £150.00-£230.00, May-Oct, bus nearby, rail 4 mls, airport 45 mls

---

Kemnay, Aberdeenshire — Map Ref: 4F10

★★ SELF CATERING

Mrs G Adam
Boatleys Farm, Kemnay, by Inverurie, Aberdeenshire, AB51 9NA
Tel: 01467 642533

Modern chalets situated on working farm with views of open countryside and the River Don. Access to Castle and Whisky Trail. Beautiful area for walking. Yet only 16 miles from Aberdeen.

2 chalets, sleeps 2-6, total sleeping capacity 12, £290.00-£500.00, Jan-Dec, bus 7 mls, rail 6 mls, airport 12 mls

---

Important: Prices stated are estimates and may be subject to amendments

GRAMPIAN HIGHLANDS, ABERDEEN AND THE NORTH EAST COAST

KEMNAY – LOGIE COLDSTONE

Kemnay, Aberdeenshire

★★ SELF CATERING

Mrs E C Riddell
Nether Coullie, Kemnay, Inverurie, Aberdeenshire, AB51 5LU
Tel/Fax: 01467 642203

Map Ref: 4F10

1 flat, 1 pub rm, 1-2 bedrms (grd flr avail), sleeps 2-4, £150.00-£200.00, Jan-Dec, bus 2 mls, rail 7 mls, airport 12 mls

Self-contained flat in stone built farmhouse on mixed farm. Own garden with riverside location and superb views of surrounding countryside, rural, yet only 17 miles from Aberdeen. Ideally situated for the Castle Trail, The Whisky Trail and Stone Circle Trail.

Kingston-on-Spey, by Elgin, Moray

★★★★ SELF CATERING

Mrs Helen Cruickshank
Drummuir, Duff Avenue, Elgin, Moray, IV30 1QS
Tel: 01343 541611

Map Ref: 4E7

1 cottage, 2 pub rms, 3 bedrms (grd flr avail), sleeps 6, min let 3 nights, £160.00-£350.00, Jan-Dec, bus nearby, rail 10 mls, airport 40 mls

Traditional fisherman's cottage built around 1910, which has been renovated and upgraded providing a comfortable cottage with a wide range of facilities. Seaside location, ideally suited to family and couples alike. Abundance of wildlife and birds in the nature reserves close by. Close to the whisky and Castle Trails. 15 minute drive to Elgin and all its amenities.

Kintore, Aberdeenshire

★★★ SELF CATERING — BRONZE

Mrs J T Lumsden
Kingsfield House, Kingsfield Road, Kintore, Aberdeenshire, AB51 0UD
Tel/Fax: 01467 632366
E-mail: kfield@clara.net

Map Ref: 4G10

1 cottage, 2 pub rms, 2 bedrms (All grd.floor), sleeps 4, £225.00-£325.00, Feb-Nov, bus ½ ml, rail 4 mls, airport 12 mls

Comfortable restored cottage on outskirts of village. Ideal touring base for castles, golf, fishing, walking and archaeological sites. Tranquil location within ½ hour drive to Aberdeen and 10 minutes to Dyce Airport.

Laurencekirk, Kincardineshire

★★★ SELF CATERING

Mrs A Mowatt
Dovecot Caravan Park, North Waterbridge,
by Laurencekirk, AB30 1QL
Tel/Fax: 01674 840630

Map Ref: 4F12

1 cottage, 1 pub rm, 2 bedrms (All grd.floor), sleeps 4, £220.00-£250.00, Jan-Dec

Recently converted castle outbuildings dating from 17c set in wooded grounds 6 miles (9 km) from Laurencekirk. All rooms on ground floor. Building situated 1 mile from A90. Ideal base for fishing, golfing or a quiet break.

Logie Coldstone, by Aboyne, Aberdeenshire

★★★ SELF CATERING

Mrs M J Booth
9 Viewfield Gardens, Aberdeen, AB15 7XN
Tel: 01224 315008

Map Ref: 4E10

1 cottage, 1 pub rm, 2 bedrms (All grd.floor), sleeps 4, £215.00-£310.00, Mar-Nov, bus post bus, rail 37 mls, airport 37 mls

Rebuilt and modernised traditional cottage with own patio area. Peacefully situated in woodland clearing a short distance from the village.

VAT is shown at 17.5%: changes in this rate may affect prices.

Key to symbols is on back flap.

LOGIE COLDSTONE – LOSSIEMOUTH

GRAMPIAN HIGHLANDS, ABERDEEN AND THE NORTH EAST COAST

Logie Coldstone, by Aboyne, Aberdeenshire — Map Ref: 4E10

SELF CATERING ★★

Mrs Craigmile
40 The Chase, Marshalls Park, Romford, Essex, RM1 4BE
Tel: 01708 726043 Fax: 01708 724284
E-mail: jic@dircon.co.uk

Traditional 300-year-old stone cottage with small cosy bedrooms in 2 acres of ground. Recently added spacious living room with log fire. Modern facilities, with many original features retained. A quiet peaceful location on edge of pine forest with Ballater and Aboyne approximately 9 miles equidistant. A lovely rural part of Royal Deeside.

1 cottage, 2 pub rms, 2 bedrms, sleeps 5, £220.00-£250.00, Jan-Dec, bus 2 mls, rail 30 mls

Lossiemouth, Moray — Map Ref: 4D7

SELF CATERING ★

Mrs Lesley Leiper
Rowan Brae, Paradise Lane, Lossiemouth, Moray, IV31 6QW
Tel: 01343 813000

Small semi-detached cottage with character, near to owner's property. Close to beaches and golf course. 0.5 mile to town centre.

1 cottage, 1 pub rm, 1 bedrm, sleeps 2-4, £95.00-£120.00, Jan-Dec, bus nearby, rail 6 mls, airport 40 mls

BEACHVIEW HOLIDAY FLATS
STOTFIELD ROAD, LOSSIEMOUTH, MORAY. TEL: 0141 942 4135

Situated on the beautiful Moray Firth, these two spacious flats sleep 6 people. Overlooking golf course, yachting station and west beach. Ideal for golfing holiday and touring Scottish Highlands.

Open April-October.
For a brochure and details contact
Mrs A Reedie, 62 Fernlea, Bearsden, Glasgow G61 1NB

SELF CATERING ★★

Mrs Agnes J Reedie
62 Fernlea, Bearsden, Glasgow, G61 1NB
Tel: 0141 942 4135

Apartments enjoying panoramic views of Moray Firth towards the hills of Sutherland. Ideal for seaside holiday and touring Highlands.

2 flats, 1 pub rm, 3 bedrms, sleeps 6, total sleeping capacity 12, £320.00-£380.00, Apr-Oct, bus nearby, rail 6 mls, airport 35 mls

---

Important: Prices stated are estimates and may be subject to amendments

GRAMPIAN HIGHLANDS, ABERDEEN AND THE NORTH EAST COAST

LOSSIEMOUTH – MONYMUSK

Lossiemouth, Moray — Map Ref: 4D7

Silver Sands Leisure Park
Covesea West Beach, Lossiemouth, Moray IV31 6SP
Tel: 01343 813262 Fax: 01343 815205
e.mail: holidays@silversands.freeserve.co.uk Web: www.travel.to/silversands

Situated alongside miles of beach and dunes, this award winning park is ideally located near the many golf courses, distilleries, castles, fishing villages and Elgin's superb leisure centre. Quality and modern holiday caravans to suit all budgets. Some double glazed and centrally heated. Excellent on-site facilities.

★★★★ HOLIDAY PARK

Silver Sands Leisure Park
Covesea, West Beach, Lossiemouth, Moray, IV31 6SP
Tel: 01343 813262 Fax: 01343 815205
E-mail: holidays@silversands.freeserve.co.uk
Web: www.travel.to/silversands

70 acres, grassy, hard-standing, Apr-Oct, prior booking in peak periods, latest time of arrival 2230. Extra charge for electricity, awnings.

Park accommodation: 505

140 tourers £7.55-11.70 or 140 motors £7.55-11.70 or 110 tents £7.55-11.70. Total Touring Pitches 140.

50 Holiday Caravans to let, sleep 4-8 £90.00-505.00, total sleeping capacity 293, min let 2 nights.

Leisure facilities:

Elgin/Lossiemouth A941, turn left 1 mile before Lossiemouth continue 1¼ miles, past RAF Camp, turn left, Park beside Lighthouse.

Macduff, Aberdeenshire — Map Ref: 4F7

★★★ SELF CATERING

Mrs G King
Glenshian, Banavie, Fort William, PH33 7LX
Tel/Fax: 01397 772174

1 cottage, 3 pub rms, 2 bedrms, sleeps 5, min let weekend, £150.00-£300.00, Jan-Dec, bus 500 yds, ferry 40 mls, airport 40 mls

Cosy fisherman's cottage. Beach location, uninterrupted sea views, peaceful yet convenient for touring coast and countryside. Countryside outdoor pursuits or relaxing.

Memsie, by Fraserburgh, Aberdeenshire — Map Ref: 4G7

★★ SELF CATERING

Judith Neish
Sandhole Farm, Memsie, Fraserburgh, Aberdeenshire, AB43 4BA
Tel/Fax: 01346 541257

1 house, 1 pub rm, 1 bedrm, sleeps 3, £80.00-£160.00, Jan-Dec, bus ½ ml, rail 40 mls, ferry 40 mls, airport 34 mls

Sympathetically restored farmhouse bothy. Walled garden. Peaceful rural working farm location. Duck lake. Many local outdoor pursuits. Fraserburgh 5 miles Aberdeen 40 miles. Dyce airport 35 miles.

Monymusk, Aberdeenshire — Map Ref: 4F10

★★★★ SELF CATERING

A Grant
Estate Office, Monymusk, Inverurie, AB51 7HS
Tel/Fax: 01467 651250

1 cottage, 2 bedrms, sleeps 4, £294.00-£370.00, Jan-Dec, bus 3 mls, rail 20 mls, airport 20 mls

Newly modernised country cottage with superb views over Donside. Rural location with woods nearby. Ideally situated for touring, walking or relaxing. Aberdeen 20 miles (32 km).

VAT is shown at 17.5%: changes in this rate may affect prices. *Key to symbols is on back flap.*

MONYMUSK – PETERHEAD

GRAMPIAN HIGHLANDS, ABERDEEN AND THE NORTH EAST COAST

Monymusk, Aberdeenshire — Map Ref: 4F10

The Lodge
THE PLACE OF TILLIEFOURE
Contact: Mr J M Uren, Priory Farmhouse, Appledore Road, Tenterden TN30 7DD
Tel: 01580 765799 or 01883 331071 Fax: 01580 766157 or 01883 331072

A charming recently modernised lodge on a small private estate known as the Place of Tilliefoure, which lies on the north bank of the river Don in Aberdeenshire, about three miles upstream of Monymusk on the road to Kieg. Salmon/ trout fishing is available on the estate.

★★ SELF CATERING

Mr J M Uren
Priory Farmhouse, Appledore Road, Tenterden, Kent, TN30 7DD
Tel: 01580 765799/01883 331071
Fax: 01580 766157/01883 331072

1 bungalow, 1 pub rm, 3 bedrms (All grd.floor), sleeps 6, £211.50-£300.00, Jan-Dec, bus 3 ½ mls, rail 10 mls, airport 22 mls

Entrance lodge with open fire in glorious wooded surroundings by the River Don. Salmon fishing available.

Oldmeldrum, Aberdeenshire — Map Ref: 4G9

★★ UP TO ★★★ SELF CATERING

Mrs Simmers
Ardmedden, Oldmeldrum, Aberdeenshire, AB51 0AG
Tel: 01651 872261 Fax: 01651 872202

2 houses, 1 cottage, 1-2 pub rms, 3-4 bedrms (grd flr avail), sleeps 6-8, total sleeping capacity 22, £175.00-£360.00, Jan-Dec, bus 5ml, rail 10mls, airport 15mls

Stone built farmhouses and spacious cottage on working stock and arable farm, 2 miles (3kms) from village. 40 miles (64kms) from Lecht ski slopes. Ideally situated for touring coast and country, whisky or castle trails.

Pennan, Aberdeenshire — Map Ref: 4G7

★★★ SELF CATERING

Mrs Anne Anderson
40 East Barnton Avenue, Edinburgh, EH4 6AQ
Tel: 0131 336 3524

1 cottage, 1 pub rm, 2 bedrms, sleeps 3-4, min let weekend, £180.00-£300.00, Apr-Oct, bus ¼ ml, rail 50 mls, airport 45 mls

Traditional fisherman's cottage in idyllic location. Modern comforts with lots of character. Awaken to the sounds of the sea. No problem with parking nearby. One dog welcome.

Peterhead, Aberdeenshire — Map Ref: 4H8

★★ SELF CATERING

Brown's Guest House
11 Merchant Street, Peterhead
Tel: 01779 838343

2 houses, 1 pub rm, 6-7 bedrms (grd flr avail), sleeps 11-12, total sleeping capacity 23, min let 1 day, £12.00 per person per night, Jan-Dec, bus 200 yds, rail 32 mls, ferry 32 mls, airport 30 mls

Two houses adjacent in central location. Well equipped. Available on nightly, weekly or long term lets. Very reasonable rates.

Important: Prices stated are estimates and may be subject to amendments

GRAMPIAN HIGHLANDS, ABERDEEN   F   PORTSOY

201

Portsoy, Banffshire   Map Ref: 4F7

★★ SELF CATERING

Mr T Burnett-Stuart
Portsoy Marble, Portsoy, Banffshire, AB45 2PB
Tel: 01261 842404 (day)/842220 (eve)
Fax: 01261 842404

Two restored houses, over 200 years old, right on picturesque harbour, in peaceful setting, yet near amenities of area.

2 houses, 1-2 pub rms, 1-3 bedrms, sleeps 2-6, total sleeping capacity 8, £140.00-£365.00, Jan-Dec, bus nearby, rail 17 mls, airport 55 mls

★★★ SELF CATERING

Mr Gary Christie
Doson, 6 Seafield Terrace, Portsoy, Aberdeenshire, AB45 2QB
Tel/Fax: 01261 842242
E-mail: enquiries@boynehotel.co.uk
Web: www.boynehotel.co.uk

Tradtional stone house in popular holiday town on Moray Firth near 17th century harbour. With large secluded, enclosed garden.

1 house, 2 bedrms, sleeps 4, min let 3 days, £150.00-£250.00, Jan-Dec, bus 200 yds, rail 18 mls, ferry 52 mls, airport 52 mls.

★★ SELF CATERING

Mrs Elizabeth Goodyear
3 Almond Close, Barby, Rugby, Warwickshire, CV23 8TL
Tel: 01788 890606 Fax: 01788 891864

Fully refurbished and attractive property on elevated site, overlooking harbour. Private garden and patio area. Ideal base for touring. Private parking. Beautiful views.

1 house, 2 pub rms, 3 bedrms, sleeps 5, £175.00-£320.00, Jan-Dec, bus nearby, rail 17 mls, airport 50 mls

---

★★★★ SELF CATERING

Mr D W Kirby
New Street Farm, Framlingham, Woodbridge, Suffolk, IP13 9RG
Tel: 01728 724488

Tastefully converted croft ideally situated overlooking Moray Firth. Close to Portsoy, perfect base for touring coast and country or enjoying the solitude.

1 cottage, 2 pub rms, 3 bedrms, sleeps 5. £200.00-£350.00, Jan-Dec, bus 1 ml, rail 17 mls, airport 55 mls.

★★★ SELF CATERING

Mr & Mrs Matthew Vaughan
36 Prospect Road, Sevenoaks, Kent, TN13 3UA
Tel: 01732 456442

Stone built cottage in residential area of Portsoy with large garden to rear, close to harbour, beach and town centre.

1 cottage, 2 pub rms, 2 bedrms, sleeps 4, £70.00-£300.00, Jan-Dec, bus nearby, rail 17 mls, airport 60 mls

---

VAT is shown at 17.5%: changes in this rate may affect prices.   Key to symbols is on back flap.

BY PORTSOY – ROTHES

F

GRAMPIAN HIGHLANDS, ABERDEEN AND THE NORTH EAST COAST

by Portsoy, Banffshire

Map Ref: 4F7

★★★ SELF CATERING

Mrs S Clements
Dytach Farm, Sandend, by Portsoy, Aberdeenshire, AB45 2UJ
Tel: 01542 840305

1 house, 2 pub rms, 2 bedrms, sleeps 4, £140.00-£250.00, Jan-Nov, bus nearby, rail 14 mls, airport 60 mls

Refurbished wing of farmhouse, with large enclosed garden set amidst rolling farmland, 2.5 miles (4kms) west of Portsoy, 15 miles from Duff House and the home of the new aquarium. Plenty of golf courses - a golfers paradise.

Rhynie, Aberdeenshire

Map Ref: 4E9

★★★★ SELF CATERING

Mains O'Noth
Rhynie, by Huntly, Aberdeenshire, AB54 4LJ
Tel: 01464 861415

1 apartment, 2 pub rms, 1 bedrm (All grd.floor), sleeps 2-4, £170.00-£250.00, Jan-Dec, bus 600 yds, rail 9 mls, ferry 36 mls, airport 34 mls

Comfortable ground floor apartment in detached house, close to Rhynie village and the Tap O'Noth. On the whisky and castle trail, fishing and golfing locally plus a variety of other sporting activities.

★★ SELF CATERING

Mrs M Wilson
Upper Balfour, Forbes, Alford, Aberdeenshire, AB33 8PS
Tel: 019755 62429

1 house, 2 pub rms, 3 bedrms (grd flr avail), sleeps 7, £175.00-£225.00, May-Oct, bus 2 mls, rail 12 mls, airport 40 mls

Detached farmhouse on working farm in isolated location on foothills of Tap O' Noth. 11 miles (18kms) from Huntly. Peaceful country holiday area central for many tourist attractions.

by Rhynie, Aberdeenshire

Map Ref: 4E9

★★ SELF CATERING

Mrs M Thomson
Belhinny Farm, Rhynie, AB54 4HN
Tel: 01464 861238
E-mail: alt@belhinny.freeserve.co.uk

1 cottage, 2 pub rms, 2 attic bedrms, sleeps 4, £150.00-£220.00, Jan-Dec, bus 3 mls, rail 13 mls, airport 30 mls.

Traditional stonebuilt country cottage retaining many original features, restricted headroom in upstairs bedrooms. Ideally located for walking, castle trail, and whisky trail. Huntly 12 miles.

Rothes, Moray

Map Ref: 4D8

★★★ UP TO ★★★★ SELF CATERING

Mrs Barbara O'Brien
Brylach, Glen of Rothes, Aberlour, Banffshire, AB38 7AQ
Tel: 01340 831355
E-mail: brylachservices@compuserve.com
Web: www.aboutscotland.com/banff/brylach.html

3 cottages, 3 pub rms, 2-3 bedrms (grd flr avail), sleeps 5-7, total sleeping capacity 14, £180.00-£320.00, Jan-Dec, bus nearby, rail 6 mls, airport 30 mls

Listed and modernised Victorian stable block with courtyard. Quietly situated near main Elgin-Rothes road, with access to River Spey, mountain and coast.

Important: Prices stated are estimates and may be subject to amendments

GRAMPIAN HIGHLANDS, ABERDEEN AND THE NORTH EAST COAST

STRATHDON – BY TOMINTOUL

Strathdon, Aberdeenshire

Buchaam Holiday Properties, Mrs E Ogg
Buchaam Farm, Strathdon, Aberdeenshire, AB36 8TN
Tel/Fax: 019756 51238

Map Ref: 4E10

1 house, 2 cottages, 2 pub rms, 2-4 bedrms (grd flr avail), sleeps 6-8, total sleeping capacity 22, £200.00-£300.00, Jan-Dec, bus 500 yds, rail 20 mls, airport 45 mls

SELF CATERING ★★

Modernised farm properties with fishing on River Don. Set amidst quiet scenic countryside, ideal for touring, hill walking and skiing. Indoor sports and putting green available June to September.

Mr Tom Hanna
Kildrummy Castle Hotel, Kildrummy, by Alford, Aberdeenshire
Tel: 019755 71288 Fax: 019755 71345

1 cottage, 3 pub rms, 3 bedrms, sleeps 6, £250.00-£475.00, Jan-Dec, bus 1 ml, rail 20 mls, airport 40 mls

SELF CATERING ★★★★★

Detached traditional stone built cottage with large South facing garden, in secluded Donside valley.

Tarland, Aberdeenshire

Mrs E Smith
Mill Cottage, Logie Coldstone, Aboyne, Aberdeenshire, AB34 5PQ
Tel: 013398 81401

Map Ref: 4E10

1 house, 1 pub rm, 3 bedrms (All grd.floor), £175.00, Apr-Oct, bus nearby, rail 31 mls, airport 31 mls

SELF CATERING ★★

Modern looking bungalow set in a quiet residential area with lovely views across this peaceful highland village to fields, woods and dark hills beyond. A gentle stroll to the village shops and restaurant approximately 1/2 mile distance. This picturesque region supports a wide range of outdoor and sporting activities.

Tomintoul, Banffshire

Mrs Michele Birnie
Livet House, 34 Main Street, Tomintoul, Ballindalloch, Banffshire, AB37 9EX
Tel: 01807 580205

Map Ref: 4D10

1 cottage, 1 pub rm, 3 bedrms (grd flr avail), sleeps 6-8, £250.00-£280.00, Jan-Dec

SELF CATERING ★★

Cosy semi-detached cottage with Rayburn and open fire. Situated in village centre with private parking. Ideal location for enjoying the magnificent scenery, outdoor pursuits, skiing or relaxing.

---

by Tomintoul, Banffshire

Alexander Turner
56 Main Street, Tomintoul, Ballindalloch, AB37 9HA
Tel: 01807 580293 Fax: 01387 580341

Map Ref: 4D10

1 cottage, 2 pub rms, 4 bedrms (grd flr avail), sleeps 8, £210.00, Jan-Dec, rail 14 mls

SELF CATERING ★★

Modern cottage 7 miles (11km) from Tomintoul. Superb views towards Ben Rinnes. 1 mile (2km) to nearest shop and telephone box.

VAT is shown at 17.5%: changes in this rate may affect prices.

Key to symbols is on back flap.

TURRIFF – WHITEHILLS, BY BANFF

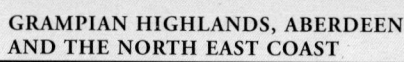

GRAMPIAN HIGHLANDS, ABERDEEN AND THE NORTH EAST COAST

Turriff, Aberdeenshire

Map Ref: 4F8

Mrs K Ferguson
Ardmiddle Mains, Turriff, Aberdeenshire, AB53 8AL
Tel/Fax: 01888 562443

★★★★ SELF CATERING

2 cottages, 1 farmhouse apartment, 1-2 bedrms (grd flr avail), sleeps 1-4, total sleeping capacity 11, £150.00-£320.00, Jan-Dec, bus 3 ½ mls, rail 16 mls, airport 35 mls

Bright, renovated, well furnished cottages situated on working farm. Ideal for activity holidays, golf, fishing, riding. Art/craft courses in farm studio, by prior arrangement.

by Turriff, Aberdeenshire

Map Ref: 4F8

Forglen Estate Ltd
Home Farm Office, Forglen Estate, Turriff, Aberdeenshire, AB53 4JP
Tel: 01888 562918 Fax: 01888 562252

★ UP TO ★★ SELF CATERING
BRONZE

8 cottages, 2 bungalows, 1-2 pub rms, 3-5 bedrms (grd flr avail), sleeps 6-9, total sleeping capacity 65, min let weekend, £106.00-£420.00, Jan-Dec, bus 3 mls, rail 35 mls, airport 35 mls

Traditional cottages set individually in beautiful private 1000 acre estate. Centrally situated in an interesting area to explore, castle and whisky trails, walls, golf, fishing villages, clean sandy beaches not far off. Wildlife haven.

Whitehills, by Banff, Banffshire

Map Ref: 4F7

Lorna Dickson
Dounepark Farm, by Banff, AB45 3QP
Tel: 01261 812121 Fax: 01261 812161

★★★★ SELF CATERING

1 house, 2 pub rms, 3 bedrms (grd flr avail), sleeps 6, min let 2 days, £240.00-£480.00, Jan-Dec, bus nearby, rail 45 mls, airport 45 mls

Very well equipped spacious house with enclosed garden at the centre of this typical fishing village. Sandy beaches, golf courses and historic Duff House nearby. On the whisky and castle trails. Garage with parking space.

Important: Prices stated are estimates and may be subject to amendments

Welcome to Scotland | The Highlands of Scotland

THE HIGHLANDS OF SCOTLAND IS RECOGNISED AS BEING ONE OF THE LAST GREAT UNSPOILT REGIONS OF EUROPE, WHOSE STUNNING LANDSCAPE HAS BEEN SHAPED NOT ONLY BY MILLIONS OF YEARS OF GEOLOGY, BUT BY GENERATIONS OF PEOPLE.

Picture postcards can never do justice to the grand scale of its awesome drama, for when you seen the mountains rivers and glens, you will surely feel the power and the spirit of this extraordinary place. Yet despite the sense of remoteness in these spectacular northlands, transport and communications are excellent, with good road, rail and air links from the south to Inverness and beyond.

The mountains around Fort William, which include Ben Nevis, Britain's highest peak, were the backdrop for the Hollywood movie Rob Roy, and the drama continues in the soaring crags of Glencoe which offer challenging walking, climbing and ski-ing. For the less energetic, a nostalgic steam train journey aboard "The Jacobite" takes you along the West Highland line, crossing the majestic Glenfinnan viaduct, past the silver sands of Morar to the delightful fishing port of Mallaig. From here you can take the ferry over to Skye or alternatively head north, stopping en-route at the famous Eilean Donan Castle, before crossing over the new bridge at Kyle of Lochalsh.

The Highlands of Scotland

The Highlands of Scotland

Superlatives cannot adequately describe the scenery on this island, from the fairy tale outlines of the Cuillin Mountains to the bizarre rock formations of the Trotternish Ridge and the hidden treasure of Loch Coruisk. The Misty Isle is rich in the romantic history and culture of the Gael, with numerous stories brought to life at the Clan Donald Centre, Dunvegan Castle, the Skye Museum of Island Life and the Aros Heritage Centre. There are also a host of pursuits to be enjoyed across Skye throughout the year, with qualified instructors and guides waiting to help you discover a vast range of activities at the many outdoor centres.

Back on the mainland, the natural gateway to the Highlands takes you through Strathspey and Badenoch where, in the shadow of the mighty Cairngorms, every sporting challenge awaits the keen visitor. The adventurous can enjoy orienteering, quad biking or abseiling, while others may simply want to explore the vast empty beauty on foot, bike or even pony.

On the shores of the Moray Firth is Inverness, the capital of the Highlands, a fast growing cosmopolitan town with fine shopping and excellent restaurants, making it an ideal centre for a touring holiday. Close by is Nairn, the "Riviera of the North" whose award-winning, pristine beaches are matched only by its remarkable sunshine hours, and championship golf courses.

To the north, the visitor will be inspired by the far-flung lands of Caithness and Sutherland which include Dunnet Head, the most northerly part of the UK mainland, the beautiful Strath of Kildonan, once the scene of a famous goldrush, and Poolewe, where the lush and exotic sub-tropical plants of Inverewe Gardens belie their geographical status. In fact, the whole region has something for everyone, and for people who like to travel this big country offers an escape that is sure to attract you back again and again.

The Highlands of Scotland

Events
The Highlands & Skye

19 Feb-11 Mar
Inverness Music Festival
Various venues throughout the Inverness area
Annual music festival incorporating competitive musical events.
Contact: Mrs M Young
Tel: 01463 232835

19 May
Highland Walking Festival
A programme of walks of all types for all abilities throughout the Highlands.
Contact: Highlands of Scotland Tourist Board
Tel: 01997 421160

26 May-10 Jun
Highland Festival
Contact: Morven MacLeod
Tel: 01463 711112

23-24 Aug
The Millennium Highland Gathering and Games Championships
Black Isle Showground, Muir of Ord, nr Inverness
Contact: Murray MacLeod
Tel: 01862 892600

21-22 Oct
Mountain Heritage Weekend
This is an educational event showing the practicalities of living and working in a mountain environment.
Contact: Tom Forrest
Tel: 014457 60234/332
web: www.cali.co.uk/kinlochewe/whatson

Area Tourist Boards

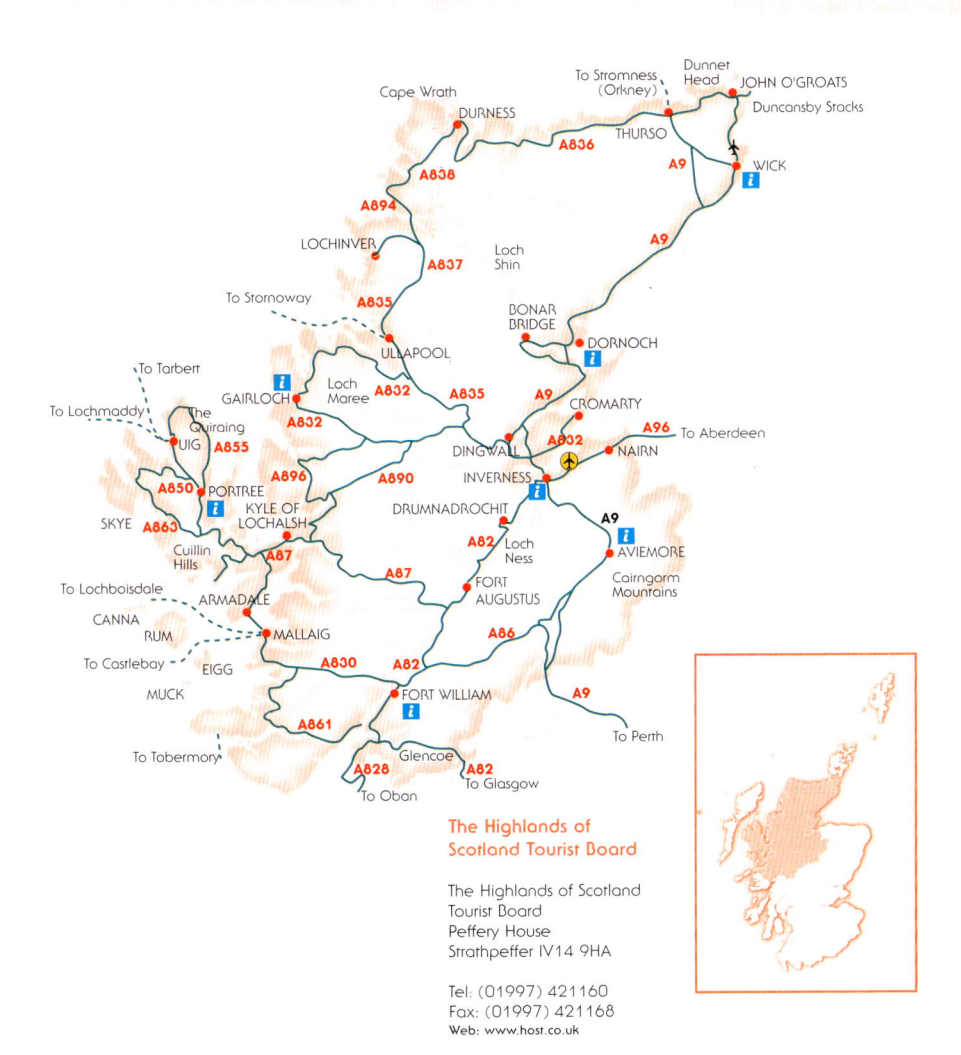

The Highlands of Scotland

209

The Highlands of Scotland Tourist Board

The Highlands of Scotland
Tourist Board
Peffery House
Strathpeffer IV14 9HA

Tel: (01997) 421160
Fax: (01997) 421168
Web: www.host.co.uk

The Highlands of Scotland

Tourist Information Centres

The Highlands of Scotland Tourist Board

Aviemore
Grampian Road
Inverness-shire
Tel: (01479) 810363
Jan-Dec

Ballachulish
Argyll
Tel: (01855) 811296
April-Oc

Bettyhill
Clachan
Sutherland
Tel: (01641) 521342
April-Sept

Broadford
Isle of Skye
Tel: (01471) 822361
April-Oct

Daviot Wood
A9 by Inverness
Tel: (01463) 772203
April-Oct

Dornoch
The Square
Sutherland
Tel: (01862) 810400
Jan-Dec

Dunvegan
2 Lochside
Isle of Skye
Tel: (01470) 521581
April-Sept

Durness
Sango
Sutherland
Tel: (01971) 511259
April-Oct

Fort Augustus
Car Park
Inverness-shire
Tel: (01320) 366367
April-Oct

Fort William
Cameron Square
Inverness-shire
Tel: (01397) 703781
Jan-Dec

Gairloch
Auchtercairn
Ross-shire
Tel: (01445) 712130
Jan-Dec

Glenshiel
Kintail
Kyle of Lochalsh
Ross-shire
Tel: (01599) 511264
April-Oct

Grantown on Spey
High Street
Morayshire
Tel: (01479) 872773
April-Oct

Helmsdale
Coupar Park
Sutherland
Tel: (01431) 821640
April-Sept

Inverness
Castle Wynd
Tel: (01463) 234353
Jan-Dec

John o'Groats
County Road
Caithness
Tel: (01955) 611373
April-Oct

Kilchoan
Argyll
Tel: (01972) 510222
Easter-Oct

Kingussie
King Street
Inverness-shire
Tel: (01540) 661297
May-Sept

Kyle of Lochalsh
Car Park
Inverness-shire
Tel: (01599) 534276
April-Oct

Lairg
Sutherland
Tel: (01549) 402160
April-Oct

Lochcarron
Main Street
Ross-shire
Tel: (01520) 722357
April-Oct

Lochinver
Main Street
Sutherland
Tel: (01571) 844330
April-Oct

Mallaig
Inverness-shire
Tel: (01687) 462170
April-Oct

Nairn
62 King Street
Nairnshire
Tel: (01667) 452753
April-Oct

North Kessock
Ross-shire
Tel: (01463) 731505
Jan-Dec

Portree
Bayfield House
Bayfield Road
Isle of Skye
Tel: (01478) 612137
Jan-Dec

Ralia
A9 North
by Newtonmore
Inverness-shire
Tel: (01540) 673253
April-Oct

Spean Bridge
Inverness-shire
Tel: (01397) 712576
April-Oct

Strathpeffer
The Square
Ross-shire
Tel: (01997) 421415
April-Nov

Strontian
Argyll
Tel: (01967) 402131
April-Oct

Thurso
Riverside
Tel: (01847) 892371
April-Oct

Uig
Ferry Terminal
Isle of Skye
Tel: (01470) 542404
April-Oct

Ullapool
Argyle Street
Ross-shire
Tel: (01854) 612135
April-Nov

Wick
Whitechapel Road
Caithness
Tel: (01955) 602596
Jan-Dec

THE HIGHLANDS AND SKYE

ABRIACHAN – ACHARACLE

Abriachan, Inverness-shire Map Ref: 4A9

★★ SELF CATERING

Achabuie Holidays
Abriachan, Inverness, IV3 8LE
Tel: 01463 861285

1 house, 2 pub rms, 3 bedrms (grd flr avail), sleeps 6, £200.00-£375.00, Apr-Oct, bus 2 mls, rail 12 mls, airport 16 mls

Two storey house in remote situation high above Loch Ness. Superb views. Roughish road for 0.5 miles (1km), owner's working croft nearby.

★★★ SELF CATERING

Mrs Irene L Coe
Purlie Lodge, Abriachan, Inverness, IV3 6LE
Tel: 01463 861295

2 studio flats, 1 pub rm, sleeps 2, total sleeping capacity 4, £165.00-£195.00, Apr-Oct, bus 1 1/2 mls, rail 7 mls, airport 12 mls

2 studio flats ideal for couples. Secluded woodland locaiton in grounds of owners home. Private parking. Magnificent views across Loch Ness to the Monadaleith mountains. Compact but fully equipped and tastefully decorated, one with stained glass window. Only 9 miles from Inverness with its many shops, theatre and Aquadome etc. Excellent for touring, walking or golf, close to the Glens of Affric, Strathconnon and Beauly Firth.

Balbeg Mill

Denwick House, Denwick Village, Alnwick, Northumberland NE66 3RE
Tel: 01665 605865   e.mail: balbegmill@cwilson.prestel.co.uk

Situated in the hills overlooking Loch Ness, this charmingly restored Cornmill is peacefully set in its own grounds of approx 5 acres bordered by a mill stream. Provides extremely comfortable accommodation for up to 6 people and is superbly equipped throughout. Log fire, linen and all heating/electricity costs included.

★★★★ SELF CATERING

Mrs Claire Wilson
Denwick House, Denwick Village, Alnwick,
Northumberland, NE66 3RE
Tel: 01665 605865
E-mail: balbegmill@cwilson.prestel.co.uk

1 cottage, 2 pub rms, 3 bedrms, sleeps 6, min let 3 nights, £240.00-£535.00, Jan-Dec, bus 1 ml, rail 12 mls, airport 25 mls

Sympathetically refurbished corn mill built around 1830. Quiet location, set in own grounds . Many walks from your own doorstep. Fishing available from lochside on Loch Ness. Central location for exploring the Highlands.

Acharacle, Argyll Map Ref: 3F12

SCOTTISH TOURIST BOARD INSPECTED

HOLIDAY CARAVAN

Mr William Cameron
Booking Enquiries: Mr William Cameron Elmbank, Acharacle, Argyll, PH36 4JL
Tel: 01967 431717

Park accommodation:

2 Holiday Caravans to let, sleep 4-6 £150.00-200.00, total sleeping capacity 12, min let 1 Week, Apr-Oct.

VAT is shown at 17.5%: changes in this rate may affect prices.

Key to symbols is on back flap.

ACHARACLE – ACHILTIBUIE

THE HIGHLANDS AND SKYE

Acharacle, Argyll
Map Ref: 3F12

★★★★ SELF CATERING

Mrs Elaine Kershaw
Cala Darach, Glenmore, by Glenborrodale, Acharacle, Argyll, PH36 4JG
Tel: 01972 500204

1 cottage, 1 pub rm, 4 bedrms (grd flr avail), sleeps 7, £250.00-£525.00, Jan-Dec, ferry 9 mls

Panoramic scenery surrounds this comfortable cottage. Situated on a small headland overlooking Loch Sunart to the Morven Hills & beyond to Mull. Set in 2 acres of ground offering complete privacy. Relax & enjoy walking, fishing & wildlife in this unspoiled location.

★★★★ SELF CATERING

Mrs Sharon Powell
Cala Darach, Glenmore, by Glenborrodale, Acharacle
Tel: 01972 500204

1 cottage, 1 pub rm, 3 bedrms (grd flr avail), sleeps 7, £250.00-£560.00, Jan-Dec

Recently completely refurbished house with garden. 5 miles (8km) from Acharacle and all amenities including shop and pub. Ideal Family base.

Achfary, Sutherland
Map Ref: 3H4

★★★ SELF CATERING

Reay Forest Estate
Estate Office, Achfary, by Lairg, IV27 4PQ
Tel: 01971 500221 Fax: 01971 500248
E-mail: elizabeth.kennedy@eeo.co.uk

2 cottages, 1-2 pub rms, 3 bedrms (grd flr avail), sleeps 5, total sleeping capacity 10, £347.00-£450.00, Easter-Oct, bus nearby, rail 40 mls, airport 90 mls

Cottages of individual character situated on large sporting estate amidst rugged scenery of N W Scotland.

Achiltibuie, Ross-shire
Map Ref: 3G6

★★★ SELF CATERING

Mr D & Mrs S Green
Stac Pollaidh Self Catering, Achnahaird, Achiltibuie, by Ullapool, Ross-shire, IV26 2YT
Tel: 01854 622340 Fax: 01854 622352

1 log cabin, 1 house, 1 turf house, 1-2 pub rms, 2-3 bedrms (grd flr avail), sleeps 4-6, total sleeping capacity 16, £210.00-£400.00, Jan-Dec, bus nearby, rail 75 mls, ferry 22 mls, airport 90 mls

Douglas Fir log cabin, detached croft house and stone turf roofed house, with mountain views in close proximity to beach.

★★★★ SELF CATERING

Gerry Irvine
Summer Isles Hotel, Achiltibuie, IV26 2YG
Tel: 01854 622282 Fax: 01854 622251

1 house, 3 pub rms, 3 bedrms (grd flr avail), sleeps 6, Jan-Dec, bus 1/4 ml, rail 85 mls, ferry 25 mls, airport 85 mls

Newly built in croft house style with excellent frontage views over Summer Isles. Large natural garden area. Walking, fishing, bird-watching available and sandy beaches nearby.

Important: Prices stated are estimates and may be subject to amendments

THE HIGHLANDS AND SKYE

ACHILTIBUIE – ARDELVE, BY DORNIE

Achiltibuie, Ross-shire

Map Ref: 3G6

★★★ SELF CATERING

Mrs Strachan
Dorevay, Birse, Aboyne, Aberdeenshire, AB34 5BT
Tel: 013398 86232

Modernised house in elevated and peaceful position. Magnificent views to Summer Isles and Dundonnell mountains.

1 house, 2 pub rms, 3 bedrms (grd flr avail), sleeps 6, £160.00-£360.00, Mar-Nov, bus 22 mls

---

★★★ SELF CATERING

Summer Isles Self Catering
Reiff, Achiltibuie, by Ullapool, Rossshire
Tel: 01854 622494 Fax: 01854 613426
E-mail: andrew.muir@masoncom.co.uk
Web: www.muirco.u.net.com/sisc

Detached modern house built to a traditional style in a peaceful setting overlooking the Summer Isles.

1 house, 2 pub rms, 3 bedrms (grd flr avail), sleeps 6, min let weekend, £200.00-£450.00, Jan-Dec, bus nearby, rail 80 mls, airport 80 mls

★★★ SELF CATERING

Mrs M Thornton
3 Baberton Mains Cottages, Juniper Green, Edinburgh, EH14 5AB
Tel: 0131 442 2324 Fax: 0131 453 6271
E-mail: info@saltiretours.co.uk

Modern chalet on high isolated site with superb views over sea to Summer Isles. Village 1 mile (2kms).

1 chalet, 1 pub rm, 2 bedrms, sleeps 4, £185.00-£350.00, Jan-Dec, bus nearby, rail 50 mls, ferry 26 mls, airport 80 mls

---

by Achiltibuie, Ross-shire

Map Ref: 3G6

★★★ SELF CATERING

Eva Campbell Whittle
Tigh na' Tilleadh, Polbain, by Achiltibuie, nr Ullapool,
Wester Ross, IV26 2YW
Tel/Fax: 01854 622448
E-mail: eva@worldski.demon.co.uk
Web: http://members.aol.com/hpsourcer/bothan.htm

A croft cottage, with magnificent view towards the summer isles, ideal for couples who enjoy a quiet relaxed holiday. Located in a small crofting and fishing community with shop close by. Ideal area for bird watching, hillwalking and touring the West Highlands. Some steps down to the cottage.

1 cottage, 1 bedrm (All grd.floor), sleeps 1-4, £150.00-£350.00, Jan-Dec, bus nearby, rail 75 mls, ferry 25 mls, airport 75 mls

---

Ardelve, by Dornie, Ross-shire

Map Ref: 3F9

SCOTTISH TOURIST BOARD INSPECTED

HOLIDAY CARAVAN

Mrs K Clark
Booking Enquiries: Mrs K Clark
Ardelve, Dornie, Kyle of Lochalsh, Ross-shire, IV40 8DY
Tel: 01599 555231

Park accommodation:

Holiday Caravan to let, sleeps 3-6, Easter-Oct.

Follow the A87, 3rd turning on the left past Eilean Donan Castle.

VAT is shown at 17.5%: changes in this rate may affect prices.

Key to symbols is on back flap.

ARDELVE, BY DORNIE – ARDNAMURCHAN

THE HIGHLANDS AND SKYE

Ardelve, by Dornie, Ross-shire
Map Ref: 3F9

CONCHRA FARM COTTAGES
Ardelve, Kyle of Lochalsh, Ross-shire IV40 8DZ
Tel: 01599 555233 Fax: 01599 555433
e.mail: cottages@conchra.co.uk

Quiet, comfortable, fully modernised farm cottages adjacent Loch Long and Eilean Donan Castle, 7 miles from Skye. Wonderful area for touring and walking. Centrally heated and fully equipped with all linen etc included in the rent together with colour TV, microwave, fridge/freezer, automatic washing machine and drying facilities.

★★ SELF CATERING

Conchra Farm Cottages
Conchra House, Ardelve, by Kyle, Ross-shire, IV40 8DZ
Tel: 01599 555233 Fax: 01599 555433
E-mail: cottages@conchra.co.uk
Web: www.conchra.co.uk

Traditional farm buildings on working farm, in secluded and tranquil lochside setting. Ideal for families, walking and activity holidays. Close to proprietors hotel with full restaurant facility.

3 cottages, 1 pub rm, 2-4 bedrms (grd flr avail), sleeps 5-6, total sleeping capacity 17, min let weekend (low season), £150.00-£395.00, Jan-Dec, bus 1 ml, rail 8 mls, airport 80 mls

★★ SELF CATERING

Mrs C Silvester
Heatherbank, Ardelve, Kyle of Lochalsh, Ross-shire,
Tel: 01599 555285

Situated overlooking Loch Duich, towards the Five Sisters of Kintail. Within easy reach of Skye, Wester Ross and Torridon.

2 cottages, 1 pub rm, 2 bedrms, sleeps 4-5, total sleeping capacity 9, £135.00-£225.00, Jan-Dec, bus 1 ml, rail 8 mls

★ SELF CATERING

Ardgay, Sutherland
Map Ref: 4A6

Mrs Gillian Smellie
Billy Hall Farm, Crook, Co Durham, DL15 9AF
Tel: 01388 765809 Fax: 01388 767871
E-mail: gsmellie@compuserve.com
Web: www.oas.co.uk/ukcottages/highlands.htm

Mid 19c watermill, sympathetically converted still retaining many of the original mill workings as features in most rooms. Peaceful location on the banks of the River Carron.

1 house, 1 pub rm, 3 bedrms, sleeps 6, £350.00-£750.00, Jan-Dec, bus ½ ml, rail ½ ml, airport 40 mls

★★★★★ SELF CATERING

Ardnamurchan, Argyll
Map Ref: 3E12

Mrs C G Cameron
Mo Dhachaidh, Portuairk, Kilchoan, by Acharacle, Argyll, PH36 4LN
Tel: 01972 510285

Cottage on seashore at south side of Sanna Bay. 1.5 miles (2kms) from most westerly point of British Isles, overlooking Eigg, Muck and Rhum.

1 cottage, 1 pub rm, 3 bedrms, sleeps 6, £250.00-£400.00, Jan-Dec, bus 5 mls, rail 30 mls, ferry 5 mls

★★ SELF CATERING

Important: Prices stated are estimates and may be subject to amendments

THE HIGHLANDS AND SKYE

ARDNAMURCHAN – ARISAIG

Ardnamurchan, Argyll

Map Ref: 3E12

★★ SELF CATERING

Mrs Brenda Neish
Barbreck Farm, Kilchrenan, Taynuilt, PA35 1HF
Tel/Fax: 01866 833292
E-mail: brenneish@aol.com
Web: http://members.aol.com/brenneish/index.html

In a uniquely remote, isolated situation, this comfortable country house offers a peaceful haven amongst some of Scotland's most dramatic scenery. The stunning location will reward the keenest of hillwalkers, anglers, ornithologists and wildlife enthusiasts. Six miles of forestry track have to be driven carefully.

1 house, 5 pub rms, 4 bedrms, sleeps 9-12, min let weekend (low season), £450.00-£775.00, Jan-Dec, bus 12 mls, rail 35 mls, ferry 24 mls

UP TO ★★ SELF CATERING

Steading Holidays
Kilchonan, Acharacle, Argyll, PH36 4LH
Tel: 01972 510262 Fax: 01972 510337
E-mail: booking@steading.co.uk   Web: www.steading.co.uk

Come to the Ardnamurchan Peninsula, Britain's most westerly point, from the heights of Ben Hiant to Sanna Sands, a place for the individual and nature lover. Islands, ferries, local nature centre, RSPB reserve and Ardnamurchan Lighthouse nearby, but above all peace and tranquility. To quote one of our many regular visitors "A safe and friendly environment for children". Our cottages are comfortable and welcoming with sea views.

3 cottages, 1 pub rm, 1-3 bedrms, sleeps 2-6, total sleeping capacity 16, £166.00-£567.00, Jan-Dec

Ardross, Ross-shire

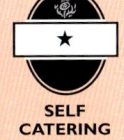

Map Ref: 4B7

★ SELF CATERING

Miss J Robertson
The Old House of Ardross, by Alness, Ross-shire, IV17 0YE
Tel/Fax: 01349 882906

Tiny traditional cottage at edge of small hill village in lovely countryside. Located 26 miles from Inverness, 10 miles from Invergordon. Ideal centre for touring, walking, golf or watching birds, dolphins and seals.

1 cottage, 1 pub rm, 2 bedrms, sleeps 3, £80.00-£190.00, Jan-Dec, bus 5 mls, rail 5 mls, airport 35 mls

Arisaig, Inverness-shire

Map Ref: 3F11

★★★ SELF CATERING

Mrs E Fleming
Tigh-An-Stor, Arisaig, Inverness-shire, PH39 4NH
Tel: 01687 450655 Fax: 01687 450676
E-mail: a.fleming@talk21.com

Smiddy house is a modern, detached bungalow set back from the main road through Arisaig, overlooking Loch Nan Ceall and with open views to the islands of Eigg and Rhum. House is 0.5 mile from village railway station where the steam train on the West Highland line passes through. Daily ferry services from Arisaig to small isles in Summer. Sandy beaches/Golf Course nearby.

1 bungalow, 1 pub rm, 3 bedrms (All grd.floor), sleeps 6-7, Jan-Dec, bus nearby, rail 800 yds, ferry 10 mls, airport 100 mls

★★★ UP TO ★★★★ SELF CATERING

Mike & Sheila Kingswood
Achnaskia Croft, Achnaskia, Arisaig, Inverness-shire, PH39 4NS
Tel/Fax: 01687 450606
E-mail: achnaskia@hotmail.com

Three chalets and one semi detached cottage set in own grounds with spectacular views towards Eigg, Rhum and Skye. 7 miles (11km) from Mallaig and ferry to Skye.

3 chalets, 1 cottage, 1-3 pub rms, 2 bedrms (All grd.floor), sleeps 4-5, total sleeping capacity 19, £180.00-£390.00, Jan-Dec, bus 100 yds, rail 1 ml, ferry 1-7 mls

VAT is shown at 17.5%: changes in this rate may affect prices.   *Key to symbols is on back flap.*

ARISAIG – AULTBEA

THE HIGHLANDS AND SKYE

Arisaig, Inverness-shire — Map Ref: 3F11

★★ SELF CATERING

Kinloid Cottages
Kinloid, Arisaig, Inverness-shire, PH39 4NS
Tel: 01687 450366 Fax: 01687 450611
E-mail: kilmartin@vacations-scotland.co.uk

2 chalets, 1 pub rm, 2 bedrms, sleeps 6, total sleeping capacity 12, £240.00-£360.00, Apr-Oct, bus 1 ml, rail 1 ml, ferry 4 mls

Two cottages attractively sited on an elevated position at Kinloid Farm commanding magnificent views overlooking Arisaig to the sea and the islands of Skye, Eigg and Rhum. 5 minutes car journey to wonderful white sands. On site launderette. Good base for walking and touring.

★★★ SELF CATERING

Brigid Moynihan
Derryfyad, Back of Keppoch, Arisaig, Inverness-shire, PH39 4NS
Tel: 01687 450667

1 house, 1 pub rm, 3 bedrms, sleeps 6, £150.00-£400.00, Jan-Dec, bus nearby, rail 1 ml, ferry 1 ml, airport 100 mls

1 bungalow with spectacular coastal views towards the Isle of Skye situated on a working croft, shop & hotel nearby, beaches 5 minutes walk & golfcourse 1 mile away.

★★★ SELF CATERING

A Simpson
Camusdarach, Arisaig, PH39 4NT
Tel/Fax: 01687 450221
E-mail: camdarach@aol.com
Web: www.road-to-the-isles.org.uk/camusdarach

2 flats, 1 cottage, 1-3 pub rms, 2-3 bedrms (grd flr avail), sleeps 4-8, total sleeping capacity 20, £200.00-£375.00, Jan-Dec, rail 4 mls, ferry 4 mls, airport 140 mls

Camusdarach Farmhouse is a Victorian stone house, with 2 spacious fully-equipped comfortable apartments. a small coastal estate near glorious white-sand beaches. Hebridean sheep, goats, turkeys and hens complete the picture. Millburn was an old shepherd's cottage situated 2 miles along the Rhue peninsula at Arisaig on the edge of its own bay - peaceful, secluded with wonderful wildlife, its own generator and water supply.

★★ UP TO ★★★ SELF CATERING

Traigh Lodges
Tigh na Bruaich, Traigh, Arisaig, Inverness-shire, PH39 4NT
Tel/Fax: 01687 450645
Web: www.road-to-the-isles.org.uk/traigh-lodges.html

2 chalets, 1 flat, 1 pub rm, 2 bedrms, sleeps 4-5, total sleeping capacity 13, £160.00-£380.00, Jan-Dec, rail 4 mls, ferry 7 mls

Holiday accommodation set in a delightful, unspoilt area on the road to Mallaig, and the ferry to the romantic isles of Skye. Excellent area for walking, climbing and exploring; glorious countryside sailing, rowing, canoeing, sea and loch fishing. Golf nearby.

Aultbea, Ross-shire — Map Ref: 3F6

★★★ SELF CATERING

Mrs J Deakin
Oran na Mara, Drumchork, Aultbea, Ross-shire, IV22 2HU
Tel/Fax: 01445 731394
E-mail: dpdeakin@aol.com
Web: http://members.aol.com/dpdeakin

2 flats, 1 pub rm, 1 bedrm, sleeps 2-4, total sleeping capacity 8, £90.00-£230.00, Jan-Dec, bus ¼ ml, rail 42 mls, ferry 44 mls, airport 85 mls

Flats peacefully situated with impressive views over Loch Ewe. 6 miles (10kms) from Inverewe Gardens. Good bird watching and walking area.

Important: Prices stated are estimates and may be subject to amendments

THE HIGHLANDS AND SKYE

AULTBEA – AVIEMORE

Aultbea, Ross-shire — Map Ref: 3F6

★★★ SELF CATERING

Mrs Carole Ann Larkin
Parkhall South Lodge Boquhan, Balfron, Stirlingshire, G63 0RW
Tel: 01360 440076

1 bungalow, 2 pub rms, 3 bedrms (All grd.floor), sleeps 6, £190.00-£430.00, Jan-Dec, bus ½ ml, rail 50 mls, airport 90 mls

Modern detached bungalow on own croft. Views to sea and surrounding hills. Close to Inverewe Gardens and Torridons.

★★★★ SELF CATERING

Mrs C MacKenzie
8 Ormiscaig, Aultbea, by Achnasheen, Ross-shire, IV22 2JJ
Tel: 01445 731382

1 house, 2 pub rms, 4 bedrms (grd flr avail), sleeps 6, from £100.00, Jan-Dec, bus 3 ½ mls, rail 40 mls, ferry 40 mls, airport 86 mls

Rebuilt traditional stone house, on elevated site. Enjoying truly magnificent panoramic views across Loch Ewe to Torridon and Dundonnell Mountains.

★★★★ SELF CATERING

Mrs C MacLennan
Eilean View, 1 Mellon Charles, Aultbea, Ross-shire, IV22 2JN
Tel: 01445 731546

1 bungalow, 1 apartment, 1 pub rm, 2 bedrms (All grd.floor), sleeps 4, total sleeping capacity 8, £100.00-£290.00, Jan-Dec, bus 1 ml

Two modern properties situated in a quiet spot overlooking Loch Ewe and Torridon mountains. Furnished and equipped with comfort in mind. Ideal for all outdoor pursuits and exploring Wester Ross. Close to safe sandy beaches and 6 miles to Inverewe Gardens.

★★★★ SELF CATERING

Mellondale Bungalows
47 Mellon Charles, Aultbea, Ross-shire, IV22 2JL
Tel/Fax: 01445 731326

2 bungalows, 1 pub rm, 2 bedrms (All grd.floor), sleeps 4, total sleeping capacity 8, £180.00-£380.00, Jan-Dec, bus 3 mls, rail 40 mls, airport 85 mls

Two comfortable modern bungalows fully equipped to a high standard with panoramic sea views, in friendly crofting community. Ideally situated for walking holidays, birdwatching and exploring Wester Ross. Just 9 miles from Inverewe Gardens.

Aviemore, Inverness-shire — Map Ref: 4C10

★★★ SELF CATERING

Bobsport (Scotland) Ltd
Ord-View House, 7 Dellmore, Rothiemurchus, Aviemore, PH22 1QW
Tel/Fax: 0131 332 6607
Web: www.bbrownlesww.com

1 house, 2 pub rms, 3 bedrms, sleeps 6, £350.00-£950.00, Jan-Dec, bus nearby, rail 1 ml, airport 35 mls

Terrace house in quiet close on ski road to Cairngorms. Ideal base for wide range of activities in area.

VAT is shown at 17.5%: changes in this rate may affect prices.   *Key to symbols is on back flap.*

AVIEMORE — THE HIGHLANDS AND SKYE

Aviemore, Inverness-shire   Map Ref: 4C10

★★ UP TO ★★★ — SELF CATERING

Genefer Clark
21 Walton Street, Oxford, OX1 2HQ
Tel: 01865 516414
E-mail: david.clark3@which.net

2 cottages, 1 pub rm, 3 bedrms (grd flr avail), sleeps 6, total sleeping capacity 12, £120.00-£345.00, Jan-Dec, bus ¼ ml, rail ½ ml

Two Victorian cottages with lots of character near shops, restaurants and public transport yet tucked away at the end of a quiet road with pleasant private gardens and Cairngorm views. Each has three bedrooms with one on ground floor. Warm, one with log fire, and well equipped, including washing machine, microwave, ideal at any time of year.

★★ — SELF CATERING

Andrea Dew
8 Ivy Lane, Boston Spa, Wetherby, LS23 6PP
Tel: 01937 844741 Fax: 01937 541631

1 house, 1 pub rm, 1 bedrm, sleeps 2-4, £150.00-£220.00, Jan-Dec, bus 1 ml, rail 1 ml, airport 30 mls

Modern 1 bedroom house with feature spiral staircase sited in quiet residential area near Aviemore, views to the Cairngorms. Parking and garden area.

★★ UP TO ★★★ — SELF CATERING

Fiona Grant
Avielochan Farm, Aviemore, Inverness-shire, PH22 1QD
Tel: 01479 810846

2 cottages, 1-2 pub rms, 2-3 bedrms (grd flr avail), sleeps 5&7, total sleeping capacity 12, min let 1 night, £250.00-£480.00, Jan-Dec, bus 3 mls, rail 3 mls, airport 35 mls

Situated on a working farm. Superb views across the loch towards the Cairngorm Mountains.

★★★★ — SELF CATERING

High Range Self Catering Chalets
Grampian Road, Aviemore, Inverness-shire, PH22 1PT
Tel: 01479 810636 Fax: 01479 811322
E-mail: highrange@enterprise.net
Web: www.aviemore.co.uk/highrange.html

7 chalets, 1 pub rm, 1-3 bedrms (grd flr avail), sleeps 2-6, total sleeping capacity 34, min let weekend, £200.00-£500.00, Jan-Dec, bus 500 yds, rail 500 yds, airport 40 mls

The chalets are part of a small complex run by the Vastano family for 23 years. Where standards and style have been influenced by continuity and continental flair.

★★★ — SELF CATERING

J Armour, Highland Holiday Homes
Station Square, Grampian Road, Aviemore
Tel: 01479 811463/810020 Fax: 01479 811577
E-mail: s-catering@hh-homes.co.uk
Web: www.hh-homes.co.uk

1 bungalow, 2 bedrms (All grd.floor), sleeps 4, min let weekend, £195.00-£395.00, Jan-Dec, bus ¾ ml, rail ½ ml, airport 35 mls

Comfortable detached holiday cottage is well located within 5 minutes walking distance of village centre and only minutes from Dalfaber Leisure Complex. With excellent views to Cairngorms, this well equipped property also has golf, fishing and watersports nearby.

Important: Prices stated are estimates and may be subject to amendments

THE HIGHLANDS AND SKYE

AVIEMORE

Aviemore, Inverness-shire — Map Ref: 4C10

★★★ SELF CATERING

Mrs Vyvienne Hosie
17 Ashburnham Gardens, South Queensferry, West Lothian
Tel: 0131 331 4941

1 bungalow, 1 pub rm, 2 bedrms (All grd.floor), sleeps 4, min let weekend, £190.00-£400.00, Jan-Dec, bus nearby, rail 1 ml, airport 35 mls

Modern detached bungalow in quiet cul de sac on outskirts of town. Well placed for access to Aviemore's many activities.

★★ UP TO ★★★ SELF CATERING

Inverdruie House
Aviemore, Inverness-shire, PH22 1QH
Tel: 01479 810889 Fax: 01479 812309

3 flats, 2 cottages, 1 bungalow, 1-2 pub rms, 2-5 bedrms (grd flr avail), sleeps 2-11, total sleeping capacity 37, min let weekend, £150.00-£695.00, Jan-Dec, bus 1 ml, rail 1 ml, airport 35 mls

Cottages and apartments of individual style and character, peacefully situated on private Highland estate, yet only 1 mile (2kms) from Aviemore.

★★★ SELF CATERING

Mrs M E Lambert
48 McIntosh Drive, Elgin, Moray, IV30 6AW
Tel/Fax: 01343 547701
E-mail: maggie@dalfaber.globalnet.co.uk
Web: www.users.globalnet.co.uk/~dalfaber

1 house, 1 pub rm, 2 bedrms, sleeps 4, £160.00-£300.00, Jan-Dec, bus 200 yds, rail 1 1/2 mls, airport 35 mls

Semi-detached house at end of cul-de-sac on northern edge of Aviemore. A quiet residential area, bordered by wooded countryside, with some lovely walks and access to the River Spey.

★★★ SELF CATERING

Mrs E M Miller
Mambeag, Lochiepots Road, Miltonduff, Elgin, IV30 3WL
Tel: 01343 540608

1 bungalow, 1 pub rm, 2 bedrms (All grd.floor), sleeps 4, min let 3 nights, £220.00-£400.00, Apr-Oct, bus 1/4 ml, rail 1/4 ml

Modern bungalow in residential area on the outskirts of town. Pleasant walkway to town centre (10 minutes).

★★★ UP TO ★★★★ SELF CATERING

Linda Murray
Glen Einich, 29 Grampian View, Aviemore, Inverness-shire, PH22 1TF
Tel: 01479 810653 Fax: 01479 810262
E-mail: linda.murray@virgin.net

3 bungalows, 1-2 pub rms, 2-4 bedrms (grd flr avail), sleeps 4-8, total sleeping capacity 18, £150.00-£695.00, Jan-Dec, bus nearby, rail 1 1/2 mls, airport 30 mls

Modern bungalows, in residential area, with views of Cairngorms. Within 1 mile (2kms) of the village's leisure centre. Ideal for families.

VAT is shown at 17.5%: changes in this rate may affect prices.

Key to symbols is on back flap.

AVIEMORE

THE HIGHLANDS AND SKYE

Aviemore, Inverness-shire | Map Ref: 4C10

★★ SELF CATERING

Mrs N Patrick
12 Braidpark Drive, Giffnock, Renfrewshire, G46 6NB
Tel: 0141 633 2656

Modern semi-detached bungalow in qiet cul-de-sac within easy access to all local amenities.

1 bungalow, 1 pub rm, 2 bedrms, sleeps 5, £150.00-£375.00, Jan-Dec, bus nearby, rail 1 ml

---

★★ UP TO ★★★★ SELF CATERING

Pine Bank Chalets
Dalfaber Road, Aviemore, Inverness-shire, PH22 1PX
Tel: 01479 810000 Fax: 01479 811469
E-mail: pinebank@enterprise.net
Web: www.aviemore.co.uk/pinebank.html

Chalets in a woodland setting adjacent to River Spey. Close to all amenities. Good food nearby.

6 chalets, 1 log cabin, 2 flats, 1 pub rm, 1-2 bedrms (grd flr avail), sleeps 2-6, total sleeping capacity 20, £287.00-£518.00, Jan-Dec, bus ¾ ml, rail ¼ ml, airport 30 mls

★ SELF CATERING

James Porter
18 Lockhart Place, Dalfaber, Aviemore, Inverness-shire, PH21 1SW
Tel: 01479 811152

Semi-detached house in cul-de-sac on edge of town, with easy access to all local amenities and attractions.

1 house, 1 bungalow, 2 pub rms, 2 bedrms (All grd.floor), sleeps 6, total sleeping capacity 6, min let 2 days, £120.00-£240.00, Jan-Dec, bus nearby, rail 1 ml, airport 30 mls

---

★★★★ HOLIDAY PARK

Rothiemurchus Camping & Caravan Park
Coylumbridge, Aviemore, Inverness-shire, PA22 1QU
Tel/Fax: 01479 812800
E-mail: rothie@enterprise.net

9 acres, mixed, Jan-Dec, prior booking in peak periods, latest time of arrival 2300. Extra charge for electricity, awnings.

Park accommodation: 89

17 tourers £9.00-11.00 or 17 motors £9.00-11.00 or 22 tents £6.00-10.00. Total Touring Pitches 39.

10 Holiday Caravans to let, sleep 4-6 £275.00-400.00, total sleeping capacity 56, min let 3 nights.

From Aviemore take B970 (Cairngorm skiroad) for 1 ½ mls, Park on right at Coylumbridge beside Lairig footpath.

★★★ SELF CATERING

Scandinavian Village
Aviemore Centre, Aviemore, Inverness-shire, PH22 1PF
Tel: 01479 810500 Fax: 01479 811604
E-mail: rentals@scandinavian-village.co.uk
Web: www.scandinavian-village.co.uk

Scandinavian themes throughout in quiet private landscaped grounds yet close to all amenities.

5 houses, 5 flats, 1 pub rm, 1-2 bedrms, sleeps 4-6, total sleeping capacity 50, from £210.00, 18 Dec-9 Nov, bus 800 yds, rail 800 yds, airport 42 mls

Important: Prices stated are estimates and may be subject to amendments

THE HIGHLANDS AND SKYE

AVIEMORE

Aviemore, Inverness-shire

Map Ref: 4C10

SILVERGLADES

Dalnabay, Aviemore, Inverness-shire PH22 1TD
Tel: 01479 810165   Fax: 01479 811246

Luxury villas nestling by the Cairngorms.

Fantastic stylish villas, sleeping up to ten. One to four bedrooms some with saunas and wood burning stoves. All with barbecues, TV, video, hi-fi, microwave, dishwasher, fully fitted kitchen and linen. Pets welcome. Superb range of amenities at foot of Cairngorms – ski-ing, fishing, golf, shooting, 4x4, hill, forest and loch walks, watersports, whisky trail, wildlife, parks, steam railway, pony trekking – if it's all too much villas have their own garden with patio. These homes are superb for larger groups or families many have ensuite. Friendly local staff will book activities for you. Colour brochure available. **Weeks from £175.**

★★★ TO ★★★★ SELF CATERING

★★★ UP TO ★★★★
SELF CATERING

Silverglades
Dalnabay, Aviemore, Inverness-shire
Tel: 01479 810165 Fax: 01479 811246

Self catering bungalows of a high standard in this popular holiday village complex. 1 mile (3 kms) to village centre and all amenities.

39 bungalows, 1-3 pub rms, 1-4 bedrms (grd flr avail), sleeps 4-10, total sleeping capacity 256, min let 3 nights, £175.00-£1695.00, Jan-Dec, bus ¼ ml, rail ¼ ml, airport 30 mls

★★★★
SELF CATERING

Stakis Coylumbridge
Coylumbridge, Aviemore, Inverness-shire, PH22 1QN
Tel: 01479 813065 Fax: 01479 811769
E-mail: reservations@stakis.co.uk
Web: www.stakis.co.uk/timeshare

The Coylumbridge Lodges are luxuriously furnished & fully equipped to provide you with everything you need during your holiday. The resort is situated in a 65 acre woodland estate just outside Aviemore under 3 hours drive from Edinburgh or Glasgow.

51, 1 pub rm, 2-3 bedrms, sleeps 4-8, total sleeping capacity 322, £700.00-£900.00, Jan Dec, bus 1½ mls, rail 1½ mls, airport 35 mls

★★★★
SELF CATERING

Mrs Sheila Walls
40 Ibis Lane, Grove Park, Chiswick, London, W4 3UP
Tel: 0181 747 1855 Fax: 0181 747 0699
E-mail: sheila_walls@msn.com

Four bedrooms and two public rooms with open fires all look to the Cairngorms across the large garden. Comfortable, centrally heated. Games room, sauna and steam bath.

1 house, 2 pub rms, 4 bedrms, sleeps 8, min let 2 nights, £600.00-£800.00, Jan-Dec, bus nearby, rail nearby

VAT is shown at 17.5%: changes in this rate may affect prices.

Key to symbols is on back flap.

THE HIGHLANDS AND SKYE

Aviemore, Inverness-shire — Map Ref: 4C10

★★★★ SELF CATERING

Mr H Weir
5 Langside Road, Bothwell, Glasgow, G71 8NG
Tel: 01698 852322 Fax: 01698 854559
E-mail: hweir@talk21.com

1 bungalow, 1 pub rm, 2 bedrms (All grd.floor), sleeps 4, £240.00-£350.00, Jan-Dec

Well equipped house in small development. 5 minutes walk from town centre. In quiet cul de sac with views to Cairngorms.

Avoch, by Fortrose, Ross-shire — Map Ref: 4B8

★★★ SELF CATERING

Mrs J Gatcombe
16 Ness Bank, Inverness, IV2 4SF
Tel/Fax: 01463 231151
E-mail: dolphcott@msn.com

1 cottage, 1 pub rm, 2 bedrms, sleeps 4, £190.00-£315.00, Mar-Oct, bus nearby

Converted terraced fisherman's cottage in historic part of Avoch. Close to sea. Dolphins and varied birdlife to be seen in the area. Ideal base for exploring the Black Isle and East Sutherland - Cromarty, Dornoch and beyond.

BURN FARM COTTAGES
Burn Farm Steading, Killen, Avoch, Ross-shire IV9 8RG
Tel: 01463 811733 Fax: 01463 811449
e.mail: burnfarm@aol.com Web: www.trad-inns.co.uk/burnfarm

Set in the beautiful rich rolling hills of the Black Isle and surrounded by the Moray and Cromarty Firths, Burn Farm Cottages are ideally suited for those who want to explore the whole Highlands. Fifteen minutes from Inverness. Set in their own courtyard overlooking the great glen. En suites.

★★★★ SELF CATERING — BRONZE

Colin & Ros Thompson
Burn Farm Steading, Killen, Ross-shire, IV9 8RG
Tel: 01463 811733 Fax: 01463 811449
E-mail: burnfarm@aol.com
Web: www.trad-inns.co.uk/burnfarm

3 holiday cottages, 1 pub rm, 2 bedrms, sleeps 4, total sleeping capacity 12, min.let 3 days, £250.00-£550.00, Jan-Dec, bus 4 ml, rail 14 ml, airport 20 mls.

Badachro, Ross-shire — Map Ref: 3F7

★★ UP TO ★★★ SELF CATERING

Caberfeidh Self Catering
c/o Mrs E Taylor, Philorth, Port Henderson, Gairloch
Tel: 01445 741244

1 house, 1 cottage, 2 pub rms, 2-4 bedrms, sleeps 4, total sleeping capacity 8, £170.00, Apr-Oct, rail 27 mls, airport 80 mls

Traditional cottages, each with its own enclosed garden and garden furniture on working croft. Breathtaking views over the Minch to the Outer Isles. Sandy beach 0.5km (1km). Sailing, fishing, golfing and walking all close by.

Important: Prices stated are estimates and may be subject to amendments

THE HIGHLANDS AND SKYE

BADACHRO

Mrs Carcas
Yarne Cottage, Tower Hill, Horsham, West Sussex, RH13 7JT
Tel: 01403 263591 Fax: 01403 211014

SELF CATERING ★★★★

Renovated crofters cottage, refurbished to a high standard. Close to shore and overlooking Gairloch bay.

1 house, 1 pub rm, 3 bedrms (grd flr avail), sleeps 6, from £210.00, Jan-Dec, bus ¼ ml, rail 30 mls, airport 80 mls

---

Mr & Mrs S A Garrioch
Old School Road, Opinan, Gairloch, Ross-shire, IV21 2AT
Tel: 01445 741206
Web: www.scotia-sc.com/51.htm

SELF CATERING ★★★

Old school converted to form large comfortable holiday accommodation. Peaceful location and lovely views to sea.

1 house, 2 pub rms, 3 bedrms, sleeps 6, £180.00-£365.00, Jan-Dec, bus 7 mls, rail 30 mls, airport 80 mls

John MacDonald
Tigh Eibhinn, Easterton, Dalcross, Inverness, IV1 2JE
Tel: 01667 462792

SELF CATERING ★★★★

Situated in a peaceful and secluded setting on the shores of Loch Sheildaig. A traditional stone house charmingly restored and decorated with superb views of the loch.

1 house, 3 pub rms, 4 bedrms (grd flr avail), sleeps 8, £340.00-£680.00, Jan-Dec, bus 5 mls, rail 30 mls, airport 90 mls

---

J MacDonald
Tigh Eibhinn, Easterton, Dalcross, Inverness, IV1 2JE
Tel: 01667 462792

SELF CATERING ★★★★★

House, refurbished to a high standard of individual character and charm. Peacefully situated with superb views and large garden.

1 house, 3 pub rms, 4 bedrms, sleeps 7, £340.00-£680.00, Jan-Dec, bus 5 mls, rail 30 mls, airport 90 mls

Mrs Alice MacKenzie
18 Port Henderson, Gairloch, Ross-shire, IV21 2AS
Tel: 01445 741239

SELF CATERING ★★★

Comfortable, well equipped bungalow 8 miles from Gairloch. Views to Skye and Torridon Hills. Ideal for a relaxing holiday.

1 bungalow, 1 pub rm, 3 bedrms, sleeps 7, £250.00-£320.00, May-Sep, bus 8 mls, rail 30 mls

---

VAT is shown at 17.5%: changes in this rate may affect prices.

Key to symbols is on back flap.

BY BADACHRO / BEAULY — THE HIGHLANDS AND SKYE

by Badachro, Ross-shire
Map Ref: 3F7

★★ SELF CATERING

Mrs C M M Thomson
18 South Erradale, Gairloch, Ross-shire, IV21 2AU
Tel: 01445 741202

1 flat, 1 pub rm, 2 bedrms, sleeps 4, £140.00-£220.00, Apr-Oct, bus 7 mls, rail 30 mls, airport 85 mls

Spacious flat with panoramic views to Skye and Torridon Hills. Use of garden. Beach nearby.

Beauly, Inverness-shire
Map Ref: 4A8

Aigas Holiday Houses
Mains of Aigas, by Beauly, Inverness-shire IV4 7AD
Tel: 01463 782423 Fax: 01463 782423
e.mail: aigas@cali.co.uk Web: www.cali.co.uk/aigas/

Lochs and fine forests with extensive hill and mountain walks are a feature of our beautiful unspoilt glens. Here country lovers will revel in the abundance of wildlife. Special rates on 9-hole PAR33 Aigas golf course. Delightful cottage, courtyard houses ideally situated for touring north, east and west coasts.

★★★ UP TO ★★★★ SELF CATERING

Aigas Holiday Houses
Mains of Aigas, Beauly, Inverness-shire, IV4 7AD
Tel/Fax: 01463 782423
E-mail: aigas@cali.co.uk
Web: www.cali.co.uk/aigas/

1 house, 1 cottage, 3 apartments, 1-2 pub rms, 2-3 bedrms (grd flr avail), sleeps 4-6, total sleeping capacity 25, £165.00-£420.00, Feb-Nov, bus 5 mls, rail 14 mls, airport 27 mls

Coach house and cottages in a courtyard setting, and a detached 19th century farm cottage overlooking the beautiful scenery of Strathglass. Situated on working farm (beef) and adjacent to 9 hole golf course. Inverness 16 miles (26 kms).

★★★★ SELF CATERING

Dunsmore Lodges
by Beauly, Inverness-shire, IV4 7EY
Tel: 01463 782424 Fax: 01463 782839
E-mail: inghammar@cali.co.uk
Web: www.cali.co.uk/dunsmore

9 chalets, 1 pub rm, 2-3 bedrms, sleeps 4-6, total sleeping capacity 40, £175.00-£545.00, Jan-Dec, bus 3 mls, rail 7 mls, airport 23 mls

A delightful retreat but only 4 miles from Beauly, winner of Britain in Bloom. A unique village with a large square dominated by the ruined 13th century priory and an excellent selection of shops and restaurants. Gateway to the most glorious glens and straths in the Highlands. All this is well documented by Pauline and Ake for their guests who also value their warm welcome and friendly advice.

★ SELF CATERING

Mrs C Guthrie
41 Barrow Point Avenue, Pinner, Middlesex, HA5 3HD
Tel: 0181 866 5026

1 cottage, 2 pub rms, 2 bedrms (All grd.floor), sleeps 4, £150.00-£200.00, Apr-Oct, bus 4 mls, rail 16 mls

Croft cottage in isolated position with magnificent views of Glen Affric and Strathglass. 4 miles (6kms) from Beauly. Former red deer hunting lodge, in isolated position etc. Hilltop position with rough road access.

Important: Prices stated are estimates and may be subject to amendments

THE HIGHLANDS AND SKYE

BEAULY – BOAT OF GARTEN

SELF CATERING ★

Mrs M M Ritchie
Rheindown Farm, by Beauly, Inverness-shire, IV4 7AB
Tel: 01463 782461

2 chalets, 1 pub rm, 2 bedrms (All grd.floor), sleeps 4-6, total sleeping capacity 12, £130.00-£220.00, Mar-Nov, bus 1 ml, rail 1 1/2 mls, airport 16 mls

Two detached chalets on working farm in elevated position overlooking Beauly and the Firth beyond.

Bettyhill, Sutherland

Map Ref: 4B3

SELF CATERING ★★★★

Mrs A Todd
Hoy Farm, Halkirk, Caithness, KW12 6UU
Tel: 01847 831544

1 house, 2 pub rms, 3 bedrms (grd flr avail), sleeps 6, min let weekend, £200.00-£300.00, Jan-Dec, bus 1/4 ml, rail 32 mls, ferry 32 mls, airport 55 mls

Modernised croft house in remote elevated position. Overlooks Torrisdale Sands and the River Naver. 0.5 miles (1km) from village.

Boat of Garten, Inverness-shire

Map Ref: 4C10

SELF CATERING ★★

Beechgrove Mountain Lodges
Mains of Garten Farm, Boat of Garten, Inverness-shire, PH24 3BY
Tel: 01479 831551 Fax: 01479 831445

5 chalets, 1 pub rm, 3 bedrms (All grd.floor), sleeps 6, total sleeping capacity 30, £100.00-£375.00, Jan-Dec, bus nearby, rail 8 mls, airport 32 mls

'A' Frame Lodges on working farm. Rural situation with fine views. Boat of Garten two miles distance.

SELF CATERING ★★

Jeremy Burr
Cam Sgriob, Boat of Garten, Inverness-shire, PH24 3BP
Tel: 01479 831604

1 cottage, 2 pub rms, 2 bedrms, sleeps 4-6, £150.00-£270.00, Jan-Dec, bus 1/4 ml, rail 1/4 ml, airport 35 mls

The cottage of traditional construction is within the village. Close to the River Spey with fine views to the Cairngorms and a short walk to local shops.

SELF CATERING ★

Mrs Margaret Dixon
Granlea, Deshar Road, Boat of Garten, Inverness-shire, PH24 3BN
Tel/Fax: 01479 831601

1 cottage, 3 bedrms (All grd.floor), sleeps 2, min let 3 days, £160.00-£230.00, Jan-Dec, bus nearby, rail 6 mls, airport 30 mls

Traditional timber built Highland cottage in grounds of owner's guest house situated in centre of village.

VAT is shown at 17.5%: changes in this rate may affect prices.

Key to symbols is on back flap.

BOAT OF GARTEN – BONAR BRIDGE

THE HIGHLANDS AND SKYE

Boat of Garten, Inverness-shire — Map Ref: 4C10

★ SELF CATERING

Mrs Dorothy C Fraser
4 Westbourne Crescent, Bearsden, Glasgow, G61 4HD
Tel: 0141 942 2717
Web: www.scotia-sc.com/639.htm

1 cottage, 2 pub rms, 2 bedrms, sleeps 6, £180.00-£270.00, Jan-Dec, bus nearby, rail 400 yds, airport 30 mls

Comfortable cottage set in quiet area of small village. Convenient for golf courses and hill walking.

★★ SELF CATERING

Mr G Keir
4 High Terrace, Boat of Garten, Inverness-shire, PH24 3BW
Tel: 01479 831262

1 flat, 1 pub rm, 2 bedrms (All grd.floor), sleeps 4, £125.00-£145.00, Mar-Oct, bus nearby, rail 6 1/2 mls

Stone built, ground floor flat situated in quiet part of village. 5 minutes walk from golf course, local shops etc.

★ SELF CATERING

Hilary MacRae
5 Brockwood Avenue, Penicuik, Midlothian, EH26 9AJ
Tel: 01968 673194
E-mail: h_macrae@compuserve.com

1 house, 2 pub rms, 3 bedrms (grd flr avail), sleeps 8, £280.00-£350.00, Dec-Oct, bus nearby, rail 6 mls, airport 30 mls

Detached, stone built house in famous "Osprey" village. Enclosed garden and plenty of private parking space.

★ SELF CATERING

Dr J Weir
Glenlora Cottage, Lochwinnoch, PA12 4DN
Tel: 01505 842062

2 cottages, 1-2 pub rms, 3 bedrms (All grd.floor), sleeps 5-6, total sleeping capacity 11, min let weekend, £110.00-£500.00, Jan-Dec, bus nearby

Tastefully appointed Highland cottages of character, with large enclosed garden, in rural setting.

Bonar Bridge, Sutherland — Map Ref: 4B6

★★★★ SELF CATERING

Mr G Ryder
53A Princes May Road, London, M16 8BF
Tel: 0171 923 3163 Fax: 0171 412 3222
E-mail: gavin.ryder@glencore.co.uk

1 house, 2 pub rms, 5 bedrms (grd flr avail), sleeps 8, min let weekend, £200.00-£430.00, Jan-Dec, bus 1/2 ml, rail 1 ml, airport 50 mls

A substantial property located 10 minutes walk from the charming village of Bonar Bridge. It's unique location offers an expanse of beaches to the east, and the lunar landscape of Sutherland to the west. Set in several acres of grounds, panoramic water front views, and is the epitome of comfort, with it's large fully equipped kitchen, traditional dining room, spacious lounge and most bedrooms enjoying superb views over the picturesque landscape.

Important: Prices stated are estimates and may be subject to amendments

THE HIGHLANDS AND SKYE

BRORA – CANNICH

★★★★ SELF CATERING

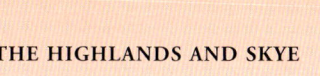

Highland Escape Ltd
Royal Marine Hotel, Golf Road, Brora, Sutherland, KW9 6QS
Tel: 01408 621225 Fax: 01408 621383
E-mail: highlandescape@btinternet.com
Web: www.host.co.uk/highlandescape

1 house, 3 apartments, 2 pub rms, 2-4 bedrms (grd flr avail), sleeps 2-7, total sleeping capacity 26, £350.00-£700.00, Jan-Dec, bus nearby, rail 2 mls, airport 70 mls

Spacious modern detached house adjacent to the 12th tee of the golf course, and well equipped apartments within the grounds of the Links Hotel, also overlooking Brora golf course. Sandy beaches close by. Hotel services and a range of leisure facilities available at the Links and Royal Marine Hotels. Maid service available.

★★★ SELF CATERING

Mary Mackay
12 Fulmar Crescent, Ardersier, Inverness-shire, IV1 2SY
Tel: 01667 462047

1 house, 2 pub rms, 3 bedrms, sleeps 7, min let weekend, £275.00-£320.00, Jan-Dec, bus ½ ml, rail 1 ml

Traditional fisherman's cottage with open sea views, close to safe sandy beaches and golf course. Fishing nearby. Ideal touring base.

Cannich, Inverness-shire — Map Ref: 3H9

★★ SELF CATERING

Glen Affric Lodges
Cannich, Beauly, IV4 7LT
Tel: 01456 415369 Fax: 01456 415429
E-mail: glenaffric@assc.co.uk
Web: www.assc.co.uk/glenaffric/index.html

13 chalets, 2 pub rms, 3 bedrms (grd flr avail), sleeps 6, total sleeping capacity 72, £190.00-£475.00, Jan-Dec, bus nearby, rail nearby, airport nearby

A warm Highland welcome awaits at this family run park. Fully equipped, comfortably furnished, three bedroom timber Lodges. Situated on the banks of the River Glass, enjoying some of Scotland's most spectacular mountains & glens. Ideal base for exploring north-west Scotland. With Games Room, Playground, Laundry. Barbecue area.

★★ SELF CATERING

Mrs J Grove
34 Stevenage Road, London, SW6 6ET
Tel: 0171 736 1533 Fax: 0171 731 4159

1 cottage, 1 pub rm, 3 bedrms, sleeps 5, £145.00-£360.00, Mar-Nov, rail 30 mls, airport 40 mls

A detached cottage, quietly situated on private estate overlooking the River Glass with far-reaching views towards Glen Affric. There are plenty of attractive woodland walks close by. Fishing available.

★★★ SELF CATERING

Hill House Self Catering Apartments
Kerrow Farm, Cannich, Inverness-shire, IV4 7NA
Tel/Fax: 01456 415300

2 apartments, 1 bedrm (All grd.floor), sleeps 4, total sleeping capacity 8, £190.00-£390.00, Jan-Dec, bus 2 mls, rail 28 mls, airport 38 mls

Well equipped ground floor accommodation attached to owners house a home farm - open views to Strathglass. Situated on the fringe of Glen Affric, 1 mile away. Loch Ness is 12.5 miles. Easy access to Munros for hillwalkers. Fishing and shooting by arrangement. Mountain bikes available in the area for hire. Post Office and local shop 2 miles.

VAT is shown at 17.5%: changes in this rate may affect prices.

Key to symbols is on back flap.

CANNICH – CAWDOR

THE HIGHLANDS AND SKYE

Cannich, Inverness-shire — Map Ref: 3H9

★★★ SELF CATERING

Kerrow House
Cannich, Strathglass, Inverness-shire, IV4 7NA
Tel: 01456 415243 Fax: 01456 415425
E-mail: stephen@kerrow-house.demon.co.uk
Web: www.kerrow-house.demom.co.uk

Two cottages, two chalets and self-contained wing of house, all of individual style and character, set amidst beautiful scenery of Strathglass. 3 1/2 miles of trout fishing available.

2 log cabins, 1 house, 2 cottages, 1-2 pub rms, 1-4 bedrms (grd flr avail), sleeps 2-10, total sleeping capacity 35, min let weekend, £200.00-£495.00, Jan-Dec, bus 2 mls, rail 26 mls, airport 35 mls

★★★ SELF CATERING

The Revd. & Mrs A M Roff
Rowan Glen, Culbokie, Dingwall, IV7 8JY
Tel: 01349 877762
E-mail: 106770.3175@compuserve.com

A modern family bungalow in a fenced garden on the edge of a village at the entrance of the famously beautiful Glen Affric and three other glens. Large sitting room, open fire, full gas central heating, airing cupboard, bathroom, separate shower room, telephone, washer drier, freezer, microwave, tv, video. Marked walks in the Caledonian Forest, lochs, waterfalls, mountains, birds of prey centre close by.

1 bungalow, 1 pub rm, 3 bedrms, sleeps 5, £210.00-£400.00, Jan-Dec, bus nearby, rail 27 mls, airport 27 mls

---

Carrbridge, Inverness-shire — Map Ref: 4C9

★★ SELF CATERING

G Carnegie
Ravendean, West Linton, Peeblesshire, EH46 7EN
Tel/Fax: 01968 660687
E-mail: 100566.2036@compuserve.com

Modern log cabin peacefully situated on the outskirts of the village, overlooking trekking centre.

1 log cabin, 1 pub rm, 3 bedrms (All grd.floor), sleeps 6, £180.00-£260.00, Apr-Oct, bus 400 yds, rail 400 yds

---

★★★★ SELF CATERING

Fairwinds Chalets
Carrbridge, Inverness-shire, PH23 3AA
Tel/Fax: 01479 841240
E-mail: fairwindsinfo@tesco.net

Wooden chalets in hotel grounds surrounded by mature pinewoods and overlooking small lochan, in 7 acres of parkland near village. Ski slopes 13 miles (21kms).

6 chalets, 1 flat, 1 pub rm, 1-3 bedrms (grd flr avail), sleeps 2-6, total sleeping capacity 32, min let 2 days, £150.00-£410.00, Dec-Oct, bus nearby, rail 1/2 ml, airport 30 mls

---

Cawdor, Nairnshire — Map Ref: 4C8

★★ SELF CATERING

Mrs A Tennant
Holiday Cottages, Cawdor Estate Office, Cawdor, IV12 5RE
Tel: 01667 404666 Fax: 01667 404787
E-mail: office@cawdor-est.demon.co.uk

Cottage tucked away on the banks of the River Findhorn. Perfect for a holiday of relaxation, scenic beauty, fishing and walking.

1 cottage, 2 pub rms, 3 bedrms (grd flr avail), sleeps 6-7, £423.00-£550.00, Mar-Oct, bus 13 mls, rail 13 mls, airport 18 mls

---

Important: Prices stated are estimates and may be subject to amendments

THE HIGHLANDS AND SKYE

CONTIN – CROY

SELF CATERING ★

Marion Greig
7 Craigdarroch Drive, Contin, by Strathpeffer, Ross-shire, IV14 9EL
Tel: 01997 421556

1 house, 1 pub rm, 3 bedrms (All grd.floor), sleeps 6, £175.00-£250.00, Jan-Dec, bus nearby, rail 8 mls, ferry 37 mls, airport 28 mls

Comfortable, furnished, terraced cottage surrounded by woodlands and hills. Excellent for golfing, fishing (booking arranged) and touring.

HOLIDAY PARK ★★

Riverside Chalets Caravan Park
Contin, by Strathpeffer, Ross-shire, IV14 9ES
Tel: 01997 421351 Fax: 01463 232502

Park accommodation: 30
30 tourers £3.00-£10.00 or 30 motors or 30 tents. Total Touring Pitches 30.

2 Holiday Chalets to let, sleep 4-6, £100.00-£160.00, total sleeping capacity 12.

2 acres, grassy, level, Jan-Dec. Extra charge for electricity.

On A835 between Inverness and Ullapool at the Strathpeffer junct.

Corpach, by Fort William, Inverness-shire Map Ref: 3G12

SELF CATERING ★★★

Snowgoose Apartments
The Old Smiddy, Station Road, Corpach, Fort William, Inverness-shire, PH33 7JH
Tel: 01397 772467/772752 Fax: 01397 772411
E-mail: info@snowgoose.prestel.co.uk
Web: www.highland-mountain-guide.co.uk

3 flats, 1 pub rm, 1-3 bedrms, sleeps 2-8, total sleeping capacity 42, from £147.00, Jan-Dec, bus 200yds, rail 50 yds, ferry 47 mls, airport 102 mls

Comfortable apartments situated at south-west end of Caledonian Canal with fine views towards Ben Nevis, Aonach Mor ski area and Loch Linnhe.

Cromarty, Ross-shire Map Ref: 4B7

SELF CATERING ★★

Mrs A G Campbell
Clunes House, Miller Road, Cromarty, IV11 8XH
Tel: 01381 600503

1 chalet, 1 pub rm, 1 bedrm (All grd.floor), sleeps 2, £200.00, Apr-Sep, bus ¼ ml, rail 23 mls, ferry ¼ ml, airport 35 mls

Charming pine chalet adjacent to owners house, a short walk from the centre of this historic village. Good sized private garden with patios; gate opening onto beach. A relaxed and tranquil setting. Dogs welcome.

Croy, Inverness-shire Map Ref: 4B8

SELF CATERING ★★★★

Mr & Mrs Robin Buchanan
Logie Estate Office, Forres, Moray, IV36 2QN
Tel: 01309 611208 Fax: 01309 611300
E-mail: jamie@logie.co.uk

1 self contained flat, 2 pub rms, 1 bedrm, sleeps 2. £245.00-£420.00. min.let 1 day, Jan-Dec, bus 1½ mls, rail 8 mls, airport 4 mls.

Situated in the beautifully maintained grounds of an historic 17th century castle and a short distance from Inverness and its airport, the Coach House has been recently converted to the highest standard to a double-bedded flat. Lots of the original features have been retained, including the original large stone arches which has given floor to ceiling windows in the kitchen and also the old hatchway to the loft.

VAT is shown at 17.5%: changes in this rate may affect prices.   *Key to symbols is on back flap.*

THE HIGHLANDS AND SKYE

CULBOKIE – DALCROSS, BY INVERNESS

Culbokie, Ross-shire
Map Ref: 4B7

SELF CATERING ★★★

Corriebeg Holiday Lodges
Culbo Road, Culbokie, by Dingwall, Ross-shire, IV7 8JX
Tel: 01349 877817 Fax: 01349 877822
E-mail: corriebeg.holiday.lodges@cheerful.com
Web: www.host.co.uk

Purpose-built bungalows, which have been well equipped. The bungalows are set in a peaceful location with views from the Black Isle towards Ben Wyvis. A host of wildlives can be seen in the area such as seals, red kites and much more. Inverness is a more 12 miles drive.

2 Lodge, 3 bedrms (All grd.floor), sleeps 6, total sleeping capacity 12, £350.00-£550.00, Jan-Dec, rail 8 Miles, airport 20 Miles

Culkein, Sutherland
Map Ref: 3G4

SELF CATERING ★★★

Mrs C MacLeod
Cherry Lodge, Kilmichael Glassary, Lochgilphead, Argyll, PA31 8QA
Tel: 01546 605204
Web: www.scotia-sc.com/95.htm

Modern bungalow set back from the shore. Superb views across Culkein Bay to the hills beyond. Hill walking, mountain climbing, birds and wildlife in abundance. Ideal base for exploring North West Sutherland.

1 bungalow, 1 pub rm, 3 bedrms, sleeps 6, £120.00-£240.00, Mar-Oct, bus 10 mls, rail 55 mls, airport 100 mls

---

SELF CATERING ★

Mrs Vicki MacLeod
7 Mount Stuart Road, Largs, Ayrshire, KA30 9ES
Tel: 01475 672931 Fax: 01475 674655
E-mail: vickimacleod@hotmail.com

Three well equipped chalets situated in an area of outstanding natural beauty. Thirty yds (27m) from a safe sandy beach.

3 chalets, 3 pub rms, 2-3 bedrms, sleeps 4-6, total sleeping capacity 15, £155.00-£310.00, Apr-Oct, bus 10 mls, rail 50 mls

Culloden Moor, Inverness-shire
Map Ref: 4B8

SELF CATERING ★★★★

Mrs K G Hornby
Drumbuie, Nairnside, Westhill, Inverness, IV2 5GX
Tel: 01463 791591 Fax: 01463 794410
E-mail: Hornby@drumbuie.freeserve.co.uk

Delightful annex to country property with panoramic views to Moray Firth and mountains beyond. 1 mile to Culloden Battlefield and 4 miles Inverness town centre. Ideal base for touring the Highlands. Peaceful rural location with private parking and gardens. Situated on a working farm, conservatory, patio and BBQ. Golf, hill walking, sailing, pony trekking, cycling etc all available locally.

1 cottage, 2 bedrms ensuite (All grd.flr), conservatory, total sleeping capacity 4, min let 7 days, £200.00-£330.00, Jan-Dec, bus 500 yds, rail 4 mls, airport 8 mls.

Dalcross, by Inverness, Inverness-shire
Map Ref: 4B8

SELF CATERING ★★★ UP TO ★★★★

Bob & Margaret Pottie
Easter Dalziel Farm, Dalcross, by Inverness, Inverness-shire, IV1 2L
Tel/Fax: 01667 462213

Tastefully decorated Victorian cottages in peaceful setting on working farm near Inverness. Short drive to Culloden, Fort George, Cawdor. 30 minutes to Aviemore. Woodland walks and open views.

3 cottages, 1 pub rm, 3 bedrms (grd flr avail), sleeps 4-6, total sleeping capacity 16, £120.00-£410.00, Jan-Dec, bus 1 ml, rail 8 mls, airport 1 ml

---

Important: Prices stated are estimates and may be subject to amendments

THE HIGHLANDS AND SKYE

DAVIOT – BY DINGWALL

Daviot, Inverness-shire

Map Ref: 4B9

HOLIDAY PARK ★★★

Auchnahillin Caravan & Camping Centre
Daviot East, Inverness-shire, IV2 5XQ
Tel: 01463 772286 Fax: 01463 772282
E-mail: info@auch.zetnet.co.uk
Web: www.auch.zetnet.co.uk

10 acres, grassy, hard-standing, level, Apr-Oct, prior booking in peak periods, latest time of arrival 2200, overnight holding area. Extra charge for electricity, awnings, showers.

Park accommodation: 100
65 tourers from £7.50 or 65 motors £7.00-9.00 or 20 tents £5.50-8.00.
Total Touring Pitches 65.
18 Holiday Caravans to let, sleep 4-6 £135.00-300.00, total sleeping capacity 104, min let 2 nights.

Leisure facilities:

Situated 7 mls sth of Inverness on B9154 off A9

Diabaig, Ross-shire

Map Ref: 3F8

SELF CATERING ★★★

Christine Duncan
13 Diabaig, Torridon, by Achnasheen, Ross-shire, IV22 2HE
Tel: 01445 790259

Traditional croft beside the road to Diabaig. Superb views over Diabaig Bay, surrounding hills and on a clear day over to Skye. Sleeping six, it is ideal for a family holiday and also well suited for climbers, walkers and nature watchers.

1 house, 3 bedrms (grd flr avail), sleeps 6, £160.00-£220.00, Mar-Dec, bus ½ ml, rail 30 mls, airport 80 mls

by Dingwall, Ross-shire

Map Ref: 4A8

SELF CATERING ★★

Mrs C Manson
Inchvannie House, Strathpeffer, Ross-shire
Tel: 01997 421436

Large T shaped bungalow with one acre of garden, split into two self contained units, quiet rural area 2 miles from Dingwall and Strathpeffer. Numerous golf courses and local walks in the area. Central for exploring the West Highlands and the far north, as well as the towns and villages of Easter Ross and East Sutherland.

2 cottages, 1-2 pub rms, 2-3 bedrms (grd flr avail), sleeps 3-5, total sleeping capacity 8, £110.00-£280.00, Apr-Oct, bus 150 yds, rail 3 mls, airport 25 mls

Fodderty Lodge

Fodderty by Dingwall, Ross-shire IV15 9UE
Tel: 01997 421393   Fax: 01997 421715
e.mail: fodderty_lodge@imride.globalnet.co.uk
Web: www.user.globalnet.co.uk/~imride

Fodderty Lodge originally built as a country manse in 1730 is located midway between Dingwall and Strathpeffer. We offer a variety of high quality accommodation to reflect the needs of families, couples and single people as a family run enterprise. We provide an excellent service to our visitors.

SELF CATERING ★★ UP TO ★★★

Mr Ian Rideout
Fodderty Lodge, by Dingwall, Ross-shire, IV15 9UE
Tel: 01997 421393 Fax: 01997 421715
E-mail: fodderty_lodge@imride.globalnet.co.uk
Web: www.user.globalnet.co.uk/~imride

Fodderty lodge offers a variety of high quality self catering accommodation. As family run enterprise, we believe in offering an excellent service to our visitors, welcome packs on arrival, advice on places to visit, local walks and home grown produce.

2 flats, 2 cottages, 1 pub rm, 1-3 bedrms (grd flr avail), sleeps 2-6, total sleeping capacity 14, £150.00-£360.00, Jan-Dec, bus 100m, rail 20 miles, airport 20 miles

VAT is shown at 17.5%: changes in this rate may affect prices.   *Key to symbols is on back flap.*

BY DINGWALL – DORNOCH — THE HIGHLANDS AND SKYE

by Dingwall, Ross-shire

★★ SELF CATERING

Seaforth Highland Country Estate
Dingwall, Ross-shire, IV7 8EE
Tel: 01349 865505/861150 Fax: 01349 861745
E-mail: seaestate@aol.com

Restored cottages on 4000 acres of richly wooded farmland. The estate offers free trout and pike fishing, garden and forest walks, shooting and stalking. Riding centre, bicycle hire. As well as local activities and attractions, the estate's location makes it an ideal base for exploring the rest of the far north and the West Highlands.

Map Ref: 4A8

2 houses, 8 cottages, 1-3 pub rms, 2-7 bedrms (grd flr avail), sleeps 4-13, total sleeping capacity 60, £150.00-£690.00, Jan-Dec, bus ½ ml, rail 1 ml, airport 20 mls

---

Dores, Inverness-shire

★★ SELF CATERING

Mr & Mrs A I Cameron
Drummond Farm, Dores, Inverness-shire, IV1 2TX
Tel: 01463 751251 Fax: 01463 751240
E-mail: aicameron@hotmail.com

Secluded site with three log cabins on farm above Loch Ness.

Map Ref: 4B9

3 log cabins, 2 pub rms, 2 bedrms (All grd.floor), sleeps 4-6, total sleeping capacity 18, £175.00-£370.00, Jan-Dec, bus 2 mls, rail 10 mls, airport 15 mls

Dornie, by Kyle of Lochalsh, Ross-shire

★★★ SELF CATERING

Zoe Macleod
23 Camuslongart, Ardelve, Dornie, by Kyle of Lochalsh, Ross-shire, IV40 8EX
Tel: 01599 555357/0468 428242 (mobile)

Traditional detached cottage in peaceful location on loch side with distant views of Eilean Donan Castle. 7 miles (11kms) from Isle of Skye bridge.

Map Ref: 3G9

2 cottages, 1-2 pub rms, 2-3 bedrms, sleeps 4-6, total sleeping capacity 10, £250.00-£350.00, Jan-Dec, bus ¼ ml, rail 7 mls, ferry 7 mls, airport 83 mls

Dornoch, Sutherland

★★★ SELF CATERING

Mrs A M Farquharson
Shuna, Westhill, Inverness, IV1 2BQ
Tel: 01463 230930

Comfortable house situated in the centre of Dornoch. Ideal for access to local shops, restaurants, the beach and the golf course is only 5 minutes walk away. A good base for exploring the Highlands. Nature reserves and forest walks are only a short drive away.

Map Ref: 4B6

1 house, 2 pub rms, 2 bedrms, sleeps 4, £200.00-£250.00, , bus ½ ml, rail 15 mls, airport 45 mls

---

★★ SELF CATERING

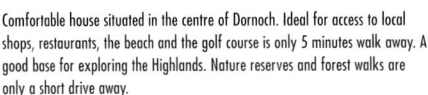

Mrs L Hartwell
17 Loch Bay, Waternish, Isle of Skye, IV55 8OD
Tel: 01470 592363 Fax: 01470 592237
E-mail: clive@skyeskyns.co.uk

Spacious detached house set in large garden, close to Royal Dornoch golf course and safe sandy beaches.

1 house, 3-4 pub rms, 3-4 bedrms (grd flr avail), sleeps 6, £300.00-£395.00, Apr-Oct, bus nearby, rail 10 mls, airport 40 mls

---

Important: Prices stated are estimates and may be subject to amendments

THE HIGHLANDS AND SKYE

DRUMNADROCHIT – BY DRUMNADROCHIT

Drumnadrochit, Inverness-shire   Map Ref: 4A9

Achmony Holidays
Drumnadrochit, by Loch Ness
IV63 6UX
Tel: 01456 450357
Fax: 01456 450830
e.mail: info@achmony.freeserve.co.uk

Enjoy your holiday in an idyllic location above Loch Ness in one of our chalet bungalows. Each chalet has 3 bedrooms, bathroom with shower, lounge with colour TV, patio door and fully fitted, well equipped kitchen.
Central for touring, Drumnadrochit has several hotels, shops, exhibition centres, pony-trekking, fishing and boat trips on Loch Ness.
Contact Mrs Elizabeth Mackintosh.

★★★★ SELF CATERING

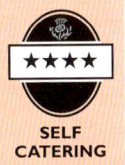

★★★★ SELF CATERING

Mrs Elizabeth MacKintosh
Achmony Holidays, Drumnadrochit, by Loch Ness, IV63 6UX
Tel: 01456 450357 Fax: 01456 450830
E-mail: info@achmony.freeserve.co.uk

House and lodges of individual style and character in a 70 acre woodland setting high above the village. Magnificent views of surrounding area and towards Loch Ness. Privacy and comfort.

10 chalets, 1 pub rm, 3 bedrms (All grd.floor), sleeps 2-6, total sleeping capacity 60, £195.00-£510.00, Mar-Nov, bus ½ ml, rail 16 mls, airport 23 mls

★★★ SELF CATERING

Mrs W D Ross
Strone, Loch Ness Side, Drumnadrochit, Inverness-shire, IV63 6XL
Tel/Fax: 01456 450351

Situated at the lower end of Glenurquhart and close to Loch Ness, the Strone Holiday Cottages command unique and magnificent views over Urquhart Bay, the legendary home of the monster. There are 2 modern cottages, Strone Cottage and Tor Na Brac (Hill of the Badger), and 1 chalet, all situated on separate sites for maximum privacy.

1 chalet, 2 bungalows, 1 pub rm, 2-3 bedrms, sleeps 4, total sleeping capacity 12, £195.00-£360.00, Apr-Sep, bus nearby, rail 15 mls, airport 20 mls

by Drumnadrochit, Inverness-shire   Map Ref: 4A9

★★★ SELF CATERING

A D MacDonald, Reservations
Borlum Farm Country Holidays, Drumnadrochit, Inverness-shire, IV63 6XN
Tel/Fax: 01456 450358
Web: www.net-trak.com/~ecs/guest/borlum

Cottage in row of three on working farm in rural setting near Urquhart Castle and Loch Ness. Riding available.

1 cottage, 1 pub rm, 3 bedrms (All grd.floor), sleeps 6, Jan-Dec, bus nearby, rail 15 mls, airport 25 mls

VAT is shown at 17.5%: changes in this rate may affect prices.   *Key to symbols is on back flap.*

DUIRINISH – DUNCANSTON

THE HIGHLANDS AND SKYE

Duirinish, by Plockton, Ross-shire
Map Ref: 3F9

★★★★ SELF CATERING

William Roe
3 Northumberland Street, EH3 6LL
Tel: 0131 556 0101 Fax: 0131 556 0801
E-mail: williamroe@sol.co.uk

1 house, 2 pub rms, 3 bedrms, sleeps 4, £290.00-£600.00, Jan-Dec, bus 5 mls, rail 1 ml

Elegant wing of large house set in 18 acres of land. Breathtaking views to surrounding area and very close to Plockton, Kyle of Lochalsh and Skye. Tastefully furnished, decorated and equipped to a very high standard. Games room and summer house available to guests also.

Dulnain Bridge, by Grantown-on-Spey, Inverness-shire
Map Ref: 4C9

★★★ SELF CATERING

Mrs Elizabeth Grant
Woodside, Skye of Curr, Dulnain Bridge, Inverness-shire, PH26 3PA
Tel: 01479 851229

1 house, 2 pub rms, 4 bedrms (grd flr avail), sleeps 8, £160.00-£360.00, Jan-Dec, bus 1 ml, rail 10 mls, ferry 30 mls, airport 30 mls

Set in a peaceful rural location, and recently built, The Cabrach lies at the very heart of beautiful Strathspey, famous worldwide for its magnificent scenery. Abundance of wildlife, fishing, its malt whisky distilleries and winter sports facilities.

★★★★ SELF CATERING

Muckrach Estate, per Strutt & Parker
St Nicholas House, 68 Station Road, Banchory, Kincardineshire, AB3 5YJ
Tel: 01330 824888 Fax: 01330 825577
E-mail: banchory@struttandparker.co.uk

1 castle, 2 pub rms, 4 bedrms, sleeps 8, £590.00-£1030.00, Jan-Dec, bus ½ ml, rail 12 mls, airport 35 mls

Restored castle dating from 16c standing in its own grounds with fine views towards Cairngorms.

★★ SELF CATERING

Peter Strother
Upper Finlarig, Dulnain Bridge, Inverness-shire, PH26 3NU
Tel: 01479 851209
E-mail: finlarig@enterprise.net

1 cottage, 1-2 pub rms, 1-2 bedrms, sleeps 4-5, £135.00-£210.00, Jan-Dec, bus ½ ml, rail 7 mls, airport 35 mls

Warm cosy cottage in a quiet, peaceful situation high up overlooking Cairngorms. With its own garden and patio. Close to local amenities.

Duncanston, Ross-shire
Map Ref: 4B8

★★ SELF CATERING

Mrs Anne Hannan
Shalom, Dunvournie, Culbokie, by Dingwall, Ross-shire, IV7 8JB
Tel: 01349 877246

1 cottage, 1 pub rm, 3 bedrms (All grd.floor), sleeps 5, £130.00-£170.00, Mar-Oct, bus nearby, rail 6 mls, airport 16 mls

Comfortable farm cottage on working farm with delightful views over the Cromarty Firth and surrounding hills. Central for touring.

Important: Prices stated are estimates and may be subject to amendments

THE HIGHLANDS AND SKYE

DUNDONNELL – EVANTON

Dundonnell, Ross-shire

Mrs A Ross
4 Camusnagaul, Dundonnell, Ross-shire, IV23 2QT
Tel: 01854 633237

*** SELF CATERING

Map Ref: 3G7

2 chalets, 1 pub rm, 2 bedrms (All grd.floor), sleeps 4-6, total sleeping capacity 12, from £200.00, Jan-Dec, rail 34 mls, ferry 26 mls, airport 60 mls

Situated on shore of Little Loch Broom. Ideal for walkers being close to An Teallach Mountain Range.

Mr M J Stott
Croft 9, Badrallach, Dundonnell, Ross-shire, IV23 2QP
Tel: 01854 633281
E-mail: michael.stott2@virgin.net

**** SELF CATERING

1 cottage, 1-2 pub rms, 1-3 bedrms, sleeps 4, min let weekend, £120.00-£250.00, Jan-Dec, bus 7 mls, rail 30 mls, ferry 3 mls, airport 60 mls

A tranquil lochshore croft overlooking the mighty Anteallach with gas lighting, peat fires and crisp linen sheets. Watch otters, porpoises, red deer, pine martins, golden eagles, seals, mountain goats and ptarmigans (in white plumage in winter). Walk in Scotland's last great wilderness or just relax with a dram in our uniquely designed warm and cosy cottage and enjoy the view. Bliss!

Eigg, Isle of, Inverness-shire

Sue Kirk
Lageorna, Isle of Eigg, Inverness-shire, PH42 4RL
Tel: 01687 482405

** SELF CATERING

Map Ref: 3E11

2 cottages, 2 pub rms, 3 bedrms (grd flr avail), sleeps 6, total sleeping capacity 12, £180.00-£380.00, Jan-Dec, ferry 3 mls

Sue and Alistair have renovated one of their two adjoining croft cottages to provide comfortable self contained accommodation. The nearby "Singing Sands" Beach, and magnificent views across the sea to Isle of Rhum are all part of the unique Eigg experience. TV on request.

Embo, by Dornoch, Sutherland

Grannies Heilan Hame Holiday Park
Embo, Dornoch, Sutherland, IV25 3QD
Tel: 01862 810383 Fax: 01862 810368
Booking Enquiries: Haven Reservations Po Box 218, 1 Park Lane, Hemel Hempstead, HP2 4GL
Tel: 0870 242 2222

**** HOLIDAY PARK

Map Ref: 4B6

Park accommodation: 421

Tourers, motor homes and tents welcome. Total touring pitches 324. £7.50-£15.00 per night approx. Contact park direct.

Holiday Caravans to let, sleep 6-8. £118.00-£509.00 per week approx. Contact reservations.

Leisure facilities:

A9 from Inverness via Kessock Bridge to Dornoch. Then left at Main Square to Embo (3 mls) beside Grannies Heilan Hame park.

32 acres, grassy, sandy, level, Mar-Oct, prior booking recommended in peak periods, latest time of arrival 2300, overnight holding area. Extra charge for electricity, dogs.

Evanton, Ross-shire

Mrs P Munro
Foulis Castle, Evanton, Ross-shire, IV16 9UX
Tel: 01349 830212

**** SELF CATERING

Map Ref: 4B7

1 house, 2 pub rms, 2 bedrms, sleeps 4, (min let 3 nights), £280.00-£420.00 per week, Jan-Dec, bus 1 1/2 mls, rail 4 mls, airport 30 mls.

Luxury apartment within Foulis Castle, sleeps four, ensuite bathrooms home of the Chiefs of Clan Munro, who have lived here since at least the 12th century. Part of the pavillion dates from the early 16th century, the rest from the 1750s. Magnificent courtyard garden. Approx 18 miles (29kms) north of Inverness.

VAT is shown at 17.5%: changes in this rate may affect prices.

Key to symbols is on back flap.

FESHIE BRIDGE – FORTROSE
THE HIGHLANDS AND SKYE

Feshie Bridge, by Kincraig, Inverness-shire
Map Ref: 4C10

★★ SELF CATERING

Wilma Adam
Blinkbonny, Milnathort, Kinross-shire, KY13 0SD
Tel: 01577 865083

1 bungalow, 2 pub rms, 3 bedrms, sleeps 5, £260.00-£290.00, Apr-Oct, bus 8 mls, rail 8 mls

Modern cottage, in quiet setting by River Feshie. Within 8 miles (13kms) of Aviemore and 1 mile (2kms) of Loch Insh.

Fort Augustus, Inverness-shire
Map Ref: 4A10

★ SELF CATERING

Mount Pleasant (Mrs C Cameron)
2 Balmaglaster, by Spean Bridge, Inverness-shire, PH34 4EB
Tel: 01809 501289

1 cottage, 1 pub rm, 3 bedrms (grd flr avail), sleeps 6, min let 3 nights (low season), £150.00-£300.00, Jan-Dec, bus nearby, rail 23 mls, airport 38 mls

Traditional cottage situated in its own grounds with burn. Views overlooking Fort Augustus village towards the Caledonian Canal. Centrally situated for touring the Highlands. Two minute walk to village and Loch Ness.

Fortrose, Ross-shire
Map Ref: 4B8

★★★ SELF CATERING

Mrs L J Grant
Fasgadh, Ness Road, Fortrose, Ross-shire
Tel: 01381 620367

1 cottage, 1 pub rm, 3 bedrms (grd flr avail), sleeps 6, £120.00-£380.00, Mar-Nov, bus ½ ml, rail 14 mls, airport 21 mls

Spacious detached farm cottage, with large garden area, situated on the edge of Fortrose village. Close to the golf course and to Chanonry Point, an excellent spot for looking for the famous Moray Firth Dolphins. Good base for exploring the Black Isle, Easter Ross and beyond.

★★★ SELF CATERING

Middleton Ross & Arnot
Mansefield House, Dingwall, Ross-shire, IV15 9HJ
Tel: 01349 862214/865125 Fax: 01349 863819
E-mail: email@middletons.demon.co.uk

1 cottage, 2 pub rms, 2 bedrms, sleeps 1-4, £180.00-£320.00, Apr-Oct, bus nearby, rail 15 mls, airport 20 mls

Comfortable modernised house close to all amenities. Great location for sailing, dolphin watching, golfing or relaxing.

★★ SELF CATERING

Mr M Strachan
332 Blackness Road, Dundee, DD2 1SD
Tel: 01382 660804

1 house, 1 pub rm, 4 bedrms (grd flr avail), sleeps 8, £200.00-£330.00, Apr-Oct, bus ½ ml, rail 12 mls, airport 15 mls

Comfortable, spacious and well appointed house, with labour saving dishwasher and microwave provided, situated in quiet residential area of Fortrose. Safe secluded garden. Fine views over the Moray Firth, close to Chanonry Point - an excellent location for dolphin watching.

Important: Prices stated are estimates and may be subject to amendments

THE HIGHLANDS AND SKYE

FORT WILLIAM

Fort William, Inverness-shire

Map Ref: 3H12

SELF CATERING ★★

Abrach House
4 Caithness Place, Fort William, Inverness-shire, PH33 6JP
Tel/Fax: 01397 702535
E-mail: cmoore3050@aol.com

1 flat, 1 pub rm, 1 bedrm, sleeps 2-4, £160.00-£220.00, Jan-Dec, bus nearby, rail 1 ml

Small ground floor flat of split level house in an elevated position overlooking Fort William and surrounding hills. Situated in a quiet cul-de-sac, private parking. Small patio area with garden furniture provided within a quiet garden. Use of laundry facilities. On bus route.

SELF CATERING ★★

Mrs E K Clark
14 Perth Place, Fort William, PH33 6UL
Tel: 01397 702444 Fax: 01397 702141

1 flat, 1 pub rm, 1 bedrm, sleeps 4, £120.00-£185.00, Jan-Dec, bus ½ ml, rail 1 ml

Modern compact flat attached to family home in quiet residential area 1 mile (2kms) from town centre. On main bus route. Walkers and climbers welcome. 5 miles from ski slope, 15 minutes walk from Fort William town centre. Own small patio area to rear. Brochure available on request.

SELF CATERING ★★★

Mrs Fiona Gibson
Glenfinnan Estate, Fort William, Inverness-shire, PH37 4LT
Tel: 01397 722203 Fax: 01397 722444

1 lodge, 3 pub rms, 4 bedrms, sleeps 8, £650.00-£750.00, Jan-Dec, bus 3 mls, rail 3 mls, ferry 31 mls, airport 80 mls

Lodge situated at the head of its own Glen, commanding spectacular views of the surrounding mountains. Solidly built and maintained as a family home, it is warm and snug in all weathers. Ideal for those seeking peace and solitude and for the active, there is Glen and hill-walking and trout fishing.

SELF CATERING ★★★

Mrs Ann Gillies
West Highland Hotel, Mallaig, Inverness-shire, PH41 4QZ
Tel: 01687 462210 Fax: 01687 462130

1 house, 2 pub rms, 3 bedrms, sleeps 6, £200.00-£305.00, Jan-Dec, bus nearby, rail 1 ml, airport 70 mls

Modern semi-detached house, with own garden, at gable-end of terrace, in residential area above the town centre.

SELF CATERING ★★★

Mrs Patricia Gillies
Ealasaid, Victoria Road, Fort William, PH33 6BH
Tel: 01397 704005

1 flat, 1 bedrm, sleeps 2, £160.00-£200.00, Jan-Dec

Self-contained studio flat with separate well-equipped quiet location and short walk from the town centre.

VAT is shown at 17.5%: changes in this rate may affect prices.   *Key to symbols is on back flap.*

FORT WILLIAM

Fort William, Inverness-shire

Map Ref: 3H12

Glen Nevis Holiday Cottages
Glen Nevis, Fort William, Inverness-shire PH33 6SX
Tel: 01397 702191 Fax: 01397 703904
e.mail: holidays@glen-nevis.demon.co.uk
Web: http://www.lochaber.com/glen-nevis/

A small select development of holiday cottages in an idyllic setting in beautiful Glen Nevis. Equipped and maintained to a high standard the cottages offer comfortable accommodation for up to five persons. Only 3 miles from historic Fort William with plenty to see and do nearby. Please request colour brochure.

UP TO ★★★★★ SELF CATERING

Glen Nevis Holiday Cottages
Glen Nevis, Fort William, Inverness-shire, PH33 6SX
Tel: 01397 702191 Fax: 01397 703904
E-mail: holidays@glen-nevis.demon.co.uk
Web: www.lochaber.com/glen-nevis/

Magnificent holiday lodges offering the utmost in comfort for up to 6 persons. 3 bedrooms (1 double and 2 twin) and two bath/shower rooms. Fully equipped kitchens. Non smokers only and regret no pets. Also modern purpose built cottages all in the midst of the best of highland scenery in famous Glen Nevis. Enjoy peaceful surroundings with lots to see and do nearby, only 4 kms from Fort William. Colour brochure available.

12 cottages, 1 pub rm, 2 bedrms (All grd.floor), sleeps 4-5, total sleeping capacity 60, £300.00-£480.00, Feb-mid Nov, mid Dec-Jan, bus 2 mls, rail 2 ½ mls

★★ SELF CATERING

Glenlochy Apartments
Nevis Bridge, Fort William, Inverness-shire PH33 6PF
Tel: 01397 702909

Two self-contained studio apartments, situated 1 mile (1.5 kms) from town centre. 1 mile (1.5 kms) to foot of Ben Nevis.

2 studio apartments, 1 pub rm, 1 bedrm (grd flr avail), sleeps 2-4, total sleeping capacity 6, £150.00-£315.00, Jan-Dec, bus nearby, rail ½ ml, ferry 8-46 mls, airport 66 mls

INNSEAGAN APARTMENTS/BUNGALOW
ACHINTORE ROAD, FORT WILLIAM PH33 6RW
TEL: 01397 702452   FAX: 01397 702606
e.mail: stewartmac@btinternet.com Web: www.lochaber.com/innseagan

Six apartments and one bungalow all beautifully furnished and maintained to the highest standards. On the shores of Loch Linnhe only 1½ miles south of Fort William, each apartment has a small balcony with panoramic views over the loch. Facilities of Innseagan House Hotel available April to October. Sleep maximum 4. Open all year. Send for full colour brochure to Highland Holidays Scotland Ltd, Innseagan House, Achintore Road, Fort William PH33 6RW. Tel: 01397 702452. Fax: 01397 702606.
Prices from £175 to £395 per week.

★★★★ SELF CATERING

Innseagan Apartments
Innseagan House, Achintore Road, Fort William, Inverness-shire, PH33 6RW
Tel: 01397 702452 Fax: 01397 702606
E-mail: stewartmac@btinternet.com
Web: www.lochaber.com/innseagan

These apartments have been designed, built and furnished to ensure a most enjoyable holiday experience and they are maintained and serviced to ensure a relaxing holiday. Only 1.5 miles from Fort William and overlooking Loch Linnhe to the mountains. Cleanliness is the watchword of the management and staff. Adjoining hotel facilities available April/October.

1 bungalow, 6 apartments, 1 pub rm, 1-2 bedrms (grd flr avail), sleeps 4, total sleeping capacity 28, £175.00-£395.00, Jan-Dec, bus nearby, rail 1 ½ mls, airport 65 mls

Important: Prices stated are estimates and may be subject to amendments

THE HIGHLANDS AND SKYE

FORT WILLIAM

Fort William, Inverness-shire

Map Ref: 3H12

★★★ SELF CATERING

Mr & Mrs A W Kimber
Calluna, Heather Croft, Fort William, Inverness-shire, PH33 6RE
Tel: 01397 700451 Fax: 01397 700489
E-mail: mountain@guide.u-net.com
Web: www.guide.u-net.com

Calluna enjoys fine elevated views across Loch Linnhe to the Ardgour Hills. Close to town (10 mins walk) yet in a quiet area of Fort William. Ideal for families touring. (Inverness-Oban-Mallaig-Aviemore-Skye are within two hours drive) or mountaineers exploring Ben-Nevis and Glen-Coe. Walkers, canoeists welcome and can have use of the best drying rooms available. Ideal for sharing families or groups of outdoor folk.

1 flat, 2 apartment, 1 pub rm, 2-3 bedrms (grd flr avail), sleeps 6-8, total sleeping capacity 22, min let 1 night, £220.00-£425.00, Jan-Dec, bus nearby, rail nearby, airport 100 mls

Linnhe Caravan & Chalet Park

Corpach, Fort William, Inverness-shire PH33 7NL
Tel: 01397 772376   Fax: 01397 772007
e.mail: holidays@linnhe.demon.co.uk
Web: www.lochaber.com/linnhe

Winner of **"Best Park in Scotland 1999"** award. Almost a botanical garden, Linnhe is unique and one of the most beautiful lochside parks in Britain. Close to Ben Nevis and Fort William, the adventure capital of Scotland. Explore or simply relax and soak up the scenery in lovely well-tended surroundings. Excellent facilities including licenced shop, children's playgrounds, private beach and free fishing. Pets welcome. Sleeps 1-8.

Luxury pine chalets from £300-£640 per week.
Thistle award caravans from £180-£450 per week.
Chalet breaks from £180, caravans from £90.

★★★★ SELF CATERING
Open: 15 December-31 October.
Colour brochure sent with pleasure.

★★★★ SELF CATERING

Linnhe Caravan & Chalet Park
Corpach, Fort William, Inverness-shire, PH33 7NL
Tel: 01397 772376 Fax: 01397 772007
E-mail: holidays@linnhe.demon.co.uk
Web: www.lochaber.com/linnhe

Comfortable Alpine chalets on beautifully landscaped lochside park. Use of all amenities. Private beach.

11 chalets, 1 pub rm, 2-3 bedrms (grd flr avail), sleeps 4-8, total sleeping capacity 70, min let 3 nights, £300.00-£640.00, 15 Dec-31 Oct, bus 1 ml, rail 1 ml

---

VAT is shown at 17.5%: changes in this rate may affect prices.

Key to symbols is on back flap.

FORT WILLIAM – BY FORT WILLIAM

THE HIGHLANDS AND SKYE

Fort William, Inverness-shire   Map Ref: 3H12

Nevis Bank Cottages and Apartments

BELFORD ROAD · FORT WILLIAM
Tel: 01397 705721   Fax: 01397 706275

Situated within walking distance of the town centre, yet only a few minutes drive from the ski slopes of "Nevis Range", the Nevis Bank Cottages and Apartments provide the ideal base for those who prefer the freedom of a self-catering holiday. Sleeping from 2-6 persons, these units come fully equipped with all essentials, including linen, central heating and TV. Guests are welcome to use all hotel facilities which include hair and beauty salon and childrens creche. Pets welcome.

Terms from £220-£525 per unit per week.

For brochure and tariff, please contact Florence Mackay.

★★ SELF CATERING

Nevis Bank Apartments & Cottges
Nevis Bank Hotel, Belford Road, Fort William, Inverness-shire, PH33 6BY
Tel: 01397 705721 Fax: 01397 706275

Terraced cottages with ample parking, 10 minutes walk from town centre. Creche facilities available.

5 cottages, 1-2 pub rms, 2 bedrms, sleeps 4, total sleeping capacity 20, £220.00-£525.00, Jan-Dec, bus nearby, rail 800 yds, airport 70 mls

★★ SELF CATERING

Mrs M Wardle
16 Perth Place, Upper Achintore, Fort William, Inverness-shire
Tel: 01397 704392

Flat on ground-floor of modern house, on upper outskirts of town, with excellent views across Loch Linnhe.

1 flat, 2 pub rms, 1 bedrm, sleeps 4, £110.00, Jan-Dec, bus nearby, rail 1 1/2 mls

---

by Fort William, Inverness-shire   Map Ref: 3H12

★★★★ SELF CATERING

Mrs E L Gray
Dolalans, 7 Blaich, Fort William, Inverness-shire, PH33 7AN
Tel: 01397 772808

Situated on a working croft on south shore of Loch Eil with superb views over loch to hills beyond. Relatively remote but peaceful location. Cosy comfortable, tastefully decorated in a modern style. Open all year for a relaxing, "get away from it all" holiday. Garden shed for storage of biking/climbing skiing equipment. Enclosed garden with seating and BBQ provided.

1 cottage, 1 pub rm, 2 bedrms, sleeps 4, £180.00-£350.00, Jan-Dec, bus 20 mls, rail 7 mls

---

Important: Prices stated are estimates and may be subject to amendments

THE HIGHLANDS AND SKYE

FOYERS – GAIRLOCH

Foyers, Inverness-shire

Map Ref: 4A10

★★ SELF CATERING

Foyers Bay House
Foyers, Loch Ness, Inverness-shire, IV2 6YB
Tel: 01456 486624 Fax: 01456 486403
E-mail: panciroli@foyersbay.freeserve.co.uk

6 chalets situated in 4 acres of grounds at Foyers Bay House overlooking Loch Ness and 20 miles (32kms) South of Inverness.

6 chalets, 1 pub rm, 3 bedrms (All grd.floor), sleeps 6, total sleeping capacity 36, £200.00-£450.00, Jan-Dec, bus $\frac{1}{4}$ ml, rail 20 mls, airport 25 mls

Gairloch, Ross-shire

Map Ref: 3F7

★★★ SELF CATERING

Mrs M Bone
Creag Beag, Gairloch, Ross-shire, IV21 2AH
Tel: 01445 712322 Fax: 01445 712310

Modern bungalows set in elevated peaceful position on southern edge of village, close to Creag Mor Hotel, sandy beaches and golf course. Small supermarket which opens late within easy reach.

2 bungalows, 2 pub rms, 2 bedrms, sleeps 4, total sleeping capacity 8, £150.00-£335.00, Jan-Dec, bus nearby, rail 28 mls, airport 80 mls

★★ SELF CATERING

Mr A Duvill
Apronhill, Primrose Cottage, Badachro, by Gairloch, Ross-shire, IV21 2AB
Tel: 01445 741317 Fax: 01445 741377

Original crofters cottage 70 yards up steep grassy hill set in 1 acre of fenced ground. Magnificent views of Gairloch and sandy bay.

1 house, 2 pub rms, 2 bedrms, sleeps 4, from £90.00, Jan-Dec, bus 500 yds, rail 30 mls, airport 76 mls

★★★ SELF CATERING

Mrs S Gerrard
Santosa, Auchtercairn, Gairloch
Tel: 01445 712023
E-mail: igerrard@aol.com
Web: www.santosa.mcmail.com

Recently refurbished ground floor flat in modern house in elevated position overlooking Gairloch. Spectacular sea views over to Skye. Close to local amenities which include Inverewe Gardens, Golf club, porpoise spotting trips, local Heritage Museum and varied eating places.

1 house, 2 pub rms, 3 bedrms (All grd.floor), sleeps 2-6, £210.00-£410.00, Apr-Oct, bus $\frac{1}{2}$ ml

★★★★ SELF CATERING

Mrs Elizabeth Jessiman
75a Craigcrook Road, Edinburgh, EH4 3PH
Tel: 0131 332 6678

Large fully equipped house in extensive secluded grounds. An idyllic location only minutes from the shops, golf course and beautiful beach. Easy access to open countryside, Inverewe Gardens and many attractive walks and drives.

1 house, 1 pub rm, 4 bedrms (All grd.floor), sleeps 7, £300.00-£550.00, Apr-Oct, bus 1 ml, rail 70 mls, ferry 60 mls, airport 75 mls

---

VAT is shown at 17.5%: changes in this rate may affect prices.

Key to symbols is on back flap.

GAIRLOCH – GLENCOE

THE HIGHLANDS AND SKYE

Gairloch, Ross-shire

Map Ref: 3F7

★★★ SELF CATERING

Mrs B Leslie
40 Big Sand, Gairloch, Ross-shire, IV21 2DD
Tel: 01445 712448

Specially designed bungalow, with disabled in mind, in a crofting township, overlooking Longa Island and Loch Gairloch to Skye and the Torridons.

1 bungalow, 2 pub rms, 3 bedrms (All grd.floor), sleeps 6, £170.00-£410.00, Jan-Dec, bus 5 mls, rail 35 mls, airport 75 mls

---

★★★ UP TO ★★★★ SELF CATERING

Mrs B J Reese
Gillymere, Horseshoe Lane, Ash Vale, Aldershot, Hampshire, GU12 5LJ
Tel/Fax: 01252 325119

We have 20 years experience of letting properties in this lovely area of mountain ranges and picturesque sea coasts. They are all in detached, individual locations, fully equipped with open fires. There are good walks and places of interest nearby including Inverewe Gardens (NT), golf course along with sea and loch fishing.

6 houses, 1-2 pub rms, 3-4 bedrms (grd flr avail), sleeps 4-7, total sleeping capacity 35, £145.00-£395.00, Jan-Dec, bus 1-7 mls, rail 26 mls, airport 85 mls

---

★★★★ HOLIDAY PARK

Sands Holiday Centre
Gairloch, Ross-shire, IV21 2DL
Tel: 01445 712152 Fax: 01445 712518
E-mail: litsands@aol.com

50 acres, mixed, Apr-Oct, prior booking in peak periods, latest time of arrival 2230. Extra charge for electricity, awnings.

Park accommodation: 250

120 tourers £8.00-9.00 and 40 motors £8.00-8.50 and 150 tents £8.00-8.20. Total Touring Pitches 310.

5 Holiday Caravans to let, sleep 6 £225.00-380.00, total sleeping capacity 30, min let 2 nights.

At Gairloch turn on to B8021 (Melvaig). Site 3 mls on, beside sandy beach.

★★ SELF CATERING

Mr J. S. Smith
26 Strath, Gairloch, Ross-shire, IV21 2DA
Tel: 01445 712064 Fax: 01445 712256

Self contained ground floor flat adjacent to owners house. Quiet location just a short walk from Gairloch shops, hotels and restaurants. Stunning sea and mountain views. Totally non-smoking.

1 flat, sleeps 2-3, £180.00-£200.00, Mar-Oct, bus ¼ ml

Glencoe, Argyll

Map Ref: 1F1

★★ SELF CATERING

Mr Peter Brown
11 Devonia Road, London, N1 8JQ
Tel: 0171 359 1281 Fax: 0171 704 1998

Ballachulish, Glencoe. Roomy, well equipped wing of stone-built house. Own entrance. Set up for hillwalkers and tourists. Near shops and pub.

1 cottage, 2 pub rms, 4 bedrms, sleeps 8, Jan-Oct, bus 300 yds, rail 15 mls, airport 85 mls

---

Important: Prices stated are estimates and may be subject to amendments

THE HIGHLANDS AND SKYE

GLENCOE

Glencoe, Argyll
Map Ref: 1F1

Carefree Self-Catering Holidays – Glencoe

Clachaig, Glencoe, Argyll PA39 4HX
Tel: 01855 811252 Fax: 01855 811679 ★★★★ SELF-CATERING
e.mail: chalets@glencoe-scotland.co.uk   Web: www.glencoe-scotland.co.uk
Well-appointed chalets located in Scotland's most famous and scenic glen. All furnished to high standard featuring a master bedroom with ensuite facilities. Fully fitted kitchen, all modern appliances. Quiet peaceful location, magnificent mountain views in the grounds of lively Inn serving imaginative food and great range of cask ales. Open all year.

★★★★ SELF CATERING

Carefree Self-Catering Holidays - Glencoe
Clachaig, Glencoe, Argyll, PA39 4HX
Tel: 01855 811252 Fax: 01855 811679
E-mail: chalets@glencoe-scotland.co.uk
Web: www.glencoe-scotland.co.uk

Purpose built timber chalets near to Clachaig Inn, enjoying stunning mountain scenery. Ideal for touring. Situated on historic site of massacre.

4 chalets, 1 pub rm, 2-3 bedrms (grd flr avail), sleeps 4-6, total sleeping capacity 12, £175.00-£550.00, Jan-Dec, bus ¼ ml, rail 18 mls

---

★★★ SELF CATERING

Mrs Christine Dawson
49 Braid Farm Road, Edinburgh, EH10 6LE
Tel: 0131 447 7689

Cosy, newly-built house in traditional cottage style with small fenced garden to rear. Superb uninterrupted panoramic views across Loch Leven to Mamores and Ardgour hills. 12 miles (19 kms) from Fort William. Ideal centre for sailing, hillwalking, skiing, fishing and touring the Glencoe area.

1 house, 1 pub rm, 3 bedrms, sleeps 5, £220.00-£320.00, Apr-Aug, bus nearby, rail 14 mls

---

★★★★ SELF CATERING

Invercoe Highland Holidays
Invercoe, Glencoe, Argyll, PA39 4HP
Tel/Fax: 01855 811210
E-mail: invercoe@sol.co.uk
Web: www.invercoe.co.uk

A choice of accommodation on the outskirts of this Highland village of either brand new lodges or refurbished two storey cottages. Built on the site of the house of Maclain, clan chief of the Macdonalds of Glencoe.

3 chalets, 3 cottages, 2-3 bedrms (grd flr avail), sleeps 2-6, total sleeping capacity 33, £200.00-£460.00, Jan-Dec, bus ½ ml, rail 15 mls, airport 100 mls

★★★ SELF CATERING

Victoria Sutherland
The Moss, Pier Road, Rhu, Helensburgh, Dunbartonshire, G84 8LR
Tel: 01436 820274 Fax: 01436 821212
E-mail: sutherland@torrencottages.freeserve.co.uk
Web: www.about-scotland.co.uk/glencoe/torren.html

3 cottages, 1 pub rm, 3 bedrms (All grd.floor), sleeps 6-8, total sleeping capacity 22, Jan-Dec, bus 2 ½ mls, rail 16 mls, ferry 8 mls, airport 80 mls

---

VAT is shown at 17.5%: changes in this rate may affect prices.

Key to symbols is on back flap.

GLENELG – GLENFINNAN
THE HIGHLANDS AND SKYE

Glenelg, Ross-shire
Map Ref: 3F10

SELF CATERING ★

Mrs Haywood
96 Viewforth (2F2), Edinburgh, Midlothian, EH10 4LG
Tel: 0131 228 8399

1 cottage, 1 pub rm, 3 bedrms (grd flr avail), sleeps 6, min let weekend, £250.00, Jan-Dec, bus 7 mls, rail 30 mls, ferry 1/2 ml, airport 70 mls

Homely cottage situated adjacent to the Glenelg Ferry road in a beautiful, remote part of the country. The summer ferry to Skye is only 2 miles away. Excellent base for those wishing to enjoy the great outdoors in peace and quiet.

SELF CATERING ★★★

Mr & Mrs M J Lamont
Creagmhor, Glenelg, by Kyle, Ross-shire, IV40 8LA
Tel/Fax: 01599 522231

5 chalets, 1 bungalow, 1 pub rm, 2-3 bedrms (grd flr avail), sleeps 4-6, total sleeping capacity 34, £110.00-£330.00, Jan-Dec, bus 8 mls, rail 25 mls, ferry 3 mls, airport 80 mls

Bungalow on working croft set amidst magnificent scenery. 3 miles (5kms) from summer ferry to Skye. Pets welcome.

SELF CATERING ★★

P J Maughan Holiday Homes
24 Whaggs Lane, Whickham, Newcastle-upon-Tyne, NE16 4PF
Tel: 0191 488 6218 Fax: 0191 488 5571
E-mail: janet@pmaughan.demon.co.uk
Web: www.pmaughan.demon.co.uk

1 bungalow, 5 pub rms, 5 bedrms, sleeps 10, min let 2 nights, £200.00-£475.00, Jan-Dec, bus nearby, rail 23 mls, ferry 1 ml, airport 50 mls

Large comfortable bungalow, pleasantly situated in elevated position in Glenelg. An ideal base for exploring much of the North West Highlands.

Glenferness, Inverness-shire
Map Ref: 4C8

SELF CATERING ★

Mrs A S D Hilleary
Logie Farm, Glenferness, Nairn, IV12 5XA
Tel/Fax: 01309 651226

1 cottage, 1 pub rm, 1 bedrm, sleeps 2-3, £125.00-£350.00, Jan-Dec, bus 10 mls, rail 10 mls, airport 15 mls

18c 'Half House' in a peaceful idyllic situation above the River Findhorn. Near equestrian centre. Trout fish available. Cosy cottage for 2.

Glenfinnan, Inverness-shire
Map Ref: 3G12

SELF CATERING ★★

R MacKellaig
Glenfinnan Cottages, Glenfinnan, Inverness-shire, PH37 4LT
Tel: 01397 722234

3 cottages, 1-2 pub rms, 2 bedrms, sleeps 4-6, total sleeping capacity 16, £170.00-£210.00, Apr-Oct, bus 1/2 ml, rail 1/2 ml, ferry 28 mls, airport 85 mls

Three adjoining self-catering cottages tastefully converted from a former farm steading. Grade 'B' listed. Peacefully situated off the main road in beautiful, historic Glenfinnan amidst the best of Highland scenery. Ideal base for exploring the romantic road to the isles.

Important: Prices stated are estimates and may be subject to amendments

THE HIGHLANDS AND SKYE

GLENMORE – GLEN URQUHART

245

Glenmore, Ardnamurchan, Argyll — Map Ref: 1D1

★★★★ UP TO ★★★★★ SELF CATERING

Mrs K MacGregor
Glenborrodale, Acharacle, Ardnamurchan, Argyll, PH36 4JP
Tel: 01972 500263/500254 Fax: 01972 500203
E-mail: info@michael-macgregor.co.uk
Web: www.michael-macgregor.co.uk

Enjoy a holiday to remember amidst stunning Highland scenery. Our houses offer fine sea views, privacy and a high standard of accommodation; including jacuzzi baths, stone built barbecues and some with open fires. Glenmore House even has a sauna!

2 houses, 1 cottage, 1-3 pub rms, 2-4 bedrms (grd flr avail), sleeps 4-8, total sleeping capacity 18, £250.00-£1000.00, Jan-Dec, bus nearby, rail 40 mls, airport 120 mls

Glen Strathfarrar, by Beauly, Inverness-shire — Map Ref: 3H9

★★ UP TO ★★★ SELF CATERING

Frank & Juliet Spencer-Nairn
Culligran Cottages, Glen Strathfarrar, Struy, by Beauly, Inverness-shire, IV4 7JX
Tel/Fax: 01463 761285

Pure magic! Come for a spell in a chalet or cottage, and this Glen will cast one over you. Choice of cottage or Norwegian chalets. Situated in National nature reserve with extensive native woodlands and wildlife. Fifteen miles of private road. Bikes for hire. Salmon and trout fishing. Guided tours of deer farm. Brochure available.

4 chalets, 1 cottage, 1-2 pub rms, 2-3 bedrms (grd flr avail), sleeps 5-7, total sleeping capacity 29, £109.00-£419.00, late Mar-mid Nov, bus 11 mls, rail 13 mls, airport 27 mls

Glen Urquhart, Inverness-shire — Map Ref: 4A9

★★★★ SELF CATERING

Mrs Doreen J Beattie
Appleton House, Errol, Perth, PH2 7QE
Tel/Fax: 01821 642412

Charming hillside cottage with log fire and sunroom, in secluded position with panoramic views over Loch Meiklie to mountains beyond. Loch Ness 6 miles. Excellent area for walking, cycling, fishing, bird-watching; riding and golf within easy reach. Plenty of space for children to play. Ideal spot for a relaxing holiday. Pets by arrangement. Nearest shopping Drumnadrochit 5 miles.

1 cottage, 2 pub rms, 4 bedrms, sleeps 7, £230.00-£450.00, Jan-Dec, airport 25 mls

---

★ SELF CATERING

Glenurquhart Lodges
Glenurqhuart, by Drumnadrochit, Loch Ness, Inverness-shire
Tel: 01456 476234 Fax: 01456 476286

Situated in country hotel grounds (barn restaurant nearby). Local attractions include Loch Ness and Caledonian Canal for watersports and Glen Affric for hillwalking and pony trekking.

5 chalets, 1 pub rm, 3 bedrms (All grd.floor), sleeps 6, total sleeping capacity 30, min let 3 days, £150.00-£400.00, Jan-Dec, bus nearby, rail 20 mls, airport 25 mls

---

★ SELF CATERING

Kenneth W Hammond
Kilmartin Chalet Park, Glenurqhuart, Inverness-shire, IV63 6TN
Tel: 01456 476371

Scandinavian chalets in peaceful birchwood setting, 5 miles from Drumnadrochit and Loch Ness. Bar and restaurant nearby. Fishing available.

5 chalets, 1 pub rm, 1-3 bedrms (grd flr avail), sleeps 2-7, total sleeping capacity 23, £100.00-£395.00, Jan-Dec, bus nearby

VAT is shown at 17.5%: changes in this rate may affect prices.   *Key to symbols is on back flap.*

GOLSPIE – GRANTOWN-ON-SPEY

THE HIGHLANDS AND SKYE

Golspie, Sutherland — Map Ref: 4B6

★ SELF CATERING

Mrs O A MacKenzie
66 Cowper Gardens, Wallington, Surrey, SH6 9RL
Tel: 0181 395 7048

1 house, 2 pub rms, 3 bedrms, sleeps 5, £150.00-£275.00, Jan-Dec, bus nearby, rail 400 yds

Semi-detached traditional cottage. Peaceful seafront location in quiet, friendly Highland seaside resort of Golspie.

★★ SELF CATERING

Mr J M L Scott
The Old School, Ann Street, Gatehouse of Fleet, Castle Douglas, Kirkcudbrightshire, DG7 2HU
Tel: 01557 814058

1 cottage, 1 pub rm, 3 bedrms, sleeps 5, £160.00-£300.00, Apr-Dec, bus 1 1/2 mls, rail 2 mls, airport 60 mls

Traditional style timber bungalow in woodland setting behind village. Superb views over sea and hills.

Grantown-on-Spey, Moray — Map Ref: 4C9

★★ SELF CATERING

Mrs G Bird
Bredhurst, The Street, Thakeham, West Sussex, RH20 3EP
Tel: 01798 813056
E-mail: gbird@wdr.co.uk
Web: freespace.virgin.net/michael.bird/grantown/grantown.htm

1 bungalow, 2 pub rms, 3 bedrms (All grd.floor), sleeps 6, £210.00-£350.00, Jan-Dec, bus nearby, rail 12 mls, airport 25 mls

Modern bungalow with sunny rear garden in quiet residential area only a few minutes walk from town centre. Many outdoor activities within easy reach. Private parking.

★★ SELF CATERING

Green (Mrs D)
3 Cobden Crescent, Edinburgh, EH9 2BG
Tel: 0131 667 6447
E-mail: sgreen5088@aol.com

1 cottage, 2 pub rms, 2 bedrms, sleeps 5, min let weekend, £100.00-£300.00, Jan-Dec, bus nearby, rail 15 mls, airport 30 mls

Comfortable cottage in excellent situation for many activities, ideal for families.

★★★ SELF CATERING

Highland Holiday Homes
Station Square, Grampian Road, Aviemore, PH22 1PD
Tel: 01479 811463 Fax: 01479 811577
E-mail: S-catering@hh-homes.co.uk
Web: www.hh-homes.co.uk

1 detached croft house, 2 pub rms, 2 bedrms, sleeps 4-5, min let 3 nights, £195.00-£395.00, Jan-Dec, bus nearby, rail 12 mls.

Original 18th century crofthouse completely re-furbished. Centrally located in a shared courtyard just off the tree lined town square. Tastefully furnished throughout, the property is only a few minutes walk from the town centre, golf course, tennis club and River Spey.

Important: Prices stated are estimates and may be subject to amendments

THE HIGHLANDS AND SKYE — GRANTOWN-ON-SPEY

Grantown-on-Spey, Moray — Map Ref: 4C9

★★ SELF CATERING

Mrs A Laing
Logie House, Forres, Moray
Tel: 01309 611278 Fax: 01309 611300
E-mail: panny@logie.co.uk

Shooting and fishing lodge and a bothy on the shores of Lochindorb. Enjoy the peace, beauty and birdlife by the shore. Close to the Moray coast.

1 house, 1 cottage, 1-3 pub rms, 2-9 bedrms (grd flr avail), sleeps 4-16, total sleeping capacity 20, min let 3 nights, £180.00-£1500.00, Mar-Dec, bus 3 mls, rail 20 mls, airport 28 mls

★★★ SELF CATERING

Mrs E A Smith
Auchernack Farm, Grantown-on-Spey, Moray, PH26 3NH
Tel/Fax: 01479 872093

Recently built spacious bungalow, on outskirts of Grantown, set amid quiet countryside with birch and pine trees. Excellent Views. Wing of farmhouse overlooking River Spey also available. Near to Loch Garten RSPB reserve. Ideal holiday for birdwatchers, fishermen and families.

1 house, 2 pub rms, 3 bedrms, sleeps 6, from £250.00, Mar-Oct, bus 500 yds, rail 15 mls, airport 35 mls

★★ SELF CATERING

Mrs M Steedman
Muir of Blebo, Blebocraigs, by Cupar, Fife, KY15 5TZ
Tel/Fax: 01334 850781

A former shepherd's cottage in remote location, with superb views to Cairngorms. Own garden area and access by farm track.

1 cottage, 2 pub rms, 2 bedrms, sleeps 4, £225.00-£240.00, May-Sep, bus 5 mls, rail 12 mls

★★★ SELF CATERING

Mrs Bridget Thomson
33 Medina Road, Grays, Essex, RM17 6AQ
Tel/Fax: 01375 370274

Modern bungalow in quiet residential area with off road parking. Enclosed rear garden area. Ideal base for touring, walking, fishing and golfing.

1 bungalow, 1 pub rm, sleeps 6, from £250.00, Jan-Dec, bus ¼ ml, rail 13 mls, airport 29 mls

★★★★ SELF CATERING

Caroline Wright
Begbie Farmhouse, Begbie, nr Haddington, East Lothian, EH41 4HQ
Tel: 01620 829488
E-mail: cwright@eyco.co.uk

Charming cottage tastefully refurbished with a modern farmhouse kitchen and log fire. Attractive surroundings and panoramic views of the Spey Valley.

1 cottage, 2 pub rms, 4 bedrms (grd flr avail), sleeps 8, £295.00-£595.00, Jan-Dec, bus 4 mls, rail 25 mls, airport 45 mls

---

VAT is shown at 17.5%: changes in this rate may affect prices.

Key to symbols is on back flap.

THE HIGHLANDS AND SKYE

BY GRANTOWN-ON-SPEY – INSH

by Grantown-on-Spey, Moray

Map Ref: 4C9

★★ SELF CATERING

Mrs P M Laing
Craggan, Grantown-on-Spey, Moray, PH26 3NT
Tel: 01479 872120 Fax: 01479 872325

1 house, 2 pub rms, 4 bedrms (grd flr avail), sleeps 7, £280.00-£500.00, Feb-Dec, bus 1 ml, rail 12 mls, airport 30 mls

A substantial, spacious, traditional farmhouse with magnificent views over Grantown to the Cairngorms and Cromdale Hills. Ideal touring base.

by Helmsdale, Sutherland

Map Ref: 4C5

★★ SELF CATERING

Sally MacKinnon
Deible, Suisgill Estate, Sutherland, KW8 6HY
Tel: 01431 831246

1 cottage, 2 pub rms, 2 bedrms (grd.flr avail), sleeps 4, £180.00-£280.00, Jan-Dec, rail 5 mls

Quietly situated former shepherds cottage, with views to the hills and the Helmsdale River. Accessible along an 'A' class road. Ideal base for birdwatching, fishing and gold panning!

Inchnadamph, Sutherland

Map Ref: 3H5

★★★ SELF CATERING

Mrs E A Miles
8 Longfield Drive, West Parley, Ferndown, Dorset, BH22 8TY
Tel: 01202 571739

1 cottage, 1 pub rm, 3 bedrms (grd flr avail), sleeps 6, £250.00-£330.00, Apr-Oct, bus 1 ml, rail 40 mls, ferry 23 mls, airport 80 mls

Modernised shepherd's cottage in remote location, near Loch Assynt. Access via unsurfaced road, rough in places.

Insh, Inverness-shire

Map Ref: 4C10

★★★ SELF CATERING

Mrs Ann Mackintosh
Annandale, Gordonhall, Kingussie, Inverness-shire, PH21 1NR
Tel: 01540 661560

1 chalet, 1 pub rm, 2 bedrms, sleeps 4-6, £140.00-£220.00, Jan-Dec, bus 2 mls, rail 5 mls, airport 45 mls

Chalet in peaceful location beside the Insh Marshes Reserve. 8 miles (13kms) from Aviemore.

★★ SELF CATERING

Mrs K Toynbee
Birch Cabin, Insh, by Kingussie, Inverness-shire, PH21 1NU
Tel/Fax: 01540 661829

1 timber clad cabin, 1 pub rm, 2 bedrms (All grd.floor), sleeps 4, £180.00-£260.00, Jan-Dec, bus 3 mls, rail 5 mls, airport 40 mls

Timber cabin set in natural birch setting. Quiet location in excellent walking, wildlife, ski-ing area. Close to Loch Insh.

Important: Prices stated are estimates and may be subject to amendments

THE HIGHLANDS AND SKYE

INVER, BY TAIN – INVERINATE, BY KYLE OF LOCHALSH

Inver, by Tain, Ross-shire

Map Ref: 4C7

★★★★ SELF CATERING

Graeme Moyes
16 Cowden Way, Eaglesfield, Comrie, Perthshire, PH6 2NW
Tel/Fax: 01764 679811
E-mail: graememoyes@compuserve.com

1 house, 1 pub rm, 3 bedrms (grd flr avail), sleeps 6, £170.00-£285.00, Jan-Dec, bus ½ ml, rail 5 mls, airport 50 mls

Very well equipped comfortable holiday home. Within easy walking distance of beaches. Ideal centre for golf and touring.

Invergarry, Inverness-shire

Map Ref: 3H11

★★★ SELF CATERING

Mrs P Fraser
Allt-na-Sithean, South Laggan, by Spean Bridge,
Inverness-shire, PH34 4EA
Tel: 01809 501311

1 chalet, 1 pub rm, 2 bedrms (All grd.floor), sleeps 4, £180.00-£360.00, Jan-Dec, bus 300 yds, rail 9 mls, airport 45 mls

Modern bungalow in a peaceful setting in the Great Glen between Loch Lochy and Loch Oich. The cottage is situated on a 16 acre croft and looking on to the Glen Garry hills, 300 yrds from the A82. There are a host of activities in the area, water sports, hill-walking, climbing, forest walks, golf, fishing and skiing. Local hotels provide good meals and there are restaurants nearby.

★★ SELF CATERING

A & D Grant
Faichemard Farm, Invergarry, Inverness-shire, PH35 4HG
Tel: 01809 501314

4 chalets, 3 bedrms (All grd.floor), sleeps 4-6, total sleeping capacity 24, £125.00-£270.00, Apr-Oct, bus 2 mls, rail 25 mls, airport 45 mls

Four chalets situated out of sight of each other all with wonderful views. In a peaceful quiet corner of a working hill farm, ideally situated for walking, bird watching and fishing. A good central base for touring the Western Highlands. Brochure available.

---

by Invergarry, Inverness-shire

Map Ref: 3H11

★★ SELF CATERING

Mrs Waugh
North Laggan Farmhouse, by Invergarry, Inverness-shire, PH34 4EB
Tel: 01809 501335
E-mail: bw001@post.almac.co.uk

1 self contained wing of farmhouse, 1 pub rm, 2 bedrms (All grd.floor), sleeps 6, £125.00-£325.00, Jan-Dec, bus 1 ml, rail 12 mls

In peaceful countryside overlooking the Caledonian Canal and Loch Oich. Ideal for hill walking. One hour's drive to Skye. Good base for touring.

Inverinate, by Kyle of Lochalsh, Ross-shire

Map Ref: 3G10

★★★ SELF CATERING

Mrs Christine Dodds
Fernfield, Nostie, by Kyle, Ross-shire
Tel: 01599 555368

1 house, 3 pub rms, 3 bedrms (1 grd flr avail), sleeps 5, £190.00-£390.00, Jan-Dec, bus nearby

Fully modernised traditional stone built cottage with scenic views of the Five Sisters of Kintail and Loch Duich.

VAT is shown at 17.5%: changes in this rate may affect prices.

Key to symbols is on back flap.

INVERINATE, BY KYLE OF LOCHALSH – INVERNESS

THE HIGHLANDS AND SKYE

Inverinate, by Kyle of Lochalsh, Ross-shire — Map Ref: 3G10

★★★★ SELF CATERING

Mrs H MacLean
Mullardoch, Inverinate, Glenshiel, by Kyle of Lochalsh,
Ross-shire, IV40 8HB
Tel/Fax: 01599 511227

1 cottage, 1 pub rm, 2 bedrms (All grd.floor), sleeps 4, £250.00-£450.00, Jan-Dec, bus nearby, rail 12 mls, ferry 12 mls, airport 65 mls

Modern bungalows situated on the shores of Loch Duich. Ideal for boating, touring; Kyle of Lochalsh 10 miles (16kms). Very well equipped to a high standard. Breathtaking views over Loch and Kintail Mountains. Private slipway.

★★★ SELF CATERING — BRONZE

Revd Roger Whitehead
116 High Street, Harrold, Bedford, MK43 7BJ
Tel/Fax: 01234 721127
E-mail: cottage@harrold.demon.co.uk

1 cottage, 2 pub rms, 4 bedrms (grd flr avail), sleeps 6, £130.00-£330.00, Jan-Dec, bus 1 ml, rail 14 mls

Traditional stone built croft cottage, tastefully modernised and well equipped. On shore of Loch Duich beneath Five Sisters of Kintail.

Invermoriston, Inverness-shire — Map Ref: 4A10

★ UP TO ★★ SELF CATERING

Glenmoriston Estates Limited
Glenmoriston, by Inverness, Inverness-shire, IV3 6YA
Tel: 01320 351202 Fax: 01320 351209

3 chalets, 1 cottage, 1-2 pub rms, 1-3 bedrms, sleeps 4-6, total sleeping capacity 20, £110.00-£320.00, Jan-Dec, bus ½ ml, rail 27 mls, airport 32 mls

Chalets and lodges on Highland estate 3 miles (5kms) from Invermoriston on Skye road. Trout fishing available on River Moriston.

★★ UP TO ★★★ SELF CATERING

Mr & Mrs E Levings
Invermoriston Holiday Chalets, Invermoriston,
Inverness-shire, IV63 7YF
Tel: 01320 351254 Fax: 01320 351343
E-mail: ihc@ipw.com   Web: www.ipw.com/ihc

15 chalets, 1 cottage, 1 pub rm, 2-3 bedrms (grd flr avail), sleeps 4-6, total sleeping capacity 66, £120.00-£425.00, Mar-Oct, bus nearby, rail 27 mls, airport 36 mls

Selection of chalet units on 23.5 acre site, some by the riverside (popular with fisher's), others in woodland, each with own BBQ and patio. Also, a traditional cottage recently refurbished and equipped. 27 miles (43kms) south west of Inverness.

Inverness — Map Ref: 4B8

★★ SELF CATERING

G Blackhurst
Highgrove, Easter Muckovie, by Inverness, IV1 2BN
Tel: 01463 792551

1 house, 1 pub rm, 4 bedrms, sleeps 8, £500.00, Mar-Oct, bus nearby, rail 1½ mls, airport 8 mls

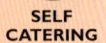

Modern house with all amenities and open views to golf course. Spacious accommodation, a quiet location, yet not too far from the town centre.

Important: Prices stated are estimates and may be subject to amendments

THE HIGHLANDS AND SKYE

INVERNESS

Inverness — Map Ref: 4B8

★★ **SELF CATERING**

Mrs K Burton
Hythe Quay, Dunain, Inverness, IV3 6JN
Tel: 01463 233230/0836 571315 Fax: 01463 233230

6 flats, 1-3 pub rms, 1-3 bedrms (grd flr avail), sleeps 2-8, total sleeping capacity 25, min let 3 nights, £210.00-£360.00, Jan-Dec, bus 500 yds, rail 500 yds, airport 11 mls

Comfortable flats/maisonettes beside River Ness. Town centre and all amenities within walking distance. Parking available. Linen, laundry, payphones.

★★★ **SELF CATERING**

Mrs A Cole-Hamilton
54 Culcabock Avenue, Inverness, IV2 3RQ
Tel: 01463 237085 Fax: 01463 718131

1 house, 1 pub rm, 1 bedrm, sleeps 2-3, £170.00-£230.00, Easter-Oct, bus 200 yds, rail 1 ml, airport 6 ml

Charming, warm and welcoming cottage in rural location beside golf course, only 5 minutes to town centre. Suntrap patio garden. Wheelchair access. Pets welcome.

★★★★ **SELF CATERING**

Mrs A Duncan
3 Connel Court, Ardconnel Street, Inverness
Tel: 01463 237086/(mobile) 07721 937942

1 flat, 1 pub rm, 2 bedrms, sleeps 4, £200.00-£365.00, Jan-Dec, bus nearby, rail nearby, airport 5 mls

Modern apartment (1989) with video entryphone. In residential area, central for all amenities. Panoramic views over city and Firth.

★★★★ **SELF CATERING**

Mrs S Ireland
Westview House, Upper Myrtlefield, Nairnside, Inverness, IV2 5BX
Tel/Fax: 01463 794228
E-mail: irelanda@clara.co.uk

1 apartment, 1 pub rm, 1 family bedroom, (grd.flr), sleeps 4, £200.00-£260.00, Jan-Dec, bus 1/2 ml, rail 3 1/2 mls, airport 5 mls

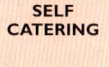

Modern, self-contained and extremely well appointed holiday apartment located on the north wing of Westview House. Tastefully decorated and quality assured accommodation. Featuring elevated panoramic views over Inverness, The Moray Firth and mountain ranges beyond. We are situated in an outstanding location to enjoy the Scottish countryside and wildlife. Near the Culloden Battlefield and close to all the facilities of Inverness.

★★★ **SELF CATERING**

Mrs Heather Lyon
Camalaig, Dunvegan, Isle of Skye, Inverness-shire, IV55 8WA
Tel/Fax: 01470 521355

1 bungalow, 1 pub rm, 2 bedrms (All grd.floor), sleeps 4, £260.00-£320.00, Jan-Dec, bus nearby, rail 2 mls, airport 10 mls

A modern bungalow on the edge of Inverness, with panoramic views over the town towards Culloden Moor and the Moray Firth. Excellent facilities within easy reach e.g. golf, dolphin watching, walking, gardens and of course Loch Ness.

VAT is shown at 17.5%: changes in this rate may affect prices.

Key to symbols is on back flap.

INVERNESS — THE HIGHLANDS AND SKYE

Inverness — Map Ref: 4B8

★★ SELF CATERING

Mrs A MacKenzie
6A Green Drive, Inverness, IV2 4EX
Tel: 01463 236763
E-mail: tom.ann@virgin.net

1 bungalow, 1 pub rm, 3 bedrms (All grd.floor), sleeps 5, £110.00-£300.00. Jan-Dec, bus nearby, rail 2 mls, airport 9 mls

Semi-detached bungalow with own garden, in quiet residential area on outskirts of Inverness. Off road parking. Centrally located for touring the Highlands.

★★★ SELF CATERING

Mrs H Ponty
Copperfield, Culloden Road, Westhill, Inverness, IV1 2BJ
Tel: 01463 792780/0411 237676 Fax: 01463 792780
E-mail: nickp@cali.co.uk
Web: www.host.co.uk

1 cottage 2 bedrooms, sleeps 4, 1 house 5 bedrooms, sleeps 9 £175.00-£550.00. Jan-Dec, bus ¼ ml, rail ¼ ml, airport 7 mls.

Converted wing of old cottage. Close to riverside and town centre. Enclosed garden and off-street parking, yet an excellent base for visitors without personal transport.

★★★★ SELF CATERING

The Revd. and Mrs A M Roff
Rowan Glen, Culbokie, Dingwall, IV7 8JY
Tel: 01349 877762
E-mail: 106770.3175@compuserve.com

2 flats, 1-2 pub rms, 2 bedrms, sleeps 4, total sleeping capacity 8, from £210.00, Jan-Dec, bus nearby, rail nearby, airport 1 ml

Two well appointed flats in a small modern purpose built block in a quiet corner of the centre of Inverness, looking to the Castle. Station, shops, restaurants, riverside walks immediately to hand. Off street private parking. Linen included. Both with two bedrooms, telephone, TV, freezer, washer drier, bath and shower. One has balcony, one has microwave, hi-fi, dishwasher, penthouse lounge.

★★★★ SELF CATERING

Mrs Evelyn Stockall
Ardvreck, Morefield, Ullapool, IV26 2TH
Tel: 01854 612028
E-mail: Ardvreck.Guesthouse@btinternet.com

1 apartment, 1 pub rm, 2 bedrms, sleeps 4, min let 3 nights, from £250.00, Jan-Dec, bus nearby, rail 2 mls, airport 8 mls.

Newly built first floor apartment situated on the outskirts of Inverness on the road to Loch Ness. Surrounded by mature woodland this property offers a very comfortable base for exploring the Highlands. The quiet and secluded location offers a great place to unwind.

Important: Prices stated are estimates and may be subject to amendments

THE HIGHLANDS AND SKYE

KENTALLEN, BY APPIN – KILCHOAN

Kentallen, by Appin, Argyll   Map Ref: 1F1

Loch Linnhe Chalets

Kentallen by Appin, Argyll PA38 4BY   Tel/Fax: 01890 781255

Our two-bedroomed chalets have been furnished and equipped with your every comfort in mind. Uniquely situated at the water's edge they enjoy magnificent views of sea and mountains. Visit us to go fishing, sailing, walking or golfing or simply come to relax and enjoy possibly the best views in Scotland.

★★ SELF CATERING

Loch Linnhe Chalets
Moorpark, Foulden, Berwick upon Tweed, TD15 1UH
Tel/Fax: 01890 781255

8 chalets, 1 pub rm, 2 bedrms, sleeps 4, total sleeping capacity 32, £200.00-£400.00, Jan-Dec, bus nearby, rail 15 mls

On private site, situated at waters edge with spectacular views over Loch Linnhe and to the mountains beyond.

★ SELF CATERING

Mrs A R Murray
39 Hesketh Road, Southport, Lancs, PR9 9PB
Tel: 01704 542360 Fax: 01704 897798

1 cottage, 2 pub rms, 3 bedrms (All grd.floor), sleeps 6-9, £300.00-£500.00, Jan-Dec

Detached cottage in secluded setting yet close to the A828. Convenient base for touring and walking.

Kilchoan, Ardnamurchan, Argyll   Map Ref: 1C1

★★ UP TO ★★★ SELF CATERING

Mrs Sue Cameron
3 Pier Road, Kilchoan, Argyll, PH36 4LJ
Tel/Fax: 01972 510321

1 house, 1 cottage, 1 bungalow, 1-3 pub rms, 2-3 bedrms (grd flr avail), sleeps 4-6, total sleeping capacity 14, min let weekend, £170.00-£570.00, Jan-Dec, bus 4 mls, rail 53 mls, ferry 9 mls, airport 130 mls

Bungalow and renovated cottages enjoying a remote setting with dramatic views of Eigg and the small Isles. Farm nearby, roughish track for 150 metres.

VAT is shown at 17.5%: changes in this rate may affect prices.   *Key to symbols is on back flap.*

KILLUNDINE – KINCRAIG, BY KINGUSSIE

THE HIGHLANDS AND SKYE

Killundine, Argyll — Map Ref: 1D1

★ UP TO ★★
SELF CATERING

Mr W Lauder
Atherton House, Atherton Lane, Totnes, Devon, TQ9 5RT
Tel: 01803 863059

3 cottages, 1 pub rm, 2-3 bedrms (grd flr avail), sleeps 4-6, total sleeping capacity 14, £92.00-£240.00, Jan-Dec, bus 40 mls, rail 50 mls, ferry 7 mls

Lodge and farm cottages in isolated setting with superb views over Sound of Mull and to Mull. Ideal for touring Mull and for walking and birdwatching.

Kincraig, by Kingussie, Inverness-shire — Map Ref: 4C10

Alvie Holiday Cottages
Alvie Estate Office, Kincraig, Inverness-shire PH21 1NE
Telephone: 01540 651255/651249   Fax: 01540 651380

Secluded and beautiful Highland Estate with breath-taking views over the Spey Valley to the Cairngorm Mountains beyond. Choose from our extremely comfortable traditional farm cottages or flats in the Estate's Edwardian shooting lodge. Activities include river and loch fishing, woodland walks and many other family activities in the surrounding area.

★★★ UP TO ★★★★
SELF CATERING

Alvie Holiday Cottages
Alvie Estate Office, Kincraig, by Kingussie,
Inverness-shire, PH21 1NE
Tel: 01540 651255/651249 Fax: 01540 651380

2 flats, 4 cottages, 2-3 pub rms, 2-5 bedrms, sleeps 4-10, total sleeping capacity 40, £160.00-£510.00, Jan-Dec, bus 4 1/2 mls, rail 4 1/2 mls, airport 40 mls

Traditional farm cottages and cedar-clad bungalow individually sited on working and sporting estate, 4 miles (6kms) south of Aviemore.

Important: Prices stated are estimates and may be subject to amendments

THE HIGHLANDS AND SKYE

KINCRAIG, BY KINGUSSIE

Kincraig, by Kingussie, Inverness-shire Map Ref: 4C10

SELF CATERING — UP TO ★★★

Lagganlia Outdoor Centre
Kincraig, Kingussie, PH21 1NG
Tel: 01540 651265 Fax: 01540 651240
E-mail: lagganlia@lagganlia.com

Self catering chalet and lodge accommodation set apart from main outdoor centre, situated in remote Glen Feshie. Nestling in the edge of the Cairngorm Mountains yet easily accessible from main routes.

9 chalets, total sleeping capacity 75, £192.53-£1120.00, Jan-Dec, bus 3 mls, rail 9 mls, airport 45 mls

---

SELF CATERING — ★★

Loch Insh Log Chalets
Insh Hall, Kincraig, by Kingussie, Inverness-shire, PH21 1NU
Tel: 01540 651272 Fax: 01540 651208
E-mail: user@lochinsh.dial.netmedia.co.uk
Web: www.lochinsh.com

Pine log chalets with fine views of Loch Insh and mountains. Access to sauna, multigym, laundry. Free watersports hire (set times) for guests in summer. Free use of ski slope (set times) in winter. 150m to lochside restaurant and beach. Mountain bikes, fishing, archery, interpretation trail, children's adventure area. Dec - April downhill skiing hire/instruction.

4 log cabins, 1 pub rm, 2-3 bedrms (grd flr avail), sleeps 4-7, total sleeping capacity 25, min let 2 nights, £294.00-£850.00, Jan-Dec, bus 1 ml, rail 6 mls, airport 35 mls

SELF CATERING — ★★★

Mrs C MacGregor
The Dairy House, Corton Denham, Sherborne, Dorset, DT9 4LX
Tel: 01963 220250 Fax: 01963 220613

A Scots Pine log house, situated in a quiet, secluded position, amongst birch trees on the approach to Glen Feshie.

1 bungalow, 1 pub rm, 4 bedrms (All grd.floor), sleeps 8, £310.00-£485.00, Mar-Dec, bus 2 mls, rail 8 mls, airport 45 mls

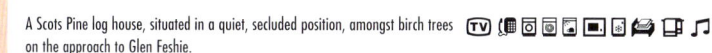

SELF CATERING — ★★★★

Roy Smart
6 Ancrum Bank, Dalkeith, EH22 3AY
Tel: 0131 654 2291

Recently built bungalow in woodland setting on edge of quiet village. Approximately 6 miles (12kms) from Aviemore.

1 house, 2 pub rms, 3 bedrms (All grd.floor), sleeps 6, £275.00-£375.00, May-Oct, bus 1/2 ml, rail 6 mls

SELF CATERING — ★★★

Nick and Patsy Thompson
Fraser & Telford Cottages, Insh House, Kincraig, by Kingussie, Inverness-shire, PH21 1NU
Tel: 01540 651377
E-mail: inshhouse@btinternet.com

Attractive timber lodges combining the traditional appearance of a Highland cottage within spacious grounds of Insh House, in good walking country. Skiing, watersports, riding, gliding and birdwatching nearby. In quiet rural area. Equidistant between Aviemore and Kingussie. Glenfeshie nearby.

2 cottages, 1 pub rm, 2 bedrms (grd flr avail), each sleeps 4, sleeping capacity 8, min let 3 days, £150.00-£300.00, Jan-Dec, bus 2 mls, rail 7 mls, airport 40 mls

---

VAT is shown at 17.5%: changes in this rate may affect prices.

Key to symbols is on back flap.

KINGUSSIE – KINLOCHEWE

THE HIGHLANDS AND SKYE

Kingussie, Inverness-shire — Map Ref: 4B11

★★★ SELF CATERING

Mrs Joyce Robertson
Rubislaw, Kingussie, Inverness-shire, PH21 1HD
Tel: 01540 661636 Fax: 01540 661013
E-mail: jkt@globalnet.co.uk

1 bungalow, 1 pub rm, 3 bedrms (All grd.floor), sleeps 6, £150.00-£395.00, Jan-Dec, bus 3 mls, rail 3 mls, airport 44 mls

Detached modern bungalows with garden area. Views across open field to Feshie Hills. 3 miles (5kms) from Kingussie. Close to RSPB Nature Reserve.

★★ SELF CATERING

Mary E Wheildon
The Old Oven, Kineton, Warwickshire, CV35 0JS
Tel/Fax: 01926 640560

1 house, 3 pub rms, 3 bedrms, sleeps 5, Jan-Dec, bus nearby, rail ½ ml, airport 40 mls

19C granite cottage in centre of Kingussie. Quiet location, close to railway station. 11 miles (17kms) from Aviemore. Ideal for all ages and sports.

Kinlocheil, by Fort William, Inverness-shire — Map Ref: 3G12

★★★ UP TO ★★★★ SELF CATERING

A G MacLeod
Altdarroch Farm, Kinlocheil, by Fort William, Inverness-shire, PH4 4PA
Tel: 01687 462346 Fax: 01687 462212
E-mail: morar-hotel@road-to-the-isles.org.uk
Web: www.road-to-the-isles.org.uk

2 houses, 1-2 pub rms, 2-3 bedrms, sleeps 4-7, total sleeping capacity 11, £275.00-£500.00, Jan-Dec, bus nearby, rail 1 ml, ferry 40 mls, airport 100 mls

A timber lodge and a semi-detached cottage, set above Loch Eil, with panoramic views.

Kinlochewe, Ross-shire — Map Ref: 3G8

★★★★ SELF CATERING

Mrs S MacLean
Duart, Kinlochewe, by Achnasheen, Ross-shire, IV22 2PA
Tel/Fax: 01445 760230
E-mail: emac@0breathemail.net

2 cottages, 1 pub rm, 2 bedrms (All grd.floor), sleeps 4, total sleeping capacity 8, £140.00-£300.00, Jan-Dec, bus nearby, rail 10 mls, ferry 50 mls, airport 60 mls

Two comfortable, well equipped semi-detached cottages with scenic views towards Torridon hills. Ideal base for hill walking and climbing.

★★★★ SELF CATERING

Mr M Madden
23 Kenmore Road, Birkenhead, Merseyside, L43 3AS
Tel: 0151 608 2663

1 bungalow, 2 pub rms, 2 bedrms (All grd.floor), sleeps 4, £130.00-£290.00, Jan-Dec, bus nearby, rail 10 mls, airport 55 mls

Modern bungalow at the heart of this small Highland village. Peaceful situation with nearby nature reserve, Torridon Mountain Range in sight, and Loch Maree with trout fishing nearby.

Important: Prices stated are estimates and may be subject to amendments

THE HIGHLANDS AND SKYE

KINLOCHLEVEN – KYLE OF LOCHALSH

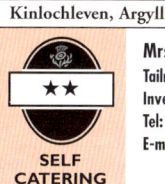

Kinlochleven, Argyll

Map Ref: 3H12

★★ SELF CATERING

Mrs Janet May
Tailrace Inn, Riverside Road, Kinlochleven,
Inverness-shire, PA40 4QH
Tel: 01855 831777 Fax: 01855 831291
E-mail: tailrace@btinternet.com

1 house, 1 pub rm, 1 bedrm, sleeps 2, £175.00, Jan-Dec, bus ¼ ml, rail 20 mls

---

Kishorn, Ross-shire

Map Ref: 3F9

★★★ SELF CATERING

Florence MacKenzie
Beinn Fhada, Lochcarron, Ross-shire, IV54 4YG
Tel: 01520 722549

Detached cottage on the shore of Loch Kishorn. Wonderful views over to Skye. Beautiful, peaceful location.

1 cottage, 1 pub rm, 2 bedrms, sleeps 4, £160.00-£300.00, Jan-Dec, bus ¼ ml, rail 8 mls, airport 70 mls.

★★★ SELF CATERING

Mrs A J Stewart
13 Kirkton Gardens, Lochcarron, Ross-shire, IV54 8UQ
Tel: 01520 722239
E-mail: ajskishorn@tesco.net

Comfortable accommodation for families up to 9 with cot. Safe seaside beach and play areas. Quiet walking trails or rugged mountain hikes. Magnificent views, friendly village location, central for day trips to Isle of Skye and north coast Scotland.

1 house, 2 pub rms, 4 bedrms (grd flr avail), sleeps 8, £160.00-£355.00, Jan-Dec, bus 2 mls, rail 9 mls, airport 70 mls

---

Knoydart, Inverness-shire

Map Ref: 3F11

★★★ SELF CATERING

Mrs V Hayward
Blynfield Farm, Stour Row, Shaftesbury, Dorset, SP7 0QW
Tel: 01747 852289 Fax: 01747 851057
E-mail: mail@virginia-hayward.co.uk

1 house, 3 pub rms, 5 bedrms, sleeps 11, min let Weekend (Out of Season), £625.00-£785.00, Jan-Dec

---

Kyle of Lochalsh, Ross-shire

Map Ref: 3F9

★★★ SELF CATERING

M J Gardiner
Kyle Pharmacy, Station Road, Kyle of Lochalsh,
Ross-shire, IV40 8AG
Tel/Fax: 01599 534206

Very comfortable first floor apartment in centre of village, close to all amenities and Skye Bridge. Ideal for larger groups.

1 flat, 1 pub rm, 3 bedrms, sleeps 8, min let weekend, £90.00-£375.00, Jan-Dec, bus nearby, rail nearby, ferry nearby, airport 85 mls

---

VAT is shown at 17.5%: changes in this rate may affect prices. *Key to symbols is on back flap.*

KYLE OF LOCHALSH – LAIDE

THE HIGHLANDS AND SKYE

Kyle of Lochalsh, Ross-shire
Map Ref: 3F9

★ SELF CATERING

M R Wright
16 Duntrune Terrace, West Ferry, Dundee, Angus, DD5 1LF
Tel: 01382 477462

1 bungalow, 1 pub rm, 3 bedrms (grd flr avail), sleeps 6, £280.00-£350.00, Apr-Oct, bus 500 yds, rail 500 yds

Bungalow situated in large, secluded garden, overlooking Kyle of Lochalsh. Near Kyle shops, swimming pool, play-park and station. Ideal centre for touring NW mainland and Skye. Photograph available on application.

Kylesku, Sutherland
Map Ref: 3H4

★★★ SELF CATERING

Unapool House Cottages
Unapool House, Kylesku, Sutherland, IV27 4HW
Tel/Fax: 01971 502344
E-mail: barry@unapoolhouse.demon.co.uk

3 cottages, 1 pub rm, 1-2 bedrms (grd flr avail), sleeps 2-5, total sleeping capacity 10, £160.00-£330.00, Jan-Dec, bus nearby, rail 40 mls, airport 90 mls

Purpose-built, comfortable cottages in magnificent setting on sea loch. Ideal for Assynt wilderness, walking, climbing, bird watching and fishing.

Laggan, by Newtonmore, Inverness-shire
Map Ref: 4B11

★ SELF CATERING — BRONZE

Mrs E A Wilson
Blaragie, Inverness-shire, PH20 1AJ
Tel: 01528 544229

1 cottage, 1 pub rm, 3 bedrms (All grd.floor), sleeps 5, £130.00-£350.00, Jan-Dec, rail 9 mls, airport 55 mls

Well equipped new bungalow with breathtaking views to Lochaber hills, beyond River Spey. Ideal for bird-watchers.

Laggan Bridge, by Newtonmore, Inverness-shire
Map Ref: 4B11

★ SELF CATERING

S M B Fleming
Saxon House, Molly Hurst Lane, Woolley, Wakefield,
West Yorkshire, WF4 2JY
Tel/Fax: 01226 383258

1 cottage, 2 pub rms, 4 bedrms, sleeps 6, £185.00-£300.00, Jan-Dec, rail 11 mls

Cosy detached cottage furnished in traditional style. Ideally situated for summer and winter pursuits.

Laide, Ross-shire
Map Ref: 3F6

★★ SELF CATERING

Arran Properties Ltd
P O Box 624, St Helier, Jersey, Channel Islands, JE4 5YJ
Tel: 01534 27264

5 chalets, 1 cottage, 1-2 pub rms, 3 bedrms, sleeps 2-6, total sleeping capacity 36, £180.00-£380.00, Mar-Oct, bus 3 mls, rail 40 mls, airport 75 mls

Hillside crofters cottage and 5 chalets overlooking sandy beach, with spectacular views towards the Summer Isles and mountains of Sutherland.

Important: Prices stated are estimates and may be subject to amendments

THE HIGHLANDS AND SKYE

LAIDE – LAIRG

Laide, Ross-shire   Map Ref: 3F6

N G A Gardner
★ SELF CATERING

5 Obinan, Laide, Achnasheen, Ross-shire, IV22 2NU
Tel: 01445 731307

Comfortable traditional stone croft cottage at head of peninsula between Loch Ewe and Gruinard Bay. Wonderful views of mountains & moorland, sea & islands. Quiet setting in secluded woodland garden. Short distance to beech & rocky coastline. Wildlife in abundance, scenic & peaceful.

1 cottage, 2 pub rms, 3 bedrms (grd flr avail), sleeps 6-8, £100.00-£375.00, Jan-Dec, bus 4 mls, rail 40 mls

---

Mr & Mrs A Gilchrist
★★ UP TO ★★★ SELF CATERING

Grassvalley Cottage, 12 Woodhall Road, Colinton, Edinburgh, EH13 ODX
Tel: 0131 441 6053 Fax: 0131 441 4849
E-mail: aandagilchrist@cwcom.net

Two detached houses in their own grounds. One a traditional croft house, fully equipped to today's standards and extended, in an elevated position with a superb outlook northwards over Gruinard Bay to the Summer Isles and beyond. The other a log constructed house built in 1992 in a uniquely beautiful situation above the shore line to Gruinard Bay with direct access to the sandy beaches and with canoes provided for tenants.

1 cottage, 1 pub rm, 3 bedrms (grd flr avail), sleeps 6, min let weekend, £220.00-£360.00, Jan-Dec, bus nearby, rail nearby, airport nearby

Mrs Catherine Macdonald
★★★★ SELF CATERING

Old Smiddy Self Catering, Laide, Ross-shire, IV22 2NB
Tel/Fax: 01445 731425
E-mail: oldsmiddy@aol.com
Web: www.scotland-info.co.uk/oldsmiddy

Superior, comfortable, spacious, well equipped cottages. Peaceful private location beside forest. Glorious views to sea and hills. Fishing arranged.

2 cottages, 1 pub rm, 2-3 bedrms (grd flr avail), sleeps 4-6, total sleeping capacity 10, £200.00-£500.00, Jan-Dec, bus 300 yds, rail 40 mls, ferry 45 mls, airport 84 mls

Mrs A MacIver
★★★★ SELF CATERING

The Sheiling, Achgarve, Laide, Ross-shire, IV22 2NS
Tel: 01445 731487

Self-contained cottage adjoining owner's house. Excellently placed for visiting Inverewe Gardens, Lochinver, Ullapool and many other beautiful areas. Watch the seals, otters and a myriad of birds closeby.

1 cottage, 1 pub rm, 1 bedrm (All grd.floor), sleeps 2, £120.00-£260.00, Jan-Dec

Lairg, Sutherland   Map Ref: 4A6

Mrs J G Johnston, Milnclarin Holiday Homes
★★★★ SELF CATERING

Woodside, Station Road, Golspie, Sutherland, KW10 6SR
Tel: 01408 634300
E-mail: Milnclarin@rsvp.demon.co.uk
Web: www.rsvp.demon.co.uk/milnclarin

Recently built, spacious and comfortable bungalows set in 3 acres of their own land. Situated on the edge of the highland village of Lairg, which lies on the shores of Loch Shin. Excellent base for trips to the rugged west coast, the far north, or to East Sutherland. Prices on application; off season short breaks available; sorry, no pets.

2 cottages, 1 pub rm, 2 bedrms (All grd.floor), sleeps 4, total sleeping capacity 8, Mar-Oct, bus 300 yds, rail 2 mls

VAT is shown at 17.5%: changes in this rate may affect prices.   *Key to symbols is on back flap.*

LAIRG – LOCHCARRON

THE HIGHLANDS AND SKYE

Lairg, Sutherland — Map Ref: 4A6

Mrs J Reid
Upper Grange Farm, Peterhead, Aberdeenshire, AB42 1HX
Tel: 01779 473116

★★★ SELF CATERING

Detached villa with own gardens and sun lounge. Walking distance of shops and small town. Ideal touring base.

1 house, 1 pub rm, 4 bedrms (grd flr avail), sleeps 6, £160.00-£320.00, Apr-Oct, bus nearby, rail 1 ml, airport 60 mls

---

Lochailort, Inverness-shire — Map Ref: 3F12

Mr & Mrs A Blackburn
Roshven Farm, Lochailort, Inverness-shire, PH38 4NB
Tel/Fax: 01687 470221
E-mail: alan@roshvenfarm.demon.co.uk

★★ SELF CATERING

Five chalets overlooking sound of Arisaig, individually sited on working sheep farm. A few minutes walk from small private sandy beach. 4.5 miles (8 km) from Lochailort.

5 chalets, 1 pub rm, 2 bedrms (All grd.floor), sleeps 4-6, total sleeping capacity 30, min let weekend, £200.00-£375.00, Jan-Dec, bus ¼ ml, rail 4 mls, ferry 20 mls, airport 160 mls

Lochcarron, Ross-shire — Map Ref: 3G9

ATTADALE HOLIDAY COTTAGES
STRATHCARRON, ROSS-SHIRE IV54 8YX
Tel/Fax: 01520 722862   e.mail: attadale@zetnet.co.uk

On the estate seen in "Hamish MacBeth" a house for 8 and three cottages for 4-6. Well furnished and comfortable in 32,000 acres of rugged beautiful country. Ideal for walking, wild-life, fishing. Transport to stocked hill loch. Boat hire. Cottages £230 to £410 per week. **Open March to November.**

Attadale Holiday Cottages
by Strathcarron, Ross-shire, IV54 8YX
Tel/Fax: 01520 722862
E-mail: attadale@zetnet.co.uk

★★★★ SELF CATERING

Croft house and three cottages a mile from the sea on unspoilt peaceful 32000 acre Highland estate. Deer, pine-martins and 75 species of birds. Hill walking, climbing and fishing hill lochs. Boat hire. Ideal base for exploring the West Coast and Skye.

1 house, 2 cottages, 1 bungalow, 1-2 pub rms, 2-4 bedrms (grd flr avail), sleeps 4-8, total sleeping capacity 23, £230-£410, Mar-Nov, rail 1 ml.

Mrs N Boyd
Ardach, Allt a Chuirn, Lochcarron, Ross-shire, IV54 8YD
Tel: 01520 722511

★★★★ SELF CATERING

Modern, well equipped bungalow overlooking Loch Carron. Private parking. Ideal centre for walking, fishing and touring.

1 bungalow, 1 pub rm, 1 bedrm (All grd.floor), sleeps 2, £80.00-£250.00, Jan-Dec, rail 3 mls

---

Important: Prices stated are estimates and may be subject to amendments

THE HIGHLANDS AND SKYE

LOCHCARRON

Lochcarron, Ross-shire

Map Ref: 3G9

SELF CATERING ★★★★

Mr M F Dennett
5 Hargate Close, Bury, Lancs, BL9 5NU
Tel: 01706 826590

1 cottage, 2 pub rms, 2 bedrms, sleeps 4-5, min let weekend, £120.00-£340.00, Jan-Dec, no pets.

A lovely traditional cottage on the shores of Loch Carron in a peaceful location with beautiful views across to Plockton and Skye. This wonderful walking area is ideal for touring and cycling. Abundant wildlife includes seals, otters and eagles. Bikes, boats and canoes can be hired locally. The cottage has central heating, a fitted kitchen and gardens down to the waters edge. No smokers or pets.

SELF CATERING ★★

Fooks Property Co
Woodgate House, Beckley, Rye, East Sussex TN31 6UH
Tel: 01797 260472 Tel/Fax: 01797 260334

1 house, 1 pub rm, 3 bedrms, sleeps 6, £250.00-£425.00, Apr-Oct, bus nearby, rail 2 mls, airport 55 mls

Modernised croft set in spectacular scenery near the West Coast in the Scottish Highlands about 4 miles (6.5kms) east of Loch Carron.

SELF CATERING ★★★★

Mrs Linda Gillespie
120 Findhorn, Forres, Moray, IV36 0YJ
Tel: 01309 690227

1 house, 2 pub rms, 3 bedrms, sleeps 5, £150.00-£395.00, Jan-Dec

A traditional Highland cottage fully modernised and located within easy walking distance of the shore of Loch Carron. Ideal for activity or relaxing holiday.

SELF CATERING ★★★

Mrs Inglis
c/o Mrs B Weighill, Craigard, Ardaneaskan, Lochcarron, Ross-shire, IV54 8YL
Tel: 01520 722257

1 cottage, 2 pub rms, 2 bedrms, sleeps 4, £200.00-£310.00, Apr-Oct, rail 2 mls, airport 65 mls

South facing cottages with wide extensive views over sea loch and beyond, at centre of this typical west coast village. Well equipped and comfortable.

SELF CATERING ★

Mr M J Knatchbull
Kelso Hotels Ltd, Newhouse, Mersham, Ashford, Kent, TN25 6NQ
Tel: 01233 503636 Fax: 01233 502244
E-mail: brabourne@newhouse.free-online.co.uk

1 cottage, 2 pub rms, 4 bedrms (grd flr avail), sleeps 8, £265.00-£450.00, Jan-Dec, bus 1/2 ml, rail 1/2 ml, airport 60 mls

Lodge attached to period house in own grounds. Beautiful Highland setting 3 miles (5kms) from village. Older style of rooms and furnishings.

VAT is shown at 17.5%: changes in this rate may affect prices.

Key to symbols is on back flap.

LOCHCARRON – LOCHINVER

THE HIGHLANDS AND SKYE

Lochcarron, Ross-shire — Map Ref: 3G9

Mrs C MacKay
Oakdale, Ardaneaskan, Lochcarron, Ross-shire, IV54 8YL
Tel/Fax: 01520 722281
E-mail: mackay@oakdale2.freeserve.co.uk

UP TO ★★ — SELF CATERING

1 cottage, 1 bungalow, 1 pub rm, 2-3 bedrms (grd flr avail), sleeps 4-6, total sleeping capacity 10, £100.00-£300.00, Jan-Dec, rail 10 mls, airport 70 mls

Two individual cottages of character on shores of Loch Carron. Magnificent views. Ideal for walkers and nature lovers.

Lochinver, Sutherland — Map Ref: 3G5

Cathair Dhubh Estate
Lochinver, Sutherland, IV27 4JB
Tel/Fax: 01571 855277

★★★★ — SELF CATERING

5 cottages, 1 pub rm, 2-3 bedrms (grd flr avail), sleeps 4-6, total sleeping capacity 22, min let 2 nights, £210.00-£650.00, Jan-Dec, bus 4 mls, rail 65 mls, ferry 37 mls, airport 97 mls

Secluded coastal estate, modern comfortable cottages all with jacuzzi baths. Near sandy beaches, an ideal base for walking, angling, hillclimbing and abundant wildlife.

Mr & Mrs N Lloyd-Jenkins
Creigard, Badnaban, Lochinver, Sutherland, IV27 4LR
Tel: 01571 844448

★★★★ — SELF CATERING

1 bungalow, 1 pub rm, 2 bedrms, sleeps 4, £195.00-£415.00, Jan-Dec, bus 30 mls, rail 70 mls, ferry 30 mls, airport 90 mls

Admire beautiful sunrises and sunsets. Panoramic views of mountains and sea. Watch fishing boats steaming to Lochinver and The Minch. The bungalow and chalet are modern, very comfortable and equipped to a high standard. They are situated 1.5 miles south of Lochinver on a private road against a backdrop of

Mr C MacKenzie
Braeside, Navidale Road, Helmsdale, Sutherland, KW8 6JS
Tel: 01431 821207

★★★★ — SELF CATERING

1 house, 2 pub rms, 4 bedrms, sleeps 6, £350.00-£650.00, Mar-Nov, bus 1 ml, rail 45 mls, airport 100 mls

Nestling in a secluded glen with glorious views of the mountains of Assynt and Wester Ross, Glendarroch house offers the perfect setting for a peaceful and relaxing holiday. Enjoy a traditional Highland home sympathetically modernised to high standards. Price includes all electricity, full central heating, electric blankets and a well stocked library. 15 acre grounds with nature all around yet less than a mile from shops.

Mrs J C MacLeod
Caisteal Liath Chalets, Baddidarrach, Lochinver,
Sutherland, IV27 4LP
Tel/Fax: 01571 844457
E-mail: caisteal_liath@compuserve.com
Web: www.scottish-highlands-accommodation.co.uk

★★★★ — SELF CATERING

3 chalets, 1 pub rm, 2 bedrms, sleeps 4, total sleeping capacity 12, min let 2 nights, £175.00-£450.00, Jan-Dec, bus ½ ml, rail 50 mls, ferry 40 mls, airport 100 mls

Wooden chalets of a good overall standard set away from the shore overlooking Lochinver Bay. 2 miles (3 kms) to Lochinver.

Important: Prices stated are estimates and may be subject to amendments

THE HIGHLANDS AND SKYE

LOCHINVER

Lochinver, Sutherland | Map Ref: 3G5

★★★★ SELF CATERING

Mr K MacLeod
37 Strathan, Lochinver, Sutherland
Tel: 01571 844631

1 bungalow, 1 pub rm, 2 bedrms (All grd.floor), sleeps 4, £195.00-£375.00, Apr-Oct, bus 1 ml, rail 45 mls, ferry 40 mls, airport 100 mls

Modern bungalow on a private site with garden and car parking area. In a peaceful location 1 mile from Lochinver. Ideal base for walking, fishing and birdwatching. Sandy beaches within easy reach. Suilven is in close proximity to the bungalow.

★★★★ SELF CATERING

Mrs Sandra MacLeod
Ardmore, Torbreck, Lochinver, Sutherland IV27 4JB
Tel: 01571 844310

1 chalet, 1 pub rm, 3 bedrms, sleeps 5, £200.00-£400.00, Jan-Dec, bus 1 1/2 mls, rail 45 mls, airport 110 mls

Modern chalet on working croft. Lochinver 1.5 miles (3kms) away with shops and restaurants. Renowned sandy beach at Achmelvich 1.5 miles (3 kms).

★★★★ SELF CATERING

Mrs Fiona McClelland
Tigh-Mo-Chridhe, Baddidarrach, Lochinver, Sutherland, IV27 4LP
Tel: 01571 844377 (eve) Fax: 01571 844766

1 cottage, 1 pub rm, 2 bedrms (All grd.floor), sleeps 2-4, min let 2 nights, £150.00-£330.00, Jan-Dec, bus 1 ml, rail 46 mls, airport 100 mls

Secluded, extensively modernised croft house with picture windows and magnificent views across Lochinver Bay to the mountains of Assynt and Coigach. Fenced garden, private parking, some steps up to cottage, village 15 minute walk.

★★★★ SELF CATERING

Mr Stuart McClelland
Baddidarroch, Lochinver, Sutherland, IV27 4LP
Tel: 01571 844377

1 cottage, 1 pub rm, 1 bedrm (All grd.floor), sleeps 2, £120.00-£320.00, Jan-Dec, bus 1/4 ml, rail 45 mls, airport 100 mls

Extensively modernised and refurbished former Cottar's Cottage. Privately situated, with garden and 1/4 acre fenced ground in hillside position. Overlooking Loch Inver with views of surrounding mountains and bay. Own drive and parking, car to door, village 10 minute walk.

★★★ SELF CATERING

Dr P McMichael
12 Craigleith Gardens, Edinburgh, EH4 3JW
Tel/Fax: 0131 332 1100

1 house, 2 pub rms, 3 bedrms, sleeps 6, £90.00-£360.00, Jan-Dec, bus nearby, rail 45 mls, airport 100 mls

Traditional cottage attractively situated in centre of village with fine harbour views.

VAT is shown at 17.5%: changes in this rate may affect prices. | *Key to symbols is on back flap.*

LOCHINVER — THE HIGHLANDS AND SKYE

Lochinver, Sutherland | Map Ref: 3G5

★★★★ SELF CATERING

Mountview Self Catering
70 Baddidarroch, Lochinver, Sutherland, IV27 4LP
Tel: 01571 844648/Fax 01571 844648
E-mail: rmac776373@aol.com
Web: http://members.aol.com/lochedge

Log cabin and cottage situated close to the water's edge, near the picturesque fishing village of Lochinver in the heart of the magnificent Scottish Highlands.

2 log cabins, 1 cottage, 1-3 pub rms, 1-3 bedrms (grd flr avail), sleeps 2-6, total sleeping capacity 12, £150.00-£520.00, Jan-Dec, bus 1 ml, rail 46 mls, ferry 40 mls, airport 100 mls

---

★★★ SELF CATERING

Mrs Mary C Ross
Tighnuilt, Inverkirkaig, Lochinver, Sutherland, IV27 4LR
Tel: 01571 844233

Modern A line chalet with own enclosed garden. Excellent position overlooking Inverkirkaig Bay, 30 yards from shore. Birds, otters and seals.

1 chalet, 1 pub rm, 2 bedrms (All grd.floor), sleeps 4, £225.00-£350.00, Mar-Nov, bus 3 mls, rail 50 mls, ferry 37 mls, airport 110 mls

---

★ SELF CATERING

Moira Stramentov
Gurrington House, Woodland, Asburton, Devon TQ13 7JS
Tel: 01364 652246 Fax: 01364 654370

Large family house, set in peaceful rural location. Ideal base for touring the West Coast.

1 house, 1 pub rm, 4 bedrms (grd flr avail), sleeps 8, £250.00-£320.00, Jan-Dec

---

★★ SELF CATERING

Tannochbrae, Mr & Mrs Dougall
22 Fife Street, Dufftown, Banffshire, AB55 4AL, AB55 4AL
Tel: 01340 820541
E-mail: tannochbrae@duff2000.globalnet.co.uk
Web: www.users.globalnet.co.uk/wduff2000/tannbrae.htm

Traditional cottage, set into the hills overlooking the village of Lochinver, the harbour and Suilven. Ideal location for hillwalking, fishing and touring the West Coast.

1 cottage, 2 pub rms, 3 bedrms (All grd.floor), sleeps 6, min let 4 days, £260.00-£385.00, Apr-Oct, bus ¼ ml, rail 68 mls, airport 100 mls

★★★ SELF CATERING

Valhalla Holdings
Inverkirkaig, Lochinver, Sutherland, IV27 4LR
Tel: 01571 844270 Fax: 01571 844483
Web: www.host.co.uk

Pine chalets set in beautiful, peaceful situation on the shores of Kirkaig Bay. Overlooking a nature reserve the area is abundant with wildlife, seals, otters, ducks and other seabirds.

2 chalets, 2 flats, 1 pub rm, 2 bedrms (All grd.floor), sleeps 2-6, total sleeping capacity 18, £210.00-£360.00, Jan-Dec, bus 1 ml, rail 40 mls, ferry 40 mls, airport 100 mls

---

Important: Prices stated are estimates and may be subject to amendments

THE HIGHLANDS AND SKYE

LOCHINVER – MALLAIG

Lochinver, Sutherland

SELF CATERING ★★

Mr & Mrs I Yates
114 Achmelvich, Lochinver, Sutherland, IV27 4JB
Tel: 01571 844312 Fax: 01571 844521
E-mail: gemsy@aol.com

Comfortable croft with open fire, excellent south-facing sheltered wooded area. Courses available in stone-cutting, photography and painting. Walks from the house. River and Loch at the back of the croft. Ideal location for touring the West Coast. 1.5 miles from safe sandy beach at Achmelvich 1.5 miles from Lochinver.

Map Ref: 3G5

1 cottage, 2 pub rms, 3 bedrms (grd flr avail), sleeps 6, £200.00-£400.00, Jan-Dec, rail 40 mls, airport 100 mls

---

Mallaig, Inverness-shire

SELF CATERING ★★★

Glaschoille Holidays
Lahill, Upper Largo, Fife, KY8 6JE
Tel: 01333 360251 Fax: 01333 360452
E-mail: lahill4444@aol.com

Spacious country house in outstanding lochside location on the remote and peaceful Knoydart peninsula.

Map Ref: 3F11

1 house, 2 pub rms, 6 bedrms (grd flr avail), sleeps 10, £420.00-£690.00, Jan-Dec, ferry 2 mls

---

ESSAN COTTAGE

Essan Cottage, Morar, Mallaig PH40 4PA
Telephone: 01687 462346 Fax: 01687 462212
e.mail: morar-hotel@roadtotheisles.org.uk
Web: www.roadtotheisles.org.uk

Trout fishing, hill climbing, boating, sailing, canoeing, bird-watching and golfing. Twice daily rail connections from London, Glasgow and Edinburgh. One double, one twin, lounge, kitchen, bathroom, small garden, double glazing. Hotel and pub 100 yards. Railway and bus station 50 yards. Cruises to Skye.

SELF CATERING ★★

Mrs M M MacLeod
Essan House, Morar Hotel, Morar, Mallaig, Inverness-shire, PH40 4P
Tel: 01687 462346 Fax: 01687 462212

Detached cottage with enclosed garden in centre of village. Ideal base for hillwalking and birdwatching. Close to owners hotel (across the road) which offers bar, meals and telephone facilities.

1 house, 1 pub rm, 2 bedrms (All grd.floor), sleeps 5, £250.00-£300.00, Jan-Dec, bus nearby, rail 10 yds, ferry 2 mls, airport 130 mls

---

SELF CATERING ★★★★

Mrs E MacPhie
Aranmore, Mallaig, Inverness-shire, PH41 4QN
Tel/Fax: 01687 462051
E-mail: emacphie@zetnet.co.uk
Web: http://ourworld.compuserve.com/homepages/rjwinters/nevis.html

Nevis Bank is situated in a secluded position at the mouth of Loch Nevis in the delightful, unspoilt country at the end of the "Road to the Isles" and the ferry to the romantic Isle of Skye. We overlook a quiet beach where otters and seals are frequently seen. Unlimited space for walking, climbing and exploring with an abundant variety of wild flora, fauna and birds.

1 cottage, 1 pub rm, 3 bedrms, sleeps 6, £293.00-£565.00, Jan-Dec, bus 1/2 ml, rail 1 1/2 mls, ferry 1 1/2 mls, airport 100 miles

VAT is shown at 17.5%: changes in this rate may affect prices.

Key to symbols is on back flap.

MELVICH – NAIRN
THE HIGHLANDS AND SKYE

Melvich, Sutherland   Map Ref: 4C3

Halladale Inn Chalet Park
Melvich, Sutherland KW14 7YJ
Telephone/Fax: 01641 541282
e.mail: jack@melvich.demon.co.uk   Web: www.melvich.demon.co.uk
Open April to October. Chalet accommodation to suit all ages. Clean beaches and golf course nearby. Salmon and trout fishing available. Bird watching and diving are recommended. Licensed bar and restaurant next to chalet park on A836, 17 miles west of Thurso, Orkney ferry 20 minutes away.

★ **SELF CATERING**

Mr Jack Paterson
Dallangwell Farmhouse, Strathy West, Sutherland, KW14 7RZ
Tel: 01641 541282/531282 Fax: 01641 541282

3 chalets, 1 pub rm, 2 bedrms (All grd.floor), sleeps 4-6, total sleeping capacity 18, £100.00-£205.00, Apr-Oct, bus nearby, rail 13 mls, ferry 18 mls, airport 40 mls

Two semi-detached sets of chalets, overlooking the sea and standing in their own ground, near a restaurant and pub. Ideal base for touring north coast.

Morar, Inverness-shire   Map Ref: 3F11

★★ **SELF CATERING**

Mrs C Finch
Glenancross, Morar, Mallaig, Inverness-shire, PH40 4PD
Tel: 01687 450294 Fax: 01687 450343

1 cottage, 1 pub rm, 2 bedrms (All grd.floor), sleeps 4, £160.00-£260.00, Jan-Dec, rail 2 mls, ferry 5 mls

Cottage forming part of courtyard, with easy access by foot to sandy beach. Mallaig and Arisaig approx. 4 miles. 9 hole golf course nearby. Private parking directly beside property. Ideal base for trips to Skye and the small isles.

Nairn   Map Ref: 4C8

★★ **SELF CATERING**

Mr & Mrs A L MacKinlay
21 Braidburn Crescent, Edinburgh, EH10 6EL
Tel: 0131 447 5294

1 bungalow, 1 pub rm, 5 bedrms (All grd.floor), sleeps 6, £225.00-£395.00, Mar-Nov, bus ½ ml, rail ¼ ml, airport 10 mls

Comfortable, spacious 1920's bungalow near swimming pool, leisure park, beach and golf course, with views over the Moray Firth. Secluded garden. Only 15 miles from Inverness, Nairn is ideal centre for touring the Moray coast, Speyside, the Cairngorms, the Great Glen, Skye and the inspiring scenery of the north-west Highlands. Golf deals are available in Moray and Grampian.

★★★ **HOLIDAY PARK**

Nairn Lochloy Holiday Park
East Beach, Nairn, IV12 4PH
Tel: 01667 453764 Fax: 01667 454721
Booking Enquiries: Haven Reservations PO Box 218, 1 Park Lane, Hemel Hempstead, HP2 4GL
Tel: 0870 242 2222

6½ acres, grassy, sandy, Apr-Oct, prior booking recommended in peak periods, latest time of arrival 2200, overnight holding area. Extra charge for electricity, dogs.

Park accommodation: 279
Tourers, motorhomes and tents welcome. Total touring pitches 45. £8.00-£15.00 per night approx. Contact park direct.
Caravans and chalets to let, sleep 4-8. £124.00-£524.00 per week approx. Contact reservations.

Leisure facilities:

From either Inverness or Aberdeen take A96. East Beach in town of Nairn adjacent Dunbar Golf course.

Important: Prices stated are estimates and may be subject to amendments

THE HIGHLANDS AND SKYE

NAIRN – NETHY BRIDGE

Nairn

Map Ref: 4C8

★★★ SELF CATERING

Mr E S Walker
1 Findhorn Road, Kinloss, Forres, Moray, IV36 0TT
Tel: 01309 691266
E-mail: vacations@walker712.freeserve.co.uk
Web: www.walker712.freeserve.co.uk

Nairn is a small coastal town with beautiful beaches and two championship golf courses. The Moorings is a modern development on the banks of the River Nairn with one of the town's golf courses beyond. A short walk to the marina.

1 house, 2 pub rms, 2 bedrms, sleeps 5, £150.00-£350.00, Jan-Dec, bus 200 yds, rail ¼ ml, airport 5 mls.

Nethy Bridge, Inverness-shire

Map Ref: 4C10

★★★★ SELF CATERING

Cairngorm Executive Ltd
Funach View, Crossroads, Durris, Banchory,
Kincardineshire, AB31 6BX
Tel: 01330 844344 Fax: 01330 844322
E-mail: cairngorm@compuserve.com

Located in Speyside's "Forest Village" on the north side of the Cairngorm Mountains, Osprey Lodge is a superb four-bedroomed house built to a traditional Highland design but with all modern facilities and comforts including its own woodland garden.

1 house, 2 pub rms, 4 bedrms, sleeps 8-10, £495.00-£795.00, Jan-Dec, bus nearby, rail 12 mls, airport 35 mls.

★★★ UP TO ★★★★ SELF CATERING
BRONZE

Mr & Mrs M T Collins
Birchfield Cottages, Birchfield, Nethy Bridge,
Inverness-shire, PH25 3DD
Tel/Fax: 01479 821613
E-mail: collins@birchcot.freeserve.co.uk
Web: www.nethybridge.com/birchfield.htm

Comfortable stone built cottage accommodation, each of individual character and style, in attractive rural setting on edge of Nethy Bridge.

3 listed cottages, 1 pub rm, 1-2 bedrms (grd flr avail), sleeps 1-5, total sleeping capacity 9, £125.00-£425.00, Jan-Dec, bus ½ ml, rail 10 mls, airport 39 mls.

★★★ SELF CATERING

John & Carina Craib
3 Albert Drive, Bearsden, East Dunbartonshire, G61 2NT
Tel: 0141 563 7830
Web: www.nethybridge.com/lorien.htm

Large timber bungalow at the centre of this delightful Highland village.

1 bungalow, 1 pub rm, 3 bedrms (All grd.floor), sleeps 6, min let weekend, £180.00-£410.00, Jan-Dec, bus nearby, rail 12 mls, airport 30 mls.

★★★★ SELF CATERING

Mrs Valery Dean
Badanfhuarain, Nethy Bridge, Inverness-shire, PH25 3ED
Tel: 01479 821642
E-mail: dv.dean@virgin.net
Web: http://freespace.virgin.net/dv.dean/

Two separately located traditional cottages, with enclosed gardens, seclusion and exceptional individual character and charm. Pets by arrangement, non-smokers preferred. Wheelchair access award.

2 cottages, 1 pub rm, 3 bedrms (All grd.floor), sleeps 5, total sleeping capacity 10, min let weekend, £250.00-£425.00, Jan-Dec, bus ½ ml, rail 10 mls, airport 40 mls.

VAT is shown at 17.5%: changes in this rate may affect prices.

Key to symbols is on back flap.

NETHY BRIDGE — THE HIGHLANDS AND SKYE

Nethy Bridge, Inverness-shire | Map Ref: 4C10

★★★ SELF CATERING

Mr John Fleming
Dell of Abernethy, Nethy Bridge, Inverness-shire, PH25 3DL
Tel: 01463 224358 Fax: 01479 821643
Web: www.nethybridge.com/dellofabernethy.htm

Warm comfortable stone built cottages in large garden of lawns and mature woodland 1 mile from village centre and marked Dell Lodge on maps. Among roe deer and red squirrels, footpaths and bicycle tracks lead into Dell Woods Nature Reserve and on to the Ospreys of Roch Garten. Central to castles, distilleries of Spey valley. Day trips to West Coast, Moray Coast and Royal Deeside. Good heated drying cupboards.

3 cottages, 3 bungalows, 1 pub rm, 2-3 bedrms (grd flr avail), sleeps 2-7, total sleeping capacity 34, £150.00-£410.00, Jan-Dec, bus 1 ml, rail 10 mls, airport 35 mls

★★★ UP TO ★★★★ SELF CATERING

A R Fraser
36 Lynstock Crescent, Nethy Bridge, PH25 3DX
Tel: 01479 821312

Modern detached bungalows situated on outskirts of Nethy Bridge, affording excellent views of Cairngorm range.

1 house, 2 bungalows, sleeps 6-8, total sleeping capacity 20, £150.00-£400.00, Jan-Dec, bus ½ ml, rail 12 mls, airport 34 mls

---

★★★★ SELF CATERING

J & F Grant
Easter Gallovie, Dulnain Bridge, by Grantown-on-Spey, Moray, PH26 LZ
Tel: 01479 851342

Innis Bhroc (Badgers Meadow) is set in a peaceful rural location in the Abernethy Forest Reserve, a paradise for bird watchers and naturalists.

1 house, 2 pub rms, 3 bedrms (All grd.floor), sleeps 6, min let 2/3 nights, £225.00-£400.00, Jan-Dec, bus 3 mls, rail 12 mls, airport 36 mls

---

★★★ SELF CATERING

Mrs I E G Hamilton
Tullochgribban Mains, Dulnain Bridge, Grantown-on-Spey, PH26 3NE
Tel: 01479 851333

Cosy, well equipped bungalow in small private development on edge of picturesque village.

1 house, 2 pub rms, 3 bedrms (All grd.floor), sleeps 5, £190.00-£400.00, Jan-Dec, bus 1 ½ mls, rail 12 mls, airport 30 mls

---

★★★ SELF CATERING

Mr & Mrs R Kunz
Ailanbeg Lodge, Nethy Bridge, Inverness-shire, PH25 3DY
Tel: 01479 821363 Fax: 01479 821841
E-mail: cottage@spey.com
Web: www.spey.com

Stone built cottage, in grounds of owner's house, recently converted and modernised to a high standard, superb views to Cairngorms.

1 cottage, 1 pub rm, 2 bedrms (All grd.floor), sleeps 5, £135.00-£285.00, Jan-Dec

Important: Prices stated are estimates and may be subject to amendments

THE HIGHLANDS AND SKYE

NETHY BRIDGE – NEWTONMORE

Nethy Bridge, Inverness-shire   Map Ref: 4C10

★★★ UP TO ★★★★ SELF CATERING

Mr & Mrs J B Patrick
Speyside Cottages, 1B Chapelton Place, Forres, Moray, IV36 2NL
Tel/Fax: 01309 672505
E-mail: speyside@enterprise.net
Web: www.assc.co.uk/speyside

Cottages and converted smithy, separately sited in Highland village, each with its own character and enclosed gardens.

2 cottages, 3 bungalows, 1 converted smithy, 1 pub rm, 1-4 bedrms (grd flr avail), sleeps 2-9, total sleeping capacity 29, min let 2 nights, £120.00-£680.00, Jan-Dec, bus nearby, rail 9 mls, airport 30 mls

★★★ SELF CATERING

Redwood Self Catering
Redwood, 4 Ross Court, Old Edinburgh Road, Inverness, IV2 3HT
Tel: 01463 729263

Traditional Highland croft with own garden, in rural situation on edge of Abernethy Forest.

1 cottage, 2 pub rms, 4 bedrms (grd flr avail), sleeps 8, Bathroom with toilet and w/h basin, separate toilet with w/h basin, separate shower room. £200.00-£400.00, Jan-Dec, bus 300 yds, rail 8 mls, airport 30 mls.

★★★★ SELF CATERING

Mrs G Robertson
Pitgarvie Farm, Laurencekirk, AB30 1RB
Tel: 01674 840219 Fax: 01674 840705
E-mail: pitgarvie@aol.com

Converted, stone built steading of original style and character, retaining some original features. Large garden. Near centre of village.

1 house, 1 pub rm with Wood Burning Stove, 3 bedrms, sleeps 7, £275.00-£440.00, Jan-Dec, bus nearby, rail 11 mls, airport 42 mls

Newtonmore, Inverness-shire   Map Ref: 4B11

★★★ SELF CATERING

Croft Holidays
Newtonmore, Inverness-shire, PH20 1BA
Tel/Fax: 01540 673504
E-mail: mmackenzie@sprite.co.uk
Web: www.newtonmore.com/strone

Ideal holiday retreat, secluded beautiful peaceful surroundings, on outskirts of lovely highland village. Refurbished cottage includes: upstairs; 2 twin bedrooms, bathroom, drying room; downstairs, ensuite bedroom; living room, open fire, TV; well-equipped kitchen, microwave, fridge freezer, washing machine. Tariff, central heating and electricity. Many local activities and attractions, central for touring, short breaks.

2 cottages, 1 pub rm, 1-3 bedrms (grd flr avail), sleeps 4-6, total sleeping capacity 10, min let 2 days, from £180.00, Jan-Dec, bus 1/2 ml, rail 1 ml

★★★★ SELF CATERING

Miss Miggi Meier/Jennifer Graham
Crubenbeg Farm Steading, Newtonmore, Inverness-shire, PH20 1BE
Tel: 01540 673566 Fax: 01540 673509
E-mail: enquiries@crudenbeg.netlineuk.net
Web: www.newtonmore.com/crubenbeg

Small complex of cosy cottages in sympathetically converted 18c steading in the heart of the Highlands. Sauna, solarium and games/fitness room.

7 cottages, 1 pub rm, 1-2 bedrms, sleeps 2-5, total sleeping capacity 24, £200.00-£360.00, Jan-Dec, bus 5 mls, rail 5 mls, airport 50 mls

VAT is shown at 17.5%: changes in this rate may affect prices.   *Key to symbols is on back flap.*

NEWTONMORE – BY NORTH KESSOCK

THE HIGHLANDS AND SKYE

Newtonmore, Inverness-shire — Map Ref: 4B11

★★ SELF CATERING

Alastair G T Troup
29 Muswell Close, Solihull, West Midlands, B91 2QS
Tel: 0121 705 4249

1 bungalow, 2 pub rms, 3 bedrms, sleeps 2-6, £170.00-£380.00, Jan-Dec, bus 800 yds, rail 400 yds, airport 45 mls

Modern bungalow, with own garden. In quiet part of village, within easy reach of shops, amenities and public transport.

★★ SELF CATERING

Mrs D J M Whymant
The Gardens, Redstone, Darnaway, by Forres, Moray
Tel: 01309 641512

1 bungalow, 1 pub rm, 2 bedrms, sleeps 4, £125.00-£210.00, Jan-Dec, bus nearby, rail 1 1/2 mls

Situated in the heart of small village, modern detached bungalow with large enclosed gardens and garage.

North Ballachulish, Inverness-shire — Map Ref: 1F1

★★★★ SELF CATERING

Mrs J Morrison
Islanders, 10 Achnalea, Onich, Fort William, PH33 6SA
Tel: 01855 821403

1 house, 1 pub rm, 3 bedrms, sleeps 7, £245.00-£395.00, Jan-Dec

In a quiet village setting close to the Ballachulish Bridge this semi-detached former ferryman's cottage provides comfortable holiday accommodation of a high standard. Bright spacious and tastefully furnished, the house sits in its own garden with spectacular views of the surrounding hills and lochs.

North Kessock, Ross-shire — Map Ref: 4B8

★★★ SELF CATERING

P A Saunders
Whin Brae, Craigton Point, North Kessock, by Inverness, Ross-shire IV1 1YB
Tel: 01463 731786

1 cottage, 1 pub rm, 2 bedrms (All grd.floor), sleeps 4, £165.00-£295.00, Apr-Sep, bus nearby, rail 3 mls, airport 10 mls

Modern terraced cottage in village of North Kessock, just 3 miles from Inverness. Ideal location for exploring the north Highlands.

---

by North Kessock, Ross-shire — Map Ref: 4B8

★★★ SELF CATERING

Mr William & Mrs Alison MacKay
Fernvilla, Halebank Road, Widnes, Cheshire, WA8 8NP
Tel: 0151 425 2129 Fax: 0151 425 2151

1 cottage, 1 pub rm, 3 bedrms (All grd.floor), sleeps 5-6, £195.00-£485.00, Apr-Oct, bus 1/4 ml, rail 4 mls, airport 12 mls

Modernised stone cottage with large private garden and driveway. Patio with BBQ. Spectacular sea views. Convenient to A9 and Inverness. Comfortable sun lounge and modern luxury kitchen. Ideal touring base.

Important: Prices stated are estimates and may be subject to amendments

THE HIGHLANDS AND SKYE

ONICH, BY FORT WILLIAM

Onich, by Fort William, Inverness-shire

Map Ref: 3G12

★★ UP TO ★★★
SELF CATERING

Ardrhu Holiday Cottages
Onich, by Fort William, PH33 6SD
Tel: 01855 821418

Ardrhu nestles by the shores of Loch Linnhe nine miles south of Fort William. 15 Self Catering properties accommodating four to ten persons with spectacular uninterrupted mountain scenery. Enjoy the splendour of the Highlands with a leisurely walk along the shoreline or for the more energetic hillwalking and climbing. Please telephone for a brochure and tariff which includes electricity and bed linen, in fact no extras at all.

14 cottages, 1 mansion, 1 pub rm, 2-4 bedrms (grd flr avail), sleeps 4-10, total sleeping capacity 80, min let 3 nights, £184.00-£894.00, Jan-Dec, bus ¼ ml, rail 9 mls, ferry 1 ½ mls, airport 76 mls

INCHREE CHALETS
ONICH, FORT WILLIAM, HIGHLAND PH33 6SD
Tel/Fax: 01855 821287   e.mail: paddy@inchreecentre1.netlink.net

The ideal centre, 8 miles south of Fort William, midway between Ben Nevis and Glencoe, for touring, walking or relaxing. Comfortable, fully equipped chalets with loch and mountain views, sleeps up to 4 or 6 persons. Licensed restaurant and pub, launderette, children's play area etc. Information pack provided. Open all year. Pets welcome. Reduced rates for couples. Short breaks. For information please write or phone.
Rates from £179 per week.

★★
SELF CATERING

Inchree Chalets
Onich, Fort William, Inverness-shire, PH33 6SD
Tel/Fax: 01855 821287
E.mail: paddy@inchreecentre1.netlink.net

Chalets on hillside in natural surroundings with views of loch and hills. Ideal for touring and hillwalking. Pub-restaurant on site.

5 chalets, 1 pub rm, 2-3 bedrms (grd flr avail), sleeps 4-6, total sleeping capacity 46, min let 2 nights, £179.00-£379.00, Jan-Dec, bus nearby, rail 8 mls, airport 70 mls

---

★★★
SELF CATERING

Mrs M MacLean
Janika, Bunree, Onich, by Fort William, Inverness-shire, PH33 6SE
Tel: 01855 821359
E-mail: janika@btinternet.com

Two apartments with own access and two modern cottages. Bunree is situated on the outskirts of Onich which is ideally situated between fabulous Glencoe and Ben Nevis - 8 miles south of Fort William. We are a small croft on the shores of Loch Linnhe at Corran Narrows. Free fishing on loch.

2 cottages, 2 apartment, 1 pub rm, 2 bedrms, sleeps 4, total sleeping capacity 16, £205.00-£375.00, Jan-Dec, bus 8 mls, rail 8 mls, airport 100 mls

★★★★
SELF CATERING

I D Graham Munro
Drumbrae, Onich, Fort William, Inverness-shire, PH33 6SE
Tel/Fax: 01855 821261
E-mail: iain@bbchalets.co.uk
Web: www.bbchalets.co.uk

Modern Scandinavian style lodges set in woodland overlooking Corran Ferry on Loch Linnhe. 8 miles (13kms) from Fort William.

7 chalets, 1 pub rm, 3 bedrms (All grd.floor), sleeps 6, total sleeping capacity 42, £200.00-£490.00, Jan-Dec, bus nearby, rail 8 mls, ferry ½ ml, airport 70 mls

VAT is shown at 17.5%: changes in this rate may affect prices.

Key to symbols is on back flap.

ONICH, BY FORT WILLIAM – PLOCKTON

THE HIGHLANDS AND SKYE

Onich, by Fort William, Inverness-shire

Map Ref: 3G12

★★ SELF CATERING

Mr & Mrs William Murray
Springwell Holiday Homes, Onich, Fort William,
Inverness-shire, PH3 6RY
Tel/Fax: 01855 821257

4 cottages, 1-2 pub rms, 2-3 bedrms (grd flr avail), sleeps 4-6, total sleeping capacity 18, £180.00-£390.00, Jan-Dec, bus nearby, rail 10 mls, ferry 2 mls, airport 100 mls

Four holiday cottages fully equipped and centrally heated. Sleep 4 to 6. Situated in 17 acres of private hillside with magnificent views across Loch Linnhe into the mountains of Argyllshire and Glencoe. Ideal location for all pursuits and relaxation.

Plockton, Ross-shire

Map Ref: 3F9

★ SELF CATERING

Lesley Burrell
43A Castle Street, Dumfries, DG1 1DU
Tel/Fax: 01387 269762
E-mail: burrell@ukgateway.net

1 cottage, 1 pub rm, 4 bedrms, sleeps 8, £200.00-£360.00, Jan-Dec, bus 5 mls, rail 1/4 ml, ferry 5 mls, airport 80 mls

Along main street in Plockton on the left hand side.

★★★ SELF CATERING

Mrs M A Byrne
27 Milner Road, Glasgow, G13 1QL
Tel: 0141 959 9439

1 house, 2 pub rms, 3 bedrms (grd flr avail), sleeps 7, £250.00-£500.00, Jan-Dec, rail 1 ml

Comfortable 3 bedroom cottage sleeping 7. In beautiful isolated location in the picturesque village of Plockton. The cottage has unspoilt views over Loch Carron to the Applecross hills. Ample garden space for children and one pet.

★★ SELF CATERING

Mrs Patricia F Heaviside
Craig Highland Farm, Craig, Plockton, Ross-shire, IV52 8UB
Tel/Fax: 01599 544205
E-mail: T_Heaviside@hcs.lochalsh.fc.uhi.ac
Web: www.geocities.com/thetropics/cabana/5734

3 cottages, to £280.00, bus 10 mls, rail 1/2 ml, ferry 10 mls, airport 80 mls

Stone built croft cottages, partly thatched and attractively modernised and Norwegian Wooden Cabins. On the shores of Lochcarron. Owner's rare breed farm close by.

★★★ SELF CATERING

Robert & Elizabeth Hogg
Aisling, 2 Bank Street, Plockton, IV52 8TP
Tel: 01599 544208

1 studio/annexe, sleeps 2-4, £150.00-£230.00, Jan-Dec, bus 6 mls

Self-contained studio at rear of owners house. Newly refurbished. Close to the shores of Loch Carron. Ideal area for touring and outdoor pursuits.

Important: Prices stated are estimates and may be subject to amendments

THE HIGHLANDS AND SKYE

PLOCKTON – POOLEWE

Plockton, Ross-shire
Map Ref: 3F9

★★★ SELF CATERING

Mrs Ann B MacLaren
34 Westbourne Gardens, Glasgow, G12 9PF
Tel/Fax: 0141 357 5152
E-mail: ann.maclaren@btinternet.com
Web: www.host.co.uk

Large detached house in centre of Plockton and on the shore of Loch Carron. Superb views in all directions. Used for the filming of the BBC 'Hamish MacBeth' series as the Police Station.

1 house, 3 pub rms, 5 bedrms (grd flr avail), sleeps 9, min let weekend (low season), £400.00-£700.00, bus 6 mls, rail 1 ml, ferry 6 mls, airport 80 mls

★★ SELF CATERING

Mrs Nicholson
Claymoddie, Whithorn, Newton Stewart, Wigtownshire DG8 8LX
Tel: 01988 500422

Secluded cottage set in its own extensive fenced grounds, 3 miles (4 kms) from Plockton, many good restaurants and shops locally.

1 cottage, 1 pub rm, 3 bedrms, sleeps 6, £160.00-£350.00, Jan-Dec

---

Poolewe, Ross-shire
Map Ref: 3F7

★★★★ SELF CATERING

Mr F Hughes
Innes-Maree Bungalows, Poolewe, Ross-shire, IV22 2JU
Tel/Fax: 01445 781454
E-mail: innes-maree@lineone.net
Web: www.assc.co.uk/innesmaree

Modern, purpose built bungalows in peaceful setting. Main bedrooms are ensuite. One bungalow suitable for disabled. Within walking distance of Inverewe Gardens.

6 bungalows, 1 pub rm, 3 bedrms (All grd.floor), sleeps 6, total sleeping capacity 36, min let 3 days, £175.00-£425.00, Jan-Dec, rail 36 mls, ferry 52 mls, airport 85 mls

★★★★ SELF CATERING

Murdo MacDonald
6 Pier Road, Aultbea, Ross-shire
Tel/Fax: 01445 731251

Modern semi-detached bungalows, furnished to a high standard. Set above a sandy beach with fine views across Loch Ewe.

2 bungalows, 1 pub rm, 2 bedrms, sleeps 4, total sleeping capacity 8, £170.00-£320.00, Jan-Dec, bus 7 mls

★★★ SELF CATERING

Mrs Hannah MacLeod
3 Braes, Inverasdale, Poolewe, Ross-shire, IV22 2LN
Tel/Fax: 01445 781434

Two recently modernised croft houses overlooking Loch Ewe. Magnificent scenery, walks, bird watching and fishing.

2 cottages, 2 pub rms, 2-3 bedrms (grd flr avail), sleeps 4-6, total sleeping capacity 10, £150.00-£340.00, Jan-Dec, bus 4 mls, rail 40 mls, ferry 54 mls, airport 90 mls

VAT is shown at 17.5%: changes in this rate may affect prices.

Key to symbols is on back flap.

POOLEWE – ROGART

THE HIGHLANDS AND SKYE

Poolewe, Ross-shire — Map Ref: 3F7

★★★★ SELF CATERING

Kenneth Mitchell
14 Croft, Poolewe, Ross-shire, IV22 2JY
Tel: 01445 781231

1 chalet, 1 pub rm, 2 bedrms (All grd.floor), sleeps 4, from £200.00, Jan-Dec, bus ½ ml, rail 35 mls, ferry 50 mls, airport 90 mls

New secluded cottage on the banks of the River Ewe. Close to Inverewe Gardens. Ideal for hillwalking and climbing in Wester Ross.

★★★★ SELF CATERING

Nicola Taylor
8 Naast, Poolewe, Achnasheen, Ross-shire, IV22 2LL
Tel/Fax: 01445 781360
E-mail: nicola.taylor@virgin.net
Web: http://freespace.virgin.net/nicola.taylor/anbothan.htm

1 cottage, 1 pub rm, 3 bedrms (All grd.floor), sleeps 5, £165.00-£340.00, Jan-Dec, bus 3 mls

Refurbished former croft house, with extensive enclosed safe garden. Superb views over Loch Ewe, and access to small beach area. Games room with dartboard, multi-gym, exercise bike and table football. Fishing rods and canoes available.

Ratagan, Ross-shire — Map Ref: 3G10

★★★★ SELF CATERING

Mr V R Vyner-Brooks
Middle Barrows Green, Kendal, Cumbria, LA8 0JG
Tel: 015395 60242/0151 526 9321/5451 Fax: 0151 526 1331

1 cottage, 4 pub rms, 2 bedrms, sleeps 6, Jan-Dec, bus 1¼ mls, rail 17 mls, ferry 8 mls, airport 70 mls

Cottage on shores of Loch Duich. Superb mountain views of Five Sisters. Great care taken over decor and furnishings. Open fire and oil fired stove.

Reay, Caithness — Map Ref: 4C3

★★ SELF CATERING

Mrs J MacKay
West Greenland, Castletown, Caithness, KW14 8SX
Tel: 01847 821633 Fax: 01847 821633
E-mail: scotno1@aol.com

1 house, 2 pub rms, 4 bedrms, sleeps 8, £150.00-£300.00, Apr-Sep, bus nearby, rail 10 mls, ferry 8 mls, airport 30 mls

Traditional, spacious stone house within walking distance of extensive sandy beach. Centrally situated for exploring the north coast.

Rogart, Sutherland — Map Ref: 4B6

★★★ SELF CATERING

Robert Mills
St Callans Manse, Rogart, Sutherland
Tel: 01408 641363 Fax: 01408 641313

1 cottage, 2 pub rms, 2 bedrms, sleeps 4, £90.00-£300.00, Jan-Dec, bus postbus, rail 1 ml, airport 63 mls

Attractively restored traditional cottage, with solid fuel stoves and full electric heating. Outstanding views down Little Rogart Glen.

Important: Prices stated are estimates and may be subject to amendments

THE HIGHLANDS AND SKYE

ROSEMARKIE – SCARFSKERRY

Rosemarkie, Ross-shire

Map Ref: 4B8

★★ UP TO ★★★
SERVICED APARTMENTS

Charles Cooper
Hillockhead Farm, Eathie Road, Rosemarkie, Ross-shire, IV10 8SL
Tel: 01381 621184 Fax: 01381 621537
E-mail: hillockhead@cali.co.uk

Five self-contained cottages central to the Highlands. The traditional sandstone and windstone barn has been carefully and sensitively converted to provide warm, comfortable accommodation throughout the year. Stunning views over the Moray Firth, recreation facilities and the freedom to roam the 160 acres, some of which is SSSI wooded land, including access to a secluded beach, provides plenty to do on travel free days. www.hillock-head.co.uk

5 cottages, 1 ground floor studio, 1-2 pub rms, 1-3 bedrms (grd flr avail), sleeps 2-6, total sleeping capacity 22, min let 3 nights, £100.00-£450.00, Jan-Dec, bus 3 mls

Roy Bridge, Inverness-shire

Map Ref: 3H12

★★★
SELF CATERING

Cottage Holidays
Kinchellie Croft, Roy Bridge, Inverness-shire, PH31 4AN
Tel: 01397 712265
E-mail: sims@holidays.force9.co.uk
Web: www.cottage-holidays.co.uk

Cottage Holidays is a 6 acre estate on the side of a hill overlooking the Grey Cories and away from the main road making it safe for children. The rural location with its tranquil setting creates the perfect holiday environment.

4 cottages, 1 bungalow, 1-2 pub rms, 3 bedrms (grd flr avail), sleeps 6, total sleeping capacity 30, min let 3 days, £160.00-£375.00, Jan-Dec, bus ½ ml, rail ½ ml, airport 60 mls

★★★
SELF CATERING

Catherine M MacDonald
125 High Street, Fort William, Inverness-shire, PH31 4AH
Tel: 01397 700178
E-mail: catherine.macdonald@btinternet.com

Modern crofthouse (built 1995) on working croft offering a comfortable base to explore the West Highlands. Glen Roy is a unique nature reserve. Wonderful walking, forestry tracks and the Great Glen cycle track. Ski at Aonach Mor (only 12 miles). Fort William 15 miles. Pub and shop in Roy Bridge 1.5 miles.

1 house, 2 pub rms, 4 bedrms (grd flr avail), sleeps 7-8, £300.00-£580.00, Jan-Dec, bus 1 ½ mls, rail 1 ½ mls, airport 60 mls

★
SELF CATERING

Mrs A MacKintosh
Druimandonich, Roy Bridge, Inverness-shire
Tel: 01397 712443

Two hundred year old traditional stone built croft home in secluded setting amid majestic scenery with uninterrupted views of the Ben Nevis range. Central for touring, bird watching, walking, climbing, skiing or just for a relaxing holiday in peaceful surroundings. Spean Bridge/Roy Bridge 1.5 miles in both directions with selection of pubs and restaurants.

1 cottage, 2 pub rms, 4 bedrms (grd flr avail), sleeps 6, £200.00-£350.00, Jan-Dec, bus 1 ½ mls, rail 1 ½ mls, ferry 47 mls, airport 60 mls

Scarfskerry, Caithness

Map Ref: 4D2

★★★
SELF CATERING

Mrs M Dixon
108 Belton Lane, Grantham, Lincolnshire, NG31 9PR
Tel: 01476 561239

Traditional stone-built croft house with open fire and central heating. Set in 4.5 acres of land, with sheltered garden and footpath access to the shore. An ideal croft house for dog owners. There is a wide variety of birdlife at all times of the year. A short drive takes you to John O' Groats where a daytrip to Orkney may be taken. Loch and sea fishing can be arranged.

1 cottage, 4 pub rms, 3 bedrms (All grd.floor), sleeps 6, £200.00-£250.00, Jan-Dec, bus nearby, rail 11 mls, ferry 8 mls, airport 20 mls

VAT is shown at 17.5%: changes in this rate may affect prices.

Key to symbols is on back flap.

THE HIGHLANDS AND SKYE

Scarfskerry, Caithness — Map Ref: 4D2

★★★ SELF CATERING

Ms Morrison
Brier Cottage, Scarfskerry, Caithness
Tel: 01847 851244 Fax: 01847 851244

1 cottage, 1 pub rm, 2 bedrms (All grd.floor), sleeps 4, min let 3 days, £160.00-£240.00, Jan-Dec, bus nearby, rail 14 mls, ferry 8 mls, airport 20 mls

Modern cottage with glorious views to the Orkney Isles. Sandy beaches and restaurant food are both within easy distance. Loch fishing available. Pets welcome. Ideal spot for relaxing and unwinding, or for exploring the far north coast of Caithness and Sutherland.

Scourie, Sutherland — Map Ref: 3H4

★★★ SELF CATERING

William J O Nicoll
3 The Logan, Liff, by Dundee, Angus, DD2 5PJ
Tel: 01382 580358 Fax: 01387 580358
E-mail: william.nicoll@virgin.net

1 house, 1 pub rm, 4 bedrms (grd flr avail), sleeps 8, £200.00-£375.00, Jan-Dec, bus 300 yds

Newly built modern house in elevated position with front views over Scourie to the bay. 2 ground floor bedrooms.

CNOCLOCHAN

DEER'S HILL, SUTTON ABINGER, NR DORKING, SURREY RH5 6PS
Tel: 01306 730331 Fax: 01306 730913 e.mail: jmwqc@dial.pipex.com

Cnoclochan is on open ground in the middle of Scourie village with views across the bay to Handa Island and over the hills behind the village. Scourie is ideally situated for fishing, bird watching and hill walking on the glorious hills of north west Scotland.

★★ SELF CATERING

Mr J M Williams
Deers Hill, Sutton Abinger, by Dorking, Surrey, RH5 6PS
Tel: 01306 730331 Fax: 01306 730913
E-mail: jmwqc@dial.pipex.com

1 house, 2 pub rms, 3 bedrms, sleeps 6, £200.00-£300.00, Apr-Oct, bus nearby, rail 43 mls, airport 100 mls

Large modern, airy bungalow overlooking village with fine views over Scourie Bay, Handa Island (R.S.P.B. reserve) and beyond.

Shieldaig, Ross-shire — Map Ref: 3F8

★★ SELF CATERING

Mrs D Birtles
Beeches Barn, Ranmoor Hill, Hathersage, Hope Valley, S32 1BU
Tel: 01433 650361

1 house, 2 pub rms, 3 bedrms, sleeps 6-8, £175.00-£300.00, Jan-Dec, bus 7 mls

Traditional cottage on shores of Loch Torridon, with views over to Beinn Alligin and Liathach.

Important: Prices stated are estimates and may be subject to amendments

THE HIGHLANDS AND SKYE

SHIELDAIG – ARMADALE, SLEAT, ISLE OF SKYE

Shieldaig, Ross-shire — Map Ref: 3F8

★★★ SELF CATERING

Mrs Singerton
94 Swievelands Road, Biggin Hill, Westerham, Kent, TN16 3QX
Tel/Fax: 01959 571469

1 cottage, 2-3 pub rms, 3 bedrms, sleeps 5, £200.00-£400.00, Apr-Oct, bus 9 mls, rail 30 mls, ferry 50 mls, airport 80 mls

Comfortable traditional crofting cottage, located in a quiet, peaceful location. Panoramic views overlooking Loch Torridon. Ideal location for those looking to "get away from it all", birdwatchers, hill and mountain walkers and those wishing to explore this interesting part of the West Coast of Scotland.

Aird, Sleat, Isle of Skye, Inverness-shire — Map Ref: 3E11

★★★★ SELF CATERING

Rhoda MacGillivray
7 Aird, Sleat, Isle of Skye, Inverness-shire, IV45 8RN
Tel: 01471 844246
E-mail: rhoda@aird7.freeserve.co.uk
Web: www.aird7.freeserve.co.uk

1 bungalow, 2 pub rms, 2 bedrms, sleeps 4, £140.00-£395.00, Jan-Dec, bus 4 mls, ferry 4 mls

Privately situated modern cottage on working croft. Elevated position with spectacular uninterrupted views across the sea to Ardnamurchan, and Isle of Eigg. 200 yards walk to interesting rocky shoreline.

Ardvasar, Sleat, Isle of Skye, Inverness-shire — Map Ref: 3E11

★ SELF CATERING

Mrs A Kennedy
32 Cedar Road, Cumbernauld, G67 3BH
Tel: 012367 25499
E-mail: ann.kennedy@ukgateway.net

1 cottage, 1 pub rm, 3 bedrms (grd flr avail), sleeps 6, £120.00-£220.00, Apr-Oct, bus ½ ml, ferry 1 1/2 mls, airport 18 mls

Comfortable cottage situated 0.5 miles from Ardvasaar, 2 miles from the Mallaig/Armadale ferry. A peaceful location with sea views, amidst the greenery of this area, Sleat, known as the "Garden of Skye".

★★ SELF CATERING

Sleat Holiday Homes
4 Calligarry, Ardvasar, Sleat, Isle of Skye, Inverness-shire
Tel/Fax: 01471 844278

2 cottages, 2 pub rms, 2 bedrms (All grd.floor), sleeps 4, total sleeping capacity 8, £125.00-£320.00, Jan-Dec, bus ½ ml, rail 6 mls, ferry 1 ml, airport 100 mls

Purpose-built self-catering bungalow. Near village centre. Elevated position with fine views over the sea to Mallaig.

Armadale, Sleat, Isle of Skye, Inverness-shire — Map Ref: 3E11

★★★★ SELF CATERING

Clan Donald Visitor Centre
Armadale Castle, Sleat, Isle of Skye, Inverness-shire, IV45 8RS
Tel: 01471 844305/844227 Fax: 01471 844275
E-mail: office@cland.demon.co.uk
Web: www.cland.demon.co.uk

6 log cottages, 1 pub rm, 2-3 bedrms (grd flr avail), sleeps 4-6, total sleeping capacity 31, min let 2 nights, £300.00-£550.00, Jan-Dec, bus nearby, rail ¼-22 mls, ferry ¼-22 mls, airport 100 mls

Spacious properties on a secluded site overlooking the Sound of Sleat. Convenient for ferry, village and nearby Visitors Centre.

VAT is shown at 17.5%: changes in this rate may affect prices.

Key to symbols is on back flap.

THE HIGHLANDS AND SKYE

BERNISDALE, BY PORTREE, ISLE OF SKYE – BREAKISH, ISLE OF SKYE

Bernisdale, by Portree, Isle of Skye, Inverness-shire — Map Ref: 3D8

★★★ SELF CATERING

Mrs K C MacKinnon
Daldon, Bernisdale, by Portree, Isle of Skye, Inverness-shire, IV51 9NS
Tel/Fax: 01470 532331

Two modern bungalows in small crofting village with private access to secluded site on shore of Loch Snizort. Portree 7 miles (10kms).

2 cottages, 1 pub rm, 2 bedrms, sleeps 4, total sleeping capacity 8, £140.00-£240.00, Jan-Dec, bus 800 yds, rail 40 mls, ferry 40 mls

Borve, by Portree, Isle of Skye, Inverness-shire — Map Ref: 3E8

★★★ SELF CATERING

Mrs M MacDonald
Moorside, Borve, by Portree, Isle of Skye, Inverness-shire, IV51 9P
Tel: 01470 532301

Modern cottages on working croft with views of hills and surrounding countryside. 3.5 miles (7 kms) north of Portree.

2 houses, 2 pub rms, 2 bedrms, sleeps 6, total sleeping capacity 12, £150.00-£250.00, Jan-Dec, bus nearby, rail 45 mls, ferry 40 mls

★★ SELF CATERING

Mrs Mackenzie
24 Borve, Skeabost Bridge, Isle of Skye, Inverness-shire
Tel: 01470 532391

Converted croft house with views to the west. Quiet location yet just off the main Portree to Dunvegan and Uig road.

1 house, 2 pub rms, 3 bedrms, sleeps 5, £160.00-£270.00, Jan-Dec, bus 800 yds

★★ SELF CATERING

Mrs M MacLeod
Chalna, Daviot, Inverness, Inverness-shire, IV2 5XQ
Tel: 01463 772239

Modern bungalow on Highland croft. Ideal home base for exploring Skye. Portree 5 miles (8kms).

1 house, 2 pub rms, 3 bedrms (All grd.floor), sleeps 6, £290.00-£350.00, Mar-Dec, bus 1 ml

Breakish, Isle of Skye, Inverness-shire — Map Ref: 3F10

★ UP TO ★★★ SELF CATERING

Anderson Self-Catering
4 Heaste, by Broadford, Isle of Skye, Inverness-shire
Tel: 01471 822388

Charming, traditional croft house recently renovated. Open fire, central heating and comfort in ideal base for visiting Skye. Price includes all bedlinen, electricity and coal. Flat also available.

1 cottage, 1 pub rm, 2 bedrms, sleeps 4, £200.00-£320.00, Jan-Dec, bus 1/2 ml, rail 7 mls, airport 100 mls

---

Important: Prices stated are estimates and may be subject to amendments

THE HIGHLANDS AND SKYE

BROADFORD, ISLE OF SKYE

Broadford, Isle of Skye, Inverness-shire   Map Ref: 3E10

★★★ SELF CATERING

Mrs Humphrey
Corriegorm Beag, Bayview Crescent, Broadford, Isle of Skye
Tel: 01471 822515 Fax: 01471 822860
E-mail: humphrey@broadbay.freeserve.co.uk

Spacious self contained apartment in quiet area of Broadford. Very well equipped to high standards and with full central heating. Ideal for touring, walking, climbing or cosy winter breaks. Sleeps 2 plus sofa bed available.

1 flat, 1 pub rm, 1 bedrm (All grd.floor), sleeps 4, min let weekend, £230.00-£250.00, Apr-Oct, bus nearby, rail 8 mls, ferry 18 mls, airport 98 mls

★★ SELF CATERING

Mrs Fiona Kennedy
12 Station Road, Blanefield, G63 9HR
Tel/Fax: 01879 230395 Tel: 01360 770756/770677

100 year old traditional croft house in peaceful location in Broadford. Open fires.

1 croft house, 2 pub rms, 2 bedrms, sleeps 4, £175.00-£250.00, Jan-Dec, bus ½ ml, ferry 5 mls

Ptarmigan Cottage
★★★★★ SELF CATERING

Ptarmigan, Broadford, Isle of Skye IV49 9AQ
Tel: 01471 822744 Fax: 01471 822745
e.mail: ptarmigan7@aol.com
Web: http://members.aol.com/ptarmigan7

15 metres from seashore and enjoying truly superb open views over Broadford Bay and harbour. Ideal bird/otter watching – telescope, binoculars and tide clock supplied. Cottage recently transformed to sleep just two people for that very special stay – many extras. Why not spoil yourselves – you will not be disappointed.

★★★★★ SELF CATERING

Mrs Doreen MacPhie
Ptarmigan, Broadford, Isle of Skye, IV49 9AQ
Tel: 01471 822744 Fax: 01471 822745
E-mail: ptarmigan7@aol.com
Web: http://members.aol.com/ptarmigan7

Totally transformed one bedroom house which commands outstanding panoramic views over Broadford Bay and situated metres from the seashore. This luxurious property for non smokers has many additional features including 'His & Her' baths, TV and Hi-fi in the bedroom and a study with personal computer, fax machine and internet connection.

1 cottage, 2 pub rms, 1 bedrm, sleeps 2, £350.00-£700.00, Jan-Dec, bus nearby, rail 8 mls, airport 80 mls.

★★ SELF CATERING

Anne McHattie
10 Waterloo, Breakish, Broadford, Isle of Skye,
Inverness-shire, IV42 8QE
Tel: 01471 822506 Fax: 01471 822465
E-mail: 106334.3425@compuserve.com

Timber built cottage, close to the shore which is rich in fossils and wildlife, looking out over Broadford Bay. A short distance from the village.

1 cottage, 1 pub rm, 2 bedrms (All grd.floor), sleeps 4-6, £150.00-£325.00, Jan-Dec, bus ½ ml, rail 9 mls, ferry 8 mls

VAT is shown at 17.5%: changes in this rate may affect prices.   Key to symbols is on back flap.

CAMUS CROISE, ISLEORNSAY, ISLE OF SKYE – CARBOST, ISLE OF SKYE

THE HIGHLANDS AND SKYE

Camus Croise, Isleornsay, Isle of Skye, Inverness-shire
Map Ref: 3F10

★★ SELF CATERING

Miss M M Fraser
Old Post Office House, Isleornsay, Isle of Skye, Inverness-shire
Tel: 01471 833201

1 cottage, 2 pub rms, 2 bedrms (All grd.floor), sleeps 3, £150.00-£200.00, Jan-Dec, bus nearby, rail 14 mls, ferry 7 mls

Cottage overlooking the Sound of Sleat and the hills of Knoydart beyond. A lovely spot for a peaceful holiday. Ideal base for touring Skye.

Carbost, Isle of Skye, Inverness-shire
Map Ref: 3D9

★★ SELF CATERING

Mr Paul Barter
118 Palace Meadow, Chudleigh, Newton Abbot, Devon, TQ13 0PJ
Tel/Fax: 01626 852266
E-mail: barter@FSBDial.co.uk

1 cottage, 1 pub rm, 3 bedrms, sleeps 6-8, £160.00-£385.00, Jan-Dec, bus 100 yds, rail 31 mls, ferry 30 mls

Modern cottage on secluded croft, with sea and mountain views.

★★ SELF CATERING

Mrs J M Brown
11 Laggan Road, Inverness, IV2 4EH
Tel: 01463 235793

1 cottage, 1 pub rm, 2 bedrms (All grd.floor), sleeps 6, £200.00-£250.00, May-Sep, bus nearby, rail 35 mls

New bungalow in elevated position with panoramic views over Loch Harport. 1 mile from Carbost and The Talisker Distillery.

★★★ SELF CATERING

Mrs Joan M Campbell
1 Carbost Beg, Carbost, Isle of Skye, Inverness-shire, IV47 8SH
Tel: 01478 640242
E-mail: graham@airdbernisdale.demon.co.uk

1 bungalow, 2 pub rms, 2 bedrms (All grd.floor), sleeps 4, £170.00-£260.00, Jan-Dec, bus nearby

Modern bungalow at side of quiet road. Magnificent views across Loch Harport to the Cuillin Hills beyond.

★★ SELF CATERING

Mrs J MacCaskill
3 Carbost Mor, Carbost, Isle of Skye, Inverness-shire, IV47 8ST
Tel: 01478 640236

1 house, 1 pub rm, 3 bedrms, sleeps 6, £180.00-£280.00, Jan-Dec, bus nearby, rail 28 mls, ferry 28 mls, airport 120 mls

Traditional cottage on edge of village of Carbost, overlooking Loch Harport. Close to Glenbrittle and Cuillins. Portree 18 miles (29kms).

Important: Prices stated are estimates and may be subject to amendments

THE HIGHLANDS AND SKYE

CARBOST, ISLE OF SKYE – DUNVEGAN, ISLE OF SKYE

Carbost, Isle of Skye, Inverness-shire — Map Ref: 3D9

★★ SELF CATERING

Dorothy Morrison
8 Satran, Carbost, Isle of Skye, Inverness-shire
Tel/Fax: 01478 640324
E-mail: dorothy.skye@lineone.net

Modern semi-detached cottage in an elevated position, at the head of Loch Harport. Ideal for walkers and climbers.

2 cottages, 1 pub rm, 2 bedrms (All grd.floor), sleeps 2-4, total sleeping capacity 8, min let weekend, £50.00-£200.00, Jan-Dec, bus 300 yds

Clachamish, by Portree, Isle of Skye, Inverness-shire — Map Ref: 3D8

★★★ SELF CATERING

Mrs Charlotte Nicolson
Drumorel, Tayinloan, Clachamish, by Portree, Isle of Skye, Inverness-shire
Tel: 01470 582215

Modern comfortable family cottage on working croft. A rural location and ideal base for all activities based in Skye.

1 house, 2 pub rms, 3 bedrms, sleeps 5, £100.00-£210.00, Jan-Dec, bus nearby, rail 40 mls, ferry 40 mls, airport 33 mls

Dunvegan, Isle of Skye, Inverness-shire — Map Ref: 3D9

★ SELF CATERING

Alistair & Helen Danter
Nuig House, No3 Edinbane, by Portree, Isle of Skye, IV51 9PR
Tel: 01470 582221 Fax: 01470 582323

3 chalets situated on riverbank at foot of 'MacLeod's Table North'. 1/2 mile (1 km) from sea. Excellent hillwalking/ wildlife area. Dunvegan 4 miles (6kms)

3 chalets, 1 pub rm, 2 bedrms (All grd.floor), sleeps 4, total sleeping capacity 12, Jan-Dec, ferry 35 mls

★★★★ SELF CATERING

Anne Gracie
Silverdale, 14 Skinidin, Dunvegan, Isle of Skye, Inverness-shire
Tel/Fax: 01470 521251
E-mail: anne@silverdalebb.idps.co.uk

Newly renovated croft house with open fire. Superb views over Loch Dunvegan. Flight of steps leads to cottage.

1 cottage, 1 pub rm, 1 bedrm, sleeps 2, £240.00-£340.00, Jan-Dec, bus nearby, rail 50 mls, ferry 50 mls

★ SELF CATERING

Mrs A I Johnson
The Beehive, Uiginish, by Dunvegan, Isle of Skye
Tel: 01470 521348

Compact 2 bedroom cottage adjoining owners house. In rural location with splendid views over Loch Dunvegan. Suitable for families with children. The shower is in the double room.

1 bungalow, 1 pub rm, 2 bedrms, sleeps 4, £120.00-£230.00, Mar-Oct, bus 3 mls, rail 48 mls, ferry 48 mls, airport 130 mls

VAT is shown at 17.5%: changes in this rate may affect prices.

Key to symbols is on back flap.

DUNVEGAN, ISLE OF SKYE – ORD, SLEAT, ISLE OF SKYE

THE HIGHLANDS AND SKYE

Dunvegan, Isle of Skye, Inverness-shire — Map Ref: 3D9

★★ SELF CATERING

MacLeod Estate Office
Dunvegan Castle, Dunvegan, Isle of Skye, Inverness-shire
Tel: 01470 521206 Fax: 01470 521205
E-mail: info@dunvegancastle.com
Web: www.dunvegancastle.com

Cottages, individual in character, close to Castle and gardens. Boat trips to seal colony available.

4 cottages, sleeps 6-7, total sleeping capacity 7, from £170.00, Jan-Dec, bus 1 ml, rail 50 mls, ferry 50 mls, airport 40 mls

---

by Elgol, Isle of Skye, Inverness-shire — Map Ref: 3E10

★ SELF CATERING

Strathaird House
Strathaird, Elgol Road, Isle of Skye, Inverness-sire, IV49 9AX
Tel: 01471 866269/01444 452990 (off season)
E-mail: jkubale@compuserve.com
Web: www.gael.net/strathairdhouse

Secluded semi detached cottage to rear of main house. Views of Cuillins and use of extensive grounds. 10 miles (16kms) west of Broadford.

1 self sufficient annexe, 1 pub rm, 2 bedrms (All grd.floor), sleeps 4, £175.00-£250.00, Apr-Sep, bus nearby, rail 20 mls, ferry 20 mls, airport 100 mls

---

Glenbrittle, Isle of Skye, Inverness-shire — Map Ref: 3E10

★ SELF CATERING

MacLeod Estates, Holiday Cottages
Dunvegan Castle, Dunvegan, IV47 8TA
Tel: 01470521 206 Fax: 01470521 205
E-mail: info@dunvegancastle.com
Web: www.dunvegancastle.com

Farm cottage in Glenbrittle. Ideal base for walking, and climbing in the Cuillins.

1 cottage, 1 pub rm, 3 bedrms (grd flr avail), sleeps 6, from £270.00, Apr-Oct, bus 9 mls, rail 45 mls, ferry 45 mls, airport 35 mls

---

Kensaleyre, by Portree, Isle of Skye, Inverness-shire — Map Ref: 3D8

★★★★ SELF CATERING

Mrs C Lamont
Corran House, Kensaleyre, by Portree, Isle of Skye, Inverness-shire
Tel: 01470 532311

Detached recently built bungalow in a quiet rural area overlooking Loch Snizort to Waternish beyond. 8 miles (10kms) from Portree and Uig.

1 cottage, 1 pub rm, 2 bedrms, sleeps 4, £230.00-£270.00, Jan-Dec, bus nearby

---

Ord, Sleat, Isle of Skye, Inverness-shire — Map Ref: 3E10

★ SELF CATERING

Mrs E White
66 Woodend Drive, Glasgow, G13 1TG
Tel/Fax: 0141 954 9013
E-mail: EMMWhite@aol.com

Spacious, homely house in a quiet, picturesque setting with sea and mountain views. A perfect base for peace and relaxation in this secluded corner of Sleat, the "Garden of Skye".

1 house, 3 pub rms, 4 bedrms, sleeps 5-9, £200.00-£550.00, Jan-Dec, bus 4 mls

---

Important: Prices stated are estimates and may be subject to amendments

THE HIGHLANDS AND SKYE

PORTREE, ISLE OF SKYE

Portree, Isle of Skye, Inverness-shire | Map Ref: 3E9

★★★ **SELF CATERING**

Mrs Marlene Grant
2 Fisherfield, Portree, Isle of Skye, Inverness-shire, IV51 9EU
Tel: 01478 612269 Fax: 01478 613553
E-mail: mgrant@ultramail.co.uk
Web: www.gael.net/seafield

A substantial Listed Georgian house on the shore in quiet area of Portree. 1 acre private grounds, spacious and comfortable traditional home.

1 house, 1 bed-sit, 1-2 pub rms, 1-4 bedrms (grd flr avail), sleeps 2-8, total sleeping capacity 10, £120.00-£500.00, Jan-Dec, rail 35 mls

★★★ **SELF CATERING**

Maureen MacKenzie
1 Heatherfield, Portree, Isle of Skye, Inverness-shire, IV51 9NE
Tel: 01478 612972 Fax: 01478 613659

Detached bungalow with double garage, overlooking Portree Village towards the Cuillen Hills. Situated in a quiet residential are yet only a few minutes walk from the centre of Portree. Very well equipped. Total heating. All electricity included.

1 bungalow, 3 bedrms (All grd.floor), sleeps 6, £180.00-£395.00, Jan-Dec, bus nearby, ferry 14 mls

---

★★★ **SELF CATERING**

Mrs Christine MacLean
4 Lower Ollach, Braes, Isle of Skye, Inverness-shire, IV51 9LJ
Tel: 01478 650246

Comfortable modern bungalow in quiet residential area, own garden. 1/4 mile from village centre and all amenities.

1 bungalow, 2 pub rms, 3 bedrms (All grd.floor), sleeps 5, £200.00-£325.00, Jan-Dec, bus 800 yds, rail 34 mls, ferry 34 mls

---

★★★★ **SELF CATERING**

Mrs C R Salt
Cedar Mount, Water End, Brompton, North Allerton, N Yorks, DL6 2RN
Tel: 01609 772433/01478 612048 Fax: 01478 612048

1 very well equipped and comfortable; Three storey Georgian house on the seafront, with magnificent views of harbour and over to Raasay. Many personal touches, 1 private parking, 2 minutes walk to Portree village centre.

1 house, 2 pub rms, 3 bedrms, sleeps 2-6, £250.00-£450.00, Jan-Dec, bus nearby, rail 30 mls

---

★★★ **SELF CATERING**

Sca View Holiday Homes
15 Edinbane, by Portree, Isle of Skye, Inerness-shire, IV51 9PR
Tel/Fax: 01470 582270
E-mail: Edinbane@hotmail.com
Web: www.destination-scotland.com/scaview/

Semi-detached bungalows with panoramic views of Loch Greshornish and the hills beyond. 14 miles (22kms) to Portree. 9 miles (14kms) to Dunvegan.

2 houses, 1 pub rm, 3 bedrms (All grd.floor), sleeps 6, total sleeping capacity 12, £180.00-£300.00, Jan-Dec, bus 1/2 ml

---

VAT is shown at 17.5%: changes in this rate may affect prices.

Key to symbols is on back flap.

PORTREE, ISLE OF SKYE – TORRIN, BY BROADFORD, ISLE OF SKYE — THE HIGHLANDS AND SKYE

Portree, Isle of Skye, Inverness-shire — Map Ref: 3E9

★★ UP TO ★★★ — SELF CATERING

Mrs Pam Simmister
Kiltaraglen, Portree, Isle of Skye, Inverness-shire, IV51 9HR
Tel: 01478 612435

1 house, 1 cottage, 1 pub rm, 2 bedrms (All grd.floor), sleeps 4, total sleeping capacity 6, £160.00-£300.00, Jan-Dec, bus ½ mls, rail 37 mls

Detached cottage and annexe to family house recently refurbished to high standard. Peaceful location, within walking distance of town centre.

Staffin, Isle of Skye, Inverness-shire — Map Ref: 3E8

SCOTTISH TOURIST BOARD INSPECTED — HOLIDAY CARAVAN

Mr John Mackenzie
Booking Enquiries: Mr John Mackenzie
Lynton, Staffin, Isle of Skye, Inverness-shire, IV51 9JS
Tel: 01470 562204/562214

Park accommodation:

Holiday Caravan to let, sleeps 8 £90.00-120.00, Apr-Oct.

By shop and BP station, facing Staffin Bay and islands.

★★★ — SELF CATERING

Mrs P MacDonald, Staffin Bay Holiday Homes
Keepers' Cottage, Staffin, Isle of Skye, Inverness-shire, IV51 9JS
Tel/Fax: 01470 562217

2 bungalows, 1 pub rm, 2 bedrms (All grd.floor), sleeps 4, total sleeping capacity 8, min let weekend, £150.00-£250.00, Jan-Dec, bus nearby, rail 50 mls, ferry 40 mls (bridge to Skye).

Three modern cottages in village of Staffin, overlooking Staffin Bay towards Outer Hebrides. Close to sandy beach and slipway at Staffin, 5 minutes drive to Quirang and Trotternish Ridge.

Tarskavaig, Isle of Skye, Inverness-shire — Map Ref: 3E10

★★★ — SELF CATERING

Mrs J MacGregor
Kilbeg House, Ostaig, Sleat, Isle of Skye, IV44 8RQ
Tel: 01471 844331 Fax: 01471 844490

1 house, 2 pub rms, 2 bedrms, sleeps 4, £150.00-£280.00, Jan-Dec, bus 6 mls, ferry 9 mls

Modernised stone built cottage in quiet crofting community. 6 miles (10 kms) from Armadale ferry terminal.

Torrin, by Broadford, Isle of Skye, Inverness-shire — Map Ref: 3E10

★★★★ — SELF CATERING

Mrs Elizabeth Bushell
Rowanlea, Torrin, by Broadford, Isle of Skye,
Inverness-shire, IV49 9BA
Tel: 01471 822763

1 bungalow, 1 pub rm, 3 bedrms (All grd.floor), sleeps 6, £160.00-£395.00, Jan-Dec, bus nearby

Well equipped bungalow in peaceful crofting village. Magnificent views across Loch Slapin to Blaven. Ideal for nature lovers and climbers. Broadford 6 miles (10kms).

Important: Prices stated are estimates and may be subject to amendments

THE HIGHLANDS AND SKYE

TOTE, SKEABOST BRIDGE, ISLE OF SKYE – SPEAN BRIDGE

Tote, Skeabost Bridge, Isle of Skye, Inverness-shire   Map Ref: 3D8

SELF CATERING ★

Mrs E Dagless
Melton Croft, 5 Tote, Skeabost Bridge, Isle of Skye,
Inverness-shire, IV51 9PQ
Tel: 01470 532251

1 flat, 1 pub rm, 1 bedrm, sleeps 2, £140.00-£190.00, Jan-Dec, bus 1 ml, rail 40 mls, ferry 40 mls

Self contained flat for two people situated on working croft. Overlooking Snizort River and Loch Snizort. Portree 6 miles (10kms).

Uig, Isle of Skye, Inverness-shire   Map Ref: 3D8

SELF CATERING ★★

D C Taylor
The Hermitage, Spey Street, Kingussie
Tel: 01540 661691 Fax: 01540 662137

2 flats, 1-2 pub rms, 1-2 bedrms, sleeps 2-4, total sleeping capacity 6, £150.00-£250.00, Jan-Dec, bus nearby, rail 50 mls, ferry 1 ml

House converted to 2 modern apartments. Magnificent views of Loch Snizort and Uig Bay.

Waternish, Isle of Skye, Inverness-shire   Map Ref: 3D8

SELF CATERING ★★★★

Mrs J L MacDonald
The Tables Hotel, Dunvegan, Isle of Skye,
Inverness-shire, IV55 8WA
Tel/Fax: 01470 521404

1 cottage, 1 pub rm, 2 bedrms (All grd.floor), sleeps 4, £140.00-£400.00, Jan-Dec, rail 40 mls, ferry 50 mls, airport 100 mls

Stone cottage in elevated quiet location with outstanding views. Fully refurbished and equipped to high standards but retaining traditional charm.

SELF CATERING ★★★

M J MacDonald
3 Ardmore, Waternish, Isle of Skye, IV55 8GW
Tel/Fax: 01470 592305
E-mail: amacdo7600@aol.com

1 cottage, 1 pub rm, 3 bedrms (All grd.floor), sleeps 5, £120.00-£300.00, Jan-Dec

Modern bungalow in crofting area, on Waternish peninsula. Outstanding views over the Minch to Outer Isles.

Spean Bridge, Inverness-shire   Map Ref: 3H12

SELF CATERING ★★★

Pam & John Pickering
Burnbank House, Spean Bridge, Inverness-shire, PH34 4EU
Tel/Fax: 01397 712520

12 chalets, 1 pub rm, 1 bedrm, sleeps 2-3, total sleeping capacity 24, min let 2 nights, £155.00-£295.00, Jan-Dec, bus ¼ ml, rail ¼ ml

A very peaceful wooded riverside site, yet within walking distance of village/restaurant. These attractive one bedroomed timber lodges are ideal for couples but 3 can sleep up to 4 on bed-settees, and are fully equipped and newly refurbished. Ideal touring base close to Nevis Range. Walking/fishing from site. Towels/microwave available on request. Drying room for walkers available.

VAT is shown at 17.5%: changes in this rate may affect prices.   *Key to symbols is on back flap.*

SPEAN BRIDGE – STRATHCONON

THE HIGHLANDS AND SKYE

Spean Bridge, Inverness-shire — Map Ref: 3H12

★★★★ SELF CATERING

Mrs Jean Wilson
Tirindrish House, Spean Bridge, Inverness-shire, PH34 4EU
Tel: 01397 712398 Fax: 01397 712595
E-mail: PJI@compuserve.com

1 house, 2 pub rms, 3 bedrms (All grd.floor), sleeps 6, £295.00-£530.00, Dec-Oct, bus 1/2 ml, rail 1/2 ml, airport 60 mls

Superbly equipped three bedroomed single storey house in grounds of historic house where Jacobite Rebellion started. Situated on outskirts of village, ten minutes drive from mountain gondolas and ideal base for touring area, many beauty spots. Terrace and major rooms including sun lounge overlook mountains.

by Spean Bridge, Inverness-shire — Map Ref: 3H12

SCOTTISH TOURIST BOARD INSPECTED
HOLIDAY CARAVAN

Mrs Catherine Cameron
Booking Enquiries: Mrs Catherine Cameron
2 Balmaglaster, Spean Bridge, Inverness-shire, PH34 4EB
Tel: 01809 501289

Park accommodation:

Holiday Caravan to let, sleeps 6 £100.00-165.00, min let weekend (low season), Jan-Dec.

Take A82 22 mls N of Fort William. Turn left at Balmaglaster, Kilfinnan road sign. Caravan at fifth house. Approx 1 1/2 mls up this road.

★★ SELF CATERING

Mrs C Kerr
Corriegour Lodge Hotel, Loch Lochy, by Spean Bridge, Inverness-shire, PH34 4EB
Tel: 01397 712685 Fax: 01397 712696

1 cottage, 1 pub rm, 2 bedrms, sleeps 4, £175.00-£370.00, Jan-Dec, bus nearby, rail 7 mls, ferry 65 mls, airport 52 mls

Cosy, traditional 125 year old highland cottage with open fire. Overlooking beautiful Loch Lochy. Eat at owners' Taste of Scotland restaurant.

Stoer, Sutherland — Map Ref: 3G4

★★★ SELF CATERING

Mrs F A Mackenzie
216 Clashmore, Stoer, Lochinver, Sutherland, IV27 4JQ
Tel/Fax: 01571 855226
E-mail: clashcotts@aol.com

3 cottages, 1-2 pub rms, 1-3 bedrms, sleeps 2-5, total sleeping capacity 11, £160.00-£320.00, Jan-Dec, bus 10 mls, rail 50 mls

Renovated croft cottages in rural setting close to Loch Clash and 3 miles (5kms) from nearest shop. Fishing and sea fishing available locally.

Strathconon, Ross-shire — Map Ref: 4A8

★★★ SELF CATERING

Mrs Jacqueline Cameron
Inverchoran, Strathconon, By Muir of Ord, Ross-shire IV6 7QQ
Tel: 01997 477252

1 bungalow, 1 pub rm, 3 bedrms, sleeps 7, £130.00-£270.00, Jan-Dec

Detached timber cottage, with an open fire, situated in beautiful Strathconon. Ideal for a quiet holiday, walking, fishing, touring or wildlife watching. Very peaceful location.

Important: Prices stated are estimates and may be subject to amendments

THE HIGHLANDS AND SKYE

STRATHPEFFER

Strathpeffer, Ross-shire | Map Ref: 4A8

★★★★ SELF CATERING

Mr & Mrs R Borrows
Fir Lodge, Blackmuir Wood, Strathpeffer, Ross-shire, IV14 9BT
Tel: 01997 421682

Detached Scandinavian style chalets situated in woodland setting about 1 mile from Highland village of Strathpeffer.

2 log cabins, 1 pub rm, 2 bedrms (All grd.floor), sleeps 4, total sleeping capacity 8, £200.00-£310.00, Apr-Oct, bus 1/3 ml, rail 5 mls, airport 20 mls

---

★★★ SELF CATERING

Mrs J Cameron
White Lodge, Strathpeffer, Ross-shire, IV14 9AL
Tel: 01997 421730
E-mail: whitelodge@vacations-scotland.co.uk
Web: www.vacations-scotland.co.uk/whitelodge.html

Detached cottage with own garden, situated in the centre of this charming Victorian Spa village. Ideal base for exploring the Highlands, Wester Ross, the far north or even the islands. Sorry no pets.

1 cottage, 1 pub rm, 2 bedrms, sleeps 4, £275.00-£285.00, Jan-Dec, bus 500 yds, rail 6 mls, airport 23 mls

★★ SELF CATERING

Mrs E MacLean
Castle View, Ardival, Strathpeffer, Ross & Cromarty, IV14 9DS
Tel: 01997 421506

Spacious bungalow with ample off-road parking, quietly situated 2 miles (3km) from the delightful Victorian Spa village of Strathpeffer. Magnificent views from the sun lounge over Strathpeffer and the valley.

1 bungalow, 2 bedrms (All grd.floor), sleeps 4-5, £200.00-£295.00, Mar-Nov, bus 1 ml, rail 4 1/2 mls, airport 28 mls

★★★ SELF CATERING

Nutwood House
Strathpeffer, Ross-shire, IV14 9DT
Tel: 01997 421666 Fax: 01997 421796
E-mail: sally@gilsmith.demon.co.uk

Exceptionally well equipped, charming wing of Victorian country house sleeping four and offering many additional features for your enjoyment and comfort.

1 wing of country house, 1 pub rm, 2 bedrms, sleeps 4, £260.00-£300.00, Mar-Dec, bus nearby, rail nearby

---

VAT is shown at 17.5%: changes in this rate may affect prices. | *Key to symbols is on back flap.*

THE HIGHLANDS AND SKYE

Stromeferry, Ross-shire — Map Ref: 3F9

PORTACHULLIN HOLIDAYS
167 Portachullin, Stromeferry, Ross-shire IV53 8UW
Tel/Fax: 01599 577267

Semi-detached cottage on shores of Loch Carron magnificent sea views to Plockton village and the Cuillins of Skye. Ideal for those with own boats or windsurfers, plenty hill walks in the area with an abundance of wildlife (otters, seals and pine-martins), lots of sea birds.

★★★★ SELF CATERING

Mr Charles R Begg
167 Portachullin, Stromeferry, Ross-shire, IV53 8UW
Tel: 01599 577267

1 cottage, 1 pub rm, 3 bedrms, sleeps 5, min let 4 days, £158.00-£310.00, Jan-Dec, bus 7 mls, rail 3 mls, airport 80 mls

Comfortable, semi-detached cottage on the shores of Loch Carron. Plockton 7 miles (11 kms). A quiet location with an abundance of wildlife, ideal for walkers.

Strontian, Argyll — Map Ref: 1E1

★★★★ SELF CATERING

Gordon Blakeway
Kilcamb Cottages, Strontian, Argyll, PH36 4HY
Tel: 01967 402257 Fax: 01967 402041

1 cottage, 1 pub rm, 2 bedrms (All grd.floor), sleeps 4, Jan-Dec, 2 bathrooms.

Cottage set in extensive hotel grounds with view to river and Loch Sunart.

Talmine, Sutherland — Map Ref: 4A3

★★★★ SELF CATERING

Mrs A Gunn
97 Kenneth Street, Inverness, IV3 5QQ
Tel: 01463 234420

1 bungalow, 2 pub rms, 3 bedrms (All grd.floor), sleeps 5, £160.00-£330.00, Apr-Oct

Modern detached bungalow with magnificent views towards Rabbit Island and Gilean Nan Ron Island. Sandy beaches in the local vicinity, craft shop and Post Office. Ideal location for touring the North Coast, or simply relaxing, enjoying the view, birds and wildlife.

Thurso, Caithness — Map Ref: 4D3

★★ SELF CATERING

Mr L R Maclean
L R M Services Ltd, Meadow Lane, Thurso, Caithness, KW14 8ER
Tel: 01847 894588 Fax: 01847 895808

1 flat, 1 pub rm, 2 bedrms, sleeps 1-6, £135.00-£185.00, Jan-Dec, bus 300 yds, rail ¼ ml, ferry 1 ml, airport 21 mls

Self-contained flat situated in the centre of the town of Thurso. A short walk from the river, and the seafront and the beach. Parking adjacent.

Important: Prices stated are estimates and may be subject to amendments

THE HIGHLANDS AND SKYE — BY THURSO – TRESLAIG, BY FORT WILLIAM

by Thurso, Caithness

Mrs C E MacGregor
Curlew Cottage, Hilliclay Mains, Weydale, by Thurso,
Caithness, KW14 8YN
Tel: 01847 895638

★★★ SELF CATERING

Map Ref: 4D3

1 cottage, 2 pub rms, 2 bedrms (All grd.floor), sleeps 4, min let 3 nights, £195.00-£340.00, Jan-Dec, bus 5 mls, rail 5 mls, ferry 7 mls, airport 20 mls

Delightful cottage with garden in peaceful country setting 4 miles from Thurso and 18 miles from John O' Groats. Warm, spacious and well-equipped with panoramic views - a superb centre for exploring the far north and for day trips to Orkney. Children welcome, cot provided, but regret no pets. Sandy beaches, puffins and peregrines, Scottish primroses, ancient cairns, flow country, 3 golf-courses, salmon and trout fishing - all nearby.

Tomacharich, Inverness-shire

Mr Alistair Smyth
24 Zetland Avenue, Fort William, PH33 6LL
Tel: 01397 702532

★★★★ SELF CATERING

Map Ref: 3H12

1 log cabin, 3 pub rms, 6 bedrms (grd flr avail), sleeps 10, £350.00-£650.00, Jan-Dec

Norwegian log house in peaceful rural setting 3 miles from Fort William. Magnificent views of Aonoch Mhor and Ben Nevis. Offering accommodation of a high standard for up to 10 people. Situated in a large, natural garden with garden shed with storage space for ski's etc.

Tongue, Sutherland

Mrs Margaret Miller
Seacrest, Braehead, Wick, Caithness, KW1 5HL
Tel: 01955 603381

★★★ SELF CATERING

Map Ref: 4A3

1 bungalow, 1 pub rm, 3 bedrms, sleeps 6, £160.00-£220.00, Apr-Oct, bus nearby, rail 40 mls, airport 65 mls

Traditional cottage, set in quiet country location, yet close to village amenities. Enclosed garden with seating area. Ideal location for touring the north coast of Scotland.

Torridon, Ross-shire

The Revd. and Mrs A M Roff
Rowan Glen, Culbokie, Dingwall, IV7 8JY
Tel: 01349 877762
E-mail: 106770@compuserve.com

★★★ SELF CATERING

Map Ref: 3G8

1 bungalow, 1 pub rm, 3 bedrms, sleeps 5, from £220.00, Jan-Dec, bus nearby, rail 25 mls, airport 70 mls

A modern property in quiet location on the slopes of Ben Alligin with open views across Upper Loch Torridon to the mountains. Otters, eagles and deer seen. Open fires and full c.h. Bathroom, separate shower room, 3rd wc. Telephone, washer drier, freezer. In one acre of fenced grounds, including woodland hillside plantation to rear, with pines, rhododendrons, eucalyptus and retreat house. 4 mins footpath walk to beach.

Treslaig, by Fort William, Inverness-shire

MacKay's Agency
30 Frederick Street, Edinburgh, EH2 2JR
Tel: 0131 225 3539 Fax: 0131 226 5284
E-mail: inv283@mackays-scotland.co.uk
Web: www.mackays-scotland.co.uk

★ UP TO ★★★ SELF CATERING

Map Ref: 3H12

2 log cabins, 1 house, 2 cottages, 2 pub rms, 2 bedrms, sleeps 4-6, total sleeping capacity 26, Jan-Dec

Two chalets, two semi detached cottages and one detached cottage, all situated in a peaceful location across Loch Linnhe from Fort William. Excellent outlook towards Ben Nevis.

VAT is shown at 17.5%: changes in this rate may affect prices.

Key to symbols is on back flap.

ULLAPOOL — THE HIGHLANDS AND SKYE

Ullapool, Ross-shire | Map Ref: 3G6

★★★ SELF CATERING

Ardmair Point Chalets
Ardmair Point, Ullapool, Ross-shire, IV26 2TN
Tel: 01854 612054 Fax: 01854 612757
E-mail: P.Fraser@btinternet.com

2 chalets, 1 pub rm, 2-4 bedrms, sleeps 4-6, total sleeping capacity 10, £175.00-£400.00, Jan-Dec, bus nearby, rail 35 mls, airport 60 mls

Well designed and constructed timber chalets. Lochside location with picture windows giving excellent views over the bay and hills beyond.

★★ SELF CATERING

Mrs P E Campbell
5 Custom House Street, Ullapool, Ross-shire, IV26 2XF
Tel: 01854 612107

1 house, 1 bungalow, 1-2 pub rms, 1-2 bedrms (grd flr avail), sleeps 4, total sleeping capacity 8, £280.00-£350.00, Apr-Oct, bus ¼ ml, rail 31 mls, ferry ¼ ml, airport 60 mls

Completely modernised, listed, sandstone houses in quiet conservation area of Ullapool. Each has its own small garden area and off road parking. Ullapool Golf Course near by.

★★★ SELF CATERING

Ms Margaret Gordon
Speyroy, Old Spey Bridge, Grantown on Spey, Morayshire, PH26 3NQ
Tel: 01479 872955/01479 872979
E-mail: denise@ddy790.freeserve.co.uk
Web: www.host.co.uk

1 house, 1 pub rm, 3 bedrms (grd flr avail), sleeps 6, £550.00, Jan-Dec, bus ¼ ml, rail 20 mls, ferry ¼ ml, airport 40 mls

Your comfort and pleasure of stay genuinely considered. Relax and absorb the ambience of the house and wonders of the area. Stunning scenery, sunsets, wildlife and outdoor pursuits. Easy access to village and it's amenities, from Sports Centre, swimming pool, restaurants and entertainments or simply the pleasure of watching the activities of the harbour. Welcome aboard! - The Skipper.

★★ SELF CATERING

Mr B Hicks
16 Ely Gardens, Tonbridge, Kent, TN10 4NZ
Tel: 01732 367827

1 cottage, 2 pub rms, 4 bedrms (grd flr avail), sleeps 8, £180.00-£375.00, Jan-Dec, bus nearby, rail 20 mls, ferry nearby, airport 60 mls

Centrally located, extensive modern detached house within its own garden. Covered garage available. Views towards Loch Broom.

Important: Prices stated are estimates and may be subject to amendments

THE HIGHLANDS AND SKYE

ULLAPOOL

Ullapool, Ross-shire   Map Ref: 3G6

Leckmelm Holiday Cottages
Lochbroom, Ullapool, Ross-shire IV23 2RN   Tel/Fax: 01854 612471

Well-equipped traditional stone cottages, lochside bungalows and timber chalets all in beautiful rural surroundings on Leckmelm Estate. An ideal base for exploring The Highlands or just enjoying the peace and quiet of this 7000 acre private estate.

SELF CATERING ★★

Leckmelm Holiday Cottages
Lochbroom, Ullapool, Ross-shire, IV23 2RN
Tel/Fax: 01854 612471

9 chalets, 7 cottages, 4 bungalows, 1-2 pub rms, 1-4 bedrms (grd flr avail), sleeps 2-10, total sleeping capacity 76, £130.00-£360.00, Jan-Dec, bus 3 1/2 mls, rail 30 mls, airport 60 mls

Compact timber chalets and cottages grouped on a hillside overlooking Loch Broom. 3 miles (5kms) from Ullapool.

SELF CATERING ★ UP TO ★★

Mrs M MacLennan
Invercorrie, Braes, Ullapool, Ross-shire, IV26 2TB
Tel: 01854 612272 Fax: 01854 613180
E-mail: mlas@globalnet.co.uk

1 chalet, 1 cottage, 1 pub rm, 3-4 bedrms (grd flr avail), sleeps 5-6, total sleeping capacity 11, £175.00-£350.00, Jan-Dec, bus 1 ml, rail 30 mls, ferry 1 ml, airport 60 mls

Original croft cottage, extended & modernised. Chalet set amidst trees on original croft land. Both have excellent views across Loch Broom.

SELF CATERING ★★★

Mr & Mrs John Macleod
Tobermory, Moss Road, Ullapool, Ross-shire, IV26 2TF
Tel/Fax: 01854 612392

1 house, 2 pub rms, 4 bedrms (grd flr avail), sleeps 10, £175.00-£375.00, Jan-Dec, bus nearby, rail 55 mls, ferry nearby, airport 63 mls

Large, comfortable house, situated in the centre of Ullapool. Ideal for families, with an enclosed garden to the rear. A good location for access to the shops, eating places, leisure centre, local attractions. Many areas to explore from here to the South, North and East. An abundance of hillwalking for the keen walker. Ground floor rooms with downstairs toilet.

SELF CATERING ★

Mrs MacLeod
Kildonan House, 19 Market Street, Ullapool, Ross-shire, IV26 2XE
Tel: 01854 612110

1 cottage, 1 pub rm, 3 bedrms (grd flr avail), sleeps 6, £250.00-£300.00, Jan-Dec, bus nearby, rail 32 mls

Well equipped house, situated close to the centre of the village of Ullapool. Many facilities within walking distance. Much to do in the area, including climbing, walking, touring, or just enjoying the breathtaking scenery in this part of the West Highlands.

VAT is shown at 17.5%: changes in this rate may affect prices.   *Key to symbols is on back flap.*

ULLAPOOL – BY ULLAPOOL

THE HIGHLANDS AND SKYE

Ullapool, Ross-shire — Map Ref: 3G6

★★★ SELF CATERING

Mr A J Macnab
13 Upper Bourtree Drive, Burnside, Rutherglen, Glasgow, G73 4EJ
Tel: 0141 634 1681 Fax: 0141 570 3901
E-mail: macnabaj@aol.com

Traditional stone built villa in Conservation area of Ullapool. Close to all town amenites.

1 house, 2 pub rms, 4 bedrms, sleeps 10, £295.00-£365.00, Jan-Dec, bus 500 yds

---

★★ SELF CATERING

Mr W G MacRae
Creggan House, 18 Pulteney Street, Ullapool, IV26 2UP
Tel: 01854 612296/612397 Fax: 01854 613396

Cottage in centre of village. Ideal for all amenities, and as base for touring North West Highlands. Private parking available.

1 bungalow, 2 pub rms, sleeps 6, £130.00-£275.00, Jan-Dec, bus 1 ml, ferry 1 ml

---

★★★★ SELF CATERING

Mrs C Mathieson
1a Rhiroy, Lochbroom, by Ullapool, Ross-shire, IV23 2SF
Tel: 01854 655229

Wonderful panoramic views from this compact cottage. Easy access to shoreline, through owners private sheep grazing land. Ullapool 12 miles (19kms).

1 bungalow, 1 pub rm, 2 bedrms (All grd.floor), sleeps 4, £190.00-£240.00, Jan-Dec, bus 4 mls, rail 28 mls, ferry 12 mls, airport 60 mls

---

★★ SELF CATERING

Mrs Pat Turner
16 West Shore Street, Ullapool, IV26 2UR
Tel: 01854 612895

Compact but well equipped and comfortable studio flat, with outlook over the shore, up Loch Broom and to the hills beyond.

1 flat, 1 pub rm, 1 bedrm, sleeps 2, £160.00-£185.00, Jan-Dec, bus 1/4 ml, ferry 1/4 ml

---

by Ullapool, Ross-shire — Map Ref: 3G6

★★★ SELF CATERING

Miss C M MacLeod
13 Mansfield Estate, Tain, Ross-shire, IV19 1JN
Tel: 01862 892178 (not Sun)

Modern bungalow in peaceful situation near end of promontory. Superb views over Loch Broom and to the Summer Isles.

1 bungalow, 1 pub rm, 2 bedrms (All grd.floor), sleeps 4, from £200.00, May-Oct, bus 3 mls, rail 35 mls, ferry 3 mls, airport 65 mls

---

Important: Prices stated are estimates and may be subject to amendments

THE HIGHLANDS AND SKYE

BY ULLAPOOL – WICK

by Ullapool, Ross-shire

Map Ref: 3G6

★★★★ SELF CATERING

Mrs L Renwick
Spindrift, Keppoch Farm, Dundonnell, Ross-shire, IV23 2QR
Tel/Fax: 01854 633269

1 house, 1 flat, 1 pub rm, 2-3 bedrms (grd flr avail), sleeps 3-5, total sleeping capacity 8, £195.00-£365.00, Apr-Oct, bus 4 1/2 mls, rail 30 mls, ferry 12 mls, airport 68 mls

House and apartment, set in peaceful, picturesque location, with beautiful views over Loch Broom and easy acess to the shore. Parking on-site. Short drive to Ullapool, ideal for touring the Highlands.

Whitebridge, Inverness-shire

Map Ref: 4A10

★★ SELF CATERING

Mrs Isabel Ross
Knockie Estate, Whitebridge, Inverness-shire, IV2 6UP
Tel: 01456 486648

1 house, 2 pub rms, 3 bedrms, sleeps 6, £320.00-£380.00, Jan-Dec, bus 3 mls, rail 27 mls, airport 30 mls

Stone built house in quiet location on Knockie Estate, deer stalking and trout fishing can be arranged. 27 miles (43kms) from Inverness.

★★★ UP TO ★★★★ SELF CATERING

Wildside Highland Lodges
Whitebridge, Inverness-shire, IV2 6UN
Tel: 01456 486373 Fax: 01456 486371
E-mail: patricia@wildside-lodges.demon.co.uk
Web: www.wildside-lodges.demon.co.uk

10 chalets, 1-3 pub rms, 1-2 bedrms (grd flr avail), sleeps 1-6, total sleeping capacity 36, min let 1 night, £185.00-£550.00, Jan-Dec, bus nearby, rail 24 mls, airport 24 mls

Situated south of Loch Ness, a small group of well-appointed Fyfestone and Cedar Lodges set along a rocky river bank in an unspoilt nature paradise.

Wick, Caithness

Map Ref: 4E3

★ SELF CATERING

Mrs Banks
Gleneagles, 33 Whitehouse Park, Wick, Caithness, KW1 4NX
Tel: 01955 602487

1 flat, 1 bedrm, sleeps 4, £120.00-£150.00, Jan-Dec, bus 3/4 ml, rail 3/4 ml, airport 1 1/2 mls

Self-contained flat on elevated site overlooking Wick harbour. Conveniently situated a short distance from the town centre. 'Frosty' the pony is a friendly resident of the garden.

VAT is shown at 17.5%: changes in this rate may affect prices.

Key to symbols is on back flap.

Welcome to Scotland

Outer Islands: Western Isles, Orkney, Shetland

THE THREE ARCHIPELAGOS WHICH MAKE UP ORKNEY, SHETLAND AND THE WESTERN ISLES HAVE BEEN ATTRACTING "VISITORS" TO THEIR SHORES FOR LONGER THAN ALMOST ANY OTHER AREA IN BRITAIN, FROM THE PICTS, CELTS AND VIKINGS, BACK THROUGH ANCIENT HISTORY TO NEOLITHIC TIMES. TODAY, HOWEVER, THESE RUGGED ISLAND OUTPOSTS OFFER THE MODERN VISITOR THE MOST WONDERFUL BLEND OF TRADITION, FOLK CULTURE AND ARCHEOLOGICAL SITES IN THE MIDST OF SOME OF THE MOST UNSPOILT ENVIRONMENT ANYWHERE.

Though set on the outer edge of Scotland they are easy to reach, with frequent ferry services and a good air network from the mainland, as well as superb inter-island connections.

From the Isle of Barra, where the Atlantic rollers crash on to deserted white shell-sand beaches, to the dramatic cliffs of the Butt of Lewis, the Western Isles offer a haunting beauty. Wherever you explore, the interplay of land, sea, light, weather and friendly people combines to create a bewitching spell. The gigantic standing stones of Callanish, second only to Stonehenge in grandeur, are an enduring symbol of a long-gone culture, whose purpose is still debated almost 5,000 years later, but you can glimpse a more recent way of life in the peat-smoky interior of the restored Black House at Arnol, now in the care of Historic Scotland.

People come to these islands for numerous reasons, for the abundance of wildlife, the spectacular wildflowers which are seen at their most colourful best on the coastal machair in the spring, for excellent angling in the thousands of lochs and perhaps most of all, for the relaxed pace of life. Space and solitude can be found in abundance, with long empty beaches running almost the length of the west coast, while heather-backed mountains and peat moors combine to create some of the finest scenery in Scotland.

Outer Islands: Western Isles, Orkney, Shetland

Outer Islands: Western Isles, Orkney, Shetland

While the people of the Western Isles are the guardians of a rich, vibrant Gaelic culture, it is another influence, the Norse legacy, which dominates the northern Islands of Orkney and Shetland. It is this Scandinavian past which influences the famous fiddle music, appears on the traditional patterns of woollens and knitwear, and distinguishes the high quality handicrafts, which often include Norse runes and Viking motifs. This unique heritage is also evidenced during the "Up Helly Aa" winter fire festival held in Lerwick, when a full-sized Viking longship is torched.

Shetland has always been a northern crossroads, its commerce bound up with the sea, and its capital, Lerwick, is a characterful town of narrow streets. The island is also full of surprises with its ancient brochs, Iron Age towers and a wealth of natural features offering some of Scotland's greatest natural features. The gentle rolling farmland of Orkney, a patchwork of brilliant greens in high summer, offers a remarkable contrast to Shetland's peat-covered hills and it holds many unusual attractions, including the Neolithic dwellings of Skara Brae, complete with Stone Age sideboards, the wrecks of the scuttled German fleet in Scapa Flow and even the world's shortest scheduled flight.

Whichever set of islands you choose to explore, you can be sure you will return from your holiday quite enchanted, having experienced somewhere completely different from anywhere else in Scotland.

Outer Islands: Western Isles, Orkney, Shetland

Events
Outer Isles

25 Jan
Up Helly Aa'
Lerwick, Shetland
Contact: Lerwick Tourist Information Centre
Tel: 01595 693434

Apr-Dec
Beo Shlaintean
Various venues in the Uists
A mobile exhibition of art and photography depicting trades and professions in Uist, as they were at the start of the Millennium and today.
Contact: Morag Ferguson, Uist 2000
Tel: 01870 602655

May-Sep
Berneray Camp Heritage Exibition
Multi-media heritage exhibition of local archaeological sites and related history, the Borve Croet Centenary and other crofting and fishing issues, island history and folklore as well as our special natural environment.
Community Halls, Isle of Berneray, North Uist, HS6 5BD
Tel: 01876 540334

16-22 Jun
St Magnus Festival
Orkney
Contact: Dorothy Rushbrook
Tel: 01856 872669

*Jul
Cedlars Music School
Music and dance summer school exploring the interconnections between Scottish traditional music, song and dance within the Gaelic community of South Uist.
Tel: 01851 704493

•denotes provisional dates

Area Tourist Boards

Outer Islands: Western Isles, Orkney, Shetland

Orkney Tourist Board

Orkney Tourist Board
8 Broad Street
Kirkwall
Orkney KW15 1NX

Tel: (01856) 872856
Fax: (01856) 875056
Web: www.orkneyislands.com

Western Isles Tourist Board

Western Isles Tourist Board
4 South Beach
Stornoway
Isle of Lewis HS1 2XY

Tel: (01851) 703088
Fax: (01851) 705244
Web: www.witb.co.uk

Shetland Tourist Board

Shetland Islands Tourism
Market Cross
Lerwick
Shetland ZE1 0LU

Tel: (01595) 693434
Fax: (01851) 695807
Web: www.witb.co.uk

Tourist Information Centres

Outer Islands: Western Isles, Orkney, Shetland

Orkney Tourist Board

Kirkwall
6 Broad Street
Orkney
KW15 1DH
Tel: (01856) 872856
Jan-Dec

Stromness
Ferry Terminal Building
The Pier Head
Orkney
Tel: (01856) 850716
Jan-Dec

Western Isles Tourist Board

Castlebay
Main Street
Isle of Barra
Tel: (01871) 810336
Easter-Oct

Lochboisdale
Pier Road
Isle of South Uist
Tel: (01878) 700286
Easter-Oct

Lochmaddy
Isle of North Uist
Tel: (01876) 500321
Easter-Oct

Stornoway
26 Cromwell Street
Isle of Lewis
Tel: (01851) 703088
Jan-Dec

Tarbert
Pier Road
Isle of Harris
Tel: (01859) 502011
Easter-Oct

Shetland Tourist Board

Lerwick
The Market Cross
Shetland
ZE1 0LU
Tel: (01595) 693434
Jan-Dec

ARDHASAIG, ISLE OF HARRIS – SEILEBOST, ISLE OF HARRIS

OUTER ISLANDS

Ardhasaig, Isle of Harris, Western Isles
Map Ref: 3C6

★★★ SELF CATERING

Mrs MacAskill
Clisham House, Ardhasaig, Harris, Western Isles
Tel: 0185950 2066 Fax: 0185950 2077

1 chalet, 3 bedrms (grd flr avail), sleeps 6, £200.00-£250.00, Jan-Dec, ferry 3 mls, airport 36 mls

Modern detached cottage looking over to Ardhasaig Bay to North Harris Hills.

Rhenigadale, Isle of Harris, Western Isles
Map Ref: 3D6

★★ SELF CATERING

Mr Alan Woodward
1a Scaladale, Harris, Western Isles, HS3 3AA
Tel/Fax: 01859 502447

1 cottage, 2 pub rms, 2 bedrms, sleeps 6, £120.00-£200.00, Jan-Dec

Isolated, fifteen minute walk from village. Fully modernised traditional stone built cottage overlooking Loch Seaforth.

Rodel, Isle of Harris, Western Isles
Map Ref: 3C7

★★★★ SELF CATERING

Mrs Norma Green
Ben View, Leverburgh, Isle of Harris, Western Isles, HS5 3TL
Tel: 01859 520300

1 cottage, 1 pub rm, 2 bedrms (All grd.floor), sleeps 4, £225.00-£275.00, Jan-Dec, bus at door, ferry 3 mls, airport 60 mls

A cosy croft cottage, tastefully modernised, with beautiful views of sea and mountains.

Scalpay, Isle of Harris, Western Isles
Map Ref: 3D6

★★★★ SELF CATERING

Mrs Donalda MacLeod
9 Merlin Crescent, Inverness, IV2 3TE
Tel: 01463 236049

1 bungalow, 2 pub rms, 4 bedrms, sleeps 6, £150.00-£250.00, Jan-Dec, bus 1 ml, airport 32 mls

Newly built bungalow, situated on a 9 acre croft, on the peaceful island of Scalpay. Ideal location for a quiet and relaxing stay.

Seilebost, Isle of Harris, Western Isles
Map Ref: 3C6

★★★★ SELF CATERING

Mrs Catherine Morrison
12 Seilbost, Harris, Western Isles, HS3 3HP
Tel: 01859 550205

2 cottages, 1-2 pub rms, 3 bedrms (grd flr avail), sleeps 5-7, total sleeping capacity 12, £260.00-£330.00, Jan-Dec, bus nearby, ferry 10 mls, airport 47 mls

Two cottages looking over a dazzling white sandy bay to the mountains of North Harris. Comfortable and equipped to a high standard.

Important: Prices stated are estimates and may be subject to amendments

OUTER ISLANDS

TARBERT, ISLE OF HARRIS – LAXDALE, ISLE OF LEWIS

Tarbert, Isle of Harris, Western Isles

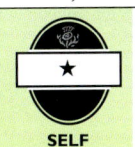

Map Ref: 3C6

★ SELF CATERING

I E Goodfellow
3 Barony Knoll, Jedburgh Road, Kelso, TD5 8JE
Tel: 01573 224791

1 bungalow, 2 pub rms, 3 bedrms, sleeps 7-9, £230.00-£300.00, Mar-Oct, bus 150 yds, ferry ¼ ml, airport 45 mls

Detached bungalow in elevated position above Tarbert. Quiet residential location. Ideal location for touring Harris & Lewis. Hillwalking, birdwatching, sandy beaches within easy reach.

Kirklea Terrace Cottages

Manse Road, Tarbert, Isle of Harris HS3 3DG
Tel: 01859 502364/502138 Fax: 01859 502578

The perfect place to base your holiday on Harris, a charming terrace of four new cottages situated in a peaceful, elevated position overlooking the village of Tarbert. Faced in Harris stone they are tastefully furnished and full of character.

Decorated to an exacting standard, each cottage accommodates 4-6 people.

★★★★ SELF CATERING

Kirklea Terrace Cottages
Manse Road, Tarbert, Isle of Harris, HS3 3DG
Tel: 01859 502364/502138 Fax: 01859 502578

4 houses, 4 pub rms, 2 bedrms, sleeps 4, total sleeping capacity 16, £180.00-£290.00, Jan-Dec, bus 400 yds, ferry 600 yds, airport 36 mls

Terrace of four cottages overlooking Tarbert. Close to ferry. Ideal for touring Harris and Lewis.

Laxdale, Isle of Lewis, Western Isles

Map Ref: 3D4

★★★★ HOLIDAY PARK

Laxdale Holiday Park
6 Laxdale Lane, Laxdale, Lewis, Western Isles, HS2 0DR
Tel: 01851 706966/703234 Fax: 01851 706966
E-mail: gordon@laxdaleholidaypark.force9.co.uk

Booking Enquiries: Mr G Macleod 6 Laxdale Lane, Laxdale, Lewis, Western Isles, HS2 0DR
Tel: 01851 706966/703234 Fax: 01851 706966

2½ acres, mixed, Apr-Oct, latest time of arrival 2400. Extra charge for electricity, awnings, showers.

Park accommodation: 43

6 tourers £8.00-9.00 and 6 motors £8.00-9.00 and 30 tents £7.50-8.50. Total Touring Pitches 42.

3 Holiday Caravans to let, sleep 4-6 £130.00-200.00, total sleeping capacity 18.

From Stornoway (ferry terminal) take the A857 for 1.5 mls to Laxdale. Turn left just before Laxdale River, park is 100m on left.

★★★ SELF CATERING

Gordon Macleod
Woodside, Laxdale Lane, Laxdale, Isle of Lewis, HS2 0DR
Tel: 01851 706966/703234 Fax: 01851 706966
E-mail: gordon@laxdaleholidaypark.force9.co.uk
Web: www.laxdaleholiday.force9.co.uk

1 bungalow, 2 pub rms, 3 bedrms (All grd.floor), sleeps 6, £180.00-£290.00, Jan-Dec, bus nearby, ferry 1½ mls, airport 4 mls

Well equipped accommodation fitted out to high standard. Located only 1.5 miles from Stornoway. Pleasing views over croft land and to Broad Bay.

VAT is shown at 17.5%: changes in this rate may affect prices.

Key to symbols is on back flap.

OUTER ISLANDS

Lochs, Isle of Lewis, Western Isles — Map Ref: 3D5

★★★ SELF CATERING

Katie McLeod
6 Calbost, Lochs, Isle of Lewis
Tel: 01851 880406

1 cottage, 1 pub rm, 3 bedrms (grd flr avail), sleeps 4, £120.00-£170.00, Jan-Dec

Traditional, modernised croft cottage, sitting on hillside with superb views to the front. Ideal for walking and trout fishing.

Point, Isle of Lewis, Western Isles — Map Ref: 3E4

★★ SELF CATERING

Norman Macfarlane
4 Fairney Edge, Ponteland, Northumberland, NE20 9EF
Tel: 01661 860515 Fax: 01661 822264
E-mail: norman@macfarlane.freeserve.co.uk
Web: www.macfarlane1.freeserve.co.uk/mvirneag.htm

1 house, 1 pub rm, 3 bedrms (grd flr avail), sleeps 6, £150.00-£270.00, Jan-Dec, bus nearby, ferry 7 mls, airport 4 mls

Comfortable well equipped house, within easy reach of Stornoway. On local bus route and near airport.

Stornoway, Isle of Lewis, Western Isles — Map Ref: 3D4

★★★★ SELF CATERING

Murdo MacLeod
31 Urquhart Gardens, Stornoway, Lewis, Western Isles
Tel: 01851 702458

2 houses, 1 pub rm, 3 bedrms (All grd.floor), sleeps 5, total sleeping capacity 10, £180.00-£225.00, Jan-Dec, ferry 2 mls, airport 4 mls

Two adjacent properties, compact but comfortable and well equipped, quietly located on the outskirts of Stornoway. Excellent sandy beaches a short distance away. Well situated for exploring Lewis and Harris - much to see and do in the area.

Uig, Isle of Lewis, Western Isles — Map Ref: 3C5

★★ SELF CATERING

Mrs MacKay
2 Melbost, Stornoway, Isle of Lewis, Western Isles
Tel: 01851 704594 (Mon-Sat)

1 cottage, 1 pub rm, 4 bedrms (grd flr avail), sleeps 6, £160.00-£210.00, Jan-Dec, ferry 35 mls, airport 40 mls

Situated in very scenic area near hills and beaches. Ideal for quiet restful holiday.

Nibon, by Hillswick, Shetland — Map Ref: 5F4

★★★ SELF CATERING

Mrs Balfour
Busta, Brae, Shetland
Tel: 01806 522589

1 cottage, 1 pub rm, 2 bedrms, sleeps 4, £110.00-£170.00, Mar-Nov, bus 2 mls

Timber chalet in isolated location overlooking sea and Isles. Safe pebble beach nearby. Ideal for walking and birdwatching. Magnificent cliff scenery makes Nibon ideal for walking, bird watching, landscape painting or just relaxing and enjoying the view.

Important: Prices stated are estimates and may be subject to amendments

OUTER ISLANDS

CLADDACH KIRKIBOST, ISLE OF NORTH UIST – **FINSTOWN**, ORKNEY

Claddach Kirkibost, Isle of North Uist, Western Isles

Map Ref: 3B8

★★ SELF CATERING

Mrs Tosh
Seabreeze, Claddach Baleshare, North Uist, Western Isles
Tel: 01876 580644

1 cottage, 1 pub rm, 2 bedrms, sleeps 4, £190.00-£295.00, Jan-Dec, bus nearby, ferry 10 mls, airport 10 mls

Cottage built on sheep rearing croft overlooking the island of Baleshare. Tidal sandy beach.

Lochportain, Isle of North Uist, Western Isles

Map Ref: 3B7

★★★ SELF CATERING

Alasdair Seale
Trinity Factoring Services Ltd, 209 Bruntsfield Place,
Edinburgh, EH10 4DH
Tel: 0131 447 9911 Fax: 0131 452 8303
E-mail: lph@trinityfactors.co.uk
Web: www.trinityfactors.co.uk

1 house, 2 pub rms, 3 bedrms (All grd.floor), sleeps 6-7, £190.00-£325.00, Jan-Dec, bus nearby, ferry 9 mls, airport 30 mls

Semi-detached cottage, former manse attached to small church in fishing/crofting community 9 miles (14kms) from Lochmaddy. Fine views over bay.

Birsay, Orkney

Map Ref: 5B11

★★★ SELF CATERING

Mrs K Reid
Orkney Self Catering, Finstown, Orkney, KW17 2EH
Tel: 01856 761581 Fax: 01856 875361

1 cottage, 1 pub rm, 3 bedrms (grd flr avail), sleeps 6, £180.00-£380.00, Jan-Dec, ferry 17 mls, airport 22 mls

Cottage full of character in idyllic lochside setting. Peat fire, antique furniture, perfect peace. Close to RSPB reserve, trout lochs and within easy reach of the major archaeological sites. Excellent base for a relaxing stay.

Finstown, Orkney

Map Ref: 5B12

★★★★ SELF CATERING

Mrs K Reid
Atlantis Lodges, Finstown, Orkney, KW17 2EH
Tel: 01856 761581 Fax: 01856 875361

13 lodges, 1 pub rm, 1-2 bedrms, sleeps 2-4, total sleeping capacity 36, £180.00-£380.00, Jan-Dec, bus nearby, ferry 7 mls, airport 10 mls

Self contained apartments at water's edge. Breathtaking views to North Isles. Wildlife to hand close by. Midway between Kirkwall and Stromness. Daily rates available.

★★★★ SELF CATERING

Mrs K Reid
Orkney Self Catering, Finstown, Orkney, KW17 2EH
Tel: 01856 761 581 Fax: 01856 875361

1 house, 3 bungalows, 1-2 pub rms, 2-3 bedrms (grd flr avail), sleeps 4-6, total sleeping capacity 18, £180.00-£380.00, Jan-Dec, bus nearby, ferry 7 mls, airport 10 mls

A novel "upside-down boat" house and five spacious chalets, situated right on the seashore with lovely open views across the Bay of Firth towards Shapinsay.

VAT is shown at 17.5%: changes in this rate may affect prices.

Key to symbols is on back flap.

OUTER ISLANDS

Holm, Orkney

M A Fox — ★★★★ SELF CATERING
Craebreck House, Holm, Orkney Isles, KW17 2RX
Tel: 01856 781220

Map Ref: 5C12

Farmhouse with views to the Southern Isles and from the kitchen window views to Scapa Flow and Hoy.

1 house, 2 pub rms, 4 bedrms, sleeps 7, min let weekend, £170.00-£350.00, Jan-Dec, bus 1 ml

Kirkwall, Orkney

Bilmaris Holiday Homes — ★★★ SELF CATERING
Glaitness Road, Kirkwall, Orkney, KW15 1TW
Tel/Fax: 01856 874515
E-mail: isabel@bilmaris.freeserve.co.uk
Web: www.orkneyislands.com/bilmaris

Map Ref: 5B12

Six holiday homes on outskirts of Kirkwall with outstanding views towards the Northern Isles.

6 chalets, 1 pub rm, 2 bedrms (All grd.floor), sleeps 4, total sleeping capacity 24, min let 4 days, £100.00-£280.00, Jan-Dec, bus 1 ml, ferry 1 ml, airport 3 mls

St Margaret's Hope, Orkney

John Holmes — ★★ SELF CATERING
42 Eglinton Road, Ardrossan, Strathclyde, KA22 8NQ
Tel/Fax: 01294 467642
E-mail: misitu@globalnet.co.uk

Map Ref: 4E1

Small traditional cottage with creature comforts. Superbly sited at water's edge overlooking St Margaret's Hope.

1 cottage, 1 pub rm, 1 bedrm, sleeps 4, £160.00-£180.00, Jan-Dec, bus nearby

Mrs J Rose — ★★ SELF CATERING
The Priory, St Olaves, Great Yarmouth, Norfolk, NR31 9HE
Tel: 01493 488609 Fax: 01493 488265
E-mail: priory@netcomuk.co.uk

Cottage peacefully situated on its own jetty by rocky shore on the edge of picturesque fishing village. Comfortable, centrally heated accommodation in which to base yourselves, as you explore the area, and the rest of Orkney.

1 house, 2 pub rms, 2 bedrms, sleeps 3, £215.00, Jan-Dec, bus 1/4 ml, airport 12 mls

Sanday, Orkney

Mrs S Towrie — ★★ SELF CATERING
Odinsgarth, Sanday, Orkney, KW17 2BN
Tel/Fax: 01857 600347

Map Ref: 5D10

Comfortable recently modernised house, situated close to a large sandy bay on the delightful island of Sanday, with abundant wildlife, walks and tranquility.

1 bungalow, 2 pub rms, 3 bedrms (All grd.floor), sleeps 6, £100.00-£180.00, Jan-Dec, ferry 3 mls, airport 7 mls

---

Important: Prices stated are estimates and may be subject to amendments

OUTER ISLANDS

STROMNESS, ORKNEY – OLLABERRY, SHETLAND

Stromness, Orkney

★★★ SELF CATERING

Mrs Sheila Moore
9 Alfred Street, Stromness, Orkney, KW16 3DF
Tel/Fax: 01856 850817

Map Ref: 5B12

Jan-Dec

Eistigar Holiday Homes consist of a 2 purpose built semi-detached bungalows, each with 2 bedrooms, living room, kitchen and bath or shower room. Both properties sleep 4 and have beautiful views of Stromness, Hoy Sound and the hills of Hoy. Ample parking for guests.

★★ UP TO ★★★ SELF CATERING

Mrs Thomas
Stenigar, Ness Road, Stromness, Orkney, KW16 3DW
Tel: 01856 850438

1 flat, 1 cottage, 1 pub rm, 1-2 bedrms (grd flr avail), sleeps 2-4, total sleeping capacity 6, £100.00-£250.00, Jan-Dec, bus ½ ml, ferry ½ ml, airport 15 mls

Cottage wing and garden cottage on owners' property. Excellent views over Stromness harbour. Adjacent to golf course and yacht club. Explore the delights of this town with its sea-faring history, or visit the many important archaeological sites of Orkney. Whatever you choose to do, you will find this a peaceful and relaxing base.

Westray, Orkney

★★★★ SELF CATERING

Mrs M Bain
Twiness, Rapness, Westray, Orkney, KW17 2DE
Tel: 01857 677319

Map Ref: 5B10

1 cottage, 1 pub rm, 3 bedrms (All grd.floor), sleeps 6, £100.00-£230.00, Jan-Dec, ferry 2 mls, airport 9 mls

Refurbished to a high standard. Comfortable, centrally heated cottage. Situated close to lovely white sandy beaches. Ideal for peaceful holiday. Birdwatching and seals nearby.

Lerwick, Shetland

★★★ SELF CATERING

Mrs I Rutherford
The North House, Gletness, South Nesting, Shetland, ZE2 9PS
Tel: 01595 890219

Map Ref: 5G6

1 flat, 2 pub rms, 2 bedrms (All grd.floor), sleeps 5, £180.00-£275.00, Jan-Dec, bus 250 yds, ferry ½ ml, airport 25 mls

Modern flat in conservation area. Close to town centre, with view over Bressay Sound. Adjacent to children's play area. A couple of hotels within a 2 minutes walk.

Ollaberry, Shetland

★★★ UP TO ★★★★ SELF CATERING

Mr & Mrs Stephen
Sunnyside, Ollaberry, Shetland, ZE2 4RT
Tel: 01806 544277

Map Ref: 5F4

1 house, 1 cottage, 1 pub rm, 3 bedrms (All grd.floor), sleeps 5, total sleeping capacity 10, £100.00-£250.00, Jan-Dec

Modern cottage and traditional croft house on a working croft, in the heart of the community of Bardister. The scenery is varied and makes good walking country.

VAT is shown at 17.5%: changes in this rate may affect prices.

Key to symbols is on back flap.

Hostel Accommodation

Aberdeen Youth Hostel
8 Queens Road
Aberdeen
AB15 4ZT
Tel: 01224 646988
min £10.25 max £12.75 (incl. continental breakfast)
★★ hostel

Dunolly House
Taybridge Drive
Aberfeldy
PH15 2BP
Tel: 01887 820298
min £7.50 max £7.50 (groups only)

Achininver Youth Hostel
Achiltibuie
Ullapool
Ross-shire
IV26 2YL
Tel: 01854 622254
min £6.50 max £6.50
★ hostel

Gerry's Achnashellach Hostel
Craig
Achnashellach
Strathcarron
Wester Ross
IV54 8YU
Tel: 01520 766232
min £9.00 max £10.00

Carbisdale Castle Youth Hostel
Culrain
Ardgay
Sutherland
IV24 3DP
Tel: 01549 421232
min £10.27 max £13.25
★★★ hostel

Armadale Youth Hostel
Ardvasar
Sleat
Isle of Skye
IV45 8RS
Tel: 01471 844260
min £7.00 max £9.00
★ hostel

Arle Farm Lodge
Aros
Isle of Mull
PA72 6JS
Tel: 01680 300343
min £11.00 max £12.00
★★★ hostel

Ardgartan Youth Hostel
Arrochar
Dumbartonshire
G83 7AR
Tel: 01301 702362
min £9.50 (jnr) max £10.75 (snr)
★★ hostel

Aviemore Youth Hostel
25 Grampian Road
Aviemore
Inverness-shire
PH22 1PR
Tel: 01479 810345
min £10.50 max £13.00
★★ hostel

Loch Morlich Youth Hostel
Aviemore
Glenmore
PH22 1QY
Tel: 01479 861238
min £8 max £9.25
★★ hostel

Ayr Youth Hostel
5 Craigweil Road
Ayr
KA7 2XJ
Tel: 01292 262322
min £8.00 (jnr) max £9.25 (snr)
★★ hostel

Cannich Youth Hostel
Beauly
Inverness-shire
IV4 7LT
Tel: 01456 415244
★★ hostel

Glen Affric Backpackers
Cannich
By Beauly
Inverness-shire
IV4 7LT
Tel: 01456 415263
min £6.00 max £7.00

Taigh Na Cille Bunkhouse
22 Baliviawich
Benbecula
Western Isles
Tel: 01870 602522
min £10 max £10

Cairnwell Mountain Sports
Gulabin Lodge Spittal of Glenshee
By Blairgowrie
Perthshire
PH10 7QE
Tel: 01250 885255
min £10 per person max £4 (per day for a group booking)

Braemar Youth Hostel
21 Glenshee Road
Braemar
Aberdeenshire
AB35 5YQ
Tel: 013397 41659
min £7.95 max £9.25
★★ hostel

Inverey Youth Hostel (S.Y.H.A.)
By Braemar
Aberdeenshire
AB35 5YB
min £5.75 (under 18)
max £6.50 (18 & over)
★ hostel

Fossil Bothy Hostel
13 Lower Breakish
Isle of Skye
Inverness-shire
IV42 8QA
Tel: 01471 822644/ 822297
min £7.50 max £8.00

Broadford Youth Hostel
Broadford
Isle of Skye
IV49 9AA
Tel: 01471 822442
min £9.00 max £10.00
★★★ hostel

Trossachs Backpackers
Invertrossachs Road
Callander
FK17 8HW
Tel: 01877 331200
min £10.00 max £15.00

John O'Groats Youth Hostel
Canisbay
Near Wick
Caithness
KW1 4YH
Tel: 01955 611424
min £7.00 (under 18)
max £8 (18 & over)
★★ hostel

Glenbrittle Youth Hostel
Glenbrittle
Carbost
Isle of Skye
IV47 8TQA
Tel: 01478 640278

Hostel Accommodation

Glendoll Youth Hostel
Glendoll
Clova, Near Kirriemuir
Angus
DD8 4RD
Tel: 01575 550236
★ hostel

Coldingham Youth Hostel
Coldingham Sands
Coldingham
Berwickshire
TD14 5PA
Tel/fax: 01890 771298
min £7.25 (jnr) max £8.25 (snr)
★★ hostel

Colonsay Backpackers Lodge
Isle of Colonsay
Argyll
PA61 7YU
Tel: 01951 200312
min £8.50 (inc. linen in dorms)
max £10.00 (inc. linen in twin rooms)

Farr Cottage Activity Centre
Farr Cottage
Corpach
By Fort William
PH33 7LR
Tel: 01397 772315
min £10.00 max £11.00

The Smiddy Bunkhouse
Snowgoose Mountain Centre
The Old Smiddy
Station Road
Corpach, Fort William
PH33 7JH
Tel: 01397 772467
min £7.00 max £8.50

Crianlarich Youth Hostel (S.Y.H.A.)
Station Road
Crianlarich
Perthshire
FK20 8QN
Tel: 01838 300260
min £7.75 (member) max £9.00 (member)
★★ hostel

Braincroft Bunkhouse
Braincroft
By Crieff
Perthshire
PH7 4JZ
tel: 01764 670140
min £7.50 max £9.50

Kilravock Castle Granary Youth Hostel
Kilravock Castle
Croy
Inverness-shire
IV2 7PJ
Tel: 01667 493258
min £5 (pppn) (minimum group 16 or £80)

Cunningsburgh Village Club
Cunningsburgh
Shetland
Tel: 01950 477294
min £4.00 max £5.00

Kendoon Youth Hostel
St John's Town of Dalry
Kirkudbright
DG7 3UD
Tel: 01644 460680
Min £5.75 max £6.75
★ hostel

Glendevon Youth Hostel
Glendevon
Dollar
Clackmananshire
FK14 7JY
Tel: 01259 781206
min £6.00 max £6.75
★ hostel

Bunkhouse B&B
Silver Fir
Carndubh
Dornie
By Kyle of Lochalsh
IV40 8EP
Tel: 01599 555264
min £8.50 max £10.00 (with bedding)

Loch Ness Backpackers Lodge
Coiltie Farmhouse
East Lewiston
Drumnadrochit
IV63 6UJ
Tel: 01456 450807
min £8.50 max £9.50

Sail Mhor Croft Independent Hostel
Camusnagaul
Dundonnell
Ross-shire
IV23 2QT
Tel: 01854 633224
min £8.50 max £8.50

City Centre Tourist Hostel
5 West Register Street
Edinburgh
Mid Lothian
EH2 2AA
min £10 max £15 (in August)

Princes Street Backpackers East
5 West Register Street
Edinburgh
EH2 2AA
Tel: 0131 556 6894
min £7.50 (dorm) £22.50 (double, long term)
max £9.50 (dorm) £24.00 (double)

Edinburgh Eglinton Youth Hostel
18 Eglinton Crescent
Edinburgh
EH12 5DD
Tel: 0131 337 1120
min £10.75 (incl. breakfast)
max £13.75 (incl. breakfast)
★★ hostel

Bruntsfield Youth Hostel
7 Bruntsfield Crescent
Edinburgh
EH10 4EZ
Tel: 0131 447 2994
min £10.00 max £16.25
★★ hostel

Cowgate Hostel
94-112 Cowgate
Edinburgh
EH1 1JN
Tel: 0131 226 7355
min £12.00 (July-September)
max £16.00 (August)

Princes Street West Backpackers
3 Queensferry Street
Edinburgh
EH2 4PA
Tel: 0131 226 2939
min £10.00 max £14.00

Belford Hostel
6/8 Douglas Gardens
Edinburgh
EH4 3DA
Tel: 0131 225 6209 (reception)
0131 221 0022 (reservations)
min £10.50 (dorm) £30 (dbl/twin room)
max £15.00 (dorm) £45.00 (dbl/twin room

Edinburgh Backpackers
65 Cockburn Street
Edinburgh
EH1 1DU
Tel: 0131 220 1717
min £11.50 (dorm) £37.50 (dbl)
max £13.50 (dorm) £42.50 (dbl)

Hostel Accommodation

Castle Rock Hostel
15 Johnston Terrace
Edinburgh
EH1 2PW
Tel: 0131 225 9666
min £10.00 max £13.00

High Street Hostel
8 Blackfriars Street
Edinburgh
EH1 1NE
Tel: 0131 557 2981
min £9.90 max £12.00

Backpackers Royal Mile
105 High Street
Edinburgh
EH1 1SG
Tel: 0131 557 6120
min £9.90 max £12.00

The Glebe Barn
Isle of Eigg
PH42 4RL
01687 482417
min £8.50 Group Booking £9.00 per person
Max £11.00 per person, Twin room

Black Rock Bunkhouse
Evanton
Ross-shire
IV16 9UN
Tel: 01349 830917
min £7.50 max £9.50

Dun Flodigarry Hostel
Flodigarry
By Staffin
Isle of Skye
IV51 9HZ
min £7.50 max £9.00

Ben Nevis Bunkhouse
Achintree Farm Guest House
Fort William
PH33 6TE
Tel: 01397 702240
min £8.50 max £10.50

Bank Street Lodge
Bank Street
Fort William
Tel: 01397 700070
min £8.00 max £13.00

Fort William Backpackers
Alma Road
Fort William
PH33 6HB
Tel: 01397 700711
min £9.50 max £13.00

Glen Nevis Youth Hostel
Fort William
PH33 6ST
Tel: 01397 702336
Min £10.25 max £12.75

Loch Ossian Youth Hostel
Corrour
By Fort William
Inverness-shire
PH30 4AA
Tel: 01397 732207
min £6.00 max £6.75
★ hostel

Achtercairn Hostel
Gairloch Sands Self Catering Apartments
Gairloch
Ross-shire
IV21 2BH
Tel: 01445 712131
min £7.00 max £8.00

Badachro Bunkhouse
Badachro
Gairloch
Ross-shire
IV21 2AA
Tel: 01445 741291 (adv bookings)
      01445 741382 (imm. bookings)
min 38.50 max £8.50 (incl linen)

Rua Reidh Lighthouse Hostel
Melvaig
Gairloch
Wester-Ross
IV21 2EA
Tel: 01445 771263
min £7.50 max £15.00

Glasgow Youth Hostel
7/8 Park Terrace
Glasgow
G3 6BY
Tel: 0141 332 3004
min £11.25 max £12.75
★★★ hostel

Glencoe Bunkhouses
Leacantium Farm
Glencoe
PA39 4HX
Tel: 01855 811256
min £6.50 max £7.50
★★ hostel

Loch Ness Youth Hostel
Glenmoriston
Inverness-shire
IV63 7YD
Tel: 01320 351274
min £8.00 max £7.00
★★ hostel

Speyside Backpackers
15/16 The Square
Grantown-on-Spey
Moray
PH26 3LG
Tel: 01479 873514
min £8.50 max £10.00

Inverness Youth Hostel
15A Victoria Drive
Inverness
IV2 3QB
Tel: 01463 231771
min £10.75 max £12.25
★★★ hostel

Dalneigh Hall
St. Ninian Drive
Inverness
IV3 5AU
Tel: 01463 239753
min £8.00 max £17.00

Inverness Student Hostel
8 Culduthel Road
Inverness
IV2 4AB
Tel: 01463 236556
min £9.00 max £10.50

Bazpackers Hostel
4 Culduthel Road
Inverness
IV2 4AB
Tel: 01463 717663
min £8.00 max £9.00

Eastgate Backpackers Hostel
38 Eastgate
Inverness
IV2 3NA
Tel: 01463 718756
min £8.00 max £8.90

Kerrera Bunkhouse
Lower Gylen Farmhouse
Isle of Kerrera, By Oban
Argyll
PA34 4SX
Tel: 01631 570223
min £7.50 max £7.50

Killin Youth Hostel
Main Street
Killin
Perthshire
FK21 8TN
Tel: 01567 820546
min £8.50 max £8.50
★★ hostel

Hostel Accommodation

Kirkbeag Hostel
Kincraig
Kingussie
PH21 1ND
Tel: 01540 651298
min £8.50 max £9.00

Kinlochewe Hotel Bunkhouse
Kinlochewe
By Achnasheen
Wester Ross
IV22 2PA
Tel: 01445 760225
min £8.00 max £8.00

Highland Trading Post
Wades Road
Kinlochleven
Argyll
PA40 4QL
min £5.00 (jnr) max £8.oo (snr)

The West Highland Lodge Bunkhouse
Kinlochleven
Argyll
PA40 4RT
Tel: 01855 831471
min £5.00 max £12.00

Kirkwall Youth Hostel
Old Scapa Road
Kirkwall
Orkney
KW15 1BB
Tel: 01856 872243
min £8.50 (15-17yrs)
max £9.50 (18yrs)
★★ hostel

Peedie Kirkwall Hostel
Ayre Road
Kirkwall
Orkney Isles
Tel: 01856 875477
min £10.00 max £10.00

Kirk Yetholm Youth Hostel
Kirk Yetholm
by Kelso
Roxburghshire
TD5 8PG
Tel: 01786 891400
★★ hostel

Ratagan Youth Hostel
Glenshiel
Kyle
Ross-shire
IV40 8HP
Tel: 01599 511243
min £7.75 max £9.00
★★★ hostel

Skye Backpackers
Kyleakin
Isle of Skye
Tel: 01599 534510
min £8.90 max £13.00

Durness Youth Hostel
Smoo
Lairg
Sutherland
IV27 4QA
Tel: 01971 511244
min £5.75 max £7.50
★ hostel

Lerwick Youth Hostel
Islesburgh House
King Harald Street
Lerwick
Shetland
ZE1 0EG
Tel: 01595 692114
min £8.00 (under 18)
max £9.25 (18 & over)

Am Bothan Leverburgh Bunkhouse
Brae House
Ferry Road
Leverburgh
Isle of Harris
HS5 3UA
Tel: 01859 520251
min £10.00 max £12.00

Achmelvich Youth Hostel (S.Y.H.A.)
Lochinver
Sutherland
IV27 4JB
Tel: 01571 844480
min £5.75 (jnr) max £6.50 (snr)
★ hostel

Lochranza Youth Hostel
Lochranza
Isle of Arran
KA27 8HL
Tel: 01770 830631
min £8.00 max £9.25
★★ hostel

Ardintigh Highland Adventure Centre
Ardintigh
Loch Nevis
Mallaig
Inverness-shire
PH40 4PA
Tel: 01687 462274
min £65 + VAT pp p week (for groups of 12-30 persons)

Sheena's Backpackers Lodge
Harbour View
Mallaig
Inverness-shire
PH41 4PU
Tel: 01687 462764
min £9.50 max £9.50

Melrose Youth Hostel
Priorwood
High Road
Melrose
TD6 9EF
min £10.00 (under 18)
max £11.25 (18 & over)
★★ hostel

New Lanark Youth Hostel
Wee Row
Rosedale Street
New Lanark
ML11 9DJ
Tel: 01555 666710
min £9.50 max £10.75
★★★ hostel

Minnigaff Youth Hostel
Newton Stewart
Wigtonshire
DG8 6PL
Tel: 01671 402211
min £7.25 max £8.25
★★ hostel

Newtonmore Independent Hostel
Craigellachie House
Main Street
Newtonmore
Inverness-shire
PH20 1DA
Tel: 01540 673360
min £7.22 (pppn groups only)
max £9.00 (pppn)

Jeremy Inglis Hostel
21 Airds Crescent
Oban
Argyll
PA34 4BA
Tel: 01631 565065
min £6.50 max £7.50
★ hostel

Oban Backpackers
Breadalbane Street
Oban
Argyll
PA34 5NZ
Tel: 01631 562107
min £8.50 (off-season)
max £10.00 (on-season)

Hostel Accommodation

Oban Youth Hostel (S.Y.H.A.)
Esplanade
Oban
PA34 5AF
Tel: 01631 562025
min £10.25 max £12.75
★★ hostel

Papa Westray Youth Hostel
Beltane House
Papa Westray
Orkney
KW17 2BU
Tel: 01857 644267
min £8.00 max £9.00

Perth Youth Hostel (S.Y.H.A.)
Glasgow Road
Perth
PH2 0NS
Tel: 01738 623658
min £8.00 max £9.25
★★ hostel

Plockton Station Bunkhouse
Burnside
Plockton
IV52 8TF
Tel: 01599 544235
min £8.50 max £10.

Islay Youth Hostel
Port Charlotte
Isle of Islay
Argyll
PA48 7TX
Tel: 01496 850385
★★ hostel

Croft Bunkhouse & Bothies
7 Portnalong
Isle of Skye
Inverness-shire
IV47 8SL
Tel: 01478 640254
min £6.50 max £8.00 (twinroom)

Skyewalker Independent Hostel and Cafe
Portnalong Post Office
Fiscavaig Road
Portnalong
Isle of Skye
IV47 8SL
min £7.00 (per bed per night)
max £8.50 (per bed per night)

Portree Independent Hostel
The Old Post Office
Portree
Isle of Skye
Inverness-shire
IV51 9BT
Tel: 01478 613737
min £7.50 max £9.50

Raasay Youth Hostel
Creachan Cottage
Raasay
By Kyle
IV40 8NT
Tel: 01478 660240
min £6.00 max £7.00
★ hostel

Rowardennan Youth Hostel
Rowardennan
By Drymen
Tel: 01360 870259
min £8.00 max £9.25
★★ hostell

Rousay Hostel
Trumland Farm
Rousay
Orkney
KW17 2PU
Tel: 01856 821252
min £3.00 (campers with tents)
max £9.00

Hairy Coo Backpackers
Torvaig House
Knock Bay
Sleat
Isle of Skye
IV44 8RJ
Tel: 01471 833231
min £9.00 (dorm)
max £25 (double/ twin room)

Sleat Independent Hostel
The Glebe
Kilmore
Sleat
Isle of Skye
IV44 8RG
Tel: 01471 844440/ 272
min £8.00 max £8.00

Ravens Point Visitors Centre (Hostel)
Kershader
South Lochs
Isle of Lewis
Tel: 01851 880236
min £6.00 (jnr groups) £7.00 (snr groups)
max £7.00 (jnr single) £8.00 (snr single)

Loch Lochy Youth Hostel
South Laggan
Spean Bridge
Inverness-shire
PH34 4EA
Tel: 01809 501239
min £7.00 max £9.00
★★ hostel/wc

Scottish Youth Hostels
7 Glebe Crescent
Stirling
FK8 2JA
Tel: 01786 891400
min £6.50 max £13.25 (incl. breakfast)

Stornoway Backpackers Hostel
47 Keith Street
Stornoway
Isle of Lewis
Tel: 01851 703628
min £9.00 max £9.00

Elsick House Youth Hostel
Strathpeffer
Ross-shire
IV14 9BT
Tel: 01997 421532
★★ hostel

Hoy Outdoor Centre
Hoy
Stromness
Orkney
Tel: 01856 791261
min £5.75 max £6.50

Thurso Youth Club Hostel
Old Mill
Millbank Road
Thurso
Caithness
KW14 8PS
Tel: 01847 892964
min £8.00 (B&B)
max £8.00 (B&B)

Tobermory Youth Hostel
Main Street
Tobermory
Isle of Mull
PA75 6NU
Tel: 01688 302481
min £7.50 max £9.50
★★★ hostel

Hostel Accommodation

Tomintoul Youth Hostel (S.Y.H.A.)
Main Street
Tomintoul
Ballindalloch
Banffshire
AB3 9HA
Tel: 01807 580282
min £5.75 (jnr) max £6.50 (snr)
★ hostel

Tomintoul Bunkhouse
the Square
Tomintoul (Adjacent to the Gordon Hotel)
Banffshire
AB38 9ET
Tel: 01807 580 206
min £7.00 mx £10.75
(incl. breakfast in the Gordon Hotel)

Tongue Youth Hostel
Tongue
By Lairg
Sutherland
IV27 4XH
Tel: 01847 611301
min £7.00 (under 18)
max £8.00 (over 18)
★★ hostel

Torridon Youth Hostel
Torridon
Achnasheen
Wester Ross
IV22 2EZ
Tel: 01445 791284
min £7.75 max £9.00
★★ hostel

Uig Youth Hostel
Uig
Isle of Skye
IV51 9YD
Tel: 01470 542211
min £7.25 (jnr) max £8.25 (snr)
★★ hostel

Ullapool Youth Hostel
22 Shore Street
Ullapool
Ross-shire
IV26 2UJ
Tel: 01854 612254
min £7.75 max £9.00
★★ hostel

Ullapool Tourist Hostel
West House
West Argyll Street
Ullapool
Ross-shire
IV26 2TY
Tel: 01854 613126
min £9.50 max £15.50

Whiting Bay Youth Hostel
Shore Road
Whiting Bay
Isle of Arran
KA27 8QW
Tel: 01770 700339
min £7.25 (under 18)
max £8.25 (18 & over)
★★ hostel

Wanlockhead Youth Hostel (S.Y.H.A.)
Lotus Lodge
Wanlockhead, By Biggar
Lanarkshire
ML12 6UT
Tel: 01659 74252
min £7 (jnr-under 18)
max £8 (snr- 18 & over)
★ hostel

Broadmeadows Youth Hostel (S.Y.H.A.)
Yarrowford
Selkirk
TD7 5LZ
Tel: 01750 76262
fixed: £5.75 (under 18)   £6.50 (18 & over)
★★ hostel

Facilities
For Visitors with Disabilities

The Scottish Tourist Board, in conjunction with the English and Wales Tourist Boards, operates a national accessible scheme that identifies, acknowledges and promotes those accommodation establishments that meet the needs of visitors with disabilities.

The three catagories of accessibility, drawn up in close consultation with specialist organisations concerned with the needs of people with disabilities are:

CATEGORY 1

Unassisted wheelchair access for residents

CATEGORY 2

Assisted wheelchair access for residents

CATEGORY 3

Access for residents with mobility difficulties

CATEGORY 1

Arlabeag Aros
Isle of Mull
PA72 6JS

Loch Ewe Holiday Cottage
17 Mellon Charles
Aultbea
Ross-shire
IV22 2JN

31 Mellon Charles
Aultbeaby
Achnasheen
Ross-shire
IV22 2JQ

Byre Cottage
Sunny Oaks
Whitefarland
Isle of Arran
KA27 8HP

Delgatie Castle
Turriff
Aberdeenshire
AB5 7TD

Eildon Holiday Cottages
Dingleton Mains
Melrose
Roxburghshire
ID6 9HS

High Range Holiday Lodges
Aviemore
Inverness-shire
PH22 1PT

Kingennie Lodges
Kingennie
Broughty
Ferry
Tayside
DD5 3RD

Miss M Brook
Lochletter Lodges
Balnain
Drumnadrochit
IV3

Northbay House
Balnabodach
Castlebay
Isle of Barra
Western Isles
HS9 5UT

CATEGORY 2

2A Laide
Laide
Ross-shire
IV22

3 Keith Row
Edinburgh
Midlothian
EH4 3NL

Appin House Apartments
Appin
Argyll
PA38 4BN

Arrochar
Well Brae
Pitlochry
Perthshire
PH16 5HG

Avon Glen Chalets
Melons Place
Melons Place Farm
Maddiston
FK2 0BT

Badanfhuarain Cottage & Flox Cottage
Nethybridge
Inverness-shire
PH25

Brewhouse Flat & Royal Artillery Cottage
Culzean Castle
Maybole
Ayrshire
KA19 8JX

Brunston Castle
Holiday Resort
Dailly
Ayrshire
KA26 9GB

Burnside Apartments
19 West Moulin Road
Pitlochry
Perthshire
PH16 5EA

Cairncross House
20 Kelvinhaugh Place
Glasgow
G3 8NH

Facilities
For Visitors with Disabilities

Caledonian Court
Glasgow Caledonian University
Caledonian Court
G4

Carden Self-catering
Alves by Elgin
Moray
IV30 3UP

Craigadam Lodge
by Castle Douglas
DG7 3HU

Crook Cottage and Elspinhope
Ettrick Valley
Selkirk
TD7 5JB

Crosswoodhill Farm
By West Calder
West Lothian
EH55 8LP

Crubenbeg Farm Steadings
Newtonmore
Inverness-shire
PH20 1BE

Deersound Cottage
Halley Road
Deerness
Orkney
KW17 2QL

Drumcroy Lodges
Mairns of Murthly
Aberfeldy
Perthshire
PH15 2EA

Dunalastair Holiday Houses
Dunalastair Estate
Kinloch Rannoch By Pitlochry
Perthshire
PH16 5PD

Dunsmore Lodges
By Beauly
Inverness-shire
IV4 7EY

East Faldonside Lodge
Melrose
TD6 9BG

Glen Tanar Estate
Brooks House
Glen Tanar Aboyne
Aberdeenshire
AB34 5EU

Glenprosen Cottages
Balnaboth Glenprosen
Kirriemuir
Angus DD8 4SA

Greenbank
Waternish
Isle of Skye
IV55 8GL

Hillhead Halls
University of Aberdeen
Aberdeen
AB24 1WU

Kilmardinny Estate
Milngavie Road
Bearsden
Glasgow
G61 3DH

Little Swinton Cottages 25 & 6
Little Swinton
Coldstream
Berwickshire TD12 4HH

Loch Tay Lodges
Remony
Aberfeldy
Perthshire
PH15 2HR

Lochland Chalets
Dounby
Orkney
KW17 2HR

Mar Lodge
Braemar
Ballater
Aberdeenshire AB35 5YJ

Mountview Self-catering
70 Baddidarrach
Lochinver
Sutherland
IV27 4LP

Mr A P Davis
Roskhill Barn Flats
Roskhill by Dunvegan
Isle of Skye
IV55 8ZD

Mr D M Buchanan
Mill Lodge & Burnside Lodge
Geddes Nairn
Inverness-shire
IV12 5SA

Napier University
Morrison Crescent &
West Bryson Road
Edinburgh
EH10 4HR

Oak Tree Cottage
Duror of Appin
Argyll
PA32 6XN

Parkmore Farm
Dufftown Keith
Banffshire
AB55 4DN

Pier North
The Pier Melfort
Kilmelford by Oban
Argyll
PA34 4XD

Pine Bank Chalets
Dalfaber Road
Aviemore
Inverness-shire
PH22 1PX

Premier Vacations
Aviemore
Inverness-shire
PH22 1PX

Rookery Nook
56 Culcabock Avenue
Inverness
Inverness-shire
IV2 3RQ

Silverglades Holiday Homes
Aviemore
Inverness-shire
PH22 1TD

Stable Cottage
Kirkton
Hawick
Roxburghshire
TD9

Facilities
For Visitors with Disabilities

Synton Mains Farm
The Davies Partnership
Ashkirk
Selkirk
TD7 4PA

Tigh an Daraich
Bridge of Awe
Taynuilt
Argyll
PA35 1HR

Tree Tops & Kestrels Nest
Laikenbuie
Grantown Road
Nairn
IV12 5QN

University of Abertay
Dundee
Bell Street
Dundee
DD1 1HG

Willow Croft
Big Sand
Gairloch
Ross-shire
IV21 2DD

Woolman Hill & Kepplestone Flats
John Street & Queens Road
Aberdeen
Aberdeenshire
AB10

CATEGORY 3

1/2 6 Valtos
Staffin by Portree
Isle of Skye
IV51

2 Burnmouth Road
Little Dunkeld
Dunkeld
Perthshire
PH8

Ailanbeg Cottage
Ailanbeg Lodge
Nethy Bridge
Inverness-shire
PH25 3DR

Aithness
Fetlar
Shetland
ZE2 9DJ

An Bothan
8 Naast
Poolewe Ross-shire
IV22 2LL

Ardgour House
Ardgour
Clovullin by Fort William
Argyll PH33 7AH

Ardmaddy Castle Holiday Cottages
Ardmaddy
Argyll
PA34 4QY

Ashieburn Lodge
Ancrum
Jedburgh
TD8 6UN

Benarty Steading Cottage
Benarty House
Kelty
Fife
KY4 0HT

Bridge Cottage & Rose Cottage
Killumpha
Port Logan
Stranraer
Wigtownshire
DG9 9NT

Caberfeidh
17 Highland Crescent
Crieff
Perthshire
PH7 4LH

Cabhalan Cottage
1 Quidinish
Isle of Harris
Western Isles
HS3 3JQ

Canon Court
20 Canonmills
Edinburgh
Mid Lothian
EH3 5LH

Cauldside Farmhouse
St Andrews
Fife
KY16 9TY

Coille nam Beithe
Dalnavert
Kincraig by Aviemore
PH21

Cologin Farm Holiday Chalets
Lergas Glen by Oban
Argyll
PA34 4SE

Corriegorm Beag
Bay View Crescent
Broadford
Isle of Skye
IV49 9AB

Courtyard Cottages
Winkston Farmhouse
Peebles
Tweeddale
EH45 8PH

Craiglyn
50 West Moulin Road
Pitlochry
Perthshire
PH16 5EQ

Croftnacarn
Loch Garten
Boat of Garten
Inverness-shire
PH24

Curlew Cottage
Hilliclay Mains
Weydale Thurso
Caithness
KW14 8YN

Egmont Shore Road
Toward by Dunoon
Glasgow
PA23 7UA

Eleraig Highland Chalets
Kilninver by Oban
Argyll
PA34 4UX

Garden Woodhead Cot. & Upper Rusko
Fmhs
Gatehouse of Fleet
Kirkcudbrightshire
DG7 2BS

Glebe Cottage
Burnside House
Burnside
Scone by Perth
PH2 6LP

Facilities
For Visitors with Disabilities

Innes Maree
Poolewe
Ross-shire
IV22 2JU

Inverawe Holiday Cottage
Inverawe House
Taynuilt
Argyll
PA35 1HU

Invermudale Annexe
Altnaharra by Lairg
IV27 4UE

Kilcamb Cottage
Strontian
Argyll
PH36 4HY

Laebrak
Gulberwick By Lerwick
Shetland
ZE1 ORJ

Lagganlia Outdoor Centre
Kincraig
Kingussie
Inverness-shire
PH21 1NG

Loch Insh Chalets
Kincraig
Inverness-shire
PH21 1NU

Lochside Cottages & Outlook
Avielochan Farm
Aviemore
Inverness-shire
PH22 1QD

Lochview Ardach
Allt a Chuirn
Lochcarron
Ross-shire
IV54 8YD

Loudoun Mains Country Holidays
Loudoun Mains
Newmilns
Ayrshire
KA16 9LG

Mr M R Fraser
Reelig Glen Estate
Reelig House
Kirkhill
Inverness-shire
IV5 7PR

Mrs C H Grant
Logie
16 Craig na Gower Ave
Aviemore
Inverness-shire
PH22 1RW

Mrs Haggart
Hillhead Cottages Bodachra Farm
Dyce
Aberdeen
Aberdeenshire
AB21 7AR

Mrs M E C Ferrier
Balvatin Cottages Perth Road
Newtonmore
Inverness-shire
PH20 1BB

Mrs M Riach
Corronich
Boat of Garten
Inverness-shire
PH24 3BN

Netherby Cottage
Bogsbank Road
Romanno Bridge
West Linton
Peeblesshire
EH46 7DB

Osprey Lodge
Dirdhu Court
Nethybridge
Inverness-shire
PH25 3EG

Roxburgh Newtown Farm
Kelso
Roxburghshire
TD5 8NN

Scottish Borders Campus Con & Hol Centre
Scottish College of Textiles
Galashiels
TD1 3HE

Seabraes Hall Duncan House and Lodge
Roseangle
Dundee
Angus
DD2 1NN

Skerryvore
66 Edinburgh Road
Peebles
Tweeddale
EH45 8EE

Speyside Cottages
Nethybridge
Inverness-shire
PH25

St Andrews Country Cottages
Cupar
Fife
KY15 4QJ

Stronchullin Holiday Cottages
Ardentinny By Dunoon
Argyll
PA23 8TP

Taigh a'Braoin
No1 Letters
Lochbroom
Ross-shire
IV23 2SD

Tanaree & Dykeside
Logie Newton
Huntly
Aberdeenshire
AB5 6BB

Templar's Cottage
Kinermony Ltd By Aberlour
Morayshire
AB38 9NR

The Chalets
Gord
Cunningsburgh
Shetland
ZE2

The Knowes
32 Riddrie Knowes
Glasgow
G33 2QH

The Old School Cottage
Pouton Farm
Garlieston Newton Stewart
Wigtownshire
DG8 8HH

The Old Stables Flats 1 & 2
Shore Street
Bowmore Isle of Islay
Argyll
PA43 7LB

Facilities
For Visitors with Disabilities

The Reed & The Toftin
Lairdie Lowes
Steading
2 Losset Road
Alyth
Perthshire
PH11 8BT

The Schoolhouse
Tombuie
Aberfeldy
Perthshire
PH15 2JS

The Shieling
Aberfeldy Road
Killin
Perthshire
FK21 8TX

The Smiddy
4 Golf Course Road
Upper Skelmorlie
North Ayrshire
PA17 5DH

The Welton of Kingoldrum
Kingoldrum by Kirriemuir
Angus
DD8 5HY

The Willows
Cambus O'May by Ballater
Aberdeenshire
AB3 5SD

Thornielee Vale
Near Clovenfords by Galashiels
Selkirkshire
TD1 3LN

Tipperwhig & Brankam
Purgavie Farm
Glenisla by Kirriemuir
Angus
DD8 5HZ

Tranew Cottages
Tranew Farm
Kirkmichael
Ayrshire
KA19 7QU

Tulloch Holiday Lodges
Rafford
Forres
Moray
IV36 0RU

Woodvale Cottage
Penifiler
Portree
Isle of Skye
IV51 9NF

Index
By Location

Area Codes

A South of Scotland: Ayrshire and Arran, Dumfries and Galloway, Scottish Borders — 2

B Edinburgh and Lothians — 39

C Greater Glasgow and Clyde Valley — 57

D West Highlands & Islands, Loch Lomond, Stirling and Trossachs — 67

E Perthshire, Angus and Dundee and the Kingdom of Fife — 128

F Grampian Highlands, Aberdeen and the North East Coast — 174

G The Highlands and Skye — 205

H Outer Islands: Western Isles, Orkney, Shetland — 294

Location	Area code	Page no.
Aberchirder by Huntly	F	180
Aberdeen	F	180
Aberdour	E	134
Aberfeldy	E	134
Aberfoyle	D	73
Aberlour	F	181
Aboyne	F	181
Abriachan	G	211
Acharacle	G	211
Acharn by Kenmore	E	136
Achfary	G	212
Achiltibuie	G	212
Aird (Sleat, Isle of Skye)	G	277
Alford	F	183
Alyth	E	136
Annbank	A	8
Anstruther	E	136
Appin	D	74
Archiestown	F	183
Ardelve by Dornie	G	213
Arden	D	75
Ardentinny by Dunoon	D	75
Ardfern	D	75

Location	Area code	Page no.
Ardgay	G	214
Ardhasaig	H	300
Ardlui	D	76
Ardnamurchan	G	214
Ardrishaig by Lochgilphead	D	77
Ardross	G	215
Ardvasar, Sleat	G	277
Arisaig	G	215
Armadale, Sleat	G	277
Arnprior by Kippen	D	77
Arrochar	D	77
Aros	D	109
Ashkirk	A	10
Auchenmalg	A	11
Auchterarder	E	137
Auchtermuchty	E	137
Aultbea	G	216
Aviemore	G	217
Avoch by Fortrose	G	222
Ayr	A	11
Badachro	G	222
Ballantrae	A	13
Ballater	F	184

Index
By Location

Location	Area code	Page no.
Ballindalloch	F	185
Ballintuim	E	137
Balloch	D	77
Ballygrant	D	94
Balquhidder	D	78
Banchory	F	186
Banff	F	188
Bankfoot	E	137
Barr by Girvan	A	13
Bearsden	C	63
Beauly	G	224
Benderloch by Oban	D	78
Bernisdale by Portree	G	278
Bettyhill	G	225
Birsay	H	303
Blair Atholl	E	138
Blairgowrie	E	139
Boat of Garten	G	225
Bonar Bridge	G	226
Borve by Portree	G	278
Bowmore	D	94
Braemar	F	188
Breakish	G	278
Brechin	E	141
Bridge of Allan	D	79
Bridge of Cally	E	141
Bridge of Earn	E	141
Bridge of Orchy	D	79
Bridgend	D	95
Broadford	G	279
Brodick	A	8
Brodie	F	189
Brora	G	227
Bruichladdich	D	95
Buchlyvie	D	79
Buckie	F	190
Bunessan	D	109

Location	Area code	Page no.
Burghead	F	190
Cairndow	D	80
Cairnryan	A	13
Calgary	D	110
Callander	D	81
Caol Ila	D	96
Cambuslang	C	63
Campbeltown	D	83
Camus Croise, Isleornsay	G	280
Cannich	G	227
Carbost by Portnalong	G	280
Carmichael	C	63
Carnoustie	E	141
Carradale	D	84
Carrbridge	G	228
Carrick Castle	D	85
Castle Douglas	A	13
Catrine	A	15
Cawdor	G	228
Cellardyke	E	142
Clachamish by Portree	G	281
Clachan Seil	D	122
Claddach Kirkibost	H	303
Clynder	D	85
Cockburnspath	A	15
Coldingham	A	15
Coldstream	A	16
Colmonell by Girvan	A	16
Colonsay Isle of	D	85
Colpy	F	190
Comrie	E	142
Contin	G	229
Corpach by Fort William	G	229
Corrie	A	8
Cowdenbeath	E	143
Craigrothie by Cupar	E	143
Crail	E	143

Index
By Location

Location	Area code	Page no.
Craobh Haven, by Lochgilphead	D	86
Creetown	A	17
Crianlarich	D	87
Crieff	E	144
Crinan by Lochgilphead	D	88
Crocketford	A	17
Cromarty	G	229
Croy	G	229
Culbokie	G	230
Culkein	G	230
Culloden Moor	G	230
Cullen	F	190
Cupar	E	145
Dailly	A	18
Dalbeattie	A	19
Dalcross by Inverness	G	230
Dalmally	D	88
Dalry by Castle Douglas	A	19
Daviot	G	231
Dervaig	D	111
Diabaig	G	231
Dingwall	G	231
Dinnet by Aboyne	F	191
Dolphinton West Linton	A	19
Dores	G	232
Dornie by Kyle of Lochalsh	G	232
Dornoch	G	232
Doune	D	89
Drumnadrochit	G	233
Dufftown	F	192
Duirinish	G	234
Dulnain Bridge by Grantown-on-Spey	G	234
Dumfries	A	19
Dunbar	B	45
Dunblane	D	89
Duncanston	G	234
Dundee	E	146
Dundonnell	G	235
Dunkeld	E	146
Dunning	E	148
Dunoon	D	89
Dunshalt	E	148
Dunure by Ayr	A	20
Dunvegan	G	281
Dykehead Cortachy	E	148
Eaglesham	C	63
Earsary	H	309
Easdale by Oban	D	90
Edinburgh	B	45
Eigg Isle of	G	235
Elgin	F	192
Elgol (Isle of Skye)	G	282
Elie	E	149
Embo	G	235
Enochdhu	E	149
Ettrick Valley	A	20
Evanton	G	235
Fairlie	A	20
Fearnan by Kenmore	E	149
Feshie Bridge by Kincraig	G	236
Findhorn	F	193
Finstown	H	303
Fintry	D	90
Fionnphort	D	112
Flodabay	H	309
Fochabers	F	193
Ford by Lochgilphead	D	91
Forfar	E	150
Forres	F	193
Fort Augustus	G	236
Fort William	G	237
Fortingall	E	150

Index
By Location

Location	Area code	Page no.
Fortrose	G	236
Foss by Pitlochry	E	151
Foulden	A	21
Foyers	G	241
Fraserburgh	F	194
Gairloch	G	241
Galashiels	A	21
Gardenstown	F	194
Gartocharn	D	92
Gatehead	A	21
Gatehouse of Fleet	A	21
Glasgow	C	64
Glenbrittle (Isle of Skye)	G	282
Glencoe	G	242
Glendaruel	D	92
Glenelg	G	244
Glenesk by Edzell	E	151
Glenfarg	E	151
Glenferness	G	244
Glenfinnan	G	244
Glenisla	E	152
Glenlivet	F	194
Glenluce	A	22
Glenlyon	E	153
Glenmore Ardnamurchan	G	245
Glenshee	E	153
Glen Strathfarrar	G	245
Glen Urquhart	G	245
Golspie	G	246
Gott Bay	D	126
Grantown-on-Spey	G	246
Greenock	C	65
Gretna	A	22
Gruinart Bridgend	D	96
Gruline	D	112
Guthrie by Forfar	E	154
Haddington	B	55
Hawick	A	23
Helmsdale	G	248
Holm	H	304
Hopeman	F	195
Houndwood	A	23
Humbie	B	55
Huntly	F	196
Inchmurrin Island of, Loch Lomond	D	93
Inchnadamph	G	248
Insh	G	248
Inver by Tain	G	249
Inveraray	D	92
Inverbeg	D	92
Invergarry	G	249
Inverinate by Kyle of Lochalsh	G	249
Invermoriston	G	250
Inverness	G	250
Inveruglas	D	94
Isle of Seil	D	99
Isle of Whithorn	A	23
Jedburgh	A	24
Keith	F	196
Kelso	A	24
Kelty	E	154
Kemnay	F	196
Kenmore	E	155
Kensaleyre by Portree	G	282
Kentallen by Appin	G	253
Kilchattan Bay	D	79
Kilchoan Ardnamurchan	G	253
Kilchoman	D	96
Kildonan	A	9
Kilchrenan	D	99
Kilconquhar	E	155
Killiechronan	D	113
Killiecrankie	E	155
Killin	D	99

Index
By Location

Location	Area code	Page no.	Location	Area code	Page no.
Killundine	G	254	Lendalfoot by Girvan	A	29
Kilmarnock	A	26	Lerwick	H	305
Kilmartin by Lochgilphead	D	102	Lilliesleaf	A	29
Kilmelford by Oban	D	103	Leven	E	159
Kilninver by Oban	D	105	Linlithgow	B	55
Kincraig by Kingussie	G	254	Loch Eck	D	106
Kingston-on-Spey by Elgin	F	197	Loch Maree	G	271
Kingussie	G	256	Lochawe	D	105
Kinloch Rannoch	E	155	Lochailort	G	260
Kinlocheil by Fort William	G	256	Lochbuie	D	113
Kinlochewe	G	256	Lochcarron	G	260
Kinlochleven	G	257	Lochdon	D	113
Kinlochspelve	D	113	Lochearnhead	D	106
Kinross	E	156	Lochgilphead	D	106
Kintore	F	197	Lochgoilhead	D	107
Kippen	D	105	Lochinver	G	262
Kippford by Dalbeattie	A	27	Lochmaben	A	29
Kirkcaldy	E	157	Lochportain	H	303
Kirkcudbright	A	27	Lochs	H	302
Kirkmichael	E	157	Lochwinnoch	C	65
Kirkwall	H	304	Lockerbie	A	29
Kirriemuir	E	158	Logie Coldstone by Aboyne	F	197
Kishorn	G	257	Longniddry	B	55
Knoydart	G	257	Lossiemouth	F	198
Kyle of Lochalsh	G	257	Luss	D	107
Kylesku	G	258	MacDuff	F	199
Ladybank	E	159	Machrie	A	10
Laggan by Newtonmore	G	258	Machrihanish	D	107
Laggan Bridge by Newtonmore	G	258	Maddiston	D	108
Laurencekirk	F	197	Mallaig	G	265
Laide	G	258	Maybole	A	30
Lairg	G	259	Melrose	A	30
Lamlash	A	9	Melvich	G	266
Lanark	C	65	Memsie by Fraserburgh	F	199
Largs	A	28	Methven by Perth	E	159
Laxdale	H	301	Millport	A	18
			Minard by Inveraray	D	108

Index
By Location

Location	Area code	Page no.	Location	Area code	Page no.
Moffat	A	31	Plockton	G	272
Moniaive	A	31	Point	H	302
Monymusk	F	199	Poolewe	G	273
Morar	G	266	Port Bannatyne	D	79
Mordington	A	31	Port Charlotte	D	97
Muasdale	D	108	Port Ellen	D	98
Muckhart	D	108	Port of Menteith	D	120
Nairn	G	266	Portpatrick	A	34
Nethy Bridge	G	267	Portree	G	283
New Galloway	A	31	Portsoy	F	201
New Lanark by Lanark	C	66	Portsonachan	D	121
Newport on-Tay	E	160	Port William	A	34
Newtonmore	G	269	Prestwick	A	34
Newton Stewart	A	32	Rannoch Station	E	167
Nibon by Hillswick	H	302	Ratagan	G	274
North Ballachulish	G	270	Reay	G	274
North Berwick	B	55	Rheinigadale	H	300
North Connel	D	116	Rhynie	F	202
North Kessock	G	270	Ringford	A	35
North Queensferry	E	160	Rockcliffe by Dalbeattie	A	35
Oban	D	116	Rodel	H	300
Old Kilpatrick	D	120	Rogart	G	274
Oldmeldrum	F	200	Romanno Bridge	A	35
Ollaberry	H	305	Rosemarkie	G	275
Onich by Fort William	G	271	Rothes	F	202
Ord Sleat	G	282	Rothesay	D	80
Otter Ferry	D	120	Rowardennan	D	121
Peebles	A	32	Roy Bridge	G	275
Penicuik	B	56	Salen Aros	D	114
Peninver	D	120	Saltcoats	A	35
Pennan	F	200	Sanday	H	304
Pennyghael	D	114	Sandhead	A	36
Perth	E	160	Scalpay	H	300
Peterhead	F	200	Scarfskerry	G	275
Pinwherry	A	34	Scarinish	D	126
Pitlochry	E	162	Scone by Perth	E	173
Pittenweem	E	166	Scourie	G	276

Index
By Location

Location	Area code	Page no.	Location	Area code	Page no.
Seilebost	H	300	Taynuilt	D	125
Selkirk	A	36	Thornhill	A	37
Shieldaig	G	276	Thurso	G	288
Skipness	D	122	Tiree Isle of	D	127
South Queensferry	B	60	Tobermory	D	115
Southerness	A	36	Tomacharich	G	289
Spean Bridge	G	285	Tomintoul	F	203
Spittal of Glenshee	E	173	Tongue	G	289
St Andrews	E	167	Torridon	G	289
St. Boswells	A	35	Torrin by Broadford	G	284
St Catherines	D	121	Tote Skeabost Bridge	G	285
St Margaret's Hope	H	304	Treslaig	G	289
St Monans	E	172	Troon	A	37
Staffin (Isle of Skye)	G	284	Tummel Bridge	E	173
Stirling	D	122	Turriff	F	204
Stoer	G	286	Tyndrum by Crianlarich	D	127
Stornoway	H	302	Uig (Isle of Lewis)	H	302
Straiton by Maybole	A	36	Uig (Isle of Skye)	G	285
Stranraer	A	37	Ullapool	G	290
Strathconon	G	286	Waternish	G	285
Strathdon	F	203	West Calder	B	56
Strathpeffer	G	287	West Linton	A	37
Strathyre	D	123	Westray	H	305
Stromeferry	G	288	Westruther by Gordon	A	38
Stromness	H	305	Whitebridge	G	293
Strontian	G	288	Whitehills by Banff	F	204
Talmine	G	288	Whiting Bay	A	10
Tarbert	H	301	Wick	G	293
Tarbert Loch Fyne	D	123	Yarrow	A	38
Tarbet by Arrochar	D	124	Yetholm by Kelso	A	38
Tarland	F	203			
Tarskavaig	G	284			

TOP QUALITY HOLIDAY HOUSES

Each Individually Inspected

———— • ————

Peaceful Country Cottages
Luxurious Country Houses
Snug Town Houses
Chalets
About 150 to choose from

Dumfries & Galloway

For free colour brochure:
G. M. Thomson & Co., 27 King Street, Castle Douglas
Telephone: 01556 50 40 30 (24 hours)
Fax: 01556 50 32 77

Please mention this guide when making your booking

Books
To Help You

THE SCOTTISH TOURIST BOARD PRODUCES A SERIES OF FOUR ACCOMMODATION GUIDES TO HELP YOU CHOOSE YOUR HOLIDAY ACCOMMODATION. THE MOST COMPREHENSIVE GUIDES ON THE MARKET, THEY GIVE DETAILS OF FACILITIES, PRICE, LOCATION AND EVERY ESTABLISHMENT IN THEM CARRIES A QUALITY ASSURANCE AWARD FROM THE SCOTTISH TOURIST BOARD.

SCOTLAND: HOTELS & GUEST HOUSES 1999   £9.50 (incl. p&p)

Over 1,400 entries, listing a variety of hotels and guest houses throughout Scotland. Also includes inns, lodges, restaurant with rooms, bed and breakfasts, campus accommodation, serviced apartments and international resort hotels. Comprehensive location maps. Completely revised each year. Full colour throughout.

SCOTLAND: BED & BREAKFAST 1999   £6.50 (incl. p&p)

Over 1,700 enties, listing a variety of bed and breakfast establishments throughout Scotland. Also incledes hotels, guest houses, inns, lodges, restaurant with rooms and campus accommodation. Comprehensive location maps. Completely revised each year.

SCOTLAND: CARAVAN & CAMPING PARKS 1999   £4.50 (incl. p&p)

Over 200 entries, listing caravan parks and individual caravan holiday homes for hire. Includes self-catering properties. Comprehensive location maps. Completely revised each year.

SCOTLAND: SELF CATERING 1999   £7.00 (incl. p&p)

Over 1,100 entries, listing cottages, flats, chalets, log cabins and serviced apartments to let. Many in scenic areas or bustling towns and cities. Caravan holiday homes included. Comprehensive location maps. Completely revised each year. Full colour throughout.

TOURING GUIDE TO SCOTLAND   £6.00 (incl. p&p)

A new, fully revised edition of this popular guide which now lists over 1,500 things to do and places to visit in Scotland. Easy to use index and locator maps. Details of opening hours, admission charges, ageneral description and information on disabled access.

TOURING MAP OF SCOTLAND   £4.00 (incl. p&p)

A new and up-to-date touring map of Scotland. Full colour with comprehensive motorway and road information, the map details over 20 categories of tourist information and names over 1,500 things to do and places to visit in Scotland

You can order any of the above by filling in the coupon on the next page or by telephone.

Publications
Order Form

MAIL ORDER

Please tick the publications you would like, cut out this section and send it with your cheque, postal order (made payable to Scottish Tourist Board) or credit card details to:

Scottish Tourist Board, FREEPOST, Dunoon, Argyll PA23 8PQ

Scotland: Hotels & Guest Houses 1999	£9.50 (incl. P&P)	☐
Scotland: Bed & Breakfast 1999	£6.50 (incl. P&P)	☐
Scotland: Camping & Caravan Parks 1999	£4.50 (incl. P&P)	☐
Scotland: Self Catering 1999	£7.00 (incl. P&P)	☐
Touring Guide to Scotland	£6.00 (incl. P&P)	☐
Touring Map of Scotland	£4.00 (incl. P&P)	☐

BLOCK CAPITALS PLEASE:

NAME (Mr/Mrs/Ms) _____

ADDRESS _____

POST CODE _____ TELEPHONE NO. _____

TOTAL REMITTANCE ENCLOSED £ _____

PLEASE CHARGE MY *VISA/ACCESS ACCOUNT (*delete as appropriate)

Card No. [ ][ ][ ][ ][ ][ ][ ][ ][ ][ ][ ][ ][ ][ ][ ][ ]   Expiry Date [ ][ ][ ][ ]

Signature _____

Date _____

TELEPHONE ORDERS

To order BY PHONE: simply call free 08705 511511 (national call rate) quoting the books you would like and give your credit card details.